Discovering Kerry

20. JAN

Discovering

KERRY

its History, Heritage & Topography

by T J Barrington

BLACKWATER DUBLIN

Copyright © T. J. Barrington 1976

ISBN 0 905471 00 8

The Blackwater Press
31 Castle Park
Monkstown
County Dublin
Ireland

Graphic design: Murphy + Kyne
Editorial and production: Daniel Sullivan
Printed and bound by W. & G. Baird Limited

Foreword

Dear Reader,

Interest in the legend and lore of our countryside has long been a feature of our culture. In ancient Ireland, "dinnsheanchas" or place-lore was held in high esteem and considered an essential study for the poet. In the course of centuries, the hills and mountains, rivers and valleys of Ireland were invested with a wealth of tradition and folk-lore. The people cherished these traditions and had a genuine interest in them long before tourism was dreamed of or developed. Such an interest is not unique in Ireland. Many other nations were equally tradition-conscious and this is particularly true of the Church.

The response to the past is deep-rooted in our nature, because the past is much more than a collection of memories that have survived the ravages of time. The past has been a powerful influence shaping the present, just as our lives will help to develop the future. The people have always been conscious of this continuity, especially when they themselves have shared the same history and hardship as their forefathers. Until recently, it was customary in West Kerry, whenever a farmer had stooked the last sheaf of oats or dug the last potato, to sit on the fence and say a prayer for the countless generations that had toiled and sweated in the same field.

This book, *Discovering Kerry*, reminds us of the struggles and events that have shaped our history. It is full of local and human interest and should appeal not merely to the tourist or historian, but to the people of Kerry whose life-story is told in these pages. I have known the author for many years and have been impressed by the genuine and enduring interest that he has long had in this subject. I wish him every success in this venture.

Yours sincerely

+ Eamonn

Eamonn Casey
Bishop of Kerry

For Aine, Ruth, Anne, Conor and Paul

who enlivened so many days

when we were

discovering Kerry.

Preface

Any group of us is, I suppose, partly the product of shared history, heritage and environment. Some places have more of these than others, and Kerry has a good deal. To understand these forces helps us to know a bit better the kind of people we are. It helps in another way. As Marc Bloch has said: 'True patriotism grows out of attachment to small territories. It is only on the small scale, where interpretation can be checked against observation and local knowledge, that definitive conclusions can be reached'.

This book has been a-writing since 1962, consuming as much time as I could spare for it from many other pre-occupations. Over such a time events and knowledge change, so I beg pardon if, despite my efforts, here and there the text shows its years.

My sources have been twofold: the printed ones, books and articles, and the topographical — journeys into every corner of the area. This book is not, therefore, that of a professional but of an amateur, in both senses of the word.

I owe great debts of gratitude to all who have helped over the years — to Most Rev. Eamonn Casey, Bishop of Kerry, for his encouragement and for writing the Foreword; to Dermot Kinlen, SC, who first set me reading; to the present and past staff of the Great Southern Hotel, Killarney; to my friend and colleague, Mary Prendergast, whose efficient charm has summoned so many hundreds of books and periodicals from the vasty deep; to Mrs. K. Browne, the Kerry County Librarian; to Raymond Kyne and Dan Sullivan for their skills in design and production and for their truly heroic work in bringing this work to (let's hope!) a timely birth. The book depends greatly on the illustrations and the maps. To these Bord Failte Eireann, the National Library, the Office of Public Works, and the Ordnance Survey Office have been major contributors. I am most grateful to the staffs of these bodies for bearing with me and for being so helpful at all times. My thanks to those I have named, and to countless others in Kerry and elsewhere whose charm and co-operation made the writing of this book such constant delight.

— T. J. B.   May, 1976

A visitor to Ireland familiar with Gaelic literature has his attention arrested everywhere in that beautiful island by many features, natural and artificial, which set him searching among his memories and clothing hill and river, rath and church and castle, with the lively and intimate colouring of long-descended tradition. And if he yields himself to the spell of that lure of recollection and summons back out of the past the kings and saints and scholars and poets whose names still cling about the places that they knew, he may be contented to recall that he is acting in the very spirit of those devoted scholars to whom that tradition owes its origin and survival. For the poets of Ireland cultivated with an unremitting assiduity a study to which they gave the name *dindshenchas*, the lore of the high places, until by the accretion of centuries there came into existence a large body of literature in prose and verse, forming a kind of Dictionary of National Topography, which fitted the famous sites of the country each with its appropriate legend. It was one of the obligations of a poet to have this knowledge ready at call, and if faced by a demand to relate the associations of some deserted rath or lonely pillar-stone he failed to render an exact and credible account, he was shamed to the very roots of his being.

— Robin Flower : The Irish Tradition (1947)

The lady answered: 'we have a means of help for thee'. 'What help is that?' he asked. 'That we should convey to Tara for thee a certain mnemonic potion of nature such that never a stream, nor river, nor estuary, nor battle, nor single combat came in thy way but thou shalt have present in thy memory'. Caeilte made answer: 'That is a helpful gift of very kinsmen and of friends'.

— Standish H. O'Grady (ed) : Silva Gadelica (1892)

Contents

List of Illustrations

Acknowledgements

My especial thanks to a number of official bodies for their splendid range of illustrations relating to Kerry and for permitting me to use so many of them — to Bord Failte Eireann for the illustrations marked BFE above; to the Commissioners of Public Works in Ireland for those marked CPWI; to the National Gallery of Ireland for those marked NGI; to the National Library of Ireland for those marked NLI; to the National Museum, Dublin, for those marked NMD. I am also indebted to the *Irish Press*; Dr. Liam de Paor; the Board of Trinity College, Dublin; Mr. K. Danaher; Dr. P. Harbison; and Mr. MacMonagle for permission to use the illustrations marked. I am also obliged to Messrs. W. Tempest, publishers of H. G. Leask : *Irish Castles and Castellated Houses;* to Messrs. Longmans, publishers of A. R. Orme : *Ireland* in the World's Landscape Series; to Messrs. Blackwell; to Messrs. Methuen, publishers of F. Henry : *Irish Art*; to Messrs. Gill and Macmillan, publishers of R. A. Stalley : *Architecture and Sculpture in Ireland 1150 – 1350*; and to the Kerry Archaeological and Historical Society for permission to use illustrations to which they hold the copyright.

I should like to acknowledge to Professor James Carney his permission to publish three of his translations from *Medieval Irish Lyrics* and one from E. Knott and G. Murphy (eds) : *Early Irish Literature*; to the Dolmen Press and to Messrs. Gill and Macmillan for permission to use translations by Frank O Connor from, respectively, *The Little Monasteries* and *Kings, Lords and Commons*; to Messrs. Gill and Macmillan, also, for permission to use an extract from Daniel Corkery : *The Hidden Ireland*; and to the Oxford University Press for the two extracts from Robin Flower's *The Irish Tradition*.

The Ordnance Survey maps are reproduced by permission of the Government, permit no. 2521.

PART 1 MEMORIES

Chapter I

Legends and Folk Tales

The earliest memories in Kerry, as in Ireland generally, are legendary. Where these overlap with historical periods they serve to enrich the austere records and, indeed, to help us to understand something of the cultural environment that moulded the historical figures.

LEGENDS

Of the rich heritage of legends, many, because of the geographical particularisms so noticeable in Irish art, are placed in Kerry. These legends enlarge, by tales of the past — most of them tall tales — the austere and uncommunicative records of tools, buildings and ornaments: they are, in fact, part of the consciousness of the race.

The periods covered by the legends fall broadly into four:

(i)   the mythological period of the 'invasions';
(ii) the heroic cycle of the Red Branch warriors of Ulster of perhaps the first century BC;
(iii) the period of Fionn and the Fiana, supposedly in the 3rd century AD; and
(iv) the period of kings, from about 400 BC to about 1000 AD.

The stories are referred to here usually only where they have a bearing on Kerry, and that summarily.

(I) THE INVASIONS

When the synthetic history of Ireland was being written about the end of the first millenium AD, the old tales of the invasions were fitted into a period of some 1250 years dating from the Flood. In the chronology of the time adopted by the Four Masters the world was 5,200 years old at the beginning of the christian era. On this chronology the Flood happened in 2958 BC and the last invasion of the legendary six occurred in 1700 BC. Surprisingly enough the archaeologists place between somewhat similar limits a series of invasions in the neolithic and bronze ages. Another surprising parallel is the persistent strain recurring through the invasion stories of an origin in the eastern Mediteranean and of a sojourn in Spain before the people invaded Ireland by way of south Kerry. As we shall see, the beaker folk who invaded by way of Kerry had some such origins, and there are some similarities to the likely behaviour of the Gaels when they came. Parallels of this kind have to be viewed with extreme caution, but, given the tenacity of folk memories, perhaps we have here some dim reflection of the memories of some of the oldest strains in Ireland, and yet another warning that there may be embodied in these memories some traditions of startling antiquity.

In any event, the compilers of the *Book of Invasions (Lebor Gabala)* identified six prehistoric invasions: of Cessair; of Parthalon and his followers; of Nemed; of the small, dark, boorish Firbolgs, or 'bag-men'; of the artistic and magical Tuatha De Danaan; and of the gaelic Milesians with their iron spears. Of these, the Firbolg and the

Milesians can be identified in some way with historical people of the iron age; that is, of course, long after the dates given for them in the old tales, but perhaps overlying similar traditions that date back a further period of 1,500 years or more.

When Noah selected his crew for the Ark he excluded his son Bith, according to Irish legend. Bith's daughter, Cessair, relapsed into paganism, took command of the party reluctant to be drowned, and built ships and set sail for Ireland which, her wizards said, being uninhabited (and thus sinless) and also free of reptiles and monsters, would escape the Flood. After a voyage of seven years — they touched at the Alps en route — three ships reached Ballinskelligs Bay just forty days before the Flood, but two ships were wrecked and their crews drowned. The third ship, with Cessair, her father Bith, two other men and forty-nine women landed on Saturday, 5th (or 15th) of the month, (but what month is not clear) in the Four Masters' dating, 2958 BC. The three men divided the fifty women between them, the pilot, Ladra, getting only sixteen and being much dissatisfied. However, he died shortly after, according to the story, of 'excess of women, or is it the shaft of the oar that penetrated his buttock'. The women were re-partitioned between Bith and the third man, Fintan, Cessair's choice. Unfortunately, Bith, taking his twenty-five women to the North of Ireland, died there, and the twenty-five widows returned to Cessair. This was too much for the remaining man, Fintan, and he fled from them all, whereupon Cessair died of a broken heart, seven days before the Flood. Fintan, in various forms, including a spell as a one-eyed salmon, survived until the arrival of christianity, and thus was a most useful source for the early history of Ireland!

Nearly three hundred years later another invader, Parthalon, came to Ireland and landed at the Kenmare River, to be precise, at Rath Strand east of Lamb's Head, and at Glanbeg cove, east of Rath on Tuesday, 14th May, 2680 BC! The party was a thousand strong and sailed from Greece where Parthalon had killed his parents. Thirty years they spent clearing the land and struggling with the one-eyed Balor and his demon Fomorians. Then Parthalon and his people, now grown to 9,000, were in a single week destroyed by plague.

The next invader was Nemed who arrived in 2350, but avoided Kerry. His people had a bad time from the oppressive Fomorian demons.

From Nemed sprang the next group, the small, dark, boorish Fir Bolg who arrived in 1934 BC in Cork. About their name there has been much speculation. The common explanation of Fir Bolg is 'Bag Men'. One reason for the origin of this name is that they exported Irish earth in bags to spread around Greek cities to protect them from snakes! As we shall see, they were probably Belgae, named after their god Bolgios. They were the main celtic invaders, the basic Iverni (or Erainn) who were to people Kerry and Cork, were (with their related peoples the Fir Domnann and the Gaileoin) to be the principal subjects of the Milesians (or Goidels, or Gaels),

Glanbeg Cove, Kenmare River

see Ireland.) With three ships he sailed there and landed in south Kerry. He spent some time in the peninsula and then made his way north to meet the three Tuatha De Danaan kings of Ireland, Mac Cuill, Mac Cecht and Mac Greine. He rashly praised the country and they, fearing he would come back with force to take it, pursued him to his ships. He was wounded in an ambush while he and his party embarked and died on the way back to Spain. This provoked his people to avenge him. In the year 1700 BC thirty ship-loads of them set sail. They included eight sons of Milesius, (Miles Espane, Spanish soldier) who had recently died. His widow Scota (which means, simply, Irishwoman) and the mother of six of the sons, sailed with them. Hence the invaders came to be called Milesians. They first saw land at Wexford but were driven off by Tuatha De Danaan magic. As they sailed westward, Erannan, the youngest of the sons, climbed the mast first to see Ireland, but fell and was drowned. Scene, the wife of the poet son Amergin, died within sight of land in the Kenmare River. Ir, a third son, was rowing so hard that his oar broke and he fell back in to the boat, died the following day, and was buried on the saddle of the Skellig where, until recently it is said, a dolmen stood. They landed near Waterville on Thursday, 1st May. As he put his foot on Ireland Amergin composed a famous incantation in which, like Krishna in the Bhagavad-Gita, he claims to subsume all being within himself. Then, a poem on the abundance of fish in the place. Erannan was buried near Kildreelig. Ballinskelligs, and Scene, reputedly, at Eightercua above Waterville.

The alignments of four stones at each of these places is supposed to mark the graves. Amergin said the estuary should always be called after her, Inber Scene. (However, some unromantic people say that Inber Scene is only the estuary of the Shannon.) Three days later they were on Slieve Mish, near Tralee, and there Banba, wife of one of the three kings of the Tuatha De Danaan, confronted them. After much magic, a battle was fought in which Scota was killed. She was buried in Glanaskagheen in the mountains and her reputed grave is to be seen. Another of the wives, Fas, was also killed and buried in Glenfash and the little christian church of Killeton is supposed to be built on her grave. The invaders won this battle, made for Tara and demanded either battle or the sovereignty of Ireland. It was represented to them that they had not given due notice of their intention — a point Amergin concurred in notwithstanding the soldierly impatience of one of the joint leaders, Donn. However, they agreed to re-embark at Waterville and withdraw 'nine waves'. When they stood out to sea a great, magic storm blew up and drove them west. At length Amergin calmed the storm and they returned to the estuary. Here the ship of the joint leader, Donn, was wrecked on Bull Rock and Donn and his shipload were drowned. They were buried on the rock which came to be called Teach Duinn (Donn's House), a synonym for the other world. At length, three of the sons of Milesius, including Amergin, landed again at Waterville. Here Luigdeach, son of Ith, was bathing naked in Lough Currane (or Lough Luigdeach) and his wife Fial was also bathing naked in the little river that runs from the lake. Husband and wife unexpectedly confronted each other and Fial died at once of shame. The great Ballybrack

to be the authors of the great Red Branch group of sagas, and to be the builders of the great stone fortresses spread around the sea coasts of the Kerry promontories. According to the legend what is now Munster west of Cork to the Shannon was divided in two, the northern part going to the Fir Domnann under their leader Geanann, and the southern part (i.e. including Kerry) to the Fir Bolg under their leader Seanghann.

The next traditional invaders were the Tuatha De Dannan, literally the peoples of the goddess Anu or Ana. They landed in a cloud of mist in Leitrim and, after some struggles with the Fir Bolg, as well as those persistent demons, the Fomorians, took over the country. This was not too difficult for them because they were gods. These people are the 'Danes' of popular speech, in Dane's grave, Dane's fort etc. Their special connexion with Kerry is with the aptly named twin mountains, the Paps (Da Chich Anand, the two breasts of the mother goddess, Anu) near Rathmore. She was also called the Mor-Righan, or Morrigan, the Great Queen, a goddess of battle. She was the mother of the three sons of Tuireann whose death story is one of the great legendary tales of ancient Ireland. These three were associated with Lug; as we shall see, the cult of the god Lug has descended to the present time in several sites in Kerry.

The last invaders were the Gaels (or Goidels from the Welsh word for Irishman). They were reputed to have moved east from Egypt and to have taken Spain. There they built a tower to protect the land. From it one fine winter's evening Ith saw Ireland. (In Galicia still there is a belief that from the top of an old Roman lighthouse one *can*, on a clear day,

16 dolmen close to Waterville house is said to be her tomb. This story is one example of the old Irish tabu on nudity. Luigdeach's daughter Tea was wife of the other joint leader of the expedition, Eremon. From her Tara (Teamhair — the wall of Tea) took its final name.

After a number of magical struggles and battles the invaders killed, at Teltown, Co. Meath, the three Tuatha De Danaan kings and their three queens Eire, Fodla, and Banba whose names, Amergin promised, would be used for the whole country. This completed the conquest. One of the party, Goiscen, came back to Kerry and built the fort of Cathair Nair on the edge of the Sliabh Mish Mountains. Later, Ireland was partitioned amongst two of the next generation of the invaders, Ir and Eibhear. Ir had the northern half; and it was from there that the Ciarraige, who gave their name to Kerry, later claimed to have come. The country was in another sense divided into halves. The Milesians occupied the land above ground, and the Tuatha De Danaan occupied that below ground where the Dagda allotted each group its *sidh,* or underground fort, the mounds of which until recently were (and, often, still are) regarded with great respect by the country folk.

(II) RED BRANCH CYCLE

The Red Branch stories, which carry many echoes of primitive indo-european times, are mainly concerned with happenings in Ulster and struggles with the men of Connacht; but there are some Kerry connexions. These stories have been held to be the special contribution of the Fir Bolg or Erainn as they held out in Ulidia against the ultimately successful attacks of the Gaels from Connacht.

Bull Rock — Teach Duinn

One of the early contenders for the kingship of Ulster was the handsome Deadhadh whose brother Duach put out his eyes. After eight battles Deadhadh and his people, a branch of the Erainn, were driven south to hold south and west Kerry. The chief of this clan was the magical (probably divine) figure of Cu Roi Mac Daire, who was Deadhadh's grandson and reputed ruler of Munster. Cu Roi lived in the great mountain promontory fort, called after him Caherconree, in the Sliabh Mish mountains near Camp.

When a dispute arose between the three great Ulster champions, Cu Chulainn, Laegaire and Conall, as to which was entitled to the 'hero's portion' at a feast and whose wife was entitled to precedence, they came south to Cu Roi to adjudicate. He put each of them, on successive nights, on guard in his fort. This fort was impregnable after sunset because it then began to revolve with terrifying swiftness. Nonetheless, ghastly beings came to attack each in turn and to hurtle Laegaire and Conall over the rampart. Out of this test Cu Chulainn emerged best, but the issue was not settled beyond dispute until all four went back north to Emain Macha, where the dispute broke out again. There Cu Roi, disguised as a giant, made a deal with each that the warrior could behead him on condition that Cu Roi could behead the warrior the following night. On successive nights each of the warriors accepted the challenge but, as Cu Roi's head rolled away, he got up and, spouting blood, tucked it, with the rest of his gear, under his arm and went out. Of the heroes only Cu Chulainn came back to fill his side of the bargain and gloomily laid his head on the block. But Cu Roi said that Cu Chulainn was indisputedly the bravest and most honourable.

On another occasion the Ulidians after a great party get blind drunk and set out on a wild dash through Ireland in their chariots. They arrive at Luachair Dedadh, near Castleisland, the capital of West Munster and, being caught in a snow storm, try to sober up there. As luck would have it their ancient enemies Medb and Oilill are on a visit there to see their son who has been fostered with Cu Roi. The Ulstermen, after some initial anxiety, are hospitably received and lodged in a metal house. Here with Medb's amiable prompting, the hosts try to roast the Ulstermen alive. This leads to much severe fighting until, thanks to Cu Chulainn, the Ulstermen win and sack the place. (Can Luachair Dedad be related to Cahercrovdarrig? Had the roasting been a success, as foreseen, one of the hosts said that all that would be left of the Ulstermen would be 'ach a mbearfadh ean uaibh ina gcrobha'.)

Cu Chulainn is associated with Anascaul Lough, west of Caherconree, in a more primitive tale of a woman Scal ni Mhurnain who was about to be carried off by a giant when she sent word to Cu Chulainn to defend her. Cu Chulainn stood on the mountain top east of the lake there and the giant on the mountain top west of it. They taunted each other in verse, and then began a week-long battle of throwing rocks across the valley. Then Cu Chulainn was hit and roared with pain. Scal thought him killed and drowned herself in the lake. On top of Cu Chulainn's mountain are three cairns called the Bed, the

House, and the Grave of Cu Chulainn. There is another House of Cu Chulainn on that mountain, in Ballynahunt.

Cu Chulainn went with a raiding party to the Isle of Man but was having no success in taking the crucial fortress until a mysterious stranger offered to help on condition that he had first pick of the spoils. The place was taken and the stranger chose the chieftain's daughter, Blathnaid, on whom Cu Chulainn had set his eye. The stranger, who was Cu Roi, outwitted Cu Chulainn and carried Blathnaid off. Cu Chulainn caught up with them on the way, but Cu Roi defeated him and shaved his head, a cruel humiliation. Cu Roi then brought Blathnaid to Caherconree. A year later, Cu Chulainn, his hair now grown, skulked below the foot of the mountain. Blathnaid found him there and persuaded Cu Roi to send his men off for big building stones for the fort. Then, when it was safe, she signalled to Cu Chulainn by pouring milk in the Fionnglas river (hence the name), and hid Cu Roi's sword. Cu Chulainn surprised and killed Cu Roi and carried off Blathnaid. Shortly afterwards, in Cu Chulainn's country of the North, Cu Roi's druid (who had helplessly watched the slaying of his master) grasped Blathnaid and flung himself with her over a cliff. Cu Roi's son, Lugaid, eventually avenged his father by hurling the magic spear that killed Cu Chulainn near Dundalk, the death that is commemorated by the sculpture in the GPO, Dublin. The Gap of Dunloe is named after Lugaid's fortress. It is most likely that this Lugaid was the god Lug. Cu Chulainn's comrade Conall Cearnach took a bitter revenge for his death and was himself killed by the three Ruadchoin of the Mairtine of Munster, who were of the Erainn, in revenge for the death of Cu Roi.

Close to Caherconree is a monument known, improbably, as Naisi's grave. Naisi was the lover of Deirdre and was killed by the jealous Conor Mac Nessa, King of Ulster. Conor persuaded Fergus Mac Roich to guarantee to Naisi and his two brothers a safe conduct. When, notwithstanding this, Conor had the three brothers killed, Fergus took implacable revenge on Conor. He went to Queen Medb and her husband Oilill in Connacht with whose help he launched constant attacks on Ulster. Medb bore him triplet sons one of whom was called Ciar, who moved south and established the kingdom of Kerry (Ciar-Rioghacht) — actually the people of Ciar — in the area originally of the barony of Trughanacmy. For this reason Kerry is often called 'the Kingdom'. Medb became the goidelic goddess of sovereignty and, by Fergus she thus provided several pre-goidelic tribes (such as the Ciarraige) with a goidelic pedigree.

(III) FENIAN CYCLE

The most popular of the Irish groups of legends in the literature of more than 1,000 years has been that based on Fionn Mac Cumhail and the Fiana. These stories first began to be popular in the ninth century, but their origin seems to be much earlier. Mac Neill suggests that the Fiana were drawn from one of the subject, pre-gaelic races of Ireland; Gerard Murphy has shown that the origin of Fionn is to be traced back to the great celtic god Lug — whom Caesar called the celtic Mercury — vestiges of whose cult, as we shall see, survive in Kerry as in other parts of Ireland. However, Mac Neill's argument that the Fionn stories were especially popular amongst the subject — that is pre-gaelic — tribes of Ireland (two-thirds of the whole) has not been controverted. The identification of Fionn with Lug suggests that the stories, while of pre-gaelic origin, give us little or no clue to the elusive pre-celtic peoples. The Fionn stories seem to have had three origins — around Tara; in Leinster; and amongst the Corcu Duibne of south and west Kerry. Thus one of the Fionn legends made him a member of the Firbolg Ivernians and had him die in their area.

In legend the Fiana were a standing army in the service of the high king of Ireland in the third century AD. The Fiana had a special duty to safeguard the ports of Ireland. When they were not on duty they spent much of their time hunting. These two activities, repelling invasions and hunting, were much engaged in in Kerry. In one of the most famous of the tale sequences, Fionn, in his young days, was a fugitive through much of Ireland and spent some time as a refugee in Killarney. Later in life, on a visit to France, he eloped with the wife *and* daughter of the king of that country who appealed to the King of Spain and the King of the World for aid. They set out for Ireland, 20 kings in all, and, touching first at Skellig, sailed for Ventry, west of Dingle, guided by a Killarney man called Glas Mac Dreamhain, who had been exiled. (Glas later switched sides.) Their fleet was so great that it choked the wide bay. For a year and a day the defenders, with great losses, could do no more than keep the invaders at bay. The King of Spain was killed in an early battle, and the King of France, in a later one, so frightened out of his wits that he took wing for Gleann na nGealt. Much humiliation was inflicted on Fionn and the Fiana by a champion of the King of the World, Dolar Dorbha, who in single combat kept on killing champions of the Fiana though not, be it noted, any of the leading figures. The thirteen-year only son of the King of Ulster heard of this and, with twelve youthful companions, escaped from his father's care and came to Ventry to aid the Fiana. While he was being restrained from fighting Dolar Dorbha his twelve young companions tackled the champion and were all killed. Dolar's roars of triumph so provoked the young prince that he insisted on taking on the champion by himself. The pair fought all day until darkness fell and the tide rose. Locked together, fighting still, boy and man were drowned on the strand. In the morning, the man's body had to be hacked away to release the boy's. Eventually, with help from the King of Ireland, the Fiana staged a great battle in which Fionn, with his poisoned weapons, killed Darach Donn, the King of the World - Ri an Domhain, the Dumnorix of the Roman accounts — his grave is in Kilvickadownig, nearby. In this contest Fionn was himself severely wounded. So great was the slaughter and the number of gravely wounded that on each side only one man stood erect. The surviving invader, chamberlain to the King of the World, swam back to the ships, followed by the survivor of the Fiana, himself gravely wounded. The invader gained his ship, but his hand was gripped in the teeth of the pursuer, and both were lost beneath the waves. So

18

ended this struggle that cost such bitter losses and that lasted a year and a day.

Also lost in this battle was a young man, Cael, who a year before, as the Fiana were marching through North Kerry, had with a poem praising her magnificent home beside Loch Cuirre on the slopes of the Paps near Rathmore and herself, wooed and won the beautiful, rich Crede, daughter of Cairbre, its king. The Fiana delayed a week to celebrate the marriage, and Cael and Crede came with them to Ventry. There she organised the feeding arrangements and the nursing of the many wounded. At the end, after the last battle, she wandered over the great strand among the piles of dead and wounded looking for her dead husband. Then the sea washed him up on the southern side of the strand and she lay beside him recalling in poetry how birds and animals sacrifice themselves for their loved ones — above her on Druim Ruithleann the continual call of the stag whose partner Fionn had long since killed — until she too died on the strand.

Another bitter invasion was centred on Knockanore, a hill above the Shannon, three miles north of Ballybunion. It has been said that the name comes from Cnoc an Air, the hill of the slaughter. Here Fionn and the Fiana, innocent for once, found themselves defending the daughter of the King of Greece who, fleeing from her husband, landed here. He came in hot pursuit, demanded his wife, and with his force killed 1,000 of the Fiana sent to stop him. Oscar, Fionn's grandson, fought him in single combat for five days and eventually killed him; whereupon the lady, rather unreasonably, died of grief upon the hill. This was bad enough until another invading party demanded satisfaction for the deaths of husband and wife. This led to a series of contests and a succession of deaths. This time it took Oscar ten days of single combat to kill the invader, whose two sons, after much slaughter, also fell. The trouble ended only when the bereaved wife and mother called it off. And so, as the old poem says, the place will always be known as Cnoc an Air, the hill of the slaughter.

Life was not always so disagreeable and the Fiana spent much of their time in Kerry, with their hounds and spears, hunting the deer that are still so plentiful about Killarney. On one famous hunting expedition from the Reeks to Ballaghabeama they killed many deer, but at Doire na bh Fian (the oakwood of the Fiana, now Derryfanga) beside Lough Acoose they aroused a sleeping wild sow which they hunted for two days, but she escaped them, after destroying many of both hunters and hounds. Pork was the favourite meat in early Ireland.

The great Irish love story — though in Irish fashion it is cased in irony — arose amongst the Erainn of Kerry. It, too, takes the form of a hunt, that lasted seven years, through the length and breadth of Ireland, the Pursuit of Diarmaid and Grainne. She was the daughter of the king of Ireland and betrothed to the now aging Fionn. She forced the gallant and dashing Diarmaid O Duibhne, a leading member of the Fiana and son of the king of Corca Duibne, to elope with her. Diarmaid had a spot, or mole, on his face that made him

irresistible to women. Fionn pursued them with implacable hatred until, long after, he encompassed Diarmaid's death, whereupon Grainne now promptly married Fionn to a great shout of derision from the Fiana. Innumerable dolmens and caves throughout Ireland are called Beds of Diarmaid and Grainne. There is a terrifying perch, so pointed out, on the edge of Binn Diarmada, west of Smerwick harbour. Diarmaid took Grainne to a cave near Glenbeigh, now destroyed by the makers of the railway line. Here he performed great deeds protecting her from bands of foreigners sent after them by Fionn, and he caught for her salmon from the rivers nearby. Notwithstanding all the 'Beds' and his reputation as a womaniser, it was not until they had been fleeing for a long time and had moved on from Glenbeigh up through the spare lands of Galway and Mayo that at length she taunted his manhood so that he lay with her. When at long last the god Oengus made peace between Fionn and Diarmaid the latter got confirmed as part of the settlement his right to his father's territory of Corca Duibne. He had six sons by Grainne before he was killed by an enchanted boar on Ben Bulben in Sligo.

Fionn had a dwarf four hands high called Cnu Dearoil, a most excellent musician. Fionn thought he should have a wife, but the little man would have no woman bigger than himself. Eventually a little woman, Blathnaid, was found in Teach Duinn, (Bull Rock), not much bigger. The Fiana took her — a fairy woman like Cnu himself — out of that place which was of course the otherworld, and the two little people were happily married.

Hunting at Killarney were the Fiana when a beautiful, golden haired girl, Niamh, came towards them on a white horse and persuaded Oisin, Fionn's son, to come with her to her kingdom. They both

Rossbeigh

mounted on the horse and galloped towards the sea at Glenbeigh. At the end of the great strand at Rossbeigh, where the legendary wave Tonn Toime roars between Rossbeigh and Inch, they took to the sea and galloped over it to Tir na nOg, the land of everlasting youth. After what seemed a short period of bliss — but was really three hundred years — Oisin was given the loan of the white horse to pay a visit to his folk, but warned not to set foot on the land of Ireland. He came in off the sea at Rossbeigh and climbed to the high peaks of Bealach Oisin (Ballaghisheen) in search of his former comrades so often to be found hunting around Glencar. Disconsolately, he sought them throughout Ireland. At Glenasmole, near Dublin, seeing a group of puny men struggling with a big stone, he leaned over, easily lifted the stone but broke his girth, fell on the ground, and immediately became a very old man. The horse galloped away.

The leader of the group helped by Oisin was St. Patrick. There followed long dialogues between the old pagan and the christian saint, by means of which the old stories of the great deeds of the Fiana came to be preserved in writing. These dialogues mirrored the long love-hatred that was to persist between the old gaelic and the new christian cultures, until a synthesis was achieved, typified in the eventual saving of the old, recalcitrant pagan's soul.

These stories were especially popular in the latter days of gaelic culture. The fourth earl of Desmond, who died in 1398, makes constant reference in his poetry to Diarmaid and Grainne and to other love tales. By the sixteenth century these tales, according to Gerard Murphy, 'had come to represent what was typically native in storytelling — and when Mairi nighean Alastair Ruadh in the seventeenth century mentions *greis ar uirsgeil na Feinne* (a period devoted to telling tales of the Fiana) as the regular ending to the feast, the board-games, and harping, which followed a day spent in hunting by a lord of the Scottish Mac Leods, the words, applied to the household of a sixteenth or seventeenth-century Irish lord, would doubtless remain equally true'. It was, of course, through this Scottish channel that the Fenian (or Ossianic) literature reached the world.

(IV) KING CYCLE

There is a series of some seventy surviving tales centred on Irish kings for a period of about 1400 years to about 1000 AD. The earlier figures were mythological; the later ones had some historical basis; the change from saga to history can be dated to about 730 AD. The stories often centre around the exploits of the high kings at Tara. As these, for eight hundred years at least, did not include a Munster man there is not a great deal of much relevance to our area. There are a number of sub-categories of these tales; two of the main ones were (1) origin tales, telling how some tribes etc. originated, and (2) *imrama,* or voyage tales.

1. Origin tales

One of the earliest kings of Ireland — of the fourth century BC — was

Labraid Loingseach who as a boy became dumb when his uncle killed the boy's father and grandfather and then fed him a piece of the heart of each and a goblet of their blood, as well as a live mouse 'as far as the tail'. The boy later recovered his speech through being hit in a hurling game, and later still was banished from Tara with the poet Ferchertne and the harper Craiphtine. They were welcomed by the king of Fir Morca, west of Castleisland. (This may well have been Armorica, now Brittany). The king had a daughter Moriath who was carefully guarded by her mother, whose two eyes never slept at once: one was always watching the girl. Craiphtine one night played such sweet music that the mother's two eyes slept and the young people came together. When the mother wakened she noticed that the daughter was 'breathing like a wife'. Labraid owned up and was accepted as a son-in-law. Moriath's father helped him with foreign aid to regain his kingdom and his revenge, which involved burning to death seven hundred of his enemies, as well as his mother, in the iron house of Dinn Rig. This story is the origin tale of the Laginian invaders, the last before the coming of the goidels, in the third century BC.

The first goidelic king of Munster may have been the invader Mug Nuadat. He was also called Eogan Mor. He was foster son of the god Nuada, hence Mug Nuadat, servant of the god. He is reputed to have landed at Kenmare and, having, like Joseph, stored food for seven years against famine, acquired the lands of two local kings. The invaders then moved north and attacked Conn of the hundred battles, but were heavily defeated and Mug Nuadat had to flee. He was hotly pursued by Goll Mac Morna, one of the Fiana. He was saved only through the love and power of the goddess Etain who changed rocks near Kenmare into the likenesses of soldiers. While Goll and his men spent their time hacking at these Mug and his party escaped to Etain on Beare Island. They then left for Spain. Here Mug married a Spanish princess, Beara, and after nine years of exile again invaded Ireland, landing at Beare Island and naming it after his wife. He then arranged to partition Ireland between Conn and himself, so that the northern part was known as Conn's half and the southern part as Mug's half.

One of Mug's descendants was Eogan from whom descended the great Munster family of the Eoganacht, to which O Sullivans, Mac Carthys and O Donoghues belonged. Eogan was killed in the great battle of Mag Mucrama in Connacht in 195 AD. Before the battle he went to Ossory to gain the help of a druid who agreed to travel with him. The druid's daughter, Moncha, went with them as charioteer. The druid knew that Eogan would die the next day, and, foreseeing the great future of the Eoganacht, arranged for his daughter to lie with Eogan. When the baby began to arrive the druid father foretold that if it could wait until the following day the child's progeny would rule over Ireland forever. To prevent delivery until the next morning Moncha sat on a stone in the river Suir. The child's head was flattened on the stone, and the mother died. The child, from whom sprang the Eoganacht, was called Fiacha Flat-Head.

Another of these origin tales is that of the Ciarraige. Fergus Mac

20

Roich was a pledge for the safety of the sons of Uisneach when they returned with Deirdre to Ireland. When Conor Mac Nessa broke this pledge and killed Deirdre's husband, Naisi, and his two brothers, Fergus fled to Connacht and, by its queen, Medb, had triplet sons. These moved to Tara and stayed there until the time of Niall Mac Eachach, and then dispersed, one to Connacht, one to Clare, and one – Ciar – to Kerry where he founded the Ciarraige and left his name.

The Corcu Duibne had a more complex origin tale. Corc was the twin son of Duben and her father (or brother) Cairbre Musc. This sin led to much scarcity and one of the twin sons, Cormac, was put to death; but Corc was taken by the druid Dinioch to Beare Island (Inis Baoi). Each day he was mounted on a cow (or bull) and his sinfulness was washed into the animal by Dinioch's wife Baoi. After a year the animal jumped into the sea and became Cow (or Bull) Rock, and Corc returned to his people. In other accounts Corc's foster mother was called Digde, Dige, or Duinech who 'passed into seven periods of youth so that every husband used to pass from her to death of old age, so that her grandchildren and great-grandchildren were peoples and races'. She was the Old Woman of Beare whose lament seems to many to be the greatest of Old Irish poems.

About the end of the fourth century AD Feidlimid was king of Munster. On a tour of his province he and his party got stuck in deep snow at Ath Lochi, near Dunloe, Killarney. In the nearest dwelling lived Gulide, formerly a great satirist and a hospitaller, that is, a great landowner required, according to Irish law, to give hospitality to travellers. Now, however, he was an old man of seven score years living alone with his daughter. When the king and his great party drew up before the old man's enclosure sounding horns and trumpets, Gulide, notwithstanding his obligations, sent his daughter 'to make a fine speech (segantus briathar) so that they may pass from us tonight'. The girl went out and made a tremendous speech about their past hospitality, present poverty and absence now of food. She apologised for her poor speech and wished that her three elder sisters might have been there to speak instead. The king, however, was delighted with her eloquence and gave her the beautiful stretch of land from Drung hill, near Glenbeigh, up to Loch Lein. At this, the girl relented and invited the party into the house where they stayed in great content for three days and three nights.

Mor Muman was the daughter of Aed Bennan, king of Iar Mumu and of Munster, who died in 619 (or 621). She became deranged and wandered through Ireland for two years, ending up tending sheep for Fingen Mor Aedo, king of Munster at Cashel. At the prompting of Fingen's wife, he went to bed with her, whereupon she was restored to her senses and to her great beauty. The king dismissed his queen, and made Mor his wife. When he died she married, it seems, his two successors.

2. Imrama

These are tales of voyages, usually into the western ocean. The main one is that of Bran who with his party travelled for long periods amongst the magical western islands, spending a presumed year on the Island of Women. Eventually they returned to their starting place, Srub Brain or Brandon Point, and one of the party, Nechtan, went on shore to collapse into a heap of dust. Whereupon the voyagers once more set sail and were never heard of again. Bran may have been a Kerry man and it seems that it was from him that Mount Brandon was named.

In the same genre is the Voyage of Maelduin which, christianised, was the immediate model for the later, medieval story of the voyage of St Brendan.

Another of these tales is that of Tadg Mac Cein whose wife was carried off from Beare island and whom he sought through magical islands.

A feature of many *imrama* is a sojourn in an earthly or ocean paradise. In christian times the journey sometimes became a *fis*, a vision of the afterworld of christian beliefs – heaven, purgatory and hell. The earliest of this genre is that of Fursa who has associations with Kilmakilloge and Cahersiveen. His visions have been reported by Bede. St Brendan in his Atlantic voyages seems to have penetrated to the next world. He was, of course, the most famous of these travellers and the one with the greatest influence on medieval Europe.

Perhaps the finest of these visions is that of Adamnan in the 7th century: it looks as if this directly influenced Dante's great poem. Nearly as popular as St Brendan's voyage was the Vision of Tundale, written in 1149 in Ratisbon by a Munster monk, Marcus, in the tradition of Adamnan. Tundale (from Tnuthgal or Tnudgal) was a soldier of King Cormac Mac Carthy who related to the monk his vision of a journey through hell, purgatory and heaven.

FOLK TALES

There is in Ireland a great wealth of folk tales. These are the remains of an old and high tradition. It was the mark of a successful poet that he should have at his command many scores of the old literary tales we have been glancing at – of old gods and mythical invaders, of kings, of Ulidians, of the Fiana. These stories were told in the duns of the old Irish chieftains and in the great stone castles to gaelic and anglo-norman lords, such as Mac Carthy Mor and the earl of Desmond in the long winter nights after days spent in hunting. It is probable that, parallel with aristocratic practice, the common folk prized similar, if less literary, tales. When gaelic culture broke down the two streams – literary and folk – coalesced in some degree and, especially in Irish speaking districts such as south and west Kerry, continued into the present time. Ireland is one of the richest sources in the world for folk tales, and Kerry one of the richest sources in Ireland.

These tales stretch back to the most primitive forms of indo-european

Gap of Dunloe

stories up through the myths we have been looking at until they engulf known historical figures. Thus in Kerry, the gaelic poet, Gearoid Iarla, the fourth earl of Desmond, is a focus for many legends; so is the gaelic lord O Donoghue of Ross castle, Killarney; another is Piaras Feiriteir, the 17th century poet and patriot; another the 18th century poet Eoghan Rua O Suilleabhain. A more recent, but major, folk hero is that great Kerryman, Daniel O'Connell.

The first collection of oral folk tales in these islands was that of T. Crofton Croker, that lover of Killarney, in 1825; but it was not until towards the end of the century that an American, Jeremiah Curtin, became the pioneer in the scientific collecting and publishing of Irish folk tales; Kerry was a major source of those he collected.

The tradition of story telling — and the pride of and respect for the master story teller — rapidly ebb away; but around the fireplaces — especially in the Irish speaking areas — in the pubs and, occasionally by a roadside ditch, one can still come across these tales. A well known collection from Kildreelig, Ballinskelligs is *Leabhar Sheain I Chonaill.* Glimpses of the tradition can be seen in the Blasket autobiographies, particularly that of Peig Sayers. She is reported to have given 375 stories for recording.

Chapter 2   The Celtic Invaders

The next chapters attempt a history of Kerry. They have to overcome great difficulties.

First, history comes from the study of written sources, and writing did not come to Ireland until about 400 AD. However, what was later written did embody a good deal of information stretching back, however dimly, to about 500 BC, that is, from early in the iron age proper. Thus, some sort of history of Ireland can be apprehended, stretching over perhaps 2,400 years. It helps to clarify the outlines if we think of the 2,400 years of Irish history divided into three periods of about 800 years apiece, each period concerned, in imitation of the ancient model, with an 'invasion' and its aftermath. Thus, we have the following periods:

I.	500 BC - 400 AD	The Celtic Invasion
II.	400 AD - 1200 AD	The Christian 'Invasion'
III.	1200 AD - to date	The English Invasion.

These are not water-tight periods. They overlap, and they must be sub-divided. Different labels might have been given to them. Nonetheless they represent meaningful groupings of the principal trends. In each of these periods there were significant occurrences in, and in relation to, that area we now call Kerry.

The second difficulty comes from the fact that the history of Ireland has not been adequately pieced together, and for those periods that have been documented it still lacks crucial insights.

Thirdly, for the earlier periods there was no such unit as 'Kerry' so that it is difficult to distinguish the area from larger parts of Munster or from the province as a whole. For the later periods the history of Kerry is not much different from the whole Irish story.

Fourthly, a big part of the story is ecclesiastical history; but there is no good history of the church in Ireland and, lamentably, no diocesan history of Kerry.

Nonetheless, there were happenings in Kerry that played a part in the development of Irish history, and some that give insights into the story as a whole.

THE CELTIC INVASION: 500 BC — 100 BC.

The considerable body of myth and legend about what happened in Kerry in celtic times throws some light on celtic history and religion in the time from the coming of the iron age invaders to the coming of christianity. Through the myths we can discern the shadowy features of that ancient life from about the 6th century BC.

The account and the dating of the 'invasions' from Parthalon downwards were attempts by gaelic writers in christian times to establish the continuity of their tenure of Ireland — notwithstanding the subject peoples — to neolithic times and, by way of spurious genealogies beyond those times, to trace the descent of the leading families from Adam. Little of this will withstand the test of criticism; but as T.F. O'Rahilly says, 'after criticism has done its legitimate utmost, there remains a modest residuum from which important historical deductions can be drawn'.

From Irish sources the archaeologists can identify the iron age influences beginning about 800 BC, some traces of iron age invaders from about 500 BC and definite evidence from about 300 BC. The philologists, working on the ancient myths, have been able to piece together an account of what took place. This is an area of much scientific infighting that the layman treads on at his peril. The account that follows rests on T. F. O'Rahilly's great book *Early Irish History and Mythology,* in effect a *Lebor Gabala Erenn.* It should, however, be recalled that other scholars would, less convincingly, put the first celtic invaders back by 1000 years or more and would relate them to the beaker invasion. One of the difficulties put forward against O'Rahilly's scheme is that he puts the Goidels as the latest invaders; but they spoke a q-celtic which is an earlier form than the p-celtic spoken by his earlier invaders. It is also argued that as Ireland was substantially goidelicised by the fifth century the process may not have had time to complete itself if they came as late as 100 BC. Another difficulty is that the earliest examples of written Irish are on the ogam stones, largely concentrated in the alleged non-goidelic areas (e.g. in the territory of the Corcu Duibne). Moreover, the goidelic language was introduced into Scotland by the Dal Riata, who were Erainn. Nonetheless, the only coherent account of the pre-historic period is, for all its weaknesses, that given by O'Rahilly.

The 'waves' of invasions in the myths are seen by O'Rahilly as successive celtic invaders in the period 500 to 100 BC or thereabouts. Four distinct groups can be identified. The first of these were the Picts (in Irish, the Cruithin) who may not have been celtic in origin; indeed, they may have constituted the people of Ireland (and Britain) before the first celtic invasion. They remained prominent to historic times, mainly in the north of Ireland and the north of Britain, but also in other parts of Ireland. They were the *Pretani* who gave their name in classical times to the Pretanic, or British, Isles. A few traces of their language survive in Scotland but have not been elucidated. It may be a mixture of early celtic and of whatever language was spoken by the bronze age inhabitants of Ireland or, even, from the stone age because the few traces suggest a non indo-european language. They were unusual in that they practised polyandry and had matrilineal succession. Mac Neill says that Queen Medb may have been of the pictish people. This would help to explain her notably free way with men. It is remarkable how many of the great centres of Irish life — Tara, Emain Macha, Tailltiu — were reputedly founded by women and, of course, the leader of the first reputed invasion of Ireland was Cessair, a woman. This suggests that the pictish system of polyandry and matrilineal succession may have been widespread, at least amongst the ruling classes. So far as Kerry is concerned, the Ciarraige, who gave their name to the county and who were supposed to have descended from Medb, may, according to Mac Neill, have been a pictish tribe.

Next, perhaps 100 years later, came the Fir Bolg (or Iverni or Erainn) who were clearly celtic and, according to O'Rahilly, can be identified with the Belgae from north Gaul who invaded Ireland from Britain. (One must point out that the archaeologists would dispute this: the Belgae invaded England in the first century BC, not the fifth, according to the archaeological evidence; and there is none that they reached Ireland much before the beginning of the christian era.) The Fir Bolg are especially associated with Cork and Kerry and it would seem that it was here that they first landed. They, of course, made their way north. They are the people of Cu Chulainn, Conor Mac Nessa, Deirdre, and, especially in Kerry, Cu Roi Mac Daire. They claimed to be descended from the god Daire through his son Lugaid who, traditionally, led them from Britain to Ireland. It has been suggested that the great Irish saga, the *Tain,* was an account of the struggle of these people against the later invaders, the Goidels. Some of the great stone forts can be identified with these people — the greatest of them, Dun Aengus and Dun Conor on the Aran Islands — are theirs. Caherconree is, of course, firmly linked with Cu Roi Mac Daire who was, possibly, their god Bolg, god of lightning, and also the sun god. It may also be that Staigue and some at least of the circle of stone forts around the coastline of south Kerry were built by the southern branch of the Fir Bolg who came to be called the Erainn and, by Ptolemy, the Iverni.

The third group of invaders were the Laginians (as well as the Gailion and the Fir Domnann) who overran Leinster and Connacht, but do not seem to have come south.

Before the arrival of the Goidels, therefore — and in practice for some centuries after they came — the country consisted of four kingdoms, roughly equivalent to the present provinces of Munster, Leinster, Ulster and Connacht. We may perhaps think of the provinces of Ulster and Munster as predominantly ruled by the Fir Bolg, with Leinster (and to some extent at least) Connacht ruled by the Laginians and their allies. There were some Picts in the north east of Ulster and scattered in other parts of Ireland as far south as Bantry; but what became of the earlier, pre-celtic inhabitants (if they were not the Picts) we do not know. No doubt they constituted the bulk of the unfree tribes referred to in the later texts.

The fourth group of invaders were the Goidels (or Gaels) who later claimed to be the Milesians. They came from Gaul in two waves about 100 BC. The earlier of the goidelic invasions was under Mug Nuadat (servant of Nuadu, or Nodens) also called Eogan Mor. He landed at the head of the Kenmare River. Here he was faced, at Carn Buide nearby, by the two Erainn kings but, with a diplomacy rare in those blood-stained times, Mug Nuadat, apparently through having abundant supplies at a time of famine, seems to have had himself accepted as king by the local people who drove out their kings. This may have been the origin of the Eoganacht kingdom of Loch Lein, later to rise into the kingdom of West Munster. Mug

Nuadat himself came to rule in some other part of the south of Ireland, possibly in East Munster. Eventually, and inevitably, he was killed in battle.

The second wave of the Goidels was to establish the kingdom of Meath in the middle part of the country. Thus, to the four traditional kingdoms a fifth was added — the gaelic word for province was *coiced,* a fifth. The early part of the *Annals of Inisfallen* point out that before the great goidelic king Conn seven kings of the pictish people ruled over Ireland.

From the earliest times, historically, we find what is now Kerry inhabited by three distinct peoples — the Ciarraige, the Corcu Duibne and the Eoganacht Locha Lein. Of these, the Eoganacht were goidelic. The Corcu Duibne were belgic Erainn. The Ciarraige were of more obscure origin. They were not unambiguously pictish; but the legend that they descended from Ciar, the son of Medb (who may have been pictish) which suggests some form of matrilineal succession, may possibly mean that they had *some* pictish origins. If so, the three ruling peoples in Kerry at the beginning of historical times incorporate in themselves three of the four major influences of those times. To these three ruling groups there were certain subject people, such as the Alltraige, the Ui Fearba, the Ui dTorna, who left their names on places — Altry, Offerba, O Dorney — but we know little of their origins.

THE RISE OF THE GOIDELS: 100 BC — 400 AD.

The Goidels came to dominate the country not by force of numbers but by their skill in war and politics and by a higher civilisation, rather like the anglo-normans many centuries later. But, as with the anglo-normans, the conquest was a slow business, and seems to have been the basis for the great sagas of the heroic age. 500 years after their arrival, at the beginning of the fully historical time around 400 AD, the Goidels had established two strong dynasties. That at Tara, founded by the Ui Neill, conquered the northern half of the country, having splintered and subjected the Erainn kingdom of Ulidia, and subjected the lesser pictish kingdoms, the northern part of the kingdom of Lagin and some part of Connacht.

They also, as the Roman empire collapsed, spread to Britain. Indeed their success as raiders to and settlers in Britain may have been the cause of their rise to power in Ireland. This certainly seems to be true of the second dynasty, the Eoganacht, that established the kingdom of Munster, based on Cashel, at about the same time. The people of Eogan, the early goidelic invaders of Kerry, had not quickly established sovereighty over the whole of Munster. Partly by peaceful penetration, partly by war, they had established several petty kingdoms in Munster and south Leinster. In the fourth century AD they penetrated the Suir valley and established, with the help of Erainn allies, the Deisi, undisputed mastery over east Munster and south Leinster. About 400 AD, after substantial conquests in Britain, they established their seat at Cashel, strong in itself and strategically

Staigue Fort

placed. Here the Eoganacht kings were to rule, on the whole very peacefully, and virtually undisturbed, for over 500 years as kings of Munster, comprising with south Leinster and south Connacht, the southern half of Ireland, Leath Mhoga, or Mug's Half.

The people of Mug, or Eogan, came to be called the Eoganacht, and it was from them that the great Kerry and Cork families of Mac Carthy, O Sullivan and O Donoghue claimed descent — 'those princes my fathers served before Christ's death', as the dying poet Aodhgan O Raithile was to claim in the eighteenth century.

Beneath the kings of Munster were the kings of East Munster and of West Munster (Iar Mumu). The latter were the kings of the Eoganacht Locha Lein, a goidelic sept that, very sensibly, settled around the shores of the lakes of Killarney. The kingdom of West Munster was considerable, stretching from Cork through Limerick to the present Galway border. This kingdom contained a number of eoganacht septs and, of course, a considerable number of pre-goidelic peoples, notably for our purposes the Ciarraige and the Corcu Duibne in what is now Kerry.

The division of Ireland between two gaelic kingdoms did not mean that Ireland became uniformly gaelic. Perhaps 1,000 years after their arrival the gaels were still only established in a third of the petty states of the country; the other two-thirds paid tribute to the gaelic kings who maintained themselves often after fierce struggles with some and with the aid of others. Thus, large numbers of the pre-gaelic, perhaps pre-celtic, peoples survived well into historical times in the greater part of the country. It has been argued that the word *baile* (town or townland) is a pre-goidelic word and that where it is widely used, as in Kerry, the pre-goidelic indigenous people of Ireland

long survived undisturbed. That the gaels, who were later so fiercely to resent anglo-norman ascendancy, could feel themselves to be an ascendancy group contemptuous of the subject populations emerges from this extract from an ancient book, quoted by Mac Neill:

'Everyone who is black-haired, who is a tattler, guileful, tale-telling, noisy, contemptible; every wretched, mean, strolling, unsteady, harsh and inhospitable person; every slave, every mean thief, every churl, every one who loves not to listen to music and entertainment, the disturbers of every council and every assembly, and the promoters of discord among people — these are the descendants of the Fir Bolgs, of the Galians, of the Lioguirne, and of the Fir Domhnann in Eirinn. But the descendants of the Fir Bolg are the most numerous of these.'

These political events were to have their effect on the artistic life of the country. A number of idols, often three-faced, with typical long celtic faces have survived and it may be that, as we shall see, the reputed head of Crom Dub in Cloghane church is one of these. But there was a sharp falling off in the great tradition of metal work. The great struggles in the north that ended in the overthrowing of the Erainn kingdom of Ulidia are, it is claimed, echoed in the wonderful stories of Cu Chulainn and his compatriots, Queen Medb, and the rest. Towards the end of this period grew up the stories of Fionn and the Fiana, so many of which had their location in Kerry. This practice of story-telling, and the memorising of long passages of genealogies and ancient laws, and knowledge of the special subject of topography, were part of the tasks of the learned men — popularly classed as druids — who orally handed down this culture in schools in which they gave extended and intensive training to young men. At this period there grew up, probably in Kerry, the first kind of writing in Ireland, ogam script.

Chapter 3 The Christian Invasion

By about 400 AD the gaelic overlords had established themselves in the kingdoms of Tara and Cashel. Under the last-named were the two gaelic sub-kingdoms of East and West Munster, of roughly equal size. For the next half millenium or so the gaelic rulers were content to hold the highest honours in the society as a whole, but for the rest to rule directly only a third of the petty kingdoms. The non-gaelic kingdoms, in general, paid tribute. Thus the area we now call Kerry was incorporated in the kingdom of West Munster that arose about the beginning of the fifth century AD and was ruled until soon after 800 AD by the gaelic sept, the Eoganacht of Loch Lein. The two non-gaelic kingdoms of the Ciarraige and the Corcu Duibne were tributaries of West Munster until it declined into a petty kingdom around Killarney. They then became direct tributaries of Cashel.

The kings of Cashel normally pursued for some centuries a peaceful policy. Of the twenty or so kings between 400 and 800 AD only three died in war. Thus the kingdom grew in wealth and civilisation and, in the seventh and eighth centuries, became the centre for the cultural and intellectual development of the country as a whole, both secular and religious. It was not until the kingdom of Meath began to break up around 600 AD and to lose its hegemony over the northern half of Ireland that the Cashel kings aimed, unsuccessfully, at the political unity, under their sovereignty, of Ireland as a whole.

We have a few indications of the rise of the Eoganacht. Their legendary ancestor in the fifth century AD was Corc Mac Luigthig who went to Scotland and there married a pictish princess by whom he had Cairpre Luachra, ancestor of the Eoganacht Locha Lein. Corc came back to Ireland, married again here and became king of Cashel. This name comes from the Latin *castellum,* and Corc may have been one of the Irish rulers expelled at this time from north Wales. Cairpre arrived from Scotland to Cashel, but was driven out and went to Killarney. His son, Maine, about the middle of the century got the stewardship of Munster, and his son again, Duach (or Dui Iarlaithe) was the first powerful king of West Munster. Duach refused allegiance to Oengus, king of Cashel, and was driven to take refuge on the Skellig. When Oengus died in 490 Duach seized the kingship of Cashel, but was killed in battle near Knockainey, Co. Limerick. His death was avenged by his warlike daughter Croinseach, but after him few kings of West Munster played any part in the history of Cashel although, in the ensuing centuries, there was constant warfare between the two kingdoms of East and West Munster.

But, of course, the main event of this period is the arrival, the acceptance and the stimulus of christianity and with it the impact, however diluted, of roman civilisation on the evolution of a gaelic nation state.

The history of the 400 years, from 400 to 800 AD, falls into two almost equal parts — the coming of christianity, to 600 AD; and the making of a christian and gaelic nation, to 800 AD. These periods are reasonably distinct, but they overlap.

About 400 AD, therefore, Kerry was part of the gaelic kingdom of West Munster. There does not seem to have been in what is now the county any significant gaelic settlement, except around Killarney, in perhaps the present barony of Magunihy. It is also possible that there was at least a gaelic presence in the baronies south of this — in Dunkerron, Glanerought and Beare. For the rest, most of the present county was held by the two subject people, the Ciarraige and the Corcu Duibne.

In the north of the county, in the present baronies of Trughanacmy, Clanmaurice and Iraghticonnor, were settled the Ciarraige. They disputed this area with another — perhaps older — people, the Alltraige, who occupied what came to be called the cantred of Altry, approximating to the present barony of Clanmaurice. About the 6th century the Ciarraige established their kingship over the whole of north Kerry. Their origin is obscure but, as we have seen, they may have been picts. Mac Neill mentions them as being of the Mugdoirn of of unknown race who may have been the aboriginal inhabitants. They seem to have originated in the neighbourhood of Tralee and in time spread over the whole of north Kerry. Ciar-raige — from which the modern 'kingdom of Kerry' comes — is supposed to mean the kingship of (the people of) Ciar. Thus was provided in the later, gaelic, times of the sixth-seventh century by the poet Luccreth moccu Cherai, an impeccable pedigree for these people, in that Ciar being the triplet son of Fergus Mac Roich and Queen Medb and she, although probably a pictish queen, being regarded as the gaelic goddess of sovereignty, any child of hers would be well found. Nonetheless, this pedigree did not save the Ciarraige from paying a stiff tribute to the kings of Cashel. In fact, -raige means 'the people of' and ciar means 'black', describing some divine ancestor or totem, 'the god by whom my people swear', as the law texts put it. Nearly all the -raige peoples were 'subject, tribute-paying peoples'.

The Ciarraige reputedly had their seat at Teamhar Luachra. O'Rahilly says there was no such place. If it did exist it must have been close to Sliabh Luachra and within striking distance of Castleisland. The Ciarraige seem to have run into trouble towards the end of the sixth century. Some time between 555 and 577 AD some at least of the Ciarraige, under Cairbri Mac Conaire, were expelled into Connacht and an old tale tells how they got land in the modern Roscommon, to the dissatisfaction of the locals. With the Alltraige they played a prominent part in the spread of christianity. Between them they contributed two leading christian saints, Brendan and Mochuda. Their missionary efforts among their kindred in east Connacht led to the establishment of two bishoprics there, Clonfert and Annaghdown, as well as to another at Lismore.

From the eighth century at least they were ruled by the O Conor Kerry family who played an active part, on land and on water, in the disorders of the eleventh and twelfth centuries. The anglo-normans confined them to the barony of Iraghticonnor, that recalls their name, centred on Ballylongford. Here they held out until the ruin of the old Irish order in the seventeenth century.

The south and west of the country were in the hands of a people of

26

the Erainn, the Corcu Duibne, that is the seed of the goddess Dovvinias, as it appears on the ogam stones, or Duben in more modern form. In historical times the Corcu Duibne were also tributaries of gaelic states. They were a gifted people. They seem to have been the builders of the great stone forts. Amongst them grew up in the 6th to 10th centuries the 'city' of Fahan, west of the modern Dingle and as populous as it. This was most unusual in pre-Norse Ireland. The Corcu Duibne contributed considerably to celtic religion in Ireland. Amongst them grew up some of the most striking of the Fenian tales. It is probable that they invented the first Irish form of writing, the ogam script. They made a notable contribution to the spread of christianity, not only in Kerry but in north Munster which then included both the present south Leinster and south Connacht. Amongst them grew up one of the most remarkable manifestations of christianity in Ireland, the eremitical movement, the little christian settlements that dot the two peninsulas of south and west Kerry. The remarkable St Fionan Cam was of this people. To them also belonged the early seventh century poetess Liadan whose love story is in some of the earliest of Irish poems.

The name of this people is now the name of the modern barony of Corkaguiney, in effect, the Dingle peninsula. But at least in its later period the kingdom had its centre at Ballycarbery near what is now Cahersiveen and incorporated into what is now the barony of Iveragh. That this expansion may have occurred in early christian times is indicated by the ogam stones. In the Dingle peninsula a number survive with the name of the tutelary goddess, Dovvinias, but not one in Iveragh.

The history of the Corcu Duibne is difficult to piece together partly because, in general, they lived in peace, although about 700 AD one of them, Mael Braccha, intruded himself into the kingship of West Munster. With a couple of exceptions it is not until the descents of the Ciarraige from the north, and of the Eoganacht invasion — both in the eleventh-twelfth centuries — that we hear of them and of their ruling families of O Falvey and O Shea — the former from what is now Corkaguiney and the latter from Iveragh. They seemed to have ruled alternately.

In the twelfth century the Corcu Duibne seem to have disappeared without a trace. In 1138 died Mahon, son of Corc, king of the Ciarraige and Corcu Duibne, and tanist of Munster. From this description it looks as if the kingdom had been annexed by the Ciarraige who were vigorous at that time. Later, their kingdom was divided between the anglo-normans — mainly geraldines — in the Dingle peninsula, and the Mac Carthys in Iveragh. The territory they had held along both sides of Dingle Bay was granted to Geoffrey de Marisco under the name of 'Ossuris' (Aes Iorruis) which suggests that by 1200 they were in complete decline.

It may have been that the baronies of Dunkerron, Glanerought and Beare, later overrun by the O Sullivans, were part of the kingdom of the Eoganachta Locha Lein. The usual sources are silent on these areas. That Aed Bennan, an Eoganacht king, had a fort at Ardea may

be of some significance; his daughter Mor was, of course, the ancestress of the O Sullivans.

THE COMING OF CHRISTIANITY

This was the framework into which christianity arrived and achieved a fine flowering. There is a persistent tradition of christianity in the south of Ireland some time before St Patrick's mission in the mid-fifth century. This, if true, arose from the close link between some of the southern statelets with Britain where christianity had been established in the third century. It would seem that this is perhaps how ogam writing came to be invented. Some christian communities in Britain may, in the troubled times after the Romans withdrew in 410, have fled for shelter to Ireland. There was also direct contact with Gaul. For example, the Corcu Loegde of west Cork were engaged in a considerable wine importing business from Gaul.

Of the four or five reputed pre-Patrician missionaires — possibly of British birth — two had some connexion with Kerry. Abban, from Wexford, came to Killarney and founded Ceall Achaidh (or Aithfe) Conchinn which, he prophesied, would come to be called after St Fionan. This may refer to Aghadoe.

The other, and more likely, pre-Patrician saint was Kieran of Saigir, 'first born of the saints of Erin' possibly as early as 357 AD, according to the *Annals of Inisfallen*. He is named after his main foundation in Offaly, but was brought up amongst his mother's people, the Corcu Loegde, on Clear Island, Co. Cork. He is said to have spent a time as a hermit in the old copper mine at Coad, near Caherdaniel, and to have composed the rule of his monastery there. He began monastic life in a small way — perhaps because christians were so scarce, and there are associated with him stories of dealings with wild animals that are such an engaging feature of early Irish hagiography. A boar was the first member of his community, and helped him to clear a site in the woods, felling trees and hauling logs. They were soon joined by a wolf, a badger and a fox, as well as a deer and her fawn. After a long time the native character of the fox got out of control and, wearying of the vegetarian life, he stole Kieran's slippers and fled to eat them in secret. Kieran sent the badger after him. The badger brought back the unwilling fox, the slippers unchewed. Kieran admonished the errant monk and ordered him to fast and do penance; and the fox settled down again to the discipline of monastic life.

The main christian mission came to Ireland under St Patrick in the middle of the fifth century. The christian was the most productive of all the invasions. Over the centuries it led to great spiritual renewal, energy and enterprise. At home it stimulated the development of language, learning and law, as well as the arts of poetry, metal work, stone carving, illumination, music and architecture. It married the old Irish with the classical worlds in a unique way and so stimulated the growth of national consciousness. It also contributed to advances in agriculture, with its stress on corn growing, which helped to finance the whole. Abroad, it contributed bravely to restoring religion and culture in western Europe.

In the early stages it went through two phases, the missionary and the monastic.

(I) MISSIONARY

The spread of christianity throughout Ireland is associated with St Patrick, brought as a boy slave from Britain to Ireland, escaped in young manhood, returned as a missionary in middle age. He died in the latter part of the fifth century — exactly when, still causes controversy.

It seems that St Patrick attempted to establish the diocesan system, that is, the organisation based on the territorial diocese under the direction of a bishop, and divided into parishes. This was based in the roman administrative system in which the european countries, but not Ireland, were long schooled and which was at that time being revived in the towns of Gaul. This system did not fit happily into the dispersed Irish political forms and rural settlements; so it was not until the twelfth century that dioceses and parishes struck roots. St Patrick's principal missionaries and their early successors were bishops. St Patrick did not come to Kerry and it is doubtful if, as claimed, one of his principal assistants, Benignus, did either. The first bishop in Kerry seems to have been Bishop Erc, usually known by that title. His main centre was in the Ardfert area, that is, in the territory of the Alltraige, later subordinated to the Ciarraige. This was to remain the seat of a bishopric.

We can think of the missionary period as lasting for something like a century or more. Indeed, Mael Cethair, of Kilmalkedar, who seems to have been an Ulster missionary there, did not die until 636. And this mission, clearly, was only a partial success. The missionary period was overlapped, until perhaps the middle of the sixth century by a full diocesan system. Of the prominent clerics dead before 549 nearly all were bishops; between 549 and 600 they were less than half of the prominent clerics recorded; and from 600 abbots are the most numerous. Christianity was received into Ireland very peacefully, and there were no martyrs. Celtic religion seems to have been geared to accept monotheism, the trinity, and an after life, and christianity could be seen, on the plane of belief, to be a meaningful development of existing religious beliefs. In particular, the higher forms of religion, as practised by the ruling classes, rapidly succumbed to christianity. But among the plain people the older forms of animism showed great tenacity. The peaceful penetration of christianity in such circumstances depended on the acceptance and christianising, or the toleration, of some pagan practices. The pilgrimages to holy wells, still so frequent in Kerry, illustrate acceptance and christianising. (It is notable that not one of the wells in Kerry is dedicated to St Patrick, though there is a townland of Kilpatrick near Clady bridge, Kenmare.) The setting up of christian settlements by pagan tombs shows how former religious practices were superseded. The survival of such pagan festivals as that of Lug and Crom Dub, of which Kerry gives several examples, as well as the

curious stones at the ecclesiastical settlement at Kilmalkedar and elsewhere in the neighbourhood, illustrate the need to come to terms with, and tolerate, some very odd practices. One of the habits of the pagan celts was head-hunting, and a great chief had the entrance to his house decorated with these trophies. There are many grisly stories about severed heads, the *tetes coupees* of the continental celts. When a distinctive style of Irish romanesque arose in the eleventh century, the great doorways were decorated with severed heads, such as on the wonderful west doorway of St Brendan's cathedral at Clonfert.

But there must have been some *odium theologicum*. Macalister argues that the defacement of so many ogam inscriptions, especially on the Dingle peninsula, shows the intolerance of such pagan relics of the dead where descent from the tutelary god (e.g. Dovvinias) was

West door, Clonfert

claimed for the deceased. The mutilation and overthrowing of the great dolmen at Eightercua, Waterville, may have had a similar reason. Certainly, the druids get the bad lines in the surviving stories and pagan and irreverent chieftains quickly get their deserts, usually by the use of miraculous powers. Christianity aimed to encourage crop husbandry, at the expense of cattle rearing with its pagan associations, so a mark of many christian sites is the bullaun and quern. The increase in food led to a rise in population.

(II) MONASTIC

The monastic movement was also introduced in St Patrick's time, but was in incubation for about 50 years. From early in the sixth century, it had great success in Ireland. A century after St Patrick's death it seems to have completely engulfed the diocesan system. Then, for some five centuries the church in Ireland was predominantly monastic. Bishop Erc, who perhaps died in 526, was the teacher of St Brendan (b. 484) who became one of the leaders of the monastic movement and founded a monastery at Ardfert which came to be known as Ardfert-Brendan, so probably beginning the transformation of the diocesan settlement into a predominantly monastic one. The monastic movement was derived from that in Egypt in the early fourth century and was spread in Gaul by St Martin of Tours, who died in 397. He became a prominent figure in Irish hagiology, comprising in himself the three leading strains in the christianity introduced by St Patrick: he had been hermit, founder of monasteries, and bishop. Monasticism fitted easily into the gaelic civil structure that was highly decentralised and rural. The transition was aided by the nature of Irish society as well as by the fact that the diocesan bishops lived in community with their clergy in special ecclesiastical settlements. Many monasteries, or groups of monasteries under the same rule, had a bishop on the staff, as it were, to administer special sacraments, such as holy orders; but the *administrative* duties now associated with the office came to be discharged by the abbot of a monastery or by the senior abbot of a number of monasteries grouped under a single rule. These included not only monasteries of men but also monasteries of women.

The rise of the monastic movement is associated with the 'Second Order of Irish Saints', that is, the native born ones, who tended to be priests, not bishops. They fall into two broad classes.

First, were the founders of the great monastic settlements — St Comgall of Bangor, St Finian of Clonard, St Ciaran of Clonmacnoise, St Kevin of Glendalough, and St Brigit of Kildare — places that were to become great monastic cities and centres of learning not only for students from Ireland but also, in the dark ages of european culture, from Britain and Europe. In Kerry the notable monastic city was at Ardfert; but there was also the important settlement dedicated to St Fionan at Inisfallen, Killarney. Kerry saints associated with foundations outside Kerry were St Brendan, St Cuimine Fota, St Mochuda (or Carthach), and St Fionan. Mochuda was the first to be called bishop of Kerry. When he as a young man was received into

the monastery of Kiltallagh, Castlemaine, it was by Carthach the Elder, who died in 580 so that probably by the middle of the century the monastic system had engulfed the diocesan one.

Secondly, were the travellers and missionaries. Perhaps because Irish society was so intensely local it was a mark of holiness to leave one's people and, if possible, country — this was called 'white martyrdom'. Hence, Irish saints did not do their main work amongst their own people and many are, indeed, notably restless. This was a time of great disorder in western Europe and the destruction of christianity in much of England because of the invasions of pagan Angles and Saxons. Of the missionaries the most famous was the missionary to Scotland, St. Colmcille (or Columba) of Iona, the archetypal Irishman who continues to haunt the consciousness of the Irish race; St Columbanus, the great missionary in France, Germany, Switzerland and Italy, the founder of an order of monks that achieved great influence; St Killian, who had a church in Lauragh and was martyred — one of the few — in Germany. It was these men who, in the late sixth and early seventh centuries, played a notable part in saving christianity in western Europe.

Straddling the two classes is St Brendan of Kerry. The principal monastic foundations of the Kerry saints were amongst the kindred of the Ciarraige of north Munster and east Connacht in the Shannon basin — at Clonfert and Annaghdown, Co. Galway; at Kinnitty and Rahan, Offaly. When he was driven out of Rahan, Mochuda established a monastery at Lismore, Co. Waterford, amongst the Desi, a branch of the Erainn.

The normal unit of Irish church government came to be the monastery, based on the territory of a powerful family, usually a *tuath*. As the movement grew other monasteries came to be founded in other areas. In this way an extensive monastic *paruchia* grew up over a wide area. In this system a bishop and some (relatively few) priests were necessary, honoured but not predominant figures. Ecclesiastical remains from this period were thus predominantly *monastic*. Irish monasticism, based substantially on its Egyptian prototype in its early period, was extremely ascetic. It became distinctive in its interest in intellectual and cultural values and in its remarkable missionary spirit. The establishment of monastic schools — as at Inisfallen — and of monastic cities — as at Ardfert — was one of the major strands in the development of christian Ireland. The great success of the monastic movement meant that the earlier structures were replaced many times so that the monastic ruins we now see do not give us glimpses of the earliest times.

From literary sources we know that the pattern was simple: within a ring (or stone) fort three main buildings — a church, a refectory and a guesthouse, with a number of round cells each holding from one to 14 monks. Perhaps the Reask site, now excavated, gives one the best impression of an early *monastery*, as distinct, or perhaps more accurately developed, from an eremitical site. Temple Martin, Lispole, is a good early example of a surviving monastic church within a ringfort — perhaps the other buildings were of wood, now

Early Irish monastery as reconstructed by Liam de Paor

perished; and Ratass, Tralee, shows the remains of a continuing church of the times. For parochial work a monastery tended to throw out small outposts, *cellae* (hence *cill* in Irish and many modern place names beginning Kill-). Each outpost consisted of a church with a small group of clerics. Perhaps a very early example is Killelton, near Camp.

At the risk of oversimplifying one can see two main trends in Irish monasticism. These trends tended to merge and their periods to overlap; nonetheless they are reasonably distinct. The first was predominantly missionary and ascetic, in the sixth and seventh centuries. The second, from the eighth century, was notably devoted to scholarly and cultural pursuits.

Out of the mists of early monasticism in Kerry four notable Kerrymen emerge in some degree. These are: St Brendan the Navigator, St Cuimine Fota, St Mochuda (or Carthach), and, in Kerry terms the most striking of all, St Fionan Cam.

Of these much the best known, as well as the earliest, is St Brendan, one of the 'Twelve Apostles of Ireland'. He was born in 484 at 'Fianann' in Alltraige Caille. This was the district around Tralee. 'Fianann' is usually identified with Fenit; but it has also been placed at Annagh, and other places. The Alltraige became a subject people of the Ciarraige about Brendan's time and the famous saint was appropriated by the Ciarraige. His father was Findlug, suggesting

that the saint's story has got mixed up with that of older gods. Brendan as an infant was fostered by St Ita at Killeedy in Co. Limerick. This was the saint associated with one of the few examples of genuine mysticism in Irish literature. She was permitted to nurse the infant Jesus in her cell and is supposed to have sung to him the poem beginning (Sigerson's translation):

Ísucán	*Jesukin*
alar lemm im dísiurtán	*Lives my little cell within*
Cía beith cléirech co lín sét	*What were wealth of cleric high*
is bréc uile acht Ísucan	*All were lie save Jesukin.*

As a boy Brendan was educated by Bishop Erc at Ardfert. Of them is told another delightful animal tale. They were short of milk: so every day from Sliabh Luachra came a hind and her fawn to be milked by the holy men. Brendan founded a monastery at Ardfert when a dove snatched his plans and flew with them to the place. His main foundation was at Clonfert, in county Galway, in 557. This was when he was already an old man. This became the seat of a bishopric that still survives. There is a famous west door in the hiberno-romanesque cathedral there. He founded, under his sister, a convent of nuns at Annaghdown, also in county Galway, which also became the seat of a bishopric that long survived. He is credited with missionary journeys to England and Scotland. He had considerable influence at the west of the Dingle peninsula. The great mountain there, Mount Brandon, is usually held to have been named after him, and there is on it an oratory that he is said to have founded, at the end of the Saints' road from Kilmalkedar. Other little settlements attributed to him are on the Blaskets on Inis Tuaiscirt, and on Inisdadroum in the Shannon.

As a young man he set out from Brandon Creek, below the mountain, on the first of his famous voyages in search of the paradisal island in the western ocean — as we have seen, a survival of pagan belief. Three skin-covered boats set out but, after a voyage covering five years, returned without finding the place. St Ita explained to Brendan that he could not hope to get to his destination in a skin-covered boat. It was not until he was a very old man that he got away for the second time, this time in a wooden boat. The voyage took two years, but he was successful. It was about this time that the keel was invented, so transforming ocean voyages: this may be the significance of the *wooden,* as opposed to the earlier skin, boat. It is on this journey that Brendan is supposed to have discovered America. The latin life of the saint and the ninth century account of the voyage became very famous, perhaps Ireland's single greatest contribution to european literature in medieval times; they are said to have inspired, amongst others, Columbus. The story of the voyages is, of course, based on a long series of Irish pagan romances, including the Voyage of Bran, another Kerryman it seems. There may have been some confusion between the two names, and it is likely that the mountain is named after the pagan voyager, not the saintly one. Brendan died, in his nineties, in 577 or 583. His feast day is May 16th. He is the patron saint of two modern dioceses: Kerry and Clonfert.

30

One of Brendan's successors as bishop of Clonfert and abbot of the monastery there was St Cuimine Fota (or Fada, the Tall). He was born in 592, the child of an incestuous union between his mother Mugain and her father Fiachna Find, king of the Eoganacht of Loch Lein. His mother, it is said, had twelve sons, six of them bishops, six of them kings. 'Mugain' in fact, means female slave. Cuimine was abandoned in a basket, *cuimine,* near St Ita's convent at Killeedy. He died in 662 and his feast day is November 12th. He played a prominent part in the controversy over the date of Easter and wrote a notable letter in latin to the Abbot of Iona in favour of the new method of dating. A number of stories link him with learning and the arts. He may have been the interlocutor of the Nun of Beare in the famous ninth century poem. He is also linked with the poet-lovers Liadan and Cuirithir. She was of the Corcu Duibne and he from Connacht. Impetuously she became a nun. Both regretted this. They put themselves under the guidance of Cuimine. At first he allowed them to converse, but not to look at each other. Later he permitted them to sleep together, with a young student between them; but the cure by ordeal does not work, and Cuirithir is sent to a monastery, and then overseas. A famous ninth century poem gives Liadan's lament for her lost lover. Cuimine also plays some part in the stories that cluster around King Guaire of Gort, Co. Galway, that famously generous man whose right hand was longer than his left from dint of giving. His brother Marban is credited with one of the most beautiful poems about the delights of a hermit's life. Guaire was a great patron of the arts and held a great hosting of the poets of Ireland. After a year they had not left for home and their exactions became so great that even his generosity could not cope with them. It was Cuimine who advised the king how to get rid of them. They were asked for the story of the *Tain,* which in that period of the eclipse of old Irish learning none of them knew. So they went off around Ireland in search of the tale. At length it was necessary, with the help of a kindly saint, to resurrect Fergus Mac Roich from the dead for three days while he dictated a first hand account of those great events.

Cuimine has left us a penitential that shows the austerity of life in a seventh century Irish monastery. It is not, however, as savagely strict as that of St Columbanus fifty years earlier. Cuimine apparently died in Kerry and his body was brought up the Shannon by boat for burial at Clonfert.

A third prominent Kerry monastic leader was St Mochuda (or Carthach or Carthage). He was born near the river Maine in the latter part of the 6th century. He seems, as a boy, to have come under the influence of the elder Carthage, a bishop in the territory of the Ciarraige, who died in 580. Mochuda was of the Ciarraige, or was appropriated by them. He seems to have been extraordinarily attractive as a boy. His first education was at Kiltallagh, close to Castlemaine. He was probably the first person to be called Bishop of Kerry; but he is mainly associated with two considerable monastic foundations — at Rahan, Offaly, in what was then north Munster; and at Lismore. After he had ruled Rahan for forty years he was expelled with some 850 monks by an alliance of other monastic and civil

leaders. Why this happened is not clear; but it may have been because he was a protagonist of the roman Easter and tonsure, the great disciplinary dispute in the early Irish-influenced church. There is a story that, perhaps for this reason, the three great neighbouring monasteries of Clonmacnoise, Clonard and Durrow resented his monastery and decided that he should be expelled. They cast lots as to which should carry out the expulsion, and the lot fell on Clonmacnoise. Within the Clonmacnoise *paruchia* the lot fell on Killeigh, and amongst the subordinate houses of Killeigh the lot fell on Cluain Congusa. In any event he *was* expelled and he went with his monks — most of whom were almost certainly tenants with their households — to Lismore where he founded a famous monastery which was for long the seat of a bishopric. He died in the following year (637).

In this struggle the 'romanising' party of whom Mochuda was one, were to gain victory on two issues — Easter and the tonsure; but they were to lose the other issues, the issue of the powers of bishops *vis-a-vis* abbots, of the monastic system versus the diocesan system. On these issues reform had to wait some five centuries. When it did come, the main monasteries of Kerry were either incorporated into the diocesan system when it was set up, as were Ardfert, Aghadoe, Kilmalkedar, Ratass, Church Island; or were taken over by continental orders, as were Inisfallen, Rattoo, Ballinskelligs, Aghavore; or just disappeared leaving little or no memory, such as the predecessor of Muckross, or Kiltallagh, or the little monastery on Dinish, Kenmare.

Of these monasteries, the most distinguished was Inisfallen. There is a strong association with St Fionan, but the actual founder was probably a disciple or associate of his, Faithliu. He was son of the king of West Munster, Aed Daman who died in 633, so we may perhaps date the monastery from the early 7th century. Mael Cethair, of Kilmalkedar, died in 636 and St Fionan seems to have died about the same time. We can perhaps put the late sixth and early seventh century as the time when christianity was consolidated in Kerry. There is an account of a convention, purportedly held in 550 AD, to justify a successful revolt by the subject people of Kerry some three centuries later. The convention, it was claimed, was attended by the chief clerics of the subject peoples: St Ciaran of Clonmacnoise, SS Brendan and Mochuda of the Ciarraige, SS Fionan Cam and Monessoc of the Corcu Duibne. The eminence of the clerics shows how much more strongly christianity had developed amongst the subject peoples.

We have some revealing glimpses of life in these early monasteries. From about the eighth century little poems began to be written about this life, though they were formally attributed to saints and hermits of earlier periods. No doubt the life led changed with the changing views on austerity. Several founders' rules and penitentials (punishments for stated offences) survive. These show an extraordinarily severe and austere rule based on incessant prayer —

especially with the book of psalms; work; mortification —
particularly fasting; and intense obedience and respect for the
superior. Robin Flower has translated some early poems that give a
glimpse of life in these places:

Cells that freeze
  The thin pale monks upon their knees,
Bodies worn with rites austere
  The falling tear — Heaven's king loves these.

We often hear of the ringing of the tongueless iron bell to mark the
hours of prayer, the bell that became almost a symbol of the
monastic life: (in James Carney's translation):

Clocán binn	*Melodious bell*
benar i n-aidchi gáithe	*that is struck in a night of wind*
ba ferr lemm dul ina dáil	*I had rather make tryst with it*
indas i ndáil mna baithe	*than with wanton womankind.*

Nonetheless, great importance was attached to hospitality. There
was teaching: the 'abcedarium' stone at Kilmalkedar survives as a
primitive textbook. There was the incessant copying of psalms,
gospels and other texts. An 11th century poem puts this in the
mouth of the 6th century St Colmcille:

Sínim me phenn mbec mbráenach
  tar aenach lebar lígoll
gan sgor, fri selba ségann,
  dian scith mo chrob ón scribhonn.

(I send my little dripping pen unceasingly over an assemblage of
books of great beauty, to enrich the possessions of men of art —
whence my hand is weary with writing.)

And we have living proof of the marvellous results from those weary
hands.

There was also scholarly work which played a part in later times in
creating a sense of nationhood by preserving the laws, myths and
traditions of ancient times. There was a great interest also in the
classics of Rome, and of Greece to some extent, as well as in the
study of grammar, mathematics, physics and exegesis. There was a
special interest, too, in the apocryphal works of scripture.

We read of the early foundations setting up in wild, uncultivated,
often heavily forested parts of the country, which have to be won for
cultivation by unremitting labour. However, land, property, wealth
rapidly accumulated. The bishop or abbot at the head of a
monastery soon became a man of real consequence, of equal 'honour
price' with the local petty king. The monastic lands acquired, and
retained throughout their existence to the sixteenth century, the
right of sanctuary (termon, from the latin *terminus;* hence the
townland of Termons, near Lough Currane) both for people and

property. They thus became primitive banks, with serious
consequences for them, if Dr A.T. Lucas is to be followed, in laying
themselves open to raiding, plundering and burning over a period of
800 years from about 750 AD by Irish, Norse, Anglo-Normans, and
English. The monastic lands were cultivated by monks but soon not
all of these were in orders; others, while being part of the community,
were in fact married laymen cultivating the monastic lands as clients
of the monastery, much as they might have been clients of a great
lord; on these clients rested the material well-being of the community.

The monasteries that acknowledged a single founder were grouped
into a *paruchia,* or federation, that might extend over extensive areas
both inside the country and abroad. The head of such a federation
became a very important person indeed, being of equal rank with a
sub-king. A sick monk might be moved, for his health's sake,
between monasteries of a *paruchia.* Monks often moved to and from
the eremitical offshoots of these monasteries.

HERMITS AND NATION BUILDERS, 600 - 800 AD.

The period 600 to 800 AD was marked, especially in Kerry, in the
early part of the period, by the extraordinary extent of the eremitical
movement, and over the whole period by a remarkable attempt at
nation building.

(I)   THE EREMITICAL MOVEMENT

One of the most striking effects of the christian invasion was in
causing the eremitical movement. For this Kerry was a main centre.
Relics of the movement are widespread throughout that part of the
county peopled by the Corcu Duibne.

In Egypt the growth of monasticism went hand in hand with the
growth of the eremitical movement. With a time-lag of about a
century the same was true of Ireland, especially in the west of the
country, and above all among the Corcu Duibne of south and west
Kerry. More than 50 eremitical sites have been identified in Kerry,
almost all in that territory. We do not know much about this
movement. It began to develop at the end of the 6th century and
seems to have had three sources. First was that of its Egyptian
origin in the Coptic church: the life of a hermit was considered to be
a holier, because more austere, one than that of an ordinary monk,
and many hermits retired to the 'wilderness' for which the familiar
word *disert* was used in Irish and survives in many placenames
Hence little settlements on islands and western promontories.
Secondly, many monasteries made provision for temporary spells of
hermitage — we read of St Fechin having one in Mayo for his
monastery in Westmeath. I am not aware that any such arrangement
was made in Kerry but, as we shall see, the career of St Fionan makes
this not unlikely. Thirdly, as the years went on the monasteries
became rich and began to fall away from their primitive austerity:
the hermits constituted a sort of reform movement which, it has
been suggested, had its origin in Munster, but where is not clear. This

32

movement was similar to that of the later Celi De, or Culdees.

A further light is thrown on the hermits by the remarkable lyric poetry they began to write in the seventh and later centuries about nature, the hermit's life, and, from the missionaries abroad, exile. These clerics inherited a well, if recently, developed literary language, but still lacking the personal passion that these men and women, their hearts overflowing with the love and goodness of God, as reflected in his creation, brought to it. Kuno Meyer says of these poems that they 'occupy a unique place in the literature of the world'. This quatrain gives an idea of the tone of the poetry, and of the contrast between the hermitage open to the natural world and the constriction of the monastery (James Carney's translation):

Ach, a luin, is buide duit	*Blackbird, it is well for you,*
cáit 'sa muine i fuil do net.	*wherever in the thicket be*
a dithrebaig nád clinn cloc	*your nest,*
is binn boc síthamail t'fet.	*hermit that sounds no bell,*
	sweet, soft, fairylike is
	your note.

Sometimes a hermit settled as a solitary and this quatrain from an early poem gives some of the flavour of his life:

M'oenuran im aireclan,	*Alone in my little cell,*
n'oenuran im-ne;	*alone like this;*
m'oenur do-lod forsin	*alone I came into the world*
n'oenur ragad de.	*alone I shall go from it.*

The Loher site must have held some such solitary.

No doubt it was in some such oratory that there occurred the delightful event told of St Kevin of Glendalough, which illustrates the austerity and self-discipline of Irish spirituality, and the love of nature of these hermits. One spring St Kevin retired to his hermit's oratory to pray with the *cros-fígil*, with arms outstretched. One hand, in the tiny place, had to be put through the window. A blackbird built a nest on it and, the saint being reluctant to disturb her, laid her eggs. The saint kept his hand there until she had safely hatched her brood.

Often, however, the hermits settled in groups, to share 'common services' as it were. Such groups did not share a common rule: each was a solitary to himself. Examples of this type of settlement may well be at Killabuonia near St Finan's Bay and Kildreelig on the south side of Bolus Head near Ballinskelligs. St Manchan of Liath (d. 665) is credited with a poem on the delights of a hermit's life, and he envisages twelve others with him. The large oratories at Church Island, Valentia, and at Killobarnaun, Cahersiveen, could perhaps have held such a number. Both the monastic and eremitical movements catered for women. The little oratory at Temple Cashel near Ballinskelligs and several sites on the Beare peninsula recall this. By its nature the eremitical movement did not flourish like the monastic movement so that, except in a few places — Church Island

(Valentia), Kilmalkedar, Reask — where the monastic movement superseded the old settlements, it has not been overlain by the relics of later developments. It seems as if the movement had died out by the end of the seventh century; certainly, so far as Kerry is concerned, there is nothing, apart from the striking exception of the Skellig and the oratory at Gallarus, to show that the movement there lasted later than 700 AD. In 664-7 there was a great plague in which a third of the population of the whole country died and in 682-3 another. Perhaps, as with the later Black Death these blows, the decline in population and presumably wealth such as it was, had the effect of severely cutting back this extensive religious activity. Perhaps the Skellig, remote as it was, excaped the infection.

As we stand on one of these eremitical sites overlooking the sea at the fringe of the western world we get some insight into the lives of these hermits, who so often chose such places of magnificent beauty, from a poem put into the mouth of St Colmcille, but written long after his time:

Meallach liom bheith in ucht oilein	*Happy I'd be on a rocky headland*
ar beinn cairrge,	*secure on some island*
bhfaicinn ann ar a meince	*to be watching the inconstant*
feth na fairrge.	*pulse of the sea.*
Go bhfaicinn a tonna troma os lear luchair,	*To watch the great waves of the brilliant ocean*
amhail chanaid ceol da nAthair	*seem to hymn the Father in their eternal surge*
ar seol suthain.	
Go bhfaicinn a tracht reidh rionnghlann (ni dal dubha);	*as they break on the rockpoint in thrilling white*
go gcloisinn guth na n-ean n-iongnadh,	*as strange bird calls float on the air.*
seol go subha.	

* *

Go ro sgrudainn ann na leabhair maith dom anmain;	*To study awhile just those books good for my soul;*
seal ar sleachtain ar neamh n'ionmhain,	*a spell contemplating heaven, a spell at psalms.*
seal ar salmaibh.	
Seal ag buain duilisg do charraig,	*a spell collecting duilisc on the rocks,*
seal ar aclaidh,	*a spell at fishing,*
seal ag tabhairt bhidh do bhochtaibh,	*a spell feeding the poor,*
seal i gcarcair,	*a spell in my cell,*
seal ag sgrudain flatha nimhe, naomhda a cheannach;	*a spell studying saintly men, holy this exchange —*
seal ar saothar na badh forrach; ro badh meallach.	*a spell at not too heavy work: at these I'd be happy.*

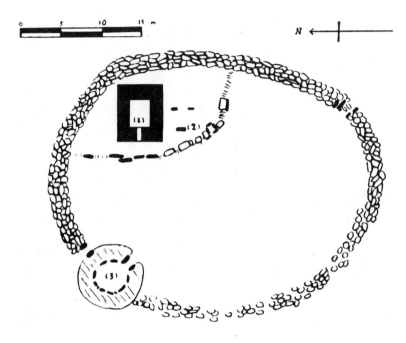

Plan of eremitical settlement at Loher:
(1) oratory; (2) cross pillar; (3) clochan

St Brendan seems to have had some influence on the eremitical movement and is represented as having spent some time as a solitary on Mount Brandon; but it is unlikely that the movement got under way until towards the end of his life near the end of the sixth century.

The monastic and the eremitical strains seem to meet in St Fionan; but here we are in a difficulty. We have no real dates for him, and there is controversy whether he was one, two or three people. The Martyrology of Donegal lists no less than nine Fionans. Only one of them seems to have Kerry connexions, Fionan Cam of Ceann-Eitigh (Kinnitty, Offaly), and of Sliabh-Bladhma (Slieve Blooms), of the Corcu Duibne, i.e., of the race of Cairbre Musc. Becnat, daughter of Cian, was his mother. He is called Cam from his squint. He also became confused with a pagan myth: he was born of a union between his mother and a red gold salmon in Loch Lein. He seems to have lived from the late sixth to the mid seventh century. According to King his dates are 560 to 630, pat and suspiciously round. Miss Hickson says he died about 655. His major foundation was at Kinnitty, Offaly, but in Kerry he is credited with monastic foundations at Inisfallen, Aghadoe, Church Island (Lough Currane), and Aghavore (Derrynane), and eremitical ones at Killemlagh (St Finan's Bay) and the Skelligs. His feast is celebrated on April 7th.

However, there was another St Fionan, called Lobhar, or the Leper.

in Leinster and it is on his feast day, March 16th, that the patron saint is commemorated e.g. at Church Island (Lough Currane). It is clear that, towards the end of the sixth century, there was a remarkable development of the eremitical movement in south and west Kerry, almost entirely confined to the territory of the Corcu Duibne, of whom Fionan Cam was one. His name is closely associated with much of this, as one would expect. We have evidence of Kerry saints moving north to christianise, and develop agriculturally, the marsh lands of the kingdom of Munster; but, apart from Mael Cethair of Kilmalkedar, we do not have during this period evidence of other missionaries moving south to Kerry. It is against parsimony to have two (or even three) St Fionans associated with this movement, these places, and this time. There are several other examples of confusion between two saints and their cults — e.g. between Pope St Gregory the Great and a local Gregory of Castlegregory. The confusion of the celebration of feast days must have occurred after one of the periods of decline in the church when such practices had fallen into disuse and records were not available. I opt, therefore, for one St Fionan, a local, in operation in south and west Kerry about this time.

If this is correct we are faced with the leader of a quite remarkable outburst of christianity. It is not necessary to credit him with every foundation; but that they should be so widely dedicated to him shows that he made a notable impact on his native area. It is clear, also, that his influence was great both on the monastic movement and on the eremitical one. There are traces of what may be more than fifty early eremitical sites in south and west Kerry; these are similar in style and seem to have been founded about the same period of the late sixth and the seventh centuries. Even allowing for the fact that some of them are very small, this shows how strong the movement was about St Fionan's time. We are faced, it seems, with a remarkable man and one who by birth, work and influence must bulk large in any history of Kerry. As one travels from Killarney out to the last vestiges of land at the Skelligs and Blaskets one cannot escape the work and influence of this man. It is likely that some at least of these settlements were places of retreat for the more austere of his monks at Kinnitty. The growth of his movement was helped by the long-standing peace of this part of Ireland and the substantial population.

One is conscious, then, of a man of energy, influence, spirituality, local patriotism and practical wisdom. He was not content to settle at his main foundation, but ensured that his native area was brought into the christian stream. He was concerned not only to establish monasteries but also that the more austere forms of spirituality be developed. He was able in this way to influence many others in his native area. He was concerned also with material welfare. The mainly silly lives that have come down to us of these men were apparently composed in the new, reformed but obviously rather uncultivated monasteries of the twelfth and thirteenth centuries. Their tall stories portray these old saints as magicians, as often malignant as beneficent, and always extraordinarily irascible. They

34

throw little, even incidental, light on the facts of the times that they purport to portray and on the personalities of what must have been remarkable men. Some of the stories have clearly got mixed up with older, magical tales of pagan gods. Nonetheless, we occasionally get from them a glimpse of something that strikes true and that tells us something about the saint's personality.

In the Irish life of Mochuda printed by Plummer there is this story:

'Once, when Finan came to visit Mochuda, he saw the monks digging, and some of them carrying bags and burdens. "It is a wretched thing" said Finan, "to make your monks into brute beasts; for it were better to have oxen for ploughing and draught, than to put such torture on the disciples of God". "We have never desired worldly possessions for ourselves", said Mochuda. "That is not well", said Finan, "for the Church to refuse alms and offerings of the secular monks [or tenants], when it gives confession and prayer in return. And let it not be so done henceforth".'

Here, indeed, is a practical man and one given to command. It is not surprising that he was able to get a great deal done, or that the important settlements at Inisfallen and Aghadoe should be dedicated to him. We mostly think of him as the leader of a spiritual movement and one of the most fascinating relics of our past are the many, largely hidden, and remote sites of the eremitical movement of those times of which he was clearly a major influence.

The most striking of St Fionan's works is the settlement on the Great Skellig. It is clear from the methods of building that this was a very early settlement, probably amongst the earliest, dating from the sixth century. It was also one of the largest and continued in use for many centuries. In all this time the original buildings and, if there was subsequent building, the original style, were maintained, except for the early medieval chapel and the (re-built) caiseal. Part of the fascination of the Skellig is that we can step directly into the unique and wholly preserved environment of the early days of Irish christianity.

One gets the impression from the simplicity of many of the sites in south Kerry that it was here that the eremitical movement began — for example, the primitive nature of the crosses at Ardkeragh and St Fionan's Well, Caherbarnagh — that it spread to the Dingle peninsula where the cross slabs were developed to a much higher level and then, perhaps, these re-acted on the sophistication of the crosses in south Kerry, as at Loher, Dromkeare, Inchfarranagleragh. It looks as though christianity had a tougher fight for survival in the Dingle peninsula.

(II) NATION BUILDING

Apart from the effects of the direct impact of christianity, the period 600 to 800 AD is notable for the attempt to develop a very ancient society into a new concept of what we would now call nationhood,

Monastic buildings, Great Skellig

especially by means of the evolution of cultural unity from many diverse strands.

1. Early Christian Society

It is commonly argued that celtic Ireland was a rural one in which, in general, there were neither towns nor villages. In this the Irish celts are considered unlike their continental ancestors who built their *oppida* in places as wide apart as Ankara, Belgrade, Milan and Trier. The general statement must be modified for Kerry at least. The early christian settlement at Fahan, west of Dingle, and possibly some others in south Kerry, was clearly a significant town.

Socially, Ireland was composed of closely knit tribes or kin groups holding territories or *tuaths*. *Tuath* means, basically, a people. There were from the 5th to the 12th centuries about 150 tuatha for a population of probably well under half a million. They were thus rather similar to a modern barony or, in norman terms, cantred. Each tuath had its king.

Corresponding to the tuath was the *tricha cet* or, in more modern form, *triochachead,* as in Trughanacmy. Tricha cet originally meant the mustering of thirty hundred fighting men (e.g. a 'legion'), and then the territory that supported them. At the outset of the historical period the tricha cet was made up of thirty units known as a *baile biatach,* or townland, or hundred. The hundred (cf. 'centurion'), like the thirty hundred, dates back to the earliest records of the indo-europeans. In Munster a hundred or *baile biatach,* which was supposed to support 300 cows, was divided into 12 ploughlands, each ploughland *(seisreach)* of 120 acres of arable land, representing 48-50 days of ploughing. In Kerry and SW Cork a ploughland could contain over 1,000 acres. Each acre corresponded to 3-4 English acres. So far as Kerry is concerned the total area of just 1.2 million acres would on this scheme demand that every acre, good and bad, be taken into account. The english acreage of a *baile biatach* in Kerry would thus come to some 6,000, a unit that came to be of significance in the Desmond plantation.

The name *baile biatach* commemorates a remarkable feature of social organisation. The country had a network of houses of hospitality where travellers were entitled to stay three days. Each was under the control of a *brugaid* or *biadhtach,* an important functionary, who held this large tract of land to support the hostel. No doubt he had a number of sub-tenants and these in later times gave the name *betagii* or *betaghs* to the serfs of feudal Ireland.

Each tuath was ruled over by a king, selected from the ruling family. The structure was highly aristocratic. There was a rigid hierarchy of birth: the nobility; the *aes dana* (professional men); freemen; serfs; and some slaves. But within these categories it was wealth of cattle and land that counted: rents, for example, were paid in livestock twice a year. The unit of society was not the individual or the family but the kin-group *(derb-fine),* all those males having a common great-grandfather. Within this group the law did not enter. It is likely that the serf and slave population of the gaelic kingdoms were the older pre-gaelic and pre-celtic populations — in much the same way as the tenants in later times were of older stock than their landlords. These unfree serfs were not declared freemen until 1605, that is, after the end of the gaelic order. The pre-celtic craftsmen and, probably, priests were honoured and free members of the gaelic society. This helped to maintain the continuity of Irish, as distinct from solely gaelic, consciousness. Moreover, as we have seen, very many of the pre-gaelic kingdoms survived. The king of a *tuath* would usually, like several others, acknowledge certain obligations to an over-king. The over-kings had obligations to the king of the province. The higher kings related only to the under-kings, and not to their people ruled by those kings. At *tuath* or higher levels there was no *apparatus* of government, no concept of a state. At the *tuath* level a king had some judicial functions, but not much. An eighth century law tract, the *Crith Gablach,* defines his occupations: 'Sunday for drinking ale, for he is not a lawful chief who does not distribute ale every Sunday; Monday for legal business, for the adjudication between *tuatha;* Tuesday for chess; Wednesday for seeing greyhounds coursing; Thursday for marital intercourse; Friday for horse-racing; Saturday for judgments'.

Each king lived in his *dun*, or royal fortress (hence the place-names beginning with Dun-). The word comes from the celtic *dunon,* which gave English the word *town;* but the first builders of organised towns in Ireland were the Norsemen, who also introduced money. In gaelic Ireland the unit of value was the *set*, the basic value of which, about 700 AD, was almost a milch cow. A higher unit was the *cumal*, or female slave, who, about the same time, was valued at seven *sets;* but it does not take much imagination to see these as shifting units of

value, too imprecise for much in the way of commerce. A basic purpose was to measure 'honour-price' or *enech*, literally 'face'. Everyone of substance had an 'honour-price' by which his status was precisely measured. The 'honour-price' of the king of a tuath was seven *cumals*, that of a *bo-aire*, a free farmer, was one *cumal.*

The basic aristocratic sport was not, of course, trading but to raid the neighbouring tribes for cattle. (The great epic of Irish literature is the Cattle Raid of Cooley). A chieftain, taking office, showed his fitness by engaging in a raid of this kind, a *creach.* This cattle raiding was to remain a feature of gaelic life to the end, and to cause loss of life in every century.

Christianity, notwithstanding its roman schooling, seems to have had no significant effect on politics or government. The roman conceptions of state, law, justice, and punishment made little impact on Irish ideas. For example, part of the tightly knit conception of Irish law, which seems to have been codified around the seventh century, was every man's 'honour price', and his close kin were caught up in this. Thus a murderer had to pay to the kin of his victim that man's honour price, or else the murderer's kin were liable. There is a suggestion that when christianity came there was an effort to change the penalty to that of death for the murderer; but this failed and, in general, the death penalty did not become a part of Irish law, except for very special crimes such as impiety and adultery. Retribution was to the injured kin who had rights, not to the injured *community,* which had none. Thus there was not achieved in Ireland, for a very long time, any conception of the public interest. Similarly, it was left to the individual or his kin to exact satisfaction for a wrong. A significant weapon for this was for the wronged one to fast against the wrongdoer, another parallel with Indian practice. In extreme cases, as when the honour price for murder was not paid, the relatives of the murdered man might kill the murderer.

The typical free commoner was the *mruigfher,* 'land-man' or *bo-aire,* who had land worth 21 cumals, well stocked with 20 cows, as well as bulls, oxen, sheep, pigs and a horse; his farm would amount to, say, 700 acres. His honour price was one cumal. The 'land of a cumal' was thus about 35 acres.

The tenants were freemen who held land on yearly tenancies, and the serfs. Sometimes a whole tribe were in this condition of serfdom.

Irish law also provided for polygamy and the ready dissolution of marriage, subject to various complex payments. There was also a custom of temporary marriages, for a year from one of the quarter days, such as Beltine or Lugnasad. Normally, all children, whether born in or out of wedlock, were considered legitimate and capable of inheriting. This led to large aristocratic families and the growth of these no doubt contributed to the general aggression and disorder of the period 900 to 1200 AD. It appears that neither the golden age of Irish christianity nor the 12th century reform, nor the post-Tridentine revival was able to eradicate these loose matrimonial habits, so they survived in gaelic Ireland a thousand years of

36   christianity and did not come to an end until gaelic civilisation itself collapsed in the 17th century.

Perhaps as a result of these complex matrimonial arrangements there was another distinctive practice, that of fosterage, by which children, from the age of seven, were sent to other families for their upbringing — to the age of seventeen for boys and fourteen for girls. This must have had some relation to the practice of giving hostages. It was a potent force in assimilating the younger members of invaders' families to the Irish way of life. For this reason it was condemned by the Statutes of Kilkenny, but notwithstanding this we find the fourth earl of Desmond, some time later, getting permission to have his children in fosterage with his relatives, the O Briens.

2. A New Nation

After about 600 AD a number of forces began to operate to create a single Irish nation. These forces were largely centred on Munster. They were aided by peace and prosperity. During the period from 400 AD to 800 Munster enjoyed, apart from sporadic local disorders, and a widespread movement and re-arrangement of peoples around 600 AD, almost continual peace. In the establishing of prosperity christianity was a significant force because of the agricultural revolution it introduced. It has been said that Munster was the most peaceful area in western Europe during the dark ages; but this may be argument from silence.

The effects of this peacefulness are strikingly evident in many parts of Kerry. Most of the ruins we now see of dwelling-houses, caher-farms, and ecclesiastical buildings date from periods after 600 AD. These show evidence of a rising, large and relatively prosperous community at this time. However, prosperity is a relative thing. There must have been riches in the community to support the craftsmen and scholars who made the period 600 to 800 AD perhaps the most striking in Irish history. But the dwellings that have been excavated at Leacanabuaile, Cahersiveen, and Beginish, Valentia, which first date from this period, show a people on the verge of subsistence. In Kerry at this time subsistence became feasible for substantial numbers of people.

In the peaceful conditions the agricultural reforms that came with christianity had a notable impact. It was church policy to encourage tillage and corn growing. These advances led to the clearing of forest land — this was a particular feature of monastic life in what was then north Munster — and the growing of grain. The interest in tillage must have led in the wilder parts of Kerry to the clearing of stones from the land and the building of cahers, which protected animals and humans from predators such as wolves. Wheat, oats, barley and rye were grown on these little farms. Ploughing was done with heavy ploughs drawn by two oxen or more. The Irish horse at the time was too small — like the present Connemara pony — and the horse's collar, invented about 900 AD, did not reach Ireland for many centuries. In Elizabethan times ploughing by horse's tail was still common. Crops were reaped by sickle — the scythe, used in

roman Britain, did not reach Ireland for many centuries.

The interest of christianity in corn growing gives a special significance to the querns that have survived in many anchoritic sites, such as Cloon Lough. Another memorial of this is the bullaun, a large boulder with a hollow or hollows in which corn was ground. A striking example is at the church site at Temple Fiachna, Garranes, Kenmare, where the larger grinding stones remain in the hollows. There is a big bullaun in Upper Main Street, Dingle, and small ones at Aghadoe and near Killarney house, as well as close to Kilmalkedar. In post-roman times in Britain a new form of barley came into use there that required to be ground to remove the grain from the husk. This practice seems to have been brought to Ireland from Britain in early christian times and the bullaun is the continuing witness of this. South Kerry is not the happiest place for corn growing; but that something led to a sharp rise in population in early christian times is evident, for example, in the Waterville area — and of course in the Fahan area — in the astonishing number of stone forts and in the clochan villages that survive. Most of the forts were farmsteads of early christian times.

Apart from grain crops there were grown flax, kale, parsnip (or carrot), onion, leek, garlic, and dye plants. The interest in cattle did not, of course, die away, notwithstanding the opposition of christianity to the pagan religious interest in them. Of the bones found at Leacanabuaile, 90% were ox; the rest were sheep and goat. The bones of only one horse were found. Leacanabuaile was clearly a substantial farm dating from the ninth or tenth century. A continuing feature of cattle farming was transhumance — under which in the summer months cattle were herded, milked and had butter made by young people on mountain sides. This practice continued in Kerry until the last century. Milk products, *banbid*, were the staple diet — milk fresh, thickened, in curds, as butter, and as cheese of various kinds.

The population must have fluctuated sharply — a steep rise after christianity came, and sharp falls after the great plagues of the late seventh and early eighth centuries, again a steady rise, and then a falling off and, it seems decline, about 1000 AD. Some glimpse of the way of life of the upper classes comes from a poem, written in the twelfth century, but harking back to the times of the Fiana, praising, in admittedly idealised terms, the home of Crede, daughter of the king of Ciarraige Luachra, at Loch Cuirre, close to the Paps mountains. 'There are a hundred feet in Crede's house from one end to the other, and twenty measured feet in the breadth of her good doorway. Her wattling and her thatch are of the feathers of blue and yellow birds; her railing beside the well to the east is of glass and carbuncle. Around each bed are fair pillars of patterned gold and silver; there is a glass gem on the top of each pillar, crowning it pleasantly'. And so on.

It is possible to give some sketch of the political history of Kerry in these two centuries. Professor **Byrne**, in his *Irish Kings and High Kings*, gives a list of the prominent **members** of the Eoganacht Locha

Lein and their relationship to the kingship of Munster.

Kings of Munster – Eoganacht Locha Lein

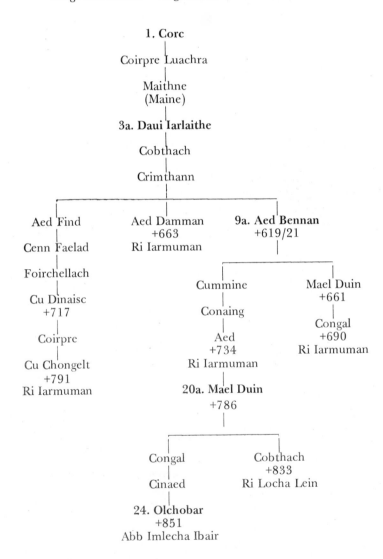

be king of Munster; but so, at the same time, was Fingen, his son-in-law. It is possible that, at this time, West Munster was in practice independent of the kingship of Cashel. Ardea (Aed's Height) castle, near Lauragh, was built on the site of a stronghold named after Aed Bennan. His nephew, Faithliu, founded the monastery of Inisfallen. Aed had twelve sons and three daughters. Keating says one of these sons was St Fursa. One of the daughters, Mor, the subject of a famous story, married Fingen, king of Cashel, who also died in 619. From her sprang the most senior and the most numerous of all the Eoganacht families, the O Sullivans, who later so widely settled on all the beautiful country one can see from Ardea. A king of Loch Lein, and West Munster, Mael Duin, became king of Cashel, succeeding the Cathal referred to below, and reigned for, it seems, 44 years, dying in 786, but it looks as if he, also, had to share his tenure. He made a couple of forays north, but without success. Mael Duin's son was Cobthach, who died in 833; he seems to have been the last king of West Munster. In 803 he fought a battle with the rising power of the Ciarraige; after this the power of the kingdom of West Munster steadily declined. Later in the century one other member of the Eoganacht Locha Lein, Olchobair mac Cinaeda (d. 851) became king of Cashel, but substantially as a compromise candidate.

The Ciarraige seem to have ruled what are now the three baronies of north Kerry — Trughanacmy, Clanmaurice, and Iraghticonnor. About the middle of the eighth century pressure from them forced the Alltraige, the people of St Brendan, to cross the Shannon and carve out a principality in Clare. The Corcu Duibne ruled what are now the baronies of Corkaguiney and Iveragh, as well as the western part of Magunihy, that is the land surrounding Dingle Bay. The Eoganacht Locha Lein held Magunihy and, possibly, Dunkerron South, Glanerought and Beare. It is to be stressed that the Corcu Duibne held of the Iveragh peninsula not much more than what is now the barony of Iveragh. To the east of them was the small kingdom of Drung — perhaps approximating to the modern barony of Dunkerron North — and to the south, the narrow territory along the Kenmare River, the mountains and the sea, now called Dunkerron South. It is not clear who ruled this and the opposite peninsula, the territories overrun by the O Sullivans at the end of the twelfth century. It may be that, dating from the time of Aed Bennan in the 7th century they had maintained some connexion there, based on the two great fortresses of Ardea and Staigue; but this, until more light can be thrown on the history of the time, is pure speculation.

The three petty kingdoms survived until the 11th and 12th centuries when the Eoganacht families from Cashel, followed by the anglo-normans, began to dispossess them.

At the national level it became clear that the decline of the kings of Tara, who had ruled the northern half of Ireland, left the way open for the strongest power, Cashel, to achieve the hegemony of the whole country and to begin the establishment of political, as well as cultural, union. Cathal, king of Munster, who twice invaded Leinster to this end, died in 742. He is styled in the later and local *Annals of*

Almost without exception the Eoganacht kings of Cashel were drawn from East Munster and the West Munster kings played little part at the highest level. Three — Daui Iarlaithe (or Duach), Aed Bennan, and Mael Duin — at best shared the kingship of Munster, and only one — Olchobair — had undisputed tenure of it. Aed Bennan, king of West Munster, who died in 619 (or 621) AD was said at his death to

Inisfallen as 'Ri hErend', king of Ireland; but this ambition was not to be achieved, and then after many disasters, for 250 years. As we have seen, Cathal's successor, Mael Duin, also made two forays north but without real success.

3. Cultural Unity

We now come to the most distinctive contribution of the period 600 to 800 AD, the achieving of cultural unity and the flowering of literature, metal-work, illuminated manuscripts and sculpture. Although, as we shall see, Munster was the principal centre for the cultural revival, the evidence does not show Kerry playing a distinctive part in all of this.

The achievement of cultural unity came from the establishment of the language of the Gaels as a single language, the adoption of writing, the outburst of lyric poetry, the impact of roman language and culture, the writing down and codification of ancient laws, the revival of topography and of literature, the building up of a synthetic genealogical system, and the beginning of the writing of a synthetic history aimed at integrating the diverse origins of the people.

As early as 400 AD Munster was the most cultured part of Ireland, and Kerry played its part in developing civilisation. There was regular contact with Britain and abroad. To this we owe the invention of the first kind of Irish writing, ogam, and Kerry was the centre for this. In the same way trade contacts, in particular the import of wine, seem to have been the means by which christianity first arrived, perhaps to west Cork. The christian settlements — especially the monasteries — reinforced these overseas contacts, and latin became the language of cultivated people. By 600 AD it seems that writing in the vernacular had begun in Munster, and from there from the preceding half century poetry has been preserved in written form.

As we have seen, the goidels ruled directly only some third of the petty kingdoms, and the others continued under the rule of the older inhabitants of Ireland, Picts, Fir Bolg, Laginians, and the rest. Under them were, in many places, the older inhabitants of Ireland dating from the metal and stone ages. It seems clear that these subject races preserved some or all of their own languages, the *iarnbelre*, up to the 7th century. Pictish was certainly spoken in Scotland in the 5th century, and later in St Colmcille's time; it is likely that something similar was true of this country. Probably, it was not until the 7th century that the everyday language of the goidels, borrowing extensively from these other languages not only words but also such features as aspiration and mutation of consonants, and greatly strengthened by the impact and example of latin, superseded its own archaic and official forms as well as the more ancient tongues. In this way the country became unified in language. This take over was much strengthened by the adoption of writing in that language. Thus, it would seem, during the 7th century the Erainn of Kerry lost their own language. In the same way their distinctive, if cumbersome, style of writing, ogam, had gone out of use by 700 AD.

Christianity, too, made for unity in the long run. Its immediate effect on Irish society had been disruptive. Up to then the learned class, who were also the priests of the old religion, had been the preservers and developers of Irish culture. They thus came into direct conflict with the christian missionaries and rapidly lost ground. Their schools were largely superseded by the monastic ones. A culture that depended on oral transmission by a class specially trained in these schools was in grave danger of sharing the fate that befell celtic culture in Gaul and Iberia. Moreover, the culture itself was fragmented because of the fragmentation of states, of language and of religious beliefs. These latter were largely superseded by a single set of beliefs and by at least the concept of a single religious organisation. Eventually, the unifying forces won out at the cultural level. The christian and the ancient cultures came to terms, as vividly illustrated by the long discussions between St Patrick and Oisin (or Caoilte), a saint's summoning of Fergus Mac Roich from the dead to tell the tale of the *Tain* to the poet Seanchain Torpeist (who died in 657), and so on. The oldest piece in Irish that can be firmly dated bears out this reconciliation, because it is a poem on the death of Colmcille in 597 by the leading poet Dallan Forgail. The extreme asceticism of Irish christianity in its early days must have put a very fine filter on the transmission of the more pagan of the tales. It was a work of near genius to think of and work out the scheme whereby so many of them were told by a *revenant* to a delighted St Patrick. There are accounts of the ignorance of tales and of topography by those who should have known better; but in the end all was well. It was at this time that the great early sagas and tales of Irish literature were first written down and some, perhaps, composed. The earliest versions that survive come from later centuries, but they are mainly written down in 8th century language.

As we have seen, Irish society shows only a slow emergence from political anarchy; but after about 700 AD the society was steadily and consciously woven together by cultural unity. Running through the whole society was a common cultural institution, the *aes dana* (literally, the gifted ones) of lawyers, poets, doctors, druids and, later, priests, as well as skilled craftsmen. These maintained and developed the common cultural values of the whole society. They were honoured within the *tuath* and welcome throughout the country across the political boundaries and received considerable pecuniary support. As late as the middle of the 16th century an English observer, Thomas Smyth, could say of them that they had all 'great plenty of cattle'. The lawyers administered an ancient, unchangeable system of law common to the whole society. The poets and story tellers maintained and developed a common language, literature and learning. Through these forms there existed a remarkable sense of nationhood which over and over again was to absorb external influences and to digest them for its own nourishment and survival. Perhaps this explains in part how, over five thousand years, one can see, at times weakly, a continuous and tenacious unfolding of Irish national consciousness.

Then began the task of unifying the people into one purportedly

Ardea Castle, Kenmare River

ethnic, i.e. gaelic, whole. After 750 AD the Cruithin, or Picts, become unpersons in Ireland and the more successful of the subject people are given gaelic pedigrees, all neatly related back to biblical characters. About the same time, around 730, saw the consolidation of the major provincial dynasties, the compilation of the first great genealogical collections, of the Annals and of the secular and ecclesiastical law codes. The heroic age was over; saga was succeeded by history.

Nonetheless the whole of the Irish cultural heritage — and with it glimpses into the pre-roman life of Europe — came to be associated with the native monasteries. As they lost their earlier austerity and became absorbed into the mainstreams of Irish life there grew up between them and the older members of the *aes dana* a productive

40 alliance from which the older professional classes began to draw
renewed strength. There began in the monasteries a long tradition of
recording the legends and history of Ireland. If we now think of the
pagan gods on Caherconree or the Fiana hunting in the hills above
Killarney the red deer that still startle us in the undergrowth, we have
these early writers to thank. The drive to create a single nation was
much aided by the artistry and scholarship that grew up in the
monasteries and by the widespread acceptance of common
institutions, common laws and common language. On these
foundations there grew up, as we have seen, a remarkable body of
lyric poetry. The marriage in the monasteries of gallican and near
eastern chant with native Irish music led to its great and lasting
development so that music throve in the following centuries and
harpers ranked with nobles in honour price. At the same time there
was the revival of the ancient Irish craft of metal work — now for
church furnishings such as the Ardagh chalice, the shrines and the
croziers. Also began that distinctive form of sculpture, the early high
crosses. The earliest of these art forms, until about 700 AD, largely
eschewed representation but carried on the abstract celtic tradition
of La Tene. In the 8th century was achieved that most marvellous of
illuminated manuscripts, the *Book of Kells,* a transcription of the
four gospels done in a monastery probably following the rule of St
Colmcille; in an associated monastery was done the earlier *Book of
Durrow.* Then was developed the dry, matter of fact chronicling of
events year by year for centuries — of which the *Annals of Inisfallen*
is a leading example — work that has been essential to understanding
our past and surviving the destruction of so much of our records.
During the same century appeared perhaps the first edition of that
great synthetic account of the pre-history of Ireland that came to be
enshrined in the later *Lebor Gabala Erenn.*

During the 8th century the monasteries were also well-known centres
of latin and greek learning. At its end and into the 9th century
Irishmen, the products of these monasteries, such as Dicuil, Sedulius
Scottus, John Scottus and many others at the carolingian court,
taught latin and greek, wrote poetry, and books on theology and
philosophy. This later, more secular, emigration was perhaps
reinforced by the destruction by the vikings of so many monasteries

when their raids began at the end of the 8th century.

At this time, just before the viking blows fell, the monasteries must
have lost most, if not all, of their earlier, terrifying austerity and
become extremely civilised places. From about the middle of the
eighth century we read of single individuals holding a plurality of
abbacies of monasteries.

Indeed, they were ripe for one of the periodic reformations of the
Irish monastic system. This time it was the Cele De movement that
arose in Munster about 750 AD and that flourished into the next
century. Notwithstanding its great contribution to poetry — and the
flowering of the sculptures of high crosses also associated with them —
it is likely that to this new outburst of austerity can be attributed
some of the falling off in Irish cultural development that was to be a
feature of the next century or more.

The great abbots played a big part in the 7th, 8th, and part of the 9th
centuries not only in acting as major patrons of the arts and
scholarship but also in legislating for the christianising and humanising
of life. By this time they had taken over the administration of the
church in full and were often much engaged in political affairs. The
same men were abbots, bishops and kings and, occasionally, a
monastic community was mobilised for battle. In the 9th and 10th
centuries it was the political ambitions of clerics that would make the
eoganacht kings of Cashel strive to achieve the political — as they
were achieving the cultural — unity of Ireland. At length, many of
the abbacies became the preserve of lay families with some
administrative ability, and the succession came to be from father to
son, or at least within the hereditary rules of the *derbfine,* just as it
was in the secular kingdoms.

It was the effects both of the internal growth of wealth, influence
and laicisation, as well as the later internal reform, coupled with the
external havoc wreaked by both native and viking raiders,that led,
after a long struggle by the reformers, to the end of the Irish form of
monasticism. But that was for the future. In the 8th century it had,
culturally, its finest hour.

Chapter 4

The Gaelic Nation
800 – 1200

The period when Ireland could be held to be clearly a gaelic nation falls into two roughly equal parts, the period of gaelic consolidation from 800 to 1000 AD and the time of troubles and of church reform, to 1200 AD.

GAELIC CONSOLIDATION, 800 – 1000 AD

The political history of the period 800 to 1000 AD is made up of three strands — the repelling of the vikings, the decline of the Eoganacht kingdoms, and the long struggle of Cashel to achieve the hegemony of Ireland.

In the 9th century the peaceful times of the preceding centuries came sharply to an end, and the notable disorder of gaelic Ireland steadily increased over the ensuing four centuries. The native Irish had recently begun the habit of raiding and looting the monasteries as sanctuaries for the goods and cattle of the neighbourhood. This practice was soon learned by the viking raiders, and they struck again and again, especially at christian settlements. The monasteries were rich sources of plunder. On the whole, however, the vikings were not a major problem in Kerry. In 812 a viking fleet of 120 vessels ravaged the southwest coast, including Valentia. The Eoganacht Locha Lein under the last king of West Munster inflicted a crushing defeat on them. There were later sporadic raids. Even so austere a place as the Skelligs was raided in 823 or 824 and again possibly before the middle of the century. Perhaps it was on a wild night on Skellig that this quatrain was written (Professor Carney's translation):

Is acher in gáith in-nocht,
  fu-fuasna fairggae findfolt;
 ní agor reimm mora minn
   dond láechraid lainn úa
   Lothlind.
	Bitter and wild is the wind tonight
	 Tossing the tresses of the sea to
	 white:
	 On such a night as this I feel at ease
	 Fierce Northmen only course
	   the quiet seas.

A poignant reminder of such terror is to find in so austere a place a souterrain, a place of refuge and of storage of whatever few goods the place possessed. Inisfallen, also, was raided in 845 and 857 in north Kerry and around the river Laune. There was no other serious action until 869 when a king of the Ciarraige, Congal Mac Mic Lachtna, with, as allies the Eoganacht Locha Lein and the Ui Chonnail Ghabhra, decisively defeated the viking leader Tomrar at Dun Main (? near Killarney). In 873 Barith from Dublin attacked the Ciarraige but was beaten off with great slaughter.

Not until the early 10th century did the norsemen get a footing in Munster — in Waterford and Limerick. The norse kingdom of Limerick was established in 922. It is possible that they also settled on Beginish, in Valentia harbour. Here have been found two traces of them, a runic stone and the remains of a scandinavian stone bowl.

The stone is one of only five found in Ireland, and has been deciphered: 'Lir erected this stone; M. . . . carved the runes'. A further memento is probably the name Smerwick. This comes from

two norse words for butter and harbour. The norse seem to have settled on both sides of the mouth of this harbour which became a centre for the export of that famous Kerry product, butter, to the norse kingdom of Limerick.

It is to be noted that the leader of the alliance that defeated the norse in 869 was the king of the Ciarraige. We have referred to an account of a convention of the subject peoples purportedly held in 550 AD and attended by famous clerics. This seems really to have been a justification for a movement of about the middle of the 9th century, led by the Ciarraige, to throw off the overlordship of the kings of West Munster (but not yet that of Cashel). The convention seems to have been an elaborate attempt to legitimise the rights of the subject peoples to throw off the intermediate overlordship of the kings of West Munster, that is, of Loch Lein at about the time of the death of Cobthach in 833 AD. His predecessor, Cu Chongelt (d. 791), was the last to be granted the title of king of West Munster. After Cobthach, described as 'rig Locha Lein', the Eoganacht Locha Lein became just one — if a privileged one because of the gaelic race — of the three petty kingdoms of Kerry. At this time the power of the provincial kings *vis-a-vis* the intermediate kings was everywhere growing.

The third strand is the struggle of Cashel, in consequence of its growing provincial strength, to achieve the hegemony of Ireland. This was to succeed, but at the price of ending the Eoganacht rule there.

We have seen that about the middle of the eighth century the kings of Munster, as the strongest and the richest of the Irish kings, began the attempt to unify Ireland under their sovereignty. The struggle was taken up in the 9th century by the king-bishop of Cashel, Feidlimid (d. 847), who did not let his cloth — nor the fact that he had been a Cele De — prevent him from becoming known as the most ferocious of the burners of monasteries. He made attacks on the Ui Neill and in 827 and 838, it is claimed, his supremacy was accepted. Feidlimid's successors were weak kings. His immediate successor, Olchobair mac Cinaeda, of the Eoganacht Locha Lein and abbot of Emly, seems to have been a compromise candidate. He ruled from 847 to 851. In 854, 856, and 858 Mael Sechnaill came south to raid Munster and took hostages. On the last expedition south, in 858, the king of Munster for the first time acknowledged supremacy, and the Osraige were detached from Munster. Another king-bishop, Cormac O Cuilleanain (in the 150 years from 800 no less than six of the kings of Cashel were clerics), took up the struggle but was defeated and killed at Ballaghmoon, near Leighlinbridge, Co. Carlow, in 908. Killed with him were the king of the Ciarraige and the abbot of Kinnitty who was also the king of the Corcu Duibne. This defeat marked the end of the undisputed prestige of the Eoganacht dynasty of Cashel and the end of one of the great scholar patrons of Ireland: he had played a great part in the development of Irish learning. To Cormac are attributed three distinguished compilations: *Cormac's Glossary,* the *psalter of Cashel,* and the *Book of Rights* — although the last is probably a later work.

The weakening of Cashel had two consequences for the history of

42

Kerry. The first was the establishment of the viking kingdom of Limerick in 922 AD. The second was the reign of a (wrongly) reputed member of the Eoganacht Locha Lein, Cellachan, in becoming king of Cashel, 920 to 954 AD. He was unsuccessful in his attacks on the Ui Neill, who imprisoned him at Aileach. When he returned in 944 he was faced by the challenge of the Dal Cais who were to bring to an end the Eoganacht dynasty. He defeated the Dal Cais contender, Cennietig, father of Brian Borama. We can assume that by this stage the Corcu Duibne and the Ciarraige had established an unacceptable degree of independence of Cashel. There is a rather fanciful book, *Caithreim Cellachain Caisil,* written by a Kerryman about 1114 AD, which *inter alia,* gives an·account of a raid into Kerry by Cellachan and his asserting of power over the Corcu Duibne and the Ciarraige. He raided Aes Iorrais for a fortnight, killed 200 and captured the king of the Corcu Duibne, Congal Mac Annrathain. Congal was later released but hostages were taken. Cellachan then raided the territory of the Ciarraige and captured Concobar, their king. Cellachan was the remote ancestor of the Mac Carthys — his great grandson was Carthach, a petty king in the Cashel area and founder of the family. The struggle of the Corcu Duibne and of the Ciarraige to maintain their independence of the kingdom of Cashel was, however, long to survive Cellachan.

Nonetheless, from Cashel was to come, briefly, the political union of Ireland, but this was not to be an Eoganacht achievement. The brunt of the struggle against the viking kingdom of Limerick was to be borne by the Dal Cais, a Clare branch of the Erainn. They seized the kingship of Cashel in 964 AD. It was from here that their most distinguished member — one of the great men of Irish history — established a single monarchy of Ireland in 1002 AD, Brian Borama, Imperator Scottorum. Brian was probably the first person in Irish history to be, in any real sense, king of Ireland. Brian was to lose his life in 1014 in the last, decisive battle against viking power in Ireland.

The drive towards nation building that had been strong in the 8th century was interrupted by the viking raids of the 9th century and the rise of the new reform movement in the monasteries; but the drive was clearly resumed in the 10th century. There was written in final form the great synthetic history of Ireland from the Flood, pushing back the gaelic invasion by some 1500 years, during which 2500 years there had been undisturbed gaelic possession of Ireland. This was done in *Lebor Gabala Erenn,* the Book of the Invasions of Ireland. In addition, pedigrees were provided for everybody of note tracing his descent from Milesius — the reputed father of the gaels — and then back to Adam. The purpose of these acts was to unify the country by obliterating the different ethnic origins of the people. The customary relationships of individuals and classes in society were codified in an extraordinarily detailed body of written law. Literature, history, craftsmanship and, later, architecture and church reform, were all encouraged and developed. For example, the art of the sculptured high crosses reached its full flowering in the 9th and 10th centuries. These sculptures, representing in relief scenes from the old and new testaments on the themes of divine intervention in

man's salvation, represent Ireland's best contribution to stone sculpture and precede by about two centuries a comparable development in Europe. Unfortunately, Kerry does not give us any examples.

Cormac's Glossary, (Sanas Cormaic) — the Cormac was Cormac O Cuilleanain, king of Munster (d. 908) — is an example of the, slightly odd, tendency towards synthesising. It lays down seven standards for road building. The principal arterial road was the *slige,* wide enough for the chariots of a king and a bishop to pass without either giving way to the other. The third in size is the *bothar,* wide enough for two cows, one lengthways, the other athwart. A *rot* will carry a one horse chariot. And so on.

The *aes dana* now take on a further development, in part independent of the monasteries; and we find in a 9th century saga the Liadan, to whom we have previously referred, presented as a professional woman poet. At that time, too, an educated or aristocratic lady might make a habit of composing verse: the author of the famous poem about the old woman of Beare may have been some such 9th century lady. If a gaelic, as distinct from an Irish, nation can be said to have been in existence it was at this time, and mainly in Munster, that it was consciously and deliberately created. (Much Irish scholarship of the 20th century has been devoted to getting behind the structure then created).

While the Fir Bolg were conceded to be distinct, the southern Fir Bolg people, the Erainn, were turned into gaels. But this nation-building movement was not brought to uneconomic lengths. The kingdom of Cashel lived on the contributions paid by the *aithechthuatha,* the tribute paying tribes. Thus, according to the *Book of Rights,* in Kerry about 1000 AD, while the Eoganacht Locha Lein being true gaels were exempt from tribute, the merely adopted gaels, the newly labelled gaelic kingdoms of the Ciarraige and the Corcu Duibne, paid substantial annual tributes of 1,000 cows and 1,000 hogs from the former, (elsewhere 700 cows, oxen and sows) and 1,000 cows and 1,000 oxen from the latter. There were reciprocal duties of the king of Cashel to give gifts to his sub-kings. In one place in the *Book of Rights* we read that he had to give to the king of Loch Lein 'seven steeds, seven drinking horns, seven swords, seven shields and seven hounds'. In another place it is ten bay horses, ten ships and ten coats of mail. Somewhat similar gifts were due to the king of the Ciarraige; but the Corcu Duibne seemed not to enjoy such favours. The king of Drung got three swords and three ships in return for a tribute of 30 oxen. Perhaps these were not as fortunate as another who was entitled to 'ten bondsmen, ten large women, and ten horns for carousing'. The acceptance of these gifts from the provincial king was also acceptance of his suzerainty. One of the rights of the king of Cashel was to maintain a *rigport,* or royal residence, in many of the sub-kingdoms. One of these residences was Cathair Meathais which O'Donovan identifies as Staigue fort, near Castlecove. On the other hand a king had some inhibitions. For example, it would be the beginning of his last days to stay at the feast of Loch Lein from a Monday to a Sunday.

One of the main patrons of the new national movement was Brian Borama, who not only restored learning and buildings at home but also sent students to Europe to study and scholars to buy books to replace the gaps left by viking and other destruction. Brian was to the Ireland of his time what Charlemagne had been on a greater stage. At home Brian, apart from making a reality of the old Munster dream of a single kingdom of Ireland, also gave considerable support to the cultural, synthesising movement, even though he was no reformer. So, Brian's pre-gaelic tribe, the Dal Cais, were given an impeccable gaelic pedigree.

At this time the monastery of Inisfallen had become an important place of learning, and Brian is reputed to have been educated there. His *anamchara*, or counsellor, was Maelsuthain O Carroll, lord of the Eoganacht Locha Lein. He accompanied Brian to Armagh in 1004 and 1006 and commemorated the event in the *Book of Armagh*. He died in 1009 and was described in the *Annals of the Four Masters* as the chief *saoi*, or doctor, of the western world. Maelsuthain, who retired to the monastery from time to time, is credited with compiling the early part of the *Annals of Inisfallen*, but this is unlikely. These end with the year 1319. The earliest version we have of these annals dates from about 1092; but it is probable that they are based on an original source that may stretch back to the 6th century.

Nonetheless, the 10th and 11th centuries were times of widespread and increasing disorder, typified in the raiding of the monasteries which became a regular practice. As we have seen the vikings were by no no means exclusively to blame for this, and Feidlimid, the king-bishop of Cashel, became one of the most ferocious raiders of monasteries. This disorder seems to have accompanied, if it did not cause, a period of economic decline. The town of Fahan seems to have been abandoned about the 10th century, as were other dwellings in south Kerry. We have no obvious remains of other dwellings of this time in equal numbers, so it must be assumed that there was a decline in population. One cause of this may have been the effects of the various plagues — afflicting both human and animal populations — that were prevalent, aggravated in their effects by severe weather; the climate seems to have begun to deteriorate at about this time. Thus we see a sharp contrast between the growth of building in the previous centuries and the limited amount of new building — although such building as there was reached a high standard — and the abandonment of existing buildings during this period.

Parallel to the decline in material circumstances was the decline in monasticism and the church generally. As we have seen, the continual raiding was a big factor in this, but there were also some forms of corruption as well. There were many abuses that arose when the monasteries became the property of the great 'protecting' families — even outside their own territories. We have seen that the abbot of Kinnitty (in Offaly) slain at the battle of Ballaghmoon was king of Corcu Duibne; three centuries before this the founder of Kinnitty, St Fionan Cam, was of that tribe, and it is clear that they maintained a proprietorial interest in the foundation. In 929 died

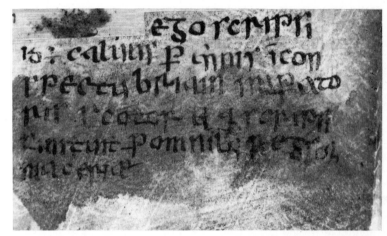

Maelsuthain O Carroll's entry in Book of Armagh

Ego scripsi, id est Calvus perennis, in conspetu Briani imperatoris Scotorum et que scripsi finivit pro omnibus regibus Maceriae

I, Mael Suthian, have written this in the presence of Brian, emperor of the Irish, and what I have written he has determined for all the Kings of Cashel.

Finnechta, son of Laegaire, King of Ciarraige Luachra, and according to the *Annals of Inisfallen,* 'chief anchorite of Ireland'. Devotion, too, seems to have slackened. The eremitical movement in Kerry had long since died out, except for the astonishing outpost on the Skellig. A new reform movement of hermits had grown up in Munster in the eighth and ninth centuries, but it is not clear where; for a time it made a considerable impact. This was the Culdee movement, its members being known as Celi De. *Celsine* was a system by which an independent freeholder gave assistance to his lord in return for protection and, without losing his independence, became his lord's *cele*. The name throws an interesting light on culdee spirituality. In any event, the movement was not able to overcome the adverse effects of the times. The scholarly and artistic centres in the monasteries were scattered by the combination of all these forces. There was a new wave of emigration to the continent; but this time the *scotti peregrini* were not missionaries, but primarily scholars, poets and teachers. However, from about the middle of the 10th century, a new missionary movement to France and Germany began, based on the reformed Benedictine order which, at that time, had itself not reached Ireland. At home, by the eleventh century, the great days of Irish christianity had come to an end, Irish monasticism was in mortal decline and many monasteries were abandoned.

44   TIME OF TROUBLES, 1000 – 1200 AD

The political and cultural unification of gaelic Ireland was to have unhappy effects in Kerry. The long centuries of peace and prosperity came to an end and the political evils that wracked the country in the 11th and 12th centuries were also to be seen in Kerry.

(I) POLITICAL DISORDER

The family of Brian Borama – the O Briens – during the 11th century were able to maintain themselves, to some extent, as Kings of Ireland and, generally, as kings of Munster. The ruling O Brien usually had difficulties with members of his own numerous and vigorous family; unsuccessful challengers were usually blinded. The last important O Brien king, Muircheartach, was a leader of church reform and gave Cashel as a seat to the bishop of Cashel. He died in 1119. During the 12th century the O Briens were to lose the kingship of Ireland to the kings of Connacht, and one of them, Turloch O Conor, partitioned Munster into Thomond (north Munster, including north Kerry) based on Limerick, and Desmond (south Munster) based on Cork. O Brien had to be content with Thomond and had to fight to maintain even part of the kingship of Munster against the Eoganacht family of Mac Carthy. During the 12th century there were 50 years of political anarchy – with armed dissensions within the ruling families; with the struggle of the O Briens to maintain their kingdom of Munster and, later, their very existence against the power of O Conor to the north and the rising power of Mac Carthy to the south; and the confusing and unprincipled alliances and treacheries of everybody. Nonetheless, these were the pains of the transition from a tribal to a feudal society; the larger visions made for greater trouble in the transition than the limited cattle-raiding of the past. However, the transition to a feudal, national society was cut short by the anglo-norman invasion.

By the 11th century there had arisen around Cashel in the modern barony of Middle Third three Eoganacht families that were to play a leading part in Kerry from that time – Mac Carthy, O Donoghue and O Sullivan. Of these, the most senior was O Sullivan, with Mac Carthy ranking second. The Mac Carthy family took its name from Carthach, a petty king of the Eoganacht Caisil, who, with many of his nobles, was burned in his house in 1045. Carthach's great grandfather, Cellachan, had been king of Munster.

The first king of Desmond was Tadhg, grandson of Carthach, deliberately taken from obscurity by Turlough O Conor in 1118 as a make-weight against O Brien. The Cormac who built the famous chapel on Cashel in 1134 was Tadhg's brother and succeeded him in 1124. Until 1138, when he was murdered by O Conor Kerry, Cormac appears as king of Desmond and, at times, king of Munster. Not until the O Brien power was finally broken after 1151 did the struggle of the two families end in the partition of Munster between them. This occurred in 1168. Desmond was left in the hands of Cormac's son, King Dermod Mac Carthy.

Kerry showed in microcosm these contentions. During the 11th century all but one of the kings of Eoganacht Locha Lein mentioned in the *Annals of Inisfallen* – O Cahill, O Carroll, O Moriarty, etc – were slain. To be king of the Ciarraige was not quite so hazardous – between 1014 and 1142 there were 14 kings of the Ciarraige, of whom seven were slain; and only one of the kings of the Corcu Duibne – but three of their royal heirs – were slain.

It was, however, the intrusion into Kerry of the Eoganacht families of Mac Carthy, O Donoghue, and O Sullivan in the 12th century that intensified in the whole county the disorder normal to Irish life at that time. For example, in 1124, the year of his accession, Cormac Mac Carthy banishes the three Kerry sub-kings – O Moriarty of Loch Lein, O Conor of the Ciarraige, and O Shea of the Corcu Duibne. In the next couple of years fleets, provided by Turloch O Conor, king of Ireland, under the command of O Moriarty arrive in Corcu Duibne and on Loch Lein and do much damage. In 1127 Cormac himself is deposed and is banished to the monastery of Lismore, from which he is taken by the O Briens and again set up, and O Moriarty is banished. And so it went on, with raids, naval battles, burning of monasteries, and treacherous killings.

The Mac Carthy onslaught, with its appropriate battle cry of 'Lamh laidir a buaidh', victory to the strong arm, seems to have concentrated on the territories of the Eoganacht Locha Lein – say, the modern barony of Magunihy; the southern part of the territory of the Corcu Duibne – the modern barony of Iveragh; and presumably the little kingdom of Drung, approximating to the modern barony of Dunkerron north. These, at least, are the areas where Mac Carthy power became paramount. The later O Donoghue intrusion into the Killarney area and the still later O Sullivan one into the modern baronies of Dunkerron South and Beare, acknowledged (or eventually came to acknowledge) Mac Carthy suzerainty as long as gaelic power survived.

The older ruling families of Kerry opposed the Mac Carthy intrusion, and the subsequent O Donoghue one. They sought support from the O Briens against Mac Carthy, and the latter invoked the aid of O Conor, king of Connacht. Of the Kerry families the most vigorous seems to have been O Conor Kerry, and their leader Diarmaid Sugach was an active and resourceful man. He built a fleet at Astee in 1146. Four years later he brought them 'on wheels' from Corcu Duibne to Loch Lein, raided Inisfallen, and established his power there. With the O Briens he devastated virtually the whole of the Mac Carthy kingdom of Desmond, and Diarmaid Mac Carthy had desperately to appeal to O Conor for help from Connacht. In the following year O Conor responded and, with the principal princes of the country, came to Mac Carthy's aid. At the decisive battle of Moin Mhor in 1151 the O Brien power outside Thomond was decisively broken and Mac Carthy was established as king of Desmond. O Conor Kerry escaped from this battle with his life, but had to abandon his ships on Loch Lein.

By the time the anglo-normans reached Kerry Mac Carthy was

Romanesque church, Inisfallen

O Donoghues drove the O Connells out of Magunihy to Iveragh. From the 13th century on the O Donoghues, reinforced by other members of the clan driven south and west by Donal Mor O Brien, the formidable king of Thomond (d. 1194), have virtually undisputed hold of the kingdom until the end of the 16th century when 'Onaght O Donoghue' is forfeited after the end of the Desmond rebellion and what remains of the ancient kingdom goes to the Browne family. There were two main branches of the O Donoghue family — O Donoghue Mor settled at Killarney, and O Donoghue of the Glens, at Glenflesk.

The third great gaelic family, the O Sullivans, came to Kerry and west Cork about the end of the 12th century. They had been settled in Co. Tipperary close to the Suir, but after 1192 were forced south by the pressure of Donal Mor O Brien or by the anglo-normans or by both. They overran west Cork and Dunkerron South along the Kenmare River. The two principal families were O Sullivan Mor, in Dunkerron, and O Sullivan Beare, in the peninsula of that name.

The ancient pre-gaelic kingdom of the Corcu Duibne was ruled by the O Falveys and the O Sheas. The O Falveys held the Dingle peninsula but were to be driven out by the anglo-normans, and they then held some property around Cahersiveen at the centre of Corcu Duibne power at Ballycarbery. The O Sheas had been the rulers of Iveragh, but so complete was the Mac Carthy conquest that, in the middle of the 17th century, Petty's surveyors could find plenty of O Sheas, but not a single landowner amongst them.

The minor Eoganacht family of O Cuilein, (Collins), of Connelo in Limerick, were also driven south by Donal Mor O Brien and went into west Kerry.

Early in the 13th century the position was that, apart from the encroachments of the anglo-normans, there was a kingdom of Desmond ruled by the Mac Carthy family, based on Cork and stretching from Kerry in the west to Waterford in the east. In Kerry, owing allegiance to the Mac Carthys were the two petty kingdoms of O Donoghue Mor around Killarney and of O Sullivan Mor along the Kenmare River. The ancient kingdom of the Corcu Duibne and the little kingdom of Drung had disappeared almost without trace. In the north were the Ciarraige, under O Conor Kerry, balanced between the rival pressures of O Brien of Thomond and Mac Carthy of Desmond. They were to bear a great part of the brunt of the anglo-norman intrusion and yet, somehow, were to survive, in reduced territory, until the general ruin at the end of the 16th century.

Thus, at the time of the coming of the anglo-normans to Kerry some sort of equilibrium had been struck after a period of great disorder. This disorder resulted in the usual plundering of churches. Even in 1114 the *Annals of Inisfallen* had exclaimed:

'Alas, indeed, we find it impossible to relate the multitude of these evils: battles and fights, raids and murders, violations of

substantially in command there; but it was not until the first half of the 13th century, after the anglo-normans had driven him from his headquarters in Cork, that the reigning Mac Carthy normally lived in Kerry.

The intrusion of the O Donoghues seems to have begun a generation after that of the Mac Carthys. Two of the O Donoghue family had been petty kings of Cashel in the 1050s. In the next (12th) century O Donoghue was lord of Cinel Laegaire, an extensive Eoganacht territory in west Cork. After a battle at Ballincollig with another branch of the Eoganacht there (who became the O Mahonys) the O Donoghues moved into Kerry overrunning the Eoganacht territory around Killarney, knocking out the ruling families of O Carroll and O Cahill early in the century; the third family, the O Moriartys, survived to the end of the century. We read in Mac Carthaigh's book that in 1158 Amhlaoibh Mor O Donoghue completed the 'great church' of Aghadoe but was, in the same year, killed in a battle between Thomond and Desmond. He is described as 'high king of the Eoganachta Locha Lein, usurper of west Munster'. The O Donoghues did not establish themselves without much struggle. In 1178 Donal O Donoghue 'king of Eoganacht and Ui Eachach' was slain by the Ui Chinnaeda, and in the same year Donal's son, Amlaib, had Lochlainn Ui Cinnaeda 'king of Eoganacht' taken from the choirs of Inisfallen and slew him. In 1195 O Donoghue killed Mahon O Moriarty of the Eoganacht. Five years later Muircheartach O Moriarty appears as king and five years later again (1205) Murchad O Donoghue died with the title of King. Amongst others, the

46

churches and holy places throughout Ireland, both of laity and clergy.'

Ratass, Tralee, is burned in 1138 by O Brien. Ardfert is burned in 1152 by O Cuilein. It was burned again in 1179 and plundered in 1180 by Mac Carthy. Inisfallen is raided in 1158, and in 1160 and 1180 plundered by O Donoghue.

The losses caused by this disorder were accentuated by the great cattle plague of 1133, the worst for centuries.

Notwithstanding all this political strife, the 11th and 12th centuries were amongst the most culturally productive in Irish history. They saw the vigorous reform of religion and the full flowering of Irish romanesque architecture, as at Kilmalkedar, Church Island (Lough Currane), Killemlagh, Aghadoe, Inisfallen. Round towers were extensively built: of the four built in Kerry — at Aghadoe, Church Island (Lough Currane), Ardfert and Rattoo — only the last-named survives intact. Some magnificent metalwork was done, of which the Inisfallen crozier is a moderately good example. The great compilations of old and middle Irish literature — such as *Lebor na hUidhre*, the *Annals of Tigernach*, the *Book of Leinster* — were made and completed, and the language itself was overhauled, modernised and standardised anew. These language forms were to survive to be incorporated in Dinneen's dictionary of 1904. Surnames came into general use. Strenuous efforts were made to maintain a great university at Armagh. About the end of the 11th century was begun the great monastic compilation of annals that were to be continued at, and named after, Inisfallen. The annals seem to have migrated to the island in the mid-twelfth century and stayed there until the 17th.

As in the rest of Europe, there grew up a class of intellectuals. In Ireland these fell into three kinds — sapientes, who were clerics or laymen attached to the monastic schools, of whom Maelsuthain O Carroll was a notable exemplar; truant scholars, who gave learning the go by and took to poetry; and the poets themselves, going singly or in bands about the country with their satires and panegyrics, levying tribute.

One wonders if it was an unduly savage satire, or exorbitant demand — both were common — that led Dermot, son of Cormac Mac Carthy, in 1160 to kill Giolla Moieda O Daly, the poet of Desmond. The O Dalys were perhaps the greatest of the poetic families.

That the poets' exactions were severe and resented is shown by many stories over the centuries, from the 7th century King Guaire at least. The great O Sullivan name is supposed to derive from the intolerable exaction of a poet. One of the mid-tenth century kings of Cashel, Eochaid, had lost an eye in battle, and a Scottish poet called Dubhan, seeking payment demanded the other eye. Whereupon the king plucked it out. This exaction caused great scandal amongst his supporters. Fortunately, there was a saint in the vicinity who took the two eyes of the poet and gave them to the king so that he could

see again. Hence the origin of the name Suilleabhain — either Suile Dhubhain (Dubhan's eyes) or Suil amhain (one eye). Either way, the famous name of O Sullivan shows how support for the arts can be carried to undue lengths.

(II) CHURCH REFORM

Notwithstanding the political disorder the old Irish missionary spirit was to revive and in the 10th century began the extensive missions in France and Germany renewing the traditions of St Columbanus at Metz, Toul, Verdun and elsewhere. The most important centre was at Ratisbon where the Irish monks adopted the rule of St Benedict. For nearly three centuries these foundations, and others as far afield as Kiev, were supplied from Ireland. Only the Benedictine *Schottenkloster* of Vienna preserves the name from those times. These 10th and 11th century Irish Benedictines were part of a reforming movement in Germany and Rome that culminated in the episcopal reforms of Leo IX (1049-54) and Gregory VII (Hildebrand) (1073-85). The Mac Carthys of Cashel had direct connexions with Germany through these monasteries, particularly with the *Schottenkloster* of St James of Regensburg. A Mac Carthy was abbot there towards the middle of the 12th century. In return, it was the mother house of, and the architectural model for, the Benedictine monastery of Cashel, which became the famous 'Cormac's chapel'. It was at Ratisbon that the famous *Vision of Tundale* was written in 1149, the journey of a soldier of King Cormac through the next world, written down there by the monk Marcus, another Munsterman.

Better known was the great, sustained and creative reform of the Irish church itself. In the 11th century the church in Ireland was in a state of depression and disorganisation that called for drastic reform. This problem had attracted the attention of reformers in England and in Rome. Indeed, Hildebrand had written to Turlough O Brien, as king of Ireland, asking him to institute reforms. But actual reform was touched off by a curious scare that linked christian Ireland with ancient paganism.

The so-called panic of 1000 AD (the 'millenium', when the world was to come to an end) seems not to have affected Ireland, but there was a severe panic in 1096 AD. In that year the feast of the beheading of St John the Baptist (August 29) fell on a Friday that, in a bi-sextile (i.e. leap) year coincided with an embolismal year (i.e. having an extra lunar month) at the end of a 19 year cycle. According to an alleged prophecy of Adamnan, when this coincidence occurred it would have fatal effects for Irishmen. The *roth rumhach*, the oared wheel of pagan mythology, would then appear, before the Judgment Day, as a punishment for the crimes referred to below. In fact, the 19 year cycle was not completed, but a great epidemic had been raging from the previous August to May. In any event, the country was gripped by panic.

Next to the crucifixion, the greatest crime in history, christian Ireland believed, was the beheading of John the Baptist. The actual

was at hand. Only a three day fast from Wednesday to Sunday once
a month and an ordinary fast every weekday to the end of the year,
plus prayer and almsgiving, saved the people of Ireland from 'the fire
of vengeance'. This scare had the effect of improving the practice of
religion and gave an impetus to the movement for church reform.

Church reform began in the last quarter of the eleventh century and
extended over the first three quarters of the twelfth century. The
rising influence of the reforming Papacy, especially associated with
Hildebrand, Pope St Gregory VII, had spread over Europe and had
begun to engage minds in this country with the need for reform. The
bishops of the norse cities of Dublin, Waterford, and occasionally
even of Limerick, acknowledged Canterbury as their superior, and
the English church came to be concerned with the reform of the Irish
church. This was to have later political consequences. Generally,
there were two main problems: the state of the church itself and the
loose marital habits of the Irish — divorce and polygamy — that had
survived from pagan times and were to continue for many more
centuries.

The main problems in the church itself arose from the decline of
monasticism and of the eremitical movements. The latter, the
'conscience' of the Irish church, as it were, had largely but not
wholly disappeared; for example, the settlement on the Skellig
continued. The monasteries themselves had declined sharply in
numbers, had become largely the private property of great families,
and a number had become corrupt; but others, such as Inisfallen,
remained centres of culture and there had grown up in the previous
century a significant missionary effort in Europe. Although there
were many bishops, there was no administrative structure of dioceses
and parishes as they are now understood.

Already by the end of the 11th century there were three territorial
dioceses — Dublin, Meath and Kildare — but the main thrust of the
Irish reform movement spread from the south to the north during
the first third of the twelfth century. The first reforming synod was
that of Cashel in 1101 at which Muircheartach O Briain, king of
Ireland, presided; the synod set the pattern of mixed clerical and lay
participation. It was on this occasion that Muircheartach gave Cashel
to the church. The problems tackled were simony, the quality of the
clergy, freedom of the church, clerical celibacy, clerical privilege, and
matrimonial law. At the synod of Rathbreasail, near Thurles, held in
1111, at which Muircheartach O Briain also presided and perhaps 58
bishops attended, the diocesan problem was tackled. There a system
of dioceses was worked out that still, substantially, survives. It
enlarged the area of the bishopric from, normally, one *tuath* to
several — the *mor-thuath* under a *rui-ri* or over-king — and thus broke
the exclusive influence of the principal family of the *tuath*. A bishop
thus became the bishop of a *place,* in the roman way, and no longer
of a tribe. A number of monastic bishoprics were thus suppressed.
For example, the Kerry bishoprics of Ardfert, Aghadoe (if it existed)
and Ratass were grouped into one, Rath Mhaighe Deiscirt, usually
taken to be Ratass. The new diocese extended, according to Keating,
from Beare island to Barrow harbour and from Feale to Valentia,

Church and round tower, Rattoo

beheading was done, they held, by an Irish druid, Mogh Roith -- the
Slave of the Wheel — who was born, lived and practised magic on
Valentia Island. (Notwithstanding that this was Corcu Duibne
territory, O Donovan says that he was of the Ciarraige). He was the
chief assistant to Simon Magus, who was the arch-sorcerer of New
Testament times, who gave us the word simony and who is claimed
to be the founder of gnosticism. This grounded black magic, esoteric
religion, and the complete inversion of christian values. One of the
most damaging arguments against the Irish tonsure (the shaving of
the back of the head instead of the crown in the roman form) at the
time of the Easter controversy was that the Irish form had been
invented by Simon Magus.

In 1096 it looked as if Ireland's hour to expiate the crime of her son

48

which seems to suggest that it excluded the most northerly part of Kerry, the barony of Iraghticonnor. At Kells, a diocese of Inis Cathay based on Scattery island, was recognised. It extended along both banks of the Shannon mouth, but by 1302 it had been partitioned between the three modern dioceses of Kerry, Killaloe and Limerick, so that Iraghticonnor was by then included in the diocese of Kerry as the rural deanery of Iriagh. Ardfert did not go down without a fight and seems to have consolidated itself at the synod of Kells in 1152 when the diocesan reform was finalised and the four archbishoprics of Armagh, Cashel, Dublin and Tuam were settled upon. There the Kerry representative was, according to Keating, 'Mac Ronain, comharba Bhreanainn, bishop of Kerry'. Perhaps Ratass did not survive its burning in 1136. (Reidy says it was the anglo-normans who made the change in 1215, but does not give reasons). The Aghadoe bishopric (if there ever was one) must already have fallen into disuse. By 1302 the barony of Beare was in the diocese of Ross but seems in penal times to have reverted to Kerry.

The bishop was to be supported by a chapter, the members of which were called 'canons', whose functions were administrative advice and support, education, and the service of the liturgy in the cathedral. They were to live around the cathedral and arrangements were to be made for their support. In this way the old monastic community was replaced by a new episcopal one of secular priests. In Ardfert this had occurred certainly by 1217. The chapter had four main officers — the dean, its head; the precentor, responsible for the church music; the chancellor, for general administration and education; and the treasurer. These were the *quattour personae* of the chapter and their stalls were at the four corners of the choir. All these officers had special provision for their support called a 'prebend'. Thus part of the prebend of the chancellor of Ardfert was half of the tithes of the parish of Kilmalkedar — so, the 'Chancellor's House' there. A fifth officer was the archdeacon, a sort of deputy and inspector of the bishop. In Ardfert, presumably because of the division of the diocese between the anglo-norman and gaelic worlds, there seem to have been two archdeacons — one based on Ardfert and one on Aghadoe for the gaelic world of south Kerry, though the papal taxation of 1302-6 seems to refer to only one, presumably of Aghadoe.

The dioceses once defined, it became the duty of the bishop to work out a system of rural deaneries and parishes. In the deanery one parish priest would have some degree of supervision over the others, but it is doubtful if this ever came to much. In Kerry the six rural deaneries were a concession to tribal feeling. As described in 1302-6, four of these were wholly in north Kerry — Iriagh (Iraghticonnor); Othorna and Offlannan (Ui dTorna and Ui Flannain), that is, substantially Clanmaurice; Hacnye (Trughanacmy); and Offerba (Ui Fearba). In south Kerry there was only one, Hacudes (Aghadoe). The sixth was divided between the two worlds (so presumably antedated that division) Ossuris (Aes Iorruis).

When the task of defining the parishes was completed is a matter of dispute; a full parochial system was in being in Kerry by the beginning of the 14th century at latest. It is argued that this was not done until the middle of the thirteenth century, or even later; but in some places at least better progress was made. A detailed study of the modern diocese of Cashel and Emly suggests that there, and elsewhere, the job was done by the date of the synod of Kells (1152). Perhaps it depends on how one regards 'parish' — as a system for the cure of souls, or one of ecclesiastical income based on tithes apportioned in a special way. Much elucidation remains to be done. In the diocese of Kerry some ninety parishes were established, almost twice the present number of roman catholic ones, so priests must have been plentiful enough. The principal churches were strategically placed — Aghadoe; Church Island (Lough Currane); Kilmalkedar; and, probably, Rattoo. All these were in the hiberno-romanesque tradition of the 11th-12th centuries, and three of them had round towers. Many of the parish churches — relatively large and in stone — date from this reform, such as at Milltown, at Annagh and at Killemlagh.

Parishes are for people and are thus based on settlement patterns. There seem to have been three main contributors to the typical parish as it emerged in the 12th and 13th centuries. First, minor tribal groupings — thus, in North Kerry, O Brennan, O Galey, O Flannan, Ui dTorna.

Secondly, from the old monastic termons (tearmon, a boundary — hence the place within a sanctuary) within which lived monastic tenants. In this way former monastic settlements such as Church

Church at Church Island, Waterville

Island (Lough Currane), Kiltallagh and Kilmalkedar became absorbed into the parochial system. The fact that these were not taken over by by the new monastic settlements, and did not become dependencies of them, suggests that they were already firmly within the parochial structure before the end of the twelfth century.

Thirdly, the manors of anglo-norman settlers. These tended to be smaller and more compact than the other two — hence 19 parishes in the Dingle peninsula, which was heavily settled. No doubt, these were amongst the latest parishes to be erected — in the 13th century.

All three arrangements made it possible for laymen to play a big part in parochial life in the choice of priests and in the economic structure of both parish and diocese — the head of the family in the familial parish, the hereditary coarb and erenagh in the monastic parish, and the new landowner in the manorial parish.

In 1171-2 was held a second synod of Cashel at the direct instigation of Henry II whose assumption of the lordship of Ireland was justified, ostensibly, by the need of church reform — this less than a year after the killing of that 'turbulent priest' Thomas à Beckett. In fact the synod, apart from attempting to tackle the marriage abuses, concerned itself with freeing the church from the financial burdens of the old Irish law system and strengthening the old provisions for the payment of tithes to parish churches — itself an indication that the parochial system was already substantially in being. Moreover, the major decision was to decree that the Irish church was to be brought in all respects into conformity with the English church, a decision that in the future was to cost the Irish church dearly.

The second major problem tackled by the reform movement was to get the monastic movement — now flowing strongly in the church as a whole — once more under way in Ireland. For this purpose the Augustinians, who were a major papal instrument of reform from the middle of the eleventh century, and in a small way the Benedictines from 1127, were introduced — the latter, under Mac Carthy influence, to Cashel in 1127 and to Rosscarbery before 1148; but these changes did not affect Kerry until the work of St Malachy began to take effect.

St Malachy was abbot of Bangor. In 1127 Irish raiders drove him and 120 of his monks out of the monastery and he took refuge for a time at Lismore where he became a friend of King Cormac Mac Carthy (the builder of the gem of Irish romanesque at Cashel) who was temporarily deposed in that year and also took refuge in Lismore. When Cormac was restored he helped Malachy and his flock to settle at 'Ibracense' which, tradition says, was Iveragh on Church Island (Lough Currane) — and build a monastery there. The main buildings date from that period. Church Island is within sight of Eighterqua where Mac Carthy — certainly some time later and probably at this time — had a seat. It was also argued that the building was at Ballinskelligs but the buildings there give no support to this. (Another suggestion is Ui Breacain near Cashel.) Some years

later Malachy became bishop of Armagh and was installed there with the support of Mac Carthy and of O Briain. Malachy was friendly with St Bernard of Clairvaux and introduced the Cistercians into Ireland in 1142. They reached Abbeydorney in 1154. St Malachy sent some Irish monks for training to St Bernard who chose one of them Christian O Connairche, to be the first abbot of Mellifont — about three-quarters of the first community of perhaps thirteen were French, but these soon withdrew. He became bishop of Lismore in 1150 and presided over the crucial synod of Kells in 1152. In 1171 Henry II travelled to Lismore apparently to see him and O Connairche presided as papal legate over the synod of Cashel in the winter of 1171-2. He died in Abbeydorney in 1186. In the next century, under norman influence, came the Augustinian Hospitallers (the Cruciferi) to Rattoo (c. 1200), and the Arroaisians there a few years later; the Augustinian canons to Killagha (1215); the Knights Hospitaller to Killorglin (about the same time); the Dominicans to Tralee (1243); and the Franciscans to Ardfert (1253). These were all new foundations.

Lastly was tackled, as part of the movement of monastic reform then sweeping Europe, the problem of winding up the old Irish monastic system. It is likely that St Malachy's own monastery had already adopted the rule of the Augustinian canons. In any event, St Malachy met on his travels the rapidly developing Arroaisian Augustinians (from Arrouaise near Arras in Flanders where in earlier times two Irish missionaries had been martyred). The Augustinian canons were secular priests who lived in community and followed a rule in some way deriving from St Augustine. The Arroaisians were much influenced by Cistercian austerity. These Malachy introduced into Ireland, and it is claimed that under his influence many cathedral chapters adopted the Arroaisian system. These Augustinian canons had for head the bishop of the diocese and were thus most apt for changing from the primacy of the abbot — which obtained in Irish monasteries — to that of the diocesan bishop. They also engaged in parochial work, so fitting in to much of the Irish tradition. These, and other forms of Augustinian canons as well as canonesses (nuns) — in time — took over everywhere and relatively soon the 200 old Irish monasteries of men and women, notwithstanding their past glories, were, with few exceptions, brought to an end, being replaced by some 100 newly founded or refounded institutions. Thus, during the last half of the twelfth century and the beginning of the thirteenth Inisfallen, Aghavore, Ballinskelligs and Rattoo (changed from the Cruciferi) became Augustinian, the two last named being Arroaisian.

It is probable that it was at this time that the Skellig was foresaken. But the old Irish monastic system was not completely obliterated. In the 14-15th centuries there were still Culdee monks in Clonmacnoise and elsewhere, and the anchoritic movement carried on until 1682 in Fore when the last Irish anchorite died. There is no evidence that either movement carried on so long in Kerry.

It seems, therefore, that by 1200 or thereabouts, the reform of the

50 Irish church had been completed and was in full running order. The secular chapter in Ardfert was certainly in operation in the 1190s. The change is symbolised by the building in 1250 of the great gaunt cathedral of St Brendan at Ardfert, superseding its Irish romanesque and earlier monastic, or *damh liag*, predecessors by the harsh early English gothic. This was the end of the romanesque style that gave us the churches at Kilmalkedar, Church Island (Lough Currane), Killemlagh, the little church on Inisfallen, and part of that at Aghadoe. In the fields of literature and scholarship the period of reform brought substantially to an end the phase in which the monasteries and churchmen generally showed a great and effective concern to conserve, interpret and develop historical, legendary and literary remains. Henceforward the new monasteries, as well as the old ones reformed, ceased to concern themselves with gaelic learning. That task was to be taken on by the great bardic families from the thirteenth century and, when they came tumbling down, by the Franciscans. Although the Augustinian canons held on to the end something seems to have been lost to the old Irish monasteries, and

their wonderful contributions to Irish spirituality, to Irish culture and and to Irish life soon came to an end. This task was later to be taken over by the new mendicant orders, especially the Franciscans, whose founder seemed closer to the traditions of Irish religion than the reformers themselves.

As we have seen, the work of reform took about a century and a half to complete. It was a long haul and the great reformers, St Malachy and later St Laurence O Toole, became convinced that it could not be achieved until the political anarchy was ended. This made them, with papal encouragement, welcome the possibility of the intervention of the king of England. When the anglo-normans did come, the back of the church reform problem had in fact been broken. Unfortunately, the invaders contributed new causes of political anarchy and injected into the church a new and most virulent ill, the struggle between the English and the Irish clerics, that was to last until the Reformation of the 16th century.

Ardfert Cathedral

Chapter 5

Feudalism 1200–1500

Ireland was unusual in Europe in that her own society had continued without outside influence for more than 1,000 years, since the time of the last celtic invaders. The overwhelming influence of the Roman empire and its civilisation had been largely avoided, except through the onset of christianity, weakly romanising at first but recently reinforced. In most unroman manner religious and secular society had continued (e.g. in relation to marriage) in their separate compartments. The great disruption of the barbarian invasions of Europe were, again, felt only in part through the most recent of these from Scandinavia. So, Irish society maintained its distinctive, and exceptional continuity throughout this great period of time. This virtual immunity to the great shaping influences of Europe was now to come to a slow, agonising end. It has been well said that 'the tragedy of the Norman invasion was not the conquest of Ireland . . . but the half conquest'.

The anglo-normans began the half-conquest of Kerry about 1200 AD. About a century later an equilibrium had been struck that lasted for another 250 years, until the conquest of Kerry began in earnest.

ANGLO-NORMAN INTRUSION

During these three centuries the history of Kerry is, normally, of two distinct areas — North Kerry, now including the Dingle peninsula, where anglo-norman influence was supreme; and South Kerry, where the gaelic way of life continued almost undisturbed. North Kerry became the county of Kerry, ruled by (to make things confusing) the geraldine earl of Desmond; and South Kerry was ruled by the gaelic king of Desmond, Mac Carthy, later Mac Carthy Mor.

When Strongbow landed in Waterford the king of Desmond, Dermod Mac Carthy, attacked him unsuccessfully. Among those killed were an O Donoghue and an O Cahill. However, when Henry II landed, also at Waterford, in 1171, Dermod was the first Irish provincial king to pay (apparently voluntary) homage to him and to promise to pay him a yearly tribute. It is suggested that Mac Carthy saw in Henry an ally against his formidable enemy, Donal Mor O Briain. If so, he underestimated both Henry and Donal. Five years later Dermod's son, Cormac Liathanach, imprisoned and deposed his father; but at Dermod's request Raymond le Gros led an expedition to Cork, Dermod was reinstated and Cormac was killed. Perhaps this encouraged Henry to forget the submission and, in 1177, to grant Mac Carthy's *regnum Corcagiense,* from Brandon in the west to the Blackwater at Lismore, to Robert Fitz Stephen and Milo de Cogan who struck west as far as Aghadoe, spent two days there, and then retired from Kerry. In the same year their ally, Donal Mor O Briain, laid Desmond waste from Waterford to Mount Brandon. It is not clear that Fitz Stephen and de Cogan ever established a 'presence' in the Kerry part of their grant. Of the 31 cantreds in Mac Carthy's kingdom they settled for seven around Cork city. Neither left male heirs. The effective anglo-norman intrusion into Kerry did not occur for a further generation. Neither did the submission of Mac Carthy to Henry prevent the followers of Theobald Walter, ancestor of the

Butlers, earls of Ormond, and companion of John, Lord of Ireland, from killing King Dermod in 1185 at a parley near Cork.

In 1177 Henry also gave the kingdom of Limerick to other adventurers; but the formidable king of Thomond, Donal Mor O Brien, had other ideas. He supported the anglo-normans whenever their efforts weakened his enemy the king of Desmond; he helped Fitz Stephen and de Cogan in their attack on Dermod Mac Carthy, weakened as he was by the struggle against his son Cormac; and, as we have seen, he laid Desmond waste in 1177. But he kept the anglo-normans firmly at bay when, returning from Cork, they encroached on his own territory. After 1178 he cleared out of his kingdom as many as possible of the gaelic and eoganacht septs. Thus the O Sullivans came to Kerry from Tipperary. Another area cleared was that of south Limerick, and in these lands he encouraged the anglo-normans to settle.

Donal Mor O Brien died in 1194 and there was the usual confused struggle for succession. This the anglo-normans fully exploited. During these struggles the eoganacht families staged a come-back, and the land around the Shannon was laid waste. Donal Mac Carthy, son and successor to King Dermod, briefly held Limerick in 1196. The rally seems to have been short-lived.

The justiciar, Hamo de Valognes, was in Limerick in 1197 and granted lands there to three sons of Maurice Fitz Gerald, one of the original invaders of Ireland, who had died in 1177. One of these sons, Thomas, was granted Shanid, near Glin, by Hamo. This Thomas was the ancestor of the earls of Desmond. The grant was confirmed by John when he became king in 1199. Shanid was in the territory of the eoganacht Coilen O Cuilein who, in defending his patrimony, was killed by the geraldines in that year. In 1200 a drive by the O Briens and the Limerick anglo-normans struck deep into Cork and contained Mac Carthy.

Now began, slowly at first, the invasion of Kerry.

John, when he became king in 1199, made Meiler Fitz Henry, one of the original invaders of Ireland and son of a bastard of Henry I, his justiciar for the ten years to 1208. In 1199 he granted Meiler the barony of Trughanacmy, the northern part of the barony of Corkaguiney called 'Offerba' (Ui Fearba) 'from Tralee to Brandon', 'Yoghenacht Lokhelen' (Eoganacht Locha Lein) 'as fully as Humuriardac (O Moriarty) had it', and it would seem 'Assurus' (Aes Iorruis), the territory of the Corcu Duibne on both sides of Dingle bay. Mahon O Moriarty was killed by O Donoghue in 1195 and Muircheartach O Moriarty, described in the *Annals of Inisfallen* as king of Eoganacht Locha Lein, was captured by Mac Carthy in 1200. It is clear from all this that the eoganacht Locha Lein were still fighting for their lands, that O Donoghue had not yet consolidated his hold in the old kingdom, and that the anglo-normans were ever ready to fish in troubled waters. And the waters were troubled indeed.

52

Dunloe Castle

As we see, the O Donoghues were still struggling around Killarney, the O Sullivans were establishing themselves along both sides of the Kenmare River, and the Mac Carthys, although now firmly established in Iveragh and much of Magunihy, were fighting for their lives on the broader front. Felled by the joint blows of Mac Carthy in Iveragh and the anglo-normans in the Dingle peninsula, the ancient kingdom of the Corcu Duibne on both sides of Dingle bay seems, about 1200, to have disappeared without trace. It is clear from the grant of Trughanacmy that the Ciarraige, too, caught between the contending forces of the O Briens and the Mac Carthys were in retreat from their rich homeland. The new gaelic kingdoms of Mac Carthy, O Donoghue and O Sullivan, under the general suzerainty of the former, were in deadly peril from the anglo-normans infiltrating from the north and from the east.

In 1200 there was an anglo-norman raid through north Kerry to the Killarney area. By 1205 Meiler had sufficient grip of part of north Kerry to grant 10 carucates of it to the Abbey of Connell which he had founded. Unless he had been by then in peaceful possession of this land, it would have been unsuitable for a monastery. He seems also to have established a branch of the Knights Hospitallers under Brother William from Dublin at Rattoo about the same year; the Arroaisian Augustinians soon took over this foundation. He was, no doubt, responsible for building Dunloe castle in 1207 in what was left of O Moriarty territory. It is possible that he also took possession of the other territories of the 1199 grant. But it was not until Meiler entered a monastery in 1215, leaving no legitimate children, that his infiltration was consolidated. This occurred as a result of a remarkable conjuncture of circumstances.

First, Donal Mac Carthy had died in 1206 and there followed a long period of dispute amongst his would-be successors. Dermod 'of Dundrinan' emerged as master but was constantly challenged by his brother, Cormac Fionn. Serious warfare broke out in 1215 with, as usual, Irish and English on both sides. This warfare gave the land hungry would-be successors of Meiler their chance to invade from Limerick.

Secondly, Geoffrey de Marisco became justiciar. He was one of the greatest ruffians of the 13th century. He had been the close collaborator of Thomas of Shanid. He had married the widow of Thomas' brother and was guardian of Thomas' younger son, Maurice. He had been granted the extensive territory of Aes Iorruis, comprising the north and south shores of Dingle bay and inland as far as Ballymalis and Dunloe on the Laune. Because Meiler had left no legitimate children his lands (with some exceptions) fell to be escheated to the Crown, whose representative was Geoffrey who had no scruple about disposing, in his own interest and that of his friends, of escheated property. Meiler had left his lands of Ui Fearba on Tralee bay to John de Clahull. (This included rights of wreck, often abused.) This grant was confirmed by the Crown, but the remaining lands were divided amongst the conspirators. King John died in 1216; his successor, Henry III, was nine years old. Geoffrey knew how to exploit the regency.

Thomas of Shanid had died at the end of 1213 and his two young sons, John and Maurice, were typical energetic geraldines, insatiable for land. From Shanid they took their war-cry — a custom borrowed from their opponents — that became the cry of the Desmonds — of 'Shanid a buaidh' — Shanid for Victory. They were joined in their enterprise by at least one of their cousins, Thomas Fitz Robert. John became the ancestor of the earls of Desmond, his cousin Thomas, by his son Maurice, the ancestor of the Fitz Maurices, lords of Kerry.

The key figure in the whole operation was Thomas Fitz Anthony to whom and to whose heirs was granted by King John in 1215 the custody, that is to be sheriff of the counties of Decies and Desmond. He was required to guard these counties at his own expense but could recoup himself out of the king's demesnes and escheats in those territories. He was also given the custody of the lands and heirs of Thomas of Shanid. He had five daughters, and three of their husbands – Gerald de Roche (or de Rupe), Stephen Archdeacon (or Mac Odo) and John Fitz Thomas of Shanid — took part in the conquest of Kerry.

Geoffrey de Marisco and Thomas Fitz Anthony bought off the Mac Carthy factions, and the whole band overran Kerry north of the Maine.

At the same time the successors of de Cogan and Fitz Stephen were pressing steadily west from Cork. They drove along the indented coast and built castles in great numbers as they went. By the time the conspirators were poised to drive from the north the Cork contingent were in position to penetrate Kerry from the east and

Shanid

establish a line along the Roughty river.

The invaders in their use of archers, cavalry and armour were able to overwhelm such of the Irish — on foot, armed with slings, swords and axes and clad in linen tunics — as attempted to oppose them. It is probable that the use of archers was as decisive in battle in Ireland as it had been in anglo-saxon England. In consequence, castles were built along the three river lines of the Maine, Laune and Roughty. These castles were built on the motte and bailey principle — a high mound of earth surrounded by a deep ditch. These are still to be seen at Aghadoe and Dunloe, amongst other places. On the mound was placed, at first, a wooden tower, usually prefabricated, and around the ditch a stockade. The tower was later replaced by a stone structure.

One string of castles was built, apparently by the brothers John and Maurice Fitz Thomas and their cousin Thomas Fitz Robert, along the valley of the river Maine at Currans, Molahiffe, Cloonmealane, Castlemaine. This was to be the line between anglo-norman and gaelic worlds for nearly four centuries. There was also built a more advanced line of castles stretching from Callanafersey, Killorglin (held by Geoffrey de Marisco), Ballymalis and Aghadoe, linking with Dunloe. The line was continued by a castle built at Irrelagh (now Muckross) by a Roche, presumably the Gerald married to Fitz Anthony's daughter. At the same time the successors of de Cogan and Fitz Stephen drove their line of castles along the Roughty to, and beyond, Kenmare — at Ardtully, Dunkerron and Cappancush — built by, apparently, Robert de Carew whose mother was daughter of King Dermot Mac Carthy and who himself was heir to Fitz Stephen. This line loosely connected with the advanced line beyond Killarney. In this way, in the period 1215 to 1228 energetic attempts were made to contain and fragment what remained of the gaelic kingdom of Desmond. Only the great peninsula of Iveragh was not overrun.

Now for the division of the spoils. The de Cogan seignory was revived in the person of Margery de Cogan and descended through her de Courcy sons. Thomas Fitz Anthony, the *custos*, fared worst of all. He was rebuked in 1223 and lost the custody of Decies and Desmond. He died about 1229, heavily in debt. The main gainer

was his son-in-law, John Fitz Thomas. The present barony of Trughanacmy went to him to hold from Margery de Cogan. He built the great castle of Tralee and founded the Dominican priory there in 1243. John Fitz Thomas married, secondly, Una daughter of O Conor Kerry now confined to the most northern barony of Iraghticonnor, and by her had the ancestors of those unexplained hereditary knights — the White Knight, the Knight of Glin, and the Knight of Kerry — which were to be the main supporting families to the future earldom of Desmond. The last two families still survive. In the four centuries of geraldine hegemony O Conor Kerry was able to survive between Lord Kerry and the Knight of Glin, often his sworn enemies, because, as Sir Nicholas Browne was to report in 1597, 'by reason of his woods and bogs he was wont to hold his own in spite of them both'.

Shanid — the keep

54

The barony of Alltraige — between Trughanacmy and Iraghticonnor — now Clanmaurice — went to John's first cousin Thomas Fitz Robert who established the Fitz Maurice family at Lixnaw. Thomas, who died after 1261, was by his son Maurice of Molahiffe, the founder of the family who later became Lords (then Earls) of Kerry. Thomas, first baron of Kerry, founded the Franciscan friary at Ardfert in 1253 and died in 1280. Next to the Desmonds, the Fitz Maurices were the most prominent anglo-norman family in Kerry and, unlike the Desmonds, they survive. In the 18th century they inherited the great wealth of the Petty family. They are now the Marquesses of Lansdowne and still have property in Kerry. (Another pedigree would trace the family to Maurice, son of Raymond le Gros, one of the ablest of the original anglo-normans. This would have brought them to Kerry before 1185 under the de Cogan and Fitz Stephen grant. The pedigree is doubtful, and it is unlikely that Kerry was invaded before 1200 AD.)

The lands at the extreme west of the Dingle peninsula went to Geoffrey's son, Robert. Geoffrey himself built the great 'Castell of the Island', now Castleisland. He also held the castle of Killorglin which came into the hands of the Knights Hospitallers. Close by was founded the Augustinian priory of Killagha, 'de bello loco'. Geoffrey is credited with this foundation which presumably replaced the older Irish monastery of Kilcolman on, or close to, this site. Geoffrey was lord of Adare and Any in County Limerick and was the archetypal bad baron. He was Strongbow's nephew. In 1207 he had been in arms against the justiciar, Meiler Fitz Henry, but was pardoned. In 1213 he had two Irish chiefs tied to a horse's tail and dragged through the streets of Dublin until they died. As justiciar from 1215 he was in trouble with the Pope over the appointment of bishops (including the bishop of Ardfert). He was in conflict with the bishop of Limerick and was excommunicated for detaining see lands and robbing church property. In 1221 he was dismissed as justiciar for appropriating the whole revenue of Ireland for the previous six years — the misbehaviour in Kerry was a big part of what was held against him. Nonetheless, he was justiciar again from 1226 to 1228. His son was accused of plotting the king's murder, was outlawed and hanged. In 1232 Geoffrey himself participated in the killing of the Earl Marshal, had to flee, and died in exile in France in 1245. He ordered his body to be buried in one of his monastic foundations in Limerick. Geoffrey's lands, including Killorglin, were confiscated in 1234 but were soon restored to him and to his son Robert, who died shortly after his father. Robert's heir was his daughter, Christiana de Marisco, a minor, placed in the wardship of the justiciar, Maurice Fitz Gerald, a kinsman of John Fitz Thomas. Over the next decades John and his successors leased or bought the de Marisco properties, such as Killorglin and Dunloe.

Geoffrey de Marisco as justiciar was concerned not only to establish armed norman power in the county but was also the instrument of a new royal policy to take over the great influence on the plain people, the church. In the 13th century bishops were elected by the appropriate cathedral chapter. The role of the pope was to sanction these appointments, and to act as a court of appeal. The English king also had a sanctioning role.

In 1217 the see of Ardfert was vacant. Although the dean and chapter elected a bishop, Gilbert, he had not yet been sanctioned at Rome, or consecrated. Geoffrey tried, as in Killaloe in like circumstances, to intrude an Englishman into the see on the new general policy that no Irishman could be permitted to be a bishop. His candidate for Ardfert was John of St Albans, an English Benedictine; that for Killaloe his nephew. The Pope, Honorius III, was not prepared to accept any such general rule, and in 1221 his specially commissioned legate had the two Irish bishops consecrated and the two Englishmen deposed; but the struggle went on. John eventually resigned and withdrew to England, but the king did not confirm Gilbert as bishop until 1225. The Irish did not press their advantage and, in the event, there came to be a *de facto* partition of the diocese of Ardfert — the english influence being usually, but not always, predominant in north Kerry, and the gaelic influence unchallenged in the south, in the archdeaconry of Aghadoe, so giving support to the impression that there had been a separate bishopric there.

At Geoffrey's foundation at Killagha it was laid down that no Irishman could be a member of the community. Notwithstanding the special emollience of life in Kerry this rule was long adhered to. We read of William Mac Gildrome as being a canon there in 1402, but the first Irishman to be formally admitted there was Alan O Lonsygh, of the diocese of Limerick, in 1411. A Florence Mac Carthy was prior there in 1476. These monasteries were not unique in their apartheid. There is reason to believe that monasteries staffed by Irishmen applied the same rule in reverse.

Although the anglo-normans were major benefactors of the church, their interest in church affairs, and their determination to keep them under English influence, posed a major problem — as Geoffrey's history shows — for the church of the 13th century and later. The conflicts between the Irish and the English churchmen were not eased in favour of the Irish until the end of the 14th century and later. They were only finally resolved when most of the English party took the reformers' side at the Reformation and the Irish party, generally forced underground, held fast to the roman connexion and kept the loyalty of the Irish people. This Irish-English tension was one of the issues that, in the 13th century, led to the sharp decline of the Cistercians. It was a special issue for their Munster houses, including that at Abbeydorney whose abbot, with four others, was deposed in 1228, allegedly leaders of a conspiracy against (probably the anglicisation of) the order. Within a century of their arrival these great reformers were rich and in decline and losing influence and recruits to the new mendicant orders.

Considerable pains were taken to keep the mendicant orders under English control and subject to the English provinces. The Augustinian friars established an Irish province only in 1457, and the Dominicans not until 1536. However, the Dominicans, from 1314, at least had a separate vicar provincial for Ireland, an Irishman with a fair degree of autonomy. The Irish vicariate might send two students each to Oxford, Cambridge and London, as well as one to Paris and other places. The Franciscans — whose founder recalls so many of the characteristics of the Irish saints, except their irascibility — were amongst the first to resolve the struggle as between the Irish and the English clerics; from as early as 1231 there was a separate Irish province. However, the king was able to establish that no Irishman could become provincial, and that the province be divided into four 'custodies', only one of which was to be Irish. It was not until 1445 that the first Irishman of native stock — William O Reilly — became provincial, but even then there was a further bitter struggle, including the deposition of O Reilly, before the Irish friars won control of the province. This long struggle led to a good deal of strife: at a general chapter in Cork in 1291 the two sides came to blows and it is said that sixteen friars were killed. In the event, the Franciscans came to be closely associated with the Irish cause. They contributed notably, at home and abroad, to Irish scholarship and in evil times stuck to their pastoral duties in Kerry and elsewhere. This is part of the reason for the great affection they still command. This is true also, but to a lesser extent, of the Dominicans. There was something familiar to the continuing Irish tradition of spirituality in the mendicant friars when the reforms of the 12th and 13th centuries had replaced the Irish tradition of monasticism with the formal, enclosed systems of the Cistercians and the Augustinian canons. These latter paid scant attention to the Irish monastic traditions of

spirituality and scholarship. So, the *Annals of Inisfallen* were discontinued and the Skellig abandoned. Nothing more in the cultural area was done than to train suitable youths in grammar and poetry, Irish and Latin, singing and rhetoric. If they showed promise as possible priests they were taught the elements of philosophy, theology, canon law, and the administration of the sacraments.

When the anglo-normans acquired a district and had it under control, they, as feudal lords, exercised rights over the churches in the territory, including the right to nominate the parish priest. The gaelic lords exercised similar rights. On occasion these rights were attached to a favoured monastery, perhaps outside the county, such as Connell and Owney. So, in later times, parishes in the Dingle and Iveragh peninsulas are found, for example, to be attached to Killagha, and the Cistercians of Abbeydorney had advowson (the right to nominate the incumbent) of, for example, the parish of Molahiffe. The holding of parishes in this way was a feature of the Augustinian canons; the Franciscans and the Dominicans did not do so.

A feature of the twelfth century romanisation of the church was the institution of tithes to support the church. This was consolidated by the decree of the synod of Cashel of 1171-2. Tithes were levied at one-tenth of the produce of the soil and of personal industry. They were of two kinds — great and small. Great tithes were levied on corn, hay and wood and, in general, went to the support of the rector. He was not obliged to live in the parish or to perform any duties in relation to it. He might hold an appointment elsewhere in

Ardfert Friary

56

the diocese or in another diocese, or be a papal or royal official, or be away studying. But if he did take the cure of souls it was necessary to provide a clergyman bound to residence. He may have been 'provided' – that is, in effect, appointed – by the bishop, but, if not, the appointee must have been acceptable to him. This clergyman was the vicar, in effect, the parish priest. He was entitled, apart from offerings, in some places, to the small tithes levied on flax, hemp, fruit, herbs, personal industry and the like, or else to a proportion – a third or a quarter – of the total tithes. Sometimes the rectorate of a parish was 'impropriate', that is, vested in a religious community of men or women, as we have seen. Then the vicar was removable at will and often poorly paid. At the end of the 14th century some improvements were made in the lot of these vicars. For example, the pope ordered the ecclesiastical authorities of Ardfert to see that the Augustinians of Killagha instituted a perpetual vicarage, with a fitting portion attached to it, for the vicar's sustenance. As a rule, five or six marks a year was regarded as sufficient – say, £300 - £400 a year. Nonetheless the vicar was independent of the rector and not subject to him. It often happened that neither rector nor vicar was a priest. If so, he was required to provide and pay a chaplain for the cure of souls. The institution of tithes was to play a big part in the later history of Kerry when the established church took over the benefits of the old system of ecclesiastical taxation. Apart from tithes, other sources of parochial income were from glebe land, as well as the offerings of the faithful for services rendered. In west Kerry, at least, the glebe land attached to a parish came to 5 to 10 acres.

On top of the general system of ecclesiastical taxation there grew up, particularly in the 13th century, an elaborate system of papal taxation – some of this to finance special ventures, such as the crusades, but some of it to finance the expenses of that great new european power, the Papacy. As part of this growth, from the election of Innocent IV in 1243, the pope began to play a much more active part in senior ecclesiastical appointments, and the king correspondingly less. As the power of the pope grew the significance of elections by episcopal chapters tended steadily to be superseded. Those appointed to the more senior offices, reserved to the pope, were expected to pay him half the first year's income from the benefice. This tax was known as First Fruits (or Annates). It was first introduced in the early 14th century, but records of its applying to Kerry begin only in 1421. It was usual to exempt from this tax when the annual income was six marks or less. It was only one of several heavy imposts.

The government of the diocese under the bishop – dean, precentor, chancellor, treasurer, canons and archdeacon – was supported by the prebendal system by which a definite source of income (usually a parish rectory and, sometimes, glebe lands) was assigned to each office as well as an allowance from a common fund, and payments for attendance at cathedral services.

The real architect of the fortunes of the house of Desmond was John Fitz Thomas who, in one shape or another, seems over the years to have gathered into his hands all the territories of the other

adventurers, save only those of his cousin. John came to be known as John of Callan, from the place of his death. Notwithstanding the invasion, he kept peaceful relations with King Dermod 'of Dundrinan' who died in 1229. Although Dermod founded a Franciscan friary in Cork, he was killed by a thunderbolt at Dundrinan 'through the vengeance of God and because of his own misdeeds'. He seems to have been the last Mac Carthy ruler to have died in the Cork area. His successor was his brother and long-standing rival, Cormac Fionn. In 1234 there was a Mac Carthy attack on Tralee, beaten off by John Fitz Thomas, in which Dermod, son of Cormac Fionn, was with others killed. The geraldine had his ambitions for more of Kerry because in 1244 he got a grant of 'free chase and warren' in Kerry, Muskerry, Magunihy and Iveragh, and in the same year he killed Donal Roe, another son of Cormac Fionn, at Shanid.

Kerry, that is the present north Kerry, was shired by 1233 – possibly in King John's original creation of shires in 1210 – and was brought into the general system of administration, taxation and justice established over a substantial part of Ireland. We have a computation by Walter Brackleyer, sheriff, for the county in 1253-4 which includes such items as 'George Fitzthomas, £20 for the castle and cantred of Killorglan and Dunlow; 71 shillings for aids of our Lord the King [Henry III] for services . . . John Fitzthomas, 1 mark for wine of whiskey, Howell de Cantelupe computation of 16s 8d for wine of whiskey. . . Adam son of Fitz Andrew of Archath [Ardfert] 20 marks for false weights and measures . . . Robert Lodele, 41s 6d – for fine of Roger Blund homicide . . .'

For nearly a generation there seems to have been peace in the area. The geraldines did not, it seems, create any great disturbance of the existing septs and they do not seem to have had appreciable difficulty in establishing themselves behind their line of castles. They seem, for all their extraordinary rapacity for land, and their lack of scruple in despoiling gaelic magnates, to have been able readily to fit in to the Irish way of life. Little in the way of atrocities is attributed to them, and none in Kerry. Yet they came of a stock which in England and Wales devised such deeds of darkness that it came to be said that God slept. Perhaps the emollience of Irish life had its effect. Moreover, the geraldines were not so much *anglo*-normans as *cambro*-normans, and this Welsh strain helped them to fit in to the related celtic way of life in Ireland. Inter-marriage played its part almost from the first. Whatever the reason the geraldines were among the first of the great norman lords who, in the words of the gaelic annalist, 'gave up their foreign ways and harshness for good manners and hospitality'.

To some extent, too, the structure of society helped this absorption. A feudal lord might hold (when he could) his lands from the king in return for certain services. The great lords had their lands divided into manors and these manors were held by the principal tenants from their lord; the local court system rested on these manors. These free tenants were often of the second rank of invaders, and paid their lords either military service or a money rent for their lands. Under them, again, were the farmers who paid rent, and also labour services. Below them were the gavillers, or tenants-at-will, who paid rent, and labour services; and below them were the cottiers and farm servants. A further class were the burgesses, who held small plots of land, and were artisans or petty merchants.

Many of these classes were colonists. In the thirteenth century there was a shortage of men and a really substantial colonization by normans, flemings, english and welsh. In Kerry, apart from the great names of Fitz Gerald and Fitz Maurice, such families as Browne, Cantillon, Ferriter, Fleming, Hoare, Hussey, Prendergast, Prenderville, Rice, Trant and Walsh date from this period.

It is likely that the anglo-norman free tenants were the lords of the Irish tenants who were, as we have seen, stratified in a somewhat similar way. Thus, the men mustered by a great lord, such as Desmond, would be a mixture of the colonists and the older Irish tenants. In the more remote areas many of the colonists did not survive the troubles of the fourteenth century; but the survival of the names we have cited shows that many of them managed to hang on. Beneath the tenants, both Irish and colonist, were the serf class, or *biataigh* (betaghs, betagii). These were legally attached to the soil, suffered various restraints and had to perform numerous services, which were by the end of the thirteenth century commuted for a money rent. The average holding of a *biataigh* seems to have been in the range 17 to 25 statute acres. These were the servile clans of celtic Ireland, and were clearly the descendants of the pre-celtic population.

In effect, one can see each wave of immigrants leaving a higher layer of society as it established itself. As one sank down the social scale one moved from the more recent to the earliest of the many settlers of Ireland.

This stratification by date of conquest — a process that was to continue — was to play a big part in later Irish land troubles. Agriculture about the middle of the thirteenth century depended on grain crops and beans, peas and onions. Root crops were practically unknown. There was a 2-3 year rotation, with the land lying fallow in the 2nd or 3rd year. Wine was extensively imported from Poitou and the Rhineland.

The forces we have been considering were played out, of course in north Kerry. But something similar occurred in south Kerry, or Desmond. Here, however, as we have seen, the invaders were not anglo-normans but gaels — Mac Carthy, O Donoghue, O Sullivan. Under Cormac Fionn Mac Carthy the Mac Carthy power came to be largely based on south Kerry — specifically the present baronies of Iveragh and Dunkerron North — and the great movements of the previous century, with all their warfare and disturbance, seemed to be coming to a close. But although at their worst the gaelic nobles engaged in much violence and killing there was not much atrocity, and there seems to be no record of a tyrant amongst Irish kings. This was, at least in part, because despotic power was not accorded to any ruler; but on occasion some of them could behave very badly.

Once the new gaelic states were established there was in them a firm system of order and taxation. Thus the Mac Carthy dynasty throughout feudal times consisted of long-lived rulers, few of whom did not die peacefully. They administered an elaborate system of demesne lands — especially around Killarney and in Iveragh — and of raising taxation, mainly in kind, from their vassal clans — O Sullivan, O Donoghue and their septs — that maintained them in reasonable affluence and that did not forfeit the consent of their subjects. The Mac Carthys, after the thirteenth century, were, unlike the Desmonds, to be blessed by having no history. Some of this came from their remoteness and their own longevity; some of it from the great lack of records of gaelic, medieval Ireland; but much of it came from the calculation of their own shrewder leaders.

However, there was to be one great outbreak of trouble before a final equilibrium, destined to last some three centuries, was struck. In the second half of the thirteenth century there was a forceful Irish rally throughout the country. The Irish leaders dropped some of their rivalries, imported hebridean mercenaries (hence such names as Sweeney and Sheehy, introduced into Kerry in later times) and established, a great innovation, their own standing armies.

The great disturbances amongst the gaelic families had yet to be worked through. Much of this was the usual hosting and raiding, with the anglo-normans on both sides; but of lasting significance were the developments in the Mac Carthy family.

The Donal Mac Carthy, king of Desmond, who died in 1206 had left three sons, two of whom Dermod (d. 1229) and Cormac Fionn (d. 1248) succeeded him; this Cormac was the founder of the house of Mac Carthy Mor. The third son was Donal God (the stammerer) who by constant warfare against O Driscolls and others carved out a separate lordship for himself in West Cork; he was the founder of the house of Mac Carthy Reagh. After Cormac Fionn's death he disputed the succession with Cormac's son who was aided by John Fitz Thomas. In 1252 John Fitz Thomas and his son Maurice killed Donal God, in Roche's house, apparently at the instigation of O Donoghue's wife. Donal's son, Fingen, a vigorous and active man, was to take implacable revenge. In the following year, he burned to death in his house at Gortalassa, Killarney, O Donoghue, his wife, his brother, his three sons and several others.

In 1259, perhaps hoping to profit from the disorder, or at least to strengthen his hand against Fingen, John Fitz Thomas induced the future king Edward I, then lord of Ireland, to give him the grant in fee of Waterford, Cork and Kerry, that is, the area forfeited by his father-in-law a generation before. Because he was accused of getting the grant by misrepresentation the justiciar refused him seisin, but John took possession by force.

In the same year Fingen twice raided North Kerry and 'made great slaughterings, plunderings and burnings of the English'. In the following year he burned no less than six castles in West Cork.

58   Hence Hanmer's vivid phrase that 'the Carties plaied the Divells in Desmond'.

It was clear that something had to be done to stop this and John Fitz Thomas induced the new justiciar, William de Dene, and a great medieval host (including Cormac Fionn's son, Donal Gall) to take the field against Fingen. This expedition was partly financed by merchants on a geraldine guarantee. On July 24th 1261 the two forces met in Callan Glen, near Kilgarvan. No doubt the justiciar and the geraldines were heading from the valley of the Roughty into Fingen's fastnesses amongst the Cork mountains. But they had gone only a few miles when they fell into his ambush in the glen where they could not display their military strength. In any event, Fingen completed his revenge. The English force was utterly routed. John Fitz Thomas, his son Maurice, eight barons and twenty-five knights were slain. Fingen overran and levelled a dozen castles, including Killorglin and Dunloe. He set out to sweep every anglo-norman from the territories of his grandfather, but overreached himself and was killed two months later that year at Rinn Roin, near Kinsale. The following year the English tried again, and there was an inconclusive but bloody battle at Tooreencormick (Tuairin Cormaic) on the sides of Mangerton. The battle field is called after Fingen's brother, Cormac, who lost his life. So did, on the other side, Gerald de Roche, the brother-in-law of John Fitz Thomas.

The battle of Callan is one of the decisive Irish battles, and *the* decisive one in the history of Kerry. It effectively partitioned Kerry between the anglo-norman and the gaelic worlds, and kept the english influence out of south Kerry (and west Cork) for over 300 years. Henceforth, the barrier between the two worlds would be the river Maine, and the castles south and east of it fell into gaelic hands.

Although Donal Rua, son of Cormac Fionn, had been on the geraldine side at Callan he became King of Desmond and ruled the territory for forty years. With him begins the most glorious period in the history of the house. Magunihy was cleared of the invaders (but not without set backs: he was routed at Ballymalis in 1270 by a geraldine and Mac Carthy alliance) and Mac Carthy power pressed along the valley of the Lee to Blarney castle, seven miles from Cork. In 1280 the Mac Carthy factions composed their differences, and made an alliance of Mac Carthy, O Donoghue, O Sullivan and O Moriarty. Killorglin and Dunloe (which must have been re-occupied by their builders) were destroyed in that year. Donal Rua was succeeded in 1302 by his grandson Diarmaid, who was murdered in Tralee in 1325. Notwithstanding this, the century was the peak of Mac Carthy power. For two centuries more the succession of the Mac Carthy lordship of Desmond passed from father to son without a break. However, notwithstanding the victory of Callan and its effects, sometime in the fourteenth century Mac Carthy acknowledged the sovereignty of the Earl of Desmond and the duty to pay him tribute.

The recovery at Callan Glen, like others by other gaelic families, was to prevent their being crushed and to give them some part to play in ensuing centuries. This period also marked the high-water mark of the King's influence in Ireland. At the end of the century, three-fourths of the land of Ireland was ruled by anglo-norman lords, and these in turn were subject to the king, Edward I. Under them many Irish families survived, and under them again the eternal tiller of the soil, the unfree biataigh. In the other fourth of the country, the great Irish families were supreme in three main areas — most of Ulster, around the head waters of the Shannon, and Desmond. The king's law did not enter these lands. Of these families Mac Carthy was one of the greatest. Butler points out that in Desmond there was an organised State with an elaborate fiscal system, providing a settled annual revenue for the sovereign and his various sub-chiefs. This revenue was definitely assessed on certain areas of land; it postulates fixed metes and bounds and a considerable amount of tillage. Every clan, every sub-sept had its own territory; and on this territory, the amounts due for the support of the hierarchy of chiefs were systematically applotted.

Nonetheless much of the detailed history of the next two centuries had to do with the activities of the Desmond geraldines.

John Fitz Thomas (John of Callan) left an infant grandson, Thomas Fitz Maurice, called Thomas an Apa, because, according to the story, a monkey had carried him as an infant along the battlements at Tralee castle. He did not become of age until 1282, but his uncle Gilbert Fitz John and his cousin the Lord of Lixnaw held his inheritance together, so far as the times permitted. In 1282 he came into possession of an enormous property in the counties Waterford, Cork, Limerick and Kerry and became hereditary sheriff of these counties except Limerick. His inheritance in Kerry was much dilapidated, great tracts of it 'lying waste amongst the Irish'. Nonetheless, he held castles at Tralee and Castleisland and some foothold at Killorglin. He spent a good deal of energy in restoring these lands, so that in 1285 Donal Rua Mac Carthy, King of Desmond, complained of him personally to Edward I. However, he got peacefully the regrant of Decies and Desmond in 1292 'with the homages and services of both Irish and English'. Three years later he was, briefly, justiciar. The following year he was in Scotland helping Edward, and was one of the magnates called to the second Irish parliament in 1297 because of the efforts to secure enormous supplies from Ireland for that war. Presumably, the abbot of Abbeydorney was also there, as well as two representatives of the county nominated by the sheriff. From 1295 until 1307, the year of Edward's death, justiciars' courts were held regularly throughout the country, including Tralee, Ardfert and Duagh.

Thomas an Apa, having in effect restored the fortunes of the family, as established by John Fitz Thomas, died in 1298. He was succeeded by his son, Thomas, who died in 1307, who was succeeded by his brother Maurice (b. c. 1293), who in 1329 became the first Earl of Desmond, and who played a stormy part in Irish politics during much of the first half of the fourteenth century.

During the reign of Edward I, that is, to 1307, the king's influence reached its highest point in medieval Ireland. The head of the government, as deputy for the king, was the justiciar. He was military chief, head of the civil administration, and supreme judge. He was assisted by a council of permanent officials and, sometimes, magnates. This constituted the central government and it was endlessly itinerant. By 1300 there were eleven shires, of which (north) Kerry was one. These came directly under the Crown government. Each shire was ruled by a sheriff who was normally appointed by the government but after 1355 elected by 24 of the best men of the county. The sheriff represented government in the area — he collected the revenue, both taxes and fines; he presided over his own county courts, which were held mainly for administrative purposes, but also had judicial functions, especially in

Ballymalis

civil cases; he was the administrative underpinning for the higher judicial courts when they came on circuit; he held prisoners and maintained the gaols and king's castles. His principal sphere of operation was the 'tourn', held apparently in the cantreds (or baronies). He had extensive military and police duties. He was assisted by a sub-sheriff, whom he appointed, and an office staff. Out of doors he was assisted (and often embarrassed) by a body of serjeants (or bailiffs), under an hereditary chief serjeant, who often acted by deputy. There was in each cantred a serjeant appointed by the chief serjeant, and these had their own sub-serjeants who often abused their duties. There was a coroner in each cantred with considerable administrative duties, and in each county a considerable number of keepers of the peace. All of these officials were under some sort of control from Dublin. For church lands, normally held directly from the Crown, known as crosses, there were separate sheriffs.

Geraldine Kerry illustrates much of this. As we have seen, Kerry became a shire by 1233, there were at least some sheriffs up to the time John Fitz Thomas got his grant in 1259; this included, it seems, being hereditary sheriff of the county. His grandson and heir, Thomas an Apa, exercised this hereditary right for a period after he came of age, but lost it. It seems that his grant of 1292 made him hereditary chief serjeant, but not sheriff. The sheriffs of Kerry were in constant trouble. When the justiciar visited Limerick and Kerry in 1295 his court had to deal with a long list of charges of violence and oppression brought against sheriffs and ex-sheriffs; but this was exceptional amongst shires, and exceptional for Kerry. Nonetheless, the second volume of the *Kerry Magazine* prints an amusing list of the charges that illustrate the hazards of the job of sheriff in the thirteenth and fourteenth centuries. When, later, Kerry became a liberty in 1329 Desmond took the place of the king and he had his own government. His chief official was the seneschal who, for that area, had the same powers and duties as the justiciar for the central government. Other officials were chancellor, treasurer, escheator, judges. The king, however, reserved to the central government the 'crosses' and the usual four pleas of arson, rape, treasure trove and forestall (assault on the king's highway). Under the lord's 'central' government was the usual local government organisation under the sheriff. As Desmond was already hereditary chief serjeant of Counties Waterford, Cork and Kerry he became, for all practical purposes, the sovereign of the latter county. In effect, therefore, the king's government had, for the next 250 years, no place in Kerry, north or south.

Miss Otway-Ruthven suggests that the population of Ireland towards the end of the twelfth century was, perhaps, a little less than 1½ m. On the assumption that, within a still rural society, the distribution of the total population did not change in over 600 years — a large assumption, of course — we can perhaps guess that the population of Kerry in our period bore the same relation to the total as it did when reliable figures became available in 1841; on this assumption the population of Kerry as a whole in the 1200s was about one-

60

twentyseventh of the total, perhaps something over 50,000, rather less than half of what it is now. As we shall see, it may have been at about the same level some 400 years later.

FEUDAL STABILISATION

In the feudal time, that is in the fourteenth and fifteenth centuries, we discern a clear overall pattern, notwithstanding the confusion of detail. The political revival of the gaelic world, that began in the latter part of the thirteenth century, continued with steadily mounting force. Ireland was politically divided into three.

First, the old gaelic world steadily regaining its power. In Kerry, for example, the Mac Carthy dynasty was at the peak of its continued power and influence during three centuries. They were supported by hereditary professional families. Thus Mac Carthy's captains were the O Rourke, his brehons (judges) the Egan, his poets the O Daly, his antiquary the O Duineen, and his physician the O Callanan families.

Secondly, the great anglo-norman lords, rich, ungovernable, gradually being absorbed by the gaelic way of life, exchanging their French language and culture for Irish. At the same time, they took occasional interest in, and charge of, the Crown government of Dublin, and kept at bay the influence of the English-born English. Of these nobles, the three most prominent during the two centuries were the earls of Kildare, Ormond and Desmond — the last named often indistinguishable from a gaelic magnate. These great nobles gradually established themselves in liberties where they in fact carried on the process of government in their own names and the substantial administrative structure by which the king's government was carried on in his name in the shires was dismantled; so Desmond became a liberty, and Kerry a county palatine.

Thirdly, the Crown government in Dublin. This was only the occasional concern of an English monarchy distracted by wars in Wales and Scotland, the Hundred Years' War in France and the Wars of the Roses at home. The Dublin government was from time to time in the hands of the Desmond or Kildare geraldines, or the Butlers. During these two centuries the Crown governed in practice only a small area around Dublin and was continually struggling both against the overbearing feudal nobles and the cultural absorption of the whole in the gaelic world. For all its formal position the Crown and its closest supporters occupied a sort of ghetto around Dublin, decimated each decade by plague, chronically short of money, the king's revenue almost disappearing as the decades wore on.

Already, towards the end of the reign of Edward I signs of the breakdown of financial administration can be seen. In 1304 writs were issued from the Treasury of the Exchequer to the sheriff of Kerry relating to the merchants of the Society of the Friscobaldis of Florence who had lent money to the king in return for exchequer concessions. The Italian merchant bankers had been introduced into

Ireland in the first half of the previous century to help with the newly established system of papal taxation. They rapidly extended their influence throughout the country. Seven years later, under Edward II, a writ is issued to the sheriff of Kerry directing the levying of customs from foreign merchants upon scarlet and other cloth throughout the ports within the bailiewick of the Sheriff of Kerry. In the following year the King, conceding that the diversion of Irish revenue to his affairs in England and Scotland had not left enough to govern Ireland, so that law and order had broken down, now directs that Irish revenue be spent in Ireland to preserve the peace. In the same year 'the King's custom in the County of Kerry is committed to Thorold del Papa, a merchant of Florence, for one year, he paying at the Exchequer 10 marks, whereof the Sheriff is directed to give him the cokets'. In the following year the Sheriff is directed to summon James Henry of Winchelsea to answer the King why he carried hides from the port of Shemery-Wyt (St Mary Wick, or Smerwick) without paying the custom dues therefrom, as Toraldus de la Papa, the Keeper of the Custom, can show. He was also to distrain James Henry for trespass. And so on. There is a constant list of complaints about sheriffs and other officers who failed to give an adequate account of funds or otherwise abused their trust. For example, the justiciar's court at Ardfert in June, 1307, was told how a local sub-serjeant and others, who were ordered to 'purvey' (that is, acquire in the king's name) cattle, returned some of them to those owners prepared to pay them bribes.

As the orderly system of central administration of the previous century began to break down in the early years of the fourteenth, there was a hastening of the process because of the rise of the great feudalists, of whom the most intractable was Maurice, the first earl of Desmond.

Also rising was the central power of the church. Increasingly, the power of appointing bishops moved from the cathedral chapters to the pope. The papal taxation system also grew. Between 1302 and 1306 the annual income of all ecclesiastical benefices in Ireland was assessed, and taxed at one tenth. The total income of the diocese of Ardfert and its parishes, priories and abbey was £178.16.6d, on which £17.7.8d became payable. This illustrates the poverty of the Irish church. A single monastic house — Furness in Lancashire — had in 1292 an income of £176, that is equal to the total ecclesiastical revenue arising in the whole diocese of Ardfert. That diocese was not exceptionally poor — of the eleven dioceses in the province of Cashel it ranked seventh. Lismore, with £711, ranked first, and Ross, with £45, came last.

Edward I died in 1307 and was succeeded by Edward II. There followed a period of considerable political confusion both in England and in Ireland. The third parliament in Irish history was held in Kilkenny in 1310 and set the pattern of those to follow — representatives of the anglo-Irish nobles, the higher and lower clergy, and two representatives each of the counties and the boroughs. It was also representative in displaying a bigoted, middle class antipathy to the 'mere Irish'. At this time Dingle and Tralee were thriving towns doing extensive trade in Irish wool and hides against French and Spanish wines and cloth. About this time, too, the *biataigh,* or unfree serfs, began to be freed from their ancient servitude and to become tenants of their lords, but their full freeing in a legal sense was not to come for three centuries.

Edward Bruce, following the victory of his brother over the English at Bannockburn the preceding year, invaded Ireland in 1315 and was crowned king of Ireland in 1316. These years coincided with a great famine, and this was a period of great hardship. For some 20 years there was very considerable disorder. Maurice, the future earl of Desmond, who came of age in 1315, supported Edward II, and Diarmaid Mac Carthy supported Bruce. There was some scattered fighting in Kerry, when in 1316 first O Brien and then Mac Carthy devastated the Dingle peninsula; but this was, no doubt, part of the local sport. Maurice was able to turn the times to good account. On the king's behalf he organised a large army but, having no subsidies for it, supported it by exacting coigne and livery, a tax — coigne i.e. cain — in kind that, apparently, he invented. This practice was execrated by the English but was maintained by the Desmonds to the end. This tax involved exacting food and maintenance for soldiers and horses. According to Sir John Davies, this exaction drove out the English free-holders from the Desmond lands, and strengthened and widened the possessions of Maurice and his kinsmen. In 1325 Diarmaid Mac Carthy was murdered in Tralee 'upon the bench before the Judges of Assize' by William Fitz Maurice, brother of the lord of Kerry, with the aid of the son of Samradhain, bishop of Ardfert, and others. Fitz Maurice was blinded by Maurice of Desmond and his men were hanged or beheaded. Diarmaid was succeeded by his brother Cormac who in 1327 welcomed to Kerry Dermot O'Mahony the member of the West Cork family who founded the important O'Mahony family in Kerry. At this time Maurice, the future earl, took on the trappings of a petty king and many of the manners and customs of the Irish. In 1326 he entered into a conspiracy with other magnates to emulate Bruce and become King of Ireland. He had to share Waterford with Arnold le Poer who insulted him in public with *enormia verba,* calling him a *Rymoure* (Rhymer) — he did write alliterative verse in French. There followed substantial military operations for four years.

In 1327 Edward II was deposed and for three years the Queen Mother and her favourite, Roger Mortimer, ruled England. These events enhanced the disorder in Ireland, which split between the English factions. In 1328 was created the great earldom of Ormond and in 1329 that of Desmond, the latter obtaining palatine rights in Kerry; but these concessions did not long keep Desmond quiet. As earl palatine he took over almost all the functions of the king in Kerry, and was in command of the full administration and revenue there. In consequence, there are no central records of the administration of the county palatine. Mortimer was overthrown in 1330 and in the following year Edward III arrived to restore the king's authority in Ireland by attempting to give the Irish equal rights under English law (Donal Cairbreach Mac Carthy, swearing fealty in French, established this in a lawsuit for himself and his chief vassals)

and by attempting to crush the unruly anglo-Irish nobles. Of these the leader was, of course, the earl of Desmond. He refused to attend a parliament in Dublin in July, 1331, but did attend it when it was summoned for Kilkenny. Later that year the justiciar arrested Desmond and he was in Dublin Castle for just two years when he was released on bail. In 1332 was hanged his principal ally, William de Bermingham. Attempts were made to deprive Desmond of his grants from Mortimer, but in 1334 Kerry was restored to him.

Without abandoning his policy of reducing the great nobles, the king decided to give priority to his interest in Scotland and so, in effect, almost abandoned Ireland. A Scottish expedition from Ireland in 1335 was headed by the two earls of Ormond and Desmond. (On this campaign, Edward used ordnance, first introduced into western Europe in 1325, but not to reach Ireland for over 150 years. This time lag gave the house of Desmond a feudal lease of 250 years.) Edward III was in continual financial trouble, and in 1340 repudiated the enormous debt of £1.4 m. This finally ruined the Italian merchants. In 1346 a parliament tried to tax the considerable revenues of the church, but the churchmen mounted a fierce resistance and won.

An Irish rising in Kerry Desmond suppressed in 1339; this revolt was aided, as was to happen many times in the future, by the current Lord of Kerry, whom Desmond captured at Currans and starved to death in Castleisland. (Desmond, having blinded one brother and murdered another, married as his second wife their sister Aveline.) However, when the justiciar's deputy, Sir John Morice, tried in 1341 to replace all the officers of the Crown in Ireland by Englishmen, Desmond and Kildare attended an adjourned meeting of Desmond's Parliament in Kilkenny where there was a united opposition to the government. A remonstrance was addressed to the king, who repealed the offending statute. In 1344 Desmond is alleged to have written from Castleisland to the kings of France and Scotland, as well as to the Pope, hoping to set on foot an international conspiracy — so setting a longstanding family tradition. The following year after a great deal of disorder, Desmond marched with thousands of men to Callan, Co. Kilkenny, where he invited the anglo-Irish lords to meet him; but they obeyed a prohibition not to attend. By now Desmond, with the help of anglo-Irish and gaelic lords (including Cormac Mac Carthy), was in open rebellion, and was outlawed and his lands declared to be confiscated. The justiciar, Ufford, mounted an expedition against him. His castle at Askeaton fell, and in November, 1345, after a two weeks' siege, his castle at Castleisland which had been held to be impregnable. The earl's seneschal, Coterel, and two others of the leading defenders, le Poer and le Grant, were hanged, drawn and quartered. Desmond fled to the Irish for protection, and the following year incited O Conor Kerry to revolt, but shortly after (June, 1346) he surrendered and was allowed to lay his case before the king in England. Again, he was nearly two years in prison, but was released on bail in 1348, was pardoned his treason in 1349, and in 1350 returned to Ireland, and in 1351 his outlawry was removed. He was a man of great personal charm and was a great success with Edward III. So far was he pardoned that in July, 1355 he became

62 justiciar for the short period until his death early in 1356. He has been claimed as being the first of the colony's Patriot Party who were to have a brief hour of glory over four centuries later; but he was in fact the classic example of the feudal lord. It is a striking feature of the history of Kerry that the real struggles of the crown in Kerry were not with the gaelic chieftains but with the anglo-normans, as long as they lasted. The Desmonds, throughout most of their history, were quite ungovernable. They met their doom when the last palatine earl, in very different times, behaved like the first.

It seems that there was a considerable growth of trade and wealth at the end of the thirteenth century, some of it through the port of Dingle. The export duty on wool and hides yielded from £5 to £15 a year in the period 1287 to 1292. This would represent an export of from 630 stone to 1,880 stone of wool, *or* 1,500 to 4,500 hides. Substantial support was given from Ireland to Edward I in his Scottish wars and Ireland yielded a substantial revenue to him. The year 1299 was one of exceptional fertility.

It is not clear why there was little or no building in Ireland as a whole, and in Kerry in particular, during almost the whole of the fourteenth century. There was, however, widespread devastation during the wars of Edward Bruce (1315-1318), accentuated by the severe famine of 1315-17 caused by excessive rainfall; this famine was a general European phenomenon. There was much loss of life, especially amongst the urbanised English, in the Black Death of 1349-50 and again in 1361 and 1370. These wars did not in any real sense reach Kerry (although Mac Carthy participated in them and was subsequently pardoned), and the Black Death which wreaked great havoc amongst the english colony was unlikely to be severe in rural areas such as Kerry. The plague was, however, but one of the epidemics of the time and there were numerous famines. For example, there was great mortality in 1363 in, amongst other places, Kerry and Desmond. For about a century from 1300 there was a sharp deterioration of the weather and this, no doubt, hit agriculture and the supply of food. Moreover, the population history of Ireland, up to the catastrophe of the mid-nineteenth century, tended to mirror that of England. There the population rose 3½ times in the 250 years before the Black Death; and this rise of population, common to Europe as a whole, provided a surplus for the colonisation of Ireland. From about 1300, however, this rise was arrested and in the fifty years to the end of the fourteenth century it almost halved from disease and hunger. It was not until about 1600 that the population of England regained the level of the early 1300s. It seems that the population had risen fast while agricultural skills remained static, and a situation not dissimilar from that of Ireland in the last half of the nineteenth century occurred. The same thing may have occurred in Ireland in the fourteenth century, so that the population of Kerry did not regain its level of the 1200s for some 400 years.

The period to about 1300 seems to have been one in which the religious reforms of the 12-13th centuries and the intrusions of the anglo-normans were being digested. The mid-fourteenth century was a period in which the mendicant friars were highly unpopular with the church authorities in Ireland. The absence of new church building in Ireland (unlike England, France and Italy) in the fourteenth century is a sign not only of the long period of economic depression that set in during this period, but also of the beginnings of a local religious decline that reflected the larger scene. It will be recalled that during this century the church as a whole suffered great harm from the Avignon captivity (1305-1378), the Black Death (1348-50 — recurring six times in the 50 years from 1361) and the Great Schism (1378-1417). The effects of this decline were also to be seen in Ireland and in Kerry.

Two of the by-products of the Avignon period were, first, an intense centralisation of church affairs in the pope, so reducing the powers of the king on the one hand and of the cathedral chapters on the other; by the end of the century all episcopal appointments were made by the pope. The second was a severe, inflexible and corrupt system of papal taxation.

One of the aims of twelfth century church reform had been clerical celibacy. To this end, the child of a cleric was debarred from holy orders. The Avignon pope, John XXII (1316-34) undermined this by giving, in return for stiff fees, dispensations from the rule. Hereditary clerical families once more became common in Ireland, both in diocesan offices and in some of the monasteries.

Already, even before the Black Death, there were complaints about shortages of priests, gross abuses were evident, and the period of decline had begun. (We have seen that in 1325 the son of the bishop of Ardfert, Nicholas O Samradain — who 'sate' 1288 to 1335 — had joined in murdering Diarmaid Mac Carthy, king of Desmond.) It is, as we have seen, unlikely that the Black Death was severe in these remote and unurbanised places and thus a significant local contributor to the decline.

A symptom of this decline was the interference of great magnates in clerical appointments which in the following century was to grow to scandalous proportions. The Fitz Maurices in Kerry, the Desmonds in Kerry and Cork and the Mac Carthys in Cork committed gross abuses.

In 1340 the chapter of Ardfert was divided on the election of a bishop — two parties elected different bishops; but the pope quashed the election and himself provided (i.e. appointed) one of the candidates, John de Valle, a member of a local family, in 1348.

The fourteenth century saw the revival of gaelic learning and literature. The greatest of Irish bardic poets — Gofraidh Fionn O Dalaigh (d. 1387) — sprung from the hereditary bardic family of the Mac Carthy Mor — could, on the one hand, urge his patron to leave the spare countryside of Kerry and the Lough Currane where he was reared and return to the ancient patrimony of Cashel — "yew-clad, swan-haunted, lovely". On the other hand, he could re-assure his other patron, the second Earl of Desmond:

I ndan na nGall gealltar linn
Gaoidhil d'ionnarba a hEirinn;
Goill do shraoineadh tar sal soir
i ndan na nGaoidheal gealltair.

(In poetry for the English we promise that the Gael shall be banished
from Ireland; in poetry for the Gaels we promise that the English
shall be routed across the sea.)

Most of the gaelic literature that survives is from manuscripts of this
time and of the following century. It was the period when the great
learned families took over the preservation of the Irish heritage from
the monasteries.

Cormac Mac Carthy Mor died in 1359 after a reign of 34 years and
was succeeded by his son Donal Og who reigned for 31 years. The
second earl of Desmond died in 1358. The third earl was an
imbecile. His guardian and successor as fourth earl, was Gerald
(b. 1338), known as Gearoid Iarla, a distinguished poet in Irish. He
wrote in French and in Irish exquisitely polished verses in the courtly
tradition of love poetry of the period. (His wife, a Butler, was
famous for her gallantries.) Gearoid may indeed have introduced the
style from the French into the already highly polished traditions of
Irish poetry — a poem of his is the first we now have of this style.
This genre was to last some 250 years — at the end of the sixteenth
century the last really powerful Mac Carthy Mor (first Earl of
Clancarre) was writing in Irish courtly poetry in the same style as
Gearoid Iarla. Gearoid Iarla was steeped in Irish literature and his
poetry makes constant allusion to it.

This was a period when the heart seemed to go out of the English
colony and it reached its lowest ebb. There was, at the same time, a
revival of Irish culture — law, medicine, history, poetry and
imaginative literature as a whole.

In 1366 were set up the Statutes of Kilkenny that attempted to set
up a system of legal *apartheid* between the English and the 'mere
Irish', proscribing all forms of the gaelic way of life in the vain hope
of stemming the rising gaelic tide. Gearoid Iarla was justiciar from
1367 to 1369. This points to the contrast there often is — especially
amongst the great — between law and practice. In this year eight
bishops excommunicated those who contravened the Statutes of
Kilkenny. The Bishop of Ardfert, John de Valle, was not among
them. It is improbable that the infamous Statutes had much
currency in Kerry. In 1370 having become involved in a dispute
between the O Briens, Gearoid Iarla was heavily defeated at
Monasteranenagh, Co. Limerick, and was captured by Brian O Brien,
King of Thomond, from whom he had to be ransomed by the king's
lieutenant. In this decade began the practice of the blackrent
whereby the colony paid gaelic magnates, such as O Brien, to leave
them in peace.

The ancient feud between Ormond Butlers and Desmond geraldines
continued. In 1381 the Bishop of Cloyne inserted this preface in a

Ballycarbery

requiem mass said before the justiciar for the repose of his wife's
soul:

Eterne Deus   *Eternal God*
duo sunt in Momonia   *there are two in Munster*
qui destruunt nos et bona   *who destroy us and our*
nostra   *property*
videlicet comes Ermonie   *namely the earl of Ormond*
et comes Dessmonie   *and the earl of Desmond*
cum eorum sequaribus   *with their followers*
quo in fine destruet Dominus   *who at length the Lord will*
per Christum Dominum   *destroy*
nostrum   *through Christ our Lord*
Amen.   *Amen.*

Not even a bishop in Ireland could with impunity take on such
adversaries and his outspoken exasperation — in which he persisted —
caused him to be proceeded against for slander, in the court of the
archbishop of Cashel so that he had to pay Ormond heavy damages,
and at Rome for schism and heresy, so that some ten years later he
was deprived of his see.

The latest record of a bishop of Ardfert being appointed with the
king's approval is from 1380. In 1382, the justiciar having suddenly
died, the same bishop of Cloyne was unable to persuade either
Ormond or Desmond to take on the by now ruinously costly job of
justiciar.

64   Some years later Desmond received the king's permission to send his son John to fosterage with another of the O Briens. But when Richard II was in trouble in 1394 with Art Mac Murrough he, unlike Ormond, gave him no aid and, indeed, later joined with Mac Murrough.

In 1390 Donal Mac Carthy died in his castle in Killarney and was succeeded by his son Tadg. Tadg was called 'of the monastery', possibly a new or revived foundation on the site of what was to become Muckross friary. According to the *Annals of Inisfallen* he was the most noted wine drinker of the English or the Irish of his time. His wife was a daughter of Gearoid Iarla. He died in Ballycarbery castle in 1428.

In 1395, Richard II, pursuing a policy of appeasement, on his first visit received the homage of most of the gaelic princes — O Neill, O Conor, O Brien and Mac Carthy — for which in return they were admitted to full citizenship and equal legal rights with the english. Tadg Mac Carthy made his (abject) submission in Kilkenny, and recognised Desmond (Gearoid Iarla) as his immediate overlord. About this time Mac Carthy ceased to style himself King of Desmond and became known as Mac Carthy Mor. In general, the title 'Ri' or 'king' was abandoned at this time. About the end of the century the royal justices ceased to sit in Munster and abandoned it to the local lords.

Gearoid Iarla died (he may have been murdered near Castleisland) in 1398 and the Four Masters in their annals said of him:

> Garrett, Earl of Desmond, a cheerful and courteous man, who excelled the English, and many of the Irish, in the knowledge of the Irish language, poetry, and history and of other learning, died. . .

He was to become a folk hero, reputedly sleeping under Lough Gur in Limerick until Ireland should need his services. He had been almost completely absorbed into the gaelic tradition. His son, the fifth earl, was drowned a year later. His daughter, Katherine, was the centre of several scandals. She left her father's home after being caught in an affair with her brother, took refuge with her uncle Ormond who raped her. She then regularised her position by poisoning his english countess and marrying him.

The sixth earl of Desmond, Gearoid's grandson, Thomas, aged 14 on his accession, was in 1411 driven from the earldom and the country by an ambitious uncle, Gearoid's son, James, who exploited Thomas' mistake in marrying a girl of the 'mere Irish' and a low born one at that. Thomas returned in 1413 and 'devastated Munster' but resigned the earldom in 1418 and died in Paris in 1420, leaving no legitimate children. His uncle, James, assumed the title of the 7th earl of Desmond. He held the title for 42 years and was the most magnificent and powerful of the line. He was all powerful in the four south-western counties. For example, in 1438 he acquired all the Cogan lands in Cork, about half the county. He commanded the

ports of Dingle, Tralee, Limerick, Youghal and Cork. He was supported by four junior branches — the Knight of Kerry at Dingle (who was the hereditary collector of the earl's rents in Kerry at a 5% commission), the Baron of Clanmaurice at Lixnaw, the Knight of Glin in Limerick, and the White Knight at Kilmallock. He founded a new branch of the Fitz Geralds in the Decies of Waterford. Unlike so many of his line he maintained an alliance with the earl of Ormond. The O Briens amongst whom he had been fostered, were his allies, and Mac Carthy Mor, Mac Carthy Reagh, O Sullivan Mor and O Sullivan Beare paid him tribute. He was married to a Clanrickard. For the law cases of his Irish tenants he introduced gaelic brehons into his lordship, and made an O Daly his court poet. For his standing army he brought in from the North the scottish gallowglass family, the Sheehys — the Sweeneys were the gallowglasses of Mac Carthy Mor. Desmond's fame reached Florence, whence in the eleventh century had come to England the Gherardini, the ancestors of the geraldines: in 1440 the Secretary of State of the Republic wrote congratulating him on being of Florentine stock. Curtis says of him that he was 'the first of the Old English to display fearlessly a power derived from feudal grants, Brehon custom and usurpation of Crown rights, to rule most of a whole province as a palatine earl, to reign over an Irish population like a Gaelic "Ri" and yet in Dublin to be of the Council and among the peers of the Anglo-Irish State'.

He was succeeded in 1462 by his son Thomas who was deputy to the viceroy, the Duke of Clarence from 1463 to 1467. (The vice royalty was usually held by a distinguished, if absent, noble: in such circumstances the effective head of such government as existed was styled, not justiciar but lord deputy.) In 1462 the Butlers had mounted a formidable Lancastrian revolt against the Yorkist, Edward IV. Desmond raised, at his own charge, 10,000 men and crushed the Butler revolt. One of the Butlers, Edmund Mac Richard, was captured, and for part ransom paid Desmond two great Irish books out of his library — the *Book of Carrick* and a copy of the *Psalter of Cashel*. Thomas was a noble-minded man who attempted to reconcile the Lancastrian Butlers, the ancient enemies of his family. He commanded the respect and affection of the gaelic princes. He spoke English. He tried to establish an Irish university in Drogheda modelled on Oxford — Irishmen had to go to England for university studies — and had an act to this effect passed at the Parliament held in Drogheda in 1465. He did establish a learned foundation at Youghal modelled on All Souls, Oxford. He was (it had seemed) the personal and loyal friend of the king, Edward IV. However, in 1467 a new deputy from England, Tibetot (or Tiptoft) was appointed. At a parliament in Drogheda that year Desmond was attainted for treason and friendship with the Irish. Desmond, not realising his danger, answered a summons to Drogheda in February, 1468, was seized and immediately beheaded, with two bastard sons. Smith has a story that one of the boys 'besought the executioner not to hurt the boil that was upon his neck'.

The decision to make the greatest of the Irish nobles 'shorter by the head' may have been a calculated act of state and it certainly ended the hegemony of the Desmond family — which in fact went in a more powerful form still for the next sixty years to the Kildare family of geraldines. It also permanently embittered Earl Thomas' successors and drove them finally 'over to the Irish': his five sons (four of whom were to succeed to the title) immediately rose in rebellion aided by Mac Carthys and O Briens, and began to ravage the Pale. Succeeding earls toyed with rebellion with foreign aid until eventually, over a century later, they rose in their fatal rebellion. There is a more romantic explanation of this act. Earl Thomas, four years previously on a visit to England, had been asked by Edward IV for advice on how to strengthen his precarious power. The earl is reputed to have said that the queen, Elizabeth Woodville, was 'too unfit a match for his majesty, shee being his subject'; adding, further 'his best course was to cast her off and to joyne and linke himself to some greate and powerful prince...' The story is that the Queen got to know of this. When Tibetot was appointed she secretly took the king's seal, sealed a death warrant for Desmond and had it sent to Tibetot. According to the story, the lord deputy, summoned before the king and council, 'shewes his commission for the execution of the earl of Desmond; yett all his excuses would not serve the turne; off goes his head from his neck to make satisfaction to the angry ear ghost of Desmond'. This was two years later when Edward IV having fled abroad, Henry VI briefly resumed the kingship. Tibetot was beheaded on 19 October 1470, the day after his trial.

Notwithstanding Earl Thomas' death, the earls of Desmond were to play some part in national affairs for another century. Thomas' successor as ninth earl, was his son James. In 1484, Richard III sent Barnet, bishop of Annaghdown, to win the Irish of the west and southwest to the peace. Of these, the chief was Desmond. Richard wrote to Desmond saying that the eighth earl had been 'extorciously slain and murdered. . . against all manhood and reason and good conscience'. Amongst other things Desmond was to be persuaded to abandon Irish array, and the bishop was supplied with a suitable wardrobe — of gowns, doublets, shirts, hose, hats and tippets, and a collar of gold — to give to Desmond should he swear allegiance. When all Ireland supported Lambert Simnel, and he was crowned in Dublin as Edward VI of England, in May, 1487, only Waterford stood out against him, and for six weeks was besieged by a force under Sir Maurice of Desmond, who was to become the tenth earl. Later that year, James, ninth earl, was murdered in Rathkeale at the instigation of his brother, Sir John, but was succeeded by his younger brother Sir Maurice, who put John to death and reigned until 1520. When Perkin Warbeck, the second impostor against Henry VII, landed in Cork in 1491 Desmond was the leader of the party that supported him. Warbeck left Cork in 1491 and came back in 1495. Again Waterford stood out and again it was besieged by Maurice of Desmond, now earl, and again without effect. Poynings, the english lord deputy, came to the city's relief bringing big guns which were first used in Ireland on this occasion. When the tenth earl was pardoned by the king for his part in the Warbeck business ('they will crown apes next') he got the revenues of the ports of Limerick, Cork, Kinsale, Baltimore and Youghal.

Apart from these futile goings on the Desmonds were, like the

Mac Carthys, to content themselves with leading the lives of great lords in their many castles with what seem to be constant forays — sometimes to collect tribute — on their subjects and neighbours. Sometime before 1500 they had adopted as their chief *ollamh,* or professor of native law, one of the famed O Maolconaire family from Connacht. Several of the great lords died violent deaths. We get some little insight into what life was like in their establishments. The nobles were, of course, devoted to all forms of hunting. When they gathered in the great halls of their castles — on the top floors of their many tower houses — in the evenings, with dim lights, huge fires blazing in the enormous fireplaces, great wolfhounds stretched before the fires, the floor cleared, the poets, the story tellers, the musicians, came into their own. We have seen what these old stories consisted in. The poetry, restricted in range but exquisitely phrased, was written and spoken by highly trained professionals. The music, robust or plaintive, still lives with us. Again, we get the occasional glimpse of a great lord tossing off a delicately, if artifically, phrased, love poem to some mistress, real or imagined. A century after this Father Wolfe the jesuit could write of Ulster: 'There are several lordly castles in Ulster, although the owners for the greater part of the time, especially in summer, live in tents and frequently change from one place to another according to the needs of their flocks'. In the sixteenth century it was reported, with surprise, that some of the Desmonds could speak English. It was an extraordinarily indrawn world. This was the period of the renaissance in Europe, of intense artistic and intellectual excitement; but Ireland remained almost wholly unaffected by the world outside, withdrawn, inward looking, steadily decaying, immune to all artistic and intellectual influences from abroad, until, in the sixteenth century, the impact of the modern world reduced it to complete and utter ruin.

The diocese of Ardfert reflected the division between the gaelic and anglo-norman worlds. It was divided into two archdeaconries, one based on Ardfert for the anglo-norman world, the other on Aghadoe for the gaelic. Of the names of the archdeacons that have survived all from Aghadoe were gaelic, nearly all from Ardfert anglo-norman. So the high line above Killarney was the line between two ecclesiastical worlds.

There was another dividing line. The popes appointed to the see english clerics — papal officials and others — who had no intention of living and ruling there. To be fair, the local clerics had, in any event, no intention of permitting them to do so! Thus, the diocese, as others at this time, shows the decline of the church as a whole in the fifteenth century. The Great Schism (1378-1417) is reflected in rival bishops of Ardfert after 1403. John Artilburgch, an english cluniac monk, apparently a papal official, secures the see in 1405; in 1408 Nicholas Fitz Maurice, brother of the Knight of Kerry, whom he forcibly expropriated, got a faculty from the Avignon pope, Gregory XII, to receive minor, subdeacon's and priest's orders and to be consecrated bishop. The anti-pope, Alexander V, supports John and orders Nicholas to be removed. Nicholas and his friends take the law into their own hands and forcibly oust John who is

66

lucky to get away with his life, and Nicholas is restored by the anti-pope John XXIII.

Nicholas was succeeded in 1449 by the scion of another powerful local family, Maurice Stack, a noted pluralist. He died in 1451 and was succeeded by Maurice Mac Conchubhair, apparently of the O Conor Kerry family. Then in 1458 John Stack was appointed bishop but was not consecrated 'for lawful impediment' and his appointment was set aside. From 1461 to 1473 an english priest, John Pigge, also apparently a papal official, was bishop; but at least for part of the time he was living in England and it looks as if he was never permitted to take up his appointment, Maurice Stack remaining in possession. In 1473 Pigge resigned and Philip Stack, Maurice's younger brother, was appointed. At age 22 Philip had been a canon of Ardfert, but was deprived of the canonry five years later (1471). A year later, in 1472, he is granted the cistercian abbey of O Dorny *in commendam* for his life, Edmund Fitz Maurice having held it for between 8 and 14 years without any title. A year later again Philip is appointed bishop. But Maurice, his brother, is not to be easily ousted and is finally consecrated in 1475. He held the see until he died in 1488. Then it is Philip's turn. He gets *in commendam* the prebend of Fenit and the perpetual vicarage of the neighbouring parish of Cuil-O-dTaidhg on the death of his brother David as well as the neighbouring vicarage of Kilmoyley because, he alleges, 'on account of the power of laymen who detain and occupy the fruits and goods of his episcopal *mensa* he enjoys them so little that he can hardly live on them and bear his other burthens and that he has no other means wherewith to maintain himself as the episcopal dignity requires'. In 1488 the lands of the bishop had been robbed and spoiled by the tenth earl of Desmond. Around this time there was much such behaviour – the bishops were treated for what they had become, rival lords: the great earl of Kildare burned Cashel cathedral because, as he afterwards apologetically explained, he believed the archbishop was in it. When Philip Stack died in 1495 it was the turn of another local notability, John Fitz Gerald, great grandson of the Nicholas appointed early in the century. He had five children by an O Conor Kerry lady, wife of the steward to the earl of Desmond.

These goings on in high places were reflected, and magnified, in lower ones. This was a feature of the church generally at this time, and Irish dioceses were no exceptions. The records, such as are available, tend to be of papal dispensations of stringent, but often readily relaxed, rules against priests who are illegitimate, against simony (buying of ecclesiastical offices), against pluralism, against holding of priests' offices by those who are not ordained priests, and of papal inquiries into complaints about these and about the marriage and co-habitation of clergy. The records thus highlight the failings rather than the strengths. An extraordinary number of clergy had to receive dispensations for illegitimacy: sometimes the father was a priest, sometimes a 'person of rank'. Almost at random one can pick from Leslie this record from the parish of Molahiffe:

1450   Thady Y'Cuyl, illegitimate, being the son of a priest, had obtained through simony the vicarage of Maghoflatym, having been presented by the abbot and convent of Kyrie Eleison [the cistercians of Abbeydorney] and was collated [i.e. appointed] by bishop Nicholas [Fitz Maurice], but afterward expelled, and
1453   Maurice O'Sullivayn, acolyte, held it in 1455 over two years without being ordained priest and is deprived, and
1455   Thady Y'Cuyl is now provided to it and confirmed in it, June 12.
1470   Donatus O Kealachayr (O'Kelliher) priest, informs the Pope that Thady Y'Cuyl above, vicar of Maghoflathymh [Molahiffe] is guilty of simony, fornication, and dilapidation of the vicarage. If true, Thady is to be deprived and Donatus provided to the vicarage, December 8.

The method of rewarding the informer, known as a Rome runner, by, other things being equal, the grant of the office held by the person complained of was a productive force making for serious, but not always well based, accusations, and fostered one of the worst abuses of clerical life in the fifteenth century. The records from other dioceses suggest that Ardfert was neither better nor worse than average of the time. This was a by-product of the extreme centralisation of appointments in the pope, especially from the time of Martin V (1417-31). It is clear from some of the decisions that irresponsibility, and occasionally fraud, governed the decisions and that this encouraged the worst types to seek ecclesiastical preferment from Rome. Large numbers of Irishmen participated in this practice.

Another problem arose from the fact that there was in Ireland no general system for educating and training priests for parochial work. The normal system was apprenticeship to a working priest. This suffered from the weakness that, once standards had slipped, there was no self-correcting mechanism for raising them again, and it facilitated the hereditary principle. A synod of Munster bishops held in 1453 issued a number of decrees aimed at limiting abuses; but one senses in the decrees a lack of real reforming spirit. Incidentally, they show that the old tradition of sanctuary within a church continued because they excommunicated anyone who prevented one in sanctuary from obtaining food. At the same time they condemned the old practice of using the church as a storage place for valuables and crops, and tried to put a stop to this and to the keeping of animals within the graveyard.

Notwithstanding all this, a fair standard of education was maintained; canon law was a specially favoured subject, usually as a result of study at Oxford. Many canonists studied the subject as a preparation for a career of pluralism. During the fifteenth century three canonists were provided to the see of Ardfert, and a sprinkling to other offices. For such general standards of clerical education as existed a good part of the credit must go to the schools attached to the friaries. It would seem that there was some vitality in the parochial system in south Kerry at least, to judge by the enlarged parish churches at Kilcrohane, Killinane, and Killemlagh.

The general decline also affected the monastic orders and especially the augustinian canons regular who were in the doldrums during this century. We read in 1479 that Donald Osulibayn had for several years held possession of the chapel of Aghavore (Derrynane) monastery, attached to Molana, and its funds against the will of the abbot, and is to be removed. Serious charges are made against the prior of Ballinskelligs, but it takes 11 years before he can be got to resign. He belonged to the O Mulchonry family which for 60 years at least continuously held the priorship; most probably they held it for over 100 years, the office descending from father to son. In 1478 the office of prior of Inisfallen has long been void, though Donal O Shea had held it for four years without title. O Shea was said to be living *in partibus montanis* and his canons in private houses outside the monastery altogether neglecting divine worship in their church. In 1494 a John O Moriarty, holder of four parishes etc. of the diocese is appointed also prior of Inisfallen — pluralism was not confined to those with norman names. In 1476 the prior of Killagha, John Fitz Gerald, was deprived and Florence Mac Carthy became prior, to be deprived himself 8 years later.

A sixteenth century moralist was to exclaim: '. . . for there is no archbishop, ne bishop, ne prior, parson, ne vicar ne any other person of the Church high or low, great or small, English or Irish, that useth to preach the word of God, saving the poor friars beggars. . . ' It is not surprising, therefore, that two gaelic magnates when, in the fifteenth century, they decided to contribute to the church, should endow monasteries for the franciscans of the strict observantine rule who were showing real vigour at this time. The observants were a reforming group within the conventual orders — they separated in 1417 — and were ruled directly from Rome. This made them appeal

South-west view of Muckross Friary

to the gaelic magnates because, apart from the abuses that existed, the Irish superiors of the conventual friars tended to be greatly susceptible to english influence. Thus Donal Mac Carthy Mor, who had succeeded in 1428, established the franciscan friary of the observantine rule at Muckross in 1448, and 30 years later O Conor Kerry established another at Lislaghtin. In 1518 the Ardfert franciscans conformed to the observantine rule.

Watt gives four main reasons for the religious decline, all evident in Kerry. These are the split between english and irish clerics, hereditary successions, monastic decline, especially amongst the cistercians and augustinians, and the complex of 'Rome-running' and trade in benefices.

About the middle of the fifteenth century there was not only some religious revival but also, clearly, an economic one too, probably helped by an improvement in the weather. This revival is shown in the quantity of building, religious and secular, that led to a remarkable revival of architecture. Many regard this period — of Irish gothic — as the highest point of Irish architecture. Kerry has very good examples — in the newly founded monasteries of Muckross and Lislaghtin, and in the re-building at the older foundations of Ardfert and Killagha, as well as at Ardfert cathedral. These buildings and additions splendidly illustrate the very fine style of late Irish gothic at its best. After a long period of gestation, as usual, the Irish consciousness had absorbed and mastered the style. The castles of Ballycarbery, Ross and Carrigafoyle are fine secular buildings of the time.

There was a revival of religious art in metal, leather and wood. The Lislaghtin cross is a very fine example. There was also a remarkable development of Irish music.

There was a great development of exports in the second half of the century, especially to continental Europe. Great quantities of hides were exported — for example, to the great leather industries of Pisa some 34,000 in the half year 1466-7 and over 24,000 in the half year 1482-3. Thousands more were shipped to Flanders, and some to France. Some meat was also exported, and horses and hawks, amongst other items. In 1500 the total population of Ireland was still only about one million, two-thirds of what it had been 200 years previously. On this basis the population of Kerry was some 30,000, not much more than a quarter of its present level.

All in all, the fifteenth century was set in an environment of anarchy, if a rather civilised anarchy. While France and England were struggling through the pains of similar anarchy to the consciousness of nationhood, and Spain was throwing off the rule of the invader, while Europe as a whole was coming alight intellectually, artistically, scientifically, Ireland remained untouched; these things passed by as roman civilisation had done. Even in politics, there was sterility, and here the anglo-irish were as sterile as the old gaelic magnates. None of the three parties in Ireland had clear-sighted long-term political

68 aims until, in the sixteenth century, the Tudors set about the conquest of Ireland in deadly earnest. In this and the succeeding centuries began that fatal fascination of Irish leaders with internal english politics and that support for the *losing* side that was to bedevil Irish history for some three centuries.

When the Desmond geraldines had fallen from power in 1468 they were succeeded by the Kildare geraldines until 1535. The earls of Kildare ruled Ireland with real effectiveness — with the help of artillery, which Garret Mor, the great earl, introduced with muskets from Germany in 1488 — until the family was destroyed, except for a child heir, in 1537. In 1520 Garret Og, earl of Kildare, marched to Kerry to compose a feud between two divisions of the family of Mac Carthy Mor and took the castle of Pallis, near Killarney, and that of Castlemaine. One of the Mac Carthy contenders had been Tadhg of the Laune who in 1514 'died in his bed, as was not expected, he being a man who had destroyed more, and about whom more had been destroyed, than anyone that came of his tribe within the memory of man'.

Lislaghtin Friary

Chapter 6

Conquest 1500-1700

These manly pursuits were about to come to an end. At the accession of Henry VII, direct English rule in Ireland covered only a small area around Dublin, some 30 miles by 20 miles. A statute of 1495 prescribed that it be surrounded by a double ditch, six feet high — the Pale. The fall of the Kildare geraldines in 1535 led to the change from indirect to direct rule, the establishment of an English government, staffed by English officials, in Dublin. A generation later began the process of establishing administrations in the provinces of Munster, Connacht and Ulster. A President of Munster, aided by a Council, was established in 1571. This administrative structure, staffed by able, determined and pitiless officials was, by the end of the century, to crush the feudal anglo-norman and the pre-feudal gaelic rulers. As the nobles fell, their lands were confiscated and for a century, as a matter of policy, given to English 'undertakers' to plant with English and protestant families. In the following century the grip of the English government was consolidated, notwithstanding two great revolts, so that by 1700 Ireland was, after 500 years, finally and completely conquered.

During these years, there grew up the fatal and futile practice of seeking foreign help to underpin Irish revolts that was to bemuse and mislead Irish patriots down to Casement's time. At this period of the early 16th century, there were off the south coasts 200 Spanish sail that fished and carried away 'beefs, hides and tallow' from the havens and harbours. Hence, there was constant contact with the Continent. In return, munitions were often imported. For example, James, 11th Earl of Desmond, who succeeded in 1520, three years later signed a treaty with Francis I, King of France, under which Desmond contracted to make war on the king of England with 400 horse and 10,000 foot for which the French were to supply equipment and munitions. The aim was to depose Henry and replace him by Richard Pole, duke of Suffolk. This came to nothing. In 1529, Francis having made peace with Henry VIII, James was in negotiation with Charles V seeking particularly artillery. At the same time he claimed to be in alliance with James IV of Scotland, and to be ready to field 16,500 foot and 1,500 horse, as well as allies. He may have had some vision of a free and independent Ireland, perhaps, the first to have one; but the account that he gave to Charles V of his wrongs suggests a vain and petty man. His hatred was, it seems, directed not at Henry but at Cardinal Wolsey. He had, however, a clear and explicit grasp of the significance of cannon, which his successors so fatally lacked. The plot came to nothing and James died shortly afterwards.

The Desmonds, like other magnates, had complex marital habits, James no less so. In 1523, in the Limerick diocesan court, his countess, Aine O Brien, sought restitution of conjugal rights — he had apparently taken up with a widow. His defence was that his marriage was null because they had been within the forbidden degree of kindred. She easily countered this by producing from her father, Turlough O Brien, bishop of Killaloe, the appropriate dispensation. *Twenty* years later, after Desmond was dead, a decision was given upholding her claim. It seems, however, that he had taken her back.

An armed revolt did take place in the years 1539–40, led by the 13th earl of Desmond and Conn O Neill. This was the revolt of the Geraldine League. Its aim was to restore the last remnant of the Kildare geraldines and to crown a king of Ireland. It was to be supported by Francis I, Charles V and James IV. In fact, no help came from abroad. There was some fighting, but the revolt collapsed and the boy earl of Kildare fled to Europe.

Then, there was injected the virulent poison of religious division. The failure of the Geraldine League led the various magnates to seek forgiveness of Henry VIII. This was given at the price of their renouncing the pope. This was done by Desmond, Mac Carthy Mor, Mac Carthy Reagh, O Sullivan Beare, and others.

At the eve of the Reformation the church was in a sorry way. There seems to have been a serious shortage of priests and many of these were ill-educated, neglected their duties, and led immoral lives. Many of the monasteries were in decline, with reduced communities; and some had been largely or wholly abandoned and their buildings were in decay.

This seems to have happened with Inisfallen and Aghavore, at least. Only the Franciscans maintained a universal zeal. Nonetheless, when the monasteries were suppressed, no charges of immorality were laid against them. The bishops, in many instances nominees of local grandees, neglected their duties and often set bad examples, leading lives little different from those led by the great nobles, their patrons. On the whole, they cut sorry figures when the Reformation did come. As a result of these abuses, the practice of religion suffered grievously. Religion was not preached, services were slovenly or wholly neglected, attendance at Sunday mass and the sacraments was lax, and widespread were illegitimacy and abuse of marriage. There seemed to be no intellectual life whatever in the church.

In 1536 the Dublin parliament legally dissolved the monasteries — of 450 no less than 114 were Franciscan — and perhaps half of the 5,000 religious and nuns were dispersed. So far as Kerry was concerned, the income from a number of the foundations went to such magnates as James, 15th earl of Desmond, Lord Kerry and Mac Carthy Mor. In 1541 Henry had himself declared by the Irish parliament King of Ireland: the former title Lord of Ireland supported the belief that Ireland was a papal fiefdom. Anglo-irish and Irish nobility hastened to make submission to Henry as king. In 1542 Desmond and others were commissioned to survey and dissolve all religious houses in Cork, Limerick, Kerry and Desmond; but in the latter two at least there seems to have been no real interference with the monasteries themselves for a further 50 years. In 1542 Henry, by exerting considerable pressure, got the Irish parliament to declare him supreme head of the church in Ireland. All the bishops but three accepted him in this role either explicitly or implicitly. Of the three, one was James Fitz Maurice, bishop of Ardfert, absent now, as he always was, from great events.

The transition from schism to full-scale protestantism, and the fluctuations in different reigns — Henry, Edward, Mary, Elizabeth — made for a whole generation of confusion, mirrored in the inconstancy

70

Signature of James, 15th Earl of Desmond

of the 15th earl of Desmond who died in 1558. He was lord treasurer of the Dublin government until his death. He rejected an offer to have his eldest son, like Ormond's, brought up with Edward VI. He nominated a reformer, William Casey as bishop of Limerick in 1551. In the same year in Cork Mac Carthy Mor took the oath of allegiance to Edward VI and renounced the pope.

It was not until Elizabeth's time that, in 1560, the Dublin parliament, against the vigorous protest of the new 16th earl of Desmond, in effect established the protestant reformation and began the long-standing — and finally futile — process of attempting to impose it on the people of Ireland. But it was in 1570, when Elizabeth was excommunicated by the pope, that the lines of battle were finally drawn between the reformation and the counter-reformation. It was then that the changes reached Kerry in the great upheavals caused by the Desmond rebellions. — which had some of their origins in the attempt to protect the old faith — and following the deaths of Desmond, Bishop James Fitz Maurice and the earl of Clancarre, formerly Mac Carthy Mor.

THE END OF FEUDALISM

Garret, 16th earl of Desmond, succeeded to the title in 1558. His father, James, the 15th earl, after the model of Henry VIII had his first wife put away and, in consequence, he disinherited their son, Sir Thomas Roe Fitz Gerald. The new earl, Garret, was son of the second of his father's four wives. He was, in many ways, a typical Desmond: in Sidney's words 'a man both void of judgement to govern, and will to be ruled'. He engaged in various types of armed forays, including putting down an attempt in arms by Thomas Roe to recover his inheritance. At one confrontation with his life-long enemy, Black Tom, earl of Ormond, at Bohermore on the borders of Limerick and Tipperary, he appeared with, according to O Daly, 4,000 men and 750 horse. Through the diplomacy of Desmond's first wife, a Butler, a clash was avoided. As long as she lived — she died soon after — she kept him out of serious trouble. His second wife, Eleanor, clearly had less diplomatic skill ; but her devotion to Desmond in all his later trials and her willingness to share his utmost miseries make a touching story. If in nothing else, Desmond was lucky in his women.

In consequence of Desmond's armed forays he was placed under

restraint in London in 1562—64. As a condition of release he promised to assist with the establishment of protestantism. He also agreed that bards would no longer be supported or encouraged in the counties Cork, Limerick and Kerry. In 1565, an attempt to collect rent from Sir Maurice Fitz Gerald of Decies led him into an armed clash at Affane, Co. Waterford, with an ancient family enemy, the earl of Ormond. Associated in some degree with Desmond were Mac Carthy Mor — again Sidney 'willing enough to be ruled, but wanteth force and credit to rule' — and O Sullivan Beare. All four were in serious trouble and were hauled off to London. Both earls entered into recognisances to be of good behaviour, and, apparently as a counterweight to Desmond, Mac Carthy Mor was made Earl of Clancarre. Further forays in which large parts of Munster were devastated by Desmond, his lack of protestant zeal and the implacable enmity of the Queen's friend, Ormond, led him with his full brother, Sir John of Desmond, again into confinement in London from 1567 to 1573. During the early part of this time the estates were managed by his first cousin, James Fitz Maurice Fitz Gerald (they were both grandsons of the 14th earl) who resisted the attempts of the earl's elder half-brother, Thomas Roe, to succeed to the title that was properly his. At the same time the earl seems to have greatly distrusted James and feared that he had designs on the earldom for himself. He made an attempt to escape from his loose confinement by sailing down the Thames, with the help of Burghley's double agent, Martin Frobisher, but this failed.

It was clear that the writing was on the wall for the feudal world that Desmond represented. The threat to religion now began to be taken seriously. There were constant attempts to undermine old privileges. The clipping of the wings of the earl, the setting up of a modern administrative structure to take over from the old feudalism — in 1571 was set up in Cork a presidency and Council to rule Munster in the Queen's name — all alarmed the upholders of the old order.

More immediately disturbing was the descent on Cork of a band of 27 adventurers from the English west country, privateers on land as their neighbours were privateers at sea: they overlapped in the cousins Humphrey Gilbert and, later, Walter Raleigh. They landed in Cork and aimed to acquire the whole area from the Shannon to Cork. They began to carve out estates for themselves, like the first anglo-normans. The most prominent amongst them was Sir Peter Carew who was joined by two Devon men, Stukeley and Danvells, who figure in the subsequent history of Kerry. Carew claimed to be the heir of the first anglo-norman conqueror Robert Fitz Stephen, whose only daughter, according to his claim, was supposed to have married a Carew. On foot of this he claimed the lands from Mount Brandon to Lismore. These were lands now held by Desmond, various branches of the MacCarthy family, and by — Ormond! Carew managed in court to establish his claim to certain lands in Leinster, including Butler lands. Ormond was in London; but his three brothers Edmund, Piers and Edward were thoroughly alarmed and took to arms. They had a battle for their lands in 1569. This sparked off the first Desmond revolt — if this could happen to the Butlers, the Desmonds must fight while there was still time. The continued detention in London of Desmond and his brother, Sir John, fed the anxieties of the Desmonds.

Already, at a meeting in Kerry Mac Carthy Mor, James Fitz Maurice and others commissioned the archbishop of Cashel, Fitz Gibbon, a geraldine, to seek an expedition from the king of Spain to restore catholicism and to ask for a Spanish prince — Don John of Austria was mentioned — as king of Ireland. Fitz Gibbon sailed from Kerry early in 1569. Mac Carthy apparently got arms from a Spanish ship. Revolt, under the leadership of James Fitz Maurice, supported by Clancarre (who renounced his English title) and the Butlers broke out and the adventurers were driven from Cork. Only monumental mismanagement by the Queen's government could have thrown together such unlikely allies. One of the adventurers, Humphrey Gilbert, was made commander of the province and told to pacify it. There was much scattered fighting, but Gilbert was able, by the end of 1569, to give an account of his methods and their success. 'Kerry is so quiet', he wrote, 'that I have but to send my horse-boy for any man and he will come'. He describes the methods of frightfulness that were to be the means of warfare henceforth adopted to cow the people of Kerry:

> I slew all those from time to time that did belong to, feed, accompany, or maintain any outlaws or traitors; and after my first summoning of any castle or fort, if they would not presently yield it, I would not afterwards take it of their gift, but won it perforce, how many lives so ever it cost, putting man, woman and child of them to the sword. Neither did I spare any malefactors unexecuted that came to my hands in any respect......

These methods pursued with ferocious energy enabled him to march almost unopposed through the wilds of Connelloe and Kerry and, without artillery, to take thirty or forty castles.

In 1570 the Pope excommunicated Elizabeth, 'deposed' her and excommunicated anyone who continued to accept her orders. Of the leaders of the revolt this was taken seriously only by Fitz Maurice who was a convinced upholder of catholicism. As we shall see, the others soon came to terms with the 'deposed' monarch. Indeed, by 1572, after a long and trying period since her accession, she was undisputed ruler of England and in full control of her country's interests at home and abroad.

In this revolt, and in the subsequent one which was to destroy utterly feudalism and Desmond power in the South of Ireland, it is difficult to detect anyone, apart from Fitz Maurice — who called the conspiracy 'the Catholic League' — any trace of idealism. Each man served his own interests — personal, family, feudal, religious, administrative — as he saw them, either by fighting or by lying low, or by alternating the two. For all the sufferings and loyalty of the common people to old ways, there was no sense in which these wars could be said to have a social or a national purpose, in present day conceptions of these terms.

Castle Magne

Notwithstanding Gilbert's successes with the garrisons of castles and with non-combatants, the county was not, in fact, pacified and much confused fighting took place, each side engaging in forays deep into the other's country without any significant effects, apart from the driving off of cattle and the destruction of homesteads. The country was thickly forested. Woods lay along the south shore of the Shannon to Ballylongford, from Listowel along the Stack mountains to Tralee, from there west to Brandon Bay, and up the Maine Valley to Castleisland, as well as, of course, in south Kerry. The country was also boggy, and in these circumstances the lightly armed and mobile

72

guerillas had substantial advantages over the English forces. There were no real roads through the forests or over the mountain passes. Such tracks as there were could be impeded by felled trees, often with their branches interlaced. Fitz Maurice had his retreat in the Glen of Aherlow in Tipperary which could only be approached through a great belt of forest. From here he made forays into the Munster counties and into Connacht, in the attempt to widen the revolt. But his main aim was to hold out until foreign aid reached him.

There was much coming and going between the west Munster ports — of which Dingle was a principal one — and France and Spain. Fish, beef, hides and tallow were exported in return for wines and arms. There was constant rumour of a large Spanish fleet that would land at Dingle; but, in fact, Fitz Gibbon, the archbishop of Cashel, had had no success in Spain and, because Ireland was a papal fief, was rebuked by Pope Pius V for going first to Philip. In 1570, Stukeley, after an extraordinary career in Leinster had gone to Spain seeking aid for Ireland and had a personal success with Philip and later with the Pope; but there was no aid from either of them.

In this position of military stalemate, the main means of reducing Fitz Maurice could not be military. The first step was to win away his allies. In 1570 also, Ormond was permitted to leave London and, with great difficulty, reconciled his three brothers and they turned against Fitz Maurice. In the winter, just to show he could make forays as well, Ormond, whose commission was to 'banish and vanquish those cankered Desmonds', drove deep into Kerry on the rumour that a French ship had landed with re-inforcements, but this was probably the ship that took Fitz Maurice's son from Dingle to France to seek directly the foreign aid he so desperately needed. Apart from the Butler brothers, there were enlisted against Fitz Maurice, Sir Thomas Roe Fitz Gerald, who considered he was the legitimate earl of Desmond, O Sullivan Beare, and several Mac Carthy groups, including Clancarre, who had been quickly brought back to cautious loyalty by promises of English favour.

The second step was to establish a modern, continuing government for Munster so that it would receive the attention a distracted central government in Dublin could not spare for it. In 1571 the long heralded Presidency and Council of Munster were set up. The first President was Sir John Perrott, reputedly a natural son of Henry VIII. He is also remembered for the libellous saying that aqua vitae might 'rather to be cald aqua mortis to poyson the people, than to comfort them in any good sorte'. The members of the council were the (reformed) archbishop and bishops of Munster and the earls of Ormond, Thomond and Clancarre. (Later, Desmond became a member). The President and council were to look after all the rights of the Crown in Munster. In particular, the liberties of Kerry were abrogated for a time. At the same time, a new county, that of Desmond, was created from South Kerry and West Cork. It was to last until 1606 when the two modern counties of Cork and Kerry were created.

With the aid of frightfulness, military resolution and of his Irish allies (particularly Clancarre) Perrott set about crushing the revolt. For five

weeks in June–July 1571, Perrot besieged Castlemaine — a likely landing place for foreign invaders — but without success. The castle over the river withstood his bombardment; he had very little powder and he had to withdraw. A year later it fell to him, for want of provisions, after a three months' siege, Fitz Maurice arriving from Connacht just too late to save it. With his Irish allies Perrott remorselessly pursued Fitz Maurice into the recesses of Aherlow until, by the end of 1572, the revolt was finally crushed. Next year, in February 1572–3 Fitz Maurice submitted prostrate in the church at Kilmallock, Co. Limerick, Perrott's sword pointed at his heart.

He was lucky, for these were bloody times. The previous August had seen the St. Bartholomew's massacre. The great revolt of the Netherlands was on. But Fitz Maurice's reprieve did not unduly limit him and he soon resumed his correspondence with Spain. He found his wife writing love-letters to his ex-ally Edward Butler, so he divorced her and promptly married the widow of O Conor Kerry. In this way came into his hands the castle of Carrigafoyle, the 'strongest and beautifullest in west Munster', and a suitable place for a foreign landing. This was to lead to its being severely damaged some years later.

To help to pacify Munster after the end of the revolt Elizabeth decided, against strong advice, to release Desmond in 1573, but to keep him on parole in Dublin. Towards the end of the year he jumped his bail and returned to his own strongholds in Limerick and Kerry where he immediately resumed the state of a great Irish chieftain and resumed his palatine rights. On Christmas eve, 1573 he surprised Castlemaine, and was not persuaded to release it until the following September. Nonetheless, the new presidency of Munster began steadily and remorselessly to invest the old palatinate of Kerry. The end was not far off. Sidney, the lord depty wrote in 1571: 'I am of opinion that the dissipation of the great lords and their countries, and the reducing of their lands into many hands, is a sound way of proceeding to perfect reformation, but the attempting of it is perilous'. Events were to force this decision.

James Fitz Maurice left Ireland in 1575 — Sir Peter Carew, the occasion of most of the trouble, died the same year — and spent weary years trying to persuade first the French government, then Philip II of Spain and then the Pope to invade Ireland and so save catholicism there. Papal policy was to get Spain to invade England and destroy the centre of protestant strength; but Philip was reluctant to get embroiled. To both, a conquest of Ireland was irrelevant. When at length the attack on England *was* made with the Armada, and failed, papal policy forsook all forms of military intervention. But in the interim, Fitz Maurice had some success with Pope Gregory XIII. He asked for, initially, 6,000 men, with arms and artillery. He got about 1,000. He had joined forces with Stukeley, who had been in and out of favour in the Spanish court, had been friendly with Don John of Austria and had, apparently, fought at Lepanto, and was a great success with successive Popes. Stukeley, with Fitz Maurice's support, was placed in charge of the expedition, which sailed from Rome to Lisbon in 1578, where he promptly went off with the young King of

Portugal and the precious papal forces on an attack on the King of Morocco, in which both kings and Stukeley were killed. Some of Stukeley's troops survived this disaster and, in all, about 600 troops were collected for Fitz Maurice's invasion.

In the meantime, Fitz Maurice, probably by now realising the folly of foreign aid, was impatient himself to begin a rising in Munster, and at length, on 17 July 1579, be came back with money, a papal legate (Sanders), some clerics, 80 Spaniards, and with the further support, to follow later, of men and arms. With three ships and three fishing vessels he landed at Dingle, and proclaimed a catholic revolt. He then went to Smerwick harbour, west of Dingle, where he strengthened a little fort, Dun an Oir, with earthen defences.

The two brothers of the earl of Desmond, Sir John and Sir James of Desmond, at once joined the revolt, beginning by murdering two officials (of whom Danvells was one) in Tralee as they were returning from inspecting the little fort at Smerwick. A month after he had landed, James Fitz Maurice, a clear sighted, dedicated and able — but, as events were to show in relation to all he held dear, a misguided — man, on the way to Connacht to rouse revolt in the catholic cause, was killed by the Burkes of Castleconnell (nephews of Desmond) in a petty squabble about two plough horses.

The revolt spread to Connacht and Leinster, but Desmond did not join it. As if sensing that this was the end, he temporised until the English officials, who failed to get him to take their side, proclaimed him a traitor in November, 1579. It looks as if it was their deliberate policy to drive him into revolt: in the previous six years he had driven them to exasperation by his persistence in leading the wild, irresponsible, feudal life of his ancestors. There were some, at least, amongst them who, fired with the spirit of colonisation in America, aimed to try it nearer home.

There was not a spontaneous rising amongst the other magnates in Kerry. Clancarre, no doubt pleased to see the noose tightening around Desmond's neck, stayed loyal and had nothing to do with the revolt. Fitz Maurice, Lord Kerry, as well as O Conor Kerry and one of the other gaelic magnates, O Donoghue of Ross, were later drawn into rebellion.

We have seen that the method of warfare common in Ireland — lightly armed (raiding) troops dodging in and out of heavily wooded places and interminable bogs — set a severe military problem for the president and his forces. The policy adopted was, first, to deny Desmond and his men use of any strong places, by resolutely storming them and mercilessly killing all men, women and children found in them. Secondly, Desmond was to be kept continually on the move by murderous forays deep into his country and by ruthlessly dealing with the common people. Thirdly, their power to support him was to be destroyed in these forays, by burning their houses and crops and so reducing them to famine; in this way Desmond's men would find nothing in the countryside to live off.

Fourthly, his allies were to be bought off, or intimidated, so as to forsake him. Fifthly, as for foreign aid, Smerwick was to be a warning to all Europe.

These cruel tactics were not pursued with complete consistency; but when they were there is no doubt as to their effectiveness. There is no doubt too, of the intolerable suffering imposed on the poor people of north Kerry and the neighbouring counties.

On the English side, Sir William Pelham, the Lord Justice, was in overall command, and Ormond came back from London to become military commander in Munster. Pelham proposed to make all the country from Askeaton to Dingle 'as bare a country as ever a Spaniard set his foot in'. In March, 1580, the first drive was made into Kerry in pursuit of Desmond and to intercept stores that, it was said, had been landed in Dingle. Everything between Castleisland and Tralee had been destroyed before them and Tralee, except for the priory, was burned. A party made for Castlemaine, and Pelham and Ormond headed for Dingle. Bad weather — snowstorms and floods — drove them back. In the meantime the ships had come to Carrigafoyle.

For the first time was to be seen the co-ordination of military and sea power in the attack on Carrigafoyle (as well as, later, Smerwick) and the effective use of artillery that was to make untenable the great castles and strongholds of the insurgents. So, almost 100 years after its introduction into Ireland, and over 250 years after its introduction into western Europe, the logic of the cannon was to make itself felt. The day of the hitherto almost impregnable castle was over and, with it, feudalism in Ireland. This was to be shown vividly when the great tower house of O Conor Kerry at Carrigafoyle was easily stormed

Carrigafoyle

74

after bombardment from sea and land in April, 1580. The whole garrison — of Italians and Irish — were put to sword or hanged. Women and children received the same fate. Not a person was spared. This policy intimidated defenders of other castles. This became the pattern of the war.

Pelham's policy was to bridle the Desmond country with garrisons, which would be strong enough to eat up the surrounding country and to fatten themselves while the rebels starved. His aim was to localise the struggle in Kerry, which was too poor to maintain it unaided. The English fleet would guard the seaboard from foreign invasion. This policy worked, on the whole, with great success for so long as it was followed.

In May, 1580, Pope Gregory XIII granted 'a plenary indulgence as conceded to Crusaders to all who take up arms against Elizabeth'. Pelham and Ormond made a second raid on Kerry in May, 1580, this time from the Cork side. Desmond and his countess narrowly escaped from Castleisland — 'a huge monstrous castle of many rooms, but very filthy and full of cowdung'. Ormond raided Glenflesk, and was joined by many of the Munster chieftains, including O Donoghue Mor. Lord Kerry was also loyal at this time. The party then made for Dingle where they met the English fleet, under Winter. The town had been burned by John of Desmond and the Knight of Kerry. Ormond went looking for James of Desmond in O Sullivan Mor's country and burned as far as Valentia. Of the gaelic chiefs only O Donoghue of Glenflesk was at this time with Desmond. The whole party camped for a while at Killarney, between Dunloe and Pallis and then went back to Cork. The geraldines were ceaselessly harried. The people were given no chance to gather their harvest. The gaelic chiefs were either interned or bound by hostages.

Sir James of Desmond was captured by Sir Cormac Mac Teige Mac Carthy, Sheriff of Cork, and executed there.

By the end of the summer, Desmond was desperate, about to sue for peace and hand himself over to Admiral Winter. His brother, Sir John, had gone to Wicklow to aid the revolt there, under Lord Baltinglas. However, Pelham was superseded by Lord Grey at the end of August, and Desmond hoped to do better under the new regime. The new commander in Munster was Bourchier and he, at this time, made the third raid of the war into Kerry. Burning, killing and driving he went from Castleisland to Dingle. The fleet was at Ventry and Admiral Winter managed to get merciful terms for the people on condition that they garrisoned Tralee and held it for the Queen. He then sailed back to England. On 13th September, 1580 the foreign aid at last arrived, some 600 men, mainly Italians but there were also Spaniards and Irish. They came with money, 5,000 stand of arms and some small guns. They landed at Dun an Oir, Smerwick, which they immediately began to strengthen. They were sent by the Pope who proclaimed the same spiritual benefit to those who fought the English as to those who fought the Turks. The invaders also carried papers naming the earl of Desmond as papal lieutenant-general of Ireland and his brother, Sir John, as commander in chief of the army.

This was the first landing (apart from Fitz Maurice's own) of foreign troops for the purpose of deposing Elizabeth on foot of the papal command of 1570. The English reacted to this special threat as might be expected.   Why the landing party stayed in Smerwick, and why Desmond, his brother and Baltinglas, who had been in the neighbourhood after their landing, did not support them is not clear. In any event, the English by early November had mounted a brilliant land and sea operation: Winter, back from England, invested the place by sea and landed some of his heavy guns; Grey, smarting from his defeat in Wicklow, surrounded it by land. The defenders' batteries were soon hopelessly outgunned and they, having little stomach for fight, decided to surrender 'at discretion'. Grey used his discretion to disarm the garrison and then massacre them, sparing only a few for ransom. Edmund Spenser participated in this operation and it is said (but it is unlikely) also Sir Walter Raleigh.

Henry Denny, later the 'undertaker' of Tralee, was knighted on the field by Grey, his relative by marriage; he was a cousin of both Sir Walter Raleigh and Sir Humphrey Gilbert, another of the west country 'privateers' who had intended to do, and did, well out of the goading and destruction of the Desmonds. He was also a connexion of Cecil and Walsingham.

The war then seems to have become even more desultory. Desmond recruited considerable forces and the English troops suffered severely from illness: one of the commanders, Zouch, lost 300 out of 450 men. Early in 1581 Elizabeth proclaimed an amnesty for all who should submit by 17 July. Only Desmond, his brother John and Baltinglas were excluded. Sanders, the papal legate, died in April. Ormond was dismissed. Grey added a further list of exclusions from pardon, amongst whom were the countess of Desmond for sticking by her husband. In fact very few submitted. Very little seems to have occurred during the whole of 1581; but in January, 1582, Sir John of Desmond was killed in a skirmish in Co. Cork. He was a leader of ability and his death was severely felt. In April of that year Lord Kerry at length joined the rebels and besieged Ardfert Abbey. Zouch soon relieved the defenders. Really serious fighting now broke out over Munster. Desmond was aided by the excesses of an ill-paid soldiery: Captain Smith and his company, who were amongst the worst offenders, were cut to pieces at Ardfert. Desmond took cruel revenge on geraldines and others who did not support him.

The war became a succession of scattered guerilla raids and encounters in the old gaelic style, with great quantities of cattle being driven off by both sides, and crops being destroyed by the English — and men, women and children butchered — to starve out the rest. This went on until 1583 when, as the Four Masters said, 'At this period it was commonly said that the lowing of a cow, or the voice of the ploughman, could scarcely be heard from Dunquin to Cashel'. The effect is vividly presented by that junior civil servant, Edmund Spenser, in a famous passage of his *State of Ireland*:

Thee proof whereof I saw suffycientlie ensampled in those late warrs in Mounster, for notwithstanding that the same

was a most ritch and plentifull Countrye, full of Corne and
Cattell that yow would have thought that they haue bene
hable to stande longe, yett err one yeare and a half, they
were brought to such wretchednes, as that any stonie harte
would haue rewed the same, out of euerie Corner of the
woodes and glennes they came crepinge forthe upon theire
handes, for theire leggs could not beare them, they looked
Anotomies of death, they spake like ghostes cryinge out of
theire graues, they did eate of the dead Carrions, happye
were they could fynde them, yea and one another soone
after in so much as the verie Carcases they spared not to
scrape out of theire graues, and yf they founde a plott of
water cresses or shamrockes, there they flocked as to a
feast for the tyme, yet not able longe to contynewe
therewithall, that in shorte space there were none almost
left and a most populous and plentyfull Countrye suddenlie
left voyde of man or beast, yet sure in all that warr there
perished not manye by the sworde, but all by the extremitye
of famyne, which they themselves had wrought.

Sir Warham St Leger wrote of Munster in April, 1582: 'There hath
died by famine only not so few as thirty thousand in this province in
less than half a year, besides others that are hanged and killed'. Their
sufferings were made worse by the European epidemic of malaria that
began in late 1580 and severely attacked Ireland. To this attack were
added outbreaks of typhus caused by the war.

It was clear that, from the English side, the war could not be
successfully prosecuted until there was a single commander once more
in Munster. Hence, the ancient enemy, Ormond, who was Desmond's
nephew, was recalled and took the war again in hand early in 1583.
He resumed the policy of confining the struggle to Kerry. By the
summer the war was over and Desmond a hunted outlaw, with a
handful of followers, and Ormond marched through Kerry without
any resistance. In the November of that year, Desmond was killed
near Tralee in squalid circumstances.

This war was notable in that it was a struggle of the centralising
English crown against feudalism in Ireland to crush the most powerful
of the Old English, who were to take a century to bring to final
subjection. It was made more complex in that it was the first main
struggle where religion was a significant issue; this it was to remain
until the end of the next century. It was not a war against the Irish
nobles — with the exception of O Conor Kerry, a minor Mac Carthy
killed at Aghadoe, and of O Donoghue Mor of Ross, who lost his life
and his lands, they kept ostentatiously aloof and on occasion helped
the Crown. *Their* turn was to come 20 years later. In short, it was
the crisis of a superseded, bewildered system faced with a new, well-
equipped, clear-headed administration. (It was not always clear-
headed, even when it was not impeded by the Queen's quite
remarkable parsimony. Ormond, of whom the English officials were
notably jealous, was the only one to show sustained ability, political
understanding and even occasional humanity.) Finally, the war

Black Tom, Earl of Ormond

illustrated what was to become the great feature of external aid to
Irish rebellions — its futility and, by raising false hopes of easy
solutions, its danger to the cause it had been hoped it would serve.

After the warfare, peace and order were restored with an iron hand.
In a short period 300 people were executed in Munster so that, in
the general loss of life, even 'malefactors' were scarce. One of those
killed in June, 1581, fighting on Desmond's side, was David Fitz
Gerald, described by Stanihurst:

usuallie called David Duffe, born in Kerie, a civilian, a
maker in Irish, not ignorant of musike, skilfull in physike,

76

a good and generall craftsman much like to Hippias......
He plaied excellently on all kind of instruments, and soong
thereto his own verses which no man could amend. In all
parts of logike, rhetorike, and philosphie he vanquished all
men, and was vanquished of none.

Little time was lost in attempting to reap a profit from Desmond's
disaster. In June, 1584 a survey of the Desmond lands and of the
lands of other fallen rebels was put in hand. Desmond had been
the proprietor of some 570,000 acres in four counties and claimed
sovereignty over something like a million acres. His estates were
forfeited by an Act of the Dublin parliament in 1586 — Dingle was
represented for the first time as a borough. In fact, because much of
Desmond's lands was held under him by landholders who could
prove their loyalty, or who had been pardoned, only some 200,000
acres were confiscated. These lands were let out to 'undertakers'
— there was a parallel with the contemporary colonisation of
America — in seignories not supposed to exceed 12,000 profitable
acres: but 'unprofitable' acres were not counted. So, Sir Walter
Raleigh and Sir William Herbert each ended up with about 40,000
acres. For these they paid a small quit rent to the Queen. Herbert,
who was highly critical of the greed of the other undertakers, tried
to dispossess some of them despite his own vast gains. For example,
the O Conor Kerry seignory at Tarbert had been granted to a John
Hollies who, in 1589, complained that the castle of Tarbert was
withheld from him by Herbert, whose explanation was that 'Sir
William desires to have a dwelling upon that river of Shenant'.
His desire was not gratified in the event.

Desmond's widow Eleanor was pardoned on condition that she
renounced all claims to the estate. She and her five children for some
time lived in great poverty until in 1587 Elizabeth granted her a
pension of £200 a year. Two (or three) of her daughters also were
granted small pensions.

One of the five surveyors of the lands to be confiscated was Sir
Valentine Browne whose two sons were to profit greatly from the
results. He was the second Sir Valentine. The first, his father, came
to Ireland and at his death in 1567 was Auditor-General. The second
Sir Valentine had two sons, Thomas and Nicholas. Thomas acquired
the main Browne lands in Co. Limerick from the Desmond
confiscation. Nicholas gained the more hazardous Mac Carthy and
O Donoghue lands at Molahiffe, Castlemaine and Ross. To survive
and prosper there, as at length he did, called for great tenacity and
resource. The two Browne families later joined by marriage and the
Killarney one — who became earls of Kenmare — were to be amongst
the greatest landowners in Ireland.

These 'undertakers' undertook to plant their lands, so depopulated
from war and pestilence, with English and protestant farmers — about
8,000 persons in all — and they were chosen because they had the
capital and a retinue of tenants, labourers and artisans that they could
bring to Ireland; but almost everywhere they, at least, partially failed
in this undertaking, failures attributable partly to the difficulty of the

task, partly to bureaucracy and partly to muddle. So, the aim of
settling these turbulent lands with substantial colonies of hardworking
loyalists, — 'loving subjects of good behaviour and account, none of
the mere Irish to be maintained in any family' — was frustrated. Thus
Sir William Herbert, who settled in the great Desmond seat of
Castleisland, should have brought with him 91 British families; but
in 1589 he had 20, with over 100 yearly Irish tenants. Other
undertakers were: the Dennys at the other Desmond seat at Tralee,
the Conways at Killorglin, the Blennerhassets at Ballyseedy — these
last were nominal tenants of Denny, at an annual rent of 'one red
rose'. Other prominent settlers at this time were the Chutes who
were granted lands near Dingle. These they lost, but marriage to a
Mac Elligott gained them lands at what is now Chute Hall, Tralee.
Here they long settled. The Crosbies of Ardfert came a few years
later. These, with of course the Brownes, were the most prominent
of the families who came to Kerry about this time and survived there
to be the leading English influence in it for three centuries.

The Desmond war set a pattern. When the great lords, Irish or Old
English, were crushed their lands were confiscated and planted, until
the old landholders were almost wholly dispossessed. The undertakers
as a rule let their estates on lease to free tenants, farmers and
copyholders, who, in turn, let them in convenient farms to the mere
Irish who, no doubt, were the continuing occupants of these farms;
they were also a valuable source of labour for the carrying out of
improvements. They paid stiff rents to the free tenants or
middlemen who then assumed the airs and importance of local squires.
In Kerry many of these were planters, but by no means all. These
were the people whose descendants earned such contempt from Lord
Kenmare and Arthur Young almost two centuries later. Sir John
Davies was to say in 1606 of Kerry that 'all our undertakers for the
most part have planted Irish tenants in their lands, and, among others,
even the sons and kinsmen of the ancient proprietors and owners
thereof.'

Apart from the undertakers, there arrived a group of wholly dishonest
officials who had no scruples about defrauding alike rightful owners,
undertakers and the Crown of land . Of these the most notable was
Richard Boyle who in Kerry, as elsewhere, acquired land by grossly
fraudulent means. He later became earl of Cork and a man of great
wealth. Another of these unsavoury types was Patrick Crosbie, an
Irishman who, with his brother, was to acquire extensive lands in
Kerry.

The plain people lived in very simple circumstances. Much of the land
was covered with forests and, of course, bogs. Communications were
poor, roads were few and bridges scarcer still. Lord Grey, of the
Smerwick massacre, is said to have introduced the first coach into
Ireland. There was a good deal of tillage, and the ancient custom
of ploughing by the tail was continued — harness, saddles and the rest
of horses' gear had not yet been adopted. The main enterprise was,
of course, cattle, and it was in 1589 that the first red cattle were
brought to Dingle from Cornwall to be crossed with the native black
Kerry breed. The ancient import of wine continued: each December

the ships from France and Spain came and took in exchange 'beeves then in best condition'. In 1569 it was reported that every year 200 vessels from Spain fished off the coast of Clancarre's country (the Iveragh peninsula) and carried away '2,000 beyffes, hydes and tallow'.

The small active cattle were well suited to the constant driving that accompanied the warfare and the usual sport of cattle-raiding. Moryson says the cattle were driven into the bawns of the castles at night to protect them from predators, human and wolves; that they were not given any hay while so pent in; and that the bawns were filthy with cattle dung. In extreme need a vein of a beast would be opened and some of the blood drunk.

The plain people lived in very simple houses, perhaps still in transition from the clochan, round, thatched, like beehives, with the fire in the middle, a hole in the roof for chimney. The women struck most observers as very beautiful, but badly dressed, wearing only a chemise and a three-cornered mantle. The men were big, and wore their hair down over their eyes — the glibbs so disliked by the English. They too wore the multi-purpose triangular mantle. Spenser says of it: ' a fit house for an outlaw, a meet bed for a rebel, and an apt cloak for a thief'. Another local witness was Sir William Herbert who wrote: 'The mantle serving unto the Irish [is] as to a hedgehog his skin, or to a snail her shell, for a garment by day and a house by night: it maketh them, with the continual use of it, more apt and able to live and lie out in bogs and woods, where their mantle serveth them for a mattress and a bush for a bedstead'. From the time of Giraldus Cambrensis to the middle of the 17th century, Irishmen wore tights. Meals usually consisted of butter and oaten bread, with sour milk. On feast days they had half-cooked meat. Hunting and falconry were much prized by the better off, and the little sure-footed hobby horses, the great Irish wolfhounds, and hawks were much esteemed abroad as presents. The principal manufacture seems to have been woollen cloth for clothing and for making the famous 16th century light rugs for laying on beds; these were considered to be fit for kings. Flax was woven into linen for the enormous linen shirts, dyed with saffron (which was supposed to repel vermin) and, according to Moryson, never taken off until they were worn out.

During the latter part of this century Ireland began to appear on printed maps. A version of Ptolemy's map of about 150 AD had appeared in 1472, but Ireland did not appear alone on a map until 1560. In 1599 Boazio (a pupil of Mercator) produced his great map of Ireland. These were followed in the next century by Speed and others.

It was in the 1580s that the gallowglasses with their axes and the kerne with their darts became obsolete and were replaced by, respectively, pikemen and musketeers. Arms and powder were imported from Scotland and the Continent. So, in Kerry, the great gallowglass families of Sheehy and Sweeney fell with the order — in particular the house of Desmond — that supported them and to which they were such support.

Irish warriors and peasants, 1521

The last of the pre-reformation bishops of Ardfert was James Fitz Maurice whose tenure of the see dated for some 50 years from 1536. He was named for the diocese by the pope, not the king. Nonetheless, he illustrates some of the abuses of the time. He belonged to the neighbouring great family of the Fitz Maurices, Lords of Kerry, or, possibly, a cadet branch of theirs, the Pierses, who would have been exceptional if they had not a proprietorial interest in the local bishopric. In 1536 he was 25 years of age and already abbot of Abbeydorney. He had to be dispensed from the qualifications of the office of bishop because he was too young and illegitimate, being the son of a cleric. He seems to have operated by omission. He was one of only three bishops who either explicitly or implicitly did not accept Henry VIII as supreme head of the catholic church in Ireland. He does not seem to have answered the writ to attend the parliament of 1560 that established the reformation in Ireland, and stayed away. On the other hand, he seems to have shown no zeal for the catholic cause. It will be recalled that the Desmond rebellion had its origin in the first two specific attempts by Sir James Fitz Maurice in 1569 and 1579 to establish a 'Catholic League' to defend catholicism from the inroads of the reformation. In 1569 the archbishop of Cashel, Fitz Gibbon, an illegitimate scion of the house of Desmond, sailed from Kerry to Spain with a petition to the catholic King to appoint a king of Ireland — Don John of Austria was suggested — to restore the catholic faith. This purported to be signed by twelve bishops, but Ardfert was not amongst them. The revolt of 1579 had considerable papal support — spiritual, material and military. The Desmond and, later, the Fitz Maurice families were deeply involved on the catholic side. However, the bishop does not seems to have taken any active part in either revolt, though it appears that he was driven from his

78

cathedral in 1579. His two sons, James and Gerald, took the Queen's side in the fighting and were killed in 1582. He may have attended the parliament of 1586 that attainted the dead earl of Desmond; although it seems he was himself posthumously attainted some years later. He died not later than 1588. He was succeeded in 1591 by Michael Fitz Walter, who may never have visited his see or else left the country after the O Neill wars and died abroad in 1610.

So it is not until 1588, after Fitz Maurice's death, that the Queen appointed Nicholas Kenan, a former sub-dean of St. Paul's, as the second protestant bishop of the united bishopric of Ardfert and Aghadoe so as to 'reduce the people to a more christian knowledge and fear of God, dutiful obedience to her Majesty' etc. He was, clearly, a conforming Irishman whose name was either O Kennane or O Kenny. He was the second such appointment because there is mention as bishop of a Davy Duke who died in 1587; but nothing is known of him and he may never have been able to exercise any functions. There was need for an active bishop if the reformation was to take hold. Outside the port towns there was not, it was reported, one protestant church standing between Dublin and the farthest part of Munster. Of the Desmond undertakers, Sir William Herbert of Castleisland almost uniquely concerned himself with religion. He provided a protestant minister to preach and conduct divine service in Irish, and had the prayers translated into Irish to be learned by the people who, he reported, were very tractable. The third protestant bishop, appointed in 1600, was John Crosbie who was an Irishman who conformed. His real name was Mac Crossan and the family were hereditary bards of the O Moores of Laois.

John Crosbie was 'skilled in the Irish tongue'. Elizabeth, with her usual realism, had grasped the significance of Irish as the spoken vernacular. But to little practical effect. She provided a press for printing religious books in Irish; but the new testament did not appear in Irish until 1603, the book of common prayer only in 1608, and it was not until 1685 that the old testament appeared. The complaints of lack of zeal by the reformers were well founded.

It was only now, after the Desmond wars, that the long agony of the monasteries began which was to last some 70 years. That of Muckross may illustrate this. In 1589 the community fled before the arrival of Crown forces; but two friars, who had gone to hide the monastery's treasures, were found, tortured and killed. In 1580 three friars of Lislaghtin had been killed by English soldiers. Until early in the next century these monasteries were abandoned.

It has been said that the most productive of all the changes made by the Council of Trent was the decision of 1563 for setting up seminaries for the education and training of aspirants to the priesthood. As the century wore on, these 'seminary priests' infused zeal and devotion into the priesthood and there was a real revival of religion. From about 1590 this was especially noted in the practice of religion both by clerics and laymen in Ireland. Spenser contrasts the zeal shown by 'jesuits and friars' with the indifference of the reformed clergy. The former came continually from France, Italy and Spain 'by

long toil and dangerous travelling thither where they know peril of death awaiteth them, and no reward or riches is to be found, only to draw the people to the Church of Rome'.

On the Kerry coast was played out part of the tragedy of the Spanish armada of 1588. Many of the ships sailed away from England round by the north of Scotland and so out into the Atlantic, there to meet fierce southwesterly storms that drove them onto the Irish coast from Donegal to Kerry. Those on board were cruelly short of food and water. This last proved crucial. Drake, in 'singeing the king of Spain's beard' the previous year, had burned all the seasoned staves for water-barrels, and new barrels were made of green wood that soon leaked. Shortage of water forced the throwing overboard of live animals, and this reduced the available food. As the voyage lengthened in the bad weather, the distress, the disease and the deaths on board sharply increased. The bad weather, too, showed up defects in the masts and rudders of the ships, and the wildly defective maps of the west Irish coast were a further hazard.

In all, some 25 ships were lost off the coast of Ireland in a period of six weeks from (n.s.) 14 September to 26 October, 1588. Three, or perhaps, four of these were lost off the coast of Kerry. There may have been one survivor out of three of these four ships — what the sea failed to kill the English did.

The English officials along the coast determined to teach once again, if they could, the lesson of Smerwick eight years before. They were not clear how far the Armada itself was intended as a continuation of that episode, and a revenge for it. Indeed, Maurice, son of James Fitz Maurice Fitz Gerald, was one of many Irish who sailed with the Armada, on the *Duquesa Santa Ana,* but died of fever on the way. This ship was to be lost off the coast of Mayo.

The first ships that arrived near Kerry were seven that anchored in the mouth of the Shannon, near Carrigaholt, on 15 September, and sheltered there a week until a favourable wind on the 22nd permitted six of them — the seventh, the 703 ton *Annunziata* of Ragusa (Dubrovnik) was so damaged that her crew set her on fire — to set off safely for Spain.

On 17 September, three ships were driven into Tralee bay, and one of them — perhaps the *Nuestra Senora del Soccorro* of 75 tons — struck, according to tradition, on the rock of Muckalagh. The crew of 24 surrendered to Lady Denny; her husband, Sir Edward Denny, blooded in the massacre of Smerwick in 1580, had all their throats cut, and pocketed some £2,000 worth of booty.

An account of events off the Blaskets has been given to us by Marcos de Aramburu, commander of the *San Juan Bautista* of 750 tons and with a complement of 243 men. On 25 September, he was tossing around off the Skelligs in atrocious weather when he saw two ships. One of these seems to have been the *Trinidad,* an 800 ton converted merchant ship with 24 guns and a complement of 302 men. She was never seen again and is assumed to have been lost 'off the coast of

Desmond' — according to tradition off Valentia.   The second proved to be the flagship of the admiral of the Armada under Medina Sidonia. This was Juan Martinez de Recalde in the *San Juan de Portugal* of 1,050 tons, with a tender, apparently a captured Scottish fishing vessel. The *San Juan* sailed west of the Blaskets, doubled around one of the islands to the north — presumably Inis Tuaiscirt — and then ran by the treacherous rock of Carraig Fhada through the narrow channel and anchored in the little harbour of 'Vicey', through an entrance about as wide as 'the length of a ship'. 'Vicey' has been identified as Inishvickillane to the south west of the Great Blasket, but this is clearly wrong. They anchored either off Beiginish or by the eastern shore of the Great Blasket. This was a formidable piece of seamanship in such weather and with such tides. The piloting was attributed to a Scot, one of six on board captured off the coast of Scotland; but there is a local tradition that there was a Dingle man on board who knew these terrible waters. Recalde himself knew this place because he had escorted the little expedition to Smerwick in 1580.   Aramburu followed Recalde into this anchorage. Recalde had had 500 men on board when he set out, but his ship had been shot to pieces in the actions off the English coast, and now some five men a day were dying of thirst and disease. Recalde despatched eight men, including a Scot, to the mainland for water, food and information. These were captured by the English. Their fate, after their examination in Dingle, is not clear, but it is most likely that they were killed. Recalde had another larger boat which, two days later, he sent out to reconnoitre the fate of the earlier party, but they came across a band of English soldiers above Dunquin and did not land there. Over the next three days this boat took on water 'but little, and that with much labour'. Aramburu had no boat, so he could not do even this.

About mid-day on the 1st October the *Santa Maria de la Rosa,* a great merchantman of 945 tons with all her sails but the foresail torn to ribbons, came through the Sound, firing her guns for help, and anchored near them. About two o'clock the tide changed and the anchor dragged.   Presumably she hit the rock called Stromboli (after a later wreck) off Dunmore head and sank at once 'about two splices of cable from us'. Then the *San Juan de Ragusa,* with her mainmast gone, came in to anchor and she, too, began to settle in the terrible tides, her crew being taken onto the other ships. Of the *Santa Maria* — one of the biggest of those lost — there was but one survivor, Antonio de Monana, the son of the ship's Genoese pilot, run through by the frenzied captain at the end. Among those lost on the ship, according to the survivor, was a natural son of the king of Spain, the Prince of Ascule: but, in fact, he was not on this ship. This was probably a fancy of the interrogator, David Gwynn, a master of a fine tale. He had been captured by the Spaniards some years previously and had been condemned to an oar in a galley. His galley, the *Diana,* sailed with the Armada but had been driven by a storm onto the coast of France, where, according to his own account, after heroic exploits he had freed the crew and captured three other galleys.

Aramburu, after the loss of the *Santa Maria de la Rosa,* then set sail

Blasket Sound

and, after a fearful battering, got back to Spain. Recalde got to Coruna on 7 October. He had been ill throughout the expedition, and died four days after his return.

After the 16th earl of Desmond's death in 1583 the government of the two parts of Kerry had been given to local worthies — the former palatinate (comprising north Kerry), and the county of Desmond (comprising south Kerry and west Cork), to the earl of Clancarre, Sir Owen O Sullivan and O Sullivan Mor. This nicely illustrates what it was had been destroyed in the Desmond rebellion — in effect, the anglo-norman intruders of the 13th century. Gaelic power, what there was of it, continued to survive — for a time. The earl of Clancarre was, of course, MacCarthy Mor who, like the other gaelic nobles — except O Conor Kerry and O Donoghue Mor — had stayed loyal to the Queen in the second Desmond war, though he had momentarily strayed from his loyalty in the first.   He had accepted the earldom in 1565 and on the usual terms had surrendered his people's lands to the Queen and had been re-granted them by her. Should he have no male heirs, the lands would be resumed by the Queen. As overlord, he claimed the O Donoghue lands around the Killarney lakes when they were confiscated in 1586 and given to Sir Nicholas Browne. In English law he had no claim, but may have had one in Irish law. In any event, thanks to the skill of his lawyers, a Kerry jury, and, possibly, for his services to the Crown, he was

80

given the lands. He then pledged them to Browne, together with the lands of Molahiffe, Glanerought and Ballycarbery that were to lead to much litigation in later times; in spite of many reverses over 60 years the Brownes held on . Clancarre was a remarkable man — shrewd, married to a sister of the 16th earl of Desmond whom he helped to destroy, profligate, a poet of some worth (some of his poetry religious), a drunkard and the last of his line. He was continually short of money and pledged much of his property to Sir Nicholas Browne which enabled the latter to hold possession of it until the loan was paid but Clancarre did not bother to pay anything. Bagwell calls him 'the wicked earl'. His legitimate son — Viscount Valentia — died before him; Clancarre also left a daughter and a favoured one of his four illegitimate sons, Donnell. He left no other legitimate male relatives and a lordship as great as that of the earl of Desmond. The undertakers, their appetites whetted by the Desmond loot — those people, as one of them Sir William Herbert called them, that 'measure conscience by commoditie, and law by lust' — were poised for a rich killing. When Clancarre should die without a male heir, the Queen would resume his lands and regrant them to the future husband of his daughter Ellen, provided that husband was English. Nicholas Browne had this in hand and, with the approval of the Queen, had signed a contract to marry Ellen. However, she had other ideas, and at midnight in Muckross friary in 1588 she was married to her handsome cousin, Florence Mac Carthy Reagh, of a cadet branch of the family. This bitterly disappointed the adventurers (and the Queen). Clancarre denied all complicity and blamed his wife. The countess, with the girl's foster father, Donal na Tubrid O Mahony, was imprisoned in Castlemaine. Florence was lodged in the Tower of London for two years, and he and his wife did not get back to Ireland until 1593.

When Clancarre did die in 1596, he should have been succeeded, under Irish law, by Donnell as Mac Carthy Mor. O Sullivan Mor, who was Florence's brother-in-law (as well as Browne's) and whose ancient task it was to inaugurate the Mac Carthy Mor by giving him the white rod at Lisbanagher, refused to do this for Donnell. Donnell got some lands conveyed to him by his father. Florence assumed the title of Mac Carthy Mor. So did Donnell. The dispute as to who should succeed to the lordship led, on Browne's suggestion, to the setting up of an inquisition into Clancarre's lands and rights. This, as analysed in Butler's *Gleanings of Irish History*, throws much light on the nature of gaelic lordship.

Both Donnell and Florence played confused parts in the O Neill wars. Early in 1600 O Neill confirmed Florence as Mac Carthy Mor; but in 1601 Florence was trapped by the English and sent to the Tower of London. He spent the next forty years of his life as a prisoner, over a third of it in London gaols, the rest on bail, estranged from his wife, whom he had taken in marriage as a young girl in what had seemed so brilliant a move. The title and substantial properties descended through his offspring until the family died out in the 1770s. By 1600 another of the six or seven great gaelic families had passed out of history.

Florence had been engaged to Julia O Sullivan, daughter of Sir Owen O Sullivan. So, Nicholas Browne, rejected by Ellen Mac Carthy, and Julia O Sullivan, rejected by Florence, were married. To this Julia can be traced the fact that the Brownes became catholic.

From the Desmond confiscations, and from the litigation over the succession to Mac Carthy Mor, as well as that between the O Sullivan Beares, we get an insight into the structure of gaelic society at the end of the sixteenth century. This, with other evidence, has been analysed in a striking paper by Professor Hayes-McCoy.

In the gaelic areas land was normally held by freemen who may have been one in five of those on the land. In Muskerry, which was Mac Carthy country, these freemen fell into five classes: (i) the septs of the Mac Carthys, (ii) subsidiary septs not Mac Carthys, (iii) 'followers'. that is, O Riordans, Mac Sweeneys and others who performed special services, (iv) inhabitants of church land, and (v) professional people. Beneath these were the various unfree people — 'churls', 'betaghs' etc. who cultivated the land and tended cattle but were not, until Hugh O Neill's time, called out on military service. It is most probable that a similar system obtained in the lordship of Mac Carthy Mor.

The free landholders were related by the old system of 'clientship' to nobles. The smallest political unit was the *tuath* in which nobles and freemen gathered together in assembly. By the sixteenth century, however, this assembly had substantially yielded political power to the ruler of the *tuath*. This chief in former times had been selected from the *derbfine* of the ruling family, but in more recent times there had grown up the institution of *tanaiste,* or designated successor, as we see in the history of O Sullivan Beare. (At a higher level, succession to Mac Carthy Mor, had, for centuries, been direct from father to son under something like a system of primogeniture).

The *tuatha* were grouped under *ur-rioghtha* as, in Kerry, O Sullivan Mor and O Donoghue Mor. These in turn owed their allegiance to the over-king, Mac Carthy Mor. Edmund Spenser gives an account of the inauguration ceremony of some such magnate:

It is a custome amongst all the Irish, that presently after the death of any of their chiefe Lords or Captaines, they doe presently assemble themselves to a place generally appointed and knowne unto them to choose another in his steed, where they doe nominate and elect for the most part, not the eldest sonne, nor any of the children of the Lord deceased, but the next to him of blood that is the eldest and the worthiest, as commonly the next brother unto him if he have any, or the next cousin, or so forth, as any is elder in that kindred or sept, and then next to him doe they choose the next of the blood to be Tanist, who shall next succeed him in the said Captaincy, if he live thereunto....

They use to place him that shalbe their Captaine, upon a stone always reserved for that purpose, and placed commonly upon a hill: In some of which I have seen formed and engraven a foot, whereon hee standing, receives an oath to perform all the ancient customes of the countery inviolable, and to deliver up the succession peaceably to his Tanist, and then hath a wand delivered unto him by some whose proper office that is: after which, descending from the stone, he turneth himselfe round, thrice forward, thrice backwards.

But how is the Tanist chosen?

They say he setteth but one foot upon the stone, and receiveth the like oath that the Captaine did... And to this end the Tanist is always ready knowne, if it should happen the Captaine suddenly to die, or to be slaine in battell, or to be out of the countrey, to defend and keepe it from all such doubts and dangers. For which cause the Tanist hath also a share of the countery allotted to him, and certaine cuttings and spendings upon all the inhabitants under the Lord.

Each of these rulers held, by virtue of his office, mensal land in the territories of his subordinates, as well as complex rights of taxation. In addition, he might be the proprietor, or landlord, of substantial areas of demesne land. For example, Mac Carthy of Muskerry held at least half of his lordship as demesne land. Mensal and demesne lands were worked directly for the lords by unfree people.

There was a system of redistributing lands as freeholders' families rose or declined, but what it was, precisely, is not clear. Redistribution under a cattle raising system where there was not a developed field system and where tillage was presumably based on what is now called rundale must have involved some complex arrangements such as still may survive in common grazing rights for mountain sheep.

Notwithstanding the earl of Desmond's easy movement between English and Irish law, his small freeholders were able, at the time of the confiscation, to produce charters to prove title under English law. The crown had alleged that they were only tenants at will because their lands had yielded Irish exactions to the earl.

The O Neill wars reached Kerry in 1598 and, within a fortnight, the county was in rebel hands. This time the old Irish rose with vigour and were supported by a number of the old English. The new English fled fast, abandoning their confiscated lands without attempting to defend them — although the capture of Browne's castle at Molahiffe called for a spirited struggle, and Castlemaine held out for the Queen for over a year.

Hundreds of planted tenants, abandoned by their leaders, fled starving to Cork and Askeaton. The dispossessed Irish resumed their lands and castles. The Desmonds had not wholly died out after 1583. The defeated earl's half-brother, Sir Thomas Roe Fitz Gerald, who had been denied the succession by their common father, and who had consistently supported the English against Desmond, had a son who claimed the title as 17th earl of Desmond. In this he was confirmed by O Neill, by now virtually king of Ireland, at Cashel in 1660. The

Catherine Fitz-Gerald (the longlived) Countess of Desmond.

81

From an engraving published in 1807 with the caption:

> *This illustrious Lady was born about the year 1464, was married in the Reign of Edward IV, lived during the entire Reigns of Edward V, Richard III, Henry VII, Henry VIII, Edward VI, Mary and Elizabeth and died in the latter end of James I or the beginning of Charles I Reigns at the great Age (as is generally supposed) of 162 years.*

The original is different from the Muckross portrait. It was in the possession of the Knight of Kerry. It seems to be based on a portrait by Rembrandt of his mother.

82 English called him derisively the Sugan (or Straw-rope) earl.

According to Lady Chatterton, a sugan is twisted to the left and was thus applied to the product of a left-handed, or repudiated, marriage. He was the principal leader of the revolt in Munster and, almost overnight, became the ruler of Munster, as his ancestors had been. For the Mac Carthy name, Donnell had raised revolt, his people rallied round him, and he displayed some ability; but in November, 1599, Florence (who had been in London about the property) arrived in Desmond to establish himself in his father-in-law's place. He ousted Donnell and tried to be on both sides at once, settling for a sort of neutrality.

The English officials in Munster were no match for this rising, and the response of the central government was slow and ineffective. By February, 1600, when Mountjoy arrived as Lord Deputy and Carew as President of Munster, Ireland was in O Neill's hands.

Carew's first aim in Munster was to sow distrust in the Irish ranks by instigating various plots for the betrayal of the leaders; this had indifferent success. He then set about subduing the province. Waterford and Tipperary were soon cleared, and then Limerick. Glin castle was besieged on 7 July, 1600, easily breached by cannon, and the survivors of the 80 defenders were butchered. Carrigafoyle was surrendered by O Conor Kerry. By the end of August Carew had swept through north Kerry. He followed the old practice of making for famine by destroying the harvest everywhere and driving off cattle. He claimed to have lost 40 against 2,000 slain 'besides husbandmen, women and children'. In September the Sugan earl was heavily defeated near Kilmallock. Nonetheless, the English that autumn were sufficiently alarmed to revive the title in favour of James, the only son of the 16th earl, who had been in their hands since 1579 and was a protestant. The Queen's earl, as he was called, landed in October, 1600, and aroused some little enthusiasm — the geraldine keeper of Castlemaine switched his allegiance to him — until in Kilmallock he went publicly to a protestant service. He left Ireland in March, 1601. By the end of the year he was dead. Florence Mac Carthy was, through a piece of gross treachery by Carew, arrested in 1601 and sent to the Tower. In May, 1601, the Sugan earl was betrayed by the White Knight and lodged in the Tower, where he died seven years later. That was the last of the Fitz Gerald earls of Desmond in Ireland and the end of their four centuries of domination in Kerry.

But not quite. There was a really remarkable figure in the family. She was countess of Desmond, originally Catherine Fitz Gerald of Dromana, Co. Waterford, who was married in the reign of Edward IV (who died in 1483) to Thomas Maol (the Bald), son of the Thomas beheaded at Drogheda who succeeded as 12th earl in 1529 and died in 1534. She was his second wife. It is suggested by those who love to spoil a good story that the ages of the two wives were aggregated. Even so, Catherine lived to a fine, active old age. After the Desmond forfeitures of 1586, Sir Walter Raleigh became possessed of her estate at Inchiquin near Youghal (subject to her life interest) and she remained in her castle;

but with Raleigh's fall from favour his property was bought for a song by Boyle, later earl of Cork, and covered by king's patent in 1604. It was to secure herself against Boyle's rapacity that she is said to have travelled to London in 1604 with her decrepit daughter to see James I about this great issue to her. (Another story is that it was Eleanor, widow of the 16th earl, who undertook this journey after the great disaster of Desmond's fall and attainder and the confiscation of his lands).

She is reputed to have renewed her teeth twice. She is said to have died soon after her return from London after a fall from a cherry tree at the age of 140. The cherry is said to have been another of Raleigh's importations into Ireland. A reputed portrait of her is in Muckross House, a copy done by one of the Herbert girls. Sainthill argues, with some force, that her portrait could not have been painted in her lifetime and that this is a much later copy of another old lady and attributed to Catherine Desmond. Lady Chatterton saw another copy in the Mac Namara house in Ennistymon, Co. Clare in 1838 : 'a face that seemed formed to survive the storms of a century — so stern, so firm and enduring, so devoid of all those susceptibilities which, though sources of much joy, are great underminers of the constitution'.

Once again, the rebels were no match for the English when they took the business seriously (and ruthlessly) in hand. On the Irish side the ambiguous — narrowly self-interested — behaviour of some of the leaders of the great Munster families, such as Florence Mac Carthy, did not make for effective action. Again, the lack of artillery was crucial. The Irish could not hold their castles against it; but when the English took the castles they were largely impregnable. In consequence, the Irish learned to undermine their castles and to destroy them when the English showed up. Thus, the reign of the castle — 400 years after it had come to Kerry — was at an end; and with it the foundation of feudalism. The Irish, in consequence, had to live and fight in the countryside, hiding in the woods and bogs, where they were vulnerable to famine deliberately induced by the English when they destroyed harvests and husbandmen, and drove off cattle to the shelter of garrisoned strongholds.

In the event, by the end of 1600, the war in Munster seemed to be over and the rebellion crushed.

The landing of a small Spanish force at Kinsale in September, 1601 — with later, smaller forces at Castlehaven and Carrigafoyle — set, after some hesitation, Kerry (apart from Castlemaine) and west Cork again aflame; but the rest of Munster did not rise. The great defeat at Kinsale in December, 1601 did not immediately bring the war to an end. In February, 1602 the English forces under Wilmot swept through north Kerry, where Lord Kerry was defeated, his castle of Lixnaw once more fell, and he himself was driven into Desmond. Then they went through the Dingle peninsula where the Knight of Kerry was defeated, his castles at Rahinnane and Castlegregory were taken, and he too driven into Desmond. Thus, the last of the old English were crushed.

Siege of Dunboy

After the Spaniards had capitulated, the great O Sullivan Beare castle of Dunboy near Bere Island was taken over by O Sullivan Beare, not the English. They attacked it by land and sea in June, 1602 and, after the most heroic defence of the war captured it, utterly destroyed, after a fortnight; not one of the survivors was spared. In the next six months there was much scattered fighting in Beare, Dunkerron and Iveragh and the gaelic names came toppling — Mac Carthy, O Sullivan Mor, O Sullivan Beare. O Sullivan Beare was the last of the chieftains to withstand the English. Eventually, with much atrocities, all was over. In December, Tyrrell gave up the contest and marched 80 miles from Castleisland into Offaly without a halt. At Christmas, 1602, O Sullivan Beare gathered a thousand of his people — men, women and children — at Glengarriff. The party included O Conor Kerry. Then began that terrible and heroic winter march of 175 miles up

through Ireland to Leitrim where the party, now dwindled to 35, of whom one was a woman, arrived at O Rourke's castle.

In March, 1603, six days after the death of Elizabeth, O Neill submitted at Mellifont, Co. Louth. At last Ireland was wholly and completely conquered. The last sustained effort of conquest had taken almost a century to achieve.

CONSOLIDATING THE CONQUEST

The seventeenth century saw the consolidation of the conquest of Ireland, but not until two great efforts had been made to assert some degree of Irish independence of English ways. One can think of the seventeenth century as divided into two almost equal parts — that of the consolidation before Cromwell, and that of the consolidation after him.

(I) BEFORE CROMWELL

The death of Elizabeth in 1603 and the accession of the Scottish and Stuart king James 1 seemed to hold out hope for a less ferocious policy towards Ireland : but Ireland had at last been conquered and, in James's reign at least, was to feel the full weight of conquest.

The main effect of the century of conquest by the Tudors was to destroy the two old traditions that had grown together — the gaelic way of life that had at length collapsed, and the 13th century feudal system. Ireland, broken and beaten, was dragged into the modern world.

Between 1604 and 1615 there was a formal period of persecution of catholics, banishing priests, preventing loyal catholics from taking high office under the Crown, and fining urban middle class catholics who did not attend protestant church services. But once the fuss caused by the Guy Fawkes plot of 1605 had died down, there was some toleration in practice, as part of a deliberate policy of reconciliation. At the same time, a determined effort was made to take over completely the parochial system for the established church. This failed to capture the loyalty of the people, but it succeeded in depriving them of all, or nearly all, their parish churches. Looking back we can see that some parish churches stayed in protestant hands, a small number probably stayed in catholic hands, and many were abandoned and fell into ruin. There were, in Kerry very few protestants — and those mostly of British origin — and no fit ministers of religion. The authorities were most critical of the so-called ministers. By 1615 there were in the county only 21 churches in use, with three clergy licensed to preach; the remaining parishes were staffed only by 'reading ministers'. Trinity College, Dublin, which came to be endowed with large tracts of land in Kerry, had been founded in 1591 to supply this lack of ministers. The failure of the established church in Kerry was notwithstanding the existence between between 1588 and 1621 of two bishops from conforming Irish families, Kenan and Crosbie. Chief Justice Saxey, reporting to

84   Cranborne in 1604, had no opinion of the bishops of the church in Munster:

> the bishops themselves ...... taken out of the basest of the
> people were fit to sacrifice to a calf than to intermeddle
> with the religion of God. The chiefest of them [Myler
> Mc Grath] ...... Another, late deceased [Nicholas Kenan]
> a poor, singing man, void of the knowledge of his grammar
> rules, advanced to the bishoprick of Kerry, who hath now
> a successor [John Crosbie] of like insufficiency.

In 1604 Brouncker succeeded Carew as President of Munster and banished all jesuits, seminarists and massing priests out of the province for seven years, and offered rewards for bringing them in. A jesuit was worth £40 but a massing priest only £5. These attractive prizes do not seem to have had any effect in the rural and village areas at least. In the same year plague swept the country from England. Brouncker died in 1607.

The catholic bishop of Ardfert, Michael Fitz Walter, who was appointed in 1591, seems to have kept away from his diocese from the end of the O Neill wars to his death about 1610; it is possible he never visited his see. Papal policy for some time had been to limit the number of bishops (so many of whom had proved unreliable) and to commit the administration of a vacant diocese to a vicar apostolic, either from Rome, or a local priest who held powers at the will of the pope or for five years. They were charged with implementing the reforms of the Council of Trent. A neighbouring bishop was given the task of supervising the vacant diocese. In this way, vacancies in the episcopal line did not impede the counter-reformation and the danger of defecting bishops was reduced. Hence, during the whole of the seventeenth century in Kerry, there was but one appointment of a bishop. From 1601 Eugene Egan was vicar apostolic. From 1611 Richard O Connell was, first, vicar general of Ardfert and, then, from 1620, vicar apostolic. In a list of November, 1613, he is recorded as vicar general of Ardfert and 'a Philosopher and Devine'. At that time there were recorded in the diocese seven regular and thirteen secular priests. O Connell was born in Ballycarbery castle in 1573, educated in Spain and either the Low Countries or Italy, and had returned to Ireland in 1603. He was appointed bishop in 1643 and died ten years later.

One of the major reforms of the Council of Trent in the middle of the previous century had been aimed at the proper education of priests in philosophy and theology, and seminaries for them had been widely established on the continent. With fleeting exceptions there were to be none in Ireland until the end of the 18th century. Irish boys were accepted at the continental seminaries and about 20 special colleges for them — at Salamanca, Lisbon, Prague, Paris, Rome etc. — were established. Hence, Brouncker's proclamation against 'seminarists'; but the students were not only for the priesthood — they studied for law, medicine and the army. The Dublin government made many attempts to penalise parents who sent their children abroad for education. Notwithstanding the local pressures, many of the

religious orders — notably the Jesuits and the Franciscans — conducted schools, as also did some laymen.

In the early years there was a good deal of tongue in cheek submission to protestantism, but by 1611 nearly all the 'converts' had melted away and a Scottish bishop wrote that it seemed the chief burden of ships coming to Ireland were jesuits and 'foreign-bred priests'.

A major social reform was in 1605 the freeing of the serfs, the betaghs or betagii. These were probably the descendants of the pre-celtic inhabitants of Ireland. Many of the English settlers tended to intermarry with these new freemen and to constitute a sort of middle class. These were the people whom the 17th century gaelic poets, their eyes glued on the decaying feudal aristocracy, wrote of with such withering snobbery.

The administrative county of Kerry came into being in 1606 when the north Kerry territory of the former earls of Desmond and the south Kerry part of the county of Desmond (now separated from west Cork) were united in a single administrative unit. Friar O Sullivan says that the curious arrangement whereby about a quarter of the Beare peninsula is in Kerry and the rest in Cork can be attributed to Sir Owen O Sullivan who dismembered the barony of Bear and Bantry from Desmond and joined them to the county of Cork 'particularly as the leading men of said counties would not grant him the convenience of Assizes and Sessions in Killarney'. This was, perhaps, a carryover from a rivalry between the two great O Sullivan families — those of O Sullivan Mor and O Sullivan Beare. However, the papal taxation of 1302 included the barony of Beare in the diocese of Ross — not as it was, earlier and later, with Kerry.

The O Neill wars had greatly disrupted the Desmond plantation, but with peace, the plantation was steadily resumed — in 1604 the undertakers were ordered back to the lands granted to them. Already Boyle, earl of Cork, had begun to pick up parcels of land, including some at the extremities of the Dingle and Iveragh peninsulas. Other relative newcomers, notably Crosbies and Blenerhassets, extended their influence.

The Crosbies (or Mac Crossans) were an interesting example of what occurred in the renewed plantation, and foreshadowed what was to come 40 years later. John Crosbie was, on the nomination of the Queen's earl of Desmond, appointed bishop of Ardfert in 1600 but was allowed to continue as prebendary of Disert in Kildare because of the poverty of Ardfert arising from the 'oppression of the Irish'. He was 'fully instructed in the Irish tongue'. In 1601 he organised a small band against Spaniards landing on the Irish coast, presumably at Carrigafoyle. He held the see until he died in 1621. He married an O Lalor, also of Laoise, and had a large family. He acquired extensive property around Ardfert. His brother, Patrick, was a trusted civil servant although he remained a catholic. For a time he was the agent for Munster patronage at court until he became too greedy. According to his enemies his fee for obtaining a grant of land was half the grant. He was granted lands confiscated after the Desmond wars from Fitz Maurices, Stacks, and Mac Elligotts in Clanmaurice and Iraghticonnor. The Crosbie homeland, Laois, had been planted from 1549 but the dispossessed Irish continually harassed the planters until their leader, Owny O More was killed in 1600. In 1607 it was decided to transplant on favourable terms 300 members of the 'Seven Septs' of Laois (O More, O Kelly, O Lalor, O Doran, Mac Evoy, O Dowling and O Deevy) mainly to 12½ ploughlands around Tarbert. Patrick Crosbie was the agent for this transplantation. The land, formerly granted to an English undertaker, Hollies, 'who was soon weary of it' was granted to Patrick Crosbie and a great part of the 300 members of the septs were settled there, and on his other lands at Clanmaurice, as his tenants in the years 1607 to 1609. He died in 1611.

Another major adventurer to establish himself in Kerry in these years was Richard Boyle, earl of Cork.   He acquired some lands by fraud, some by marriage, and some by purchase, when he acquired the vast estates of Sir Walter Raleigh for £1,000, including the lands of Molanah Abbey, the head house of Aghavore, Derrynane.

Plantation towns — Killarney with 40 English houses, Tralee with 32 — were established as market towns. Dingle, a borough, was still an important port. There was a substantial trade in timber and iron. For example, in the early part of the century nearly all the wine of France and much of that of Spain was casked in Irish timber, especially from Munster. The province also supplied the timber for the hulls of many of the East Indies ships. In the new plantation there was a steady economic exploitation of the resources of the country, helped in part by government action. For example, in 1617, the Presidency of Munster, concerned that the land was in open ranches, required all farmers with leases of seven years or more to enclose all meadow and arable land 'with hedges and ditches with double course of quicksett'. It seems that the practice grew up of doing this annually and throwing down the hedges in winter. On another level, six years earlier, the President forbade both English and Irish farmers to shoot 'deare, hare, partridge and feazant' which 'principall games of pleasure' were to be reserved for the landowners. Nonetheless, by 1622 much of the damage caused by the wars twenty years previously had not been remedied — for example, Sir Henry Denny's house in Tralee, built in the ruins of the Dominican priory. The total number of English planters, while substantial as compared with the contemporary English or Spanish colonisation of the Americas, was still less than it had been before the war. This is all the more surprising when we consider that during these same years the Ulster plantation was carried through with such success.

By 1600 the population of Ireland as a whole was about 1.4 million, a rise of some 40% in the preceding 100 years, giving a population for Kerry of, perhaps, 50,000.

In 1615 a statute was passed requiring the parishes in a barony to provide labour to improve and maintain the roads of the barony;

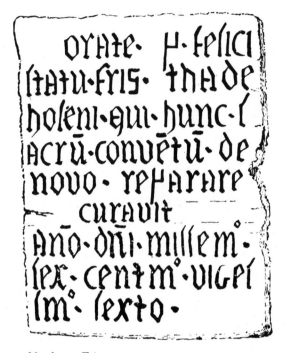

Plaque at Muckross Friary

*Orate p (pro) Felici
statu Fris (Fratric). Thade(i)
Holem qui hume s-
accru(m) convetu (conventum) de
novo reparare
   curavit
Anno Dominc millesimo
sexcentesimo vigesimo sexto.*

*Pray for the happy state
of brother Thadeus
Holenus, who superintended
the rebuilding or repairing
of this sacred convent.*

A.D. 1626

but there was no administrative underpinning to the concept of the barony: all depended on local magnates, appointed as justices of the peace, to be responsible not only for law and order but also for such rudimentary public services as there were. There is much evidence that, particularly for south Kerry, very little was done about roads and communications. This problem was not tackled until some 150 years later, when grand juries were given the task.

In 1613 it was necessary to call a parliament in Dublin and, in preparation for this, to ensure a majority in favour of the government, steps were taken to lay the foundations of the corrupt system of Irish parliamentary representation. Out of this Kerry emerged with seven (later eight) seats that were to remain until the Union: there were two Knights of the Shire; two representatives of the borough of Dingle, recreated in 1607; two representatives from the newly created (1613) borough of Tralee; and one (later two) representatives from the obscurely erected borough of Ardfert, fief of the Crosbies.

86   Notwithstanding the attempts to pack it, this parliament, in its two years of life, put up a spirited defence of the practice of catholicism; from this period, toleration became general and there was a steady revival of religious life. For example, in 1612 the Franciscan community of Muckross was formally re-established; but some re-occupation and restoration had begun in 1602. From 1617 to 1626 extensive works were done on the building, as a plaque in the chancel there shows. In the following years the church seemed to be returning to normal despite occasional scares, such as in 1629 when there was a sharp bout of persecution of regular, but not of secular, clergy and the Muckross friars had to go into hiding. It seems that Ardfert friary had never been fully abandoned, and Lislaghtin was re-established in 1629. In that year O Sullivan Mor wrote to Rome that no bishop had visited the diocese for 28 years, and two years later a long list of Kerry worthies — including ten burgesses of Ardfert — urged the appointment of a distinguished Kerry Dominican, Daniel O Daly (from Kilsarkan, Castleisland, a member of the ancient bardic family of the Desmonds). He was a founder of the Dominican friary at Lisbon and of a convent of Dominican nuns at Belem, also in Portugal.

He published in 1655 the well-known short history of the southern geraldines. He was confessor to the Queen of Portugal. He was Portuguese ambassador in Paris. However, he did not become bishop in in Kerry and died in 1662 shortly after being nominated to a bishopric in Portugal. In 1633 the vicar apostolic, Richard O Connell was recommended for the bishopric, but did not become bishop until 1643. An account of the diocese for the year 1633 is available, being an account of O Connell's stewardship as vicar apostolic. There were 80 parishes, five priories of Canons Regular (Aghavore, Ballinskelligs, Inisfallen, Killagha and Rattoo), one abbey of St. Bernard (Abbeydorney), one Dominican priory (Tralee) and three Franciscan friaries, (Ardfert, Lislaghtin and Muckross). Of priests there were 52 diocesans (of whom six were doctors of theology), and 31—2 regulars (12 Dominicans, 12 Augustinians, 7 Franciscans besides lay brothers, one or two Cistercians). (In 1970, for comparison, there were 134 diocesan priests and 11 regulars). It is clear from these figures that, given the limited population of the time — most likely less than 60,000, or about half the present population — the church was in a healthy state, although the orders apart from the Dominicans, were under severe pressure. However, another return of 1636 gives a less happy picture of the diocesan structure — under O Connell, 12 diocesan priests, 13 Dominicans, eight Augustinians, eight Franciscans — three being described as guardians, three Jesuits and one Cistercian, described as abbot. In all of this Kerry was typical of Ireland as a whole at this time when there were as many religious as at the peak of the medieval period.

These years saw not only the revival of the formal structure of the church, but also it seems, an intensifying of pastoral work. One of the scandals of christianity in Ireland had been the extraordinary laxity in relation to marriage, the ease through the centuries with which wives could be put away (or exchanged), new and annual marriages contracted, and plurality of wives tolerated. This derived from old gaelic custom and a thousand years of christianity had not wiped

it out. In the same way, all children, whether born within or without wedlock, were, with few exceptions, considered legitimate and capable of inheriting. These practices, e.g. amongst the Desmonds and Mac Carthys helped to confuse still further the confused history of Kerry in the 16th century. In 1634 the Irish parliament passed an act outlawing polygamy which the Irish house of lords in 1640 made a strenuous, but unsuccessful, effort to repeal. The decay of the gaelic way of life and the revival of pastoral religion at length during this period of rising puritanism brought these ancient, pre-christian practices to an end.

Scandal was caused, also, on a lesser scale by Irish habits of dress — mainly the wearing by men of a sort of tights called *braccae*. The 1630s were to see the assimilation of the Irish people generally to European notions of decency in dress. In 1644 le Gouz described the dress of the typical Irishman as consisting of:

> a head-dress a little blue bonnet, raised two fingers breadth in front and behind, covering their head and ears. Their doublet has a long body and four skirts and their breeches are a pantaloon of white frize which they call trousers. Their shoes, which are pointed, they call brogues with a single sole. For cloaks they have five or six yards of frize drawn round the neck, the body and over the head and they never quit this mantle, either in sleeping or in eating. The generality of them have no shirts.

Other habits — drunkenness and gambling — remained more ingrained. Nonetheless, we must look on this period as one of a substantial revival in the practice of religion.

The revived church, and above all the Franciscans, were to play a major part in another sphere.

During this period most of the Irish way of life was destroyed; but some of the old scholarly and artistic traditions were by heroic efforts continued. The monastic tradition of secular scholarship, abandoned after the twelfth century reforms, was revived under cruel difficulties. In early christian times the tradition of scholarship was taken over by the monasteries from the old pagan secular order. Then, when the old Irish monasteries themselves came to an end in the twelfth century, the tradition was taken over by the newly revived secular order of learned and bardic families. When they themselves collapsed in the social and material ruin of the sixteenth century, there still remained a number of the old bardic schools, including some professional schools of leech-craft, law and history, but these eventually collapsed about the middle of the seventeenth century. As in earlier times, the monasteries, now above all the Franciscans, took over the burden of maintaining this long cultural tradition. Between 1630 and 1636, in the Franciscan friary of Donegal, a Franciscan lay brother Michael O Clery, with the whole gaelic world falling in ruins about him, set about, with three companions, completing the *Annals of the Four Masters,* the attempt to keep a living accurate memory of what had occurred in Ireland to his time. This was part of an immense

Franciscan scheme to preserve all that could be recorded of Irish culture, of Ireland's antiquities, religious and secular, that was organised by Irish Franciscan exiles from Louvain in Belgium. As Plummer says: 'There is, indeed, hardly to be found in the history of literature a more pathetic tale than that of the way in which Colgan and his fellow workers ...... strove amid poverty and persecution and exile to save the remains of their country's antiquities from destruction'. Other collectors, also in exile in the Low Countries, assembled books of poems.

A secular priest from Tipperary, Dr. Geoffrey Keating, combined a number of these traditions — he composed religious works in Irish, bardic poems in praise of the great Butler lords, more popular verse, and, in the 1620s, the first history of Ireland in Irish, based on the fast disappearing relics and tales of the past.

From the 'establishment' in Dublin, also came this practical concern for preserving the past. Archbishop Ussher and Sir James Ware at this time greatly encouraged the study of Ireland's past. By 1624 Ware had acquired for his great library the country's oldest surviving manuscript, the *Annals of Inisfallen*.

The terrible economic effects of the Desmond wars, and of the later O Neill one, continued. In 1634, in return for a promise to redress some of the grievances of those who had lost the earlier wars, a substantial sum was paid to Charles I. The total sum paid by Munster was £11,200 to which Kerry contributed only £874. This suggests that the county was, half a century after the Desmond wars, still in great poverty and depopulated. In general, the country steadily revived economically during the first forty years of the century. This was notable in agriculture. For example, the practice of saving hay for winter fodder was introduced and gradually became general. Exports also rose in spite of the prevalence of pirates. One of the principal export items was pipe staves for barrels, and the woods of Kerry became a significant source of supply. At this time the technique of barelling butter reached Cork and permitted the beginning of the great export trade in butter that was to mean so much to Kerry in the following centuries.

The spectacular rule of Wentworth (later Strafford) had little impact on Kerry; but Miss Hickson quotes an entry from the diary of Sir Edward Denny of Tralee : '23rd Julye, 1633. The Lord Viscounte Wentworth came to Ireland to governe ye kingdom. Manie men feare'. Six years later Wentworth required Denny to take out new letters patent for the estate his grandfather had acquired in the Desmond confiscations. This required him to pay £500 and to bring in eight new British tenants. According to Miss Hickson, it was those new tenants who suffered in 1641, the longer established ones being undisturbed.

Wentworth also engaged the arch-predator, Richard Boyle, earl of Cork, in 1635 in a great Star Chamber case. Amongst other charges, Boyle was accused of having obtained an improper lease of the parsonages of Kynard and Ballinacourty and the vicarage

of Mynard from the incumbent he had presented to them.

John Crosbie, the third reformed bishop of Ardfert and Aghadoe, had a numerous family. Of these the most distinguished was Col. David Crosbie, who was later to complain that Wentworth forced him to pay, in respect of Bishop's lands at Killiney etc. a rent increased from £1.15s. a year to £10. However, one of Strafford's most implacable enemies in Ireland was David Crosbie's cousin, Sir Piers, who had fought as a colonel under Gustavus Adolphus and been at the siege of Rochelle. His father, Patrick, the bishop's brother, had also acquired substantial lands in Kerry, including the abbey lands of Odorney and a seignory at Tarbert. Sir Piers Crosbie, a member of the Irish Privy Council, fell foul of Strafford by siding with the catholics — like his father he seems to have been a catholic — in the Irish parliament

Richard Boyle, 1st Earl of Cork

88

to frustrate Strafford's reforms against bigamy, being accessory to murder, etc. and was jailed. He escaped from jail and, later, accused Strafford of being responsible for the death in prison of a sea captain struck by Strafford, who then sued Crosbie before the Star Chamber which eventually heavily fined Crosbie (and others) and awarded severe damages against him. Crosbie had sold his Odorney property to cover his costs but these penalties were ruinous. However, a year later, Strafford was on trial, Crosbie was one of the witnesses against him, and it may be that in the confusion Crosbie escaped the penalties imposed by the Star Chamber.

Some insight into the effects of confiscation and the reality of the 'undertakers' comes from evidence about the Herbert estate at Castleisland. This seignory, the heart of the Desmond possessions in Kerry, of about 12,000 profitable acres, was undertaken by Sir William Herbert in 1587, and by 1589 he had planted 20 British tenants. The estate went to his daughter Mary who married a kinsman, later the first Lord Herbert of Cherbury in Wales, the first of a line of absentee landlords. About 1608 he leased the estate – against his wife's wishes apparently – to Sir Thomas Roper, later Viscount Baltinglass (Constable of Castlemaine from 1605) for a period of three lives, in return for a fine that financed a two-year grand tour of Europe. In 1622 there were 18 tenants of British birth or descent. In the mid 1630s, Roper had let the castle fall into ruin and had devastated the woods. The third life ended in 1640 and the estate reverted to Lord Herbert. This was the period when Wentworth was inquiring into titles of such estates as these. Apparently, Herbert was able to avoid any real inquisition, but the uncertainty of title was to last for fifty years.

In 1640 at least half the seignory was held by three tenants – two Fitz Geralds and a John West. One of the Fitz Geralds, Garret, also held adjoining lands from the Earl of Cork, and the tenants under him, on both estates, numbered about 350 persons. The parson of the seignory, Mr. Cooke, was at that date willing to resign into Lord Herbert's hands two parish churches, Ballincuslane and Killeentierna, both worth £100 a year, no service having been read in either for 20 years. They are, respectively, just east and just south of Castleisland.

Towards the end of October, 1641 rebellion broke out all over Ireland. In the north and west there were many massacres of protestants. Miss Hickson prints depositions that allege that at Easter, 1642, seventeen protestants were taken from the shelter of Ross Castle, Killarney, stripped, confined in the market place of the town, and then taken two miles outside the town and murdered. Several of these were aged, one pregnant and others were children. Protestants were pressed to become catholics and many in Kerry did so. (There is some reason to doubt the genuineness of many of these depositions. By January, 1653 the Cromwellians, despite hard swearing by witnesses, had secured the execution of 52 persons in all Ireland convicted of the murder of protestants).

Kerry was almost at once in the hands of the rebels. During the rebellion there was an uneasy alliance – such as had long existed in

Kerry – between the Irish and the old English. Florence Mac Carthy of Ardtully, called Captain Sugan, was governor in the rebel interest until he was killed in action in 1642, and the leaders of the revolt were the old Irish – Mac Carthys, Owen O Sullivan Mor, and other O Sullivans, as well as lesser names. Several of the newer protestants, such as some of the Crosbies and a Blennerhasset, were either implicated or remained neutral. The only prominent Catholic who remained neutral – he was excommunicated by the new bishop – was the Knight of Kerry, of old English stock. Lord Kerry, head of the Fitz Maurice family was in charge of the county for the government, but had little stomach for this and departed for England, never to return. He had committed the county to a number of captains, who rapidly went over to the rebel side. Castlemaine fell to one of the Mac Carthys after a siege of a few days, and the booty contained two old cannon, much prized but not used in the principal actions.

Of the captains who went with the rebels one of the most interesting was Piaras Ferriter, a distinguished poet in Irish, from west of Dingle, where he has become a folk hero. He was in charge of the single substantial action of the war in Kerry, the siege of the two castles of Tralee. The main castle was the old castle of the Desmonds, restored by the Dennys in the 1620s, now commanded by the husband of Denny's widow, Sir Thomas Harris. Also invested was the nearby short castle of the Rices. The siege lasted from January 1641–2 to July or August of that year when, Harris having died, it was yielded on terms, honourably kept. Amongst those investing the castles were O Donoghue of the Glens and his three sons, the eldest of whom Geoffrey was to succeed him in 1643. So this action involved two of the four major Kerry poets.

A curious attempt to relieve the castle led to the fitting out of two ships in Youghal, the *Flower of Youghal* and the *Lion of Youghal*. At Cork at end May they took aboard Sir Edward Denny and a foot company, had a little skirmish with O Sullivan Beare's men at Durrus, and another with O Sullivan Mor's troops somewhere in the Kenmare river. They landed at Ballinskelligs, where there was another small skirmish that led them to burn the village and the surrounding places. They then sailed to Dingle and being opposed there on 3 June went back to Ballinskelligs where four score men, raiding for cattle, were ambushed by O Sullivan Mor's men and all but three were killed. The following day they raided Kilmackilloge for salt, remaining there until Monday the 6th, when eight men again landed, again ran into an ambush by O Sullivan Mor, and were all but two of them (who were captured) stoned to death. This seems to have been the end of this disastrous and incompetent expedition.

The other notable siege of the war was that of Ballingarry castle on a peninsula at the mouth of the Shannon. This was held by Colonel David Crosbie until 1645 but was betrayed by three of the defenders. Crosbie was saved by his nephews, Mac Elligott and Mac Gillacuddy on the Irish side and his niece Katherine Mac Gillacuddy. In 1649 Cromwell made him governor of Kerry, when he was able to repay past favours. In 1643 Richard O Connell, who had been vicar apostolic since 1620, was appointed bishop, the only bishop appointed to Kerry in the 17th century. He lived at Muckross and established a seminary at Tralee.

The papal nuncio, Rinuccini, landed at Ardea castle near Kenmare on 21-22 October, 1645. On the six day voyage from France he had been hotly pursued by an English naval vessel under an Irishman, Plunkett; but the English ship, after a nine hour chase, just failed to catch him because its cook house went on fire. Rinuccini brought substantial sums of money and quantities of arms. He spent his first night in Ireland in a shepherd's hut near Ardea. The next two nights were spent at Ardtully castle, the home of Mac Fineen Mac Carthy, one of the leaders of the rebels in Kerry.

One of the party with Rinuccini, who was archbishop of Fermo, was Dionisio Massari, dean of Fermo, who has left an account of the journey into Limerick. He was much taken by what he saw. He was impressed by the religious fervour of the people around Ardea and the high level of religious instruction among young people there. They went by Ardtully near Kilgarvan, to Macroom, Killmallock and Limerick. The mountainy country was:

> most abundantly stocked with cattle of every kind.... The men are fine looking and of incredible strength. They are stout runners and bear every sort of hardship with incredible cheerfulness.... Those who apply themselves to the study of literature are most learned, and such persons are to be found of every profession and in every branch of science.

> The women are remarkably tall and comely, and display a charming union of gracefulness with modesty and devotion. Their manners are marked by extreme simplicity, and they freely mix in conversation without surpise or jealousy. Their costume is different from ours and somewhat resembles the French. They moreover wear a long cloak and profuse locks of hair, and go without any head-dress, contenting themselves with a kind of handkerchief, almost Greek in fashion, which displays their natural beauty to great advantage. The families are very large. There are some that have as many as thirty children all living, and the number of those who have fifteen or twenty children is immense, and all these children are handsome, tall and robust, the majority being light-haired and of clear white and red complexion. The entertainments were superb and consisted of flesh and fish, together with butter, which was used on all occasions.

Lady Fanshawe, who fled from Cork to Limerick to Galway a few years later, has a similar, if shorter, account: 'The country exceeds in timber and seaports, and great plenty of fish, fowl, flesh; and by shipping wants no foreign commodities'.

When Rinuccini left Ireland he organised Capuchin priests to write an account of his unsuccessful mission. The chief of these was Robert O Connell of Ballycarbery castle, a kinsman of the bishop.

The most curious story of the war in Kerry is that of the young Englishman, Rev. Devereux Spratt, tutor in Tralee to Sir Edward Denny's three sons. He was caught in the siege and his mother and eight-year old brother (he himself was 22) died there. At the surrender he went with the other protestants to Ballingarry castle and from there to Youghal on his way to England. At sea, and while they were in sight of land, the crew and passengers were captured by an Algerine pirate. In Algiers he met and ministered to many of his compatriots. He was ransomed soon after but, at the request of his flock, he stayed. Two years later he, with others, was required to leave because he had been ransomed. He ended as rector of Mitchelstown, Co. Cork.

At a later stage of the wars, military posts were established at Kenmare (Cromwell's Fort) and at Valentia. From the former of these a number of raids were made on O Sullivan Mor's territory along the north side of the Kenmare river. There were attempts, reinforced by massacre, to depopulate the whole area.

The final action of the war, and the only significant attack in Kerry, was the siege of Ross castle, Killarney in 1652. This was surrendered on 28 June to Ludlow on the usual terms of permitting the commander (Lord Muskerry) to bring his soldiers to any European country at peace with the Commonwealth. Some local resistance continued in Kerry. Ross castle was put in the command of Captain James Nelson who did not feel unduly constrained by the terms of the surrender. Cornelius Mac Carthy, a diocesan parish priest, was hanged in 1652. Piaras Ferriter, Thaddeus Moriarty — prior of the Dominican house in Tralee who refused to leave the country — and Teigue O Conor Kerry, having been separately captured, were hanged in Killarney on 15th October 1653. Francis O Sullivan, provincial of the Franciscans, was killed on Scariff island in the same year. Bishop O Connell, now a very old man, had to flee from his home in Muckross but was captured. On paying a fine of £300 he was released and permitted to live with a relative and namesake in Killarney. He died in July 1653 and was buried in Aghadoe.

The ten monasteries that had been boasted of twenty years previously all were now suppressed and finally abandoned. As we shall see, however, the Muckross and Lislaghtin Franciscans and, in part, the Tralee Dominicans clandestinely survived. Franciscan records show that there were guardians (that is, superiors) of the Muckross community from the Restoration of 1660 right down to 1873; something similar was true of the Lislaghtin community. It was the general practice of the religious communities to live near their old foundations, to dress in civilian clothes and to recruit and train young people locally, occasionally (but not frequently enough, it seems) sending them abroad for education. Hence, the continuity was discreetly maintained. The Cistercians and the Augustinians now drop out of Kerry history; but it is likely that some, at least, of the Augustinian communities revived after the Restoration.

90

Landfall at Ardea Castle

(II) AFTER CROMWELL

The Cromwelliam period — 1649-1660 — is remembered with great horror in Ireland. This was for four reasons : the brutality of Cromwell's own campaigns in 1649-50 — he did not come to Kerry; the intense persecution of catholics — and some protestants; the wholesale confiscation of land; and the organised deportation to the West Indies and to Europe of thousands of destitute people. These miseries were made worse by severe attacks of bubonic plague in 1650 and again in 1652-53, which may have killed up to one-third of the population.

Many thousands of able-bodied were shipped by Bristol merchants as slaves for the tobacco planters of Barbados. Petty mentions 6,000 Irish boys and girls — as distinct from young adults — being shipped to the West Indies.

The confiscation, based on a statute of August, 1652, was in conception — though not always in execution — an attempt at a 'final solution' of the Irish problem. The defeated proprietors — virtually all of them — were to lose their own lands; up to two-thirds of these would be confiscated and they were to be compensated for the remainder with property in the under-populated province of Connacht, which, at that time, included Clare. The places reserved for the Kerry dispossessed were the baronies of Burren and Inchiquin in Clare, and Artagh in north Roscommon — oddly enough, places associated with the ancient migrations of the Ciarraige. Those transplanted were to be, under penalty of death, removed by May, 1654. There were extensive

confiscations in Kerry. For example, O Conor Kerry's lands at Carrigafoyle went to a Cromwelliam settler, Sandes. Miss Hickson prints long lists of the Kerry dispossessed, with the members of their extended households, the properties of which they were dispossessed, their stock, etc. Sixty-six travel certificates were issued in Kerry covering no less than 4,981 persons, or about 75 persons in each extended household. In this way, a branch of the O Connell family was moved from Iveragh to west Clare. In all, it seems as if twelve land *owners* were actually transplanted. Allowing for their extended households, it is nonetheless highly unlikely that anything like 5,000 people were driven out of Kerry in this way. The period of transplantation was postponed to the time from 1 May, 1654 to 30 September, 1657. As there was little administrative underpinning to these savage laws, and as there was a great deal of inefficiency and at least some corruption, they were not as rigidly enforced as their authors — the chief of whom was Cromwell himself — intended. Many families managed to evade them, often staying on their own lands, according to the ancient pattern, as tenants of the new proprietors. In this way, O Sullivan Mor survived in Killarney until the last of the name died over a century later. The new proprietors needed, of course, the native population to work the land. Others returned after the Restoration of 1660, and some before that date. In general, the actual tillers of the soil were not to be disturbed, but were to be grouped in villages of not less than 30 families, sited away from bogs and woods.

The county as a whole was still, proportionately, as poor as a generation before: in the parliament of 1661 Kerry was assessed at £550 out of a total Munster contribution of £8,000, marginally a smaller proportion than in 1634.

At this time, there emerged Dr. William Petty, possessed of a genius for practical affairs. Petty (1623—1687) was one of the most remarkable men of the century, and he left a considerable mark on Kerry as well as great possessions there. He was of humble origin, but became a doctor and professor of medicine at Oxford at twenty-seven years of age and a professor of music at Gresham College, London. He came to Ireland as an army physician in 1652 primarily to seek his fortune; and he was not disappointed.

The cost of the war in Ireland was from 1642 partly financed by 'Adventurers' who were to be repaid with five million acres of Irish land confiscated from the Irish rebels. In addition, the 35,000 soldiers were to be given land in lieu of arrears of pay. The land was to be valued at a quarter of its value at the outbreak of war. This land was to be made available, above that left empty by war and plague, by transplantations to Connacht, the shipment of able-bodied men and destitute women and children to the West Indies and the Continent, and the emigration of soldiers to continental armies. The net effect of this, in Petty's calculation, was to cut the population by one-third in the period 1641 to 1652.

To meet the demands for land, it was necessary to survey it completely, accurately and promptly. This Petty volunteered to do on a contract basis. He received crucial support from Sir Hardress Waller, who had married into a Limerick property in the 1620s, had lost all in the rebellion, had become a major-general in Cromwell's army and a regicide. He was at the siege of Ross castle; after the Restoration he died in the Tower. Petty later married his daughter. The Wallers still have property in Kerry. Petty's Down survey of 22 Irish counties began early in 1655 and was finished in 15 months, a truly remarkable feat of organisation. His basic surveyors were 1,000 foot soldiers. To this we owe a splendid set of maps. There is a Petty map of Kerry as a whole, and of each of the baronies. (The originals of the Petty maps were captured by a French ship and lodged in the Bibliotheque Nationale de Paris; hence the attribution on modern prints of them).

Ten counties were set aside to meet the claims of the adventurers and soldiers. Six other counties, including Kerry, were set aside as additional security for the soldiers, but they showed extreme reluctance to be allotted any land in Kerry. The soldiers fell into three categories, those in the second of which had to take about one-sixth of their compensation in Kerry land. Moreover, the baronies of Iveragh and Dunkerron and, it would seem, Glanerought, were excluded from the count as being 'unprofitable', to be used to meet claims that could not otherwise be met. Although Petty's survey was done with such speed, no comparable arrangements were made for distributing the spoils so surveyed. Many of the soldiers sold their claims to land at about a quarter of their nominal value which, as we have seen, was itself about a quarter of what may have been their true value. Petty bought many of these claims. The land in Kerry was not good for agriculture, and those who were allotted it were glad to sell it; but Petty saw the value of the landlocked harbours, the forests, the quarries, and the mines, and added to his own allotment by buying the land allotted to others. He was not paid in full for his survey and other duties, and he was permitted to take land in exchange for his claims. In this way he acquired about 3,500 acres in Glanerought — in the Tuosist and Killmare (Kenmare) parishes against £900 of his claim. He also bought very cheaply 2,000 acres in the same area. Aubrey described him in 1661 as able 'from Mount Mangerton in that county to behold 50,000 acres of his own land', much of it waste. The Restoration did not abate his acquisitions. In 1662 he was given 30,000 unprofitable acres in Glanerought, and in 1668—69 he obtained almost 60,000 acres in Dunkerron and Iveragh.

Petty did not confine himself to Kerry. He used much of the gains from his survey to employ cash to acquire for a song land throughout Ireland. One complex transaction gave him 10,000 acres for £600. He was also one of the commissioners for the distribution of forfeited lands, and became the sole commissioner in practice. He had estates, it was claimed, in every county in Ireland, but his most extensive, if not so profitable, lands were in Kerry. He was one of the trusted assistants of Henry Cromwell, ruler of Ireland from 1655 to 1660; but his economic and administrative skills were underpinned by his political skills at the time of the Restoration. These led to his being knighted in 1661 and his getting large grants, as we have seen, of 'unprofitable' lands in Kerry — this, while he still remained one of the

trustees for the Cromwell property.

He became possessed in Kerry alone of 270,000 acres, about one-quarter of the whole county; of the nine baronies of Kerry, he was the owner of the greater part of four: Glanerought, Dunkerron North and South, and Iveragh. These were mainly the territories of O Sullivan Mor and O Sullivan Beare. Much of this was mountainy land, but it had good small harbours, good sea fisheries, salmon fisheries, marble quarries; it was extensively wooded, and there were a number of iron and copper deposits. Iron was in increasing demand and fuel for smelting it scarce in England. Petty opened, or re-opened the iron mines. Timber from the valleys of the Carra, the Finnihy, and the

Sir William Petty

92

Blackwater, all supplied his ironworks. When coin was scarce for his piece rate wages he struck his own iron coins. Several of these coins marked Glanerought Iron Works, dated 1667 and 1669, are extant. He smelted pig-iron with charcoal from the woods. It is said that so extensive were the clearances in consequence that at least one mine (at Blackstones, Glencar) was deprived of fuel and had to close. He also exported timber for the Royal Navy, for pipe staves and for other purposes. In another part of the country a poet was bewailing, in a famous poem, the same process:

Cad a dheanfaimid feasta gan admad?	*What shall we do without timber?*
Ta deire na gcoillte ar lar	*The last of the woods is felled . . . .*

Until the mid 18th century the Kerry woods were to feed these iron-works and to give bark for tanning at Killarney. Then, as in the rest of the country, the woods were all consumed and the countryside was left bare.

Petty was notable for the scale and modernity of his operations; and he threw himself with passion into the economic development (and exploitation) of his Kerry property. He established salmon, herring and pilchard fisheries at Killmare (Kenmare), Ballinskelligs, Dursey and Kilmackilloge. The big seine boats still used in the bay were his introduction. He introduced the special local system of 'sweeper' nets used to surround salmon by means of a seine boat and a smaller boat, a 'follower'. Seine boats are now used also for the local sport of seine boat racing. He founded the town of Nedeen (now Kenmare) for the English miners he induced to settle there. Two years after his death in 1687 they were so harassed by the Irish that they returned to England but came back after the williamite wars. Petty's property descended through his daughter to the Fitz Maurice family, Lords of Kerry, from Lixnaw. Anne Petty's husband became the first earl of Kerry. Her eldest son, childless, disposed of all the lands in north Kerry. Her other son, the founder of the Petty-Fitz Maurice family, became the second earl of Shelburne and his son first marquis of Lansdowne. The last named laid out the modern form of Petty's town of Nedeen and renamed it Kenmare, after his friend Lord Kenmare of Killarney. The Lansdowne family still have a seat at Lauragh on the south side of the Kenmare river.

The great landowner displaced in Kerry by Petty was Owen O Sullivan Mor who had played a prominent part in the recent rebellion and forfeited the lands his family had acquired four and a half centuries before. He was not transplanted. Instead, he managed to acquire some lands formerly held by the Brownes at Tomies, Killarney and, here, in much reduced circumstances, an O Sullivan Mor held out for over a century. Petty let the O Sullivan Mor lands to the descendants of an ancient family, the O Mahonys, who now began a steady rise to wealth and influence so that, by the end of the century, Donal O Mahony was a man of power and wealth holding state like a medieval chieftain. Not only English adventurers profited

from the disturbed times.

Again, we get some insight into events from the *Herbert Correspondence*. The effects of the war, the destruction of man and beast by sword and pestilence and, no doubt the flight of protestants at the early stages, made the Castleisland estate profitless for a long period. It was necessary to re-stock it with tenants. No less than 150 persons were brought from Wales — one of them Andrew Ellis, with 200 beasts, 1,000 sheep, 20 breeding mares 'and other considerable goods'. However, these were not enough to repeople the estate and permission was sought and granted to re-tenant it with Irish tenants. The agent for all this was Lord Herbert's remote kinsman, Thomas Herbert, the founder of the Herbert family of Muckross. In 1656, twenty-three of the new tenants petitioned the landlord: of these a dozen had Irish names (Mac Fineen, O Daly, etc.) or the names of old English long settled in Kerry.

The Cromwellians decreed the union, under a single parliament, of the three kingdoms of England, Scotland and Ireland, and accepted the logic of a common market between them. This led to some revival of Irish exports and growth in the export of Irish cattle to England.

The Cromwellians were, of course, protestants but not episcopalians and harshly treated the senior clergy of the Church of Ireland. However, the bishop of Ardfert and Aghadoe, Thomas Fulwar, survived the Commonwealth. At the Restoration, the diocese was united with that of Limerick where it remains.

What survived of the old Irish system of education was finally destroyed at this time but love of education was not extirpated and there grew up, at this time, those 'hedge schools', popular, informal groups of students around an (often itinerant) schoolmaster. These schools were to give great service to — and to be almost the sole means of schooling for — poorer people for over a century. Kerry was a notable centre for these schools.

At the Restoration in 1660 when Charles II returned as king, there were strong hopes that Irish landowners who had lost their lands to Cromwellians would get them back. They were to be sadly disappointed. Two Kerry magnates who were with Charles on his travels — the young Sir Valentine Browne and the Mac Gillacuddy of the Reeks were, however, restored to their lands. So also was Piaras Ferriter's son, Major Dominick Ferriter.

Economically too, hopes were to be disappointed. The common market was undone, and the export of cattle to England was forbidden in 1663 and 1666. The Navigation Acts were applied to Irish imports so that they could be shipped from the colonies only through England.

However, if cattle could not be exported alive, they could be exported as meat and, as the century wore along, there grew up an extensive trade in provisions to the continent, to America and the West Indies. This helped the long-standing export trade in hides. If there were restrictions on legitimate shipping, there were plentiful small harbours — especially in Kerry — where long-standing trade with France, Portugal and Spain could be maintained and developed. As the trade in cattle developed, the little oxen ceased to be used as draught animals and were replaced by little garrons. It seems that, in general, there was a substantial rise in trade and in wealth in the latter part of the century.

At the Restoration, the country as a whole was well supplied with priests. In 1661 there were about 2,000 of whom, it seems, nearly half were regular clergy of whom about half were Franciscans and a quarter Dominicans. In that year a synod held at Fethard, at which there was no bishop (the two surviving Munster ones were in exile and during the 1660s there was only one bishop active in all Ireland) arranged for the appointment of an administrative vicar in the dioceses of Ross and Ardfert. Cornelius Daly seems to have been vicar apostolic from 1677 to his death in prison about 1699. About 1680, according to Petty, there were 3,000 priests. In 1673 the county (of south Kerry) 'aboundeth with unnecessary priests and officers and friars, exacting large allowances from the people and with youth learning of needless Latin, instead of useful trades'. Petty also certifies that knowledge of Latin 'is very frequent amongst the poorest Irish, and chiefly in Kerry'. However, the friars — Franciscans and Dominicans — suffered at this time from the break-down of such educational system as had previously existed in Ireland, and several bishops complained of having to ordain uncouth and uneducated friars.

From the time of the Restoration, there was a regrouping and substantial reduction of parishes of the established church. Ardfert cathedral had been burnt in the wars of the 1640s and had fallen into disuse. A part of it was eventually retained for parochial services. The established church had two bad frights — from the catholics and the Cromwellians. After the Restoration, and the eclipse of the Cromwellians, there were energetic attempts to keep the catholics down, on the plea that the pope, by maintaining the claim that he could depose a sovereign, necessarily made all catholics disloyal to the king. However, this intolerance in high places was not supported by pastoral zeal in low ones.

On the Restoration, Petty had had two ministers established for the four parishes on his lands — one at Nedeen and Kilmakillogue, and one in Templenoe and Kilcroghane. One of the ministers died in 1673 and the other in 1676 and from that year there was but one minister officiating 'without Churchwardens or Service books' only intermittently in the four baronies of Beare, Glanerought, Dunkerron and Iveragh. This minister died in 1701, and the livings were annexed by Dean Richards of Tralee, so compounding the neglect. It was possible to maintain what was largely an empty structure because of the levying of tithes on the inhabitants of these parishes. This continued even though few, and in some places perhaps none, of the inhabitants were protestant. In such places, of course, there was real difficulty in collecting tithes for the support of ministers of religion who were totally irrelevant to the religious lives of the tithe-payers. Petty reported that the minister referred to 'is now ready to perish for want of maintenance'. Many of the landlords laid claim to a proportion — one-third, half, two-thirds — of whatever tithe rents were collected and thus much of the income was not available for the upkeep of church buildings.

For the catholics, the restoration of their religion in practice seems to have restored the movement, begun before the wars, toward higher standards of general morality; but this seems not to have affected the hold of alcohol on the people.

The second of the four major Kerry poets lived at this time: he was Geoffrey O Donoghue of Glenflesk who died in 1678 whose parties in the tower house, the ruins of which are still to be seen at the opening of the glen, were famous. A feature, perhaps, of this intermission of softer times is the attractive poem he wrote on the death of his little spaniel. This was when the old bardic order finally collapsed, so liberating Irish poetry from the more intense of the ancient prosodic rules. This freedom led to an outburst of lyric poetry, especially in Kerry. A similar liberation seems to have occurred with music. This, married to the new popular lyric poetry, was to be a big part of the cultural sustenance of the people for nearly two centuries.

Mac Lysaght quotes from a manuscript of 1682 a passage that strikes a not unfamiliar note:

> The inhabitants of the county of Kerry, I mean those of them that are downright Irish, are remarkable beyond the inhabitants of the other parts of Ireland for their gaming, speaking Latin and inclination to philosophy and disputes therein. For their gaming, they are so exquisite that they generally make a prey of whatever stranger comes amongst them, who will venture his stock or money at cards or dice; and even the very cowherds and shepherds will be under a hedge with each other at tables..... When they can get no-one to game with them you shall often find them alone with a book of Aristotle's or some of his commentators' logic, which they read very diligently, till they are able to pour out nonsensical words a whole day about: *universale a parte rei, ens rationis,* and such like stuff, and this they do pretty fluently without such hesitation, though all the while their Latin is bald and barbarous and very often not grammatical....Those that are loathe to be called the inferior sort are generally very litigious among one another and they will go to law about the least trifle, and this is the reason (or, perhaps, the consequence) of this county's abounding more than ordinarily with men that are (as they term it) towards the law.

In 1673 Lord Herbert and others sent the Lord Lieutenant a report on the state of south Kerry. It depicts the partially dispossessed O Sullivans and Carties attempting to carry on their old ways in their nearly impenetrable fastnesses, 'the waies... the worst of all Ireland,

94 impassable in the winter time, and requiring an hour's riding, with much trouble and danger,for each mile'. The country was very thinly peopled and the inhabitants were wretchedly poor. There was no administration of English justice and in the whole vast area no military post — obviously the Cromwellian garrisons at Kenmare and Valentia were no more — so that ships could 'infest' the place and get supplies without trouble, and malefactors survive safely. Apart from Petty's enterprises there was 'no industry of fishing (but of oysters, low water) even in this place, which, before the discovery of Newfoundland, was the fishery of Europe; and no employment but the grazing of small cattle in summer-time without making any hay for winter'. 'From the year 1657 to 1668, it is manifest that there hath been a strange destruction of woods, and vast number of pipe, hhde and barrel staves exported'. They conclude by saying that the rest of the county of Kerry, and part of the county of Cork, are more or less in the same condition.

In 1672 the government had been centralised in Dublin and the Presidencies of Munster and Connacht abolished after a life of 100 years. In effect, this committed government to the local land-owners and their agents. We get a vivid insight into such activity by one of these agents, Richard Orpen, for whom Petty had built a house at Killowen near Kenmare. Orpen was to complain of rough treatment by the Irish in the williamite wars but his own exploits must have made him unpopular. He lists the malefactors he brought to justice. There was a Mac Carthy who in 1680 had robbed and murdered a smelter in open day. There was Owen Sullivan (a loose gentleman) who, in the same year, had run Orpen through the back on a dark night for seeking to recover a debt. In 1685 there was Teague a Glauna who had murdered a poursuivant for trying to arrest papists. The following year there was David Mac Dermot who, with half a score more, had robbed some French protestant fugitives who, after the revocation of the Edict of Nantes, had taken refuge in the Kenmare River. In the following year, Daniel Croly and seven more Tories attacked Orpen and his brother, who shot three of them. 'The greatest part of all these malefactors were severely prosecuted by Richard Orpen ; some of them were hanged; some burned in the hand; some remained in gaol and the rest dispersed and fled out of the country'.

Petty gives us an insight into the conditions of the plain people at about the same time:

> Men live in such cottages as themselves can make in three or four days; Eat such Food (Tobacco excepted) as they buy not from others; wear such Cloaths as the Wooll of their own Sheep, spun into Yarn by themselves, doth make..... The Housing thereof consists of ...nasty Cabbins, in which neither Butter nor Cheese nor Linnen, Yarn nor Worsted, and I Think no other can be made to the best advantage; chiefly by reason of the Soot and Smoaks annoying the same; as also for the Narrowness and Nastiness of the Place; which cannot be kept clean nor Safe from Beasts and Vermin, nor from Damps

and Musty Stenches of which all the Eggs laid or kept in those Cabbins do partake.

He goes on:

> But their Clothing far better than that of the French peasants or the poor of most other Countreys. The Diet of these people is Milk, sweet and sower, thick and thin, which is also their Drink in Summer-time, in Winter, Small-beer or Water... Their Food is Bread in Cakes, whereof a Penny serves a Week for each; Potatoes from August till May, Muscles, Cockles and Oysters, near the Sea; Eggs and Butter, made very rancid, by keeping in Bogs. As for Flesh, they seldom eat it , notwithstanding the great plenty thereof, unless it be of smaller Animals..... Their Fewel is Turf in most places; and of late even where Wood is plentiful, and to be had for nothing, the cutting and the carriage of the Turf being more easy than that of Wood.

The Milk — sweet and sower — was no doubt the famous bonney-clabber — milk left standing and then mixed with sweet fresh milk. Wentworth in 1635 said it was 'the bravest, freshest drink you ever tasted... the drink of the Gods....'.

Petty also tells us that the daily wage of a labourer was 4d, half of the English rate. Notwithstanding the instructions of the Presidency of Munster, there were, in general, as yet no fences in the fields, all cattle had still to be herded all day.   There continued the practice of booleying — of driving the cattle in summer onto high ground and herding them there, the herds living at night in little shelters on the mountainside, remains of which are still to be seen. But, in general, a more settled, less nomadic agriculture began to take over.

By now, it is clear, the potato was beginning to be well established as a main article of diet, but not yet as the predominant food it later was to become. Petty's account of the Nasty Cabbins is similar to that of Arthur Young, a century later; or of Tomas O Criomhthain, on the Blaskets, nearly a century later still. The absence of a chimney was a main cause of the Nastiness. It is probable that the use of the chimney became general in the late 17th century; but, clearly, not yet in Kerry.

It is possible to get our first indication of the population of Kerry in the post-cromwellian period. From 1662 each hearth was taxed and the returns give an idea of the number of households; but these are usually held to be unreliable in understating the number of households. There is some reason to heed the returns for 1692 which show just under 12,000 households in Kerry. It is usual to multiply the number of households by five to get the total population; so it looks as if the population of Kerry was at least 60,000 in 1692. These are the returns of Philip Anderson, and we have the returns for each barony. The first really reliable census of population was in 1841, and it is a striking fact that the percentage distribution of the then total Kerry population (almost 300,000) between each of the baronies in 1841 was almost precisely identical with the percentage distribution of households given by Anderson. Calculations of what the population was in the next century would suggest that the Kerry population in 1692 was about 80,000. Sir Richard Cox in 1687 says 'This County is supposed to contain sixty thousand souls...' We can reasonably assume that the population of Kerry at the end of the 17th century was in the neighbourhood of 80,000. At the end of the cromwellian wars, which were not very destructive in the county, the population may have been in the range 50-60,000. It is just possible that in the latter half of the 16th century, before the Desmond wars, the population may have been about the same. After those wars it may have been about one-third less. And we have already seen that the population at that time was probably about the level it had reached in the 13th century.

The century from the time of Galileo had been one of remarkable scientific and philosophical advance, but nearly all of this passed Ireland by. Petty who had been one of the first fellows of the Royal Society, and had associated with Hobbes and Newton, was one of the founders of the Philosophical Society of Ireland in 1682 and of the Dublin College of Physicians. But, once again, one of the great intellectual movements of Europe failed to influence Irish life.

The country towards the end of the century was prosperous and relatively peaceful but it was not until well into the next century that the ruling classes in Kerry ceased to live in fortified houses and castles, as witness the Browne addition to Ross Castle, finished in 1688.

In 1689, when James II as a catholic, was deposed, most of Ireland stayed loyal to him. Kerry, under Sir Valentine Browne who had been in exile with Charles II and whom James in 1689 made Viscount Kenmare (from a Browne property in Limerick) was no exception. Apart from the expelling of Petty's English settlement near Nedeen at the beginning of the troubles, and the burning of Orpen's house at Killowen, the county saw no action until near the end of the troubles, when Killarney and Tralee were burned and there was a skirmish near Lixnaw. Kenmare had died in 1690. His son, the second viscount, went with the other Wild Geese into exile and, a heroic drinker, died in 1720 in the Low Countries, his estates confiscated for his lifetime. Another forfeiting magnate was Lord Clare who had acquired by purchase the seignory of Tarbert formerly held by Sir Piers Crosbie. This confiscated property was granted to the Leslies, the only scottish williamite grantees in Kerry.

Although it was necessary from time to time to take cover from the storms, the old faith continued, and with it its priests – a Kerry Dominican priest was killed in Listowel in 1691, and two others died in London early in the next century, one in jail and the other by hanging. The vicar apostolic for the diocese, Cornelius Daly, died about 1699 in prison in Cork. Fifty-four priests were identified by the customs officer in Dingle, twelve of them regulars but it is not clear how many of these were tracked down and transported, though some, at least, of them went abroad for a while.

95

One-roomed cabin, Mountain Stage, c. 1900

By the end of the 17th century, two of the three great issues had been settled, it seemed, for good. Politically, the conquest of Ireland had been thoroughly consolidated, and the local government in the hands of English and anglo-Irish officials and representatives wholly submissive to English government. The transfer of ownership of land, and thus in theory and practice of economic power was, after 150 years, complete – of 540 Catholic landowners in Kerry in 1641 scarcely one remained.

The third great problem, that of religion, was never even temporarily solved, for here the rulers of Ireland were faced with the resistance — passive as it was — not of great feudalists fighting for the preservation of a privileged and outmoded way of life; not of new and old landowners threatened with the loss of their lands; not of bewildered politicians seeking to maintain an English political system twice rejected by the English themselves, but of the great mass of the ordinary people of Ireland cleaving to their common religious beliefs and practices.

So, in the 1690s bishops, 'dignitaries', monks, friars and nuns were banished from the country. In 1698 over four hundred regular clergy were transported to the continent, and by the beginning of the 18th century only two (perhaps three) bishops remained in the whole country. With the regulars banished, and no bishops permitted, no new secular priests, it was hoped, could be ordained. In this way the clergy would die away and with it the practice of catholicism. But this was to reckon without the single-minded, passive, patient resistance of the ordinary people, and the courage of their priests dertermined to minister to them. Already, by the end of the century, they were flooding back to their posts, despite the severe penalties enacted against those who returned.

Chapter 7 Death and Rebirth 1700–

At the beginning of the 17th century Ireland had been conquered, but not crushed. Twice during the century she had given her conquerors a bad fright. By the end of the century she had been crushed.

During the 18th century Ireland went through a living death; then early in the 19th began the process, despite the appalling setback of the Famine, of rebirth, slow at first, gradually gaining momentum.

THE EIGHTEENTH CENTURY

During the 18th century the people of Ireland were to know what it was to be in the hands of a ruthless ascendancy. The gaelic rulers were gone or ruined. The old English feudalists were destroyed. The country was in the hands of English protestant settlers who held the great part of its property, were loyal to the English interest, and submissive to the English government. In return, they were given a free hand in running the country, except where their interests clashed with English interests. So, during the first half of the century, the Irish people were bound down by the heavy chains of penal legislation intended to reduce them to serfdom; in the second half, this began gradually, and reluctantly, to be relaxed.

(I) THE PENAL SYSTEM

The one clash of interest between the English and the Irish ascendancy interests was in trade. At the end of the previous century the woollen trade had been destroyed. Irish interests must be subordinated to English interests even where, as usual, this hurt the protestant ascendancy. However, as had happened earlier in the 17th century, if cattle could not be exported alive they could be exported as meat, and if land was not to support sheep for wool it could, even on the mountains, carry more of the hardy breed of Kerry cattle. Thus a substantial dead meat trade had grown up by the end of the 17th century. The 18th century saw the great growth of Cork as an export centre for some half of Ireland's exports of butter and beef. This trade grew steadily during the 18th century and was spread, in roughly equal parts, between Britain, the continent, and America, particularly the West Indies. In the early part of the century a series of acts of parliament regulated the quantity and quality of butter sold in barrels, and this helped the trade. Much of the butter came from Kerry. During this period it became the practice for ships crossing (in convoy, for fear of pirates) to and from America to call at Cork. The special import there was, of course, tobacco. The growth of trade through Cork meant a great deal for the economy of Kerry. Thus, except in such places as the Kenmare River where the old connexion with France and Spain continued, the focus of trade shifted to America. Butter was carried from Kerry to Cork on horseback, with rum and groceries being taken on the return journey. From Muckross the costs were 9d a firkin for butter and 1s 8d a hundredweight for carriage back from Cork.

There was, however, little growth of industry and wealth derived otherwise than from land. Catholics were deprived from the ownership of land whenever possible and, where this was not possible, were required to divide inherited land equally amongst their sons. The Kenmare family remained catholic and resumed ownership in 1720 of one of the greatest properties in Ireland. They were able to keep this because during the whole century each generation of the family had only one surviving son. Catholics were forbidden to acquire land for a lease longer than 31 years or at a rent less than two-thirds of its full value. Where they succeeded in doing this – the O Mahonys, the O Connells (another old family that now began the long climb back to wealth and influence) – they lived in constant fear of being betrayed by informers whose reward would be the propery. The purpose was to keep catholics poor and to reduce to poverty those already not poor enough.

At the same time, a century of peace and the increased use of that remarkably efficient food, the potato, led to a steady rise in population, increased demand for land, rising agricultural prices, and higher rents. Agricultural prices seem to have risen in the first three-quarters of the century by from twice to four times. Rents doubled and trebled in the period; Lord Kenmare, in the first half of the century, would often renew a lease at double the previous rent. In general, the increased wealth of the country was siphoned off by the landowners. This economic development in Kerry had a severe setback in the famine of 1740, when severe frost destroyed crops and there was acute distress and many deaths. (The frost had set in about Christmas, 1739, and lasted for six weeks, destroying the potatoes *in the ground*). From Dunloe, on the Kenmare estate, it was reported in April, 1741, 'there is not a tenant in Lower Lahard able to pay 20s, most of them being dead'. The mortality was made worse by a typhus type infection that spread amongst the population. Typhus and smallpox were endemic.

Those who paid hearth tax in Kerry in 1733 numbered 14,346; in 1744, about 10,000. The danger of this narrow economic base was not heeded, although it foreshadowed the enormous disaster of a century later. At the usual rate of grossing up, 14,346 households would give a population in 1733 of 72,000; but this shows a slow rate of population growth. In Ireland as a whole the population increased by over one-third in the period 1692 to 1732, and there seems to be no reason why Kerry should not have grown at a comparable rate. If so, the population in 1732 would be of the order of 110,000. There is some reason to accept this figure, which is very similar to the present-day one. As it happens, the ratio of Kerry households to the total number in Ireland that year (14,346 : 386,902) is the same as the ratio in 1841 of the population of Kerry to that of all Ireland. Connell has shown that the population of Ireland in 1732 must have been just over three millions. On that basis the 1732 population of Kerry should have been 110,000.

Catholics were forbidden entry to the country's one university, Trinity College, Dublin, which was supported by grants of much of their land, including substantial areas in Kerry. They were also forbidden to send their children abroad for education; this was widely evaded, but in Kerry in 1714 five parents called Connell, two called Rice and two called Pierce were prosecuted for doing so. For the great majority who could not go abroad there were very few educational chances at home — popish schoolmasters were forbidden to teach in public or in private on penalty of being treated as popish regular clergymen. Again in 1714 five of them were prosecuted. Nonetheless there is a constant reference to the tradition of classical schooling in Kerry — Petty had noted it in the 1670s and Story, a williamite chaplain, in 1691: ('every cow-boy among them can speak latin, on purpose to save them from the Gallows, when they come afterwards to be tried for theft'). There was a man who claimed a knowledge of Greek gained from a woman who read Homer with him in a retired spot near the lakes of Killarney. Smith, in the middle of the century, comments on the tradition of classical learning — he met a Peter Kelly near Sneem 'who was a good Latin scholar but knew no English'. Holmes, in 1801, said that 'many' were to be met of this kind. Arthur Young comments on the hedge-schools, both for children and young men in the 1770s, and Weld, more guardedly, at the end of the century associated with the hedge-schools some classical teaching. Carr, early in the 19th century, found a boy holding his horse who was well schooled in Latin authors. But these schools at best could benefit only a minority. This minority included 'poor scholars' from other counties who came to study before going to the Continent to become priests. The rudiments of a catholic secondary education had been developed by the hedge grammar schools, but an adequate system began only at the end of the 18th century when the penal system was being dismantled. The effect of all this could be measured in the next century. In 1861, when the national education system of primary schools had been in operation for a generation — but had had the effect of displacing the old classical masters — no less than 48% of the population of Kerry was found to be wholly illiterate.

Because of the educational lacks, and by positive enactment, catholics were debarred from the more remunerative professions and from municipal corporations. For most of the century they were denied the franchise. They had been made poor and ignorant and were to be kept poor and ignorant. In 1714 there were six charity schools in the county. From elizabethan times there had been a statutory obligation 'to provide in each parish a schole for to learn English' and a central diocesan free school: but in Kerry in 1738 there were only three schoolmasters so provided, and in 1755 only two. A few grammar schools were, however, started by individual clergymen.

The penal system enacted by the Dublin parliament has usually been thought of as a system of persecuting religion; but the persecution, except in isolated instances calculated to buttress the protestant ascendancy, had substantially ceased since the time of Cromwell. In fact, the practice of religion was not significantly interfered with, but the church like its flock was desperately poor. The penal system was basically one of *economic* discrimination against a conquered people. Religion was simply a convenient badge of discrimination, as

Ross Castle

skin pigment was elsewhere to become. However, these catholics, especially landowners, who chose to conform to protestantism were freely accepted within the fold. If they chose not to be absorbed into the ascendancy they stood to lose lands, education, access to the professions, and civil rights. The one area where there was a sustained, and largely successful, effort to spread protestantism was amongst the catholic landowners. Thus old families like Falvey, Mac Gillacuddy, O Mahony of Dromore, the knight of Kerry, conformed in the first decades of the 18th century. Religion is easier to change, when there is a will, than skin.

The Mac Gillacuddy Papers illustrate how an old gaelic family were able to hold their lands but were eventually brought to conformity. They were a sept of the O Sullivans and drew their patronymic — Mac Giolla Chuda — from Ailinn O Sullivan, bishop of Lismore, who died in 1253. Lismore was the monastery (and bishopric) founded by Mo-chuda in the 7th century. In the Desmond wars, Donald Mac Gillycuddy was killed and his lands, which were mainly near Killarney, were confiscated. They were conveyed back to the family in 1598. Various grants were made in 1604; but the lands seem to have been held all along by the family. Donogh Mac Gillycuddy lost these lands after Cromwell and served Charles abroad. His lands were restored to him in the 1660s and he was even able to fend off the covetousness of Petty. Donogh's son, Cornelius, took the side of James II and forfeited some of the Mac Gillycuddy lands and mortgaged others. His nephew, Denis, succeeded to a partially restored estate, married a Blennerhasset, and conformed to protestantism in 1718.

It is important that one remember that at this time lay catholics were not persecuted for practising their religion. The Recusancy

98

Act of 1560 which required them to attend protestant service on Sundays had by the end of the 17th century fallen completely into disuse, and during the 18th century no efforts were made to require catholics to attend protestant, or refrain from attending catholic, services. The policy was, instead, to concentrate on cutting off the supply of clergy. The contrast is nicely illustrated in the actions of two military commanders early in the century.

This is from a letter, printed by Burke, from the commandant in Dingle in March 1702:

> The Mass house being so nigh the Barracks heir, the Suffreine and I have ordert the Preist to say noe more mass there but will in another place further off from my guards. The Barracks is a long defenceless house within 20 yards of the mass house to which 3 or 400 persons resort Sundays and other Holydays and therefore there is danger of a surprise.

Five years later the commandant of Ross castle announces the arrest of one priest and the impending arrest of six more. Those whose loyalty was doubtful were required to take the oath of abjuration of the Stuart succession, and in 1708 the commandant asks that the following local worthies, who had refused to take the oath, be transferred from prison in Tralee to Ross castle where they could be better supported by their friends: Lord Kenmare, Colonel Maurice Hussey and his two sons, Mac Carthy Mor, and others.

However, the main line of government policy was clear enough. At no time had there been *effective* legislation proscribing diocesan priests as such — much of the traditional lore about 'mass rocks' must be received with this in mind. In 1703 an act required all catholic parochial clergy, on pain of expulsion, to register before the clerk of the peace before a certain date in 1704, to say where they were ordained, and to specify the parishes under their care. There was to be but one priest in each parish. Each was required to give two sureties, in the penal sum of £50, of 'peaceable behaviour' and that he would not leave the county where he lived. Registered priests were not impeded in their normal work. No priest subsequently arriving, who was not registered and no regular priest, would be tolerated. In this way, coupled with the lack of, and impediments to, the education of young catholics, it was hoped to kill the church by inanition. In 1710 the registered priests were required under penalty of banishment, and on return death, to take the oath abjuring the Stuart succession, but few took the oath and the penalties were not invoked against the rest.

Severe penalties were prescribed for banished **clerics** who returned to Ireland. Large numbers of regular clergy returned but the laws against them were not rigorously enforced. Lecky quotes a magistrate from Castlemaine who complained in 1714 that, although magistrates signed warrants for the apprehension of many priests in the area, it was found impossible to execute the warrants. So the Franciscans of Ardfert, Lislaghtin and Muckross seem to have survived unscathed. No bishop or cleric was in fact executed

during the 18th century for unauthorised return, although some were imprisoned, a few died in gaol, others transported, and many priests and popish schoolmasters had to lead underground lives. It was a beastly system of government but it usually lacked the inhumanity (or efficiency) to live up to its cruel pretensions. In 1726 a statute punished with death any priest who married a catholic and a protestant; in the same year in Limerick a priest was hanged for that offence. In 1727, at the beginning of the reign of George II, the penal laws reached their peak.

The 1704 registration showed that three-quarters of the Kerry diocesan priests had been ordained abroad, a higher proportion than in most other dioceses, reflecting the greater ease of communication with the Continent. Thirty-six parishes were shown to be in existence, as against about 90 in pre-reformation times (as well as the monasteries). Part of the reduction was simple rationalisation: in the barony of Corkaguiney there had been no less than 19 parishes, as against eight in 1704 and four today. Against the 36 parishes in 1704 there were 45 in 1837 and 51 today. The ratio of the number of parishes today to that of 1704 is about the same as the ratio of the respective populations, but nowadays a parish often has two or more priests and communications are so much better. Nonetheless, the church, at parish level, was clearly holding its own so far as its organisation and manpower were concerned. Its physical 'plant' was another story. All, or virtually all, of the parish churches, were lost to the reformed church and most were in ruins. The absence of ecclesiastical buildings of the time is silent witness. Where there were mass houses they were rude buildings, thatch roofed, mud floored, whitewashed inside, devoid of furnishings, used on week days as schoolhouses and, occasionally, as threshing barns.

As the registered priests died off they were replaced by unregistered ones in defiance of the intention of the law. The freedom with which young men could be shipped abroad from such little ports as Derrynane, for the education denied them at home, and the great generosity with which they were received and supported in the territories of Spain, Austria and France meant that the church could be supplied with eager, educated young men for the priesthood. They were ordained abroad and came back to staff the parishes at home.

In 1713-14 the government issued an instruction to local magistrates — who were under heavy penalties for failing to enforce the registration law — to do so. This led to a flurry of activity in Kerry, and about two-thirds of the priests were prosecuted for not being registered, for failing to take the oath of abjuration, and the like. It is not clear what happened next because there are no further records; but the magistrate in Castlemaine who complained that orders were not enforced may have been typical. One suspects that the flurry soon died down.

Although many of the old surviving landowners had conformed to protestantism, the Church of Ireland fell on evil times in Kerry: by the middle of the century only eleven churches were in use.

The Catholic vicar apostolic from 1699 was O Leyne, who still held the office ten years later. From 1707 the pope began to restore the episcopacy: indeed, in 1697 the archbishop of Cashel and two other Munster bishops had proposed, and in 1703 James II, now of course in exile, had nominated, Denis Moriarty, parish priest of Dingle, as bishop. Partly because of the complexities of Stuart politics, partly because of the danger to himself, but mainly because of intense local opposition, he did not, in fact, become bishop until 1720. The line has since been unbroken. The Stuarts continued to nominate bishops until James III died in 1766.

The steady re-establishment of the episcopacy, the re-organisation of dioceses and parishes, the tightening of ecclesiastical discipline, the building of mass houses and chapels, all show the rise of the church in this, formally unpromising, time. By 1731 when the government ordered a special inquiry on the state of popery, there were over 1,400 known parochial clergy in the country — the true number was probably higher: for some reason no returns were made from the diocese of Ardfert and Aghadoe — as against some 1,000 registered in 1704.

There were over 900 known places of catholic worship, mostly mass houses. In 1742, the pope, at the instance of the bishops of Cork and Kerry, ordered a restriction on the number of ordinations to twelve for each bishop. By 1812 the total of parochial clergy had risen to some 1,900. Against this rise must be put the sharp decline in the number of regular clergy — from a peak of 800 in 1750 to 200 in 1803: the Dominicans, for example, had by then died out in Kerry. It so happened, therefore, that by the end of the 18th century there were probably fewer priests in all than there had been 50 or 60 years before: this at a time when the population had sharply risen. In 1785 Bishop Moylan of Kerry reported that he had 64 secular priests in the 41 parishes of his diocese, and four regulars — two Franciscans and two Dominicans. In 10 years he had lost 29 priests by death and had ordained only 21 some of them before they had finished their studies; so in Kerry also there was a manpower problem.

Nonetheless, by the end of the 18th century, the church was still ill-equipped: a few churches — Moylan claimed he had built two fine churches in Tralee and Killarney — the simple mass houses, few religious houses and little or no schools of its own. All this was to be dramatically changed in the ensuing century. A turning point came with the founding, with government help in 1795, of Maynooth College — the continent by then not being available for the higher education of priests.

In 1753 Lord Chesterfield was to say that the time had come to 'make Connacht and Kerry know that there is a God, a king and a government, three things to which they are at present utter strangers'. Not much progress was made. At that time, as we have seen, less than one-fifth of the pre-reformation churches were in repair.

In 1708-10 Louis XIV drove out of the Palatinate in Germany a number of protestants. Queen Anne received some of these refugees and many were sent to Ireland as tenants and farmers on the estates of protestant gentry, displacing Irish tenants. In 1709 some 800 families came to Limerick and Kerry. In Kerry they settled with government grants around Castleisland; about the middle of the century the Blennerhassets settled a number of Palatines at Ballyseedy. These like other protestant farmers tended gradually to become catholics.

The day to day business of government was carried out by the British government using the Dublin government — which was not accountable to Parliament — as its agent; but from early in the century power had to be shared with cliques in parliament who controlled the votes necessary for supplies and legislation; they were normally kept amenable by a massive use of patronage. In general, government was minimal and economical. For example, in the whole of south Kerry there were but two military posts, that at Dingle and that at Ross Castle, Killarney — the latter was so ill-supplied that a commander complained that he had to buy powder at his own expense. At intervals, during most of the century, there were frequent raids on the Iveragh peninsula by privateers, but the government took no action to protect the inhabitants or to permit them to protect themselves with arms.

The absence of any catholic unrest at the time of the Old Pretender in 1715 confirmed government and ascendancy in their sense of security.

The government of the county was the responsibility of the county lord lieutenant, appointed by the Crown. He appointed the high sheriff who appointed the grand jury who were responsible for such county administration as existed. The enforcement of what went for justice was in the hands of a local magistrate, appointed by the Irish lord chancellor usually on the advice of the county lord lieutenant. Until the end of the century all these functionaries were drawn from the small group of protestant landowners. In the absence of any significant military force or of a paid police, the enforcement of law and order was in the hands of the local gentry, who maintained local militias. Those who violently resented the loss of their property or who committed serious crimes were outlawed, and tracked down and killed by the local gentry. These outlaws were called rapparees or tories and gave their name to the English political party. Glenflesk was a great haunt of such outlaws.

The government of Kerry was in the hands, mainly, of those families who had arrived in Kerry after the Desmond plantation — Blennerhasset, Crosbie, Denny, Godfrey and Herbert — to whom were added such lesser familes as Bland and Chute.

As we have seen, Kerry returned eight members to the Irish parliament — two from the county (the 'knights of the shire') and two each from the boroughs of Ardfert, Dingle and Tralee. Dingle had been a borough from 1586; Tralee became one in 1612; and Ardfert about the same time. There was an election for the county members: but the electorate was, from 1727 to 1793, confined to protestant freeholders. The protestant population was around the 5,000 mark; but the number of electors in the county seems to have been in 1791 about 1,160 of whom, perhaps, half had voted in a previous election. We read that in the middle of the ·

100 century the family estates of Sir Thomas Denny, of Tralee, had been planted with '173 substantial freeholders ...... to elect representatives to serve in Parliament' and that there were not 'in the whole county besides above 220'. This limited electorate and public voting led to some exciting contests in the county. From 1692 to 1800, when the Irish parliament came to an end, there was never a time when the county was not represented by either a Blennerhasset, a Crosbie or a Denny, often by two of them. John Blennerhasset sat in parliament for sixty years. These families and some others, were intermarried again and again, so giving rise to the expression 'Kerry Cousins'.

In the boroughs the election was in the hands, nominally, of the sovereign and burgesses, just over a dozen people, plus honorary Freemen. These electors were in the hands of the great proprietors. In 1790 Dingle had a total electorate of 177, of whom 150 lived outside the county. In Tralee the electorate numbered 13. Dingle and Tralee were at least towns of some degree of significance, but Ardfert was a rotten borough wholly in the hands of the Crosbie family who nominated both members; in 1770 the electorate numbered 18. From 1703 one of the members was married to a Crosbie, and from 1713 to 1783 one Crosbie (and often two) represented the 'borough'. During the greater part of the century the head of the clan was Sir Maurice Crosbie, who had married a Fitzmaurice. He was able to represent to a corrupt government often pressed for votes that 'we are four', and became Baron Brandon, Viscount Crosbie and Earl of Glandore. He died in 1781. A cousin of his — Robert Day — represented Ardfert from 1790 to 1801 and voted for the union. During the whole period he was a judge and in the latter part a High Court justice.

Dingle was very much in the control of a branch of the Desmond family, the Fitzgeralds, Knights of Kerry, who had conformed to protestantism. One of them represented it for much of the century. Up to 1761 Tralee was normally represented by Blennerhassets; for a generation, the family held the two seats between 1727 and 1761, but the controlling power were the Dennys, one of whom, Sir Barry Denny, was killed by a Crosbie in a duel in 1793 arising from an election dispute. Many members bought their seats in the hope of gaining official posts, or of improving on those they already held.

There was a famous scandal implicating members of several of these families which throws a revealing light on the times. In October, 1730 a Danish East Indiaman, *The Golden Lyon,* was wrecked in Ballyheigue Bay. The crew were rescued and with them silver bullion and coins valued at £16,000, together with other valuables. Danes and bullion were lodged at the Crosbie house at Ballyheigue. For some reason they were still there in June, 1731, when armed men with blackened faced raided the place, killed two Danes, and took the silver. In the ensuing five years, there was a hanging, a suicide, a possible murder and several trials in which an Archdeacon Lauder of Ardfert, two Crosbies, a Blennerhasset and a Cantillon were charged with responsibility for what took place, but (Lauder may have been the ringleader) were acquitted either by local or Dublin courts. The local juries were made up of the small groups of protestant ascendancy families; Miss Hickson's suggestions are that the Dublin proceedings and court officials were much influenced by the power of John Blennerhasset, Sir Maurice Crosbie and their friends, as well as by offerings of the Danish silver.

The other great post-Desmond family were the Brownes, Viscounts of Kenmare. They were catholic and thus held no offices. The existence of such a catholic magnate perhaps explains in part the notably good relations that existed in Kerry in matters of religion. There is a story that the Dublin government sent an inspector to investigate a report that friars were to be seen walking in Killarney in full habit. The local (protestant) magistrates clapped him in jail as a spy and the government had to appeal to the (catholic) Lord Kenmare to get him released.

The Kenmares show how, partly by good luck, a great catholic family could survive the hazards of the times.

The Browne family descended from Sir Valentine Browne, an English civil servant, appointed Surveyor General of Ireland in 1559. He set a family fashion of second marriages. By the sons of his second marriage the family acquired three extensive estates in Limerick, Cork and Kerry. Two of these were acquired through marriage. The Killarney estate, the former Onaght O Donoghue, was bought by Sir Nicholas Browne, who married a daughter of O Sullivan Beare, from Mac Carthy Mor, Earl of Clancarre, after O Donoghue Mor had lost it at the end of the Desmond rebellion. The family became and stayed firmly catholic. They married into the great Gaelic and old English families — Mac Carthy, O Sullivan Mor, Plunkett, Desmond, Butler. The first Viscount was a friend of James II, the title being given in 1689 after James had been expelled from England, and thus, subsequently, regarded as a courtesy title. The second viscount succeeded in 1690 and went into exile with James. He died in 1720, still in exile. He had married the heiress of the Limerick and Cork estates, and became the proprietor of 130,000 acres, one of the largest properties in Ireland. This was confiscated for his lifetime, but was restored much ruined — trees to the value of £20,000 were cut down on the Kerry property — and encumbered with lawsuits to his only surviving son, Valentine, the third viscount. He, and his only surviving son, the fourth viscount — a leader of the catholic party towards the end of the century — raised the value of the property to a considerable amount. The fifth viscount became the first Earl of Kenmare at the time of the passing of the union of the Irish and British parliaments in 1800.

The ruin of the Gaelic way of life is epitomised in the life of one of the greatest of Irish poets, Aodhgan O Rathaile (Egan O Rahilly). His father seems to have been an O Reilly from Cavan who married an Egan, one of the hereditary gaelic bardic families in Kerry. The son was born about 1670 at Scrahanaveal near Barraduff, lived all his life in the Killarney area (except for a period in the 1720s when he seems to have been in Limerick practising as a scribe), and died at Knockoorah, near his birthplace, about 1728. He wrote the most perfect of *aisling,* or vision, poems, 'Gile na gile do chonnarc ar slighe i n-uigneas'. He bewailed the passing of the great gaelic houses where

Muckross Friary church. O Rathaile lies in nave under plaque on right; O Suilleabhain in chancel behind plaque.

Egan O Rahilly when his only cow was appraized last winter, 1726, by James Curtoyne, for composing songs for Master Thomas Browne and the rest of his Lordship's children as per song appears as voucher ..... At John Rierdane's prayer and request : £1. 10. 0d.' Master Thomas, if he was the future fourth viscount, was then just 18 months old! The song, being a voucher, has not survived. O Rahilly, come to death in great poverty a year after this entry, began his last poem (the translation is Frank O'Connor's);

Cabhair ni ghoirfead go gcuirtear me i gcruinn-chomhrainn	*I shall not cry for help until they coffin me*

and his last lines were:

Stadfad-sa feasta, is gar dom eag gan moill	*Now I shall cease, death comes, and I must not delay*
O treascradh dreaguin Leamhain, Lein is Laoi	*By Laune and Laine and Lee, diminished of their pride,*
Rachad-sa a haithle searc na laoch don chill,	*I shall go after the heroes, ay, into the clay —*
Na flatha fa raibh mo shean roimh eag do Chriost.	*My fathers followed theirs before Christ was crucified.*

The last enduring pride of a servitor who was a great poet. So, he lies, in the nave of Muckross abbey, his head almost at the feet of those great heroes of the Eoganacht — Mac Carthy Mor, O Sullivan Mor, O Donoghue Mor — who lie above him in the chancel. Also in the chancel of Muckross, as became an O Sullivan, lies another of Ireland's leading poets, born at Meentogues twenty years after O Rathaile's death, in 1748, a few miles away from O Rathaile's birthplace in Sliabh Luachra: Eoghan Ruadh O Suilleabhain (Owen Roe O Sullivan). In 1784 he died close to his birthplace. In the meantime, he had travelled much in Ireland and as far as the West Indies while he was in the British navy. At eighteen he had opened a school at Gneevegullia, but within three years had to flee the wrath of the parish priest; one of Owen's most perfect lyrics is a lullaby he wrote when a local girl came into his school and left with him their baby, whose crying had to be stilled. For the rest of his life, except for the spell in the navy, succeeded by a short one in the army, he was a travelling labourer cum schoolmaster with joint gifts of leading women astray and of composing delicate lyrics. This, from a request to put a handle on a spade (again, O Connor's translation):

Iar gcaitheamh an lae mas treith no tuirseach mo chnamha,	*And whenever I am feeling low at the end of the day*
Is go n-abrann an maor nach eachtach m'acfuinn ar rain,	*And the ganger comes around and accuses me with dodging it well,*
Labharfad fein go seimh ar eachtra an bhais,	*I'll drop a few words about Death's adventurous way*
No ar chathaibh na nGreig 'san Trae d'fhuig flatha go tlaith	*And of the wars of the Greeks in Troy, and the kings that fell.*

poets like him were once honoured and supported. In great poverty he called on the great landlord Valentine Browne, third viscount of Kenmare, to aid him and, rebuffed, wrote a lamentation for his and his country's wrongs that echoes, like Jeremiah, in the imagination. In the Kenmare papers there is an entry for August 1727: 'Allowed

102 Freed of the army, he opened, for a few months, his last school at
Knocknagree. In a fever hut there he died aged 36, after a tavern
brawl in Killarney. His memory and his poems remain vividly
amongst the Irish speaking people of the countryside with whom he
threw in his lot. By contrast, the poems of O Rathaile, the would be
servitor of the fallen great, have no such continuing life amongst the
people.

These poets were nourished by a court of poetry that encouraged
many lesser poets in the Sliabh Luachra neighbourhood, the last
remnants of those bardic schools that may have reached back to
pre-Christian times. According to Daniel Corkery, nowhere else in
Ireland were so many sweet singers gathered together as in this
place, 'the south-west corner of Munster was the Attica of Irish
Ireland and Sliabh Luachra its Hymettus'.

As one travels through this rather commonplace countryside
perhaps one may recall the flickering out of a thousand years of
gaelic culture as these courts of poetry drifted to their end. The
words of that brilliant, gallant book, Corkery's *The Hidden Ireland*,
sum it up:

> In some hidden spot, it is likely, some long-established Court did
> outlive all others, not knowing itself to be the last: on some
> wintry night, perhaps, its few remaining old gabblers of verse rose
> up and bade each other good night, thinking to meet again,
> thinking a vain thought. The strange thing would be if in breaking
> their little gathering that night, it was given them to know that it
> had fallen to their humble and withered labouring hands to roll up
> forever the Druidic scroll of the bards, that in closing the door
> that night they were leaving the 'booths of the poets' to desolation
> for evermore: had the thought struck them one imagines that they
> could hardly have survived the vast and lonely wailing that must
> have begun to re-echo in their souls.

At Bird Hill near Kilgarvan was another nest of singers, also
O Sullivans — three brothers and a son, who lived and composed
through the first half of the century. They were minor poets but
pleasing. Their poems were collected and published by Risteard
O Foghludha.

A few of the gaelic families survived during the eighteenth century
but in reduced circumstances: Mac Carthy Mor at Pallis, Killarney —
to 1770; O Sullivan Mor nearby at Tomies — to 1762; O Sullivan
Beare near Eyries; and a branch of the O Donoghues at Glenflesk.
But the most colourful figure of the first half of the 18th century in
Kerry was from another old family, O Mahony, that had come to
Kerry from Cork in the early 14th century. The O Sullivan Mor properties held from Petty passed by marriage to John O Mahony who
died in 1707, the founder of the Dunloe and Dromore families. His
son, Donal O Mahony of Dunloe, was a remarkable figure, 'a Willfull
Man without Remorse of Conscience'. He revived for a time the feudal state of a gaelic chieftain, mainly by taking intermediate tenancies

Dunloe Castle

from the great absentee landlords. He had, it was claimed, 4,000
tenants whom he could mobilise at will. With these white-robed
bullyboys he could terrorise the area in the early part of the century
They were known as O Mahony's 'Fairesses'. (A generation later
similar white-robed groups were known in Tipperary as 'fairies').
O Mahony's men raided even the military post at Ross castle and
recovered stolen goods seized by a too conscientious customs officer.
Donal died in 1729. His brother Denis had Dromore castle, near the
mouth of the Blackwater; his family conformed to protestantism in
the middle of the century.

(II) THE BEGINNINGS OF REBIRTH

From about 1750 began the long, slow haul, progress and regress, of
the Irish people from utter subjection. The easing of religious bigotry,
the absence of political activity by what seemed an utterly crushed
people, the growth of economic wealth, all these permitted some
green shoots to appear above the frozen earth.

The rise in population and in rents made the landowners wealthy and
led to a demand for luxuries — wines, brandies, tobacco and silks.
To pay for these, wool, hides and butter were exported. It is also
said that there was a firm practice of wrecking — of luring passing
ships onto the rocks. One means was, at night, to attach a lamp to
a horse's head — the bobbing up and down to suggest a boat on the
water, so confusing the navigator. A major hazard for sailors was the
absence of lighthouses. One of Lord Shelburne's advisers was
Dominic Trant who wrote to Shelburne in 1782 that ships frequently
get driven into bays on dark winter nights and almost always
perished , 'and the savages of the neighbouring cliffs plunder
without mercy'. 'Within my memory of 25 years', he goes on,

'above 30 valuable vessels, most of them West Indiamen, have been totally lost on one spot — the peninsula of Inch....' For smuggling, the indented coast, the scarcity of naval patrols, the firm local practices in dealing with unduly zealous or incorruptible customs officers when they appeared, above all, long tradition, — all made for a thriving trade with the Continent and, later, with America. Dingle and Valentia were great smuggling centres: Port Magee, facing Valentia, commemorates the name of a famous smuggler from the North of Ireland who married a Kerrywoman and died in Lisbon in 1727. This was added to by the constant recruitment of soldiers to fight in European armies, the sending of children to be educated, the coming and going of priests. Reference is made elsewhere to FitzGerald of Gallarus, and to the remarkable figure of Morty Og O Sullivan Beare in the first half of the century with his eight-gun brigantine sailing up and down the Kenmare River, more than a match for any naval cruiser. James Mason, Robert Emmet's grandfather, had in Killarney an exclusive wholesale business in brandy and other smuggled goods. But the principal family in the import-export business was the O Connells.

Here was an old catholic and pre-gaelic family that would rise to riches during this century through carrying on an extensive import-export business with the Continent. The O Connells had been hereditary seneschals of the great Mac Carthy Mor castle at Bally-carbery, Cahersiveen, but were dispossessed after the Cromwellian wars. A branch of them took a lease of Derrynane, Caherdaniel, from the earl of Cork, and were landlords and smugglers there throughout the eighteenth century. In the second quarter of the eighteenth century, Donal Mor O Connell, grandfather of the famous Daniel, built a Georgian house there, since demolished. It was the first slated house in south Kerry, resolutely faced north, as was the practice. In the younger Daniel's time hideous victorian additions were built: these now constitute the museum there. The wife of Donal Mor was an O Donoghue of Glenflesk, Maire ni Dhuibh, mother of 22 children of whom 12 survived birth, possibly a great granddaughter of Piaras Feirteir, a personality in her own right, a wit, mistress of a vast household and of extempore verse in Irish, surviving to her nineties. Of the five boys, Andrew was hanged in Cork in 1754 as an accomplice of Morty Og O Sullivan Beare; on the eve of his execution he wrote a rather touching poem in Irish. Another boy, Connell, was drowned at sea in 1765. The other boys were Maurice, who became head of the family, Daniel, 'the last colonel of the Irish Brigade' and a French count, and Morgan, father of the great Dan. Of the girls, Eileen became famous in her own right. Married off at fifteen to an old man, O Connor of Firies, she was widowed in six months. Some nine years later, in 1767, she eloped with a handsome, reckless Corkman, Arthur O Leary, formerly a captain in the Hungarian Hussars of the Austrian army. Because he would not, under one of the now increasingly disused penal laws, part with a favourite horse when offered five pounds, he was outlawed and shot at Carriganimma, Co. Cork, in 1773 at the age of 36. Eileen wrote on his death a poem in an ancient Irish genre, the *caoineadh*. It is a living, moving poem and the highest artistic point of the style. It has been beautifully rendered by Frank O Connor. This is a stanza:

Mo chara go daingean tu!	*My mind remembers*
Is cuimhin lem aigne	*That bright spring day,*
An la brea earraigh ud,	*How your hat with its band*
Gur bhrea thiodh hata dhuit	*Of gold became you,*
Faoi bhanda oir tarraingthe,	*Your silver-hilted sword,*
Claiomh cinn airgid —	*Your manly right hand,*
Lamh dheas chalma —	*Your horse on her mettle*
Rompsail bhagarthach —	*And foes around you*
Fir-chritheagla	*Cowed by your air;*
Ar namhaid chealgach —	*For when you rode by*
Tu i gcoir chun falaracht,	*On your white-nosed mare*
Is each caol ceannann fut.	*The English lowered their head*
D'umhlaidis Sasanaigh	*before you,*
Sios go talamh duit,	*Not out of love for you*
Is ni ar mhaithe leat	*But hate and fear,*
Act le haon-chorp eagla,	*For, sweetheart of my soul,*
Ce gur leo a cailleadh tu,	*The English killed you.*
A mhuirnin mh'anama.	

Eileen's brother, the famous 'Hunting Cap' (from his favourite headgear) became head of the family and over a long lifetime made a fortune. Childless himself, he supported brothers, numerous nephews and relatives in the vicissitudes of their careers. From the little, concealed harbour of Derrynane there was a constant sailing of small ships laden with goods, to return with contraband. From this remote place the imports were sold to all the leading families of Kerry. Hunting Cap fully appreciated the value of this remoteness. When Dr Smith, in the 1750s, offered to give them a favourable mention in his history in return for one of the surefooted hobby horses he so much admired, Hunting Cap urged his father to give the horse on condition that *no* reference to them was made because 'our safety lies in our obscurity'.

About the same period, in 1758, Pococke in one of his letters writes: 'I must give you some idea of a Milesian feast and manner of living'. He does not say that the O Connells of Derrynane were the 'Milesians' but the context leaves this in little doubt.

We had a dram offer'd before dinner & had at the upper end Bacon & fowls & cabbage, at the lower a large roasted Turkey, on one side a leg & Lyon of mutton boyl'd & cabbage, on the other a boyl'd Cod, pease on one side, Lobster on the other & 2 dishes of Potatoes on each side below, & a large dish of stew'd apples in the middle; all succeeded by a large bowl of punch & wines. The Breakfast the remnants of the day before, cold Turkey, chickens, minced Turkey, a dish of fryed mutton & of Boyl'd Salmon, a large wooden bowl of potatoes at a side table cover'd with a cloth to keep 'em warm, boyl'd eggs at the tea table & a dram before they sat down.

The business of smuggling continued throughout the century and seems only to have been curbed at its end. In 1787 it was reported

Maurice 'Hunting Cap' O Connell

that there were 10 vessels in Kenmare River wholly engaged in smuggling. A customs ship specially assigned to the Kenmare River had no effect. When pursued, the smugglers ran into the hidden harbours of Sneem, Nedeen, and Kilmackillogue in the river, or in Ballinskelligs Bay and Valentia, where they had agents ready to store the contraband.

Eventually a customs post was established near the modern Waterville. 'In consequence', wrote Beresford in 1782,

> we have had several battles in every one of which we have been defeated except one, which was actually a siege when our people landed their guns and brought them to bear on Mr O Connell's house [at Derrynane] before they would give up the goods. We have twice been beaten at Nedeen, where they now land most of their goods; on one occasion they took our two principal

officers and were going to hang them; in the other they killed one of our officers, and rescued a whole cargo of tobacco....

In 1765 the death penalty was introduced for customs officers who allowed themselves to be corrupted by smugglers and, twenty years later, for smugglers who forcibly resisted. The O Connells seem to have given up the business about this time; but smuggling spirits was still rife at the end of the century.

There were other cargoes, of young men and women. In this remote place, always concerned with education there were two cruel deprivations, education and its consequence, jobs. There were no advanced schools available to catholics. So the boys were sent off at an early age to school on the Continent, to be supported there for many years. Many came back as priests to minister to their people. Others came back, subalterns in the French, Austrian, Spanish armies to see their people and to seek wives. Unless they could inherit land there was no future for these educated catholic boys in their own country. Strictly, as catholics they could not hold land and were always open to the risk of being delated or of having to conform to protestantism. The older professions were quite closed to them. Trade and industry were minimal. Unless they could fit in to the colourful life of an 'exporter-importer agent' i.e. smuggler, these young men had to seek their fortunes elsewhere which many of them did with great distinction. A Daniel O Connell, brother of Hunting Cap, became the last colonel of the Irish Brigade in France and, after the Revolution, arranged for its transfer to English service. After the restoration he became a French general and a Count. An O Sullivan from Dunkerron was a close adviser of the Young Pretender in 1745. And so on.

One of the O Connells was later to sum it up 'their faith, their education, their wine and their clothing were equally contraband'.

The most famous of all these young men was Daniel O Connell, nephew and heir of Hunting Cap, who went to France and Flanders for his education and, in the altered times after the French Revolution, to England for his profession.

But more surprising than this middle class movement to the Continent was that of the ordinary people. Early in the century it was reported: 'when they have sown their summer corn in the spring, many [Kerry] families will take a vagary of going into Spain, and there spend the summer in begging and wandering up and down in the northern side of that kingdom'. There is a story of a woman in Ballinskelligs who asked a neighbour for a loan of a mantle. Being asked how far she proposed to go she replied, 'Only to Spain'.

The last man to bear the title Mac Carthy Mor, Charles, died unmarried in London in 1770 and was buried there. He left the extensive Mac Carthy properties to his mother's people, the Herberts; but, after litigation, other relatives, the O Donoghues

Kerry played little part in the political history of Ireland in the eighteenth century. Whatever the poets might say — and the Kerry poets said a lot — the Old and Young Pretenders made no impact on the county, though an O Sullivan from Dunkerron is blamed for the latter's bad generalship at Culloden and Morty Og O Sullivan Beare was not only at Culloden but at Fontenoy — that great victory of the Irish Brigade — the previous year.

The O Sullivans were to be the heroes of the first history of Kerry — *The Ancient History of the Kingdom of Kerry* — written about 1750 by Friar O Sullivan of Muckross Abbey. This book, not without marvels and inaccuracies, was dedicated to the glory of the O Sullivans.

In 1756 Dr. Charles Smith published his *Present and Antient State of Kerry,* (recently republished), much more to the modern taste and still an important book. There emerges very clearly a picture of underdevelopment and of wretched communications. Just over twenty years later, Arthur Young was in the county and we get some vivid glimpses of life at that time — the grinding poverty of the ordinary people, the occasional improving landlord, and the agricultural state of the county — the little black Kerry cows, still so ubiquitous; the surprising fewness of sheep; the herds of goats on the mountains; the importance of cider; the frequency of flax. The great product of the county was butter, all sent to Cork. He gives the total rental of the county at about £90,000 a year (out of over £5 million for the country as a whole). The great Kerry absentee landlords — the Shelburnes and Fitz Maurices, Lords Kerry, Kenmare (at that time), and Valentia — drew rents at that time (but not necessarily solely from Kerry) of £55,000. Young points out that some of them, notably Lord Shelburne, returned some of this by way of improvement. In 1775 believing that Nedeen meant 'nest of thieves', he changed the name to Kenmare, to honour his close friend and host at Killarney. He laid out a plan for the town, and for the rest of his life took an interest in its development: a market house, a courthouse, a bridewell, and an inn were built. It still shows the mark of his care. A broker named Peet was introduced to organise spinning for the Manchester market. Twenty years earlier, Lord Kenmare, a much poorer man, had tried to get something done about Killarney, but, as is still obvious, failed. The *Cork Journal* in 1754 carried the following advertisement: 'Lord Viscount Kenmare has determined to enlarge his town of Killarney by additional streeets. Will give leases at a reasonable rent for 31 years or 3 lives of sites and 6 to 10 acres of land each'. Before these improvements 'there were not six slate houses in the village, but mostly mud cabins, low and ill-thatched'. Nonetheless, Pococke in 1758 is enthusiastic about what Lord Kenmare had done for the place in the previous decade — the setting aside of a salmon fishery for public works, a road and dining place in Inisfallen, encouraging tenants to build three or four streets, a market house, a tower and steeple for the church, roads, boats to attend all strangers. 'I saw this place ten years ago, a miserable village and now there are good Inns, Lodgings, & Accommodations for Strangers who come to see this place, mostly during the month of July and August'. Smith confirms that the rise of the Killarney tourist trade began in the 1750s. Lord Kenmare

General Count Daniel O Connell

acquired some of them.

Eight years previously, Donal, the last O Sullivan Mor, died in Tomies, Killarney and was buried in Muckross. He was the last representative of the most senior of all gaelic families. The property at Tomies had come to them in 1694 when Sir Nicholas Browne had forfeited. Ross O Connell gives a vivid account of how some of the records of our past were lost. O Sullivan Mor left an illegitimate son whose grandson was a boatman in Killarney. When the grandfather died, the grandson saw a great pile of old papers 'maybe three feet high, mostly written on skins in Latin and Irish; and, faith, I was in dread they might fall into the hands of the Mahonys or some other *new* people in the country, and they might get more of the old O Sullivan estates, so I burned them all myself'.

106

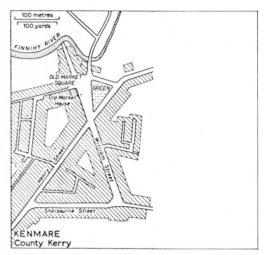

Plan of Kenmare

also introduced linen and woollen manufacturing. However, a Customs and Excise report of 1733 describes Killarney as 'a large and well inhabited market town' with 'three very good inns'; but this may have been to point up the miserable yield of excise on beer and wines — 17s. 1d. in the previous month! In general, however, these great landowners have left us in Kerry little to compare with the monuments of earlier times — the Blennerhasset hous house at Ballyseedy, something of Tralee, and the Muckross estate at Killarney — laid out with loving labour by the Herbert family when they finally inherited it from Mac Carthy Mor in the 1770s. It is remarkable that three of the principal towns were in the ownership of great families — Tralee, of Denny; Killarney, of Kenmare; and Kenmares of Shelburne.

One of the curses of Ireland at that time were the middlemen who held from these great landowners and sublet to cottiers and small holders. Young, thinking of the country as a whole, says of them — 'the class of little country gentlemen; tenants who drink their claret by means of profit rents; jobbers in farms; bucks; your fellows with round hats, edged with gold, who hunt in the day, get drunk in the evening, and fight the next morning'. Twenty years earlier Lord Kenmare, complaining that heavy expenditure by him on trying to bring about improvements in Killarney, had, if anything, made things worse, wrote in his private notebook:

> This is in great measure owing to the pride, drunkenness and sloth of the middling sort among the Irish. Every one of them thinks himself too great for any industry except taking farms. When they happen to get them they screw enormous rents from some beggarly dairyman and spend their whole time in the alehouse of the next village. If they have sons they are all to be priests, physicians or French officers; if daughters they are bred up to no kind of industry but become encumbrances on their parents and the public and thus sloth and beggary are transmitted from generation to generation'.

These middlemen let not only land but cattle also. Young noted of the district around Castleisland : 'Great farmers hire vast quantities of land in order to stock with cows and let them to dairymen; one farmer, who died lately, paid £1,400 a year for this purpose, but £300 or £400 [is] common'. Dairymen paid rent in money, butter, calves and pigs.

An american manufacturer, Joshua Griffin, visited Ireland in 1796. He describes a week's trip from Cork to Killarney and Ross island. He summed up his impressions:

> The inhabitants of these hills are few and poor, their chief employment is to tend ye Cattle and to cultivate some few spots in potatoes or oats; no Indians could possibly appear wilder in their aspect nor more wretchedly clouthed, yet they are smart, intelligent and healthy, they speak and most of them read English, tho' Irish is the language they use to each other.'

On the other hand, Weld, a few years later, agreed with Petty that they were, relatively, well dressed.

After 1760 the problem of making road and bridges was tackled. In each county the grand jury was required to encourage the submission of proposals for improving roads and authorised to raise taxation to cover the cost. As a result, in the next two generations or so the existing road system of Kerry was laid down. This is referred to in more detail elsewhere. In 1765 the rudiments of a public health service began when each grand jury was required to build a county infirmary. In Kerry this was done in Tralee towards the end of the

College street, Killarney, c. 1900. Probably little changed from 1750

century. From the same period began the system of dispensary doctors throughout the country required to give medical attention to those too poor to pay for it. This system was for long in the forefront of public medical services.

From 1760 there grew up a widespread agrarian agitation and severe atrocities were perpetrated. This began amongst dissenters in the North who protested against forced labour on the roads and against tithes. In the south the movement began in Tipperary but soon spread. The export of cattle, prohibited for a century, was permitted in 1765 and this led to a sharp rise in price. This in turn made profitable the enclosure of common land. In the period from about 1750 to 1850 were established the hedges and ditches around these fields. Part of the agrarian unrest was to protest against the enclosure of these fields and to knock down the fences erected around them; hence, the agitators came to be called 'Levellers'. They affected for uniform a white cockade and a white shirt worn outside everyday clothes; hence the well-known name of 'Whiteboys'. Other causes of the unrest were county cesses and competition for land.

Whatever the diverse origins of this movement, the main aim came to be to end the levying of tithes for the support of the established church. These were paid overwhelmingly by catholics who did not, of course, get any spiritual services in return. Tithes were charged at a specially high rate in the south of Ireland. Moreover, they were levied on crops but not on cattle. They thus fell heavily on the poor cultivator while the more affluent dairy and grazing farmers were substantially free of them. In 1800 the tithes in Kerry on potatoes and wheat were £1 an acre and on hay 5s. Those who were required to pay the tithes lived on the margin of subsistence, especially in the 'hungry months' of July and August, before the main crop potatoes came in. Lecky quotes the saying 'Kerry cows know Sunday' from the weekly bleeding given to these animals, fattened on summer grass, to feed their half-starving owners. In 1779 the Knight of Kerry reported that the common people of Kerry were in despair. Apart from occasional economic depressions, the system was such that the full benefit of whatever economic growth there was tended to be siphoned off by the landowners, and the actual cultivators of the soil lived on the edge of destitution.

Whatever about rents, the tithes were fiercely resented. A number of factors aggravated this sense of grievance. There was, as we have seen, the unfair incidence of this tax. It was for the support of a church that had nothing to offer the bulk of those paying the tax. There were many abuses attached to the system. For one thing, over 2,500 parishes of the Church of Ireland, the rectorial — but not the vicarial — tithes of almost a quarter were in the hands of laymen. Most of the senior protestant clergy, who benefited from the tithes, were absentees, indifferent to their duties but exigent in their demands for money. Lecky says a 'contagion of rapacity' affected the protestant clergy of Munster and livings doubled and even trebled in value. The tithes were levied by proctors, or by those who farmed them from proctors, and gross abuses occurred. The

levying, on those required to pay, was most arbitrary. Even Froude described the tithes as 'abominable extortions'. To those who could not pay the tithe-farmers advanced the money at extortionate rates of interest, often to be paid by personal services. From their prevalence in Kerry, these arrangements came to be known as 'Kerry bonds'.

The collectors were intensely hated. Many were killed or mutilated. Some of the junior clergy, who themselves were victims of the system, were attacked. The Whiteboys constituted a very tight-lipped conspiracy, and there was great difficulty in defeating it. Whiteboys broke open the gaol in Tralee and released the prisoners. In Kerry many Whiteboy leaders were protestants. But, in the end, brutality and ruthlessness by government won the day. In Kerry the volunteer corps under Sir Barry Denny acted as a police force and they made successful forays against Whiteboys in the Killorglin area and in the barony of Clanmaurice. Again, in 1786 disorder broke out. This time the disorder began in Kerry. There was a phantom leader called 'Captain Right'. An underground taxation system was set up and a very rough form of justice and punishment. One effect of this was to send the junior clergy fleeing from the rural areas. This time firm methods were rapidly adopted. In Kerry, Lord Kenmare, although himself a catholic leader, hunted down the insurgents 'dragging them from the very altars of the Popish chapels to which they had flown for concealment and protection'. For his efforts the protestant clergy, assembled in Tralee, voted him thanks. For the best part of a year there were serious disturbances throughout the country, but the Irish parliament rejected all attempts to remove the real cause. More disturbances and forty years were to pass before this was done. So was established a long tradition of agrarian agitation that has not had its historical due as a sustained, if often ill-led, attempt to tackle the basic economic and social problems of the time. These arose from the charges on land held by tenants.

The tithes issue was but one part of the whole system of land tenure, economically inefficient and socially unjust. O Brien, writing of Kerry at the end of the century, said it was the habit of proprietors generally to let land to middlemen for three lives or 31 years, These let parcels of the land on short leases — sometimes for one life, sometimes for 7, 10 or 21 years. At the expiration of the lease, the tenant, unless he paid the highest current rent for a new lease, was evicted without compunction. To try to keep the value of the land down, the tenants neglected it, and this neglect was a main cause of the lack of farming progress. The middlemen in Kerry were very snugly housed, but the under tenants very badly so. The labourers, when they could get work, were paid six and a half pence a day in Corkaguiney and were wretchedly housed indeed. But part of the trouble also arose from archaism, in the survival of the rundale system of tenure, dating, perhaps, from prehistoric times, by which all the inhabitants of a townland held the land in common, each cultivating isolated patches. This facilitated further subdivision. In the latter part of the 18th century, holdings began to be consolidated, but into the next century rundale was widespread around Kenmare and Iveragh generally.

108

The Irish parliament got legislative freedom in 1782 because the American war of independence had weakened and frightened the British government and because of the establishment of an Irish volunteer force, ostensibly to protect the country from America's French allies. The force was strong in Kerry. There were picturesque groups — Tralee Corps, Killarney Foresters, Milltown Fusiliers, Laune Rangers, Glanerogians, Kerry Legion, Clanmaurice Cavalry, etc. They were colourful — the Kerry Legion had a scarlet uniform faced black, edged white, silver epaulettes and white buttons. Lord Kenmare and his agent Gallwey were prominent in the Killarney Foresters, thus bringing catholics into a predominantly protestant movement. However, by 1794 it seems to have virtually died out in Kerry. The actual legislation freeing the Irish parliament was handled by that Kerry magnate, the earl of Shelburne (later marquis of Lansdowne), then Secretary of State in Rockingham's administration and, subsequently, for a short time prime minister.

In these years began a great revival of the linen industry. In Kerry it was especially concentrated in the Dingle peninsula, with flax-growing, spinning and weaving. There were factories in Dingle and Killarney. This was to continue until the 1820s when competition from English factories aided by the dropping of the 30% import duty led to its decline and abandonment.

Water wheel for
Kerry carding mill

From 1774 began to appear, often with a short life, a number of Kerry newspapers, of which the earliest and most long-lived was the *Kerry Evening Post,* which appeared twice weekly.

The practice of making prints — elegant but often wildly inaccurate — of views of Killarney and its surroundings began about this time. The first artist of note seems to have been Jonathan Fisher, a Dublin draper, who published six copper plate engravings of Killarney in 1770. Some time later the technique of aquatint printing was invented and Fisher produced 20 of these for Killarney. In the 1790s lithograph printing began. From about 1795, Thomas Walmsley, also born in Dublin, produced many very romantic views that were printed by this method. Fisher and Walmsley were the forerunners of many.

During the period of legislative independence (1782—1800) there was constant agitation for catholic relief, much of it eventually granted in 1793, freeing catholics from nearly all their legal disabilities, economic, social and cultural. From this time, the catholic church in Ireland began to revive vigorously, especially in physical form: churches were built to replace the mass houses, primary and secondary schools were established, parishes were reorganised and convents founded. Gerald, Teahan, bishop of Kerry from 1787 to 1797, was persuaded by Lord Kenmare who had the advowson of the parish of Killarney, to move from Tralee to Killarney, and there the see has since been. A small group of catholic peers discreetly took part in the agitation for catholic relief. Of these the leader was Lord Kenmare who, for all his conservatism and lack of political drive, was a man of real distinction. He died in 1795.

One of the most bigoted parliamentary opponents of these efforts was Sir Boyle Roche (d.1807) member for Tralee and descendant of the de Rupe who overran Kerry in 1215. His mother was, apparently, a Browne, and he was thus a nephew of Lord Kenmare's. He was also the immortal master of the Irish bull : 'What has posterity done for us?' ; 'I smell a rat ; I see him forming in the air and darkening the sky ; but I'll nip him in the bud'. His name is, of course, perpetuated in the expression 'Boyle Roches Bird' — for how could he be in two places at the same time unless he was a bird?.

It was not until the aristocrats were put aside by middle class activists — Keogh and Wolfe Tone — that real progress towards freeing catholics was made. Wolfe Tone was to lose his belief in constitutional action and, abortively, brought two French invasion fleets to Ireland, one of them in 1796 to Bantry Bay, referred to elsewhere. During this time there was much political unrest in Ireland, but Kerry remained loyal. This did not change even under the stimulus of French invasion or of actual rebellion elsewhere in the country. In 1793, legislation had formally banned the volunteers and established county militias. The Kerry Militia, nearly all (except for their officers) catholics, with much atrocity defeated the French and local insurgents at Killala in 1798. In Kerry itself there was some disturbance in Castleisland, and three soldiers were killed in their barracks. There survives, unusually, a pastoral letter in Irish that Bishop Teahan sent his flock in 1794 warning against whiteboyism and the dangers of French godlessness: in June of the previous year a party of 40 soldiers had opened fire on a group of whiteboys in Dingle, killing fourteen.

The rebellion of 1798 clinched the decision to abolish the Irish parliament, an incredibly corrupt body. Of those who supported Castlereagh in this enterprise one of the ablest was the Knight of Kerry. Catholics saw the departure of the Irish parliament with an equanimity lulled by promises of full political participation through complete catholic emancipation. Of the catholics, only a small group of lawyers, headed by the young Daniel O Connell, opposed the Union. For all its failings, the Irish parliament in the last decades of its life made some contributions to governing the country in the interests of the country, a benefit it was not to enjoy again for many decades, and then only spasmodically, in response to extreme political pressures.

Of the eight Kerry members of the Irish parliament, seven voted for the Union and opted for the share-out given to those who voted the right way. Of the seven, two had been, it seems, replaced by the patrons of the boroughs of Ardfert and Dingle. The one surviving anti-unionist, and, therefore, clearly an uncorrupted one, was Arthur Moore of Tralee, a lawyer who afterwards became a jovial and bibulous judge. An effect of the Union was to reduce the number of parliamentary seats: Ardfert and Dingle, amongst 80 disfranchised boroughs, lost their members and the Crosbie family and Townshend (heir and nephew to the 16th Knight of Kerry), the respective proprietors of these boroughs, each got the standard rate of compensation, namely £15,000. Tralee was one of 34 boroughs entitled to send one member to the Union parliament: one member to that parliament was reckoned to be as valuable as two members to the Irish parliament, so the Dennys got no compensation for the loss of the seat. Tralee was to lose this seat under a reforming act of 1840. Viscount Kenmare who, as a catholic, was not a member of the house of lords, and whose title had been regarded as a courtesy one, but who, like his father, was accepted as a catholic leader, in 1798 got an indisputable viscounty — the first catholic to do so since the time of James II — and, two years later, an earldom. As Castlereagh, on whom it chiefly fell, the task was 'to buy out, and secure to the Crown for ever, the fee simple of Irish corruption'.

The century opened with the members of the protestant ascendancy climbing firmly into the saddle. It ended with the leaders selling themselves — and the saddle — for hard cash.

THE NINETEENTH CENTURY RESURGENCE

The nineteenth century in Ireland is divided sharply by the great catastrophe of the Famine that occurred about the middle of the century that, of course, caused such terrible social and psychological havoc for nearly another century. Nonetheless, the nineteenth century considered as a whole shows a long, accelerating re-creation of the Irish nation in the context of the modern world. It illustrates, too, what was becoming apparent at the end of the eighteenth century, that there were three main forces in Irish national life — the parliamentary, the revolutionary, and the agrarian — that, separately, could not force Irish problems towards solution but, together, could get results.

(I) BEFORE THE FAMINE

So it seemed in the first half of the century that there would be steady, slow but uninterrupted progress towards a self-sustaining Irish society.

In 1803, the grandson of a respected dealer (James Mason) in smuggled goods in Killarney led an abortive rising in Dublin — he was Robert Emmet. His rioting mob got out of hand and killed a distinguished judge, Lord Kilwarden, who, as Arthur Wolfe, had briefly, in 1798, held one of the Crosbie Ardfert seats in the Irish parliament.

The end of the 18th century and the early part of the 19th saw a great part of the most inaccessible areas of the county opened up by roads. The circulation this evoked, and the prosperity brought to an agricultural county by the long drawn out foreign wars, led to the rise of towns: such a town as Cahersiveen began its existence early in the century. In 1815 it had five houses; but soon others were built. Along the roads could be seen the constant jogging of farmers on their famous hobbies having descended from their mountains, each laden with two firkins of butter for Cork, the great centre for its export. Weld, in the early part of the century, could sing the praises of this butter which, desalted, was sold in London as the produce of Epping. The small, black Kerry cattle — still to be seen grazing on the mountainsides — yield high butter fat. It was perhaps a memory of all this that made the modern Irish butter marketing organisation label its product 'Kerrygold'. The locals exported their butter and for themselves milked large herds of goats, keeping few sheep. Weld, like Petty a century and a half earlier, found the people living on milk and potatoes and surprisingly well clothed. He points out that good food and clothing and plentiful fuel, as well as neat ways, offset the appearance of wretchedness given by bad housing.

In 1810 a four-horse mail began from Cork to Kerry, and in 1825 the Limerick mail coach began. But in 1830 the post was carried between Dingle and Tralee by two boys who jogged from each town, met half way, and exchanged post bags. In 1836 began the coach service to Cahersiveen. Things steadily improved. Nonetheless, it was said that it used to take Daniel O Connell, later in the century, some two weeks to get from Derrynane to Westminster. The lakes of Killarney were a main thoroughfare and old prints show them crowded with sail. The ore and iron from Muckross were carried across the lake and down the Laune by Colonel Herbert's ships.

Muckross House

The war led to the re-opening of the mines on Ross island. The new earl of Kenmare — an absentee short of funds — sold all the trees on the island, as well as those on Tomies mountain, much to the distress of those concerned with the rising tourist trade. There were three not very good inns in Killarney, and the people of the town also took in guests. Two Lancashire men had a scheme for Lord Kenmare to empty the Lower Lake, so putting all that space to a useful purpose; but the outlet at the Laune was found to be much shallower than the lake. This irresponsibility was much contrasted with the constant improvements made by the Herberts of Muckross who were, however, severely criticised by the local gentry for spending their money so rather than on drink. In 1843, the great, if rather undistinguished, Herbert house at Muckross was built, the Portland stone facing being specially imported through Cork and carried over the bad roads.

Some technological improvements occurred in the period 1815 to 1845. Perhaps the most important was the replacement of the old Irish wooden plough, that barely scratched the surface of the soil, by the iron swing plough from Scotland. By 1845, the scythe had begun to replace the sickle.

There had been a tanning works and a linen factory in Killarney and in some other places, but the slump that followed the end of the European wars and the removal of protection under the Union led to their disappearance. But tourism progressed. In 1828, a German visitor actually praised the inns at Killarney, saying that the 'incessant resort of English tourists has also introduced into the inns an English elegance and English prices'.

The legislative union had also provided for the union of the Church of Ireland with that of England. As a consequence of the evangelical movement early in the century there were substantial reforms and a notable church building programme got under way. Some 80% of the churches then in use in Kerry — about 40 in all — were either rebuilt or, more often, built anew. These churches, some now again in ruins, are easily recognisable — grey, gloomy, with a square tower at the west end. What is to be noted is that so many as 50 Church of Ireland churches were in use in those decades. This shows the vigour that had come into the church for the first time in its history in Kerry. In 1824, Bishop Jebb said that there were 42 benefices in Ardfert and Aghadoe and 21 incumbents were resident. This vigour led to its one isolated success with the plain people of the county which underlines the chances that for three centuries had been missed. In 1831 began an energetic mission in four parishes west of Dingle. From 1833, the Rev Charles Gayer, an Englishman, was to be the main force behind the movement. By 1836, 20 teachers were employed. In 1840-42 was established the 'colony' in Dingle of 25 houses (with 10 others at Ventry), as well as Kilmalkedar, Dunquin and other places, to house the converted. In 1838, a former catholic native of Dingle, Thomas Moriarty, became a priest of the Church of Ireland and in 1839 worked in Ventry and other places preaching in Irish. In 1840 there were 80 children in the protestant school in Ventry. He and his helpers had much success for a time, but this died away against a determined catholic counter-movement. Gayer himself died of famine fever in January, 1848. Some success was also achieved in north Kerry, in Brosna, and in south Kerry, in Kilgarvan.

Ireland's basic problem was the economic one. How was a rapidly increasing population to live without an economic base other than land? How was that land to be made more productive when it was being divided into ever more uneconomical holdings under a system of land tenure so atrocious that it impeded investment, management and improvement? Incompetent and improvident landlords for the most part let their land to unscrupulous middlemen who recklessly sub-let at increasing rents in sub-divided holdings to ever more impoverished cottiers without the capital, the means or the incentive to improve the land.

The system was described in 1847 by Peter Fitzgerald who owned practically all of Valentia island, let by an ancestor in 1795:

> My estate was let .... on thirteen leases of 3 lives to
> thirteen substantial middlemen — those tenures average
> four to five hundred acres each. The [middlemen]
> tenants, after building houses and performing nominally a
> few other covenants violated their engagements of improvement
> and became nearly altogether absentees, sub-dividing and sub-
> letting their lands, the fruit of which has been the augmentation
> [of the population] from something like 400 to 3,000 persons.

Of the leases originally granted, but three have fallen in after a lapse of 52 years.

Later in the century, some landlords were able to get rid of the middlemen and began to provide improvements directly - houses, barns, convenient sized fields, ditches, dykes, access roads and so on. This policy was followed by Sir John Walsh in North Kerry and by the earl of Kenmare, amongst others. Nonetheless, in 1850, nineteen of the twenty-three townlands on Kenmare's estate in Killarney union were held by middlemen. As these leases fell in large sums were spent on drainage, houses and farm buildings on the vast estates in Cork, Kerry and Limerick.

Because of the failure of other forms of economic development to take root anywhere other than the north-east, the problem reduced itself to the familiar terms of undoing the 16—17th century conquest of Irish land, that is, of getting rid of the protestant ascendancy who owned the land, and of the middleman system that battened both on owners and tenants alike. This meant also that the great growth of population had to be stopped and reversed. Both of these were done — the second by the Great Famine in the middle of the century, the first by successive British governments towards its end.

There was a foretaste of the great famine in 1816—17 and 1822 when, in Kerry, there was much distress from hunger and typhus — a disease that was to remain endemic in Kerry until the next century, one of its last outposts in Western Europe. Again in 1832 cholera entered the country through Belfast from Britain, having spread from the Far East by way of Russia.   This caused much loss of life, a foretaste of its recurrence during the famine.

In the light of this analysis, there is a curious sense of unreality about Irish history up to the Famine. Only the Whiteboys and the other agrarian agitators had, in their bewildered way, a grasp of this basic issue of the land which evaded the understanding of most parliamentarians and revolutionaries alike. In north-east Kerry the famine of 1821—22 provoked serious disorder. The long agitation against tithes —in 1821 Knockane protestant church near Killarney was severely damaged by being set on fire — was a symptom that culminated in the bitter seven years' Tithe War. In this Kerry played a continuing part. The tithes in 1832 amounted to an, at least, nominal £500,000, and the other income of the Church of Ireland to £250,000. Eventually, in 1838 this grievance was substantially eased. But within the framework of law and order the issues of the early 19th century were merely the unfinished business of the 18th. It was the crucial weakness of the Union that it gave Ireland no really relevant government until it was too late.

One slightly ludicrous attempt to do this — typically in a repressive sense — was the founding of the coastguards in 1822 and the building of stations around the coast. This was to finish off the business of smuggling. From 1836 the coastguard were given the added duty of stamping out illegal distilling, without, be it said, complete success.

The early decades of the nineteenth century were marked by the curious phenomenon of faction fighting, usually after fairs when drink flowed freely. This was a kind of tribalist throw-back, family fighting family and village against village, from fair to fair, occasionally with loss of life. Croker refers to a couple of these encounters at the end of the 1820s — one in Muckross and one in Killarney, the protagonists being the Moynihans and the O Donoghues. There were fights in Dingle, Kenmare, Killorglin and Tralee; but they seem to have been most widespread in the north of the county. For forty years, from about 1794, the two great rivals here were the Cooleens and the Mulvihills. This rivalry culminated in a faction fight in Ballybunion in 1834 that cost at least sixteen lives. After this, large scale faction fighting was steadily suppressed and had effectively ended by 1839.

The protestant ascendancy had sold political power in 1800 for hard cash. The catholics, having less to sell, were paid by cheque — one that continued to bounce for a generation. This cheque was the promise of catholic emancipation, that is, full and equal civil rights. In effect, this meant the right to sit in the union parliament and to tackle the problems of Irish government. Regularly, until his death in 1820, Grattan tried to persuade parliament to grant this reform. He and his successors made some progress, but parliament would grant nothing until it was forced to do so, a lesson Ireland was to learn many times.

In 1826 the two seats for Kerry were contested by three candidates, the sitting members, the Knight of Kerry and Col. James Crosbie, both long-time supporters of catholic emancipation, and William Hare, grandson of the first earl of Listowel, who also declared himself on the side of emancipation. There were gross abuses at the election, apparently in Hare's interest, and a riot broke out in which soldiers killed sixteen people. In the event, Hare won Crosbie's seat. It became known as 'Hare's election'.

It was the struggle to achieve popular support for the parliamentary effort for emancipation that made Irish democracy. This was under the leadership of, possibly, the second greatest man in Irish history, Daniel O Connell, a Kerryman, born near Cahersiveen in 1775, who inherited his uncle's home in Derrynane and much of his wealth in 1825. He had, at this time, a highly successful practice at the bar but was to enchange the title of 'Counsellor' for that of 'Liberator'. Evoking the help of priests all over the country by means of the 'Catholic Rent ' — a penny a month subscribed by great numbers — he built up an enormous disciplined agitation. At first they concentrated on getting protestant sympathisers into parliament; but at length O Connell himself stood at a by-election for Clare and was elected. Faced with this, and his backing by overwhelming support in Ireland, the British government capitulated, and catholic emancipation was granted in 1829.

In this struggle O Connell, from 1823, evoked the support of the catholic clergy as the local leaders of his campaign. Thus developed an important force in the 19th century — the political power of the

111

112 clergy. It also helped to sharpen the anti-catholic feelings of protestant orangemen, so storing up trouble for the future. But, in any event, the catholic church was in full resurgence from this time. Then began the revival of one of the great glories of its past in the sending abroad of large numbers of missionaries. This time they went mainly to countries under English influence. The first catholic missionary to Australia, Jeremiah O Flynn (b. 1788) was educated at the Franciscan school in Killarney. Already, by 1832 there was an Irish bishop of Madras, south India. There began too at home the great outburst of church building — typified in that at Caherdaniel, beside O Connell's home — to replace the crude churches and mass houses of the previous century. The striking monument of this in Kerry is, of course, the great Pugin cathedral at Killarney. The winning of the battle for denominational schools further consolidated the position of the church, though it meant that desperately poor catholics had to find further money for building. Thus emerged the special features of the modern catholic church in Ireland — distrustful of government, missionary, pre-occupied with building and with education.

In the decade 1831—40, O Connell and his supporters often held the balance of power in parliament. O Connell's price for supporting the whigs was that Ireland be governed. Now, perhaps for the first time in its history, Ireland began to be governed in the interests of the people as a whole.

A first fruit of O Connell's new power was the national system of primary education established in 1831, completely superseding the old hedge schools. After a long struggle to prevent the schools becoming under undue protestant influence, it was settled that each denomination would manage its own schools. The primary school system has often been blamed for destroying Irish as the vernacular in rural areas, but not all the blame lies there. Already 'English' schools, that is where that language was to be learned, were popular. In 1806 Weld had commented on seeing them 'amid some of the wildest mountains of Kerry'. Clearly, the tide of anglicisation was already rising. Gradually, after 1831, the country was covered by a network of grey primary schools. The size of these buildings, now mostly abandoned and replaced, shows how the population of children has declined.

About the same time, the Board of Works was constituted and a formidable programme of road building was engaged in by the State through this agency. Most of the really attractive Kerry roads were built at this time. The linking up of the various road systems in Kerry enabled the great Italian carrier, Bianconi, to open up passenger routes to and in Kerry with his long, horse-drawn cars. He linked Mallow with Killarney, Cahersiveen and Tralee; and these towns with Limerick. He also linked Cork with Tralee. There was another, later, link in that his daughter married an O Connell, Morgan John, and wrote a fascinating book about the Derrynane family and its ramifications *The Last Colonel of the Irish Brigade*.

Already, from 1827, the Ordnance Survey had been established and

Daniel O Connell

this became the nursery of a remarkable generation of public servants, some like Drummond and Larcom being British, others like O Donovan and O Curry being Irish; all destined to play a big part in Ireland's history, but the latter two a crucial part in its cultural history.

Under Melbourne, with Thomas Drummond as under-secretary and O Connell as champion in parliament, there began a five year period of reform from 1835. In 1836 was organised a comprehensive police force, the Royal Irish Constabulary, the gaunt ruins of whose barracks are still to be seen, often in odd places, such as at Ladies View, Killarney.   The Irish parliament in 1797 had provided for full-time constables in every barony, and in 1814 Peel had established a police force (the 'peelers') for disturbed districts. A county constabulary was established in 1822. But it was not until 1836 when Drummond took the matter in hand that Ireland got a proper police force. In 1838 it was possible to get through parliament a measure settling that constant source of disorder and coercion acts, the tithe question. In the same year the English poor law system was extended to Ireland. It was in part wildly inappropriate to Irish conditions but it did give to Ireland its first genuinely democratic institutions, the poor law unions. Kerry was divided into six of these, based on Tralee, Killarney, Listowel, Cahersiveen, Dingle and Kenmare. These were ruled by boards of poor law guardians popularly elected on a property suffrage — big property owners had up to six votes— and financed by local taxation. A remarkable national programme of workhouse building was got going in the next decade, and Kerry had a workhouse erected in each of its six unions. Also democratised from 1840 were the corrupt and unrepresentative borough corporations, and Tralee, Dingle, and Ardfert ceased to be boroughs, the last two losing all pretence of local government.

The effort to govern Ireland was to prove too little and it was not sustained but it was a beginning.

O Connell's power depended on winning seats in parliament. For example, in the elections of 1832 and 1835 he won all three Kerry seats in the Repeal interest, two of them gained in 1835 by his nephew and his son. The electorates were desperately narrow — 1,200 for the two seats in the county and about 175 for the seat in Tralee. With the restricted electorate and open voting, pressure, bribery and intimidation were widely used. As an inspector of police in Kerry put it : 'The priest has got excommunication and the landlord has got ejectment'.

After 1840, with Melbourne fallen and Drummond dead, and the parliamentary road to reform substantially blocked by the Tories, O Connell began the last great crusade of his life — for the repeal of the Union, so that Ireland could be governed in the interests of her people. Again he called on the help of the catholic clergy. He assembled enormous meetings — as many as three-quarters of a million people — whom he thrilled with his oratory and yet kept disciplined and orderly. This great democratic phenomenon made him famous in Europe. He was in a real sense the founder of christian democracy — 'king of the beggars' his enemies called him. But this agitation failed just before the Famine, and O Connell died

in the midst of it in 1847.

113

The Famine was the great traumatic event in Irish history. A hundred years afterwards it was still raw in the consciousness of the Irish people. Only in recent years has that wound begun to heal.

The population of Ireland rose very fast from 1780. At the turn of the century it was about five million. Forty years later it was three million greater. This was during a period when such Irish industry as had existed at the Union had, outside the north-east, nearly all succumbed to free trade, economic slump and better communications with Britain. There was thus no way of employing the people except on the land. This became grossly overcrowded, but the rural people were, for the most part, content to live in the most extreme poverty — in 1841 two-thirds of the rural population of Kerry were living in one-roomed mud cabins. The poorest people lived almost exclusively off the potato. There is an account on the eve of the Famine of part of O Connell's own country, Derrynanebeg:

> The distress of people was horrible. There is not a pane of glass in the parish, nor a window of any kind in half of the cottages. Some have got a hole in the wall for light, with a board to stop it up. In not one in a dozen is there a chair to sit upon, or anything whatever in the cottages beyond an iron pot and a rude bedstead with some straw on it; and not always that. In many of them the smoke is coming out of the doorway and they have no chimney ...... the poor creatures are in the lowest degree of squalid poverty'

The previous year, in 1844, the Devon Commission found that wages in Kerry were 6d to 8d a day.

Between 1821 and 1841 the population of the whole country increased by just under 20% but that of Kerry by 30%. In the early 1840s, over two million people — one-quarter of the population — were living on the verge of destitution. What the Famine did was to destroy these people — killing half of them by hunger and disease and sending the rest — starving, half naked, fever-ridden, destitute, panic-stricken, embittered — across the Atlantic.

What happened was that in the summer of 1845 a great part of the potato crop in Ireland was destroyed by blight, a fungus disease then not understood. Thanks to the prompt action of Peel, grain was imported and the people were fed. This gave Peel the opportunity to get the Corn Laws repealed, but he lost office in consequence. From 1846 a Whig government, under Lord John Russell, was in office, incompetent, heartless and unwilling to deal with an Irish catastrophe in the terms that a similar disaster elsewhere in the Union would have evoked. The 1846 potato crop failed everywhere. In 1847 the crop was not affected by blight, but because of the shortage of seed, was much too small. The crop failed again in 1848. An inadequate Irish administration, harried and denied money from London, did its

114 best, helped by private charity. At one stage 700,000 people were employed on public works — on those improbable 'famine roads' that are a mute testimony of the time. They were made in a freezing winter by starving, half-naked wretches, continually urged — from London — to increase their productivity. At another time, three million people were being fed. But, in general, the country was ruled for three years by uncontrolled hunger and disease. A great part of the deaths that occurred were from the 'famine diseases' of typhus, relapsing fever, dysentry, cholera, and the rest for which starving people were no match.

It was a terrible vindication of Malthus, and the Irish people learned the lesson. In the previous fifty years, the Irish population had doubled; in the subsequent fifty years it halved. Emigration and postponed marriages did this. One will still see pointed out high on the Kerry hillsides grass grown ridges where the potatoes failed and from which the cultivators — forced by the pressure of population up into this sub-marginal land — had died or fled at this time.

Overall, Ireland, if one allows for the natural increase between 1841 and 1846, lost in the subsequent five years about one-quarter of her population from death and emigration. This was true, also of Kerry as a whole; but the losses were much above average in Clanmaurice (in the Lixnaw area), in Corkaguiney and in Glanerought. Indeed, by the end of the next decade, these three baronies had lost over 40% of their population, as against a loss of just over 30% for Kerry as a whole. Some calculations of excess mortality in the years 1846 to 1850 show that the five western counties — Galway, Clare, Mayo, Kerry and Cork — suffered most. In the first two, the excess mortality was between 15% and 17½% and in the other three, 12½% to 15%.

We have not a great deal of detail about what happened in Kerry during the Famine years, but a few vivid glimpses come to us. In the autumn of 1846 relief works were slow to get under way. In October, 1846 there was a threat in Castleisland that work must be started or there would be plunder — the men of Castleisland could not 'bear the cries of hungry children any longer'. In February, 1847 after it had been decided to set up soup kitchens to feed the starving, there was in Killarney one kitchen for 10,000 people, and in Tarbert two small places for 18,000. At this time the parish priest of Kenmare found a man, still living, lying in bed with a dead wife and two dead children, while a starving cat was eating another dead infant. Relief works and soup kitchens ended in the summer and autumn of 1847. In that autumn, the idea was that, instead of relief works and soup kitchens, the workhouses should be cleared of the infirm who were to be given cash relief in their homes, and that the able-bodied would be relieved only in the workhouses. In Tralee this was impossible for two reasons. The first was that the infirm had no homes to go to, because the landlords usually pulled down their houses as soon as they were vacated. The second was that, even emptied, the workhouse could not hold all the able-bodied who applied for entry. In December 1847, Tralee workhouse, which held 1,400, was full and able-bodied people were arriving in masses to be refused, 700 to 800 at a time. The previous month a mob of them had tried to break into the workhouse by force, bearing a black flag marked 'Flag of Distress'.

The parish priest of Kenmare, Father John O Sullivan, pressed the government for general outdoor relief. He played a major part in relief work in the Kenmare area, helped financially by the great local (if absentee) landlord, Lord Lansdowne, who was a member of Russell's government. Shiploads of grain were imported into Kenmare. Hunger was only part of the problem. The famine enabled endemic diseases, such as typhus and relapsing fever, to break their normal bounds, and relatively new ones, like cholera, to get a grip. The public health services were pitifully inadequate. There was delay, for example, in Dingle in providing a fever hospital so that infected people could be removed from their homes. There was, of course, inadquate knowledge of how to treat the diseases and the existing doctors were overwhelmed. Lice were big carriers of the main fevers, and in 1847 relief committees were empowered to cleanse houses, persons and clothing. In Kenmare union over 5,000 cabins were whitewashed inside and out. This was claimed to have saved 'innumerable lives'. Nonetheless, by 1849, over 5,000 people had died in the union of Kenmare, this out of a total in 1841 of just 30,000.   In the summer of 1849 over 10,000 people were getting relief in Kenmare union. Trench, who came on the scene in 1849 as Lord Lansdowne's agent, claimed that this disaster in Kenmare was caused by bad management: the landlord was willing to finance the import of whatever grain was needed to feed the people, but this was only intermittently arranged. So, he said:

> they died on the roads, and they died in the fields; they died in the mountains and they died in the glens; they died at the relief works, and they died in their houses; so that the little "streets" or villages were left almost without an inhabitant; and at least some few, despairing of help in the country, crawled into the town, and died at the doors of the residents and outside the Union walls. Some were buried underground, and some were left unburied in the mountains where they died, there being no one able to bury them.

By 1850 there were still 30,000 people receiving relief in Kenmare union, chargeable to the Lansdowne estate which was about a third of the whole area of the union. Between 1851 and 1853 the estate organised and paid for the emigration (not all of it willing, it would seem) of 4,600 persons from the estate at a cost in 1851 alone of £14,000 — for each a free passage and a few shillings over. Another landlord in north Kerry, Sir John Walsh, had, as he said, 'very great difficulty' in persuading his poorer tenants to go to Quebec, but considered the trouble worthwhile because of the restoration of tranquillity.

It was also an economic operation. The emigrants lost their tiny patches of land and their cabins and had, in any event, little stomach for returning to them. They were supported in the work-

Famine funeral, 1847

houses and on outdoor relief from rates levied on the landlord's land. In Kenmare it struck the new agent, Trench, that it would be more economical — and humane — to pay their passage to America and give them a little money for clothes than to continue to support them as paupers in Kenmare. So, at the peak, weekly, for many weeks, they were shepherded off in batches of 200 at a time to sail from Cork. It was later alleged that many of them arrived in New York in poor health and that there was a special Lansdowne ward for them in a New York hospital; but this was denied. In all, 4,600 penniless emigrants were thus launched into the new world, and the lean mountainsides around Kenmare were emptied of people. The census figures for the parish of Tuosist tell the tale of death and emigration. In 1841 a population of 7,485; in 1851 it was 4,034, a loss in 10 years of 46%. In 1966 it was 899. In west Kerry the tale was equally grim. In 1841 there were 215 people in the townland of Gallarus; in 1851, ten years later, there were 84. Ballyferriter had 183 in 1841 and 63 in 1851. These are extreme figures, but they illustrate how hard hit some places (and people) were.

(II) AFTER THE FAMINE

After the Famine Irish life entered a doldrum period while the population melted away by emigration. Nonetheless, there were some dynamic forces. One of the most striking was the vigour of the catholic church. The ecclesiastical centre around Pugin's cathedral in Killarney dates from this time, as well as many churches and schools. But perhaps the story of the establishment of convents of nuns is the most striking feature of this vigorous growth. There were no nuns in Kerry in medieval times. Now there are 27 communities. Perhaps the story of the growth of the 11 Presentation convents in the Kerry diocese succintly tells the tale. The Presentation nuns were founded by a Cork woman, Nano Nagle, at the end of the eighteenth century when, for the first time, women began to play a significant part in religion. The Kerry convents are all educational institutions, founded as follows:

Killarney, 1793; Tralee, 1809; Dingle, 1829; Milltown, 1838; Millstreet (Co. Cork), 1840; Cahersiveen, 1840; Listowel, 1844; Castleisland, 1846; Lixnaw, 1877; Rathmore, 1888; Tralee (Oakpark), 1925. In 1825, of just over 6,000 girls in convent schools in Ireland as a whole, three-quarters were in Presentation convents, 350 of them in Killarney, 180 in Tralee. From 1850 dates the romanising movement in the Irish church when the first synod of Irish bishops since the reformation was held.

The railways reached Kerry in the early 1850s and the trans-atlantic cables later in the same decade. The long isolation of the county began to be breached, and the tourist trade to Killarney began to rise sharply. This was boosted by the visit there of Queen Victoria, the Prince Consort, the Prince of Wales, and three other of their children in August, 1861. They stayed, with a train of over 100, one night in Kenmare House and for the rest of their stay in Muckross with the Herberts. Henry Arthur Herbert had married a Balfour and was chief secretary for Ireland in 1857-8, the first Kerryman to play a significant part in the Irish government since the days of the earls of Desmond, four centuries before. His glory was brief, and he died in 1866. In the next generation, the family were to go down into financial ruin, just over 100 years after they had inherited the property to which they devoted such unremitting care.

The Famine was not over when, in July, 1848, the Young Ireland revolutionaries began rising in that home of disaffection, Tipperary. After a futile attack on a house at Ballingarry held by a number of police, the revolt, led by William Smith O Brien, was over. The police fired one volley and killed two of their besiegers and lightly wounded another, James Stephens. He went 'on the run' for some two months in the Cork and Kerry mountains. He spent a period in the Glengariff-Kenmare-Killarney area. Stephens' companion was Michael Doheny (whose *Felon's Track* describes their adventures) until they separately escaped to Paris, Doheny equipped with a clerical outfit and breviary given him by a curate in Tuosist, Fr M. O Leary. That was the end of revolution for 10 years.

During the 1850s there was some parliamentary effort to improve the lot of the tenant holders of land, but it came to nothing. From the 1840s to 1871, the two parliamentary seats for the county of Kerry were allotted without election to the two great Killarney families — the Brownes in the Whig interest, and the Herberts in the Tory interest.

In 1856 Stephens came back from Paris and travelled much of the country. He was in Killarney in 1856 and attended the installation of David Moriarty as bishop of Kerry. He taught French and other languages for two terms there in that year in Miss Morris's School for Young Ladies. From 1858, he organised with great ingenuity the oathbound, revolutionary society, the Fenians, named after the Fiana of old. He had great success in winning over the rural agitators, the former whiteboys now called Ribbonmen, and in inducing them to forsake land agitation for the cause of revolutionary, disciplined

116 nationalism. The Fenians incorporated the Phoenix Society founded
by O Donovan Rossa. The Phoenix clubs were very numerous in the
area between Skibbereen and Kenmare; in the mountains there was
much drilling. This was an area in which the sufferings of the
Famine had been much publicised, and the memory was now a force
for revolution. A good part of this area is in the diocese of Kerry,
and the clergy there, under the leadership of the bishop, David
Moriarty, coadjutor since 1854, and the parish priest of Kenmare,
Archdeacon John O Sullivan (the locally favoured candidate for the
see), soon came to denounce the oathbound secret organisation and
to refuse the sacraments to its members. Early in October, 1858,
the archdeacon, apparently through the informer O Sullivan Gowla,
learned of the local conspiracy and informed Dublin Castle and the
local magustrate, Trench, of what he had learned. This was the
beginning of a long and bitter story. In December, 1858, nine
members of the Phoenix Society were arrested in Kenmare and four
in Killarney. Daniel O Sullivan, a schoolteacher, was sentenced to
10 years, but was released in October, 1859; the others had been
released some months earlier.

This was the end of Fenianism in Kenmare, but it revived in
Killarney and became strong in south Kerry. The Fenians were
strongly supported by exiles in the United States whose implacable
hatred of England was to be a big factor in Irish history for two
generations. The membership of the Fenians was considerable, and
included many Irishmen in the British army. The Government, with
the help of informers and *agents provocateurs,* arrested many of the
leaders. Nonetheless, a rising was fixed for 11 February 1867.
Almost at once it was postponed to 5 March.

News of the postponement did not reach Kerry, and on the night of
Tuesday, 12 February, two groups took to arms, one at Cahersiveen
and the other nearby at Kells Bay. They were under the leadership
of J.J. O Connor, a Valentia man, aged 23, who had been a colonel
in the American Civil War. The Cahersiveen group of about 30 men,
with the help of the sergeant of the police, were to take the police
barracks, and so arm themselves; but they did not attempt this
because there was a gunboat in the harbour. Apparently, Head
Constable O Connell's four sons and daughter were in the plot, and
it was to save him that one of the Fenians, Noonan, apparently
alerted him just in time. In consequence, the Cahersiveen group
marched on to join the group at Kells Bay, who had captured some
guns at the coastguard station. This exploit gave rise to a well-known
local ballad. It had been planned that a group from Valentia would
capture the cable station, from which a proclamation of
independence was to be sent to the outside world; then the party
would march on Killarney, join the Killarney group and set up a
headquarters there. The Valentia groups seems not to have activated
itself, and the leaders of the Killarney group were arrested. In the
event a party of about 60 marched on Killarney, shooting and
wounding at Esk, near Glenbeigh, a solitary mounted policeman,
Constable Duggan, who refused to halt. Duggan's life was for some
time despaired of, but he recovered. The policeman's messages
showed that the plot was discovered, that the Killarney leaders had

Colonel J. J. O Connor

been arrested, and that the rising had, in any event, been postponed.

Many of the insurgents took to the mountains around Glencar, but a
number persevered and camped at Dunloe. After a couple of days,
after the situation was clearly hopeless, they took to the hills.
Soldiers were poured into Kerry to put down the rising. A handful
of Fenians were captured and one (Joseph Noonan) was transported.
O Connor managed with much hardship to escape to the United
States; he died in 1870. Abortive as this outbreak was, it was one
of the most considerable manifestations of the great and widespread
Fenian conspiracy. The parish priest of Cahersiveen, Fr Healy,
complained: 'That cursed Fenian outbreak left the farmers in no
spirit for matchmaking in Cahir'!

The following Sunday David Moriarty, bishop of Kerry, preached
on these events in Killarney cathedral. In a mixture of rebuke, irony,
humour and scorn, he gave an account of the events of the previous
days, and then ended with these words that have never been forgotten
or forgiven to him:

If we must condemn the foolish youths who have joined in this conspiracy, how much must we not execrate the conduct of those designing villains who have been entrapping innocent youth and organising this work of crime....but beyond them there are criminals of a far deeper guilt. The men who, while they send their dupes into danger, are fattening in the spoil of Paris and New York. The execrable swindlers who care not to endanger the necks of the men who trust them, who care not how many are murdered by the rebel or hanged by the strong arm of the law, provided that they can get a supply of dollars either for their pleasures or for their wants. O God's heaviest curse, his withering, blasting, blighting curse is on them. I preached to you last Sunday on the eternity of Hell's torment. Human reason was inclined to say — 'it is a hard word and who can bear it?' But when we look down into the fathomless depth of this infamy of the heads of the Fenian conspiracy, we must acknowledge that eternity is not long enough, nor hell hot enough, to punish such miscreants.

Some particularly unsavoury characters had infiltrated the higher ranks of the Fenian movement and had helped to organise it while betraying it. Several of these gave evidence in the various trials of the time. It was these men who led astray simple young men and then betrayed them, not the honourable patriots, that, Bishop Moriarty later explained, he had condemned; but it is difficult to accept that, consciously or subconsciously, he had not Stephens particularly in mind. This terrible saying came to be believed to be aimed at all Fenians, and so intensified the long-lasting bitterness that had grown up between the church and the Fenians. It also marked a significant difference between the increasingly romanised, self-confident and conservative bishops and the lower clergy who in sentiment remained much closer to the ordinary people.

Moriarty's conservatism had commended him to Cullen who had ensured his appointment as bishop of Kerry over the favoured local candidate, John O Sullivan, parish priest of Kenmare. The same conservatism had commended him to the British government as a future archbishop of Armagh. He was a main influence on the disestablishment of the Church of Ireland in 1869. At the first Vatican Council of 1870 he, with by no means his natural ally Archbishop Mac Hale, fought vigorously against the proposed doctrine of papal infallibility, but did not finally vote against it. He wrote to Newman at this time: 'The majority represents the *Curia Romana*....it is composed of men who have not come into conflict with the unbelieving mind or into contact with the intellectual mind of the day'.

He was a very active bishop and did a great deal for the religious and educational development of his diocese. It was he who restored two old religious communities to Kerry by inviting the Dominicans to return to Tralee in 1861 and the Belgian Franciscans from their Gorey house to establish a house in Killarney in 1859. (This last was to end the long survival of the Muckross and Lislaghtin communities. There was no further Guardian cf Muckross after 1873, and the last of the Muckross friars, James FitzGerald, died in 1881. He seems to have been the last connexion with the Franciscan school founded under

Bishop David Moriarty

the auspices of Bishop Sugrue. The present Franciscan church was opened in 1867). Moriarty had opened a secondary school — for catholic and protestant boys — in Tralee in 1855, and was patron of two more — in Tralee, opened 1855, and Killarney, opened 1857. The famous St Brendan's seminary was founded in Killarney, as part of the cathedral complex, in 1860, apparently succeeding an earlier seminary. Another diocesan secondary school, St Michael's, was founded in Listowel in 1879. Moriarty died in 1877, probably the most notable of all Kerry bishops.

Moriarty was not only a conservative: he was a unionist who believed the union to be in the best interst of Ireland. In 1871, the earl of Kenamre died and his son's succession left a vacancy for member of parliament for Kerry. For thirty years the two Kerry seats had been allocated without contest to a Herbert in the Tory interest and a Browne in the Whig. It was intended that the new earl's cousin, a Dease from Westmeath and a catholic, should succeed to the seat. However, the newly emergent home rulers decided to contest the seat with a protestant Kerryman, Rowland Blennerhasset of Kells. Moriarty tried to mobilise the full power of the church

118

behind Dease, and the landlord interest — a combination of Brownes, Herberts, O Connells, O Donoghues — coined the slogan 'Property versus communism'. This by-election of 1872 was the last example of open voting in the United Kingdom and tenants were subjected to extreme pressures. Nonetheless, they voted three to two for Blennerhasset. This gave a great fillip to the home rule movement. Blennerhasset did not, however, prove to be a stalwart home ruler.

In the decade to 1880, the new earl of Kenmare laid out great sums in improving the estates, and in improving Killarney. He built 300 cottages for his labourers and spent possibly £100,000, or more, on building Killarney House (since burned down). Notwithstanding raising in 1882-3 some £11,000 in fines for long leases towards the cost, he borrowed £146,000 from the Standard Life Assurance Co. His rental in 1880 was about £38,000, a rise of one-third since 1850. About £5,000 of this was due to six years' work of his new agent, Sam Hussey, through raising rents, calling in leases, and so on.

Already, the Fenian unrest had persuaded Gladstone that Irish problems had to be tackled. The fenian tradition of bitter irreconcilability to British rule in Ireland, and American based, was to continue through the Land War and to be the crucial influence on the rising of 1916. Gladstone began his long involvement in Irish affairs with the disestablishment of the Church of Ireland in 1869; from then on, except in a few places where there were protestant populations, the clergy were withdrawn — protestants number less than one per cent of the present population of Kerry — and many protestant churches fell into disuse. Bishop Moriarty, in urging disestablishment in a public letter to his clergy in 1867, had paid a notable tribute to the 'estimable and edifying' protestant clergy of the time.

Gladstone's second effort was the Land Act of 1870. This was at least an attempt to tackle that most obdurate of Irish problems. So long as there was little or no industry in Ireland — and free trade principles forbade its being fostered — the only economic resource of the vast mass of the people was the land. Irish landlords were, on the whole, a worthless and frequently a heartless lot, so there was not adequate agricultural development. Thus a poor, desperate people seemed forever stuck in the wrongs of the 16th and 17th centuries. In 1870 Gladstone tried to protect tenants' tenure or to compensate for the loss of it; but this did not meet the problem. From the Famine to the mid-1870s there was a steady rise in agricultural prosperity and great pressure from tenants to subdivide farms. This the landlords strongly resisted. In the mid-1870s, however, the prosperous trend sharply reversed and there was a severe period of agricultural depression culminating in the famine of 1879 which in Kerry was severely felt.

A remarkable woman, Mary Frances Cusack, a Dublin-born convert to catholicism, a nun in the newly founded carmelite convent in Kenmare, a prolific writer with a flair for publicity, established in 1879 a famine relief fund and collected £15,000. Five to six hundred men and women frequented her relief stores in Kenmare

Killarney House

until they were closed down by December, 1880. She became very well known as the Nun of Kenmare, and joined in the attacks on the marquis of Lansdowne who was drawing rents from starving tenants in Kenmare. These attacks became a significant propaganda effort for the Land League, and led to the raking up of old charges about the Lansdowne scheme of assisted emigration after the Great Famine.

The Land War was on. It had two phases — under the Land League, from 1879 to 1882, and under the Plan of Campaign, from 1886 to 1890. Both phases were associated with severe agricultural depression, the first with actual famine — in 1879 the potato crop, on which so many poor people still depended, was only a quarter of what it had been in 1876. Because the depression lasted over several years, tenants used up their reserves, their stocks fell, rents fell into arrears, and they were ruthlessly evicted in large numbers. Both phases of the Land War arose from the attempt to protect tenants in arrears, and those evicted; but the basic issue became the destruction of landlordism and the changing of tenants into peasant proprietors. In both phases Kerry played a prominent part.

The Land League was founded in August, 1879, with Parnell as president and with Davitt and Dillon as driving forces. The first Kerry branch was founded in Tralee on 25 September, 1879, the second in Castleisland a few days later. The chairman of the Tralee branch was Timothy Harrington, editor of the *Kerry Sentinel* which he and his brother Edward, both natives of Castletownbere, had established in Tralee. This paper, first under Timothy and then, when he became secretary of the Irish National League, in 1881, under his brother Edward, was a forceful voice on behalf of the Land

League. Timothy was later to be, it is believed, the main author of the Plan of Campaign. Both brothers were to become MPs in the Irish party; both remained loyal to Parnell after the Split, and Edward lost his West Kerry seat in consequence. Under the Land League a formidable agitation was established and in this the priests, especially the more junior ones, took an active and leading part. A major weapon of the League was to establish unofficial land courts at which fair rents were fixed for tenants beyond which they should not pay.

Whatever about the parliamentary and political side of the agitation, the old practice of agrarian violence rapidly extended. By the end of 1880, Kerry, with Mayo and Galway, were joint leaders in the league table for agrarian violence. North Kerry was particularly affected. It had a large proportion of single young men, because of a sharp decline in marriage coupled with the general slump in emigration — the population of the county actually rose by over 2% between 1871 and 1881. Butter prices fell sharply and the number of cows and pigs also fell sharply. Kerry had the highest eviction rate for the first nine months of 1880. So, incomes were severely reduced, disorder rapidly increased, and there were many young, unencumbered men to express forcibly their discontent.

The agrarian agitators followed their own long tradition which had been firmly established in the Tithe War. On the one hand landlords were shot and intimidated. On the other, security of tenure was maintained even against forced evictions by imposing a fierce discipline on local people. Those who attempted to take holdings from which people had been evicted and those who — when shortly afterwards a rent strike was declared — paid any rents at all were mercilessly intimidated — by boycott, by shooting (usually in the leg), by murder, by the maiming of animals. Castleisland was a centre of really serious and prolonged disorder. The first outrage nearby occurred on 10 September, 1879, when a band of armed men reinstated in her holding the evicted Widow Leary. The hated land agent Sam Hussey retorted, in future, by burning the houses of those evicted. Fire was met by fire. Eventually, in 1884, Hussey was himself burned out. As a foreshadowing of things to come, 11 policemen in the district, disgusted by the evictions, resigned. This agrarian disorder was the work of groups, in the whiteboy tradition, called 'moonlighters'. It is claimed that the first group of moonlighters was formed in Castleisland in 1879. It was necessary to institute nightly patrols by some 140 soldiers and police to limit moonlighting in the area. A special police tax was imposed on the Castleisland area until the worst of the trouble had ceased early in 1884.

Tim Healy, at the political end, threw himself into the fray. One of his special targets was the earl of Kenmare, and along the whole of the Beare peninsula, all payment of rents was, in the autumn of 1880, apparently interdicted. In December, 1881, four Rathmore tenants of the Kenmare estate were shot in the legs for paying rent.

Gladstone, back in power, fell back on the classic British policy —

Eviction

repression under a Coercion Act, and redress. Under the first, the Land League was suppressed, and Parnell and others imprisoned. Under the second, the Land Act of 1881 at last gained the three 'F's — fair rent, free sale, and fixity of tenure. New rents were judicially fixed, that is, reduced on average by 20%. Sam Hussey, perhaps not an unprejudiced witness, says he heard Gladstone introduce the bill in a speech without notes lasting five hours but, notwithstanding much interruption, did he once lose the thread of his discourse or 'as far as I could judge he never even by accident let slip one word of truth'.

This act was a milestone in the struggle for the land in Ireland; but it did not meet the problem of tenants fallen into arrears and threatened with eviction. They were dealt with in the 'Arrears Act' of 1882 which in effect meant that the Government paid their arrears. Those measures, and the improvement in prices that occurred, took the force out of the land agitation — for the moment.

Unfortunately, another slump occurred in the mid-eighties. Between 1881 and 1886 agricultural prices fell by 30%, but judicial rents by only 20%. Trouble began once more. Again Kerry was one of the most disturbed counties, this time with Limerick and Tipperary. The political response — already broached by Tim Healy in a speech in Killarney in August, 1885 — was the Plan of Campaign launched in October, 1886, by Dillon, William O Brien and Timothy Harrington, but with little or no support from Parnell. This Plan involved offering the landlord what the tenants considered a fair rent. If he refused, the rents would be used instead to support evicted tenants. This involved, in addition, raising substantial sums abroad, a

120   difficult task. By mid-1886 there were on the Kenmare estate
eight National League branches adjudicating on tenants' grievances
and laying down courses of action. Locally, evictions were met with
boycott, intimidation and violence. In Kerry, as elsewhere, the
landlords, taking a lesson from the tenants, joined in landlords'
associations for mutual help, but nonetheless in 1886 reduced rents
by from 20% to 35%. In consequence, the Kenmare estate — now in
the hands of trustees — was able to impose its own terms in 1889,
but on a Lansdowne estate in Laois both sides suffered crippling
losses.

Castleisland was the centre of widespread and sustained violence that
continued to 1889. There was also trouble in the west of the county
— a large force of police sent to carry out evictions in the
Ballyferriter area met such a determined local mobolisation that they
were forced to retire. Generally, Kerry was the most lawless county
at that time, with Clare close behind. In consequence, civil and
military affairs in these two counties were put under the command
of General Redvers Buller in 1886.

Buller was soon siding with the tenants against the landlords: 'you
must alter the law if you are to have peace'. Early in 1887 occurred
the famous 'Glenbeigh evictions' on the Headley estate, which even
some unionists called cruel and unnecessary. These evictions
became a big issue for English radicals and, of course, Irish
nationalists. They were a source of considerable embarrassment to
the government.

The Tories were now in power and the Irish chief secretary was
Balfour, Salisbury's nephew, an able, active and tough antagonist.
Again repression under a Perpetual Crimes Act and the suppression
of the most troublesome National League branches in Kerry and
Clare. Again, redress under the Land Act of 1887. Balfour seems to
have been able to engineer a rescript from Rome condemning the
Plan of Campaign and its support by the clergy; but the Irish
bishops managed to gloss it over. The Plan dragged on until the
end of 1890, with some success to its credit. Then, the Parnell
split absorbed all Irish political energies.

Landlordism assailed on two sides — by the bullets and buckshot of
tenants and by the law that sharply reduced its profitability — soon
collapsed and in the next forty years almost completely disappeared
as the tenants got the right to buy their land with money advanced
by the state. But it did not go down without a fight, especially in
Kerry. Michael Davitt, the founder of the Land League, said in
Castleisland in 1886 that in just over the three preceding years,
1600 families had been evicted in that county.

One of the landlords shot in Kerry was Arthur Herbert of
Killeentierna, Castleisland. He was a magistrate, turbulent and
contemptuous of the people. At petty sessions at Brosna he
regretted publicly that he was not in command when a riot occurred
in the village when he would have 'skivered the people with
buckshot'. He was killed three days after giving a decisive vote

against a home ruler as chairman of the Tralee board of guardians.

Shooting landlords has been the subject of many good stories. There
was a famous landlord in Tipperary called Carden who was called
'Woodcock' for having so often missed being shot. Another
Tipperary landlord from the famous, or infamous, family of Scully
stood for election in Kerry. Inquiries were made of a Tipperary
man about him and got the answer: 'I don't know this gentleman
personally, but I believe we have already shot the best of the family'.

That is one of the innumerable stories in Sam Hussey's
Reminiscences of an Irish Land-Agent — he was perhaps the most
considerable in Ireland — who was also called after the woodcock.
He replaced Thomas Gallwey as the agent of the earl of Kenmare's
119,000 acre estate in Cork, Kerry and Limerick in 1874. In 1882
he personally received rents of almost £81,000 from 4,600 tenants
in Kerry and adjacent parts of Cork and Limerick. He was senior
partner in the firm of Hussey and Townsend which collected
£139,000 a year from 4,800 tenants all over Munster — one of the
leading businesses of the time. Hussey tells the story of the priest
inveighing against whiskey drinking: 'It's whiskey makes you bate
your wives; it's whiskey makes your houses desolate; it's whiskey
makes you shoot your landlords, and' — with emphasis, as he
thumped the pulpit — 'it's whiskey makes you miss them'!

A hated agent in north Kerry was George Sandes. In one episode,
in 1881, he refused his permission for a tenant to marry unless he
were paid £200 of the wife's £300 dowry. He was also a noted
womaniser and according to local report, given to Fr Gaughan,
died 'the gander's death'.

So ended the long struggle for the land. In Kerry it had taken a
century to despoil the people of their only economic resource. For
another century they had been the helpless victims of the landlords.
At the end of the third century and after the atrocious catastrophe
of the Great Famine, they had at length won back the land and
their landlords were almost completely dispossessed.

Balfour, as part of the policy of 'killing home rule with kindness',
took an interest in western development. One example of this was
his encouragement of the baronial railways that led to Dingle and
Cahersiveen being linked with the national system. Another
example, a by-product of the Land Act of 1891, was the setting up
of the Congested Districts Board whose work in establishing piers,
accomodation roads and housing earned great praise. The CDB's
inspectors calculated that west Munster was the least distressed of
the congested areas — that a good farm in the Dingle peninsula
might earn an annual income of £60, against £40 on Aran and £20
in Connemara.

Already, another struggle had begun, that for independence.
Gladstone's two home rule bills, of 1886 and 1893, had failed.
Parnell had been broken; (61 Kerry priests had in 1891 protested
against his leadership on 'moral and political grounds') and he had

Sam Hussey

died. In the election of 1892 the anti-Parnellites took the four Kerry seats. The lesson of the conjuncture of three traditions — parliamentary, revolutionary, and agrarian — had to be learned again before progress could be made. This time a fourth, the tradition of the old gaelic culture, was to make a big contribution.

As the century wore on the numbers speaking Irish as a vernacular sharply declined and its literature of a thousand years was coming to an end. At the same time there had grown up a scientific curiosity about Ireland's past. Much of this was stimulated by the ordnance survey of Ireland from 1827, and the brilliant group involved in it, especially Petrie and O Donovan. The survey made clear the great quantity of antiquities that were in the country, and the surveyors wrote letters to headquarters about their discoveries. Most of the Kerry letters were written by O Donovan. Two of the pioneers of the revival of the interest in Irish archaeology and early architecture

after the middle of the century were Charles Graves, bishop of Limerick, Ardfert and Aghadoe, who had a house at Parknasilla, and the earl of Dunraven, at Garinish, Sneem, nearby, whose magnificent book of photographs of ancient Irish buildings was edited by Miss Margaret Stokes. Archdeacon Blennerhasset Rowan made a significant contribution to the concern with Kerry's past, especially from the cromwellian period, and the *Kerry Magazine,* 1854-6, which appeared monthly, had him as editor and major contributor; it was a most valuable paper. In the same tradition, somewhat later, was Miss Mary Agnes Hickson who did most valuable work on the 17th and 18th century history of Kerry. A *History of Kerry* was published in 1871 by Miss M. Cusack, the famous 'Nun of Kenmare'. J.A. Froude contributed, to the annoyance of many, to the rising interest in Kerry's place in Irish history. Other writers, such as du Noyer of the Geological Survey, and Windele, of Cork, brought to public attention the wealth of archaeological interest in Kerry.

This growth of scholarship culminated in enthusiasm for Irish literature and a determination to save the old language, so leading to the founding of the Gaelic League in 1893. In this effort, the Irish speaking areas were believed to be crucial because here was preserved — for example at the end of the Dingle and Iveragh peninsulas — the unbroken, pre-literate culture of gaelic Ireland, a well from which the whole movement could be irrigated. This concern with old Irish values also spilled over into writing in English.

A main contributor to this cultural and national revival was the Gaelic Athletic Association founded in 1884. Its aim was to revive and develop the playing of old Irish field games. For Kerry its significant achievement was the evolution of a brand of football, a cross between association and rugby. Kerry soon became the county where this game, gaelic, was played to best and widest effect, and the county team has long been the champion at this game, winning nearly a third of all-Ireland county championships since then.

In the concerted effort based on these four traditions, Kerry was to play a big part that, especially in that county, was to end in most bitter tragedy.

The foundations of the major economic resource of the county began to be extended. From the 1750s, Killarney had been a famous tourist centre, but a century later the coming of the railway and of Queen Victoria put it firmly on the map. In the 1890s the county as a whole began to be opened up, and railway lines were laid to Dingle, Cahersiveen and Kenmare. The railway company built, or acquired, hotels at Killarney, Caragh Lake, Waterville, Parknasilla and Kenmare.

From 1898 a fully democratic system of local government applied to the whole of Ireland. The nominated, landowning grand jury was, for the most part, replaced by the elected county council — the landlords were replaced by the rising middle class. Underneath the county council continued the elected boards of guardians concerned with health and assistance problems. Other local problems were dealt with by nine district councils. Already, the three urban areas of

122 Tralee, Killarney and Listowel had acquired democratic local government. Now also were constituted six rural district councils coinciding with the poor law union areas less the urban districts.

So, looking back over the century, to set against the appalling catastrophe of the Famine, was a record of revival. The basic issue that Ireland needed disinterested government, and with it appropriate institutions, was being grasped. The great problem of the land was well on the way to being solved. The cultural distinctiveness of the country was being articulated. Even the political issue had seemed to be within the grasp of being solved.

Perhaps the most remarkable example of this rebirth was to be seen in the rise of the church during the century. It emerged from its long eclipse, purified and strong. It re-established its full organisation. It built extensively — churches, schools, institutions. It enjoyed great political power. It opened widespread and notably successful missions, especially in English-speaking countries — Britain, Australia, the United States. It had, in a thousand years, perhaps its finest hour.

TWENTIETH CENTURY INDEPENDENCE

The nineteenth century had seen completed the undoing of the sixteenth and seventeenth century conquest of Irish land, and had seen the removal of the last vestiges of religious discrimination under law. The century had also seen the strengthening of three facets of Irish nationalism — the parliamentary, the popular agrarian, and the revolutionary. During the same century there had grown up a fourth strand, the scientific interest in Ireland's old civilisation, antiquities, and language. These four strains became the weave of twentieth century Irish nationalism, each in turn strengthening the others. With them began the great interest in the economic development of the country by forward thinking members of all groups, from unionist to revolutionary. There was severe labour unrest, especially in Dublin. Finally, there grew up a distinguished literary movement. In Kerry there was founded in 1907 the Kerry Archaeological Society which published an annual magazine of high quality until 1920. From the beginning of the century, Fr Patrick Dinneen edited the poems of the main gaelic Kerry poets and played a big part in re-kindling the old literary traditions.

(I) THE STRUGGLE FOR INDEPENDENCE

After 1911 the Irish party held the balance of power at Westminster and the Liberal government introduced a home rule bill that was held up by the House of Lords and was not due to become law until 1914, by which time the Great War was about to break out and the measure was further postponed. (Of the then marquis of Lansdowne, who ceased to be Foreign Secretary, it was said — 'he was of such eminence that when he fell, he fell upwards'). Home rule had been bitterly opposed by Ulster protestants, who saw it as Rome rule. They were vigorously supported and, at times, stimulated by English unionist politicians.

Early in 1913 they set up a defending force, the Ulster Volunteers, with ample German rifles and strong support by the Tory party and highly placed army officers. This led, in November 1913, to the setting up of a counter force by those of nationalist sentiment, the Irish Volunteers, soon with 200,000 men. Most of the members of this force followed John Redmond's line in supporting Britain in the war and many thousands of them enlisted. However, about 20,000 of them maintained the Irish National Volunteers under the leadership of revolutionaries in the fenian tradition. It was this small group of revolutionaries — now called the Irish Republican Brotherhood (IRB) — with help and encouragement from Irish-Americans, who determined on having a revolution to force Ireland's freedom, if not from Britain while she was at war, at least from the peace conference that would follow the end of the war. The 20,000 were armed with some 1,500 German rifles and inadequate munitions.

Recruiting for the volunteers began in the 1913—14 period in Kerry, and Austin Stack became their leader. In 1913 two young men who were to play prominent parts in the first Irish native government — Ernest Blythe and Desmond Fitz Gerald — came to live in the Dingle area to learn Irish — Blythe in Kinard and Fitz Gerald in Ventry. Blythe was a member of the IRB and enrolled Fitz Gerald. They organised and drilled volunteers in the Dingle area until, late in 1914, Blythe was assigned IRB duties in Dublin, and Fitz Gerald was 'exiled' by police order to Co. Wicklow.

The Kerry coast saw played out another of those tragi-comedies of which Irish history is full. The Rising was eventually fixed by the IRB and their Irish-American supporters for Easter Sunday, 23 April, 1916. Through the German embassy in Washington, it was arranged that the Germans would land 20,000 rifles, 10 machine guns and ammunition at Fenit harbour in Tralee Bay in time for the Rising which was to extend to the whole of Ireland. From Fenit the guns were to be sent by a captured train towards Cork, to Limerick and to Athenry, which was to be the centre of the whole rising. Even if the guns could have been landed, a formidable undertaking in itself, the distribution in this way would have been a major undertaking and unlikely to have succeeded. Nonetheless, the northern unionists had landed 24,000 guns at Larne, Bangor, and Donaghadee on 24th April, 1914, and within 24 hours had distributed them throughout Ulster. The effect of success in this enterprise would be to have a rifle for every member of the volunteers. There were in the country only 6,000 troops and 10,000 police, so the two sides, if the guns were distributed, would have been reasonably well matched. Unfortunately, the difficulties of communication led to doubt about the date fixed for the arrival of the arms — the Germans working to Holy Thursday — Good Friday, April, 20—21, the Irish to Easter Sunday, April 23.

There is doubt about how confusion arose on the date the arms were to arrive. The accepted story is that the Dublin leaders changed their plans for the landing date. The rising was fixed to take place on Easter Sunday and Volunteers generally were to parade on that day.

In Tralee Bay that week-end two rendezvous had to be made. First, the *Aud* and the U–19 carrying Casement, Monteith and Bailey had to meet at about midnight on 20/21 April close to Inishtooskert. The submarine was there but the *Aud* seems to have been anchored some eight miles off near Castlegregory.

The second rendezvous was with the pilot in Fenit whose instructions were that the ship would arrive on the night of 23rd and show green lights. When he saw a ship arrive on 20th and show what he held to be blue lights — Spindler says green, but the colours may have been confused on land — he took no action, even on the following morning when the ship could still be seen. The *Aud* remained in Tralee Bay until Friday afternoon. Then because of movement by British patrol ships, set for the open sea.

Whatever the failure on shore, it appears that British naval intelligence knew all about the *Aud,* though they did not in advance tell the government authorities in Dublin, but picked it up easily that afternoon eighteen miles west of the Skelligs. It has been suggested that the British did not do this sooner because of the propaganda value of having 'German guns' landed from a German ship off the Irish coast. This would have discredited the Volunteers amongst Allied opinion. Moreover, the amount of guns was not relatively considerable, the logistics of landing and distributing them formidable and their quality was poor. They were made in Orleans for the Russians in 1902 and captured by the Germans in the war. The ammunition was incompatible with most of the other arms held by the Volunteers.

So the guns sailed away in the *Aud,* to be captured about 6 pm that afternoon and scuttled next morning in Cork Harbour.

Sir Roger Casement with two companions, Monteith and Bailey (or Beverly) had the ostensible task of supervising the landing of the arms. Casement had been in Germany on a fruitless errand of recruiting Irish members of the British army, prisoners of war in German camps, to join an Irish Brigade to fight for Irish freedom. His real, apart from ostensible, purpose in arriving now was, it seems, to dissuade the leaders against the projected rising, because there would be no effective German intervention on their behalf. The submarine was at the place appointed ten minutes after midnight and spent a couple of hours vainly searching for the *Aud* which was not at the rendezvous. The submarine then went across the Bay to within two miles of Banna Strand. Here at about 1.15 am GMT Casement and his companions were put in a dinghy and they landed, after once capsizing, on Banna Strand between Fenit and Ballyheigue. There is now a memorial near this spot. They were armed but buried their guns in the sand.

Casement, who had been ill before leaving Germany and was unable to continue further, took refuge in a secluded rath, called Mc Kenna's fort, near Ardfert. Monteith and Bailey struggled on to Tralee to seek the aid of Austin Stack, an IRB man, and leader of the

Sir Roger Casement

Florence O Donoghue argues persuasively that the Irish leaders' plans were to have the guns arrive on that night so that the gun-running would be synchronised with the actual rising; the Volunteer commanders in Kerry, Cork, Limerick, Clare and Galway were not — except possibly for Stack — told of the rising; but they were told of the planned landing of guns, each to have his men mobilised to accept his quota; and it was obvious what the outcome would be. The German planners, given the difficulties of getting the ship through the Allied blockade, required some flexibility and suggested April 20 to 23rd. This was accepted by Devoy in America, but rejected by the Dublin leaders whose countermanding messages reached the Germans after the *Aud,* which had no radio, had sailed. As luck and good seamanship would have it, she reached her destination at the earliest date, the 20th. The crucial problem was that of communications — not well developed in 1916 and much disrupted by the war. Whatever the reasons, the Volunteers who had been mobilised in, e.g. Cork and Kerry for a major gun-running effort, were dismissed on Easter Sunday evening and took no part in the rising that had been re-fixed for the following day.

The German arms ship under Karl Spindler and disguised as the Norwegian freighter *Aud* arrived, after astonishing adventures, at the rendezvous of Inishtooskert, the most exposed of the Maharee islands off Castlegregory, on the afternoon of Holy Thursday and spent that afternoon and part of the night vainly cruising around the bay looking for the lights and pilot agreed upon for the landing at Fenit. Eventually, she anchored in Tralee bay, but where is a matter of controversy.

124 Volunteers in Kerry. They took refuge in Spicer's shop in Tralee and sent messages to Stack to seek them out. After what seemed great delay, he came with his deputy, Con Collins. A car containing Stack, Collins and Bailey, as well as Miss Spicer, immediately set out to collect Casement. By this time he had been arrested by the RIC in Ardfert. Stack and Collins were also arrested and so, later that day, was Bailey, who told the whole story. During all this time the *Aud* was still in Tralee Bay, but no one seems to have attempted to seek it out.

Monteith, a soldier of some experience, found himself in command of about 320 volunteers who assembled in Tralee on Easter Sunday. The general plan seemed to be – but in Stack's absence no one seemed to be sure – to capture the military barracks, the police stations, telegraph offices and railway stations, to unload the arms ship at Fenit, and dispatch special trains to Killarney, Limerick and Galway; but according to Monteith no detailed plans were available, the Volunteers were outnumbered by the militia and the police, and the element of surprise had been lost. Nonetheless, the men paraded on the Sunday, but when Mac Neill's order countermanding the rising was received about noon, the men dispersed. Monteith escaped with a group of volunteers from Ballymacelligott and then, for the next week, moved from house to house in the Glounageentha area until he was at last spirited by car to his home ground in Limerick, and eventually escaped to America.

On Good Friday morning, five Volunteers set out from Dublin for Killarney by train. Two cars from Limerick met them there and they set out for Cahersiveen to take two wireless installations from there and erect one at Ballyard, Tralee, to help with the arms landing, and the other at Athenry. One of the cars, with the only wireless expert on board, took two wrong turnings at Killorglin and ran out over Ballykissane pier into the sea, and three of the four occupants – including the radio man Con Keating – were drowned. The other car got to Cahersiveen to find the police there on the alert and it returned to Killarney by way of Ballaghusheen.

The nominal leader of the volunteers, Eoin Mac Neill, heard only on Holy Thursday of the rising planned for the following Sunday. His scruples were overcome by news of the German arms on their way. By this means the Volunteers would be armed, and 20,000 armed men in a national uprising would make some sense. On Holy Saturday, when the news came that the arms were gone and Casement arrested, Mac Neill's scruples were again aroused and he issued an order countermanding the 'manoeuvres' announced for Easter Sunday. This prevented the national uprising on Easter Sunday. What took place on Easter Monday was an uprising by the hard core of less than 1,000 men almost entirely confined to Dublin. Thus, the failure to contact (and empty) the *Aud* in Tralee Bay on Holy Thursday and Good Friday had a decisive effect on the events of the time. There was another effect.

That week-end without any intervention by the Tralee Volunteers, Roger Casement took the journey to London, to trial as the only

Austin Stack

British 'traitor' in the war, and to a high place in the gallery of Irish heroes.

Bernard Shaw, writing a petition to save Casement's life, pointed out that Casement had not become a national hero in Ireland:

There is, however, one infallible way by which that can be

done; and that is to hang him. His trial and sentence have already raised his status in Nationalist Ireland; but it lacks the final consecration of death. We urge you very strongly not to effect that consecration......[Reprieved] Casement will be harmless, disabled by his own failure. On a British scaffold he will do endless mischief.

He died on that scaffold on 3 August, 1916. Later, it was an embittered IRA man in Frongoch internment camp who said : 'Casement's ghost haunts Kerry'. To commemorate the first anniversary of Casement's execution, some 12,000 people assembled at McKenna's Fort where he was arrested. Thomas Ashe, himself soon to die, made a memorable speech. Now at 'loney Banna Strand' there is a memorial near the place where Casement landed.

In comparison with the drama of Casement and the *Aud*, the remainder of Kerry's part in the struggle for Irish Independence was humdrum enough.

Three Kerrymen played a prominent part in the national scene. First there was the brave, gallant, talkative The O Rahilly (born 1875 at Ballylongford). He was editor of *An Claidheamh Soluis* and invited Eoin Mac Neill to write the famous article 'The North Began' — organising for independence. It was The O Rahilly who convened the meeting at which the Irish Volunteers were founded in November 1913. He was killed in the withdrawal from the General Post Office in Easter week 1916.

Second, was Thomas Ashe (born 1885 at Kinard, Lispole) a teacher in north county Dublin, a prominent 'political' in the Gaelic League and a well-known piper. He was the leader of a party from Co. Meath and Co. Dublin which attacked the RIC barracks at Ashbourne, Co. Meath and ambushed a party of reinforcements of fifty-six police in seventeen motor cars. Ten police died and fifteen were wounded. The reinforcements after five hours surrendered. Two days later, thirty-two volunteers surrendered to the military. This was one of the very few actions — and the most important and successful of them — outside Dublin during that week. It was to set a headline — little comprehended at the time — for much of the guerilla activity in later years. Ashe was condemned to death, but reprieved. He wrote from prison of 'the happiness I felt while awaiting sentence of death in Kilmainham prison. It was a beautiful experience'. Ashe wrote a rather mawkish poem 'Let me carry your Cross for Ireland, Lord'. He was released in June 1917 and became acting President of an interim group to re-organise the Supreme Council of the IRB. After eight weeks of freedom he was arrested again in August 1917. With others — including Austin Stack and Fionan Lynch — he went on hunger strike so that they might be treated as political prisoners, and, after forcible feeding, died of neglect. His death and spectacular funeral, and the strong condemnation by the inquest jury of the manner of that death, contributed to the big swing in public opinion away from the British connexion.

Third, was Austin Stack (born 1879 near Tralee) who played the not very distinguished part in the Casement and *Aud* stories. He served terms in various jails and underwent many hunger strikes. He was the leader of the prisoners who smashed up Belfast Jail in November, 1918. He escaped from jail in Britain in October, 1919 and became Minister for Home Affairs in the government set up by the second Dail in 1921. He was one of the two members of the seven-man cabinet who followed Mr. de Valera in opposing the Treaty. He took part in the fighting on the republican side during the civil war and was deputy chief-of-staff. He died in 1929.

The O Rahilly

126

During 1917 the tension began to rise. Volunteers paraded and drilled and the police harassed their leaders. In July, a volunteer, Daniel Scanlon, was shot in a riot outside the police station at Ballybunion. In August there was the Casement Commemoration. Then there was the death of Thomas Ashe. In early 1918 there was the great agitation to fight the extension of conscription to Ireland. Tension heightened at every incident. The stage was being set for widespread and bitter conflict.

Kerry illustrates much of the military tactics of the struggle that ensued; but little of its positive or creative side.

Thomas Ashe

Elections were held at the end of 1918 and the Sinn Fein revolutionary party received a large majority in Ireland as a whole. They gained all four seats in Kerry: the sitting Irish party members did not go forward. The elected Irish members of Parliament opposed to the Union met in Dublin on 21 January, 1919 and constituted the First Dail, or Irish Parliament. This parliament elected a government which set up a rival administration to that of the British, and one that was largely successful in reducing British government in Ireland to impotence.

On the same day as the first Dail met, but unconnected with that event, two policemen were shot dead in Tipperary. This was the beginning of the military struggle. The major military objective on the Irish side was to make the country ungovernable. One means of doing this was to make life intolerable for the main agent of government, the police. Thus, their barracks were attacked and burned — especially the outlying ones — they themselves lived in mortal danger, they were publicly ostracised, and great pressure was put on them, as Irishmen, to resign. From early in 1920 this policy was followed with great resolution in Kerry. Thus, a lot of the fighting consisted of attacks on police barracks and the disarming of police, so as to have arms for more attacks. For example, the police inspector at Dingle had responsibility for the police barracks at Anascaul, Ballyferriter, Camp, Castlegregory and Cloghane. All of these had to be evacuated, and they were destroyed. (The Dingle barracks went in the civil war). Coast guard stations were also objects of attack; and their gaunt remains, as well as of the curiously placed police barracks (such as at Ladies View), are reminders of these struggles. There were also ambushes of military parties and, of course, of Black and Tans and Auxiliaries. Big houses were also raided for arms.

By 1919 the IRA in Kerry was organised in two brigades — one based on Tralee for north and west Kerry, and the other based on Killarney for the rest of the county. Each was divided into battalions, and these into companies, being fifty or so activists from three or four neighbouring parishes.

It is claimed that the first police barracks in Ireland to be attacked since Ashe's exploit in 1916 was that at Gortatlea in April, 1918, that is nine months before the real struggle began: the attackers had been beaten off after two of them had been killed. Over a year later, in June 1919, two policemen were disarmed at Meenascorthy, Camp. In January and February, 1920 began the first of the attacks on 'big houses' when the Stoughton house, Ballyhorgan, near Rattoo was twice attacked and damaged. It was later destroyed.

However, the real struggle in Kerry did not begin until March, 1920 In the sixteen months to July, 1921 — when the Truce that ended the fighting with Britain took effect — there were numerous similar 'incidents', as well as many isolated killings on both sides. The constabulary, although armed with carbines, had not been recruited for such work, and in June, 1920 there was a highly significant and, in some ways, crucial 'mutiny' of fourteen of them in Listowel. This followed a pep speech by the Munster RIC Commissioner, Col Smyth, who told them 'the more you shoot, the better I like it'. He was himself soon afterwards shot dead in Cork. Similar trouble occurred with the constables in Milltown. A number of constables resigned. Disorders, resignations, and scarcity of recruits for the police led to the recruitment from March 1920 of the Black and Tans and, from August 1920, the Auxiliaries. Both of these were intended to stiffen the police. The Auxiliaries were Churchill's idea. Both forces did much to free Ireland, because their unbridled behaviour stiffened popular support for the rebels, the essential ingredient of successful guerilla activity. Reprisals led to counter-reprisals and in Tralee a headline in atrocities was set — that was to have grim echoes in the civil war — when two Black and Tans were flung alive into a flaming gas retort. In October, 1920, after a number of constables had been killed and wounded, two in the Tralee area were kidnapped. In an abortive attempt to force their release, the military from October 31 to November 10, kept the town under a state of siege. The County Hall and a number of business premises were set on fire, and to this we owe the very attractive Thomas Ashe Memorial Hall — the head-quarters of the county council — that now graces the town. In December 1920, all Kerry was put under martial law.

The most severe of the attacks on the military in Kerry was that at the railway station of Headford Junction on 21 March, 1921. A party of thirty British soldiers from Kenmare was attacked at the junction while they waited for a train to Killarney. They suffered twenty-six casualties before the engagement was interrupted by the arrival of the Killarney train full of soldiers. In April, 1921, the Gun Mahony home, Kilmorna House, was destroyed and the ageing tenant, Sir Arthur Vicars, was found shot dead in the grounds, apparently for being a spy. He had been Ulster King of Arms in Dublin Castle when the Crown Jewels, in his custody, had had been stolen in 1907: he was sacked for negligence. He was a brother of Gun Mahony, owner of the house and had, at least, been foolhardy in entertaining Black and Tans, despite a warning of the possible consequences. In May, Ballyheigue castle was also destroyed.

At the civil level, two crucial steps were taken to give effect to the establishment of a rival government. These were the setting up of district and county courts, supported by a republican police force, with the consequent boycotting of British courts and the switching of allegiance of the local authorities from the King's government to that of the new republic. Both these steps earned widespread public support. At the local elections of January, 1920, the Sinn Fein candidates won extensive majorities. Kerry (and West Limerick) returned the same eight Sinn Fein members in the general election of 1921 to the Second Dail. Two Kerrymen were members of the subsequent cabinet — J.J. O Kelly (Sceilg) was minister for Education, and Austin Stack, minister for Home Affairs, responsible, under its secretary, Dan Browne, a Listowel solicitor, for setting up a rival court and police system to that of the British. This achieved considerable success in diverting 'business' away from the British system.

Fighting against Britain ceased with the Truce of July, 1921. There followed the Treaty of December, 1921. Many of those who fought in the struggle, headed by Mr. de Valera, who had been president of the revolutionary government of 1919, and who was supported by Austin Stack, believed that the terms negotiated with the British and accepted by the majority were not favourable enough. Those who had fought for freedom split into two armed camps. During this period of the Truce and its aftermath, the practice of setting fire to the 'Big Houses' was consolidated; Derreen went up in flames, and Derryquin, near Sneem, and Headley Towers at Glenbeigh, remain as gaunt reminders of the social and agrarian undertow of the political struggle. It was during this period, too — in March, 1922 — that Mr de Valera made those speeches long held against him, including that at Killarney when he said that those committed to defend the Republic 'will have to wade through Irish blood'. The same eight deputies were returned to the Third Dail in 1922; but now they had split: three for the Treaty and five against.

(II) THE CIVIL WAR

Eventually civil war broke out — on 28 June, 1922. For a while the lightly armed Irregulars (as the republicans were called) held the whole south of Ireland against Government troops. On 30 June, the Government troops in Listowel, after a fight, surrendered to the Irregular commander, Humphrey Murphy, who now had command of all Kerry. However, the main group of the Irregulars was defeated near Kilmallock after a 14 day battle on 5 August. Shortly afterwards the Government was in substantial control of the whole country. Thus, on 2 August, Government troops from Limerick, under Brigadier Patrick O Daly, landed at Fenit and with little opposition occupied Tralee. On the following day, 240 troops from Kilrush landed at Tarbert and took Ballylongford and Listowel. A third column from Newcastlewest linked up with these and the troops soon overran north Kerry.

South Kerry was, as usual, more difficult, and was approached by sea. On 10 August, two small ships sailed from Limerick and arrived in the Kenmare River early next morning. A sortie on the coastguard station of Lackeen, at Blackwater, led to its evacuation and firing by the republicans. The troops, under a local man, Brigadier Tom (Scarteen) O Connor, marched to Kenmare, their ships meeting up with them again at the pier. Kenmare was abandoned by the republicans without a fight; they retreated into the nearby mountain fastness. On 23 August, O Connor, with 100 men, sailed from Kenmare to Valentia and, the following day, with little trouble, occupied Cahersiveen, and on the 25th, Waterville. O Connor, with his men thus widely dispersed, returned to Kenmare. On 9 September, the republicans surprised Kenmare and, taking O Connor and his brother John from their beds, shot them dead. The republicans, under the command of John Joe Rice, were to hold the town until nearly Christmas. It was in September that there occurred the curious incident when HMS *Barrington*, probably

127

Memorial at Ballyseedy

unwittingly, landed marines at Lackeen Pier, Blackwater, and found herself attacked by a hail of bullets before she retired to Castletownbere. Later in the month a determined, but unsuccessful, attempt was made to recapture Killorglin.

From August until May, 1923, when the fighting stopped, the Irregulars waged guerrilla warfare on the troops. They held out in hunted groups in the wild mountain countryside stretching from the Dingle mountains to Waterford, and in this area there were many inconclusive skirmishes reminiscent of the Desmond wars of over three centuries previously. One of the main Irregular centres was in the wild country above Lough Guitane, near Killarney. During the months of disorder many old scores against landlords were worked off, and the 'Big Houses' were looted and set in flames.

The civil war was fought in Kerry more bitterly than anywhere in Ireland. In general, the majority of the people of Kerry sympathised, at least, with the Irregular side. In the spring of 1923 there were a number of 'incidents'. The troops, hurriedly recruited and ill-trained, subjected to the strain of guerrilla attacks, got completely out of hand and, eventually, their acting commander, Brigadier O Daly, was removed. The breaking point came in March, 1923. A Lieutenant O Connor from the Castleisland area, accused of torturing prisoners in Castleisland, was with four others blown up by a booby trap at Knocknagoshel on 6 March. One of the methods of government in

those days — borrowed from British practice — was the 'reprisal', and in the early hours of 7 March, at Ballyseedy Cross near Tralee, nine prisoners from Tralee were roped around a land mine; one was, miraculously, blown free. Later that night, five prisoners from Killarney were led to a similar fate at Countess Bridge. Again, one of them escaped. On 12 March, five prisoners were blown up at Bahaghs, Cahirsiveen. Later in the month, and in April there was a good deal of indiscriminate shooting of prisoners and others. In April occurred the episode of Clashmealcon caves in the cliffs above Kerry Head. Six irregulars were besieged in the caves by troops for three days and two nights. In the end, two irregulars were drowned, one fell down the cliffs, and the three who surrendered were executed in Tralee.

Casualties amongst the troops were relatively heavy — sixty-nine were killed and one-hundred-and fifty-nine were wounded.

All these events left an intense undercurrent of bitterness in Kerry. However, the fine memorial at Ballyseedy transcends all this and commemorates the names of more than one-hundred Kerrymen volunteers who, in Ireland as a whole, died in the fighting in the seven years 1916—23, about half of them in the civil war. All over the county one sees the (now) rather dingy memorial crosses for those who died by the roadsides in those years. These memories, particularly of the civil war, for long nourished a tradition of violent revolutionary politics in Kerry, a tradition still not wholly spent.

(III) INDEPENDENCE

In the first permanent government of the independent part of Ireland, there served one Kerryman as minister, Fionan Lynch, minister without portfolio; he afterwards served, until 1932, as Minister for Fisheries. Another Kerryman, Professor John Marcus O Sullivan, later became minister for Education. Since 1932 no Kerryman has reached ministerial office. In the 1923 election Kerry, now without West Limerick and with seven seats, returned three pro-Treaty members and four anti-Treaty ones.

When Mr. de Valera returned to politics after the civil war and won political victory from military defeat, Kerry gave him solid support, usually in the 1930s with five of the seven Dail seats for the county. But the revolutionary tradition did not die, and the Irish Republican Army, when it developed an active policy in the late 1930s and the 1940s, first by bombings in England and later against Mr. de Valera's policy of neutrality during World War II, had Kerrymen prominent in its leadership and support. Its leader for a time, until he was interned, was Sean Harrington from Ballyduff. Two famous IRA leaders, Frank Ryan, released from a Spanish jail, and Sean Russell sailed by U boat for Smerwick harbour in August, 1940 but Russell died on the voyage and the U boat returned to Germany where Ryan later died.

Six IRA activists were executed by the Dublin government during World War II. Of these, two were Kerrymen — Michael O Neill from

Cahirsiveen and Charles Kerins from Tralee. O Neill was executed in 1942, convicted by a military court of being implicated in, but not actually, shooting a policeman in a Dublin police raid of November, 1942. Kerins was chief of staff of the IRA and was executed for being implicated in the murder of police sergeant O Brien outside his house in Dublin in September, 1942. It is said that this shooting was in punishment for revealing to the Northern Ireland police that a supply of arms had been sent from Kerry through Dublin to Belfast. This led to a police raid in Belfast in which one policeman and one IRA man were killed, and to the subsequent execution of another IRA man. Kerins evaded capture, but was executed in December, 1944. The executions of O Neill and Kerins led to major political storms and alienated many Kerrymen from Mr de Valera's government.

There seem to have been seven German spies at work — some very briefly indeed — in Ireland during World War II of whom four had some connexion with Kerry. The most famous, Herman Goertz, arrived in Ireland in May 1940, and tried to escape by trawler from Fenit in February 1941, but the Irish police picked up his IRA collaborators and a British patrol boat waited outside the three-mile limit. Another spy, Karl Anderson, landed by U boat in Dingle Bay in June, 1940, but was arrested in Dublin a day later. The third, Gunther Schuetz, escaped from jail in February, 1942, and was to have sailed by trawler from Dingle a month later; but on the day fixed for sailing, the skipper and crew were arrested. The fourth, Willy Preetz, landed in Dingle Bay early in the same month, got to Dublin, and was arrested a few weeks later.

Much of Kerry's local spirit is now worked out in the extraordinary prowess on the football field. Much of it also went into the intense missionary effort of the 20th century Irish church, so that for every two priests working at home there was another in the missions overseas. Many Kerrymen achieved distinction in this field, paralleling, as it did, the most famous period of the Irish church. Indeed, the growth of the numerical strength of the church in the 20th century has been remarkable. In 1901, for the country as a whole, priests numbered just 3,500 and brothers and sisters, just over 9,000. By 1970 these figures had become just over 6,000 and just over 17,000 respectively — this for a virtually static population. In Kerry diocese where the decline in catholic population in the period was just 30%, from 175,000 to 125,000, the number of diocesan priests rose by almost the same percentage, from 120 to 153. This is a rise in the ratio of diocesan priests to people of 80% approximately.

Much of the local spirit too is applied to the solid work of building a new society at home. So the potentialities of Kerry's great economic resource, tourism, are steadily developed, towns and villages — notably Sneem — cleaned and brightened up, and the stirrings of economic development reaching places whose economies had hardly changed for four or five thousand years. Institutions are being adapted and changed. In the 1920s the poor law unions and

the rural districts were incorporated in the county council. In the 1930s special committees of the county council were set up to develop agricultural advisory services and vocational education.

Tralee has its own vocational education committee. Kerry is now divided into two parliamentary constituencies, each returning three members to the Dail — North Kerry (the traditional north Kerry, less the Dingle peninsula), and South Kerry, including for this purpose the Dingle peninsula.

From the uttermost part of this peninsula came the last brillant flame of a doomed society. In 1925 Tomas O Criomhthain published in Irish his autobiography of a Great Blasket islander, *An tOileanach,* one of the most notable books written in Irish. (It was translated as *The Islandman* by Robin Flower who has also written a book about the island). In the late 1930s came another fine book in the same genre from the island, *Fiche Blian ag Fas* by Muiris O Suilleabhain (translated as *Twenty Years A-Growing*). In the next decade came one from that queen of story tellers, Peig Sayers, *Peig* (translated under the same title. A decade later the island was deserted — the remaining people being moved by the Land Commission to less unproductive holdings on the mainland, still, in that strip facing the islands, Irish speaking. But that strip is itself declining fast. In 1841, in the five civil parishes that form the official Gaeltacht of the Dingle peninsula, the population was over 8,300; by 1961 it was only a quarter of that figure. In that 120 years, the population of Ireland as a whole fell to a half; but the population of this place fell to a quarter. Nonetheless, it maintains a considerable intellectual

Peig Sayers at home

130

and artistic vitality and a number of books continue to be written from there and published — some fifty in as many years.

Kerry has two fine writers in English, both living in Listowel — Bryan Mac Mahon, short story writer and novelist, and John B Keane, principally a playwright.   Two earlier writers from there were George Fitz Maurice and Maurice Walsh.

The work of preserving and presenting the records of Kerry's past was continued. Exiled gentry from Kerry organised in London, the County Kerry Society, the annual reports of which, mainly of geneaological interest, appeared between 1922 and 1940. In the 1930s and 1940s major work on the place names of Iveragh, Trughanacmy and, notably, Corkaguiney was done by Padraig O Siochfhradha (An Seabhach) who also edited for publication *An tOileanach*.   Between 1936 and 1940, Commander D.B. O Connell organised the County Kerry Archaeological Survey and voluntary workers throughout the county brought to light many treasures of the past, the most curious being a bronze age basin still in use for feeding hens. In 1967 was founded the Kerry Archaeological and Historical Society which has produced annually since 1968 a distinguished journal. Much detailed work has also been reported in various learned journals. In 1963 Muckross House, Killarney became a Kerry museum under local trustees, and in 1970 Derrynane, the ugly home of Daniel O Connell, shed of his grand-father's appealing house, became a museum under the Office of Public Works.

A striking demographic change has been the sharp decline of the protestant population of Kerry. Between 1881 and 1961 it fell from just under 6,000 to just over 1,300, from just under three per cent of the population to just over one per cent. The latter proportion has not much changed since 1926. The decline has led to a reduction of the parishes into eight unions. In recent years, the decline has been caused, according to an analysis by H. W. Robinson, by deaths exceeding births, by emigration (though this has been less severe than in the Kerry population as a whole), and by mixed marriages with catholics, where the children are brought up as roman catholics. The distribution of occupations of protestants in Kerry differs little from that of protestants in the Republic as a whole and this, contrary to popular belief, is little different from that of the population as a whole. Nearly half of the Church of Ireland population in Kerry — and its heart — are farmers in the area between Tralee and Killarney, the continuing descendants of English and Palatine farmers brought into the rich land of Trughanacmy by landlords now gone. Of the Church of Ireland surnames nearly a quarter are comprised in four — Blennerhasset, O Neill (including Neill), Boyle and Fitzell, this last a Palatine family; and about a sixth in names more to be expected — Mason, Parkinson, Stephens, West and Wharton. In recent years some reinforcement of the protestant population has come from the influx of Germans and English concerned with establishing new industry in Kerry and future growth of the population will, perhaps, depend on this and related kinds of immigration. But

of the great protestant families -- Crosbie, Denny, Chute, Bland, Headley — all are totally gone. and of the Godfreys and Herberts there are but two each.   The names of only the Blennerhassets (55) and the Days (11) survive.

Some insight into the general social and economic state of Kerry during the 1960s can be gleaned from the south west regional plan of the Industrial Development Authority, 1972. These insights are limited because the results of the 1971 census are not fully available.

The most striking fact is that the long and calamitous decline in the population of Kerry has been stopped; but only barely: between 1966 and 1971 the total loss was 13 persons. In only one decade since the Famine has there been an actual increase in the population — between 1871 and 1881. The figures for 1961, 1966 and 1971 are:

	Males	KERRY Females	Total	STATE
Population				
1961	60,838	55,620	116,458	2,813,341
1966	58,674	54,111	112,785	2,884,002
1971	58,404	54,368	112,772	2,978,248
Change 1961—66				
Number	-2,164	- 1,509	-3,678	+65,661
Percentage	-3.4%	- 2.7%	-3.2%	+2.3%
Change 1966—71				
Number	-270	+257	-13	+94,246
Percentage	-0.5%	+0.5%	-0.01%	+3.3%

The improvement has been brought about by little change in birth and death rates but by a sharp fall in movement out of the country, especially by women.

The following table shows annual rates per 1,000 of average population 1961—66 and 1966—71:

employ all those who left agriculture. The structure of employment was as follows:

Numbers Employed in Kerry 1961—71

	1961	1966	1971*
Agriculture, forestry and fishing	22,820	20,128	17,000
Industry:			
Manufacturing	3,091	3,666	5,000
Other	1,443	2,532	2,800
Services	12,112	12,534	12,900
Totals	39,466	38,860	37,700

*   estimated*

	Kerry	State
Births		
1961—66	18.1	21.9
1966—71	17.9	21.3
Deaths		
1961—66	13.3	11.7
1966—71	13.2	11.2
Natural Increase		
1961—66	4.8	10.3
1966—71	4.7	10.1
Net Emigration		
1961—66	11.2	5.7
1966—71	4.7	3.7
Population Change		
1961—66	-6.4	+4.6
1966—71	-0.01	+6.4

In the first category shown in the table, almost all the employment is in agriculture proper. In 1971, the 20,000 acres of State forests in Kerry employed some 130 people. Full-time employment in sea-fishing seems to be of the same order of magnitude, with, perhaps, a further 200-300 employed part-time. Total seafish landings in the three harbours of Dingle, Fenit and Valentia in 1970 came to just under £200,000. Of the county as a whole, just under half was in crops and pasture. Of the farms, almost two-thirds were under 50 acres. Of the farmers, just over one-third were in 1966 over 55 years of age.

In the services sector, direct employment in the hotel business is surprisingly small despite substantial growth in hotel accommodation:

	1966	1971
Hotel employees	1,213	1,726*
Hotel bedrooms	2,194	3,533

* in 1970

The total rate of emigration from Kerry in 1966—71 was not much more than that from the State as a whole; but a lower birth-rate and a higher death-rate reduced Kerry's rate of natural increase to about half of the national rate. A striking feature was that the big short-fall of women in the county began during the decade to be slowly reduced, and the population of women began to rise.

Over the decade, the total number at work in the county declined — the rise in industrial and service employment was not enough to

Two other features of the work force are the high level of unemploy-ment ranging from nearly seven per cent to over nine per cent over the decade; and the high dependence rate — the number in the dependent age groups (0-14 and 65 and over) for each hundred in the active (15—64) age group; so that in Kerry in 1961 and 1966 for every four in the active age group there were three dependants.

Some idea of what all this comes to in money can be gauged from a paper on county incomes prepared by Miceal Ross.

O Connell museum, Derrynane

Some of the figures show Kerry's standing in relation to Irish agriculture. (Unfortunately comparable figures are not available for the other economic sectors). The gross output (that is, before £6m expenses are deducted) of agriculture in Kerry was £18m, giving Kerry the fourth highest agricultural output (after Cork, Tipperary and Limerick) in the State. This gross production figure was made up of £9m for livestock, £7m for milk and £1.5m for crops. These gave Kerry rankings of 4th, 4th and 16th respectively.

What is one to make of figures of this kind? If, demographically, the State had turned the corner by the mid 1960s and decline was succeeded by growth, Kerry (just barely) did the same five years later. If a reasonable rate of economic growth was achieved for the State as a whole during the 1960s, then income per head in Kerry is improving reasonably well. If the numbers in agriculture are due to fall in accordance with the general trend, then Kerry will need much more jobs in industry and services. Notwithstanding Kerry's large share of the tourist trade and long coastline, a rise in direct employment in hotels and sea-fishing seems to be a relatively small part of the solution of the problem of maintaining the people at work.

Culturally, the county continues to enrich itself. The Gaeltacht at the end of the Dingle peninsula may decline but its output of books continues: the county has a folk museum at Muckross since 1967 and an O Connell museum at Derrynane. In the 1960s, there grew up a new folk theatre movement, Siamsa, and in 1974 was opened at Finuge the first of what is hoped will be a network of Siamsa theatres. Again, Listowel continues its literary tradition with an annual Writers' Week. Tralee has its great Rose of Tralee festival, and almost every town and village an annual festival of its own.

If one thinks of history in terms of a special kind of people inhabiting a special kind of place, then the history of Kerry has a curious durability. For every five Kerrymen in Kerry over a century ago there are two today, and it may just be possible to maintain that number. But for every two today it was one three centuries ago, and perhaps the same three centuries before that again. Three centuries earlier, as we emerge from the mists of history, it was, just conceivably, the same.

As the men and women of Kerry look back on the long perspective of their history they can at least congratulate themselves that, like the Abbe Sieyes, they have survived. But, as they look around them at the vast debris of their history, they face, in the times to come, a great challenge to reconstruction — social, cultural and economic — and the development of a society worthy of that heritage, tattered as it is.

In 1969 the total of personal incomes in Kerry was just short of £40 million, of which just one-third (£12m) was from agriculture, a sixth (over £6m) from industry, and rather more than one-eighth (£5.5m) from the State. As a proportion of income this last was seventh highest in the twenty-six counties and compares with an average if just one-tenth for the state as a whole
average of just one-tenth for the State as a whole.

These figures are available for the three years 1960, 1965 and 1969. If we take income per head at 1969 prices for the three years and compare Kerry's showing with that for the other twenty-five counties, we find that Kerry's ranking has risen from 16th to 12 place over the period and that average income has risen over the same period by 39%.

Per Capita Income (1969 prices)

	1960	1965	1969
Kerry	£251	£291	£348
State	£293	£353	£419
Kerry's ranking	16	13	12

PART 2 THINGS

Chapter 8

The Physical Scene

In a countryside as beautiful as that of Kerry one is everywhere surrounded by 'scenery'. This is a compound of rock and soil, plants and animals, and climate. So, first, a layman's impressionistic account of these large subjects so far as they show themselves in the scenery of Kerry.

SHAPES

The geophysicists put the age of our earth at some 4,500 million years, but the recognised geological periods go back only some 2,000 million years. Of the first two-thirds of this period of 2,000 million years — the pre-cambrian — little is known. The last third, that is from some 600 million years ago, is divided into numbered periods of geological time. We know that some 600 million years ago, after a long period of evolution, life was flowing on something recognisable as our earth. The earth consists of a crust some 37 miles thick on average that rests on a 'Mantle' that flows like hot fudge under pressure. The crust is constantly being worn away by weather, and earth, sand and rocks are washed into low-lying places. Over immense periods of time these settle as new rock and, because of their great weight, cause the crust to sink into the mantle. This causes the mantle in other places to burst up through the crust where, perhaps, it has been stretched thin by the drifting apart of continents. So there is a constant movement of the landscape — erosion from high places, deposits of silt in lower ones and occasional subsidences and upheavals great and small. The geology of Ireland, and of Kerry, gives continuous examples of this attrition, of great rises and falls, of disappearance and reappearance, in the long struggle with the sea.

The various kinds of rocks reflect this constant movement. The *sedimentary* rocks are the results of past deposits: such are the sandstones and limestones that are so common in Kerry. The *igneous* rocks, such as granite and basalt, are the result of the upsurge of molten rock from the mantle. The *metamorphic* rocks, such as slates and grits, have been changed from sedimentary or igneous rocks by the pressures of gigantic disturbances.

The geological history of Ireland has been exceptionally troubled, and much of the story cannot be read because so much of what once was Ireland has been carried away. We now witness only the 'skeleton of a departed country'. The North East of Ireland has most to show of the many changes of geological time, but Kerry has its interest, with the Dingle peninsula having the longest story to tell.

From the first two-thirds of geological time, the vast period known as pre-cambrian, date the gneiss and schist of the conglomerates at Inch (e.g. along the roadway between Inch and Anascaul).

The three principal eras of geological time proper are, in order of remoteness, the *Palaeozoic* of 360 million years, the *Mesozoic* of 135 million years, and the

Sybil Head, Dingle Peninsula

Cainozoic of 65 million years. Each of these eras is divided into ages.

(I) THE BIRTH OF THE LAND

The great part of the surface of Kerry dates from the earliest of these eras, the palaeozoic. The oldest layers of rock in Kerry are the Ordovician ones of 500 million years ago stretching between Anascaul and Slieve Mish. But the county as a whole was formed in a period some 400 to 200 million years ago, substantially by two great convulsions: the Caledonian near the earlier date and the Armorican near the latter one.

At the earlier date Ireland was mainly beneath the sea flanking the great continent of Atlantis and the wreckage of that continent can be seen in the Silurian outcrops of dark-grey and bluish shales with bands of bluish and greenish

Shapes
(I) The Birth of the Land
(II) The Age of Reptiles
(III) The Long Erosion

Things   Part 2

135

grits — believed to be some 6,000 feet deep — at the west of the Dingle peninsula, which was near and under the edge of that sea. In the middle of the Silurian period — about 415 million years ago — this was part of a coral sea: the stones at Sybil Head contain, amongst others, fossils of coral. In the Silurian rocks are, also, fossils of early shellfish, the brachiopods. About this time plants first began to grow on land. Clogher Head near here was a volcano that at this time emitted large quantities of ash and lava. This was unusual for the time. Relics of this are the outcrops of the extreme western islets of the Blaskets group, as well as Inishvickillane, Beginish and Clogher Head, comprising an area of twelve miles by four, one of the most extensive lava fields in these islands.

The constant deposits caused the bottom of the sea to sink. Sometimes the deposits accumulated faster than the sinking, so the bed rose above the water; sometimes the sea bed sank faster. This pressure seems to have forced the land elsewhere to rise and so, in the great Caledonian convulsion, roughly 400 million years ago, most of what is now Ireland rose from the sea. It became part of a high continental desert.

This was worn away by sun and torrential rains until the sand accumulated in large fresh water lakes and piled high in the folds of the wrinkled earth, in the Devonian age. This became the old red sandstone that constitutes much of the high land of Kerry — perhaps to a depth of 10,000 to 17,000 feet — and gives the landscape that distinctive melting quality. The rock is brown, red or purple, but the upper (later) layers in the south are often yellow and green. The Kerry-Cork highlands are one of the two old red sandstone areas in Ireland — the other is near the Sperrin mountains. At this time, perhaps 300 million years ago, because of the weight of the deposits, the volcanoes between Lough Guitane and Loo Bridge, both near Killarney, came into violent eruption.

The sea steadily encroached on this land and in the moderately deep and tranquil waters countless organisms lived and died and left their limy substance until great deposits of limestone were built up in the carboniferous age. These deposits, for example, covered the old red sandstone of what is now south Kerry. In central Kerry, from Tralee east and from Ballybunion in the north to Killarney in the south is a belt of limestone land that gives Kerry its one fertile farming area. The tattered remnants of this limestone are still to be seen around the Middle and Lower Lakes, Killarney; it has, with great quantities of sandstone as well, been eroded from the higher places. Between Cork and Kerry later pressure has turned the limestone into slates and grits.

Gradually great deltas were formed and in a hot, moist and uniform climate these became vast swamps in which giant ferns 100 or more feet high grew and decayed, to be reduced by bacteria and pressure into coal measures. These covered almost the whole country, and in Kerry have survived in the dull lands of the north. Fortunately for the beauty of Kerry, ruthless erosion has removed them with nearly all the underlying limestone from south Kerry. In north Kerry, where the underlying limestone occasionally leaks through, the seams of coal are less than a foot thick, are impure, and so folded by the pressure from the north as to be largely unworkable.

Towards the end of the palaeozoic era, over 200 million years ago, came the great Armorican upheaval with tremendous pressure from the south that formed the east-west lines of mountains in Cork and Kerry, and valleys between that, flooded by the sea, became the bays of Tralee, Dingle, Kenmare, Bantry and the rest. This pressure from the south was so great that in some places the older rocks were forced over the newer ones — near Clogher Head where the silurian rock was forced over the old red sandstone, and in the northern flanks of the mountains south of Muckross Lake and Lough Guitane where the old red sandstone was forced over the limestone. A further effect of these pressures was to form the copper and other metals that came to be mined in Kerry.

In a period of 200 million years Kerry was formed, and for the past 200 million years the mountains of Kerry seem to have stayed above the sea and serenely watched the rise and fall of lands and continents.

(II)   THE AGE OF REPTILES

Of the mesozoic era — that time of the great reptiles — there now remains, with one exception, no record in Ireland outside the North East. Kerry, unlike most of the rest of Ireland, stayed above the sea. The exception is a tiny deposit of flint-bearing chalk at Ballydeenlea, Killarney. In the North East it was from flints of this kind that some at least of the earliest Irishmen made their tools.

(III)   THE LONG EROSION

Of the early part of the cainozoic era there remains little record in Ireland. In the middle of this era — perhaps 30 million years ago — the great mountain ranges of the world were formed in the Himalayas, Alps, Andes, Caucasus, Appenines, Pyrenees, etc. — so that, by comparison with the great age of the Kerry mountains, these are but gigantic striplings. This was an era of great volcanoes — such as the Giant's Causeway — and such eruptions occurred off the coast of Kerry.

In this long mesozoic-cainozoic period of 200 million years, Kerry was subject to ceaseless erosion, and the mountains that remain are but the worn stumps of great ranges. The debris of this spread in the various 'peneplanes', deposits left by long-vanished rivers, their careers ended abruptly by the shifting of land and sea. Some of the highest of the Irish peneplanes, of over 2,000 feet, can be seen abruptly broken by one of the features of the Kerry landscape, the Cirques (or coums). The lower peneplanes, in the 600-800 foot range and at 200 feet, are of later date. The great bays, or 'rias', of the county represent largely submerged rivers of the cainozoic era. The newly born Atlantic ocean beat on the coast and dissolved the limestone to form the semi-circular bays of Tralee and Brandon. Nonetheless, and notwithstanding the long erosion, the mountains that remain are the highest in Ireland. The highest peak is Carrantuohill (3,414 ft) in the MacGillacuddy Reeks above Killarney, and in the Reeks there are five other peaks of over 3,000 feet. Ireland's second highest mountain is Mount Brandon (3,127 ft) in the Dingle peninsula. In the county there are 88 peaks in the 2,000 to 3,000 foot range, and in

136 all 190 over 1,500 feet. Other relics of this period are the pre-glacial raised beaches of the Dingle peninsula — at Ballydavid, just south of the slipway; at the western tip of Ventry harbour intermittently between Pointanskoh and Parkmore Point; and at the eastern side of Dingle harbour, almost to the lighthouse.

(IV) THE AGE OF ICE

During most of her history Ireland has had a warm and tropical climate, but during the cainozoic era the climate cooled. Eventually, over a million years ago, glaciers began to form. One sheet of ice drove south from the midlands. Another drove north from Bantry. What is now the Kenmare River was a vast mass of ice. Ice also accumulated west of Kenmare and centred on Templenoe. It passed north through the Reeks and the mountains around Killarney and formed a

Lough Fadda, Sneem

series of moraines, in the shape of crescents, in the lowlands facing Dingle bay. The ice accumulated in the hearts of the mountains, but did not cover summits above 2,000 feet. The striations of the ice 'shod' sand, mud and boulders are to be seen on the mountainsides, as well as whale-back rocks (or *roches moutonnées*), and the debris of boulders and pebbles shed by them is scattered over the landscape, for example east of Lough Currane. Rocks have been rounded by the wearing of ice — at Lough Fadda near Parknasilla, at Moll's Gap, along the Upper Lake and Long Range, Killarney. The ice withdrew into the coums in the hearts of the mountains, and scooped out the Upper Lake, Killarney. A great glacier spread over the plain about Killarney and along the northern foot of the mountains from Headford Junction to the head of Dingle bay. It shrank back into the Reeks, shedding its debris in mounds, such as those that encircle the Gap of Dunloe. Ice

withdrew south through Glenflesk and, for a time, created a lake above Kenmare. Glaciers also barred the valleys in the Reeks, so forming wild mountain lakes. It played a geological joke near Kenmare when it left a great block of sandstone lying on top of a block of limestone. The height of Turner's Rock, due east of the tunnel on the Kenmare-Glengariff road shows groovings made by the passage of ice. The most striking result has been the lowering of such cols as the Gap of Dunloe — this by as much as 1,000 feet; the creation of the great coums on Brandon, as well as around Killarney and in the Iveragh peninsula; and the formation of dark, spectacular loughs as well as, in particular, the three Killarney lakes — the Upper Lake, as we have seen, by direct action; the Middle and Lower lakes indirectly from the dissolving in water of the layers of limestone that remained. The Kerry peninsulas show every type of mountain glaciation from past times — such as may be found today in the Alps and the Scandinavian and Alaskan mountains. The beauty of the county is a direct result of this glaciation.

The glaciers passed away 20,000 years ago but severe conditions lasted longer. The melting of the ice removed a great weight from the land so raising it in relation to the sea. Thus, about 7000 BC, Ireland was part of the European landmass, joined to Scotland, the Iberian peninsula and Denmark, but separated from England and Wales by a large river. The melting of the ice also had the effect of raising the level of the sea, and an up and down struggle between land and sea was to continue for nearly another 5,000 years. About 5600 BC, Ireland, after a considerable subsidence, became an island — but a contrary shift of a mere 600 feet would restore it as part of the continent. After lesser ups and downs, Ireland settled in its present form about 2500 BC.

PLANTS

The plants (and to some extent the animals) of a country are determined by the climate, the soil, and of course the work (and neglect) of man. Climate — which comprises temperature, moisture, and wind — governs what will or will not flourish in a given soil.

LONG LAKE, SNEEM. 2758. W.

Shapes
(IV) The Ages of Ice
Plants
(I) Climate
(II) Soil

Things   Part 2

137

The constituents of the soil are the products of geological change. The work of man determines the extent to which the advantages and disadvantages of climate and soil are used and transcended.

(I) CLIMATE

From an arctic climate at the end of the last ice age, the weather slowly improved. This permitted the growth of a tundra-like scrub and the arctic willow.

From about 5500 BC to about 2500 BC, there was the warmer 'Atlantic' climate in which birch and hazel appeared, and then the great oak forests, with holly, brambles and thorns. The weather was stormy and moist, and there was much waterlogging and peat began to grow in the hollows and around the stumps of the oak forest. Evidence of this period can be seen around Cahersiveen where tree roots embedded in peat can be seen below what is now the high water mark of the sea. Other evidence is the growth of the plants *Silene maritima* and *Asplenium marium* along the lakes at Killarney.

From about 2500 BC to about 500 BC, there was a warm, dry period, the sub-Boreal. This was the great age of forests in Ireland — pine, oak, elm, birch, alder, and hazel grow freely, and up the mountain sides.

For the next 500 years the climate was harsh. This was the sub-Atlantic period when the rainfall was higher than at present. This led to the virtual disappearance of the forests and to the great growth of peat, formed from rushes and various species of mosses. From this period date the upland — or blanket — bogs so widespread in Kerry; the oakwoods around Killarney survived this period.

Finally, for the past 2000 years, there have been no dramatic changes in climate. But the climate sharply disimproved about 1000 AD, and then sharply improved until about 1300 AD when it reached a peak, and then went into a long decline until after 1600 AD.

The present climate of Kerry is dealt with later in this chapter. The significant point

Killarney Woods

is that the mild, wet winters barely impede growth so that vigorous plants like rhododendrons get little check in winter, and mosses, ferns and liverworts continue to grow. Freeman says of the Killarney woods:

> The general impression of these natural and semi-natural woods is that their very richness makes them practically useless: in them one species preys upon another and there is little good timber available, for beauty of scene and fascination of detail are combined with perpetual decay.

(II) SOIL

The soil is the product of geological change.

The significant feature for plants is the division between the lime and the acid soils — in large measure the difference between much of north Kerry and all of south Kerry. Other soil divisions relate to sea-coasts and to marshes. These divisions also govern the overland travel of plants.

According to Lloyd Praeger, the south west (comprising west Cork and south Kerry) 'is from almost every point of view the most interesting region in Ireland for the botanist and is the area where the special features of the Irish climate and vegetation attain their most pronounced expression'. He goes on to describe Killarney, where the lime and acid soils meet, as 'a paradise for the botanist'. According to Scully, about a quarter of all the rare Irish plants are to be found in Kerry.

What is striking about the plants of western Ireland is the mingling of the Mediteranean-Lusitanian plants with American ones, a mixture not to be found elsewhere in the British Isles or in Europe. Moreover, although there are in Ireland only about two-thirds of the number of species that there are in England, a number are to be found in Ireland, including Kerry, that are not to be found in England. For this reason it is believed that the south European plants must have travelled overland before the great severance of 5600 BC' Four of the Lusitanian plants have their headquarters in Kerry — *saxifraga geum*, *saxifraga spathularis* (London pride), *arbetus unedo* (strawberry tree), and *pinguicula grandiflora* (large flowered butterwort). Of the American plants the special ones in Kerry are *sisyrinchium angustifolium* (blue-eyed grass), and *juncus tenuis*, a member of the rush family. There are, of course, many more Lusitanian and some more American plants.

The special botanical glory of Killarney is *arbutus unedo*, a Mediteranean shrub that grows there to be a fine tree — the Halls say that it grew even bigger on Mount Athos. It is plentiful in the Muckross estate and around the Upper Lake. It may have survived in the Reeks above the 2,000 foot line where the glaciers of the ice age could not reach it. Of Kerry generally the great glory is the large-flowered butterwort (*Pinguicula grandiflora*), according to Scully the most beautiful of the Irish flora. It grows in some profusion in very wet, marshy places such as mountainsides, from light-green leaves like a starfish, up to about four inches in diameter. Its flower, rather like a Parma violet, but an intense blue, (very occasionally white or lilac), grows on a stem six to nine inches tall. It is in flower from late April to early July. Other treasures

138

are the saxifrages, especially *s.spathularis* and *s. geum*. The former is the so-called 'London pride'. It is very common in Kerry, in damp rocky places. It has thick, leathery, toothed leaves, with stems six to twelve inches high bearing a panicle of numerous flowers with petals, each with a number of pink spots. It is in flower from May to July. *S. geum* is much rarer, and has hybridised itself with other forms. Its leaves are kidney-shaped and hairy, often with rounded (crenate) edges, and its petals are narrower than those of *s. spathularis* and have only one or two spots. It is in flower at the same time. The Irish spurge (*euphorbia hibernia*) is an erect herb, one to two feet high, with simple leaves and bright yellow-green flowers, grown in tufts, with very warty fruit. It is found mainly in banks. Fairly plentiful in damp meadows and marshes is the blue-eyed Canadian grass, six to twelve inches high, with its blue flowers open only in sunshine. Along damp roadsides are to be found the other American curiosity, the slender, wiry, lush *juncus tenuis*, in south Kerry, especially between Kenmare and Lauragh. The Lusitanian plants are in flower in May, June and early July, which is the best period for the botanist, the American flowers in July and August.

There is an orchid named the Kerry Orchid found in Kerry and west Cork, an erect spike four or five inches high, with a head of dense flowers; the normal colour is deep purple. It is found in pasture land.

There are many varieties of ferns, liverworts and mosses, especially in the Killarney area. Here, in the woods of Derrycunnihy, on Ross Island and around Muckross Lake, are many opportunities for the botanist. Perhaps the most striking plant in the Killarney area — especially along the Kenmare road — is *rhododendron ponticum*, introduced about

1880 and now a major problem to foresters and others; but very beautiful in flower early in May. Other places of special botanical interest recommended by Webb are Cloonee Lakes (south west of Kenmare); Derrynane; Glencar; Mount Brandon; Castlegregory; the marshes near Lixnaw; and the coast between Fenit and Ballyheigue.

(III) HUMAN ACTIVITY

For the first 2,000 years of human activity in Ireland — to about 4000 BC — there was little interference with the forests and natural growth. Then, with the first farmers, who practised shifting cultivation, the forest began to be invaded by axe and fire; elm declined and hazel, ash and birch scrub developed. Two thousand years later, metal axes began to be used and the clearance became more efficient, and heath and bog plants began to invade the exhausted soil. About 2,000 years later, perhaps because of the turmoil caused by the celtic invasions, the great forests began to spread again. With christianity came the heavy iron plough so enabling the rich soils to be cultivated, and iron axes enabled the oak trees growing there to be felled. Nonetheless, it was not until the 17th century AD that the great oak woods — that covered much of the lowlands of Kerry — were finally consumed, mainly for smelting iron, and the country reached its present appearance.

From the 16th century AD the open fields began to be enclosed and sycamore to be grown around planters' homes. The hedgerows we now see date from that time. The hawthorn, blackthorn and elder, whose white flowers so enliven the spring, owe much of their prominence to this enclosing and planting movement.

In the 18th century began to be laid out the great demesnes around landlord's houses, the most beautiful of which is, of course, that around Muckross House.

At present, the land of Kerry falls into three main classes — 594,000 acres of lowland mineral land; 440,000 acres of mountain and hill; and 129,000 acres of bog.

Fuchsia and rhododendron, such prominent features of the Kerry hedgerows, were specially introduced and liked what they found. The growth of rhododendrons introduced around Killarney and of fuchsia in the Dingle and Iveragh peninsulas is really spectacular. The fuchsia is a native of Brazil brought to England in 1778 and introduced into this country, in south west Donegal, only at the beginning of this century. It rapidly made itself at home all along the western coast.

More recently, in the latter half of the present century, the forestry service has planted large areas with conifers — pine, larch, spruce and fir — and these are growing in south Kerry with great vigour.

Amongst the most beautiful sights in spring and autumn are great tracts of golden gorse and purple heather, thriving on over-grazed hillsides and on acid soils exhausted by human malpractices.

However, those interested in wild flowers need not take all this too seriously. There is to be seen a great *variety* of plants and shrubs: about three-quarters of all the Irish plants are to be found in Kerry. A walk along the hedgerows in summer reveals a great variety of striking flowers — as obvious as fuchsia, meadowsweet, many kinds of vetch, woodbine, loosestrife, cornflower, foxglove, gorse, heathers, lings, etc., etc., etc. — easy and fragrant to gather and calling for little knowledge of plants.

(IV) GARDENS

For the lover of plants and trees in a more formal setting, much pleasure is to be obtained from two of the great gardens of Ireland set in Kerry — Muckross and Rossdohan — and a third just outside its borders, Garinish.

Muckross, near Killarney, needs no praising. It is the famous garden set in the famous grounds of the house of the Herberts on which they lavished such care for over a century until they disappeared at the end of the last century. After some vicissitudes it came into the hands of the Commissioners of Public Works who are now bestowing great care on it. To visit the garden on a fine May morning is to enjoy a rare experience.

Rossdohan, Sneem, is a much less formal affair, and it has suffered cruelly from near hurricanes that have uprooted many trees. It was begun by Samuel Thomas Heard in 1870 and is remarkable mainly for its richness of Australian and New Zealand

Plants
(III) Human Activity
(IV) Gardens
Living Things
(I) Fish

Things   Part 2

plants and great trees. It is now owned by the brothers P. and R.J. Walker.

Garinish, just off Glengariff, is a formal, Italian style garden begun by Annan Bryce in 1910 with the advice of the great gardener, Harold Peto. It contains an extraordinary richness of plants and is, of course, in an exquisite setting. It was left by Bryce's son, Roland, to the nation and is now being managed and developed by the Commissioners of Public Works.

The gardens of *Derreen*, Lauragh, are open to the public on three afternoons a week during the summer months. These gardens also date from about 1870.

Two notable private gardens, apart from Rossdohan, are those at *Garinish*, Sneem (not to be confused with the Glengariff Garinish) and *Glanleam*, Valentia.

LIVING THINGS

(I) FISH

As our world evolved geologically, so, after long periods, did various forms of life. About 400 million years ago, marine forms of life began to develop into fish as we know them. Fish are plentiful in and around Ireland, and especially in the rivers, lakes and seas of Kerry.

Kerry, especially south Kerry, is well supplied with game fish — salmon, sea trout, brown trout, a special variety of char, and unusual freshwater shad in the Killarney lakes known as Killarney shad. Perch, pike, rudd and bream, which require rich water, are virtually absent from Kerry. The fishing season is from 17 January (in some places February or March) to 12 October. Fishing in the large lakes (Killarney, Currane and Caragh) is free; generally in the smaller ones and the rivers it is preserved: but it is usually possible to rent fishing from an hotel or angling association. A licence is necessary for salmon and sea trout fishing. The brown trout, also numerous on the Dingle peninsula, tend in acid waters to be small. Indeed, none of the record Irish freshwater fish have been caught in Kerry. Nonetheless, between 1955 and 1971, Kerry waters — the Killarney lakes, River Laune,

Muckross Gardens

Glanleam Gardens, Valentia

Garinish Gardens, Glengariff

and Lough Currane — have yielded 21 'specimen' brown trout, that is, over 10 lbs in weight. Top weights have been 17¼ lbs, 12 lbs, 14 ozs, and 11 lbs, respectively. Excluding the two great limestone lakes of Mask and Corrib, where half the 'specimens' were taken, the Kerry aggregate is about one-eighth of the remainder. Overall, it ranks next to Mayo and Galway — but a long way behind them — in the county totals.

The famous fishing centre is Waterville and it is quite a sight to see in the hallway of the Butler Arms Hotel there, a day's good catch laid out for inspection and admiration. The Glenbeigh-Glencar system, and the Killarney area are also great angling centres. Fishing is for the people of Killarney a major pre-occupation and one gets the impression that nearly everyone in the town has a blue-grey boat nestling in some small creek of one or the other of the lakes. When the fish are rising, on a Sunday, and indeed on many other days, the lakes are dotted with boats.

At many places along the Kenmare River from the Inny to the Roughty, salmon and sea trout are in the summer months taken in nets, and those who like to eat these fish rather than catch them can, with some trouble, buy an occasional fish at reasonable prices.

Sea fishing is much less a pre-occupation, although a number of people in Kerry have it as a wholetime or part-time way of life. Dingle is one of Ireland's major fishing centres, but for the rest of the coast fishing is almost exclusively a very part-time occupation of a dwindling band of inshore fishermen. These catch considerable quantities of shellfish — chiefly delicious lobsters and crayfish, but also exquisite scallops, sea urchins, and crabs. (The Dingle boats also fish for the most succulent prawns.) There is a major mussel purification plant at Cromane, and there is oyster fishing there and at Fenit.

About 200 species of sea fish are known to visit the shores of Ireland. All around the Iveragh peninsula, along both sides of the Kenmare River, at Dingle, Fenit and Ballybunion are sea angling centres. From the shore it is possible to fish for bass, pollack,

140

mackerel and flat fish. From small boats larger fish can be taken close to the shore — the foregoing, as well as coalfish, cod, conger, dogfish and tope. There is also considerable scope for deep sea fishing for large fish — skate, ray, shark, larger conger, tope and halibut. A number of record fish have been taken along the coast of Kerry — four at Valentia: conger (72 lbs), halibut (152¾ lbs), mackerel (3 lbs, 6 ozs), and red sea bream (9 lbs, 6ozs); two at Fenit: sting ray (51 lbs), and undulate ray (15 lbs, 2 ozs); and a 16 lb bass at Waterville. In addition, a large number of 'specimen' fish are taken. A 'specimen' tends normally to be a fish at least two-thirds the weight of the record for the species, but for some species it is a bit less. For the year 1971, just under 300 'specimen' sea fish were registered for the whole of Ireland, of which over one-third came from Kerry waters. Species where the Kerry proportion was significantly higher than this were: cod (four out of seven); greater spotted dogfish (17 out of 21); garfish (eight out of thirteen); red gurnard (eight out of seventeen); haddock (18 out of 30); monkfish (two out of three); undulate ray (seven out of seven); red sea bream (four out of four); and common skate (12 out of 24). Of the Kerry total, Valentia supplied almost 60%, Fenit almost a quarter, Dingle just 15%, with Sneem, Inch and Cahersiveen making small showings. Of the 19 'interesting' fish listed by the Irish Specimen Fish Committee as taken in Irish waters in 1971, the Kerry coast provided eight.

Those who engage in under-water diving, for example in the Kenmare River, are much impressed by the teaming and colourful fish life.

In the deep waters off the Blaskets and Skelligs are frequently to be seen the huge basking sharks and the sluggish sunfish.

The waters off the coast also have a number of sea mammals. Occasional whales are to be seen, even close to land, and, very occasionally, a school of them. Seals are very numerous along the rocky parts of the coast, and so are dolphins and porpoises. From time to time numbers of whales, dolphins and porpoises get stranded on the beaches.

Gannets on the Little Skellig

The most notable of these strandings was in November, 1965, when no less than 63 pilot whales were stranded at Cloghane. Twelve of them were measured and ranged in length from 20½ feet to 11 feet. In October, 1967, eight white-sided dolphins were stranded, five at Ventry and three in Brandon Bay. Six were measured and ranged in length from eight and one-half feet to six feet. It seems that on 28 July, 1918, a school of porpoises were stranded also at Cloghane, but there are no records of numbers, sizes, etc.

(II) AMPHIBIANS AND REPTILES

About 300 million years ago the first vertebrates, the amphibians, began to leave water for land. After the ice age many of them travelled overland to the north. When, nearly 8,000 years ago, Ireland became an island not many of these slow travellers had reached this country; so, of the 2,500 species of amphibia, only three are to be found in Ireland — the common newt, the common frog, and, a Lusitanian relic, the natterjack toad. This is referred to further below.

From the amphibians evolved, about 200 million years ago, the reptiles; but of the 6,000 species of reptiles only one is native to Ireland, the viviparous lizard (viviparous because the young lizard is born alive). We do not know what was the nature of the magical 'serpents' that seem to have been worshipped in Ireland in pagan times and that were banished by the success of christianity.

(III) BIRDS

Some 150 million years ago birds evolved from reptiles. Of the 8,600 species of birds

Living Things
(II) Amphibians and Reptiles
(III) Birds
(IV) Animals
1 Extinct Animals

Things   Part 2

141

some 350 are found in Ireland. Kerry is one of the most important counties in Ireland for bird watching. Most of the birds on the Irish list have been seen, or are to be found, in the county. The mild and sheltered valleys of the south of the county are an important winter refuge for many species of birds, for example warblers like the chiff-chaff; the chough is common in the cliff regions. There are two sub-species of bird special to Kerry, of the tree-creeper and the stone chat. Kerry shares with Cork and Limerick a special species of chaffinch.

Killarney was once a great centre for eagles — the golden eagle and the osprey, both now vanished.

However, for now the main interest in the county is in water and sea birds.

The seabirds are found mainly on islands off the coast, which hold some of the most important colonies in Europe. The most spectacular place is the Little Skellig, on which it is difficult to land. It has over 1,000 pairs of kittiwakes and over 500 pairs of razorbills. But, especially, it is one of the three gannetries off the Irish coast and incomparably the most important. Indeed, it is the second largest in the northern hemisphere with over 20,000 pairs of gannets on its bare ledges. The second of the three gannetries is the Bull Rock, south of the Skelligs, with about 1,500 pairs. The Cow Rock nearby has a great concentration of guillemots, some 2,000 pairs.

The islands generally hold over 50,000 pairs of storm petrels, probably the greatest concentration in the world. Many thousand nest in the Great Skellig in the walls of clochans and under the stone steps. On this island, too, are some 5,000 pairs of Manx shearwater. The island seems to have been, at the beginning of this century, the original breeding ground for fulmar. From there they have spread to the other islands and to the mainland. There are now some 2,000 pairs on the islands. Razorbills and guillemots are numerous on the Great Skellig and some 6,000 pairs of puffins breed there.

Other notable breeding stations are the nearby Puffin Island for puffin, shearwater and razorbill and, especially, the lonely Tearaght (the most inaccessible and westerly of the Blasket islands) for puffin, for razorbill and for kittiwake. It is probably the greatest breeding station in the world for storm petrel. Also important is the nearby Inishvickillane: over 10,000 pairs have been seen there.

Many kinds of tern — common, arctic and sandwich — breed in Tralee bay.

The water birds — principally the swan, goose, duck and wader — are more widely distributed. Important places are Castlemaine harbour, Dingle harbour and Dingle bay generally; Brandon bay; Tralee bay (Blennerville is a famous centre, as is Lough Gill, Castlegregory) and Barrow harbour, near Fenit.

North of this, about two miles due south of Ballyheigue, between the road and the sea, is the small Akeragh lough which is a remarkable centre for various types of duck (such as gadwall) and for such American visitors as waders. Many more common birds are to be seen there, as well as ruffs, various types of sandpipers, and the spotted redshank. There is here an unusual combination of brackish and fresh water.

Many herons are to be found along the coast on both sides of Sneem.

(IV) ANIMALS

Mammals also evolved about 150 million years ago. Of the 5,000 species of mammal 56 are to be found in Ireland, the latest to appear a bank vole in 1964 near Listowel.

1. Extinct Animals

Before man arrived in Ireland, and for thousands of years after that time, animal life abounded in the country. The most striking of these creatures was the Irish elk (*cervus giganteus*) whose remains have been found all over Europe, but especially in Ireland. It had great horns measuring as much as fourteen feet from tip to tip. A smaller example is in Muckross House. These horns must have much impeded its movements as the forests began to grow and bogs became

Antlers of Great Irish Elk, Muckross

plentiful in the worsening climate. It seems to have died out about 6000 BC.

Bears in small numbers also existed in the country until the bronze age at least. The tooth of a bear was found in a shore site in the sandhills near Castlegregory.

Much more plentiful was the wild boar which was to survive, in degenerate form, until the 17th century. In crannog sites, boar bones and tusks, often of great size, have been found. There are many stories of the Fiana hunting these boars around Killarney and the Reeks. It was a magical boar which killed that great Corkaguiney hero, Diarmaid O Duibhne. In iron age times at least they seem to have been cult objects.

The wolf, too, was plentiful. This was the great predator, and it is likely that many, if not all, of the stone forts so plentiful in Kerry were erected to protect cattle and humans from this danger. Smith says the last wolf in Ireland was killed in Kerry, apparently in the Mac Gillacuddy Reeks, about 1710, but Lloyd Praeger gives an account of one killed in Carlow in 1786.

Extinct, too, unless he survives as the Irish wolfhound, is the great hunting hound of the Fiana. Two of the most famous of these — Bran and Sgeolmhaidhe — ended their days in Kerry. Hounds of this kind must have had, in earlier times, totem significance from the use of the word 'hound' (*cu*) in the names of great heroes — Cu Roi, Cu Chulain, etc.

142 *2. Surviving Animals*

(a) Deer

Of these the most beautiful and evocative are the red deer. They came comparatively late to Ireland but were nonetheless here before man. They survive in native form only in Kerry, in the Killarney area — in the high country between Cromaglan and Mangerton, in Derrycunnihy, at Glena, and in the high land of Tomies and Purple mountains — indeed they are the only surviving large native mammals in Ireland. There are about 200 of them. As one travels the Kenmare road, with Muckross lake on the right, there are, on the left, many valleys heavily shrouded by oak and rhododendron where the red deer come for shelter in wild weather. In the rutting season the wild valley above Torc waterfall echoes with their dry cries. These are the descendants of the deer that Fionn and his companions hunted here nearly 2,000 years ago, but their survival is due in part, not only to the wild country but also to the careful management of the great landowners, the earls of Kenmare and the Herberts who kept the herds culled and imported breeding stock from Scotland. The herds do not now get this management and their freedom of action is being much encroached upon by high fences around new forestry plantations — between foresters and deer no love is lost. The deer can still be stalked under controlled conditions. In Muckross House are to be seen many antlers of deer shot by Herberts, Balfours, Vincents and others. The male deer casts his antlers every year and new ones grow again. The points on the antlers, or the 'tynes', increase every year. The maximun on a deer shot in Killarney is 16. This would be a magnificent specimen and rare. The more usual maximum is 10. It is said that antlers, once dropped, are eaten by the hinds.

A small number of fallow deer survive in the Killarney area. It has been claimed that this species was introduced into Ireland by the anglo-normans; but it is not clear when they were introduced into Killarney.

There are also to be seen in Killarney the smaller, hardier, darker Japanese, or *sika*,

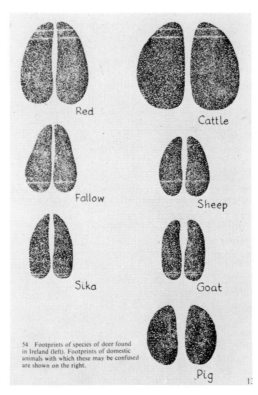

54 Footprints of species of deer found in Ireland (left). Footprints of domestic animals with which these may be confused are shown on the right.

Footprints of deer and domestic animals

deer, especially in the Kenmare estate. They are much more numerous, much less beautiful, and much more destructive to young trees than the red deer. They were introduced — it is said two does and a buck — by the earl of Kenmare a little over a century ago.

(b) Cattle

The most striking and visible of the Kerry animals are the Kerry cattle, the small, dark, elegant and hardy beasts that are capable of living off the poor fare offered by the Kerry hills. The breed, with its long, poetic face, derives from the asian *bos longifrons* which came here in the late stone age. These became the staple of the Irish economic, monetary, and sporting system. Eventually, as other breeds were imported and crossed with the native breed, the small, black, silken coated breed survived unscathed only in the uplands of Kerry and west Cork, prolific and

durable providers of good milk from these ungenerous pastures.

About the middle of the 18th century, their special merits began to be publicly recognised, but it was not until 1890 that a herd book was established to protect the purity of the breed. In judging, marks were awarded for 'quick, active movements, deerlike expression and pose; picturesque appearance'. The bull 'should show a fine, masculine appearance, with a gay and active carriage'. Those who early developed fine herds of Kerries were 'gentlemen who are fanciers of pretty animals' — the Knight of Kerry in Valentia, the Butlers of Waterville, the Mahonys of Dromore castle and Kilmorna. The Mahonys of Kilmorna were evangelists of the breed in England where a Kerry Cattle Society was formed some years before one was formed in Kerry. The breed in Kerry now gets a good deal of official support in money, regulations and general encouragement and it may be that this 'silk of the kine' will be secure in Kerry for some time to come. A splendid herd of Kerries can be seen at the farm attached to the Bourn-Vincent park at Muckross — the farm buildings are almost opposite the entrance to the folk museum.

(c) Horses

Another breed of animal of special interest in Kerry is the rather shaggy pony, the Kerry hobby. This animal has been, perhaps, taken too much for granted, unlike say, the Kerry cow or the Connemara pony, but its special qualities require to be better known. It may be that, like the Kerry cow, it is a survival of the small native Irish animal, dating from neolithic times, which was so agile through the forests and over bogs in struggles with the anglo-normans. Its praises have been on record for two centuries by Dr Smith, and there is little to do but quote what he says about it as he travelled on its back through Dunkerron and Iveragh:

The little hobbies of the country are the properest horses to travel through it; and a man must abandon himself intirely to their guidance, which will answer much better than if one should strive to manage and direct their footsteps; for these creatures are a kind of automata or machines. . . . which naturally follow the laws of mechanics, and will conduct themselves much better on those occasions, than the most knowing persons can possibly direct them.

And again:

I have already observed, that the horses in these baronies, are naturally very sure-footed; they are small, but an excellent breed; they climb over the most rugged rocks, and both ascend and descend the steepest precipices with great facility and safety; are so light, as to skim over waving bogs and morasses without sinking, where heavier horses would certainly perish. They are strong and durable, easily supported, and not ill-shaped; so hardy as to stand abroad all winter, and will browse on heath, furze and other shrubs; add to this their gait is ambling, which is extremely easy.

However, one must not overlook that a great interest of the people of Kerry is horse-racing, and the county is one of the few in Ireland with three race courses — at Killarney where there is a two-day meeting in the fourth week of April and a three-day meeting in the fourth week of July; at Tralee where there is a two-day meeting in the third week of June, a four-day meeting in the first week of September, and a one-day meeting in November; and at Listowel where there is a four-day meeting in the last week of September. There are also 'flapper' meetings, such as the hilarious two-day one at Rossbeigh at the end of July or beginning of August.

(d) Sheep

It looks, too, from the records of excavations that the small mountain sheep one sees in Kerry also date from neolithic times. The larger, lowland sheep are later importations.

(e) Donkeys

Plentiful, too, are the attractive donkeys — near Dunquin little bands of them make a great fuss of visitors, especially if they bring lumps of sugar. Donkeys are such a part of

the scene that it comes as a surprise to learn how much they are newcomers to Ireland. No record of them in Ireland has been found before 1780 AD.

(f) Dogs

Although none of the great hounds of the past survive in Kerry there are two breeds of dogs special to the county — the Kerry beagle and the Kerry blue terrier. The beagle is to be seen all over south Kerry, large (20 to 22 inches), tan coloured and black. This dog may originally have been a small Irish hound crossed with Spanish and French hounds and bloodhounds. Packs of beagles were kept by some of the leading Kerry families — O Connells, Herberts, Chutes. They were followed on foot over the wild countryside — as in the time of the Fiana and their great dogs. The famous stag hunts of Killarney were based on beagles and beaters. Beagling above Derrynane was a favourite sport of Daniel

Coming on to rain, Conor Pass, Dingle

O Connell. The breed was specially developed from the end of the 18th century at Scarteen, Co Tipperary, origin of the famous hunt, the Scarteen Black and Tans who gave their name to Lloyd George's militia. Ownership of these hounds is now widespread in south Kerry and west Cork. They are used for hunting hares in the winter and for draghunts in summer. These latter are dog races, often with 60 or more entries, over 12 or 15 miles of mountains and valley, drawing large crowds of watchers from Kerry and Cork.

The Kerry blue terrier is a more famous animal though much less frequently to be seen. It is much bred in the Tralee-Castleisland—Listowel area. It is a well coated terrier about 18 inches high with a reputation as a remorseless fighter, with some kindly qualities but with the possibility of developing a very nasty streak indeed. The breed, according to an old story, originated when, towards the end of the 18th

144 century, a ship was wrecked in Tralee bay and a blue dog swam ashore and mated with the native wheaten bitches. The development of the breed is attributed, in Kerry, to Robert Madgett of Ballymacadam, Castleisland. It was allotted a class at Crufts in 1922 thanks to the efforts of the earl of Kenmare, himself a noted breeder of Kerry blues.

(V) CURIOUS CREATURES

1. Natterjack Toad

This Lusitanian amphibian is to be found in the Mediteranean, in England, in south west Scotland, but in Ireland only in Kerry, and in Kerry only in the area around Castlemaine harbour between the great sandbanks of Inch and Rossbeigh. Its precise distribution is not certain. Mac Dougald says it is centred on Glenbeigh on both sides of the Caragh river where it enters the sea, notably at Dooks golf links on the east bank of the estuary. It is normally to be seen only at night; by day it goes into burrows in the sand. Locally, it is called the 'black frog', but it is in colour golden to olive, spotty or warty, with lumpy, prominent eyes. It is ¾ inches to 2¾ inches in length. It runs rather than jumps. It has also been reported in the Derrynane area, but this has not been confirmed. One suggestion is that the natterjack first came by ship to Castlemaine harbour, but this is unlikely. However, when it did at last get to Ireland, it seems to have lost all further interest in travel.

2. Greater Spotted Slug

Another Lusitanian visitor unique to Kerry is the greater spotted slug, or Kerry slug. This is quite a handsome beast as slugs go, shiny black with silvery spots. It is to be found only in Portugal, part of Spain, and Kerry — and possibly also in west Cork. Having travelled so far, it, understandably, confined itself to Killarney and Dunkerron. It is readily to be seen in moist weather.

Another little beast of interest to naturalists is the fine grasshopper, *mecostethus grossus*, special to the Killarney area. But here we begin to move into specialised areas.

CLIMATE

Climate is the behaviour of temperature, wind, rainfall, sunshine and humidity over a period of years. Weather is their behaviour at any time of day. Generally in Kerry there is little change from season to season and from year to year. What seems to be a great deal of change occurs from day to day and hour to hour, but within narrow limits. In the simplest terms, Kerry has little climate but much weather.

A good deal can be known about the climate of Kerry because it has had since 1867 a meteorological observatory. Until 1892, it was on Valentia island but was then moved to Cahersiveen, the name 'Valentia' not being changed. In addition, throughout the county a network of stations keep rainfall records, some from the last century. A few of them have kept other meteorological records over long periods.

The geography of Kerry affects the climate in two main ways — through the sea and through the mountains. The sea influences the temperature and the mountains the rainfall.

The influence of the sea is pervasive because of the long indented coastline. The sea accepts and loses heat much more slowly than the land so that the heat stored in it falls very slowly during the winter. The range of temperature of the sea is much moderated by the Gulf Stream and the Atlantic drift. So, off the west coast of Ireland the temperature of the sea does not vary much — from a low of eight degrees in March to a peak of 16 degrees in August (Celsius). Hence in Kerry higher winter temperatures, earlier and longer growing seasons, and less severe frosts than in most other parts of Ireland. Along this warm sea blow winds from the south and west that stay warm but moisture laden.

The mean annual temperature at Cahersiveen over the 30 years 1931-60 was 10.8 degrees

This is typical of — perhaps marginally warmer than — the rest of south Munster, south Leinster and Connemara, as well as west Wales and south England. The annual variations around this mean are small. Within each year

there is at Cahersiveen a steady range of monthly mean temperatures around 7-8 degrees C in December, January, February and March, to 15 degrees C in July and August, with April and November showing 9 degrees C, May and October showing 11.5 degrees C and June and September showing 14 degrees C. The January temperature in Kerry is higher than in any part of the British Isles except, marginally, around Penzance and the Scilly Isles. The average temperature over 24 hours fluctuates over the whole year 5.5 degrees C, and this is fairly steady from month to month.

In these moderate conditions the level of rainfall is significant. This is much influenced by the mountains so that the variation in annual rainfall between the mountainous areas and the flat lands of north Kerry is as much as three to one. The average rainfall for the British Isles is 1050 millimetres. For Ireland it is 1100 mm. For Scotland and Wales it is 1275 mm each, and for England 950 mm. Not only is Ireland fairly typical of the British Isles as a whole, but of the four countries it is the one that deviates least from the average. Within Ireland, Kerry, with a mean deviation of 10% from the normal of annual rainfall, is almost typical of Ireland as a whole. Contrary to popular belief Ireland of all four countries has least extremes of wetness. Kerry falls into three main regions for rainfall — roughly the three northern baronies with annual rainfall of 1250 mm or less; the high mountains of the Iveragh and Beare peninsulas and Mount Brandon with a rainfall of 2000 mm to over 3000 mm; and the rest of the county in the 1250 to 2000 mm range. The average annual rainfall at Cahersiveen is just below 1400 mm with an average range from 74 mm in April to 168 mm in December. Less than 100 mm falls on average in April, May, June and August. Over 150 mm falls in November, December and January. February and July have 107 mm.

For most purposes total rainfall is less important than how often it rains and for how long the rain lasts. The meteorologists define a 'rain day' as one on which 0.2 mm of rain has fallen. On this basis the number of rain days in Kerry as a whole is typical of the west of Ireland, namely, in the 225 to 250 day range. The two northern baronies and Corkaguiney do better than this: they are in the 200 to 225 day range. As might be expected, the Killarney area does worse with over 250 rain days. The average daily duration of rain in Cahersiveen on those days when it does rain is 3½ hours. This fluctuates just over 25% up and down in individual months, with April showing 2.6 hours of rain on each rain day at one end of the scale and June with 4.3 hours at the other. The average for the whole year is just about one-third higher than for London.

Another major feature is wind. The range of monthly mean speeds at Cahersiveen is from 14.6 mph in January to 10.1 mph in June

(these may be understated somewhat), with calm as a percentage of the time varying from 12% to 16% in nine months, 18% in September and 11% and 9% in December and January respectively. The table shows the ranges of wind given by Bilham for Cahersiveen over 19 years. For about half of the year there is no more than a gentle breeze and for almost the whole of the rest of the period the wind is moderate to fresh. On average, only one day in twelve (twice as frequently in January) is the wind stronger than this. Over 38 mph is gale force. In the period 1909 to 1935 there were on average 16 hours of gales each year at Cahersiveen. The direction of the wind is also important: the northerly winds tend to be less agreeable than the southerly ones. The winds from

the north, north west and north east blow on average on one windy day in three. In the winter months of December, January and February they blow on one windy day in four. The southerly coasts of Corkaguiney and Dunkerron are usually sheltered from these winds.

Wind Speeds at Cahersiveen (mph)

| | Percentage more than | | | | |
	38 +	25-38	13-24	4-12	0-4
January	0.6	18	44	29	8
July	0.1	2	41	44	13
Year	0.2	8	43	37	11
Beaufort Scale	8 +	6-7	4-5	2-3	0-1

Source: Bilham

Decaying Limestone, Dundag Bay, Muckross Lake

What about sunshine? The sun shines on average at Cahersiveen, as over elsewhere in Ireland, just under four hours a day. The proportion of actual to possible sunshine over the British Isles as a whole varies from 24% in Shetland to 39% at Dover. At Cahersiveen it is 31%, and at Dublin it is 32%. The monthly average of sunshine at Cahersiveen ranges from 6½ hours in May to 1.3 hours in December. The December average is about typical for Ireland as a whole, and few places in the British isles have more December sunshine than this. The May average at Cahersiveen of over 6½ hours is above the average of 6 to 6½ hours for most of Ireland, and is better than the average for most of Britain. Sunless days at Cahersiveen average 21%, ranging from 11% in May and June to 38% in December and January. On the other hand those days giving more than half the maximum of bright sunshine there ranged from 37% in April to 11%-12% in December-January. This shows Cahersiveen as fairly typical of six stations throughout the British Isles, though a good way behind Falmouth, only coming second to it in the sunniness of March and April.

There is little to say about humidity. The

146

mean relative humidity averaged over the whole year is much the same throughout the British Isles. Where Cahersiveen is a bit exceptional is that the relative humidity varies little either from month to month or from hour to hour. Thus the summer months are marginally more humid than at most other stations of the British Isles.

Snow has been observed at Cahersiveen on average on five days a year, and lying on the ground only once in every two years. Frost is also infrequent – the coldest temperature recorded at Cahersiveen is −7.2 degrees C in 1958. Cahersiveen is, however, relatively prone to hail with an average of 23 days on which hail falls; this is one of the highest in the British Isles. The hail falls almost entirely in the period Novermber to March and the showers are relatively mild. Fog is exceptionally infrequent – with an average of three days a year.

How typical is Cahersiveen's experience of that of Kerry as a whole? It seems to be fairly typical of the coastal areas. In the inland areas, other than the mountains, rainfall and temperature are similar to those on the coast. For example, the Cahersiveen annual rainfall of 1400 mm compares with figures of under 1300 mm for Killarney and over 1700 mm for Kenmare; but at the western tip of the Dingle peninsula and in the two northern baronies the rainfall is under 1250 mm. Around Lixnaw it is just under 1000 mm but at Ballaghabeama it is over 3200 mm. Nonetheless, the Cahersiveen experience is reasonably representative of Kerry as a whole.

So far as the British Isles are concerned, the rainfall in Kerry is higher than average but this is accompanied by a winter temperature comparable to that of Cornwall and a proportion of bright and extended sunshine that it is fairly typical. Moreover, there is little deviation from these norms so that the Kerry climate is notably free from extremes. The mildness of the winters is exceptional: the mean January temperature is the same as that of places on the northern coast of the Mediteranean. The hours of sunshine are, of course, a good deal less.

One effect of this mild climate is the length

of the growing season. At Cahersiveen in the period 1954-1968 the season began on average on 17 February and continued until 6 January, that is, for 323 days. This is the longest in Ireland, some 10 or 11 weeks

longer than in the Irish midlands.

The following table shows some weather statistics for Cahersiveen ('Valentia'):

Valentia Observatory 1931 - 1960

Temperature (C)	Jan.	Feb.	Mar.	Apr.	May	June	July	Aug.	Sept.	Oct.	Nov.	Dec.	Year
Average	7.0	6.8	8.3	9.4	11.5	13.8	15.0	15.4	14.0	11.6	9.1	7.8	10.8
Daily Maximum	9.4	9.3	11.1	12.5	14.8	16.8	17.7	18.2	16.8	14.2	11.5	10.1	13.5
Daily Minimum	4.5	4.3	5.4	6.3	8.1	10.8	12.3	12.6	11.2	8.9	6.6	5.5	8.0
Monthly Maximum	12.5	12.6	15.2	17.2	20.6	22.8	22.4	23.0	20.4	17.6	14.5	13.1	25.2
Monthly Minimum	-1.9	-1.8	-0.6	0.9	2.6	6.1	8.0	7.3	5.7	2.2	0.3	-0.7	-3.4
Extreme Maximum	13.8	16.8	19.9	23.9	26.1	27.2	29.6	29.8	26.7	23.5	18.2	15.7	29.8
Extreme Minimum	-7.2	-5.4	-3.3	-1.8	0.2	1.7	6.2	4.4	1.7	-2.1	-2.3	-4.8	-7.2

Rainfall (mm)													
Average	164	107	103	74	86	81	107	95	122	140	151	168	1398
Rain Days (0.2m)	24	20	18	18	17	17	22	21	21	21	22	25	246
Wet Days (1.0m)	20	15	14	13	13	13	15	15	16	17	18	21	190
Most in a Day	47.5	75.9	41.4	47.2	47.9	43.6	55.8	37.4	59.7	84.5	58.8	58.7	84.5

Sunshine													
Hours per day	1.6	2.5	3.5	5.2	6.5	5.9	4.7	4.9	3.8	2.8	2.0	1.3	3.7
Percent of possible	18	27	30	38	42	35	30	33	31	27	24	16	31

Source: Irish Meteorological Service

9

Pre-Christian Remains

Kerry is littered with the debris of the past. This is especially true of the ends of the Dingle and Iveragh peninsulas. As, for some six thousand years, age succeeded age it left distinctive ruins. There is much to see and much to stimulate the imagination. In this chapter we try to classify the ruins before christianity came to Ireland, and, in the next, those from after that time.

Because Ireland was for so long at the end of the world, the various cultures that reached it were already old and weakened and, far from blotting out, had come to terms with what was here before them, so that a process of absorption and interaction took place. There is thus a more continuous cultural tradition in Ireland than in most other places.

Bit by bit we can build up some idea of the past by classifying this debris into distinctive groups. There is, first, the silent witness of the archaeological remains yielding grudging account of, in Kerry, over 4,000 years of human occupation in the stone and bronze ages. For the next 1,000 years — from about the beginning of the christian era — to fill out the archaeological remains, comes the linguistic evidence from the iron age invaders yielded by the philological study of the old mythological and quasi-historical tales, supplemented by a still living tradition of folklore. The written evidence begins in the ogam stones of the late pagan and early christian centuries. Overlapping this we have the manuscript material in Latin and Irish that has survived the depredations of centuries, filled out by the evidence of christian settlements. Finally, for the last 1,000 years reliable, if inadequate, historical records exist.

What follows in this and the next chapter is an attempt to group what survives in and about Kerry into meaningful categories and thus, insofar as Kerry is typical of Ireland generally, to slice through a cross-section of Irish buildings to use what strikes the eye in Kerry to give a meaningful account of much that is distinctive about Ireland. This is a layman's account; but it tries to give a comprehensive picture of man's works and buildings in Kerry.

For the present chapter almost all the evidence is archaeological. It is possible to relate nearly all the material to periods or ages; but seldom is there enough material to give a clear account of any age. Moreover, the ages overlap. One can say, roughly, when an age began, but the preceding age then by no means came to an end. Sometimes there may have been regression or degeneration when the skills of the earlier times may have been lost. Irish archaeology is not in an advanced state, although it is developing. Relatively few archaeological sites have been excavated, and very few in Kerry. Many of those excavated elsewhere in Ireland in the past were unscientifically done. Much of our knowledge, therefore, depends on accidental finds. These seldom yield enough to reconstruct the life of which the sites are the tattered remains. In particular, an archaeology of Kerry remains to be written. Indeed, important archaeological areas in the county have not been adequately surveyed.

Within these severe limitations one can, however, make some sense of the jumbles of ruins.

It is convenient to divide the past doings of man in Kerry into periods — the pre-christian ages of stone and metal (from the materials from which tools and weapons were made), and then the christian ages, early, medieval and modern. The dates of these periods tend to get later as one moves north and west across Europe from the womb of civilisation. The earlier ones also tend to get pushed further back as improvements are made in techniques of dating. However, for Ireland one can broadly date these periods as follows: *stone ages:* to 2000 BC; *metal ages:* to 400 AD; *early christian* and *gaelic periods:* 400 AD to 1200 AD; *medieval period:* 1200 AD to 1600 AD; *modern period:* from 1600 AD. There are in Kerry distinctive sites for each of these. For the stone ages we have the great stone tombs. For the metal ages, the great stone forts. For the christian period, the little monasteries and isolated churches. For the medieval period, the great monasteries and castles. For the modern period, virtually the rest of the buildings one sees.

THE AGES OF STONE

It is usual to divide the stone ages into three periods — early, middle and late, called respectively the *palaeolithic*, the *mesolithic*, and the *neolithic*.

(I) EARLY STONE AGE

As the ice melted away the bare plains of Europe were inhabited, from about 50,000 BC to about 9000 BC by a free-ranging hunter called palaeolithic (early stone age) man who lived in caves. From 30,000 BC lived upper palaeolithic man whose cave paintings in France, Spain and Italy still delight us. It now seems (after much dispute) that two skeletons found in a cave in Kilgreany, Co. Waterford, are of upper palaeolithic man who reached Ireland and hunted here the reindeer and the great Irish elk before 9000 BC. But no other evidence of palaeolithic man has so far been found in Ireland.

(II) MIDDLE STONE AGE

After about 9000 BC the weather became warmer, dense forests began to grow, the great sub-artic animals on which man had lived by hunting began to die away, and human populations began to rise sharply. These changes forced a new way of life adapted to fishing, on the coasts and rivers, and to hunting, on the edges of the forest. As a hunter and food collector man shifted from place to place. That is to say, he had not yet become a farmer: he seems to have domesticated but one animal, the dog. Thus evolved mesolithic (middle stone age) man. He came to Ireland about 6000 BC, probably from Scotland and, ultimately, from north western France. He centred around Larne, Co. Antrim, and his traces — tools of roughly shaped flint — have been found as far south as Dublin. Mesolithic man continued to survive the later invasions, to be affected by them, and to constitute a basic part of the Irish population. The fact that flint has been found in chalk near Killarney opens up the possibility that traces of mesolithic man may be found in the area.

Some traces of what may have been a

148

Sandhills at the Maharees, Castlegregory

mesolithic culture in its stark poverty survived long into subsequent ages. It may have been in those ages that the sandhill people came to Kerry. They lived in light shelters among high sandhills and fed almost entirely on shellfish, leaving great quantities of shells to be seen in their middens. Apart from the piles of shells their blackened hearths can be seen buried in the sand and subsequently exposed. Rough stone tools, hut sites, animal remains — red deer, horse, bear — and human burials in long cists have been found in Kerry — at Ballyeagh, Ballybunion; at the Maharees near Castlegregory; and at Inch. These sites long continued to be used — iron age pins and roman coins were found at Ballyeagh. There also were found 17 stone cists with recumbent skeletons, but these have not been dated.

(III) LATE STONE AGE

The cradle of civilisation was in the eastern

Mediteranean. Gradually traders and colonists spread west from there until they opened the Atlantic trade route along the western coasts of Iberia and of Ireland as well as up the Irish sea. They then sailed around the north of Scotland to Scandinavia and northern Europe. These routes remained active for perhaps 3,000 years to 1000 BC. Ireland was in the middle of these routes and was thus affected by the trading and cultural influences from the south and, later, also from the north.

The late (or neolithic) stone age begins in Ireland some time before 4000 BC, it would now seem. Neolithic man differed from his predecessor in being a settled farmer, so we may think of Irish agriculture as beginning over 6,000 years ago. The improvement in the efficiency of food production led to sharp rises in population.

The relics of neolithic man are, mainly, the

megaliths (megalith: great stone) that are so striking a part of the Irish scene. They, of course, continued into the bronze age. These megaliths comprise, notably, stone tombs for the collective burial of aristocrats, and scribed rocks, and, from bronze age times these and standing stones, stone circles and alignments. There are many of these monuments in Kerry; but the Kerry relics do not give a complete picture of the four main groups of megalith builders. These megaliths are found in the Mediteranean area and stretch along western Europe to Scandinavia. It is from assessing the changes in these monuments (mainly tombs) and in their surviving furniture of pottery vessels, polished stone tools and (later) metal objects that a picture of Ireland's past and its relationships with the rest of Europe can be made. Unfortunately, this picture is still very sketchy.

The tombs can be grouped into four main classes, within which there are many variations. These are: court cairns; single chamber tombs (or dolmens); passage graves; and wedge shaped tombs and gallery graves. Normally, these are constructed of great stones and are covered by earth (the tumulus, or barrow) or by stones (the cairn), usually confined within a ring of large, sometimes decorated, stones, a round covering for a passage grave, an elongated one over a gallery grave; but in many obvious instances the covering has been worn, or dug, away. Because of the dense growth of trees in so many places and the poor tools for felling them, these tombs tend to be built on the fringes of now vanished forests some 500 feet above sea level, or in especially bare lowland places.

Apart from the great graves the surviving remains of neolithic man in Ireland are the *polished* stone tools, notably axes — unlike the rough flint of the mesolithic — and the pottery, some of it elegantly decorated — woman's great gift to the technology of the time.

One must think of the two thousand or so years of the neolithic — which of course overlapped the succeeding ages of metal — as possibly receiving two major invasions, or if not invasions, major cultural influences.

There were also minor influences. The picture is at best confused because there is no single agreed interpretation, and drastic changes of view have occurred and are likely to recur. In particular, dates are receding fast. Generally, the main sources of information are the graves where these people left the remains of their leaders and the gods they left with them to ease their journey to the next world. In Ireland these human remains were usually cremated, unusual for the Europe of the time, where the normal practice was inhumation, that is, the body was not burned.

The first of these invading groups (if they were invaders) was the Western Neolithic which either came from Scotland to Connacht or from Iberia through Connacht to Scotland. Their distinctive work was the court (or horned) cairn, a gallery grave with two, three or more chambers linked together, and a stone semi-circle (or court) radiating from the first chamber and facing east. These tombs are largely concentrated in the northern third of Ireland. The remaining two-thirds was colonised by people whose origins are obscure and whose graves are mainly unpretentious cists. Some of them settled around Lough Gur in Co. Limerick in the

Four types of megalithic tomb

COURT CAIRN

Fig. 1. Groundplans of the four main types of megalithic tombs.

MOYTIRRA EAST

PASSAGE GRAVE

CARROWKEEL - Cairn K

WEDGE-SHAPED
GALLERY GRAVE

BALLYEDMONDUFF

DOLMEN

CARROWMORE

period 2700 to 2100 BC; but similar remains have not been found in Kerry. (There is a multiple cist at Knockane, Anascaul). These people also used the most striking of the great single chamber tombs (or dolmens), large capstones resting on smaller stones, also facing east. These are the so-called portal dolmens which are normally associated with the court cairns, but also exist in south east Ireland. Portal dolmens are not found in Kerry (unless there are remains of this kind in Glanmore, near Lauragh). So it looks as if this strain did not reach Kerry.

The second strain dates in Ireland from about 3500 BC. These people came in two streams, from Iberia and western France, and through central France reaching Scandinavia. Both streams were from an ultimate origin in the Mediteranean region. Their work was the passage grave, and they constructed the magnificent ones at Newgrange and at Knowth, Co. Meath, after 3000 BC.

No passage graves have so far been found in Kerry, but the marks of these people nonetheless survive in the county. The most notable of these marks consists in the great dolmens, or single chamber tombs (other than portal dolmens). These seem to be simplified versions of the passage grave. Examples of these large dolmens are to be found in south Kerry at Coumatlakane, Caherdaniel (where one can see the remains of the tumulus and at least one small dolmen in the inner of the two circles of stones that surround the mound); at Ballybrack, Waterville; and at Eightercua, Waterville, where the dolmen seems to have been defaced and cast down; it was surrounded by a number of stone circles. Dolmens have been found in Japan, India, Syria, east and north Africa, western Europe, Denmark, and Britain, as well as in Ireland which is a principal source. They have also been found, less frequently, in other European countries.

The notable features of the passage grave proper are their *corbelled* chambers and their hieratic art. Corbelling is a technique of building in undressed stone without mortar. The stones are laid horizontally in circular courses, with each succeeding course in a smaller circle than its predecessor until the

Modern clochans at Coumeenole

final course can be closed by a flat stone placed at the top. Kerry is full of the inheritance of this technique in the shape of bee-hive huts — the *clochan* — which continued to be built in living memory. Most of these old houses, which were a special feature of early christian Ireland, are now in ruins; the Fahan area is a major site for them; the perfect examples are on the Great Skellig; but these are both remains from christian times.

At the passage graves of Newgrange and of Knowth the hieratic art has considerable variety. The designs are pocked out on large stones with a stone chisel. The major design is the spiral, which is a formalised version of the human face, but, further back, the unfolding of the life principle. There are other common designs, such as concentric circles and lozenges. In Kerry the range is less but there are examples of concentric circles on one of the outliers in Lissyvigeen, Killarney; of spirals and other representations of the human figure at Tullakeel and Dromtine, Sneem; and notably, on the principal of the 15 stones at Derynablaha, Ballaghabeama.

The 15 stones at Derrynablaha are probably the most notable collection in Kerry. According to Anati the several cases of superpositions and the different degree of wear of the carvings, show that they were executed at different times over a long period.

150

Scribings at Derrynablaha, Sneem

People must have come back again and again to make their marks. One of the marks has a complex pattern, but the others are variations on three basic themes — the cup, the groove, and the ring. It has been tentatively suggested that these may be anthropomorphic — the cup and several rings, the breast; the cup, groove and ring, the female sex organ; and the cup and groove, the male. At Derrynablaha over half the marks are cup marks, and three-quarters consist of these and ring marks; but there are 17 basic types — a cup mark with up to four rings, a groove and cup mark with up to five rings, a groove with one or two open rings, etc. There are other designs, the 'Galician' ones, that have been related to the ages of metal; but it may be that both antedate the passage graves.

All of these motifs are in megalithic art. It may be that both in Ireland and in Galicia (see below) this art developed separately and that they inter-reacted in later, metal-using

times. In general the neolithic rock scribings are not as numerous in Kerry as the bronze age (or Galician) scribings referred to later; but they are more puzzling because, unlike corbelling, they did not become absorbed into the Irish tradition and it is not clear why these marks should have been made on remote boulders scattered around the county far from burial places. Designs of this kind are found amongst primitive people all over the world, and in some cases are associated with totemism.

From time to time in these relics we get a picture of, as Estyn Evans has pointed out, a ' peasant culture deeply concerned with religious ideas, with votive offerings and magic ceremonies at wells, in lakes and on hill-tops'. Perhaps only in the surviving stone age cultures of the world can we now get a real glimpse of life as lived in Ireland 4,000 to 6,000 years ago. However, the absence of fighting weapons, fortifications, defended homesteads all suggest a peaceful body of farmers trying to bring the forested land into subjection, growing some grain and beginning to domesticate animals, such as cattle, ponies, sheep and pigs. A small number of human skeletons survive from these times and we get a glimpse of what sort of people they were. They were predominantly dolichocephalic (long, narrow skulled) and rather short — a man of five feet six inches would have been considered tall. These neolithic people no doubt mixed with the existing mesolithic inhabitants setting up complex processes of interaction.

THE AGES OF METAL

The beginning of the use of metal tools and of the mining and working of copper, tin and gold can be related to major invasions, perhaps before 2000 BC by the Beaker people (named from the elegantly decorated bell-shaped pottery beakers found in their graves). They arose on the northern shores of Africa and established a main culture in Iberia based on the mining of copper. They spread in two waves, one along the west coast of Europe, and the other through central Europe, where they fused with other elements, to north western Europe and Britain. It seems that both waves reached Ireland, the first arriving

via Britain, both in the north of Ireland and the area around Dalkey island, the second through these places but also at, and settling in, the copper producing areas of the south west of Ireland. In Ireland these invaders settled as miners, metal workers and traders over a wide area. In the years around 2000 BC, south west Ireland, especially Kerry, was an important trading and metal-working area for Europe as a whole.

The beaker people were brachycephalic (round-headed) and some inches taller than the native folk. The invasions seem to have been substantial and military and, from the scanty evidence of surviving skeletons, the invaders do not seem to have brought women with them. This would have facilitated their absorption into the existing population amongst whom they continued in a position of power during most, if not all, of the bronze age. What remains to us therefore are their considerable cultural contributions while they themselves succumbed to the osmosis of Irish life.

Early in the metal age, therefore, the Irish were an amalgam of four main groups — the mesolithic (themselves incorporating whatever, if anything, there may have been remaining of the upper palaeolithic), the western neolithic, the passage grave people, and the beaker folk. It was this amalgam that constituted something like an Irish nation that moved into the age of metal with such conspicuous success.

The Irish people, as they emerged following the beaker invasions, were a mainly pastoral one. This trend was reinforced by the natural bent of the country as well as by a change in climate. The change from stone to metal tools, gradual as it must have been, must have greatly increased productivity and this, with the new export trade in metal goods, no doubt gave the extra resources to enable the society to demand and support a supply of goods that represented conspicuous consumption indeed. The increased wealth was not evenly spread. It seems that the northern part of the country continued poor; but the south and west, with minerals, became prosperous. The growth in wealth also led to growth in civilisation.

It seems that until the iron age invaders of after 800 BC there were no further significant invasions of Ireland; but this is disputed. If there were no invasions, the period from 2000 BC to about 800 BC was a period of strong cultural influence both on and by the Irish. We see during this time the development in the Irish people of that curious capacity, so often to be used, to absorb influences from abroad and, while remaining within the scope of those influences, to produce from them something characteristically Irish. There was a need for these external challenges and, especially in the cultural field, the capacity to respond creatively to them.

The new amalgam of the Irish people left, especially in Kerry, notable marks of their way of life; but they are chiefly to be remembered as miners of copper and gold, and workers of great skill in copper, bronze and gold, as well as extraordinarily pervasive traders: their goods have been found throughout Europe.

One can think of the ages of metal in three stages — the copper age to about 1800 BC; the ages of bronze and gold to about 800 BC; and the iron age to about 400 AD. The dates given represent not when a preceding age came to an end, but when a subsequent age began to overlap it.

We know little of the kind of life the Irish people led at this time, apart from what one can deduce from the silent remains. It is normally assumed, as we do here, that the kind of Ireland portrayed in the ancient sagas is an iron age Ireland, that is, from after 800 BC when the later invaders began to arrive; but it has been argued on linguistic, not on archaeological, grounds that the metal users were the first celtic invaders and that what we see reflected in the sagas is a life that stretches back to these remote metal-using times. While it does not seem that the celts could have arisen as a people, or could have reached Ireland, so early as this, the sagas have certainly incorporated religious values and social customs of at least bronze age times.

There are to be seen four striking remains of the beaker folk invasion in Kerry — the wedge shaped tomb and gallery grave; the stone

Wedge grave, Coom, Ballinskelligs

circle; the pillarstone or *gallan*; and the rock scribings. The wedge grave has usually been taken as a relic of the beaker folk; but there is no *direct* evidence of this: one find of beaker fragments is reported in Kerry — from an unnamed tomb in the Dingle peninsula.

For the wedge-shaped grave Kerry is a main centre. The wedge faces in a direction from west of south to north of west and tapers both in width and height from the opening to the back. (The wedge design may have been suggested by what was one of their principal tools for clearing woodlands). A good example of a wedge-shaped grave on the Iveragh peninsula is at Caherlehillan, Cahersiveen; others are near Ballinskelligs — at Meelagulleen and Coom — and at Kildreenagh, Valentia, and there are four at Coumatlakane, Caherdaniel. There are others on the Dingle peninsula — several at Maumnahaltora, Camp; one (with cairn) at Doonmanagh, Minard; one (possibly three) at Ballyhoneen, Cloghane; and one (possibly two) at Ceann Tragha. On the Beare peninsula there may be two in Glanmore. The wedge *gallery* grave is much scarcer; but there is a curious ruined one (with alignment) at Glanlough, between Sneem and Caherdaniel.

(The megalithic tomb tradition survives into present-day Kerry. Observe the great concrete strong-boxes at Ardfert, Aghadoe and elsewhere. The megalithic tradition has no doubt reached its apotheosis in the strong-box on Abbey Island, Derrynane, faced with white, glazed bricks in the late victorian style for men's lavatories. If 4,000 years

hence, as 4,000 years ago, our civilisation is to be judged by the more notable of our tombs, then we shall leave some curious impressions to posterity).

The second major relic of the beaker invasion is the stone circle, although this may also have had other origins. The stone circles are mainly open air temples, but some may have had secular, ceremonial use. They seem to have derived from the circles built around passage graves. Aristotle says of them: 'Amongst the Iberians, who are a military people, it is the custom to set around the tomb of a deceased warrior a number of obelisks corresponding to the number of enemies he has killed'. Examples of stone circles are at Lissyvigeen, Killarney, where there is a small circle rather unusually surrounded by a bank, with two outliers, one with a neolithic concentric ring (perhaps a stone appropriated for another purpose); at Kenmare, where there is a central recumbent boulder; at Eightercua, Waterville; near Ballyferriter; and in the Beare peninsula, where there are several. Cork and Kerry give the larger of two concentrations in Ireland of a special variety of these circles — the recumbent or 'axial'. There are 83 of these, less than 10 of them in Kerry. Of these less than half (and none in Kerry) have five stones and are 'D' shaped. The rest range from seven to 19 stones (always an uneven number) with sometimes one or more outliers and one to three central boulders. Typically, there is a flat boulder or recumbent slab in the western semi-circle: this is the lowest stone of the group. In the eastern semi-circle, directly opposite, stand two portal stones, the highest of the circle. The circle may have a diameter of three metres to 50 metres. Sometimes one or more of the stones is cup-marked. Some of of the circles seem to be oriented to major points of the horizon, such as the sunrise at midsummer and the sunset at midwinter, and may have been used to determine the time of solstice and equinox. Others seem to be oriented to various bright stars. They are all oriented within the 100 degrees from west of south to north of west, like the wedge graves. It is argued that the greatest of these circles, at Stonehenge in England, was an elaborate astronomical computer and that the much simpler Irish ones had a similar purpose. Recent studies in Britain suggest that these are not true circles but are made up of arcs of circles of different radii struck from collinear centres so that adjacent arcs merge smoothly the one into the next.

All this suggests a people possessing a good knowledge of geometry and astronomy. Linking this with the exquisite Irish gold work that dates from these times we must deduce that these people had a significant degree of civilisation and of culture.

Apart from these speculations there is one small piece of hard evidence about the recumbent or 'axial' stone circle. In the late 1950s one of these, at Drombeg, Glandore, Co. Cork was excavated by Dr E.M. Fahy. There were 17 stones in the circle but no outlier or central recumbent. Within the circle the ground had been levelled to the subsoil, gravelled and kept clean. Almost in the centre, under the gravelled pavement, was the ritual burial of a cremated adolescent. The axis between the recumbent boulder of the circle and the two portal stones opposite it was almost precisely that of the midwinter sunset. Two of the stones, carefully arranged, suggest fertility symbols, one phallic, the neighbouring lozenge female. No satisfactory dating emerged. The evidence suggests anything from the early bronze to the early iron ages. The probability is that these circles date from the early ages of metal.

The third mark of these people is the stone alignment and single pillarstone (gallan, menhir). Alignments of pillarstones seem to have had some ritual significance, but what we do not know. There is an alignment of four stones at Eightercua, Waterville, associated with a stone circle; at Kildreelig, Ballinskelligs; at Doory, Waterville, with a fifth some distance away and others now fallen; at Ballynacarrig, Killarney, associated with a great gallan; and of three stones at Dromtouk, Kenmare (the central one has ogam markings) and at Glanlough, Caherdaniel, at a gallery grave. There is an alignment of six stones at Garrough, Caherdaniel — these are almost certainly a signpost from the harbour at Derrynane to the copper workings at Coad. A somewhat similar alignment (though some

Stone circle, Drombeg, Co. Cork

of the stones are now missing) led to the wedge grave at Ballyhoneen and a complex one at Gallarus. However, there are in Kerry no alignments to compare with the enormous ones in Brittany.

Gallans, or single pillarstones, are widely scattered in Kerry. Some marked bronze age graves. Others had cult significnce, possibly representing gods — the pointed ones the male principle, the flat-topped ones the female; sometimes one of each is found together, as at Ballyferriter. Some recall the Hindu *yoni* with a hole through them some six inches in diameter — as in Kilmalkedar, Reask, Aghacarrible, Doonbeg. Some marked boundaries. Others marked routes, such as the tall one in the ringfort at Dromtine, Sneem. At Ballycrovane a tall gallan was set up as a beacon for the hidden harbour. They are typically eight to twelve feet above ground, but may be as high as 20 feet or as

low as four to six feet. A stone 10 feet high or more will date from early bronze age times even though much later ogam markings may have been added, or a christian cross. They continued to be erected into historical times with ogam markings, or christian crosses, or both. As a general rule, the smaller the later and *vice-versa*. They are grouped in three main areas in Kerry — in the Dingle peninsula; along the outer rim of the Iveragh peninsula; and in a ring centred on Castleisland. But individual ones are scattered throughout the county.

The fourth major relic of the beaker invasion, the rock scribings, is referred to below.

(I) THE COPPER AGE

As we have seen one branch of the beaker folk worked along the Atlantic coast and seems to have arrived in Kerry and west Cork,

The Ages of Metal
(I) The Copper Age

impelled at least in part by tne need to prospect for copper. (Bright quartz boulders are a good indication of the presence of copper). They arrived sometime before 2000 BC. We may have some racial memory of this invasion in the legendary account (referred to already) of the Milesian invasion from the same origin, to the same place and ascribed by the old writers to something like the period now in question. The south west of Ireland was one of the richest sources of copper in north western Europe. A mark of these people was the tanged copper dagger, the first weapon to be made of the metal; one of these triangular copper daggers, of unusual shape, as well as hatchet heads and fragments of a later weapon, the halberd, were found at Killaha East, Kenmare. The dagger is perhaps a fragment of the remains of these miners and craftsmen from Iberia. An axe of Killaha style was found at Newgrange in a settlement dating from 1935 BC. Another hoard was found at Knockasarnet, Killarney.

From this early metal period nearly 2,500 metal objects have been found, suggesting a considerable metal industry. All the Irish hoards (unlike the central European ones) are small — this suggests they were the stock-in-trade of a travelling smith or tinker. For example, tne Killaha hoard contains some roughly cast objects and one that is a casting failure, suggesting that the whole was the property of a casting smith.

Some of the old mines first used by these people continued to be used until relatively recent times. Near Killarney — at Muckross and on Ross Island — these mines were still being used in the 19th century. On Coad mountain, near Caherdaniel, are ancient copper mines, one of which became a christian hermit's cell; beside it are workings of the 17th-19th centuries. Across the Kenmare river, at Allihies in Cork, are workings first opened by the beaker folk and used in the present century.

Intriguing relics, which may be of these people, are rock scribings, of which Kerry is a major source, with the heaviest concentration in south Kerry. The scribings are pock marks on large boulders and rocks, often in remote places, but none of them far

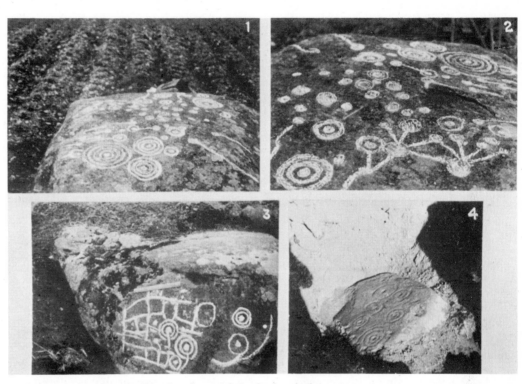

Scribings at Gortboy, Ballynahowbeg and Coolnaharrigal

distant from the coast. It is probable that from Kerry the scribings spread, along the usual trading route, to north Britain and Scandinavia.

The scribings fall into two classes — those that, as we have seen, hark back to the passage grave art of Newgrange and elsewhere; and those that are called 'Galician'. The Galician scribings are the more widespread. Whether they represent the work of existing people or whether they were designs brought afresh to Ireland, or whether they were in the common fashion an interaction of the two traditions is not clear. They were so called because they are paralleled in Galicia, in north west Spain, and in north Portugal. Similar scribings are to be found in Scotland. Some of the designs seem to have very old association with the eastern Mediteranean. Complex scribings can be seen at Ballynahowbeg, Cahersiveen; at Coomasaharn, Glenbeigh; at Derrynablaha, Ballaghabeama; at Staigue bridge;at Poulacopple, Kenmare;

at Ardcanaght, Castlemaine; and at Milltown, Dingle.

The basic scribing, as with the neolithic people, is the cup mark, a small, round hollow pocked in the stone; in many sandstone rocks this occurs naturally. There are also circles, concentric rings, triangles, etc., and lines linking the basic designs into complex patterns. Generally speaking, one is supposed to see in the scribings in simplified form the human face, figures squatting, perhaps the ribs in a human frame, stylised flowers, and men and skirted women with hands raised over their heads. Whether this is true of any of the Kerry scribings is a matter of considerable doubt — as indeed whether these are bronze age remains at all. For example, there are cups and circles on the upper surfaces of roof slabs at the great neolithic grave at Newgrange. Again, they have been found on early bronze age cists. For these, not in themselves convincing, reasons, they have been dated to the period

154 2300 BC to 1500 BC; but this problem of dating is but one of the problems here waiting to be cracked.

It is not clear why these representations should be made in these places which normally are devoid of monuments or remains. Whether these scribings, or the earlier neolithic ones, were made for cult reasons or for their own sake or are a form of pictograms and ideograms associated with an aborted evolution of writing, they have a curious interest and are continuing evidence of the place of south west Ireland on the great trade route from the Mediteranean to Scandinavia.

(II) THE BRONZE AGE

Copper began to be mixed with tin, in a ratio of about nine to one, to make the much harder metal, bronze, from about 1800 BC. Sometimes the copper ore was exported. It has been claimed by Smith, and before him by the Irish Nennius, that there was some tin in the Killarney area close to the copper workings, so that bronze could be readily cast locally. Some traces of tin have been found at Allihies and tin was also mined to some extent elsewhere in Ireland. But for the most part it seems that tin was imported and the bronze was mixed and worked here by itinerant craftsmen and traders. From this there grew up a substantial and remunerative export business.

Gold began to be mined in Kerry and west Cork about 2000 BC. The most striking relic of the bronze age is the beautiful metal work, especially in gold, that began to be produced and to be exported all over Europe from these times.

The bronze age, which began to be overlaid by the iron age perhaps as early as 800 BC, is traditionally divided into three periods — the early (to 1350 BC), the middle (1350 to 950 BC), and the late (950 to 300 BC); but another classification would give *two* periods — before and after 1200 BC. Of the three periods the most brilliant in Ireland as in Britain was the early bronze age of some 400 years centred on 1550 BC. There were made fine bronze weapons — daggers and rapiers,

axes, and halberds (daggers mounted on poles) — exquisite gold ornaments, and some pottery. A substantial find of bronze age weapons was made at Carhan, Cahersiveen. Of the gold ornaments the most striking was the *lunula*, or collar of beaten gold, with its zig-zag designs. Five of these found in Kerry are in the National Museum, Dublin. Three fine lunulae — a small, a medium, and a large — were found at Banemore, Abbeydorney. A large one and one of the finest now extant was found on Mangerton, Killarney. Another large one, but rather cruder than the others, was found at Ballingroun, Anascaul. Other gold ornaments found in Kerry were an unornamented fibula found in 'the parish of Templenoe' and a bent, pennanular ring at Carhan, Cahersiveen.

Irish goods of this kind are to be found all over Europe. Similarly, articles from north, south, west and central Europe are to be found in Ireland. This shows how active the Atlantic trade route continued to be. In particular, the axes found show the influence of the Battle Axe culture, the indo-europeans, who reached central Europe but so strongly influenced all of it. It must be borne in mind that metal objects were at all times during the bronze age scarce and dear and that in effect the great stone monuments and stone tools continued to be made.

As we have seen, the gallan and stone circle continued to be erected at this time. Round cairns on hilltops — as on the Paps mountains — may perhaps be dated to the early and middle bronze age. These cairns cover short cists that contain beakers in which have been found traces of strong drink; barley was the main crop in the bronze age; but it happens that Kerry is the only Irish county in which no bronze age cist has yet been found.

Stone beehive huts — some of which have been erected in Kerry in living memory and most of which are associated with christian sites — also began to be built in the early bronze age; they seem to have been an adaptation of the round, wooden hut. The normal house was rectangular, round or oval, with wattled walls and thatched roof. As well as barley the farmer grew wheat, oats, flax, and possibly, rye. He gathered wild

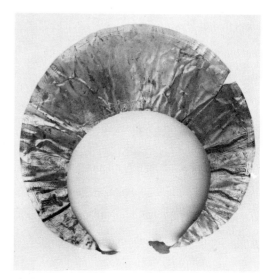

Ballingroun Lunula

plants — apparently some kind of cabbage (claimed to be a native of this country) and parsnip.

There were, as we have seen, groups of miners, smiths and traders, engaged amongst other things in an import-export trade. Perhaps it is not fanciful to picture such a community on Coad mountain bringing their ore and finished goods to the little harbour at Derrynane and importing there tin from Allihies and Cornwall and, for the farming folk, salt from central Europe. There is on Coad mountain the remains of a house that dates from these times.

The middle bronze age in Ireland stretches from about 1350 BC to about 950 BC. As in Britain in the same period there was a falling off from the brilliant and diversified culture of the earlier period. Nonetheless, a widespread material culture existed. Perhaps, as in other times, increasing affluence led to disorder. There was a substantial increase in the number and kinds of weapons in this period. To earlier weapons are joined the dirk, thrusting sword and spear which, in particular, became in number and variety an important weapon.

Perhaps for these reasons there arises sometime during this period the ringfort; (however, there is also some reason to believe that it began in the early bronze age). It certainly became widespread during the middle bronze age. The earliest kind seems to have been the *earthen* ringfort. This is called *dun, lios* or *rath*, hence placenames beginning with these words. *Dun* and *lios* have been held to be pre-goidelic words and *rath* to be a later term. (Strictly, the *rath* was the ring, the *lios* the place enclosed; but the terms came to be interchangeable). There may be, according to the importance of the place, one, two, or three rings, with a fosse outside each, but sometimes (as at Rahinnane, Dingle) it is inside the ring. The ring was often topped by a wooden palisade or a hedge of bushes or trees. There was a gap in the ring filled by a large wooden door. Builders of ringforts were highly regarded in later times at least: this was one of the attributes of the father of the gods, the Dagda. We read of a ringfort builder being paid, for a trivallate fort, as much cattle as the fort would hold.

In general, in later times, a bi-vallate ringfort was the home of the king of a tuath — thus Lissaree (of the king), near Sneem. Inside the ring was a number of houses, round or rectangular, built usually of wattles, whitewashed; but sometimes of stones. The houses were thatched, smaller ones with conical roofs. Outside the rings of the important forts (e.g. of kings) were the houses of dependants. The ring and fosse, apart from being useful enclosures (e.g. for farm animals) were also a protection against predators — wolves were plentiful: premiums for their capture were paid in Kerry until 1710 AD. These ringforts were mainly about farmsteads — the absence of wells indicates their peaceful purpose; but some, with substantial earthworks, (perhaps to guard against that new weapon, the sling) were defensive and places of refuge; these latter may date from later, more disturbed, times. Ringforts were used by the principal families until, in anglo-norman times, they built castles. Ringforts were most extensively used in early christian times (from the sixth to tenth centuries) and their use, and construction, continued for some centuries later — to elizabethan times, and in Co. Clare, to the

19th century. One can still see in use the ringfort, with round, conical roofed houses within, amongst the pastoral Masai tribesmen of Kenya and Tanzania. (Stone ringforts, promontory forts and hillforts date from periods later than the middle bronze age).

Examples of earthen ringforts in Kerry are (near Kilgobnet, Killarney) Lisnagallaun and Lispadrickmore. These have three and one rings respectively and each has a souterrain, with three and five chambers respectively.

At Ballynavenooragh, Brandon Creek, is a ringfort with the ruins of three clochans. (There are also stone forts nearby). At Glen, St Finan's Bay, is a small ringfort with an easily entered souterrain. At Temple Martin, Lispole, is a church inside a ringfort. Whether this was an appropriation of an existing one or the the building of, rather unusually, a special earthen ring is not clear. Almost 30,000 ringforts are marked on the ordnance survey maps. Of these, a third are in Munster and just 2,000 in Kerry. They are thickly concentrated in the Dingle area and around the Castleisland area, as well as in the coastal lands north of Tralee to the Shannon.

They have been preserved often because of superstition: the 'good people' who still live within them could perhaps turn nasty if disturbed. However, aerial photographs now reveal that this risk has been extensively taken and that many ringforts have been ploughed back into tilled land.

The wooden houses inside the ringforts have now wholly disappeared but in the stonier and poorer places the houses were built of stone and a number of these ruins remain to us.

A feature of many ringforts is the souterrain, an underground passage from a place inside the fort to one not far outside. A souterrain in Kerry usually consists of one, two, three or more chambers, normally corbelled — in effect underground clochans — in which adults can stand, approached by passages through which adults must wriggle. Sometimes the main passage is disguised, as at Dromavally, Anascaul, a side passage leads to a chamber cut off by a porthole that can

be closed by a moveable stone. They were thus clearly places of refuge and easily defended. They also seem to have been used as cool, if often dark, places of storage. They were still being used for this purpose during the anglo-norman invasion, according to Giraldus Cambrensis. A ringfort to which they were attached, therefore, normally had a defensive purpose. That they continued to be made in Kerry in christian times is shown by the ogam stones with crosses that were found as part of the construction of souterrains at Whitefield and at Coolmagort near Killarney, and at Aghacasla, Castlegregory. Souterrains without ringforts are to be seen at Muckross; at Glenderry, on Kerry Head, are a number of such souterrain systems. Champneys refers to a souterrain with up to 11 chambers at Ventry and Macalister to one with nine at Cloghane.

Another relic of the middle (and indeed early) as well as of late bronze age times is the outdoor cooking place, or *fulacht fiadh*. They were of two kinds — a wood lined trough in the earth to hold water and a stone lined hole. In the former meat was boiled in these holes. The water in them was brought to the boil by throwing in large quantities of stones heated in a great fire, the meat being wrapped in straw and immersed in the boiling water. In the stone lined holes the hot stones were used to roast the meat. In the old stories the Fiana typically cooked the fruit of their hunting in this way. The method was used at least as late as the time of Brian Boramha. Sites in Kerry are at Milleens, Cloghane and Rossanean. Several are said to exist in the sandhills at the Fenit end of Barrow strand.

With the late bronze age, from about 900 BC to 300 BC, we come to a fresh flowering of artistic activity and, clearly, wealth. There is a relatively tremendous output of often elaborately decorated weapons, to which shields have now been added, and of magnificent gold ornaments. Gold was worked at this time near Cahersiveen and near Kenmare. Gold fasteners and bracelets of this period were found at Staigue fort; in Templenoe, Kenmare; Headford; and, in a hoard, at Kilmoyley North, Ardfert. There

156

are many bronze trappings for horses showing that these animals had at last found a place where they were appreciated. The designs have clearly been influenced by continental models, whether from invasion or by the importation of smiths. As this period of the late bronze age wore on, trade routes between northern and central Europe on the one hand and the Mediteranean countries on the other were opened through the Alps, and the old Atlantic trade route via Ireland was by-passed. For this reason, after about 700 BC the main influences on Ireland were from northern and central Europe and the Iberian influence was much diminished. This reflects the rise of the celtic nation in central Europe which was to have profound effects on the history of Ireland.

Apart from weapons there was a considerable output of bronze cooking cauldrons — a generation ago one was found in Kerry as a feeding pot for hens — sickles and tools for bronze working. There have been substantial finds of hoards of bronze and gold products, suggesting insecure times. The armaments manufacturers — whose output was reaching its peak — were feeling the effects of their own work!

The striking mark of this in Kerry is the number of stone forts, mainly in the Iveragh and Dingle peninsulas, which began to be built from this period. Many, but by no means all, of these places were for defence, suggesting perhaps both a substantial rise in population forced out into these beautiful if rather barren places and the extension to peaceful areas of the need for defence. An alternative — or perhaps supplemental reason — is that these stone forts, as well as the somewhat later promontory forts, were the footholds of invaders from the sea. The magnificent Staigue fort at Castlecove, the best preserved and one of the most striking in the country, which may later have been a royal residence of the kings of Cashel, was clearly a military position of consequence; but the forts at Caherdaniel — there are two, an earlier and a later one side by side in a strong position — the defensive line of stones, or *chevaux de frise,* around one of the forts at Loher; the strong position of the fort at Caher Geal, Cahersiveen; the fosses around,

and the steps inside, the fort at Cahersavane, Waterville — all suggest military positions, perhaps from early periods. The building of these forts was of course made easy by the abundance of stones in these places; in some cases it may have been a handy way of using stones cleared from the fields.

However, not all these forts were military or early. That excavated at Leacanabuaile, Cahersiveen, showed that the houses inside were occupied by farming and fishing folk in the sixth to tenth centuries AD, that is, during the peak period for building ringforts generally. Indeed, Mr Rynne argues that Leacanabuaile dates from after the anglo-normans. It appears that stone forts of this kind were being built up to the 16th and 17th centuries. Mlle Henry has identified no less than five stone forts in a small area of Loher, and there are many close to the Finglas river between Loher and Waterville. These must

Staigue Fort, Castlecove

have been part of a farming settlement. Sometimes a caher will be very small, like the ruined one at Fermoyle, Ballinskelligs. On the Dingle peninsula there are, in the Fahan area, many stone ringforts with clochans, etc; but these are the remains of a big town of christian times. At Cahercrovdarrig, Rathmore, is a fort that may possibly have been the royal seat of Teamhair Luachra, if such ever existed. A stone fort is called *cathair* or *caiseal.* Hence the place names beginning caher or cashel. The second word comes from the latin *castellum,* hence a 'castle'.

The best of these forts, as at Staigue, show great skill in building. No mortar was used and the stones were not dressed. The facing stones, inside and out, were laid with great skill and the space between them filled with rubble, to make a wall some 18 feet thick. Inside again were built sets of stairs leading to

a ledge near the top. This skill in drystone building, the great flat lintel over the entrance, the sloping jambs, the 'batter' of the walls, — and the corbelling of the chambers inside the walls — that inside the entrance was the standard retreat for the guard dogs — all these were to be the dominant features of Irish building until well into christian times.

Another type of late bronze age dwelling is the crannog. This is an artificial, defended island made in a lake — like a rath set in water. I am not aware of any in Kerry. The little island in Cloon Lough has a stone wall around it and so has the christian settlement on Church Island, Valentia harbour. These recall, in part, the principle of the crannog which continued in use to the 16th century.

Another relic of bronze age times is the field boundaries now largely but not wholly obliterated. The fields tend to be square and to range in size from a half acre to two acres. They can often be discerned from a height or from an opposing hill. Above Cloon Lough are, in addition to ruined houses and field boundaries, some striking examples of terraced fields. Another example is on the low hill east of Dromtine Lough, Sneem. The existence of these old fields shows that there must have been private property in animals and, at least, in the products of the fields.

To be discerned amongst the relics of old farming folk are the old roadways. To follow these roadways is often the best way of stumbling on ancient settlements. One can think of the landscape at this time of the late bronze age as an untidy patchwork of tillage patches, pastures, dwellings and trackways lying amongst abandoned clearings, secondary scrub and virgin woodland.

Some time in the latter part of the late bronze age the weather got much cooler and wetter, inhibiting the growth of pine and elm, favouring birch, oak. alder and hazel, and flooding the bogs, causing them once more to grow. It was in such a bog as this that someone, perhaps a travelling goldsmith, buried in a wooden box in Kilmoyley, Ardfert, his golden treasures, to save them from such great danger — no doubt iron age

invaders — as he was not himself to survive. So came to an end the bronze age and with it for 1,000 years the age of gold and golden exports.

(III)   THE IRON AGE

The iron age in Ireland dates from perhaps 800 BC and spans the gap to the opening of the christian age sometime around 400 AD.

We have seen that the Irish people from stone age times consisted of an old mesolithic stock, a group of western neolithic peoples, and the beaker folk. These, in bronze age times were at least influenced by the battle axe indo-european culture from the east. In central Europe something of the same sort happened. The beaker folk from the west overlapped with the battle axe people from the east, and both overlaid older stocks. From this amalgam emerged the first recognisable historical nation north of the Alps. This occurred some time after 1000 BC. These people were the Celts who were also called Gauls or Galatians. (Dillon and Chadwick say in their book *The Celtic Realms* that the celts could have arisen 1,000 years before the date given here, and that the celts thus reached Ireland long before the dates that follow. If so, this would upset the chronological order of the celtic invaders given in Part I of this book. On this showing, the beaker folk were early celts, who may have been the Goidels and this would explain why the latter spoke a more ancient form of celtic.)

The Celts appear in history — as distinct from linguistics and archaeology — in the sixth century BC. Some centuries after their rise as a people they were to overrun Europe — east as far as Asia Minor (where in later times St Paul was to write to them), south as far as Sicily, and west as far as Ireland. Their homeland was in the area north of the Alps. At the end of the bronze age, and at the beginning of the iron age, that is, perhaps in the eighth century BC, there grew up amongst them a remarkable material and artistic culture. They were notably skilled in building vehicles and, in consequence, roads. Perhaps because they were early to use iron tools they

could grow more food and they became very numerous. They were remarkably skilled in metal work and the finds at their cemetery of Hallstat, in the Salzkammergut, Upper Austria, dating from the seventh century BC are a cornerstone in European art. The Hallstat culture was to affect both Ireland and Britain with its brilliant, but geometrical, designs.

Because of their increasing wealth, the celts engaged in extensive trade with the south — particularly for wine — and absorbed many southern and eastern cultural influences. Hence the zoomorphic and interlacing motifs in their metal work, called La Tene after the place on Lake Neuchatel, Switzerland, where a notable find, dating back to the fifth century BC was made. This, from about the first century BC, was the greatest single influence on Irish art, and on celtic art in Britain. As the Czech writer, Jan Filip, says:

And once again we see documented the Celtic ability to recast foreign elements in the melting pot of their own concepts. The abstract principle in Celtic ornament reached its culmination in the insular art of this period. It is not a mere stylisation of natural forms, but a new expressive art working with forms independent of nature and reality.

This power to absorb foreign influences and to create something new and distinctive is to be seen over and over again in Irish history. This influence survived in Ireland — Jacobsthal's summary of celtic art could be a reference to Joyce's writing:

It is attractive and repellent; it is far from primitiveness and simplicity; it is refined in thought and technique, elaborate and clever, full of paradoxes, restless, puzzlingly ambiguous; rational and irrational; dark and uncanny.

(Joyce himself referred *Finnegans Wake* back to the *Book of Kells*, itself perhaps the most remarkable product of celtic art).

The celts settled in strength in what is now northern Italy, France, Spain and Portugal. It took the Romans some three centuries to

158

crush them. They left behind them much craft work and some monuments, but no records or literature. This is because these last were the preserve of the druid class who insisted on their oral transmission through the strict discipline of the druidic schools. This exclusively oral transmission continued even when they came into contact with latin and greek writing. Eventually, the oral records and the celtic social system were overwhelmed by the force of the culture and institutions of their conquerors. The result is that little remains of celtic thought and religion and nothing of their literature. Such fragments as remain are contained in the not always comprehending comments of latin and greek writers. Occasionally, however, one reads a comment that strikes a familiar note. The celts, we are told, were notably fond of horses, talk, drink, hospitality and feasting. 'The whole nation', says Strabo, '. . . is war mad, and both high spirited and quick for battle although otherwise simple and not uncouth'. The elder Cato says the celts 'have two great passions, to be brave in warfare and to speak well'.

The first of the main celtic invasions of these islands — there were several — may have been as early as the 6th century BC, although modern opinion tends to favour a date several centuries later. These invasions were part of the natural overflowing of the race. This was followed at a later date by the pressure from behind of the rising German peoples. This pressure seems, in particular, to have influenced the movements of the Belgae, who inhabited the most easterly of the three parts into which Caesar divided Gaul. It is probable that the iron age proper came to Ireland with this group. Lastly came the roman pressure that drove celtic refugees to Britain at least.

Some theories of how the celts came to Ireland have been referred to in Part I; but, however they came, here they remained, distinctive, untouched by roman power, the main and almost the only surviving remnant of the first of the 'barbarian' nations of Europe. When one hears, at the tip of the Dingle or Iveragh peninsulas, native speakers of Irish one can hear, in unbroken line, the descendants of the language that grew up in

central Europe almost 3,000 years ago, itself enshrining many ideas and concepts dating back to the common stock of indo-europeans. It is believed that nearly all the European languages had a common origin, the language of the indo-europeans of about 2000 BC. In the next 1,000 years this language split into distinctive groups — slavonic, germanic, italic, common celtic, etc. Each of these divided into the modern language groups. With the others, common celtic broke into the present-day celtic languages — Irish, Welsh, Breton, etc. One of the puzzling features of this is that Irish seems to have broken off from common celtic at an early stage although the gaels, whose language it was, were latecomers to Ireland.

We have seen that the celtic learned class refused to record in writing the traditions, ideas and literature of their peoples and that they perished in the tide of roman culture. This did not happen in Ireland because the romans did not directly come here. When their influence came indirectly by way of christianity the habit of writing and recording was freely accepted by a people intensely conscious of their heritage. Eventually, the christian monastic schools took over from the old oral druidic schools and it is to these monasteries that we owe the writing down of Irish literature — itself stimulated by the impact of latin and greek — from about the 8th century AD. Much of this literature was screened by the monastic writers and, in Ireland, literature has always been intensely localised; but behind all this we can reach back in some way into the old celtic consciousness. Next to the latin and greek literatures, Irish is the oldest in Europe and through it we can penetrate into a strange, fascinating and curious world. Irish as a language has been retreating for centuries, and the extremities of Kerry are amongst the few places where it has survived in everyday use; but much of what surrounds one in Kerry harks back to these ancient times of the early iron age. Moreover, it is becoming increasingly clear that this tradition stretches right back into indo-european times — to the common ancestors of both celts and Indians — thus making it the oldest of all European traditions. Writers have pointed out significant similarities between the two

priestly castes — the celtic druids and the Indian brahmins. The metres in the *Rigveda* can be echoed in the earliest Irish poetry. There are some striking parallels in the ancient Irish and Indian law books, relating to marriage, property, fasting as a symbol of getting redress. Some characteristic survivals of Indian religion remain in Ireland — such as the Turoe stone in Galway and the holed stones at Kilmalkedar, Dingle. Macalister claims that there is evidence from earlier grave sites that *sati* was frequently practised in Ireland.

In Kerry the striking remains of the celtic iron age are the promontory forts — of which Westropp counted 43 in the county — which are a constant feature of north Kerry and of the Dingle peninsula. In these places considerable numbers of promontories have each a fort cut off from the mainland by an earthen or stone wall and fosse. Indeed, over large areas of the south and west of Ireland nearly every promontory is defended in this way. Probably the most striking and complex of these forts is at Dunbeag, Fahan, which has a souterrain and is made of large stones. There is an interesting promontory fort at Cooseenadagallan, Valentia; there are others in the mainland nearby; and many others in north Kerry, especially above Ballybunion. The most considerable inland promontory fort in Ireland is Caherconree high on the mountain of that name between Inch and Camp, cut off on three sides by conglomerate cliffs and cut off from the main part of the mountain by a wall of *small* stones that were to play their part in the downfall of the owner of the fort, the magical Curoi mac Daire. Promontory forts were a special mark of the Belgae in Gaul.

Another early iron age remain (if it does not date from the late bronze age) is the hillfort, with a rampart round the whole top of the hill. These are common in Britain and relatively scarce in Ireland. There is an example, but not a very striking one, at Dunkilla, Sneem.

At Dromtine, Sneem, are the remains of an iron age mine.

We have to imagine the ruling classes —

certainly in celtic times — living in ring, stone and promontory forts. Outside these, in scattered clusters through the open fields were the unenclosed, wattle and daub houses of the serfs, the subject populations. These farm clusters are related to the present-day townland, the *baile;* it is believed that this is a pre-celtic word. These clusters survived until fairly recently and traces of them, still partly inhabited, can be found west of Dingle.

EARLY WRITING

(I) OGAM

A major iron age relic is ogam writing which overlaps the end of the iron age and the beginning of the christian period. We have seen that a mark of the bronze age is the gallan, often a very large stone, but with no inscription on it.

So, at last towards the end of the iron age we come upon written records. Ogam is called after the celtic god of eloquence, Ogmios, but the surviving ogam inscriptions are anything but eloquent: they are austere and uncommunicative, mainly names on gravestones, often giving also the descent of the deceased. They are written in a form of script peculiar to Irish. It is based on the roman alphabet. In this it resembles, as well as partly influenced, runic script; but that began earlier and continued to be used much longer — moreover, the runic stones are usually much more communicative. Ogam script may have begun about the fourth century AD or a little earlier and continued in use until the seventh century by which time cursive writing, under the influence of the missionaries, had become common in Ireland. Thus the inscriptions cover the transition from a wholly pagan to a mainly christian Ireland. Ogam has been used occasionally, no doubt in a spirit of antiquarianism, up to the 19th century.

The principle of ogam is simple — cross lines are related to a single spinal line. The script may have arisen from cutting notches on a stick — like a tally stick — so as to send messages. It may have been invented in Ireland by an Irishman who had spent time in Britain where he had learned latin and its

alphabet; but Professor Carney has recently (1973) argued that it was a cipher imported directly from Gaul, perhaps as early as the first century BC. Its use for *epigraphic* purposes on gallans may not have begun until 400 AD. In any event, the ogam stones in Ireland are written in a very archaic form of language, with forms like those of Gaulish, bearing the same relation to those of later Irish as Latin does to French. The numerous mistakes make it possible that the archaisms may have been a deliberate use of old, but imperfectly understood, forms, as Latin is still used for inscriptions.

Over 360 ogam stones survive, about 60 of them in Britain in places of Irish influence, mainly in Wales. Of the stones in Ireland, just five-sixths of them are found in Waterford, Cork and Kerry, in the territory occupied by the pre-goidelic race of the Erainn (or Ivernian or Firbolg). Of all ogam stones a third are in Kerry alone and of the Kerry stones about three-fifths are found in the territory formerly occupied by the Corcu Duibne. It may be that this people, gifted as we know them to be, were the originators of this style of writing. Ogam stones are clearly descendants of the pillarstone or gallan. Ogam writing has been put on some existing bronze age gallans.

The ogam alphabet has twenty principal letters divided into four groups of five, no doubt based on fingers, as follows:

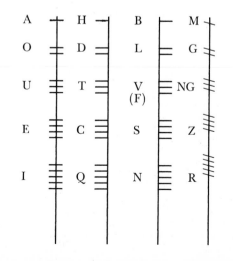

The first column is of five vowels; sometimes these appear as dots. In the second column the letters *H, D, T, C* are the initials, in old Irish, of the numerals one to four; but *Q* is not the initial for five. Six rare complications (diphthongs, etc.) have been omitted. Professor Carney argues that the order in which the letters are grouped is part of the cipher system.

The cross lines are usually related to a straight spinal line. This is usually the left, as one faces the writing, corner of the pillarstone. One reads from the bottom up. Occasionally a long inscription is continued over the top and down the right side. Sometimes the spinal line is implied and the characters may wander over a rounded stone, as on Ballintaggart IX below.

Some of the stones are fairly well preserved and it is of interest to try to read them. This is not always easy. The characters are 'pocked' on the stone in a manner that dates from neolithic times: a good example of the neolithic technique of pocking is given on the principal stone at Derrynablaha, Ballaghabeama. Pocking was done with another stone; metal chisels were seldom used until crosses were incised on early christian or christianised slabs. Because of this, because of the natural forms of the stone, the weathering of sandstone, the growth of lichen, and deliberate defacement, many stones are hard to read accurately, and there has been dispute between the scholars on this point. The defacing of stones is of interest. Macalister, noting that the part defaced so often relates to the ancestry of the deceased, argues that this claims descent from a pagan god and the obliteration marks the struggle of the christian missionaries against old beliefs. For example, of the 71 stones in the baronies of Corkaguiney and Iveragh, the territory of the Corcu Duibne, only five now bear the name of the tutelary goddess, Dovvinias. Many ogam stones have crosses carved on them, as well as other figures, perhaps to 'convert' the stone and to christianise its power. Sometimes the cross is later than the ogam, sometimes earlier. A striking example of ogam superimposed on a cross can be seen on the stone found on Church Island, Valentia, and now in Cork

159

160 Museum. There are some curious, perhaps magical, ogam inscriptions, now meaningless. The stones, before they come to an end in the seventh century, mark the change from a pagan to a christian society. A small number of names from the early historical period have been identified from the markings. It is clear that much more analytical work needs to be done on the remains. This may lead to revision of Macalister's work.

Ogam stone at Coolmagort, Killarney

There are, in Kerry, two convenient places for studying ogam stones. (The most convenient place is, of course, the first volume of Macalister's remarkable book, referred to below). The first place is the group of seven stones set up at Coolmagort, near Dunloe castle, Killarney, after they had been rescued from a nearby souterrain — where they supported the roof — and so preserved from severe wear. They are thus, in the main, easier to read than most. Only one has a christian sign — a tiny cross in a circle — so that they may be from late pagan times, that is from the fifth or sixth century AD. The example on the left reads, from the bottom up, across the top and down the right hand side (but here shown straight for simplicity):

MAQI TTAL MAQI VORGOS MAQI MUCOI TOICAC

In the original the vowels (that is, those lines that cross the spine strictly horizontally) are shown as dots on the spine. In each instance 'The stone of' is to be understood before the inscription. *MAQI* means 'of the son' and *MUCOI* means 'of the kindred'. Thus the inscription reads in English: 'The stone of the son of Ttal the son of Vorgos the son of the kindred of Toicac'. Two of the other stones relate to this kindred. Sometimes a single name is inscribed.

In Macalister's numbering and decipherment the Coolmagort stones read as follows:

197. I *DEGOS MAQI MUCOI TOICACI*
198. II *MAQI RITEAS MAQI MAQI — DDUMILEAS MUCOI TOICACI*
199. III *CUNACENA*
200. IV as above

201. V   too damaged to be read
202. VI *NIOTTVRECC MAQI (. . . .) GNI*
203. VII *MAQI DECEDA MAQ (. . . .)*

There is an eighth stone here, a recumbent, brought from the old parish church of Kilbonane a short distance away. This is unusual in having three inscriptions, one at each side and one, in two lines, on the face, and in the nature of one of these inscriptions. Macalister deciphers the two inscriptions on the sides as follows:

241. *B [AID] AGNI MAQI ADDILONA NAGUNI MUCO BAIDANI*

The letters in brackets are conjectural.

On the face of the stone he reads:

*NIR *** MN [I] DAGNIESSICONIDDALA AMIT BAIDAGNI*

The three asterisks represent three unknown 'W' like characters around the letter 'B'. Mac Neill, to some scepticism, renders them *ABAA.* This would give a sentence:

   NI RABA AMNI DAGNI, ESSE CONIDD ALA AMIT BAIDAGNI

reading 'let it not be thus he makes it, but let him compose it thus 'Baidagni'. If this is correct it is a criticism of the spelling in the second inscription, and an unusual example of a message, other than a mortuary inscription, on one of the stones.

The second place for studying these stones is the little cemetery at Ballintaggart, Dingle.

The Ballintaggart stones number nine and the little cemetery is off the Tralee-Dingle road close to the race-course. Eight of the stones are some three or four feet long; one is shorter. They have been rounded by the sea into broadly egg shapes and it is claimed that stones of this sort do not naturally occur nearer than Minard strand some six miles away where they are plentiful. Several of the stones have crosses inscribed and thus seem to date from early christian times, say the sixth to seventh centuries.

Macalister's numbering and renderings are:

155. I   *AKREVRITTI*

156. II *MAQQI–IARI KOI MAQQI MUCCOI DOVVINIAS.* This stone has a plain cross incised in the middle. It uses a rare symbol, *X,* for *KOI* meaning *the* (i.e. principal) descendant of . . . The unnecessary duplication of bulky consonants, a general practice, is because, it is suggested, the stone cutter was paid by piece rates! (A stone at Rathduff should read *LONOC* in 15 strokes, but was cut *LLONNOCC* in 26). Dovvinias, or Duben, was the tutelary goddess of the Corcu Duibne.

157. III *DOVETTI MAQI CATTINI.* Macalister in the second edition of his *Archaeology* cites this inscription as, not a commemoration but, an embodiment of the dead Dovettos in the stone. To chip off the name is to destroy the personality.

158. IV *SUVALLOS MAQQI DUCOVAROS*

159. V *MAQI–DECCEDA MAQI GLASICONAS*

160. VI *TRIA MAQA MAILAGNI.* This, Macalister says, is to be understood as *TRIAM MAQAM MAILAGNI,* 'of the three sons of Mailagnos'. This is a first inscription. The stone has incised on its back a probably later one: *CURCITTI.* The stone has also incised, on its centre, a curious cross with triple, expanding ends, an early version of what was to become known as an 'Irish' cross. Is it so 'fanciful' as Macalister says, to take this triple cross as a comment on the lost three sons?

161. VII *INISSIONAS.* There is a plain cross on the stone.

162. VIII *CUNAMAQQI AVI CORBBI. AVI,* which has become Ua or O, means 'granson'.

163. IX *NETTA LAMINACCA KOI MAQQI MUCOI DOVIN [IA] S. See* 156. *NETTA* means 'nephew'. The centre of the stone has an incised cross with expanding terminals. It is, in relation to the writing, upside down and was, presumably, added later.

There is a large stone some eight feet high at Crag, Currans, near Castleisland. This bears a word on each side, the epitaph *VELITAS LEGUTTI* which Macalister has rendered, to some scepticism, as 'of Leguttos the poet'. If he was so, his works are unknown, but that he was of some significance in the fourth or fifth century can be seen from the size of this memorial which, Macalister claimed, is perhaps the oldest and the greatest memorial to a poet in northern Europe. His monument is, however, a second hand one — earlier inscriptions have been hammered away.

(II) RUNIC

Runic writing seems to have been influenced in some degree by ogam and was in vogue in the same period, but began a century or so earlier and continued in use for several centuries longer. Only a few of these stones have been found in Ireland, one of them used as a lintel of a 12th-13th century house on Beginish beside Valentia Island. It commemorates the men who erected and carved the stone. It has a small cross carved on it. There may have been a viking settlement in this place.

RACIAL TYPES

For long periods in Ireland the dead were cremated, and thus there are scanty human remains to give some idea of the kind of people who inhabited this country in early times. Even for periods when cremation was not the rule the skeletons and skulls that survive are few indeed. This is a field of study where scanty evidence and dangerous generalisations are not unusual. Nonetheless,

162 some sort of picture emerges.

(I) SKULLS

Skulls can be classified into various shapes — the simplest classification is into long and round; but there are others: width, height, capacity, etc. These can be related in some way to predominant sub-racial groupings in other countries. The argument is that where a single feature, such as long-headedness, exists in a substantial part of an existing population, that feature is likely to persist even if there are considerable invasions by, for example, round heads. If a particular racial type is spread fairly consistently throughout the population it is likely to have been the basic, or oldest, one and this can, of course, be checked against finds in ancient tombs. If other types are found to have concentrations in special areas they may be the relics of invasions into those areas. So far as can be made out, invasions after the iron age — that is, by vikings, anglo-normans, English and Scots — do not seem to have much altered the physical features of the existing 'mix' of the population, so the study of the distribution of sub-racial groups in Ireland may conceivably be related to archaeological, legendary and historical evidence about the earliest Irishmen.

It is of interest to see whether the distribution of sub-racial types in Ireland falls into categories and whether Kerry is in any way different in the distribution of the vestiges of the layers of settlement from the most ancient times. It is often said that the people of Kerry, and of the west generally, being often short and dark, show evidence of Spanish ancestry. However, it is possible to take this discussion further as a result of a most curious book by Hooton and Dupertuis based on a 1934-36 survey of over 10,000 Irish men and almost 2,000 Irish women taken in the western counties. The results can be related in some way to archaeological and other remains.

The most common type in the Irish population, and the most evenly spread, is the Nordic-Mediteranean — 29% of Irishmen as a whole, 26% of Kerrymen. They have long skulls, are shortish, with darkish hair and

eyes of mixed colour. Palaeolithic man (so far as he is represented in Ireland) and mesolithic man were long-headed and short, and the neolithic people — except possibly the passage grave people — were of somewhat similar build. It may be therefore that by the end of the stone age there had been an amalgam of the rather similar peoples of the early, middle and late stone ages into a basic Irish population type that still survives in rather more than one in four of present-day Irishmen.

The invaders of the age of metal were round-headed and can be related with a little more assurance to the two leading round-headed groups in the present Irish population. These are the Dinarics, who seem to have been the beaker folk, and are 19% of Irishmen and 26% of Kerrymen, and the Nordic Alpines (18% and 25% respectively). To these as perhaps a segregation of a rufous strain in these invaders can be added the East Baltics (1% and 2.5% respectively). Thus the bronze age population strains represent almost two in five of present-day Irishmen; but over half of present-day Kerrymen. The Dinarics are round-headed with long faces and usually long, hooked noses, and are of various colourings. The Nordic Alpines have round heads, broad faces, relatively broad noses and darkish colourings. The East Baltics are round-headed with blond or red hair and mixed eyes.

Thus, two-thirds of Irishmen can be said possibly to incorporate the stocks of the Irishmen of the stone and bronze ages, and four-fifths of Kerrymen.

The most distinctive type in Ireland but not the most common — 25% of Irishmen but only 15% of Kerrymen — is the Celtic, long-headed with darkish or red hair, and blue eyes. Of the four groups of celts which, according to O Rahilly as we have seen already, overran Ireland in the iron age, only one — the Laginian — conform it seems to this type. The other three — Picts (or Cruithin or Pretani), Fir Bolg or Erainn, and Goidels — conformed, it would seem, to the existing types of Nordic-Mediteranean, Dinaric-East Baltic, and Nordic-Alpine. Thus, on this analysis, Kerry did not get any special

infusion from the Laginians or Picts because their respective types are scarcer than in the population as a whole. But it did most decisively get infusions from the Fir Bolg and the Goidels, because these types are more numerous in Kerry than in the population as a whole.

For what it is worth, the following table summarises the position:

Type	Distribution (% of population)		Period
	Ireland	Kerry	
Nordic-Mediteranean	29	26	Stone (Pictish)
Dinaric-East Baltic	20	29	Bronze (Erainn)
Nordic-Alpine	18	25	Bronze (Goidels)
Celtic	25	15	— (Laginian)
Others	8	5	—

The general conclusions of Hooton and Dupertuis about Kerry are:

Kerry is the leading brachycephalic (round-headed) county and shows the highest index of East Baltics. The other round-headed types — Dinaric and Nordic Alpine — also markedly exceed there their normal proportions. . . . Here the strongest Irish types, Nordic-Mediteranean and Keltic, fall far below their expected occurrence.

Of Kerrymen as a whole:

Large, heavy, sub-brachycephalic men with broad faces, square jaws and long, narrow noses are, then, the hypothetical average for Kerry. The most notable morphological feature of Kerry is the enormous excess of blue-brown eyes.

Amongst other excesses is freckling.

Kerry peasant, c. 1900

(II) BLOOD GROUPS

Other evidence comes from blood groups. Generally, racial groups can be related to dominant genetic groupings of blood. These tend to be very stable in any population and therefore to reflect invasions by people of different genetic groupings. In this way different racial origins can be glimpsed.

In Ireland the National Blood Transfusion service has collected evidence of some 120,000 blood donors in the 1950s and 1960s, and their blood groupings have been related to the counties in which the donors were born. The following figures contrast, for the 26 counties of the Republic of Ireland and for Kerry, the distribution of the frequencies of the three genes in the most common classifications of blood groups.

	Distribution of genes (%)		
	O	A	B
Ireland (26 counties)	75	18	7
Kerry	77	15	8

The overall Irish figures contain a remarkable vertical striping effect: an extra concentration of group O genes in the western counties from Kerry to Donegal; a similar concentration of group A genes in the counties along the east coast; and a concentration of group B genes in the midland counties, with the addition of Cork and Kerry.

The concentration of group O genes in the west of Ireland, of which Kerry is fairly typical, is probably the highest in Europe, and the shift to group A genes as one moves eastward is a typical European pattern. This suggests that an early population of Europe belonged predominantly to group O, but a people in which group A genes were prominent overran Europe, perhaps from its centre; at the extremity, in the west of Ireland, its effect on the native stock is least. Group A genes are a prominent feature of the population of Britain, and the high concentration of this group along the east coast of Ireland can closely be related to the import of anglo-normans and English stock from the 12th century AD. (The earlier Scandinavian invasion seems to have been of people with genes similar to the native Irish). It is probable that the pre-12th century Irish had an O concentration of about 78%, as compared with a concentration of 68% in England, so that in this respect the present Kerry population is of a stock similar to that of much of Ireland 1,000 to 2,000 years ago. Kerry has an infusion of something over 10% of English stock, compared with 26% for the 26 counties as a whole; so that Kerry has not much more than a third of the English infusion. Unfortunately, the published figures do not distinguish between north and south Kerry or, for our area, by names. We know from historical evidence that, following the geraldine occupation of north

Kerry, there was a considerable import of settlers, an experience that south Kerry did not share. Is there a different incidence of group A genes north and south?

Even more intriguing is the incidence of group B genes. Dawson deduces that this group invaded Ireland from the east (and perhaps the south?) but were overlain by the later English A invaders so that the B group are now evident only in the south and midlands where the A group did not become dominant. One is tempted to see in this intermediate group B the relics of the celtic, especially the goidelic, invaders of the iron age whose centres of power were the south and the midlands, centring on Cashel and Tara, overlaying, as a significant minority, the older O stock. Here again, closer study of distributions, in baronies and by names, is needed.

In fine, one can say that the evidence of skull types and blood groups, so far as it goes, gives some support to the archaeological, legendary and historical evidence of the origins of Kerrymen.

PAGAN RELIGION

From other scanty evidence — physical remains and strange survivals — we can glean some glimmering of the nature of old Irish religion, and therefore of some of the modes of thought of the earliest Irishmen. As each great ethnic or cultural wave passed over the country it must have blotted out much of what existed before it; but it also preserved a little, sometimes consciously, sometimes unconsciously. No doubt there were common features in the various faiths and these served to reinforce each other. Some of the great natural features — mountains and rivers — were often associated with deities and may have preserved their ancient names.

Wood-Martin makes an important point in distinguishing between the religion of the common people and that of the official cults. These latter would be much more vulnerable to the invasion of new official faiths while the popular devotions could carry on at least an underground and local existence through

164

great periods of time. There would also tend to be more primitive forms of religion, such as animism. Looking backwards, therefore, we can discern two broad layers of pagan religion in Ireland — the local, popular and primitive cults, and the official religions of the conquering aristocracies.

(I) WELLS AND TREES

Of course the local cults would have to make some concession to the prevailing official religion. Thus we find the striking survival to our own times of animism. This is shown in the veneration given to holy wells and holy trees, and through them to ancient local gods now disguised as (often dubious) christian saints. This survival has withstood the denunciation of the fifth century council of Arles of those 'who offer vows to trees, or wells or stones', These popular devotions may carry some memories of intervening official cults — such as of the celtic religions — but it is most likely that we see in these popular practices the survival of the faiths of our earliest stone age ancestors. Paradoxically the need of the later religions to come to terms with these popular devotions helped to preserve them, as often when a christian settlement was established at one of these pagan sites.

Some of this may be illustrated by devotions at Kilcrohane, Coad. Here there was a sacred tree — for which there is the special word *bile* — and no less than three holy wells. The ancient form of the devotions suggest that they derive from the earliest, stone age, times. The remains of the bronze age mine beside one of the holy wells suggest that the miners practised these devotions. A pattern is held here — now in much attenuated form — at the end of July showing that it became appropriated to the celtic god Lug. The devotions became attached to a St Criomhthain, who may have been the pre-patrician missionary, Kieran of Saigir, whose hermitage is at the old mine. The medieval parish church now in ruins is dedicated to this St Criomhthain. When we see on a summer's day people making the 'rounds' at this place — the *bile* was standing in the middle of the last century — we see something that has continued, no doubt, from the earliest Irish

men and women. In later times the literature mentions some famous ash, oak or yew known by name. Chieftains were often inaugurated beneath a special tribal tree.

The cult of the wells is very extensive — over 3,000 have been listed in Ireland. For Kerry, Mr O Danachair has listed in the three baronies of north Kerry some 44 wells and no less than 59 in Corkaguiney. There is some doubt about some of these wells. In the other baronies such wells are also numerous. The wells are now dedicated to God himself, the Virgin, or a saint (but never, in Kerry, to St Patrick). In former times great patterns were held at some of the wells but these have either died out or have lost their vigour. Only a minority of the wells are still visited, and by declining numbers. Some are visited on the patron saint's day, but others are visited at all times. At the wells certain prayers are said; 'rounds' are made, a clock-wise circuit of the well, an associated grave, mound, etc. — this is the *deisiol*: to go anti-clockwise, or *tuathal*, against the sun is to invoke black magic; and water is drunk or otherwise used. The wells are often believed to have healing qualities. Sometimes these are attributed to the waters themselves; but more often the cure is believed to be granted to pilgrims who perform the prescribed ritual with good intentions. A number of wells are believed to cure sore eyes, others to cure headache, backache, toothache and rheumatism. A few, it is claimed, will cure any ill. An offering is often believed to be part of the exercise — hence coins dropped into the well or strips of clothing or rags tied to the bushes around it. The rag is a sort of scapegoat on which the ill to be cured is placed. It is thus not only an offering but a riddance. Similar customs have been reported from India and, indeed, from all over the world.

A number of wells have slabs or stones, incised or carved in relief with a cross. Wells tend to be close to what are now christian sites, such as St Buonia's well at Killabuonia; but occasionally they are close to other remains. The most important of the wells is perhaps Wether's well near Ardfert where St Brendan was baptised; the name comes from the three wethers that sprang from the

well when the baby saint was brought to it. Here one may see the rags tied to the bushes that recall its very early origin.

A main feature of this traditional observance, much to be seen in Kerry, is the pilgrimage and patron. This is held once a year on the feast of the patron saint of the well. The well, sometimes beside a parish church now in ruins, maintained a special prominence at the site as the centre around which the patronal meeting (or pattern) was held. As we have seen, the religious observance at a pattern consisted almost always of rounds with a prescribed set of prayers at the well, with possibly other rounds at nearby stations. After the rounds, sports, dancing and general sociability took over so that the word 'patron' has come to mean an outdoor rural festive gathering with a religious core.

Apart from the sacred tree, or *bile*, special veneration has always been given to the whitethorn tree, special to the 'good' people, or fairies. Widespread acceptance of the existence of these people — who could turn nasty indeed if crossed — can be found in the folk mind, together with many superstitious beliefs and practices.

That so much of this should have survived through such periods and so many upheavals illustrates yet another of the astounding continuities of Irish life.

Apart from this popular observance there can be seen remnants of the 'official' religions of stone, bronze and iron age Ireland.

(II) CULT OF THE DEAD

The first of these is the cult of the dead. It is clear that from neolithic times at least, when grave goods of one kind and another were interred with the deceased, that there was a strong belief in life after death. The cult of the dead was at its strongest in the earliest periods, and many of the most striking monuments we have are the tombs of neolithic princes. The strain goes through the bronze age monuments, the ogam monuments, to the christian saints' tombs. It is striking that many of the christian sites in Kerry should be beside ancient tombs.

Pagan Religion
(I) Wells and Trees
(II) Cult of the Dead
(III) Stone Circles
(IV) Celtic Gods

Things   Part 2

165

It seems as if, in Kerry, popular devotions, in early christian times, were associated with a widespread cult of the dead and that the christian missionaries found it necessary to cash in on the devotions. But that the principle of life was also served as well as that of the dead can be seen, as we have noted, in the surviving cult of wells. The cult of the dead also in some sense survives: it has been said that the only ritual at which the Irish nowadays excel is the funeral. Whether this is so or not, there is a striking dignity in the line of canoes, as described in *An t-Oileanach,* bringing a dead islander from the Blaskets to the mainland or, still, the line of mourners walking across Derrynane strand at low tide, led by a dark-clad figure with a white sash, to the graveyard beside the old monastery at Aghavore.

(III) STONE CIRCLES

From the bronze age times we have, as noted, the continuing cult of the dead. We have also the stone circles, sometimes about a tomb; but the rites practised here are not clear. Macalister quotes an ancient poem about the destruction by St Patrick of 'Crom Cruaich and his sub-gods twelve', clearly a stone circle. This poem makes clear that Crom was gilded and that human sacrifice — especially of children — was practised there as well as of self-mutilation. Also associated with these circles is the practice of dancing around them in the sunwise direction — the *deisiol.* The purpose of these exercises was fertility of crops and safety in battle, the circling being intended to keep the sun on course. This is a widespread practice amongst primitive people. (Croker recounts a story of the stones at Lissyvigeen dancing on May eve). This practice is associated with the use of the bull-roarer — a wooden lath on the end of a string — which, when swung, gives strange sounds as it flashes in the sun. Macalister links this primitive instrument with the *roth ramhach* (oared wheel) that is a feature of Irish religion for 3,500 years, from Newgrange to 1096 AD. The Buddhist prayer wheel is still turned in a sunwise direction. It is widely suggested that the circles were devised for the worship of the sun and that they were designed to compute or commemorate such heavenly events as solstices. If this were the purpose

of the circles we may see some continuation of it in the early christian practice of orienting the church to the sunrise on the patron saint's feast day, and in the continuing practice of the sunwise 'rounds'. The excavation of Drombeg circle in west Cork, discussed elsewhere, shows the possibility at least of the ritual, dedicatory killing of a young adolescent. The orientation of the axis suggests some ritual of midwinter and perhaps of rebirth. Two of the stones suggest the practice of a fertility cult.

It is possible that the oldest Irish gods we know of derive from this period of the stone circles — the Dagda, the good god; Aengus; Midir; Anu; and others who have been represented to us as living in the passage graves. In the terrifying preternatural forces that pervade some of the old tales, in the demons embodied in the Fomorians under their baleful, one-eyed leader, Balor, we perhaps get some dark shadows of bronze age beliefs.

Some of the earliest gold ornaments we have —

Holed Ogam stone, Kilmalkedar

the sub discs — give some further indication of sun worship.

Apart from the circles, we have from these times the gallans, commemorating not only the dead but also some sex cults, with their male (pointed top) and female (flat top) connotations. Even more striking are the holed stones, with their echoes of indo-european religion, surviving notably at Kilmalkedar.

Perhaps a further survival from ancient times was totemism when a tribe identified with, and was named from, an animal — horse, boar, badger etc — which it was *geis* for a member of the tribe not to kill.

(IV) CELTIC GODS

From the iron age the paganism of celtic Ireland is less obscure. Some of the Irish gods can be related to the celtic gods of Gaul, Britain and elsewhere, to whom reference is made by latin writers. They stress that a feature of celtic religion in Gaul was human sacrifice. There is no direct evidence that this was true of celtic Ireland, but it is likely. Of these celtic gods, Lug was the most prominent but Nuadu (Nodens), Ogma (Ogmios), and Macha (Epona), were others. The last named harks back to the indo-european origin of the celts. It is through the language of the goidels, screened by the christian recorders in the monasteries, that we get some pre-christian glimpses of Irish, and specifically celtic, religion. The celts had their own pantheon, but they incorporated into it much of the gods of their predecessors. It is likely that each wave of celtic invaders had its own special gods. For example, in Kerry the pre-goidelic celts were the Erainn, a branch of the Fir Bolg, or Belgae. The Fir Bolg were called after Bolg, or Bolgios, the god of lightning and, ultimately, the sun. Near the presumed burial place of Daire Donn, close to Ventry, is Caherbullig, presumably named after Bolg.

Celtic religion in Ireland was based on the acceptance of a single, all embracing god, with a male and a female principle. He was the sun who raced his chariot across the sky, loosed bolts of lightning, took the forms of sacred animals — hound, wolf, bull, horse, salmon — and presided over the other otherworld where

166

all went after death, and where there was perpetual feasting. So we have Eochaid Ollathair – the universal father; An, Anu, Aine – the sun; and so on. The gods, goddesses and sacred animals could take numerous shapes and names, but they could all be related to this single sun-god. A special feature of Irish thinking was the use of triads. Thus, this single god had triadic forms and some of the few idols that have survived are tri-cephalous ones. Collectively, the gods were Tuatha De Danaan – the people of the goddess Anu whose Paps dominate Rathmore. This underlines the high prestige of women at this time: through them the dead came to rebirth.

If O Rahilly is to be followed, a central theme of Irish religion was the struggle between the Hero – Lug, Cuchulainn, Fionn – against the sun-god, in the shape of Balor, Cu Roi, Donn, Goll. A mark of the first and last of these is that they were one-eyed, a mark of the sun itself. Of these forms of the sun-god, the one special to Kerry was Cu Roi whom Cuchulainn killed in the mountain fortress of Caherconree; but earlier it had been necessary to kill Cu Roi in the shape of a salmon and a dog. Cu Roi is given as the son of Daire, but is really another manifestation of that god, who after took the form of a sacred bull. He it was, in the form of Daire Donn, king of the world, that Fionn killed at the battle of Ventry. Donn was buried nearby at Kilvickadownig; that the tomb, now ruined, was venerated up to christian times is shown by the christian settlement beside it. Diarmaid O Duibne, from the Corcu Duibne, is also called Diarmaid Donn he lost his life because Fionn would not, from old enmity, save him. Donn is specifically the god of the other world, and the entrance to that world, to which all must go, is Teach Duinn, Donn's house, or Bull Rock, off Dursey. Here, in the form of a head he presides over the perpetual feasting. We shall see shortly the survival of an ancient cult in Kerry and its relationship to feasting, with the head of a harvest god, Crom Dub, improbably surviving as a cult object – for toothache! – in an old church at Cloghane. This is one of only two or three idols that have survived in Munster.

The sun spinning across the heavens is likened also to a wheel; the sun-god in Gaul is shown with a wheel. When the sun set Cu Roi's fortress each night began to spin with terrifying speed. On Valentia lived the famous one eyed druid, the chief druid of Ireland, who typified the struggle between paganism and christianity. He was called Mug (or Mogh) Roith, the servant of the wheel. He is associated not only with a brilliant sky-flying chariot, but also with the Roth Ramhach, the oared wheel, which appears when the setting sun shines through the clouds. With these he was able to make magical divinations. So could his daughter who went with him to the East to learn magic. This motif of the oared wheel goes back, as we have seen, in Irish religion to the great passage grave at Newgrange. Mug Roith it was who actually beheaded John the Baptist, and was chief assistant to Simon Magus in his contest with St. Peter and the apostles and, as we have seen, was ultimately responsible for the great panic of 1096 AD.

The great antagonist of the one-eyed sun-god was Lug, or Lugaid, who was a specially venerated deity of the Erainn – hence such places as Loch Lugdech (Lough Currane) and Dun Loich (Dunloe). He also appears as Fionn. Traces of his cult as Lug survive in many places in Kerry, as we shall see.

We have some inkling of a Kerry goddess, Duben, (or Dovvinias as she appears on the ogam stones of the Dingle peninsula). From her come the Corcu Duibne (or the people of Duben) and her name survives in the barony name Corkaguiney (Corca Dhuibhne). She is given as a granddaughter of Conairi More, a king of Ireland in the mid second century AD, and daughter of Cairbre Musc by whom and/or her brother Corc she became the ancestress of the Corcu Duibne. She was the mother of Donn, the god of the other world. Given her marital habits, it is not surprising that so many of the ogam stones claiming descent from her have been defaced by zealous early christians. In the promontory fort of Dun Mor, near Dunquin, is an ogam stone – called gallan an tsagairt, after the priest, Fr. Casey, who re-erected it in 1839. Originally, there were held to be two inscriptions of which one was read as *[A]NME DOVINIA*, the name of Duben. Westropp suggested that this may have been a shrine of the goddess. Macalister holds generally that to write the name in this way

is to embody the goddess. The slight fortifications here suggest that the promontory fort was not defended militarily. However, Macalister's definitive reading of the inscription as one – *ERC MAQI MAQI* – *ERCIAS MU DOVINIA* explodes that theory.

Dun Mor – if it does not mean the big fort, and it is big – may be called after Mor, wife of Lir (or Lear), the sea-god. They landed here. Her husband went north, but she stayed here and the place was called Tigh Mhoire na Greine, the house of Mor of the sun. Another version of the story says Lir was buried here.

(V) FESTIVALS

There were four main religious festivals held quarterly. These were Samain (1 November) Imbolc (1 February), Beltine (1 May), and Lugnasad (1 August). Of these, the two principal ones (as in Gaul) were the essentially pastoralist ones – Samain and Beltine. The year was thus divided into two – the cold half and the warm, the end of the grazing season and its beginning. Samain marked the beginning of the year and was the most important feast. Then surplus beasts, that is those not needed for breeding, were killed for winter (because the saving of hay for winter feed did not reach Ireland until the 17th century AD). At Samain the barrier between this world and the other world was removed and contact with the gods and the dead was close. On the previous night magic powers were liberated and magic warrior bands came from caves and hillsides. Some of this still survives in rural Ireland and Halloween (31 October) is a time for many traditional games, dressing up, etc. (The memory is, of course, reinforced by the christian festivals of All Saints and All Souls (1st and 2nd November, respectively). The slaughter of cattle led to much feasting at this time for the re-uniting of the people at an *oenach*. In pre-christian times many important events occurred at this time. Sacrifices were offered, and it seems to have been basically a festival for the renewal of the fecundity of the earth, its inhabitants and the society as a whole.

An example of the celtic religious connexion of Samain with the earth, fertility and birth can be seen in Kerry in the twin mountains near Rathmore, the Paps, in Irish, Da Chich dAnann,

Pagan Religion
(V) Festivals

the two breasts of Anu. As we have seen, Anu, or Ana, was a mother goddess of the mythical Tuatha De Danann, that race of gods who are called her people. The old writer, Cormac, says she was the mother of the gods and that she fed them well. Three of them she had by her own father, the Dagda, from a union at Samain, so perhaps incorporating some of the older pantheon into the celtic one. Anu is also to be seen as an earth goddess, and to be contrasted with the sea god Mananaan, son of Lir (or Lear, the sea) who, as we have seen, has connexions with the Dingle peninsula.

It was at Samain that the feast of Tara was held — apparently once in each reign celebrating the king's ritual marriage with sovereignty. This has been a continuing Irish theme, right up to recent times, that sovereignty was a female supernatural force — sometimes disguised as a hideous hag, also personified in the great queen Medb, but in recent times appearing as the beautiful but forlorn Eire — to which a king, if his reign were to succeed, must be wedded. It was called *banais rig,* the king's wedding, and was similar to the sacred marriage of Greek tradition and was a fertility rite. Giraldus Cambrensis reports an account, now accepted to be reliable, that he had heard of in the twelfth century AD of the inauguration of an Irish king involving a symbolic marriage with a mare, a rite that recalls the ancient horse sacrifice of the Hindus and harks back to a common indo-european tradition of formal inauguration to which great importance was attached in ancient and medieval times. We find a great overlord like Mac Carthy Mor being inaugurated by his chief subject O Sullivan Mor, who presented him with the white rod of sovereignty. This ceremony took place from the thirteenth century at Lisbanagher near Cahersiveen, and, at the end of the 16th century, it was the refusal of the O Sullivan Mor to do this for the expected heir that helped to bring the Mac Carthy Mor title to its effective end.

The second most important festival was that of May Day, Beltine. This word incorporates the name of the celtic god Belenus, much honoured in Northern Italy and south-eastern Gaul, and the celtic word for fire. Great fires were lit on this day well into christian times.

The Paps, Rathmore

About Imbolc (1 February) little is known. It is now the feast-day of the great St. Brigid of Kildare; but before that the day was dedicated to the goddess Brigit, daughter of the Dagda, who can be associated with a Sanscrit goddess.

The fourth festival that of Lugnasa, (1 August), is less shadowed in mist, thanks to the researches revealed in a fascinating book *The Festival of Lugnasa* by Maire Mac Neill. Lugnasa is the gaelic word for the month of August and comes from the word *nasad,* a commemoration and Lug, the name of a well known god whom the Romans considered to be the celtic Mercury who gave his name to several European cities — Lugudonum (Lug's town), such as Lyons and Leon in France, London, Leiden in Holland, and Liegnitz in Silesia. (Under his other name, Find, or Vindonnus, he is remembered by Uindobona or Vienna). Lug, in Irish mythology, was on his father's side the son of one of the Tuatha De Danaan and on his mother's, the grandson of the terrible leader of the demon Fomorians, Balor, whom Lug eventually killed. Lug was young and brilliant and was called Lamfada (the long-armed) and Samildanach (the many-gifted). He seems, however, to be a late arrival in Ireland —

possibly brought here by the goidels in the first century BC.

The great annual festival of Ireland up to almost 1000 AD was the Games of Tailtiu, held at Teltown, Co. Meath. This festival was originally held in honour of Lug, for the two weeks before and after 1st August, Lug's Day. This was one of the quarter days in Irish reckoning. This date became, in places, affected by the calendar reform of the 18th century putting it back to 12th August. Miss Mac Neill, with the help of literary remains and living folk memories, has been able to trace no less than 195 places in modern Ireland where festivals of this kind were, or are, held, now of course frequently overlain by christianity. Of these places, eight are in Kerry, the most famous being Puck Fair at Killorglin.

It is clear that the festival was to celebrate the beginning of the harvest and the opening up of the riches of the year to come, wrested from a niggardly fate that grudgingly doled out its great resources. This was personified by an older chief god, Crom Dub, and the triumph over him during the festival by Lug. This was often signalised by taking a head representing Crom Dub from its sanctuary to a neighbouring

168 height, there temporarily burying it. Miss Mac Neill ends (p 426):

> The pagan rites of the festival, according to these speculations, may be summarised as follows: a solemn cutting of the first of the corn of which an offering would be made to the deity by bringing it up to a high place and burying it; a meal of the new food and of bilberries of which everyone must partake; a sacrifice of a sacred bull, a feast of its flesh, with some ceremony involving its hide; a ritual dance-play, perhaps telling of a struggle for a goddess and a ritual fight; an installation of a head on top of the hill and a triumphing over it by an actor impersonating Lugh: another play representing the confinement by Lugh of the monster blight or famine; a three-day celebration presided over by the brilliant young god or his human representative. Finally, a ceremony indicating that the interregnum was over, and the chief god in his right place again.

We have seen that the eternal feasting in the otherworld was presided over by a head, representing the chief god. Perhaps, the non-stop drinking at Puck Fair is the nearest christian Ireland can get to this eternal revelling of the pagan afterlife!

Of course this struggle came to be christianised in the popular mind. St. Patrick, or a local saint, took the place of Lug and Crom Dub was converted. It is the origin of the widespread 'Garland Sunday' (the last in July) and of a number of fairs. It is possible that this Crom Dub can be seen in the in the form of Donn, god of the Corcu Duibne.

In Kerry Miss Mac Neill has identified four sites on the Dingle peninsula and four on the Iveragh peninsula. Of the Dingle ones, the most interesting is the Mount Brandon — Dingle — Cloghane complex. As we have seen, in the ruined church of Cloghane is what is believed to be a stone head representing Crom Dub. Of interest, too, is Anascaul which brings Cuchulainn into the story. Of the survivals, one of the most vigorous of all is Puck Fair, Killorglin, affected by calendar reform and

now held 10—12 August.

Lug has other connexions with Kerry, such as that of Dunloe (Dun Loich or Dun Lugaid). This Lugaid was the son of Curoi Mac Daire who was killed by Cuchulainn and in turn it was Lugaid who hurled the spear that fatally wounded that terrible little man. On another level, however, Cuchulainn can be related to Lug. Lough Currane, Waterville, was formerly called Loch Lugdech, also presumably after the god Lug. The cult of this god must have been remarkably extensive. It is said that St. Comgall had at Bangor no less than 50 monks named Lugaid.

That these gods died hard can be inferred from the reputed father of the greatest of the Kerry saints, St. Brendan. He was called Findlug. Is it significant, too, that the remarkable south Kerry saint, Fionan, should be so closely associated with Loch Lugdech?

(VI) ANIMALS AND TOTEMS

Animals, no less than heroes, were venerated and the great Irish saga — the Tain Bo Cuailgne (The Cattle Raid of Cooley) — is about a sacred bull. Hounds were also venerated — hence, Cu Chulainn and Cu Roi — cu is the word for hound. Fionn had several half magical hounds and there is a cairn over the reputed grave of one of them — Sgeolmhaidhe — near Glenbeigh. The most famous of his hounds was Bran, lost in Lough Brin near Ballaghabeama and still said to be manifesting himself. There is also a record of magical boars — one of which killed Diarmaid O Duibne. Most notable is the interest in serpents, which certainly played some part in religion in Gaul. As every schoolboy knows, serpents are not found in Ireland because St. Patrick banished them from the country and there is a vivid account, given elsewhere, of their being driven by his power over the cliffs of the Great Skellig. Brash says that this was a centre of serpent worship. There is a legend of a magical serpent in Corkaguiney that grew to great size and engulfed large quantities of victims. There is also a legend of a serpent — the 'Caraboonkle' — in a lake under Mount Brandon. There is a tradition of a 'carbuncle' in Muckross lake and of another being trapped in one of the lakes in the Gap of Dunloe.

Some of the serpents were able to hit back. Below Knockanure, at Kilconly, is Lisnapeestia, from which a 'piast' or serpent emerged and killed or was killed by St. Chonla there. Perhaps, the banishing of snakes refers to a fairly severe struggle between the cult of serpents and the new religion.

At Kilcatherine in the Beara peninsula, there is over the door of the ruined church an effigy that has been held to be the head of a cat and It has been suggested that it is from the veneration given to this cat, not to St Catherine, that the name comes, but this is almost certainly fanciful. However, there are no less than three cahers called caher na gcat in the Ballyferriter area — near Ballyheabought, near Ballywickeen and near Gallarus — suggesting a tribal settlement there with this totem. However, the Seabhac is sceptical of this. There is some reason to believe that totemism may have been widespread, especially amongst the aboriginal tribes, who called themselves after animals and fish.

(VII) OTHERWORLD

We have seen that celtic religion provided for an otherworld to which all returned, the gateway to which was Teach Duinn, the house of the god Donn, namely Bull Rock, off Dursey island. Some of the most beautiful of the old stories relate how a living hero is invited, as Oisin was at Killarney, to come to this otherworld pictured as a paradisal island in the sea, 'where there is naught but truth, where there is neither age, nor decay, nor gloom, nor sadness, nor envy, nor jealousy, nor hate, nor pride'. This notion of a paradise in the great western ocean seems to have been an inspiration for the island-seeking hermits of christian times.

Many sacrifices were held in sacred woods and at sacred trees. (In Gaul, at least, one of the methods was to hang the victim from a tree in one of these groves). The veneration of trees, rivers and wells must represent the incorporation into celtic religion of older, primitive forms of animistic religion. Seneca says: 'Where a spring rises, or a river flows, there should we build altars and make sacrifices'. Something similar must have been true in Ireland.

Chapter 10 Christian and other Buildings

Christianity came to Ireland sometime after 400 AD. Most of what strikes the eye in Kerry dates from after that time. Broadly, the artefacts one sees are christian buildings, castles, houses and public buildings, and roads and railways.

ECCLESIASTICAL BUILDINGS

For six or seven centuries after the introduction of christianity most of the physical relics now left to us are ecclesiastical, mainly the remains of ecclesiastical settlements. Indeed, for a thousand years they constitute the most striking physical relics of Irish living. Although there are many christian remains in Kerry, the county produced none of the treasures of the early times; but there is much of interest and some of the later ruins are very fine. They fall, broadly, into three periods: the early christian — 1200 AD; the medieval — 1600 AD; and the modern.

There is a great number of these buildings, especially for the early period. The second edition of the Ordnance Survey map of monastic Ireland identifies no less than 42 monastic or eremitical sites in Kerry. Half of these are shown at the tip of the Iveragh peninsula, thanks to the remarkable survey of Mlle Henry. There are others, not shown, on that peninsula. The Dingle peninsula must have as many sites, but these have not been systematically surveyed. Even when one allows for the smallness of most of these foundations they add up to a remarkable total. A number of extant remains of some historical or artistic interest are not now in the county.

It helps to make clear the significance of the ecclesiastical remains to recapitulate the outline of Irish church history — already given in some detail — with special reference to Kerry and then to classify the most significant of the Kerry remains. Most generalisations about Irish history are suspect, and this may be especially true of Irish church history; but a few main trends can be discerned in the fifteen hundred years of christianity in Ireland.

The three main periods of Irish church history fall into five sub-periods: the early christian had a primitive and a monastic sub-period in succession; the medieval was not so divided; but the modern period began with a troubled sub-period and was succeeded by a revivalist one. Church buildings in Kerry fall fairly readily into these five sub-periods.

From the primitive period we have the large number of tiny eremitical settlements dating from the sixth and seventh centuries and abandoned mostly in the eighth, so that the original buildings were never replaced.

From the same period date many of the monastic settlements but their success was such that the early, simple buildings were several times replaced, so that from none of the monasteries have we now anything of their early days.

By the medieval period the old Irish monasteries were in decline and were being reformed. There grew up a full diocesan and parochial system (hence cathedrals and, relatively, large parish churches) and large monasteries of continental orders of monks and friars. From this period, therefore, date the large ruins.

In the troubled or Reformation period, the formal structure of the established church became protestant and the monasteries were suppressed: but, as the great mass of the people would not become protestant, many cathedrals and parish churches were abandoned. In the more settled times of the 19th century, many new protestant churches were built, often close to the sites of pre-reformation parish churches. These, in the rural areas, are now being abandoned.

In the modern period of the 19th and 20th centuries, there was a notable catholic revival and cathedrals, parish churches, monasteries and convents were built in the new centres of population.

From the earliest times, three broad levels of building can be seen in Europe. The simplest was the *megalithic*, the use of large, undressed stones, often one on end. This, until very late, was the only influence on Ireland, and in the pagan Staigue Fort we can see the exemplar of much building of the early christian period. The second level of building was the *cyclopean*, large blocks of stones placed flat on one another, common in Mediterranean countries, but slow to reach Ireland. Examples are to be found on some very early churches, e.g. on Aran; in Kerry some influence of it can be seen in the large stones used in Ratass church, Tralee. The third was the east Mediterranean technique of chisel dressed stone, *ashlar,* with, later, the use of mortar and the arch. This third development did not begin to reach Ireland until the 7th century.

There is, in Kerry, a range of churches that incorporate in some degree the foregoing styles. It should be remembered, however, that the principal churches in early christian Ireland were, like other buildings, of wattle construction, or built of wood — usually oak — that normally was so plentiful. The wooden structures have, of course, disappeared. It was not until the 11th–12th centuries that substantial churches were built of stone. Only in the poorer, more barren and stony places were early christian churches built of stone, and even there some of the earliest churches may have been wooden — as at Church Island, Valentia and at Reask.

A broad rule for dating churches is, thus, size. A large church (except Christ Church, Dublin) will be later than 1100 AD and a very small one, with a single chamber, likely to be earlier than 800 AD.

It is likely that in pagan worship in Ireland the congregation remained in the open air (e.g. at stone circles). It is also likely that in early christian times the congregation continued to remain in the open — as happened, e.g. in Latin America — so that only tiny churches were normally necessary. This practice of remaining outside the church continued in rural areas to some degree until recent times.

Generally, the 16 centuries of christian building in Ireland can be broken into eight groupings of two centuries each, with, of course, some overlapping.

(I) EARLY CHRISTIAN PERIOD

1. Primitive Churches
(a) 5th — 6th centuries

What is, perhaps, the oldest ecclesiastical site

170 in Kerry has no building. It is the abandoned copper mine on Coad mountain, Caherdaniel, reputed to be the hermitage of the pre-patrician St. Kieran of Saigir in the early 5th century. The many eremitical sites that do have buildings date from the 6th century to the end of the 7th. These long abandoned, neglected places are full of interest.

We have seen that the main prototype for Irish buildings is to be found at Staigue Fort (close to Coad) and its lesser fellows. Staigue illustrates (i) the unmortared stone external ringfort, (ii) the batter — the sloping back of the stone wall, (iii) the flat lintel, and (iv) the slated door openings. Other stone forts illustrate (v) the internal house, the corbelled *clochan*, a form that stretches back to the passage graves. These are 5 of the features of the earliest christian buildings that survive to us in Kerry from the little eremitical settlements that dot the extremities of the county. These are : the external ring (called a *caiseal*) as at Loher; Kildreelig; Ilauntannig; and within this *clochans,* illustrating batter, flat lintel, slanted door openings and corbelling, almost perfectly preserved on the Great Skellig. The clochan was a corbelled structure, circular courses, roughly dressed, of unmortared stones slanting inwards until at length the whole can be capped by a large, flat stone. On the whole, the local sandstones were a suitable shape and material for corbelling. The clochan evolved into the boat shaped oratory, the best example of which is at Gallarus.

It is the eremitical strain, grown in the 6th century into a remarkable movement, especially in Kerry, that has given us some of the most fascinating of christian remains. They are mostly to be found in very beautiful places, but their main interest is that we find in them married three leading traditions : the ancient Irish systems of building; coptic and gaulish asceticism; and latin and greek christian triumphalism.

Those sites have a standard, but not universal pattern, as at Loher. They are surrounded by a *caiseal*; it is noteworthy how the quality of building these rings has deteriorated: compare the remarkable stone work at Caher Geal and Staigue with the crudity of the caiseal at the little monastery of Kildreelig, Bolus Head. Inside the circle is a small, raised segment, the laura, within which the hermit's clochan, a tiny boat shaped oratory, a tomb shrine and a cross-pillar are placed. On the remainder of the site were other clochans, a quern or two and, now, miscellaneous burials.

The oratory, like an upturned boat, is a 6th century evolution of the clochan. The perfect example of this is at Gallarus; but this seems to be at the end of the evolution — partly because of the skilful construction, the dressing and hammering of the internal stones, the use of some mortar (for pointing and possibly for primitive plastering) and the arched window. Gallarus thus possibly dates from the late 7th or the 8th century; but

Interior of Temple Cashel Oratory

Dr Harbison would date it much later. However, it is, I think, best understood as the full development of a style that began in the 5th-6th centuries. There are two earlier, but preserved, oratories on the Great Skellig. Here we can see the evolution of the style. There are big, perfect clochans, round outside, evolving inside from round to square. Other examples are at Church Island, Valentia, and at Dunbeag, Fahan — this last a secular example. At the ancient nunnery of Temple Cashel the oratory has become elongated inside and outside, the perfect transition to the fully rectangular form at Gallarus. Many of these oratories were built, but nearly all of them, from the great weight of their uncemented roofs of undressed stones, have fallen in. There is one, less ruined than most, St Brendan's oratory, close to Gallarus at Kilmalkedar; but in greater or lesser state of ruin they are a constant feature of the eremitical sites. An attempt to obviate the danger of collapse by the brute mass of a relatively large structure can be seen at Church Island, Waterville; but this has been plausibly argued to be a much later storehouse.

When the use of mortar and cement became extensive in the late 8th century this boat shaped style was developed, in other parts of the country, but not in Kerry, into the barreled vault ceiling supporting a pitched stone roof, as at the 9th century St Kevin's 'House', Glendalough, Co. Wicklow. This, in turn, became a special feature of 12th century romanesque structures. The supreme example is the 12th century Cormac's Chapel at Cashel.

Gallarus Oratory

Clochans on Skellig

That at Kilmalkedar seems to derive from the Cashel model. This evolution of the corbel, by way of the oratory to the barreled roof may well have been a distinctive Irish contribution to the technology of building.

The corbelled rectangle is not unique to Kerry. Mlle Henry points out that there are examples — some of relatively recent construction — in nearly all the limestone plateaux of France and Spain, in parts of Italy, Istria, Crete, in the Caucasus, and in various parts of Africa. They are all, perhaps, independent developments of megalithic corbelling.

Inset above the doorway of the oratory was a rough cross — still to be seen at Illauntannig — in lighter, quartz stone. In the *Book of Kells* this upturned boat style was evolved into a representation of an ark with finials such as one sees on Temple Geal (or Temple Manachain) and on the much later Kilmalkedar church. This ark itself was to be represented in the shrine tomb referred to below.

In Killabuonia — next to the Skellig the site that gives one the best flavour of these settlements: at Kildreenagh Valentia; at Killoluaig; and, probably, at Kilpeacan, Cahersiveen, are relics that remind one of the origin of this eremitical movement, the tomb shrine, like a tiny high-pitched house or ark. Coptic in origin, it travelled from north Africa to Spain, from Spain to south Gaul, from south Gaul to Kerry, from Kerry to west England and Scotland. It is remarkable that all of the examples that have been reported in Kerry should be confined to a narrow radius of Cahersiveen.

Monasticism began in the Egyptian desert, and led to the subsidiary eremitical movement for those to whom the desert monasteries were not austere enough. This was mainly a Coptic movement that spread to south Gaul. It was from there that monasticism and the eremitical movement spread to Ireland. A place of hermitage, preserving its desert memories, came to be called *diseart* in Irish; hence many placenames. One mark of all this is the coptic tomb shrine. Where one sees it at an Irish site it is presumably the

Coptic Tomb Shrine at Killabuonia, Ballinskelligs

shrine of the first saintly hermit — his body having decayed his washed bones were placed in the shrine. Pilgrimages were made to this. A hole in the base of the shrine at the narrow end permitted the hand to touch the relics: a cloth so touching them itself became a relic. This shrine became a smaller version of the oratory, as if recalling in death the prayers offered in life. It also, of course, recalled the promise of the Ark of the Covenant.

In most of the sites there is no tomb shrine, but there is a small, standing cross incised pillar (sometimes more than one) that marks what is presumably the founder's grave. It seems that here daily prayers were said. This veneration of the dead must, in some places at least, be linked with pre-christian practices. It can be no accident that so many of these eremitical sites contain, or are beside, ruined chamber tombs of pagan times. The

pillar itself is a link with a widespread cult in the Middle East of Nefech in which the pillar represents, in a sense embodies, the spirit of the deceased and becomes a cult object.

Apart from the cross incised on these pillars there are a number of other marks and symbols. The iconography of these pillars is of exceptional interest and is discussed separately later.

From the detailed discussion of these cross-pillars we get evidence of the existence of these little communities heavily influenced by roman triumphalism and by the coptic and gaulish churches in the 6th and 7th centuries. It would seem that they were mostly abandoned by the end of the 7th century; the Skellig community, of course, lasted much longer as did some others, such as those at Church Island, Valentia, and Reask.

We are reminded that this christian movement also led to an agricultural revolution in the growing of grain, especially a hard-shelled barley, by the querns to be seen at these sites, such as Cloon Lough. (There is a perforated slab at Kilpeacan, Cahersiveen, which may also be a quern, if it is not a degenerate grave shrine). Even more striking is the larger and cruder grinding 'plant' of the bullaun, to be seen at Temple Fiachna, Kenmare, and in Dingle.

Lastly, nearly every one of these sites is in a christian burial ground called *cillin* or *ceallurach* (usually pronounced in Kerry as 'ceallunach') and sometimes marked on the map as (unbaptised) children's burial ground. Some of these burial grounds have, now at least, no trace of an oratory and may represent a transition from pagan to christian times, as at Ballintaggart, Dingle, which seems to have have been a special place with rounded ogam grave stones, some invoking the tutelary goddess of the Corcu Duibne. In the eremitical sites, many of the common people came to be buried about the founder's grave, so transforming each into a ceallunach. One of the effects of this is that the stones of the oratory and of the original cell were used as headstones, so ruining the site for later eyes. What is so exciting about the Skellig site is that while it lacks the coptic

172 shrine and the most fascinating of the cross-pillars, almost everything else is there and almost perfectly preserved. Amongst what is left on the Skellig is what can safely be described as a sun-dial. Two other sites — Kilmalkedar and Ballywiheen nearby — also have what have been described as sun-dials but are almost certainly relics of fertility cults of pagan times.

2. Monasteries

(a) 7th — 8th centuries

The second stage of early christian architecture, typical of the 7th and 8th centuries, is the use under roman influence of dressed stones for doorways and of some mortar, often as grouting, i.e. poured wet on a dry stone wall. As this technique developed the facing stones were dressed and laid, both beds and joints, in tolerably fine mortar; a grout was then prepared of hot lime, sand and gravel and the heart of the wall was then filled with it; stones of various sizes

'Sundial' at Kilmalkedar

were then packed into the grouting. These innovations were brought back from Europe by Irish missionaries of the 7th century. Thus a new building tradition was established, overlapping with, and then largely superseding, the old. So corbelling was perfected, as at Gallarus, and then superseded until it was later developed into the barreled roof; but we still have the horizontal lintel and the inclined doorways. In the new style, the building stones, usually unsquared, are often astonishingly large and are laid in very rough courses indeed.

The normal structure was a simple perpindicular rectangle containing a nave simply. It is difficult to find original examples of this style because an arch and chancel were usually later added to the original nave. Perhaps the earliest Kerry example is at Killelton, near Camp; though Lynch says, wrongly I think, that it is an oratory. Another example is at Templenacloonagh, near Ballyferriter. Another early example, cyclopean in part, using no mortar and now much ruined, is Templenakilla, Waterville. A good — perhaps late 8th century — example is at Glendaghalin, near Ballyheigue; here the east window, according to the Ordnance Survey Letters and to Westropp, had a true arch, now fallen. Another is on the Great Skellig, an oddly ruined building there amongst the perfect clochans and oratories, perhaps underlining the newness of the technique in comparison with the long-standing mastery of corbelling. The rectangular church much resembled the rectangular house of the richer classes, while the monks continued to live in the clochans of the poor. An impressive example is at Temple Martin, Lispole, now much ruined. It was built in an earthen rath, with moulded doorway and large stones. Ratass, which was clearly later extended, gives examples of the use of big stones in building of this period. This practice died out in the 12th century. The churches were, in general, modelled on the wooden frame churches of the country as a whole, narrow, high structures with projecting constructional timbers, or antae, to be seen still on Ratass and the (much later) Kilmalkedar. Brash suggests that all these churches were so small because they were stone-roofed and the art of making large stone

Doorway at Temple Martin, Lispole

roofs was not mastered until the 11th century. Again, Kilmalkedar is an example.

At this period the doorways maintained the slanting jambs which were indeed to remain a feature for many centuries. They also kept the flat lintel. The doorways now, as at Temple Martin, began to be moulded. The same features are to be seen on the window opes. Perhaps early in this period the flat window lintel is replaced by an arch scooped out of the lintel stone. Perhaps towards the middle of the 8th century the true arch began to appear in the window opes.

(b) 9th — 10th centuries

Another of the later feedbacks from Irish missionary activity was the introduction of the full romanesque arch into Irish building: this is to say, how to lay stones vertically as well as horizontally. As we have seen a beginning of the arch was made with window opes which show many examples over a long period of botched attempts at the arch: closing the gap by corbelling, carving the arch in a single block of stone. Examples of these, and of messy building generally, can be seen in the 9th century monastery at Aghavore. This monastery is of special interest in that it missed the two great periods of Irish building (and re-building), the Irish romanesque and the Irish gothic. So we get from it something of the flavour of Irish

173

monastic building in one of its less distinguished periods — the 9th century. But the best impression can now be got at Reask, the excavations at which show how an eremitical settlement seems to have evolved into a significant monastery of this period, and then stopped.

The typical 9th and 10th century church consists of a small nave and chancel joined by a fully romanesque arch. Examples of this arch and chancel are at Ratass and at Temple Martin, earlier churches to which the chancel was later added; but if the east window at Ratass is original, then the chancel was not added until the 12th century. The arch in the 9th and 10th centuries began to be used in doorways and to replace the flat lintel. I have not seen in Kerry a doorway of this period except on the round tower at Rattoo. The third general mark of the building of this period is the use of cement.

Towards the end of this period, and at the beginning of the next, the round towers began to be built. There were four in Kerry — one on Church Island, Waterville, now disappeared; one at Ardfert, also gone; one at Aghadoe, largely destroyed; and one at Rattoo, wholly preserved. There were four successive styles of these towers. Rattoo is of the third — well dressed stones set in horizontal courses and in good mortar. Aghadoe, the building of which was begun in 1027, with the earlier part of the present church still there, is one of the fourth style — ashlar masonry or sandstone in squared masonry.

(c) 11th — 12th centuries

The fourth period of Irish church architecture covers the 11th and 12th centuries. It saw the great flowering of Irish romanesque that synthesised in much larger buildings all the best of the foregoing influences. The style began about 1000 AD and reached its peak in the chapel of King Cormac Mac Carthy at Cashel (1127-1134) and in the cathedral at Clonfert (1166) built at the monastery founded by St Brendan the Navigator. In Kerry itself the best examples fall far short of these, but Kilmalkedar — which, though now much ruined — was among the half-dozen

Doorway at Kilmalkedar

best of the style. It was stone-roofed in the manner of the much earlier Gallarus nearby; this must have given it a most elegant appearance; it must also have helped to save it from being burned, as was the fashion of the time. Roofing in stone on so relatively large a church became possible because of the development from the corbelled to the barreled roof. The west wall of Ardfert cathedral — observe one of the latest uses of large stones in building; the west door at Aghadoe; the little church on Inisfallen; the church on Church Island, Waterville; and the parish church at Killemlagh, Ballinskelligs, give some idea, in spite of the re-building and some insensitive restoration, of the beauty, charm and artistic quality of this style. The doorway at Temple na Hoe at Ardfert shows the transition from the small, plain doorway arch of the previous period to the more elaborate doorway of the fully developed style.

A noteworthy example of the survival of tradition is the decoration on these romanesque doorways. The slanted jambs remain,

but the arch head springs from chamfered imposts, the arches are elegantly proportioned and decorated, with several recessed arches. This is the continuation in stone of a style that reached its peak in the great illuminated manuscripts of the 7th-8th centuries, itself a continuation of the decorated metal work of the late bronze age. Paradoxically, a most distinctive part of this decoration — the pointed chevron and the bead, as on the door shafts at Aghadoe — are an import from England of the norman style. The decoration with severed heads is a relic of old pagan celtic practices with real heads. There are no noteworthy sculptures — apart from those on church buildings — of this period.

The development of the Irish romanesque coincided with the great efforts to reform the Irish church in the 12th century after the disorganisation caused by the Scandinavian invasions and much internal anarchy. Then, after this long period of development, this

Temple na Hoe, Ardfert

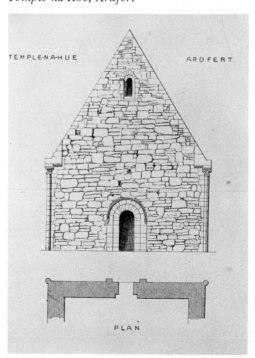

174 beautiful style of architecture suddenly disappeared after the building of Ardmore cathedral in 1203. One reason for the disappearance was the problem of the stone roof which even with the greatest ingenuity as at Cashel, could not give a greater span than 20-21 feet. When the rise in population and the taste of the anglo-normans demanded larger churches the stone roof, and thus a major feature of the style, could not be used.

(II) MEDIEVAL PERIOD

1. 13th — 14th centuries

The fifth stage, of the 13th and 14th centuries, reflects the import of the great monastic orders of the church and of the anglo-norman invasion. Under these influences the gothic style succeeded the romanesque. Now began the building of really large churches, so leading to problems of architecture that had not been posed by the smaller churches of the previous period. The Cistercians, as part of the reforms of the Irish church, came to Ireland (to Mellifont, Co. Louth) in 1142. Twelve years later they

Doorway at Aghadoe Church, Killarney

reached Abbeydorney in Kerry — though the present (undistinguished) ruins there date from the 15th century. The main thrust of church building shifted from wooden to stone churches and the import of foreign technology permitted these to be large. At first the new style was transitional, an amalgam of romanesque and gothic, with rounded and pointed arches together, as was to happen again in the 15th-16th centuries. However, early gothic in Ireland was, when it established itself before 1250, nearly indistinguishable from the early English style. The eastern part of the present structure at Aghadoe was built in this style, giving the whole building a curious discontinuity. The two great mendicant orders, the Dominicans and the Franciscans, arrived in Kerry in the 13th century. The Dominican priory in Tralee, a geraldine foundation of 1243, is now wholly destroyed; but of the Franciscan friary of Ardfert, founded by a Fitz Maurice ten years later, there remain of the original building the 13th century early gothic — or early English — nave and chancel. The whole building reflects the fairly standard plan for friaries of this time. In the same way the new influences can be seen in Ardfert cathedral, the main building of which dates in the same style from 1250. This is a simple, austere building, big but plain, clearly erected with limited resources as compared with the freer, more affluent style of, say, Kilkenny cathedral, of about the same period. All during this period poverty helped to reinforce the extreme austerity of the building style. The main building is in some sense a monument to a series of styles — from the Irish romanesque in the west gable through the transitional to the late Irish gothic of the transept and battlements.

As part of the reforms of Irish monasticism the old Irish monasteries became the care of Augustinian canons and they took over the surviving ancient foundations from 1205. Ruins dating from this period can be seen at Inisfallen, Killarney — the main buildings were finally destroyed in 1652. Better preserved, but undistinguished, ruins of the same kind can be seen at Ballinskelligs. At Killagha, near Milltown, is a norman foundation of the Augustinian canons of

Romanesque door, Transitional windows, and late Gothic battlements at Ardfert Cathedral

1215. The present fine building was restored and enlarged in 1445.

Close beside Killagha is a parish church of about the same period as the foundation of the monastery incorporating much of the Irish romanesque tradition. It is an example of the building of parish churches undertaken in the 12th and 13th centuries as part of the establishment of a parochial system following the reforms of the 12th century. Many of these medium-sized buildings, covered with ivy, are to be seen close to parish churches of the Church of Ireland, themselves falling into decay.

Nearly all the church building of this period was done in the 13th century. In the 14th widespread disorder, the Black Death, economic depression, and perhaps some unidentified factor, prevented all types of building in Ireland. This was exceptional, because in England, France and Italy church building continued during this period.

2. 15th — 16th centuries

The sixth stage of Irish church building is that of the late Irish gothic, one of the great periods of Irish building. The style was a distinctly Irish adaptation, with pointed and rounded arches being built together. It is especially marked in Kerry by the foundation of two Franciscan friaries, and by the

Muckross Friary, Killarney

highly ornamented mouldings on capitals; and brackets with pointed bases.

A feature of the Pale at this period was the magnificently sculptured tombs — as in Kilkenny cathedral or the old church at Lusk. Nothing of this quality was achieved in Kerry. In Ardfert cathedral are two examples of fairly simple sculptures, effigies of bishops. Two tomb lids with delicate tracery are to be found in the nave of Ardfert friary.

(III) MODERN PERIOD

1. Time of Troubles (17th - 18th centuries)

These two centuries represent a blank in the history of over a 1,000 years of Irish church building. In the 17th century buildings were destroyed or fell into decay, while the Irish church and with it Irish church building passed through a dark night. However, the little Church of Ireland church at Sneem, still in use and restored, may date from the early 17th century, as did Ballynahaglish parish church at Church Hill near Fenit; but the Sneem church is more probably a piece of 18th century antiquarianism. During the 18th century many catholic 'mass houses' were built in inconspicuous places. In the latter part of the century and in the 19th these were all replaced and I have not come across the ruins of even one of them.

Why are nearly all the old churches in ruins? The main reason was the reformation which, when at length it reached the people of Kerry at the end of the 16th century, was not accepted by them. On the one hand the monasteries were, by the 17th century, finally suppressed and wholly, or partly, abandoned. On the other, the catholic church lost its cathedral and parish churches to the reformed church of Ireland which, in a county where protestants were few, was unable to keep them up or to repair those damaged in the wars of the 17th century, such as Ardfert cathedral. When religion, both catholic and protestant, began to revive in the 19th century many parishes were amalgamated, there had been shifts of population, new churches were built in new places, and the old churches were left in ruins.

extensive building and re-building at several other places.

In 1448 Donnell Mac Carthy Mor founded Muckross friary, completed about 1500. Additions were made in the 17th century. There are fine cloisters — two sides with pointed arches, two with round — and a good east window. Generally this is a very pleasing building. In 1470 John O Conor Kerry founded another Franciscan friary at Lislaghtin, Ballylongford. This also is a very pleasing building, but more ruined now than Muckross. Marks of monasteries of this period are cloisters, the building of domestic buildings to the north, with the nave to the south and a transept south of that, and the curious *addition* of battlements. These two foundations are good examples of the style. To these can be added the additions made to Ardfert friary and to Killagha, as well as to Abbeydorney. In the later cloisters note

the marks of the wattles with which the mortaring of the barreled roofs were centred.

Temple na Griffin at Ardfert and the south transept of the cathedral were built in the 15th century. Close to Kilmalkedar is the ecclesiastical dwelling, St Brendan's House, also of the 15th century and in a fair state of preservation.

This is the period of the late Irish gothic and is the second of the notable periods of Irish church building — some would claim its highest point — and another example of the Irish capacity for accepting an external influence and, after a period of gestation — much extended here — turning it into something distinctively Irish and beautiful. Features of Irish gothic, apart from those mentioned above, are finely wrought and jointed masonry; window mouldings on top, sides and bottom;

176

Church of the Transfiguration, Sneem

2. Revival (19th — 20th centuries)

The earliest sign of religious revival in the 19th century is to be seen in the Church of Ireland, a by-product of the evangelical movement of those years which put a new vigour and zeal into the church. Helped by advances by the Board of First Fruits — a by-product of the Union — and, later, by the Church Temporalities Fund, the stock of churches in Kerry was completely overhauled. Of 50 then in use, 40 were reconstructed or replaced. These are usually of a distinct style, a grim grey colour, with a gaunt square tower at the entrance. The churches at Cloghane, Aghadoe and Templenoe are typical examples. It is usually close to these churches that one must go to find the ruins of the pre-reformation churches of those parishes where the old church has not been incorporated into the new, as at Cloghane. In other places, where the Church of Ireland did not maintain

a parish, the pre-reformation churches may be associated with traditional graveyards. In one or two places, such as at Kilcrohane, Coad, and at Killemlagh, St Finan's Bay, and no doubt in other remote places, the old churches may have continued in catholic use.

The catholic church building revival was a bit later. At Fossa, Killarney, is a fairly typical example of the kind of plain catholic church built in the early 19th century. A more pleasing example is that built at Caherdaniel about 1828. From about 1829, the year of catholic emancipation, can be dated the real growth of catholic church building. In the following century no less than 24 cathedrals and pro-cathedrals and over 3,000 substantial churches were built in Ireland as a whole. Kerry participated fully in this movement. There were two main periods of church building in that century — those of the neo-gothic and the neo-romanesque styles.

The most striking example of the reorganisation of religion in Kerry in the 19th century is the very fine neo-gothic cathedral at Killarney. This was A. W. Pugin's first commission, and most outstanding work, in Ireland. The collection of funds for the cathedral began in 1828 and it was built between 1842 and 1855, later extended, finished in 1914, and extensively repaired in 1972-73. This is probably the finest example of the neo-gothic revival in Ireland. It is set in a splendid complex of stone buildings of matching design. Pugin and his son were in partnership with George Ashlin and the firm were responsible for the churches at Kenmare and Castleisland and the Dominican priory in Tralee. Killarney shows another good example of the gothic revival in St Mary's church, a Church of Ireland church reconstructed in the 1870s. Here, in a succession of churches, worship has been continuous for probably seven or eight centuries.

Ashlin alone was responsible for a fine church built towards the end of the 19th century, the O Connell Memorial Church at Cahersiveen, built only when the parish priest had appealed over the head of his bishop and archbishop to the pope: there was some dispute whether O Connell, born just outside of Cahersiveen, bore a name

suitable for attaching to a church. Ashlin also designed the church at Brosna. Another fine gothic style church is that at Castlemaine, designed by W.G. Doolin.

There is in Kerry no outstanding example of the neo-romanesque, but a fine example of 19th century church building is St John's, Tralee, recently well restored but for an ugly baldacchino.

In 1869 the Church of Ireland, which since the reformation had been charged with the care of the old ecclesiastical buildings, was disestablished and the care of those buildings not still used for worship came to the state, through the Board of Works, as national monuments; with what melancholy effect the visitor can see. A major, and frequently disgusting, feature of the present dismal situation has been the Irish belief that to be buried in a holy site, no matter how over-crowded, is of great importance and, perhaps to be buried with one's ancestors, more important still. This done, the survivors are exempt from any form of maintenance other

St Mary's Cathedral, Killarney

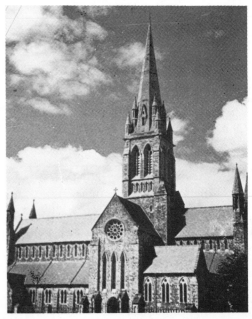

Cross Pillars, High Crosses, Cross Slabs, etc.
(I) Cross Pillars
1 Latin Cross

Things   Part 2

177

than, in families of bourgeois splendour, the erection of some hideous tomb. By patient action by local authorities the old burial grounds in and around ecclesiastical settlements are being closed to further burials and soon, we may hope, they will be left undisturbed, to be engulfed by thorns and nettles until the dawn of the day of enlightened responsibility by their official guardians.

Church design in the first half of the 20th century has not been impressive. But since World War II there has been a great deal of church building in Kerry. Most of it has been the work of Rupert Boyd Barrett. Small, economical, cleanly designed churches have been built all over the county. The best of them is, without a doubt, Muckross church, near Killarney. This church has also been furnished with great taste. Particularly to be noted are the stations of the cross by Ian Stuart. Unfortunately some of the simple lines of some of the other churches have been spoiled by repository art. Interesting examples are Cloonkeen church, at the Cork border on the road to Cork from Killarney; the little church at Glen, St Finan's Bay, presented to the parishioners by a family in America; and the little church in the Black Valley.

A more uncompromisingly modern church is that at Knockanure, a few miles north of Listowel, designed by Michael Scott. There is a fine carving of the Last Supper by Oisin Kelly, and tapestry stations of the cross by Lesley McWeeney.

There is a Harry Clarke stained-glass window in the Franciscan church in Killarney and in the church at Castlegregory. There are four small Sarah Purser windows in the Chapel of St. Brendan's seminary in Killarney. There are Michael Healy windows in the sacristy of the Dominican priory in Tralee.

CROSS PILLARS, HIGH CROSSES, CROSS SLABS, ETC.

(I) CROSS PILLARS

As we have seen, there are at the ends of the Dingle and Iveragh peninsulas over 50 eremitical sites. In most of those sites,

where there is no tomb shrine, a small, standing cross-incised pillar marks what is presumably the founder's tomb. Sometimes there are two of these pillars. It seems that here daily prayers were said. Apart from the cross there are other incised marks often on these pillars. The iconography of these pillars is of great interest. Mlle Henry points out that part of their charm lies in the contrast between the clear, incised designs and the rough sandstone on the pillars. It is as if the clear christian symbols were being seen to be imposed on the rough material of pagan Ireland. It is to be remembered that these are relics of the missionary period in these areas.

There are many examples. Crawford's list of early cross slabs and pillars noted in 1912 fifty-five sites in Kerry, some with several examples. Since then several other sites have come to light.

From the fourth century the cross was the main symbol of christianity. In Kerry there are four basic designs of the incised cross that recall similar designs from south Gaul, but which came to develop Irish forms. There is, first, the elongated latin cross. Secondly, there is the greek cross, with members of equal length. Thirdly, there is the maltese cross, also with members of equal length, but with each broadening out from the centre in leaf form, the so-called 'marigold'. Fourthly, there is the syrian cross which, instead of one horizontal cross member, has three.

The greek and the maltese crosses came to be enclosed in a circle; but on the latin cross the circle — often a double circle — was cut around the intersection of the four members. In the typical Irish cross these members developed finials.

1. Latin Cross

Three simple latin crosses are to be found on

Cross Slab at Loher, Waterville

Cross Slab at Inchfarranagleragh, Waterville

178 the Skellig, one on a figure shaped stone and two on cross slabs. But what is perhaps one of the earliest examples of the developing form of the latin cross in Ireland is at the little settlement at Loher; but see below. This cross is relatively large and is chiselled showing that the transition from pocking and grooving to chiselling had at long last been made.

An early stage of the development of the plain latin cross to the enlarged member ends of the Irish cross is on the cross-pillars at Dromkeare and Inchfarranagleragh, Waterville, at Killogrone, Cahersiveen, and at Kildreelig, Ballinskelligs.

Another stage can be seen on one of the round ogam stones at Ballintaggart, Dingle (no. 160 in Macalister's numbering) in the development of the triple open ends, itself a development of the expanding, coptic style finials, common in early christian Egypt, and to be seen on the little cross at Ballywiheen. There is a variation of this on one of the cross pillars at Caherlehillan, Cahersiveen, and another on the Inishvickillane stone now in Trinity College, Dublin. Perhaps the most complex of these is on one of the slabs at Templenacloonagh, Ballyferriter. Another stage in the transition is the incorporating of the Irish iron age, that is pagan, motif of the divergent spiral, or trumpet, with the enlargement of the ends of the cross members — as at Kilshannig — to reach a later, fully developed form on the cross slabs of the 9th and 10th centuries. A development in the other direction is the 'crutched' or 'potent' cross (without the top piece) to be seen, according to Crawford (but I failed to find it), at Ballynacarrig, Killarney. At Kilvickadownig is a latin cross with expanding finials surrounded by a motif that recalls the Reask one, referred to below.

Compared with these the Loher cross is relatively large. It is noteworthy, too, because incised under the arms are the first and last letters of the greek alphabet, alpha and omega, signifying the complete power of God. It is one of the marks of triumphalism, recalling the words from the Apocalypse: 'Then the One sitting on the throne spoke: "... I am the Alpha and the

Omega, the Beginning and the End. I will give water from the well of life free to anybody who is thirsty; it is the rightful inheritance of the one who proves victorious; and I will be his God and he a son to me" '. The motif of the alpha and omega is still frequently to be seen in modern catholic churches. It hails from merovingian times — it is on the tomb of a French bishop who died in 603 AD. We think of the late 6th century and early 7th century as seeing the peak of the eremitical movement; so perhaps the founder of Loher died about the middle of the 7th century; if so, the motif was not slow in reaching this remote spot.

2. Greek Cross

The greek cross did not get anything like the same development: two simple examples are at Spunkane and Termons, Waterville, and at Keeldarragh, Cahersiveen. Perhaps the simplest of all is at St Finan's Well, Caherbarnagh, Waterville. It may be that the

eremitical movement began in south Kerry and that these little greek crossses were the earliest ones. The latin and maltese crosses tended, on the whole, to be much more sophisticated. There are many very simple greek crosses, and a good proportion of them are in the Waterville area.

There are a number of ogam stones with very simple greek crosses without adornment. At Kinard is a large greek cross in an incised square; in each of the top quarters of the square is another greek cross. A greek cross with expanding coptic style finials enclosed in a circle above a curious kite shaped figure is at Killabuonia. At Kildreelig, not far away, a simple greek cross is enclosed in an egg shaped oval, with four small egg shaped ovals between the arms and a squiggle, perhaps representing a soul bird, above.

A development of the greek cross is the swastika, with lines at right angles to the members at their ends. There are two

Cross Slab at Cloon Lough

Cross Slab at Gallarus

swastikas on the pillar at Aglish, and a sort of one on the Inishvickillane pillar. On this latter the elongated swastika may have been an attempt to unsuccessfully work out an Irish cross which elsewhere on the pillar is successfully achieved. The most elegant of the crosses is the little shattered one at Cloon Lough, with its striking development of the swastika. This may be one of the earliest, though it is one of the most sophisticated, of the crosses. The swastika was a pagan design used by the early christians as a disguised cross and thus represents a very early stage of the triumphalist movement.

At Gallarus and at Kilfountain are cross pillars each with a pocked and grooved greek cross in a single circle. There is even a simpler one at Ardkeragh, Waterville. Sometimes, as at Rathduff, Anascaul, it is a double circle, extending from the central one. This circle represents, as Miss Roe convincingly argues, the *scutum fidei*, the shield of faith. This derives from the trophy shield of a victorious roman general and later became the frame for the bust of the victorious emperor.

The Kilfountain (Cill Fiontain) pillar also has the name of the founder, Finten, incised on it. It also has the motifs referred to below.

3. Maltese Cross

However, it is with the maltese cross that the most interesting developments have occurred. At Reask, Ballyferriter, is a maltese cross in low relief in a circle with a complex incised motif underneath. Between the cross members remain, in high relief, four 'leaves' (or marigold design) themselves decorated. Beneath the cross is incised the word 'dne' signifying the latin invocation of a prayer for the deceased. This use of a latin form, rather than the Irish 'or' or 'oroit' is very early and unusual — though there are a couple of other examples in the neighbourhood. The incised motif below the cross, like that on the 'leaves', shows the La Tene trumpet design. This incorporating of the native pagan style is a small illustration of the compromises of the time. But the complex design has a more fascinating message. Miss Roe has pointed

Cross Slab at Reask, Ballyferriter

Cross Slabs at Caherlehillan, Cahersiveen

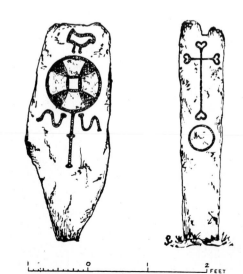

out that in roman times a victor hung his trophies on a pole with a cross-piece. This was to become the symbol of the all-conquering christians — 'in hoc signo vinces'. The four members of the cross became equated with the four axes of the cosmos.

This motif, known as the trophy of the cross, became widely popular in the 4th to 6th centuries and is seen mainly on sarcophagi of the 4th-5th centuries around the Mediteranean coasts of Italy, France and Spain. In its full version it shows a standing latin cross — the original trophy stand. Immediately above the cross-bar is a wreathed shield displaying the chi-rho monogram; at each end a soul bird perches. Below the arms of the cross are the defeated guards of the sepulchre, crouched and conquered like barbarians. The full design celebrates the resurrection. At Reask we have the most developed of these cross pillars incorporating in a formalised way the triumphal motif, although we do not have the chi-rho. We do, however, have the trumpet motif signifying the incorporation into the christian the native pagan traditional design. At the bottom of the design is another motif: it may be the dolphin, appropriate to these parts and emerging at this period in the illuminated manuscripts as another symbol of the resurrection. An extremely complex version of all this — with a crude version of a a glorified Christ — is to be seen on the ogam stone at Caher Murphy, Glenfahan.

The greek initials for Jesus are P (chi) and X (rho). The emperor Constantine in 313 changed the emblems of the roman standard from the invincible sun to the chi-rho. From this time on, the cross, in its various forms, became the main christian symbol. So, when we see the chi-rho on these little pillars we see one more example of christian triumphalism. The chi-rho appears, often in formalised and degenerate form, on a number of cross pillars, especially on the Dingle peninsula. At Kilshannig, it appears merely as a loop out of the top member of a latin cross, at Arraglen similarly on a maltese cross, and at Knockane, Anascaul, on a cross that is a compromise between these two and a dagger. At Kilfountain there is a pattern broadly similar to that at Reask and above it an elaborate, if formalised, chi-rho.

180

1

2

Trophy of the Cross

One of the pillars at Caherlehillan shows a maltese cross in a circle mounted on what looks like a standard for bearing. Above the cross is, most unusually, a bird, and beneath the circle two squiggles, perhaps stylised version of the sepulchre guards, perhaps of serpents, perhaps of both. The serpents recall a passage from St John's gospel: 'And as Moses lifted up the serpent in the wilderness, so must the Son of man be lifted up that whoever believes in Him may have eternal life'. This passage recalls that from the *Book of Numbers*: 'So Moses made a

bronze serpent, and set it on a pole: and if a serpent bit any man, he would look at the bronze serpent and live'. Again the theme of the triumph of the cross.

A number of cross pillars have ogam markings. Sometimes the ogam is earlier than the cross, as at Dromkeare. Sometimes it is early christian, as at Arraglen, where it reads: 'Ronan the priest son of Camogann', with a chi-rho monogram above and, on the other side of the pillar, a greek cross in a circle. Sometimes, as on the fine cross pillar found on Church Island, Valentia, and now in the Cork Museum, the ogam markings are later than the cross. As ogam had gone out of use by 700 AD we have a late date for the full development of the cross pillar.

4. Syrian Cross

The fourth style of cross is the syrian, with three cross members — one for inscription, one for arms, and one for feet, a mark of syrian, greek and coptic churches. What

Cross Slab at Farrantooreen, Killorglin

seems to be a syrian cross, with the end broken off, is on a cup and circle inscribed rock near the Caherlehillan ceallunach, and there is an unmistakable one, with degenerate chi-rho, on a rock at Farrantooreen, Killorglin. It is curious that both of these should be on recumbent rocks, and not on pillars or slabs. However, at Templenacloonagh, near Gallarus, there is a pillar with a syrian cross and odd, coptic style finials. On the Skellig is a syrian cross having one of the members enclosed in a double circle.

In a few places the carving is representational. As we have seen, at Caher Murphy, Fahan, is a representation of Christ in glory and, in Caherlehillan, a bird. In the oratory of Church Island, Valentia, and also in that at Templenacloonagh, were carved stones, now much worn, with animals similar to those found in the early illuminated manuscripts of the 8th century.

(II) HIGH CROSSES

The 7th and 8th centuries saw the development of a most distinctive form of Irish art, the high cross, sculptured all over with, in the best examples, scenes from the bible. Kerry illustrates how that art form failed to develop in the south west. At the little site of Baslickane, Waterville, is the beginning of an attempt to develop a cross inscribed pillar into a cross. This development can be dated towards the middle of the 7th century. In all, there are some two dozen more or less unsuccessful attempts at crosses. There are two, relatively tall ones, of nine and six feet respectively, at Killiney and Illauntannig, Castlegregory; one of eight and a half feet at Kilmalkedar, and a fine one of six feet at Reenconnell nearby; and small ones of one and a half feet to three feet at Kilvickadownig and Inishtooskert, (Blasket Islands). On the Skellig there are three crude crosses of seven feet, five feet, and two feet high, as well as others. On Valentia there are three at St Brendan's well. On the mainland nearby there are others at Garranbane, Killabuonia, and at Reenard. The tallest (11 feet) and the nearest to a high cross, but with a short arm on one side and no decoration, is at Tonaknock, Abbeydorney. Quite the best of these is at Reenconnell, in proportion, style and finish.

A few of these crosses are incised — with a square at Kilmalkedar, a cross and double circle at Reenconnell, simple crosses at St Brendan's well and Skellig; but they have little of the interest of the cross pillars. So there was a second failure of development here. By the end of the 7th century we have the cross pillar at Fahan Mura, Co. Donegal, being lavishly decorated in full development towards the fine crosses of some 50 years later; but the iconography of the Kerry cross pillars did not develop in this way. It looks as if the great, basically Corcu Duibne, eremitical movement was already largely spent by the end of the 7th century.

It seems as if the successful monasteries at, for example, Ardfert, Inisfallen, Aghadoe, took no interest in the especial Irish art

Cross Slab at Templenacloonagh, Ballyferriter

Cross Slab at Reenconnell, Dingle

form of the high cross and turned their backs on the exciting beginnings in the eremitical sites all around them. So the cross pillar is the symbol, too, of the failure in Kerry of the whole eremitical movement to develop into a significant feature of Irish christianity. The future was with the missionaries and with the big monasteries involved in education, agriculture, scholarship and the arts.

(III) CROSS SLABS

A feature of the 9th and 10th centuries which affected Kerry to a small degree was the practice of placing large, undressed recumbent slabs on graves near churches. On these slabs crosses, and variations of crosses, were incised, with a reference in cursive script to the dead person.

On Church Island, Lough Currane, there is a fine slab with:

Bennacht F [ar] Anmain Gille in Chomded
I Buicine Adbur Ri Ciarraidi

('A blessing on the soul of Gille in Chomded O Buicine, royal heir of the Ciarraige'). We have no other reference to him. It is of interest that a prominent member of the Ciarraige should have been buried here, and not in, say, Ardfert. There is another slab on the island with:

Bennacht F [ar] Anmain Anmchada

There was a bishop of Ardfert Anmchad O hAnmchada who died in 1117 AD, but it is not clear what connexion there may have been between the two.

The use of the form 'Bennacht' shows that the slabs date from later than 850 AD up to which time the form would have been 'Bendacht'. The shape of the cross is a late form.

At Gallarus, in the graveyard around the old oratory, is a slab, now standing that reads 'Colum Mac Dinet'. On Inishvickillane, in the Blaskets, is a slab of this form at the ruined oratory there reading, in scratched

181

182

letters:

> Or do Macrued U Dalach

On the Skellig there is a simple roman cross incised on two slabs, and on another a complex, syrian type cross, the cross members inside a double circle; but there is no inscription.

(IV) BULLAUNS AND QUERN STONES

The bullaun is a recumbent stone with hollows in it in which small round or oval stones ground corn. It is associated with the introduction of christianity and of corn growing of a special hardshelled variety. The best example of a bullaun is at Temple Fiachna, Garranes, Kenmare. Another is at Upper Main Street, Dingle.

The bullaun is a version of the saddle quern brought to these parts by neolithic farmers 5,000 to 6,000 years ago. An example is at the little eremitical settlement at Cloon Lough.

The main relics of quern stones are rotary querns, basically two circular discs rotating on a spindle between which the corn was

Gallowglass (?), St John's Church, Tralee

ground. These date in this country from about 500 AD and were in regular use up to the last century. There is a distinctive, if minor, variant of them known as the Kerry quern. The greatest collection of quern stones

in Ireland, outside the National and Ulster museums, is that of the Godfrey family at Ballingroun, Anascaul.

(V) MEDIEVAL SCULPTURE

Sculpture had a revival in Kerry with the arrival of the anglo-normans in the 13th century. In Ardfert cathedral are two late 13th century sculptures of an abbot and a bishop or abbot. This last has been claimed to be of St Brendan and (by Smith) of Bishop Stack; but the three bishops of that name were some two centuries later. Another bishop or abbot of the early 14th century is portrayed in the Franciscan friary of Ardfert. At St Brendan's well is part of an early 16th century tomb chest. Also probably from a tomb chest is the figure of a knight or gallowglass at the Dominican priory in Tralee. This is notable in being one of the very few sculptures of the period 1350-1450. If it represents a gallowglass it is one of only three in the country. These all show the remains of some good carving. Some of the old parish churches — such as Annagh, Castleisland, Kilnanare, Kilsarkan — all in the same general area, also have good carvings of the period 1200-1600. There is also an attractive fragment at Aghadoe. This medieval sculpture is discussed by Dr Peter Harbison in the sixth volume of the *Journal of the Kerry Archaeological and Historical Society*, as well as in John Hunt's book.

(VI) MEDIEVAL RELIGIOUS ART

Apart from architecture and sculpture, three examples of medieval religious art in Kerry have come down to us. These are the Inisfallen and Aghadoe croziers and the Ballylongford processional cross.

The Inisfallen crozier was found in the river Laune, near Beaufort bridge, in the last century. It is now in the National Museum in Dublin. It is of wood, covered in silver, much of it gilded, and beautifully ornamented. It has, of course, suffered from its long immersion, but it must have been, originally, a magnificent work. Mlle Henry says that of all the Irish art work of the romanesque era that has come down to us it is probably the most perfect in execution and **structure**.

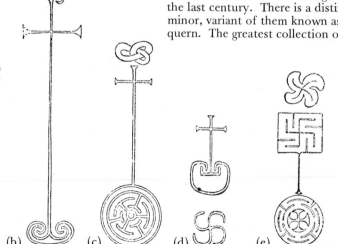

Designs on Cross Slabs:
(a) Caherlehillan   (b) Kilshannig   (c) (d) (e) Cloon Lough

(IV) Bullauns and Quern Stones
(V) Medieval Sculpture
(VI) Medieval Religious Art
Medieval Castles

Things   Part 2

183

Aghadoe Crozier

be mentioned here. These buildings had a period of five centuries — first built by anglo-norman intruders after 1200 AD; most destroyed by Ludlow's cromwellians in 1652; but some built up to the end of the 17th century. Artillery was first imported into Ireland only in 1488; but the logic of artillery — mainly because the weapon was so scarce — took more than a century and a half to establish itself in Kerry. The castles were often effective against the Irish who lacked artillery; but whenever the English could muster it — and the cromwellians were well supplied — the castles easily succumbed. In other parts of Ireland the castle was being abandoned for the unfortified manor house in the 16th century; but this transition seems not to have begun in Kerry until a century later, and then exceptionally.

(I) DATING

The great period of castle building in Ireland, when the really large structures were built, was from 1180 until 1310. Kerry does not give us examples of these great castles; but we do find examples of 13th century round

Inisfallen Crozier

Lislaghtin Cross

The Aghadoe crozier is of carved ivory. It is incomplete. It was found in the church at Aghadoe and was sold, about 1922, to the Stockholm Museum, where it is now. It dates from the 12th century and is thus a century or so younger than the Inisfallen crozier. It has a complex zoomorphic design that re-echoes the design on the portals of Aghadoe church itself.

The Ballylongford processional cross is much later in date. It comes from Lislaghtin friary, so dating from the 15th century. It is a fine example of its kind. It is now in the National Museum, Dublin.

MEDIEVAL CASTLES

The third group of ruins of the christian period is of castles and fortified houses. These are fairly numerous in Kerry — a count in 1909 gave 68 of them; Leask gives a total of 89. Less than a third of these can

castles at Aghadoe and Barrow, and of the further development of the fortified gatehouse of the same century at Ballingarry.

It is not easy to give simple rules for dating Irish castles. The use of sandstone for moulding around doors and windows, and for pillars, capitals and bases is a sure mark of a date before 1260. Afterwards limestone was used for those purposes.

Arches that are segmental pointed (two segments of a circle meeting at a point) and trefoil pointed (four segments meeting at three points) are marks of the next period — to about 1310.

There was, as we have seen in relation to churches, little or no building in stone in Ireland during the 14th century and the early part of the 15th.

The third period is thus that of the 15th

184 and 16th centuries. The marks of this period in Ireland are arches that either narrow in steps or are ogee arches (that rise to a very sharply moulded point). This was a period during which some splendid castles were built — such as Ross castle and Ballycarbery.

The mark of the fourth period in Ireland, of the 16th-17th centuries, is the flat, elliptical three-or four-centred arch. Many of the tall slender tower houses were built at this time.

A common feature of Irish castles is the *bawn* or enclosure around the castle. This begins as a motte but is also a continuation of the ring around the ringfort. Just as with them the cattle were enclosed at night within the bawn and Joyce says the origin of the word comes from this practice — bo-dhaingean or ba-dhun, literally cow-keep. Writers of the 16th and 17th centuries make clear that the bawns were very dirty places.

1. 12th — 13th centuries

The first late twelfth and early thirteenth century castles were wooden — often pre-fabricated — towers and palisades. These castles were of the motte and bailey style — built around a mound of earth (still obvious at Dunloe, Killarney) with a raised earthen courtyard, surrounded by fosse and moat. Such castles were built not only at Dunloe, but also at Dunkerron, near Kenmare; at Castleisland; at Tralee; etc. No remains of these early structures survive, although castles continued to be built on their sites. Bridging the river Maine at Castlemaine the anglo-normans built a castle in 1215. This was to guard the marches between geraldine and Mac Carthy territories. It often changed hands until, in elizabethan times, it was given to the charge of a royal constable. It was destroyed in the cromwellian wars. The round stone castle at Aghadoe dates — as does the other round castle in Kerry, that at Barrow — from later in the 13th century. The Aghadoe castle is rudely built of boulders and rubble, and is surrounded by a fosse and moat. Round castles were held to be safer than the former square keeps because, with these, the enemy could hack out the corner stones and the walls could collapse; with round castles this was more difficult.

When the geraldines were driven from south Kerry after their defeat at the battle of Callan in 1261, Dunkerron and, intermittently, Dunloe became strongholds of O Sullivan Mor. In 1280 the Cantillons built a strong castle on a rock of the sea at Ballingarry north of Ballyheigue: this was in the style of the time basically a strong gateway with adjoining curtain walls and no keep, so making it the more resemble a modern version of an iron age promontory fort. In the cromwellian wars Col D. Crosbie, a loyalist, held out there for four years until the stronghold was betrayed. Killorglin castle, a norman foundation held by the Knights Hospitallers, dates, most probably, from the 13th century. It was later called Castle Conway, after its elizabethan restorer, Jenkin Conway.

2. 15th century

The main surviving castle ruins date from the 15th century. These include the magnificent Mac Carthy Mor castle at Ballycarbery, Cahersiveen — of which Daniel O Connell's family were the hereditary keepers. Mac Carthy Mor also built the great castle at Blarney in 1446. The beautifully sited castle of Mac Carthy Mor at Castlelough, Killarney, also no doubt dates from that period; but few traces of it remain. From

Medieval arch and window forms

(*a*) Round or semicircular (Trim).
(*b*) Pointed (many castles and all dates).
(*c*) Segmental (Trim).
(*d*) Segmental pointed (Ballymoon).
(*e*) Four-centred (Donegal, fireplaces).
(*f*) Semi-elliptical (Kanturk, Mallow, Carrick).
(*g*) Trefoil-pointed (Athenry, Ferns, Lea).
(*h*) Ogee and (*i*) Cusped ogee (many XVth and XVIth century examples).
(*j*) Pair of ogee-headed lights with square hood-moulding.
(*k* and *l*) XVth century stepped and shouldered forms (Askeaton).
(*m*) the "Caernarvon" arch (early XIV century, Ballymoon and Ballyloughan).

Round Castle, Aghadoe, Killarney

Medieval Castles
1 16th-17th Centuries
2 15th Century
3 15th-17th Century Tower Houses

Things   Part 2

185

Ross Castle, Killarney

the same period also dates the exquisitely sited O Donoghue stronghold of Ross castle, Killarney, to which a late 17th century house was added and it was then transformed into a military barracks. The castle was surrendered on terms to Ludlow in 1652 when he brought artillery by boat up the Laune and across Loch Lein — the last strongpoint to yield in the cromwellian wars. Another fine 15th century structure was the Fitz Maurice castle at Listowel. This has a feature in common with the well-known (and restored) Bunratty castle in Clare in having an arch between the turrets. It was the last place to surrender in the Desmond wars. It was taken again in 1600 by the elizabethan commander, Sir Charles Wilmot.

3. 15th — 17th century Tower Houses

In the two centuries from about 1430 a number of fortified houses, called tower houses, were built. These consisted of a single tower of four storeys, usually with an enclosed yard or bawn. The tower houses were usually of a standard plan and were erected all over the country — in the Pale with the help of a £10 government grant. A small turret above the staircase at one corner leads to the roof with two ridges of the roof within the parapets. The dimly lit ground floor rooms were used as stores and cellars. The floor above has wall cupboards and loop windows; in the floor of one of the rooms will be a 'murdering hole' overlooking the entrance so that intruders can be kept under fire. Above this floor are

two rooms with, in the wall, a garderobe or privy. This floor will be well lighted and will have a fireplace, and will have been occupied by the master of the house. The whole top storey is taken up by a large, well lighted room, with a large fireplace and a slop stone delivering through a wall below a window. This was the general living and cooking place. Off it there may be a secret chamber, its entrance disguised as a garderobe seat. Above this floor are roof walks.

The room had little furniture, and the inhabitants slept on rushes in summer and on straw in winter, perhaps a foot deep. Within these rude surroundings lavish hospitality was shown to visitors. Drink, of course. 'First, the ordinary beer, then aqua vitae, then sack, then old-ale'. Before the fire 'you may solace yourself until supper-time. You shall not

want sack or tobacco. By this time the table is spread and plentifully furnished with variety of meats; but ill-cooked and without sauce. When you come to your chamber, do not expect canopy and curtains'. Thus Luke Gernon in 1620.

A Spanish agent wrote to Philip II in 1579: '. . . every petty gentleman lives in a stone tower, where he gathers into his service all the rascals of the neighbourhood (and of these towers there is an infinite number).'

The Ferriter castle near Ballyferriter, built in 1460, is one of these tower houses. But the really striking example is the O Conor Kerry tower house at Carrigafoyle, near Ballylongford; this also dates from the late 15th century. It is, relatively, very well preserved. It was built of small limestones,

Carrigafoyle: 'The beautifullest castle in all Munster'

186 giving it an appearance almost of grey brick. It is on the seashore between the high and low tide marks of a channel between the mainland and an island shielding it from the mouth of the Shannon. The wall surrounding the bawn enclosed part of the sea, making an anchorage for boats. This is believed to be unique; it is now much silted. In 1580, in the Desmond wars, Carrigafoyle was besieged by Sir William Pelham whose artillery reduced it in two days. Pelham hanged all the survivors — the Italian captain, the 16 Spaniards and the 50 Irish who were the defenders. It figured in the elizabethan and cromwellian wars and was severely slighted in 1652 but not destroyed. A tower house of Mac Carthy Mor is on the small island at Ballinskelligs.

From the 16th century dates the attractive, unfinished tower house at Castlecove. It is said a wife began it to emulate a neighbour at Ballycarnahan, Caherdaniel — while her husband was away, but when he came back he banned further work. The tower house at Killaha, Glenflesk, is a late example. This was the home of the O Donoghues of

Rahinnanex Castle, Dingle

Glenflesk, and here the poet, Seafraidh O Donoghue, gave those parties for which, amongst other things, he was famous. Another late example is that of the Knight of Kerry at Rahinnane, near Ventry, where a ringfort with souterrain was used as a bawn. Ballymalis, near Beaufort, Killarney, is an example of a variation in the standard tower house plan, built close to the end of the 16th century. A special feature is the 'bartizan' built at a second storey angle. This was used for firing at those who attempted to undermine the tower. This was a home of the Ferris family, guardians of the line of the Laune. From the 17th century dates Gallarus castle, near Ballyferriter, a stronghold of the Knights of Kerry. This was the great period of the destruction of castles by the cromwellians. Normally, because gunpowder was scarce, they did not blow them up, but 'slighted' them, by throwing down the parapets from the walls and breaching some part, so as to make them indefensible (and even more uncomfortable to live in!). Carrigafoyle well illustrates this.

4. 16th — 17th century Manor and Unfortified Houses

Kerry gives us no example of a 16th-17th century manor house, but there are two good examples of a domestic wing attached to an earlier castle, a feature of the period 1600-1640 but that lasted well into the last quarter of the century. Of these the better is that attached to a tower house at Kilmurray, Cordal, Castleisland. This is a fine house, now much ruined, that shows in striking manner the transition from the castle to the great house, but still heavily influenced by the castle tradition. It is typical of a style dating from the first half of the 17th century. Attached to Ross castle, Killarney, are the remains of a strong house, finished in 1688, to provide less cramped quarters for the Browne family. However, it was taken over almost immediately as a military post in the williamite wars and remained the home of a garrison through the 18th century to the beginning of the 19th, the Brownes having to build elsewhere a house now destroyed. Later, the 17th century windows were reduced to 15th century slits.

Kilmurray Castle, Castleisland

Of the occasional elizabethan or jacobean style home built in Ireland in the 17th century there appears to be no example in Kerry.

HOUSES AND PUBLIC BUILDINGS

(I) BIG HOUSES

A feature of the 18th century in Ireland is the 'big house', some of them very fine buildings indeed. Unfortunately, Kerry has no memorable example of this style. In the 1730s Ballyheigue 'castle', home of Thomas Crosbie, was a 'long, low thatched mansion of the old fashioned Irish type, having an orchard, gardens and bowling-green at the rear and eastern side and a walled courtyard with gates in front'. In the middle of the century Donal Mor O Connell, grandfather of the Liberator, built a smallish, rather attractive house at Derrynane — the 'first slated house in south Kerry' — facing as was the georgian fashion inflexibly north. The Liberator built hideous extensions to the place and, when it recently became a national monument, the original house was demolished. John Blennerhasset, father of the Irish House of Commons because a member for 60 years, built a large house at Ballyseedy, also added to, that has now become a hotel. Sir Maurice Crosbie, later earl of Glandore, built a large house at Ardfert, now in ruins. About 1760 James Leslie, bishop of Limerick, Ardfert and Aghadoe, built Tarbert House. A pleasant, but presumably later, georgian style house was the Butler home at Waterville; recent extensions have spoiled its flavour. So, there

Medieval Castles
4 16th-17th Centuries
Houses and Public Buildings
(I) Big Houses
(II) Public Buildings

Things Part 2

187

is little to show of the third great building period in Ireland, the georgian. The town of Tralee, rebuilt at the beginning of, and growing throughout, the century has some of the style of the georgian period. Kenmare, laid out towards the end of the century, has some attraction.

The main building period in Kerry was the 19th century, not the most distinguished of our building periods. Early in the century began that concern with the neo-gothic style that led to the building of a number of 'castles', now all in ruins. Some of these are Coltsman's castle, Killarney, built by a Londoner of that name; Ballyheigue castle, and Ardfert castle, designed by Sir Richard Morrison and burned down in the troubles, both Crosbie dwellings; the Bland castle at Derryquin, near Parknasilla, also burned during the troubles; the neighbouring Dromore castle of the song; the Orpen castle at Ardtully; the later, gaunt Headley Towers at Glenbeigh, designed by one of Ellen Terry's lovers; and a number of others. Also in the neo-gothic style, but the finest building in Kerry is, of course, as we have seen, the cathedral in Killarney, designed by Pugin.

Later began other revivals, neo-romanesque (in churches) and neo-tudor. The greatest house in Kerry is Muckross House, now a museum, built by the Herberts in 1843 in this neo-tudor style at a cost of £30,000. It is faced with portland stone specially imported and brought by cart over the wild roads from Cork. About the same time, the Herberts built the attractive Dinis Cottage, across Muckross lake, as accomodation for their guests.

An attractive early victorian house is Kilmurray house, east of Castleisland. Another, later victorian style house is Oak Park, Tralee, built in 1857-60 by Maurice Fitz Gerald Sandes, and later a Presentation convent. In 1877 was built Cahernane, Killarney, by a cadet branch of the Herberts, in what has been described as a 'hybrid' style. It is now an hotel.

(II) PUBLIC BUILDINGS

An act of 1765 authorised the setting up of

Flesk (or Coltsman's) Castle, Killarney

a public infirmary in each county and the Kerry county infirmary was set up in Tralee towards the end of the century. The classical county courthouse in Tralee was designed by William Morrison, son of a pupil of Gandon's, Sir Richard Morrison, and was erected about 1830. In Tralee also is the headquarters of the county council in the fine Thomas Ashe Memorial Hall built to replace the headquarters destroyed by the British army in 1920. From 1838 were set up workhouses in Tralee, Killarney, Dingle, Listowel, Kenmare and Cahersiveen. The Tralee building is now the county hospital. That at Killarney is the county home, basically a geriatric institution for the whole county. Also in Killarney, opened in 1852, is the grey, rather attractive county mental hospital, designed by Sir Thomas Deane; about a quarter of the population of Killarney is made up of those in the mental hospital and the county home. There is also a small hospital there. Small hospitals have superseded the Dingle, Listowel, Kenmare and Cahersiveen institutions. These are all local government institutions. The central government has built little in Kerry, except for the large number of clean-cut primary schools built in recent years to replace the grey, sad

buildings of the 19th century.

Relics of more colourful times are the coastguard stations. The coastguard was established in 1822 to put a final end to smuggling, and from 1836, poteen making. At the beginning they had 11 cruisers off the coast of Ireland. In 1856 the coastguard was handed over to the British navy, to be disbanded in 1923. During the war of independence many of the Irish coastguard stations were destroyed — as at West Cove; but others survive, as does the gaunt station at Knightstown, Valentia.

Another relic is the Martello tower, miscalled from a Saracen watch tower at Mortella (myrtle) Point, Corsica, which for strength, economy of garrison and equipment much impressed the British who built towers modelled on it from South Africa to America. There are none now extant in Kerry, but three overlook Bantry Bay. That at Garinish, Glengariff, was the first to be built in the British isles against the expected Napoleonic invasion of 1804-05. The other two, on Beare island, were built soon after. Square watch towers, as at Valentia, were built somewhat earlier.

188   (III) FARM HOUSES

It is an irony of history that the houses that survive to us from the remote past are the houses of the poor, because they were built wholly or largely of stone. The houses of the great, described in some detail in the sagas, were of wood and have perished. So what remains to us now does not give us a full picture of the past.

The first farmhouse we know of in Kerry is the clochan dating, in its technique of corbelling, back to neolithic times. It seems also to have been the style used for Kerry farmhouses in bronze age times. The style certainly derived from the tent. Some of the earliest houses were in sandhills, e.g. at Ballybunion, but the houses are now so ruined that nothing can be learned about them, except that they were round, whether beehive shaped or the earlier jampot style we cannot say. In other parts of Ireland in these periods rectangular houses were used but, apart from that on Scariff island, I am not aware that any of the style are to be found among the bronze age remains in Kerry. Perhaps there were wooden houses of the type, but if so they have not been excavated. It is likely that a great fort like Staigue contained a significant village of wooden houses now gone when lesser forts — such as Leacanbuaile — with their round and rectangular houses showed how they were occupied.

From early christian times a development of house types can be seen. On the Skellig the clochans began to develop more and more pronounced rectangular interiors. On Church Island, Valentia, there was a round house with a thatched roof, and on Beiginish close by another but later example. This style, the walls built of stone or of wattles and clay with a conical thatched roof — a style still very prevalent in African places — persisted into elizabethan times; but it is not clear whether this was true of Kerry: if so, the houses were easily destroyed in the great firing forays of the Desmond wars. In any event, another style, linking with that on the Skellig, begins in early christian times. At Leacanbuaile, Cahersiveen, is a square stone house, that was thatched-roofed, built on the

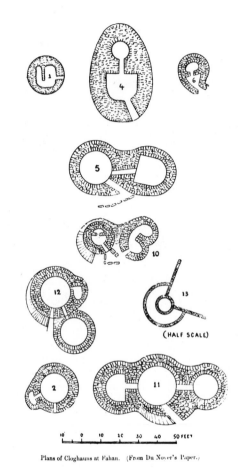

Plans of Cloghauns at Fahan. (From Du Noyer's Paper.)

Plans of clochans at Fahan, Dingle

remains of two circular ones. At Church Island, Valentia, is a rectangular house, that had a hipped, thatched roof. At Fahan are a number of oval ruins which once, no doubt, bore the same kind of roof. At the monastery at Reask was at least a large oval building of the same sort. At Fahan are also a number of multi-chambered clochans, with one, two or three rooms, as well as an enclosure for the dog. Some are round, some rectangular, some segmented.

It is probable that amongst the users of stone houses the better off had rectangular ones — for example the 15th century Chancellor's and St Brendan's Houses at Kilmalkedar — on the model of the wooden house, and the

poorer classes the round or oval ones. The distinction can be seen in the round cells of the early christian monasteries and the rectangular church. The poorer classes did not have enclosures around their houses — such as the eight houses set in small fields at Beiginish.

In the latter part of the 17th century Petty refers to the houses as 'nasty Cabbins', cottages that can be made in three or four days, with everything inside destroyed by 'Smoaks'. This must have arisen from the absence of a chimney, noted as usual in cabins by Arthur Young, a century later. This despite the fact that the chimney had been introduced from the 16th century, and was certainly introduced in the reconstruction of Muckross friary early in the 1620s. Young says a small house could be built for £2.

However, by early in the next century the chimney must have arrived in Kerry for, while Weld comments on the poverty-stricken and dirty looks of the houses in the Iveragh and Dingle peninsulas and makes several references to blazing fires, he does not complain of smoke.

If Aalen is to be followed, the evolution of the farmhouse in the west of Ireland developed from the oval type of house with a hipped, thatched roof and the fire in the middle. No doubt, to have the smoke going through a hole in the roof was a distinct advance from Petty's time. Then was created

St Brendan's House, Kilmalkedar

Houses and Public Buildings
(III) Farm Houses
(IV) Booleys
Roads and Railways
(I) Roads

Things   Part 2

some kind of chimney breast; then the moving of the fire somewhat to one end of the house and the opening of two doors, facing each other, in opposite walls. Behind the fireplace grew up a separate room, a bedroom for the parents; at the other end of the house there was shelter for animals, poultry, etc. as, for example, Tomas O Criomthain describes of the Blaskets in the middle of the last century. Nonetheless, the census of 1841 reported that 67% of the rural population of Kerry lived in mud, one roomed cabins. From these conditions evolved the long, gabled, thatched house with three separate rooms and a loft over that remote from the fireplace. And, of course, separate cabins for the livestock. Before the Famine Sir John Walsh was building farmhouses for his tenants at a cost of £20 each, and farm buildings for £15. Danaher's survey of house types in Iraghticonnor suggests that the oval and the rectangular models can be seen to draw together in surviving house types there — the oval house leading to the hipped, thatched gable, the rectangular to the stone gable, the latter a better proposition in exposed places. Some of the older, simpler houses there were made of mud or sods.

The thatched farmhouse, though longer, but still one storey and white-washed, is very frequent in north Kerry; but it has been superseded in south and west Kerry by houses reconstructed or rebuilt mainly in the present century. Those in south Kerry, with their second storey, their roofs slated, and dormer windows upstairs, often with coloured walls, are curiously attractive. Similar houses are to be seen in the Beare peninsula. On the Dingle peninsula, however, the reconstructed two storey houses are much less attractive, while those at the Irish speaking end of the peninsula, erected with extra and special Government help, are hideous.

Traditionally, the houses fall into four main classes — the one room cabin, the two to four roomed house of the small farmer, the five to nine room house of the large farmer, and the large landowner's house.

A feature of the houses in south Kerry is the grouping of two or three of them together at the head of an otherwise deserted coum. The

Two types of rural house, c. 1900

pot plants — mainly geraniums — are an engaging feature of many of these houses. In the Dingle peninsula can be seen somewhat larger clusters of houses, constituting an ancient hamlet, or *baile*.

Typical of Ireland as a whole is the absence in Kerry of good wooden furniture in the normal rural house.

(IV) BOOLEYS

Spenser in 1595 makes what is perhaps the first reference to a practice that was a major feature of Irish life. It seems that in his time, and in Kerry well into the 19th century, there was the practice of rundale, cultivation on the open field system. The people lived in small, disorderly groups of houses, a *baile*, in the middle of such arable land as was available, and distributed, and redistributed, the patches by lot. This method of

cultivation, the crops having been sown, made no provision for cattle which otherwise would wander over the open fields. They were, in consequence, driven up the grassy mountainsides for the summer months and some or all of the family went with them to herd them, milk them, and draw off their blood, as was the custom. This transfer was known as 'booleying', or, by the technical name of 'transhumance'. High up on the hills primitive huts — beehive, oval or rectangular — can still be found, ruined, in sheltered places, beside the head waters of streams. These were shelters for humans and also, no doubt, for butter and cheese. Considerable numbers of these ruins are still to be seen on high ground on the Dingle and Iveragh peninsulas. The summer over, animals and humans came down again, the crops being gathered. This practice seems to have died out after the great famine of the 19th century.

ROADS AND RAILWAYS

(I) ROADS

One of the most fascinating relics of the past, so often taken for granted, are the roads.

The celts are credited with a considerable interest in roads. Their chariots called for paved roads. The romans borrowed most of their words for wheeled vehicles from the celtic languages. In Ireland there is a long tradition of road building and, even of a national road system, from gaelic times. Tara in its period of power in the early part of the christian era, was the hub of a road system for the northern part of the country. Earlier still, we must assume that some system of roads throughout the country existed from the evidence of the drunken expedition of Cuchulain and his friends travelled by chariot from Ulster to Teamhar Luachra, ostensibly near Castleisland, on one wild night. The 7th century life of St Brigid by Cogitosus tells how an over-king sent out an order *per plebes et provincias* for a road or causeway to be built over boggy ground, constructed of logs laid over a stone foundation and suitable for the passage of horses, wagons and chariots. The labour was distributed through the kindred groups through whose lands the

190 road should pass. When the *Book of Rights* was compiled at the end of the first millenium AD it included national standards for four classes of roads. There was a main road — Slighe Dala Meic Umhoir, the road of Dala son of Umhor — from Dublin to Tarbert, much as the present road. There was also an 'itinerary' from Limerick to Castleisland to Tralee, also much as at present. There is no early record of any other road in Kerry.

Kerry was , of course, at the periphery of any systems there were, and we do not come across any of the old great roads. There was, however, a reputed road leading to Teamhar Luachra, and traces of it, it is claimed, between Taur Hill in Co. Cork and Ballahantauragh, near Castleisland.

We do not find a large number of traces of local roads. One of the best ways of finding old settlements is to discover these — often still in use as boithrins — and to follow them.

For example, from the ancient copper mine on Coad mountain there is a road, no doubt improved in the 17th century, that finds its way down to the harbour at Derrynane: this may be 4,000 years old. There are magnificent signposts along it in the shape of standing stones at Garrough, Caherdaniel. Again, towards the end of the present roadway at Cloon Lough there is a branch right into an old farming settlement, with remains of houses and field systems going back perhaps to bronze age times. At Dromtine, Sneem, is another old system picking its way through dry and wet ground, with relics of bronze age and iron age times. Between the bridge over the Finglas river, in the area of Baslickane and Ballybrack, Waterville, and the sea is an extensive system of wide roads with remains scattered about from at least early christian times. There is the famous Saints' road from Kilmalkedar (perhaps Ventry) to the top of Brandon and down to Cloghane that might date from pagan times. These examples could be multiplied.

There are also the roads across the mountains, now often partly washed away, the 'green' roads that lead from old, now abandoned hamlets, to centres of some kind. The old

church at Kilcrohane is the nub of such a system where people from the wild wet mountainsides, and glens and coums still inaccessible, came to worship almost certainly throughout penal times as before. In the 17th and 18th centuries improved roads were laid down to link the mines on Coad mountain with Derrynane and Castlecove.

After the Desmond wars a crude, and apparently unfinished, road across Sliabh Luachra to Castleisland was begun.

In 1615 an act was passed to improve highways. Each parish was levied labour to make and maintain roads, and there was compulsory power to take small stones and underwood for this purpose. But this and subsequent compulsory attempts were failures. However, there remain from this period some examples of trunk roads joining what are now appreciable centres of population. Some of these were used in whole or in part in later times; but others have been superseded and can sometimes be seen following the general direction of the new road, but displaying much greater abandon and attack. Thus there was a road from Glenbeigh to what is now Cahersiveen that, in the early 18th century, terrified the ladies, mounted on the famous hobbies of the district, as they travelled to Derrynane. Where the modern road turns cravenly right beyond Mountain Stage, we can see the old road march bravely up the 1200 foot shoulder of Drung Hill, with what seems, when the swirling mists momentarily reveal it, a precipitous drop into the sea.

From 1690 we have an account of a road that ran from 'Corke to Ardfert, via Eglish, Macroom, Balinary, Killarney, Aghadoe, and Trally'. This linked up with a road shown by Smith running to Lixnaw, Listowel, Carrigafoyle, Tarbert and Limerick.

Not until early in the 18th century was there a real attempt by government to take the road problem in hand. Between then and the middle of the 19th century the existing road system was laid down. Three main expedients were adopted, and there are still to be seen the results — most wasteful in a

country cruelly short of capital — of the differing use of these expedients and the changing conceptions of what a road ought to do. The three expedients were: the grand juries of nominated landlords; the turnpike trusts; and relief works that came to be administered by the Board of Works. From the middle of the 19th century the grand juries took over completely, and these were, at the end of the century superseded by the rural district councils, and then, in the present century by the county councils.

The grand jury system provided that a landowner had to 'present' for a road work. If this were approved he carried out the work directly and was recouped the cost by the grand jury which raised the amount by local taxation. The system was in full force from 1759 to 1836, and for all that there were gross abuses, it had a dramatic effect on the quality of the roads. Some private landowners, notably Lord Shelburne, made special contributions up to half the cost of building a new road. Smith mentions (1756) the 'new' road from Killarney to Kenmare (i.e. that over the shoulder of Torc mountain) and a road through Dunkerron to Iveragh. In 1776 Arthur Young was most enthusiastic about the effect on the new road system — a much better one than in England — of this enlightened self interest which had the effect of fitting the country with a network of roads for which both the materials and the labour were freely available: 'I could trace a route upon paper as wild as fancy could dictate, and everywhere I found beautiful roads without break or hindrance, to enable me to realize my design'.

Earlier in the century a more planned attack had been made by the setting up of turnpike trusts to link the main centres. These were not a success because the volume of toll-paying traffic was not enough to cover the annual charges for construction and maintenance. The Cork-Kerry turnpike, linking Cork-Millstreet-Castleisland-Listowel, with a branch to Killarney, got going in 1748; but 20 years later it had met little more than half its cost. Poor income led to bad maintenance and this in turn to less traffic. Young said that the turnpikes were almost the only **bad roads** in Ireland.

The striking thing about the turnpikes is their *straightness*. They paid little regard to gradients. A later standard became a gradient of one in thirty-five; these turnpikes tackled gradients of one in seven or eight. (Some amateur road builders were even more enthusiastic). It is suggested that one reason for this affection for gradients was that the hills gave secure foundations for less cost. In the early years this direct approach was somehow feasible because cars and their loads were very light; but in the latter part of the century the use of heavy cars and the transport of grain made these gradients impracticable. This concern for straightness was a mark of all the roads of the early 18th century. Arthur Young, travelling between Macroom and Kenmare in 1776, says:

> The road leads directly against a mountain ridge, and those who made it were so incredibly stupid that they kept the strait line up the hill, instead of turning aside to the right, to wind around a projection of it. The path of the road is worn by the torrents into a channel which is blocked up in places by huge fragments, so that it would be a horrid road on a level; but on a hill so steep that the best path would be difficult to ascend, it may be supposed terrible; the (six) labourers, two passing strangers, and my servant, could with difficulty get the chaise up. It is much to be regretted that the direction of the road is not changed, as the rest from Corke to Nedeen is good enough.

He had to take this more inland road because the later main road, over Priest's Leap — itself a formidable gradient — was not then fully finished.

The Cork-Kerry turnpike went from Millstreet to Rathmore to Knocknaboul Cross to Castleisland to Listowel in straight lines cut across the map. Charles Smith tells us: 'The principal undertaker was one Mr Murphy, a man who by the meer dint of genius hath extremely well executed several new roads here, and taught others to do the like, and carry them on, through very difficult, and almost impracticable, bogs and mountains'. The fashion was taken up by the local landowners in their own co-operatively

financed and 'presentment' roads. So the map shows straight line roads from Castleisland to Abbeyfeale, to Killarney, and Tralee; from Killarney to Tralee (superseding an older one); and from Killarney to Castlemaine to Tralee and Dingle. Thus, from 1750 or so Killarney became relatively accessible with, as Smith says, 'four great new roads' radiating straight from it — to Cork, to Kenmare, to Castleisland and Limerick, and to Castlemaine. The extreme example of devotion to straightness was shown by Lord Ventry in his 1759 road south west from Kilmore Lodge to the Connor Pass. This went in two straight drives for the pass, until 200 feet from the summit, it succumbed to zig-zags in a one in three gradient. A really straight road, therefore, can with great confidence be dated to the mid-eighteenth century.

At the end of the 18th century the postal service began to be organised in Kerry. In 1812 a mail coach road was built between Cork and Tralee, and Tralee-Listowel-Limerick. These roads used some of the old turnpikes; but because of the concern to avoid undue gradients a wholly new road — the third in a century — was built between Killarney and Tralee: this is, substantially, the present main road.

Also at the end of the 18th century the great fastness of the Iveragh peninsula began to be opened up and a presentment road was made from Glenbeigh to Cahersiveen to Waterville. Old Hunting Cap O Connell was able to bring his dead butler, Andrew Connell, by cart from Tralee to Waterville; but from there to Derrynane the body had to be carried up the steep green road, still to be seen, that so boldly makes for Coomakista.

O Brien in 1800 complains of the state of maintenance of the roads and of the dishonesty of those paid to make and maintain minor roads who spent little or nothing on them.

In the post-war slump of 1817 there was much distress that led, in the following decade, to considerable disorder. This provoked extensive government relief works.

That great public servant, Richard Griffith, built a number of roads in north Kerry between 1823 and 1829, including the road from Castleisland to Newcastlewest and from Abbeyfeale to Newmarket and Charleville, crucial for opening up the delivery of butter from north Kerry to Cork. After the foundation of the Board of Works in 1831, these works were directly administered by the Board. There was much praise for their engineer, Mr Nimmo, and his roads. So, at the end of the thirties, was built the present road between Waterville and Caherdaniel, at the expense it would seem from Lady Chatterton's observations, of the destruction on the Waterville side of Coomakista of a great dolmen, matching that at Coumatlakane on the Caherdaniel side of the pass. Also built at this time (1838-39) was the striking 'Tunnel' road between Kenmare and Glengariff as well as that between Tralee and Dingle, and many others. Later was built the, scenically, splendid road from Muckross by the Upper Lake to Moll's Gap and Kenmare, and the two roads from Sneem — that to Kenmare and that back to Moll's Gap. In the 1840s a road, superseding a more inland one, was built between Kenmare and Clonee, between Clonee and the Cork border and, later, by the coast to Derreen.

Also built were piers at such places as Cahersiveen and Portmagee, and feeder roads into Cahersiveen, which grew from nothing to a town at this time. In the same area the 'old inhabitants of the hill left their cabins and built new ones along the new road sides'. Piers were also built at Dingle, Dunquin, Cloghane and Kilmakillogue.

Between 1834 and 1845, 233 miles of roads were made in the county, 140 of them by the Board of Works at a cost of £123,000. The county surveyor wrote that, as a result, 'every horse has now his car instead of his baskets'.

By the middle of the 19th century the road system as we know it was complete. This system is being steadily improved as motor traffic increases; but the same traffic is leading to the break-up of a number of roads that pass over bogs and thus have poor foundations.

During the famine of 1845-47 many unlikely

191

192 roads were started for relief works. Since
then, there has been some official concern to
help with roads into bogs, to facilitate turf
saving. 'Accomodation and cul-de-sac roads'
serving two or three farmhouses gain grants
for co-operative repair: these roads are usually
to be known by being cut off by a gate.
There is a steady pressure for roads into
the coums to be taken over and maintained
by the county council. As a result of all this
the not too intrepid motorist can now
penetrate into the wildest places and the
walker finds firm footing on abandoned
roads.

An ancient earthwork, the Cladh Rua or Red
Ditch, may have had some connexion with the
road system. This ran from Kerry Head to
Athea, Co. Limerick, where it linked up with
another earthwork, the Black Ditch, which
ran to Rath Luirc. There are a number of
these in Ireland, but only one is reported from
Kerry. It is not known what was their purpose.

(II) RAILWAYS

The second half of the 19th century saw the
opening of Kerry by railways. There were
two main lines into Kerry — the Mallow-Tralee
and the Limerick-Tralee lines.

The first of these was the Mallow to Tralee
line. This was built by the Killarney
Junction Railway. The line from Mallow as
far as Killarney was opened in July, 1853.
It reached Tralee in 1859. It was connected

Lartigue Railway, Listowel

Glinsk Railway Viaduct, Cahersiveen

with the Limerick, via Newcastlewest, line in
1883.

Three branches from the Mallow-Tralee line
were made. A branch from Headford Junction
for the 20 miles to Kenmare was opened in
1893, and closed in 1960. From Farranfore
a branch to Killorglin was opened in 1885
and extended to Cahersiveen and Valentia
Harbour in 1893; this was also closed in
1960. From Gortatlea a five mile branch to
Castleisland was opened by the Castleisland
Railway in 1875 — the single and original
locomotive (XW 90) of this line is preserved
on the platform of Mallow station.

The second main line was the Limerick-Tralee
line of 70 miles. It reached Newcastlewest
by 1867, and the Newcastlewest-Tralee section
was opened in 1880 by the Limerick and
Kerry Railway, and linked with the Mallow-
Tralee line in 1883. There were no branches
on this line. It was closed to passengers in
1963.

Three other local lines were opened: Tralee-
Fenit; Tralee-Dingle; and Listowel-
Ballybunion. In 1887 the Tralee-Fenit line
was built by the Tralee and Fenit Railway to
capture the fish traffic from Fenit. The

Tralee-Dingle line was opened in 1891 by the
Tralee and Dingle Light Railway; it was a
three-foot gauge line of 37 miles. It had a
branch to Castlegregory. It had some
awkward gradients and, because of accidents,
speed was cut to a minimum. It was closed in
1953.

The third line, the Listowel-Ballybunion one,
was the most remarkable line built in Ireland.
This was a monorail devised by a Spaniard
with a French name and domicile, Charles
Francois Marie-Therese Lartigue (1834-1907),
and the line was alwys known as *The Lartigue*.
It was nine miles long, opened in 1888 and
closed in 1924. The monorail was at about
the level of the passengers' heads, with a
double boiler locomotive, and passengers'
coaches slung each side of the rail. This had
two special features — the noise the passengers
had to endure close to their ears, and the
problem of balance to ensure that the same
weight (not number!) of passengers was on
each side of the rail. Sacks of sand were
available in the stations to correct imbalances.
Lartigue tried similar systems in the Argentine
and France. Both were almost immediate
failures. He built another railway in Algeria
worked by mule power! His fame remains in
Ireland.

PART 3 PLACES

194 Kerry lies between 51°40' and 52°34' of north latitude, and 9°8' and 10°42' of west longitude. These are distances of 63 miles and 67 miles respectively. The extreme points are Hungry Hill in the south (E76 N50 on the National Grid), the Tiaracht in the west (E18 N95), Tarbert point in the north (E108 N150) and just east of Mullaghanish (E124 N84) in the east. The centre of the county is about half way between Killorglin and Kilgobnet, so that the whole county lies within a radius of 40 miles from that point.

The modern county of Kerry, which dates from 1606, consists of nine baronies, 87 civil (ie. pre-reformation) parishes, and some 2,300 townlands. It is bounded mostly by the Shannon and the sea, and is cut off from the neighbouring county of Limerick by, mainly, the river Feale, and from the county of Cork by great highlands. Of the inhabitants of these areas 99% are catholics. The catholic *diocese* of Kerry — the protestant diocese is united with Limerick — comprises the county plus the whole of the Beare peninsula and a few other places in Cork. In this diocese there are 51 modern parishes. In this topography we cover virtually the whole of this diocese because it is a homogeneous area. We deal with parishes as they are now in present-day catholic use.

The two territorial units that have day to day significance are the parish and the townland. The townland (baile-fearainn) is the basic geographical unit. It is a very ancient division; but it has been subdivided on such irregular lines that it is now a most confusing one. Some townlands may contain only two small farms and others may cover several square miles; the average is 500 acres, that is, somewhat less than a square mile. However, the townland is invariably used for postal addresses and for naming historical and archaeological sites. It is thus a significant division, but hard to locate on the maps readily in circulation. (Townlands are grouped into district electoral divisions and these into registrars' districts; but these units are almost exclusively of administrative significance; they have their own maps).

But both parish and townland are small units.

After a good deal of experiment, we decided to deal with the topography of the county and diocese on the basis of the barony. With this as a unit it is possible to get a detailed grasp of the topography of Kerry.

The nine baronies of Kerry represent the pattern of control after the upheavals of the twelfth and thirteenth centuries. The four baronies of north Kerry comprised the county of Kerry as the anglo-normans defined it in the thirteenth century and this became the county palatine of Kerry from 1327 when the first earl of Desmond got virtual sovereignty over it. The Desmond power was centred on the rich barony of Trughanacmy, with the two great castles of Castleisland at the eastern end and of Tralee at the western. With this went the beautiful, if poor, barony of Corkaguiney. The other geraldine house

The Baronies of Kerry

of Fitz Maurice settled in the barony of Clanmaurice, called after them, the wedge of good farming land to the north, centred on Ardfert, with Listowel as a northern outpost. The older rulers of Trughanacmy and Clanmaurice, the O Connor Kerry house, were pushed north into the less profitable area of the barony of Iraghticonnor between the Feale and the Shannon, centred on Ballylongford.

In south Kerry which, with west Cork, was to constitute for a short time (1571-1606) the county of Desmond, gaelic power became supreme under the MacCarthy dynasty. This, from the end of the thirteenth century, rested on the beautiful barony of Magunihy centred on Killarney, with which went the barony of Iveragh. The other gaelic intruders, the O Sullivans centred on Dunkerron, near Kenmare, ruled the great baronies of Dunkerron — later divided into North and South — and Glanerought.

In north Kerry, *Iraghticonnor* is defined by the Shannon, the sea, the river Feale and the Limerick border. South of the Feale, *Clanmaurice* runs as a wedge from the sea between the mouth of the Feale and Barrow harbour to a point just below Abbeyfeale on the east.

Beneath this runs the rich limestone barony of *Trughanacmy*. The western line is from Barrow to Cromane and the southern line runs almost due east from the base of the Cromane peninsula to the Cork border just south of Ballydesmond except where, just east of Killorglin, it runs north to the Maine river, and follows the river, with two salients north of it, until, just west of Farranfore, it turns south again. At its western end it comprises Castlemaine, Miltown and Killorglin, clearly a mark of the compromises made over the march lands and the sea access around Killorglin.

The rest of the Dingle peninsula, west from the summits of the mountains of Baurtregaum and Caherconree, is the barony of *Corkaguiney.*

In south Kerry, the barony of *Magunihy* is bounded by the west banks of the Killarney lakes, on the north by the Maine and the line of hills west to Ballydesmond, by Mangerton on the south and the Cork border on the east. Lying west of Magunihy is *Dunkerron North*, between the Killarney lakes and Caragh lake and river, and between the Laune on the north and the line of mountains intersected by Ballaghabeama on the south. *Iveragh* runs from Caragh lake to Lough Currane and Valentia.

Dunkerron South runs south west between the line of mountains from Kenmare along the Kenmare River to Lough Currane. *Glanerought* comprises the valley of the Roughty River from the Cork border east of Kilgarvan, and the northern half of the Beare peninsula to just west of Kilmakilloge harbour.

There were older patterns of settlements than the baronies. It is natural to think of Kerry as a series of peninsulas because the modern road system makes travel easier that way. But each of the peninsulas has a spine of high mountains cutting off contact between the two sides. In earlier times, before there were adequate roads, contact *between* peninsulas was easier than contact across them. So the county should be seen, in an historical sense, as a collection of bays separated by mountains. For example, from the earliest historical times, the Corcu Duibne did not occupy all of the peninsula now named after them — they lived in the narrow strip of arable land on the south side of the peninsula and, equally, on the strip across Dingle Bay in the modern barony of Iveragh. In the same way the Alltraige — the people of St Brendan — occupied the shores of Tralee Bay below Kerry Head to what is now Tralee, and the Ui Fearba occupied the shores of Brandon Bay and that part of Tralee Bay west of Annagh. Later, both Alltraige and the Ui Fearba were overwhelmed by the Ciarraige. Later still, the O Sullivans descended on what was left of the kingdom of West Munster and settled on both sides of the Kenmare River (and of Bantry Bay). But historians are only beginning to open up the history of these areas. For our purposes we cleave to the medieval patterns of settlement and the modern road systems. For this the barony is the crucial unit.

What follows assumes that the traveller in Kerry has the constant use of a car, the occasional use of not only a second driver but also of a second car, and, very occasionally, the use of a boat.

The other essential piece of equipment is boots.

Because the rainfall in Kerry is heavy, and because of the boggy nature of the ground, most places tend to be very wet, notwithstanding all the rivers and lakes and the general air of water running everywhere. This is so, even after long periods of drought. If one wishes to walk it is highly desirable to be well-shod. Climbing, or rubber, boots are best; strong shoes are a minimun: in many places the water oozes over the tops of shoes.

It is necessary, also, for sight-seeing to adapt oneself to the weather that prevails at any time. The weather in Kerry is analysed in chapter eight. It emerges there that, on average, rain on a rain day lasts about 3½ hours, with little variation throughout the year. This bears out the old saying that normally in Ireland any kind of weather seldom lasts more than half a day, taking that as something of the order of four hours. A fine half-day in this sense may be the full morning, or the full afternoon, or the full evening; but it is just as likely to be from mid-morning to mid-afternoon, or mid-afternoon to mid-evening. One must be ready to seize fine weather, as it comes, even if this is to cut across mealtimes, etc. Adapting oneself to the caprices of the weather is essential if one is to get the best value from one's sight-seeing; but it is precisely these caprices that give the wonderful effects of colour, mobility and variety. There are so many things to see that one should relate one's trips to the minimum weather conditions for each. One should also be quick to take advantage of spectacular turns in the weather, such as really heavy rainfall in mountainy places. As Boll has said of this in Mayo: 'The rain is absolute, magnificent and frightening. To call this rain bad weather is as inappropriate as to call scorching sun fine weather.' However, a major hazard in sight-seeing by the sea is to run into mist; very often this does not penetrate inland.

195

196   **FINDING PLACES**

County Kerry, after Speed (1610)

It is a major hindrance in seeing the county in detail that the map situation is so bad. The whole of Kerry is given on the ¼ inch Ordnance Survey map, Sheet 5; this gives the broad outlines, but little detail, especially in relation to minor roads. Bartholomew's ¼ inch map (Sheet 4, Cork—Killarney) gives much more detail (including some not on the much bigger ½ inch and 1 inch Ordnance Survey maps); but it omits details they give, and reading it calls for very good eyesight.

The ½ inch Ordnance Survey maps (Sheets 17, 20, 21 and 24), bases of the maps I to VI used in this book, are essential, but they suffer from four main defects. The first is that they are not up-to-date, and are often quite misleading about minor roads: some are not given at all; others are shown as in poor condition that are relatively good; others as no worse that are impassable. The second defect is that they are printed as part of an overall scheme for the country as a whole and not for the understanding of specific areas: thus, while the bulk of the Iveragh peninsula is given on Sheet 20, the southern part of the peninsula appears on Sheet 24; and north Kerry calls for pieces from three maps. The maps in this book give the essential features of the Ordnance Survey ½ inch maps, by permission of the Government, but they are pieced together so as to give a clear impression of the principal areas of the county. The third defect relates to townlands: they mark only a few of these. The fourth defect is related to the third: some sites are specially marked, but most are not marked at all. The cumulative effect of all these defects is that they are not much use in helping to find places of special scenic, archaeological or historic interest.

The 1 inch maps are not much better in this respect. First, they are not readily available, except for a slightly eccentric compilation labelled 'The Killarney District', the only one available in colour. Secondly, they are even more out of date than the ½ inch maps. Thirdly, they are only a little less unhelpful about townlands and sites. Fourthly, they are necessarily bulky and when cut up and pieced together to give a coherent view of,

County Kerry Enlarged from Speed's
KINGDOME OF IRLAND
1610 A.D.

say, the Iveragh peninsula, make an unmanageable (and expensive) sheet. There is a series of maps called the townland index (of 6 inch maps) showing the townlands and the baronies, but they also need piecing together if one is to understand any area.

There are, of course, 6 inch and 25 inch maps that give a great deal of detail, but these (where they are in print) are too bulky for other than specialist use. There are also some other maps, also of specialist interest.

The net effect of all this is that it is difficult, time-consuming and exhausting to *find* a specific place. In this book three devices are used to ease the finding of sites. A few sites have, however, defeated me.

The first device, adopted throughout this Part III of the book, is to describe as precisely as possible how to get to a particular site. Thus, to take an extreme example, the Coolnaharrigal scribed stone is on the Glenbeigh—Cahersiveen road. As one goes to Cahersiveen one passes the crossing of the old Mountain Stage railway station and bears left along the former main road. It is at the third house on the left under the flower bed in the extreme right hand corner of the flower garden. Clearly, there are a number of variables in any such description — and no normal map could be expected to mark such a site. Moreover, some sites are in such featureless places — such as mountain sides — as to defy precise description.

So, the second device is to divide the county into baronies, and to give a map for each barony or, more usually, two neighbouring baronies. In this way coherent neighbourhoods can be established. These maps are based on the Ordnance Survey ½ inch maps and maintain the scale of ½ inch to the mile. The barony boundaries shown are not precise: they are near approximations.

The third device is to base the reference for sites on the National Grid. The Grid has three indices — a lettered zone, an easting co-ordinate and a northing co-ordinate. In this book the index letter is replaced by a roman numeral showing which of the six barony maps — I to VI — in this Part of this

book applies. The easting co-ordinate is always shown first: it is the vertical line *east* of the site. The northing co-ordinate is the horizontal line *north* of the site. The ½ inch maps as generally supplied do not show the co-ordinate lines in less than units of ten. So, there is supplied with each book a transparent plastic square breaking the tens into numbered units. Each unit defines an area approximately 0.6 miles square. For the purposes of this book that square is *notionally* divided into four sub-squares indicated as a, b. c and d. Each unit square on the map is thus to be visualised as follows:

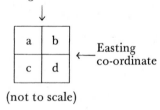

Northing co-ordinate

Easting co-ordinate

(not to scale)

Within a sub-square as indicated one should not be more than about ¼ mile of the site and, on average, a fair bit less.

This is relatively easy for a site that is marked on the map. Thus, the index of places in this book gives the location of Temple Martin as: III. 52.102.c (Lispole). This is to be understood as follows: III is for the Corkaguiney map in this book; 52 is the easting co-ordinate, that is the vertical line east of the site; 102 is the northing co-ordinate, that is the horizontal line north of the site; c is for the bottom left sub-square west and south of the two co-ordinates. Thus

is pinpointed the 'Ch' marked on the map. Lispole is the nearest town/village referred to in the text, and the remaining figure is the page number in this book where one can find directions to locate the site.

The same system applies where the site is not marked on the map. For example, the Ballynahowbeg rock scribing has in the index of places the reference V.54.83.c Cahersiveen. This is the fifth, or Iveragh-Dunkerron South, map in this part of this book; 54 for the easting co-ordinate; 83 for the northing co-ordinate; and c for the bottom left sub-square west and south of the co-ordinates. The precise instructions for getting there from Cahersiveen are given on the page cited.

A careful following of these instructions will not remove all the drudgery from site-finding, but will much reduce it. Perhaps one should add that the easy option of asking one's way assumes amongst the local people a degree of knowledge of archaeological or historical sites that it is unusual to find. Where, for some reason or another, I have not been able precisely to locate a site I have given the closest reference possible. These defeats are few.

Chapter 12

The Killarney Area: Magunihy and Dunkerron North

MAGUNIHY

The western boundary of Magunihy barony runs south-west from the River Maine at a point just east of Castlemaine to the River Laune just east of Killorglin. It follows the line of the Laune to the Killarney lakes and then south along the western shores of the lakes to a point just south of Looscaunagh Lough. It then runs east along the top of Mangerton mountain and reaches the Cork border a short distance north east of Morley's Bridge. From the Cork border just south of Ballydesmond it runs generally west along the line of the Sliabh Luachra mountains and the River Maine, with two narrow salients north west of Firies, almost to Castlemaine.

Magunihy comes from Magh O gCoinchinn, the plain of the (?) hound head family, possibly from their totem. The main part of the barony consists of flat country between the Maine and the Laune, bounded on the south west by a line of high mountains. This is a populous part of Kerry. Much of the barony consists of relatively good limestone land — one of the attractions of of Castlelough and of Muckross Lake is to see the last remnants of this lakeside limestone being eaten away — typified in the very large farmhouses in the otherwise rather dull northern part of the barony. There is some industry around Killarney, but the great economic resource is the tourist trade centred there. While Magunihy contains the **Lakes of Killarney** and the mountains to the east of the lakes — Torc, Mangerton and the rest — it does not contain the great mountains to the west—Tomies, Purple and the Mac Gillacuddy Reeks: these are in Dunkerron North. They form, of course, an essential part of the astonishingly beautiful place we call 'Killarney'.

If the derivation of the name Magunihy suggested above is correct, it is a very old one, most likely pre-goidelic. Killarney figures largely in the legends of the Fiana. There is in the *Pursuit of Diarmuid and Grainne*, an account of a gigantic but inconclusive, hurling match between the Tuatha De Danaan — virtually the whole pantheon turned out — and the Fiana. The game lasted three days.

It was played over the flat stretch of ground between the Flesk and the Laune. Neither side scored. Killarney was the centre of the goidelic kingdom of West Munster, ruled by the Eoganachta Locha Lein, the descendants of the goidel invader Eogan who established a kingdom based probably on Kenmare about 100BC. The kingdom of West Munster collapsed in the early 9th century, but the Eoganacht Locha Lein continued as local rulers for perhaps another 200 years when, after sustained struggle, they were overthrown by other eoganacht families from the Cashel area, O Donoghue and MacCarthy. From about 1200 these had to fight off anglo-norman intrusion, which was eventually beaten back after the decisive battle of Callan in 1261. It was not until after the killing and overthrow of O Donoghue Mor in the Desmond disaster of 1583 that the english got a permanent foothold in Magunihy when Sir Nicholas Browne acquired the O Donoghue castle of Molahiffe just south of the Maine, and also the O Donoghue seat at Ross castle. With the effective end of the MacCarthy Mor dynasty at the end of the 16th century the Brownes — eventually earls of Kenmare — became the great power in this area until they, too, died out in the present century.

(I) KILLARNEY TOWN (I.97.91).
(Pop. 1971: 7,541)

Killarney comes from Cill Airne, or Cill Airine. The first name means the church of the sloes, an unlikely name. The second means the church of Airin, whoever he or she was.

Killarney as a town was a product of the resumed plantation of Munster after 1604. It was made a market town with 40 english houses, but seems not to have thrived. The new county of Kerry in 1606 lost the baronies of Beare and Bantry to Cork, according to Friar O Sullivan, because Sir Owen O Sullivan would not be given 'the convenience of Assizes and Sessions in Killarney'. By 1642, when it was alleged that the protestants were massacred there, the number of men, women and children was put at 17, three or four households.

A military post was established at Ross castle in 1652 and a number of victims of the Cromwellians were hanged in Killarney in the following year.

Although in 1733 Killarney was a 'well populated market town' and had 'three very good inns', its real growth began about 1750 when Viscount Kenmare began to develop the tourist business, encouraging the establishment of inns, of the building of houses, of the provision of boating facilities for tourists, roads, and some industry. Almost at the same time 'four great new roads', according to Smith, were built radiating from it — to Cork, to Kenmare, to Castleisland, and to Limerick. The growth of Killarney as a tourist centre was consolidated by the arrival of the railway a century later, and of Queen Victoria and her family in 1861. It became the seat of the bishopric in the 1780s, also on the initiative of Lord Kenmare. He had established the right to nominate the parish priest of the town and nominated the fifth 18th century bishop, Francis Moylan (1775-1787) who moved here from Tralee.

Killarney has formidable advantages as a tourist centre. Foremost is the extraordinary beauty of the surroundings, and the great variety of places to see. Secondly, it is very central: a fifty mile radius of Killarney comprises all Kerry and West Cork, and there are half a dozen long, memorable forays that can be made, apart from the more local runs. There is no other centre so well placed for exploring those places, amongst the most beautiful in Ireland. Thirdly, there is a wide variety of hotels and guesthouses, a hostel, and caravan and camping sites, and a traditional skill and charm in coping with the tourist that few places possess. Fourthly, the weather is more strongly varied than in other parts of the south-west, and flexibility by the tourist can enable him to turn this to good account.

Killarney town has a bad reputation, partly from its scruffy appearance — poor architecture and layout and the smell and dirt caused by so many horses — and partly from what other Kerrymen say about Killarney people. It is commonly held to have been destroyed by the 'tourist mentality' which is said to have undermined the personal independence of the people and make them prone to overcharging. This stereotype is almost entirely false. The people of Killarney possess a great deal of charm, and a great deal of skill in the arts of hotel-keeping, shop-keeping and generally coping with the tourist. Both the hotels and the shops are extremely well-run; the service is very courteous, and there is no evidence of overcharging in any of these. Enjoy the ritual of being given discount in the drapers' shops.

Where the people of Killarney can be criticised, is that they appear to lack a collective sense. The overall appearance of their town and the neglect of obvious tourist amenities amply illustrate this. The faults of

Killarney are obvious to the most unobservant eye. The town shares most of the failings of Irish towns, and has few redeeming qualities. However, it has some. New Street, and the group of ecclesiastical buildings around the fine Pugin cathedral, are attractive by any standards. Less obvious are the large number of lanes off the main streets which are, usually, filled with small, gaily-painted houses, displaying flowers. This, at its best, is something distinctive to Killarney. At its worst, one has the risk of walking straight into a slaughter-yard. These houses arose in the early nineteenth century when the first earl of Kenmare gave 500 year leases of houses set up in neat blocks, with gateways between to gardens and stables. The locals soon turned these accesses into a means of private development unforeseen by their landlord.

The Franciscan Friary is built on a hill, variously called Martyrs Hill or Gallows Hill. It was there that the distinguished Irish poet, Piaras Ferriter, was hanged in 1653. There is a Harry Clarke stained-glass window in the Franciscan Church, and some interesting wood carving there. There are murals in the enclosed cloister of the Friary, and overhead, some curious legends in Irish. St Mary's Church, the Church of Ireland Church, is a fine building reconstructed in 1870, one of a succession built on the site of a fifteenth century church, which itself may be on the site of the original Cill Airne. The Catholic Cathedral was designed by Pugin, the main part was built between 1842 and 1855, and was extended in length, and the magnificent spire added, some 50 years later. It is the finest example in Ireland of the gothic revival style. Collectors of genuine Irish bulls may

Barony of Magunihie
County of Kerry
Enlarged from Petty 1683.

Magunihie Barony, after Petty

200

be interested in the stone at the West Door which solemnly announces 'The foundation stone of the completion of this Church . . . ' The Cathedral has a haunting set of chimes. It was extensively repaired in 1972 notably by revealing and pointing the internal stone work. There are four small Sarah Purser stained glass windows in the newly, and pleasantly, renovated chapel of St Brendan's Seminary. Of public buildings there is a wholly undistinguished town hall (but with a theatre), a gaunt but impressive mental hospital, a geriatric hospital and a small hospital. Close to the complex is a rather striking Convent of Mercy. Otherwise the town of Killarney has not much to offer in the way of buildings or remains.

(II) THE KILLARNEY AREA

The Killarney area is particularly beautiful in Spring, when the azaleas and rhododendrons are in flower from mid April to mid June, when there is much bright, showery weather, and many rare and beautiful wild flowers, such as the butterwort, the Irish spurge and the saxifrages are in bloom. It is also very beautiful in Autumn, when the leaves have turned: the birches are especially striking. There is debate as to which is the better of the two seasons. The Winter is very attractive, and notably mild. In Summer, to set against the bright weather, are the large numbers of visitors, the incidence of muggy weather and the call of the sea.

In some ways, the Winter is the best, because the most unexpected, of these seasons. The mobility of light and shade at that time is remarkable indeed. The weather seldom ceases to be mild: frost is unusual and harsh winds are few.

What makes the Killarney area exceptional is the richness of the gifts with which it has been endowed. There are four main ingredients, each contributing to the others. They are the geology — the strangely shaped and jumbled mountains; the water — in lakes, streams and cascades, and in the air; the light — continually changing; and the vegetation — lush and colourful. Add to these the mildness

of the climate, the antiquities, and the sheer extent of the whole. All of this, mixed by some miracle of combination, accounts for the fame of the place.

The fact that some of the mountains lie so steeply, and that others have strange contorted forms, with bare rock jutting out of bracken, grass and heather, give the place its distinctive shape. These rocks, old red sandstone for the most part, but limestone in lower places, give a reddish hue to many of the mountains and water that is distinctive. The Reeks, on the other hand, are usually an intense, dark blue. Around the lakes are the remains of the former limestone cover, pitted and eroded, white-grey.

The second feature of the landscape is the quantity of water, in the air, down mountain streams, in torrents and cascades, in rivers, and in the lakes. The sight of water in its many colours and shapes, and the sound of it, are everywhere.

The sunlight, through the moist air, with frequent rainbows, combines with the unusual shapes and colours of the mountains, and reflected by the various stages of water flow, to give most striking light effects. It throws delicate colours about in the oddest way.

Bright, decayed bracken, rhododendrons in flower, beeches and oaks leafing, birches with blazing leaves in Autumn and shining silver trunks, mosses, lichens, liverworts and ferns under and on the trees, larches dry against a winter sky, or fresh green in spring, the ever green rhododendron, holly and arbutus leaves, at all seasons these contribute to the variety of colour and shape.

These factors contribute to the various moods of Killarney, infinitely tranquil, or delicate, melting, mobile; or grim and glowering, or stormy; or misty in wisps. A view is seldom the same for more than an hour or so, and will often change several times within that hour. Add to all of this the considerable extent of the area and the fact that — when one comes to know where to go — it is possible to enjoy and obtain a remarkable variety of vista. Perhaps a small

addition, is the abundance of deer to be startled on many walks.

The special thing about Killarney is that it enables one to widen one's range of appreciation of natural beauty, because of the remarkable variety and mobility of the scenery, which can be beguiling, terrifying, and serene almost in turns.

Killarney town lies at the junction of two roads that contain nearly all the lake district — The Muckross-Moll's Gap road to the south-west and the Killorglin road to the west. There is occasional use of the Cork road to the east; but, normally, all sightseeing trips from Killarney will use or lie close to either the Muckross-Moll's Gap road or the Killorglin road.

For most activities in Killarney, apart from the standard jarvey-runs, a car is necessary. The town itself is some distance from the beauty spots. These are extraordinarily numerous, and cover a very large area. Even for short walks, it is best to take the car through the tedious preliminaries, and devote the whole of the walk to beauty spots.

However, a genuine sense of frustration can build up in the visitor from the great area to be covered, the frustrations of transport, the absence of information, and the local indifference on this issue. Killarney cannot be taken by force: one must work hard at uncovering its almost illimitable beauties, and one must be patient until place, time and weather give one a momentary insight into how landscape can embody beauty.

One of the important things is to adapt one's sight-seeing to the varying moods of the weather. There is so much to see that selections of this kind can be made. The obvious example is to view the many cascades during or after heavy rainfall. Another is to see the flat areas around the Lower Lake in still mist. Some trips through trees and rhododendrons have an attraction in rain. The savage country above Lough Guitane or at the Eagle's Nest gains from equally savage weather; and so on. This calls for much time in Killarney, and at all seasons. But where better to spend one's time?

Killarney is geared to giving the tourist three set trips, each superb in its way.

The most spectacular, if the weather is settled, is the trip to the Gap of Dunloe by jaunting car, through the Gap by pony, and down the three lakes by boat. This is not to be missed. This takes from the early forenoon to the late afternoon and is normally an organised trip. It is available, usually, from May to October.

Next, there is the half day trip by jaunting car through Muckross and Dinis island. This can be taken in mixed weather. It is not accessible to the motorist.

Thirdly, there is the 100 mile trip around the Ring of Kerry. One has a better view if one goes by way of Killorglin to Waterville to Sneem and back by Moll's Gap. This demands a good day.

Killarney from Aghadoe

There is also the 100 mile trip around the Dingle peninsula. This demands a brilliant day. If a choice must be made and the day is brilliant (but *only* if it is) then the Dingle run is the better bet.

For the motorist who wants to make his own way, there are suggestions in what follows.

But, first, a few words about the Lakes of Killarney.

It is perhaps unnecessary to say that the lakes of Killarney are three. The largest is the Lower Lake (Lough Leane) nearest the town. It lies to the south west of the town, and runs north-west south-east. From the shore one can be confused by the peninsula of Ross 'island'. Running west of the Lower Lake is the spine of the Mac Gillacuddy Reeks. One does not get an easy view of the Lower Lake

from any of the principal roads: but there is the fine panorama, just off the Killorglin road, at Aghadoe. Due south of the Lower Lake is the Middle (or Muckross) Lake, which is surrounded by the Bourn Vincent Memorial Park. The Middle Lake runs directly into the Lower Lake at its western end, at Brickeen Bridge. Good views of this lake can be had from the Muckross-Moll's Gap road. The Upper Lake is separated from the Middle and Lower Lakes by the Long Range, a stretch of river about two and a half miles long. It lies to the south and west of the other two lakes. A number of views of this lake can be had from the Muckross-Moll's Gap road. The fourth principal lake is Lough Guitane, due east of the Middle Lake. This can be seen easily from the road running from Muckross Village to the Cork road. There are, of course, countless other small lakes in the area.

Boating on the lakes is a source of great delight, and the early travellers give lyrical descriptions of it when, before decent roads were made, the lakes were a main thoroughfare. However, the lakes can be rough, and the level of water fluctuates widely. There are some nasty sharp rocks in the water. For this reason boatmen are reluctant to let inexperienced oarsmen hire boats from them and much prefer to row the sightseer. But for the experienced there is no great hazard. Boats are plentiful on the Lower Lake, and may be obtained, with more or less trouble, on the Middle and Upper Lakes, and on Lough Guitane.

If one has a boat of one's own it is possible to take the Lakes piecemeal. It is easy to launch a boat on the Lower and Upper Lakes, but a bit troublesome to do so on the Middle Lake. It is very easy to find a launching place along the Kenmare road where it touches the Upper Lake, and from here one can readily explore that lake, and the Long Range. Under the Old Weir Bridge there is a tricky race (where there have been drownings) so it is safer to turn back here. Under the Eagle's Nest there are wonderful echoes, and when there was a garrison in Killarney, cannon used be fired here for special visitors, making the most remarkable echoes; but this was stopped after a 'frightful accident'. Buglemen used also be

202 hired with boats for creating echoes; in 1819 we read of 'bugleman's bill — 16s 3d'.

The Lower and Middle Lakes are better taken together, from the former. A famous sight is the hanging woods of Glena. Weld has a wonderful description of boating on the Lower Lake at night. An interesting trip is to go down the Laune as far as Killorglin.

1. *Aghadoe — Mahony's Point — Ross Castle — Castlelough — Muckross — Ladies View.*

To begin to know Killarney from the land the first step is to get a bird's eye view of the whole complex. Take the Limerick road and the second road (after New Road) left and then left again. After a dull run one comes to a churchyard on the left. This is *Aghadoe*, (I.94.93.b), from which the best panoramic view of Killarney can be obtained — unless one climbs the high mountains. But, first, a look at the antiquities here.

Aghadoe (Achadh da Eo, the enclosure of the two yews) was probably a pagan religious settlement — yews are often a sign of this.

By the south wall of the church is a poor example of an ogam stone from this period which reads 'BRRUANANN', and a pleasant sculptured fragment. It was perhaps here (no wonder!) that St Abban, a pre-patrician missionary from Wexford established in the 5th centry his Ceall Achaidh (or Aithfe) Conchinn. Certainly a monastery was established here in the 6th-7th century and dedicated to St Fionan. It was here in 1010, that Maelsuthain O Carroll, king of the Eoganacht Locha Lein, chief doctor of the western world and friend of Brian Boramha, died.

A generation later, in 1044, O Cathail, heir to the kingship of Loch Lein, was taken from sanctuary here and slain. A church was begun here in 1027, the damh liag Maenig (who died here in1045); part of the church is incorporated in the north-west wall of the present nave. The round tower, now a stump, was begun in the same year.

During the eleventh century, there *may* have been a bishopric here, incorporated in the

diocese of Ratass by the synod of Rathbreasail in 1111. The memory of this is incorporated in the title of the protestant diocese comprising Kerry which was, before it was added to Limerick, called Ardfert and Aghadoe. Hence, the continued use of 'cathedral' for the church. But the only documentary evidence of a bishopric are three references in the calendar of Papal Letters for 1218 AD, 1257 and 1289. These are almost certainly mistakes for Annaghdown, in the province of Tuam; indeed two of the entries refer specificially to Tuam.

The present nave of the church, with its fine romanesque west door, was a replacement for the damh liag, by Auliff Mor O Donoghue. It was finished in 1158, and he was buried in his great church eight years later.

In 1177 Milo de Cogan and FitzStephen, having taken Cork, came here for two days and nights, perhaps the first anglo-normans to reach Kerry which was not to be invaded until a generation later.

Perhaps in the thirteenth century was built the severe transitional style chancel to O Donoghue's romanesque 'great church'. At some later time, chancel and nave were separated by a wall which is not bonded into the side walls; it may be that part was used as living quarters.

Aghadoe became an archdeaconry of the diocese of Ardfert. Because the seat of the bishopric of Ardfert was in the centre of anglo-norman influence it was convenient to have a vicar-general, as it were, for the gaelic areas and all the names of the archdeacons which have come down to us are gaelic ones. The Papal Taxation of 1306 refers to the deanery of Aghadoe. This probably supported the tradition that Aghadoe had once been an independent bishopric.

Observe the strong box tombs. Buried in this place is Richard O Connell, who became bishop of Ardfert in 1643, the only roman catholic bishop in Kerry for over a century. He died in 1653. Also buried here is James Gandsey (1769-1857) the blind piper whose

piping caused such enthusiasm amongst visitors to Killarney. The Halls' praise of his playing was ecstatic and Crofton Croker printed several of his tunes. One of his patrons was Lord Headley — of Aghadoe House nearby (now the youth hostel) — and he described himself as Lord Headley's piper.

Below to the right of the church, in a square bailey with double ditch that enclosed a moat, is a circular stone anglo-norman castle, no doubt built in the thirteenth century to replace the wooden, prefabricated one erected by the geraldine invaders when they came here in 1215. Circular castles are not unusual in Ireland, but I know of only one other in Kerry, at Barrow near Fenit. Two storeys now remain here, with the remains of a fireplace in the upper storey, so it was presumably occupied in the seventeenth century when fireplaces reached this part of the world. In 1581 the rebellious earl of Desmond, with his followers, all in deep sleep, were surprised here by the English captain Zouch and a number killed before Desmond was put to flight.

Move up the road to the Aghadoe Heights hotel. From here there are splendid views. First, of course, the Lower Lake and its islands, constantly changing colour and form. Directly before one, across the lake, is the tiny arc of Brickeen Bridge, the bright spot framed by it the only evidence of Muckross, or the Middle, Lake. The Upper Lake lies to the right of this between the two lines of mountains. To the left in the flat plain is Killarney, and behind it the line of mountains bordering the barony to the Cork border. One is looking due south from here and the horizon is framed by a line of mountains running east and west. This line is broken by three great passes — Glenflesk, on the way to Cork; the Upper Lake, on the way to Kenmare and Sneem; and the Gap of Dunloe. To the east (that is, left as one views them) are the Cork mountains, then, in Kerry, the aptly named Paps (2,273 ft. and 2,284 ft.); then the divide at Glenflesk; then the volcanic Crohane (2,162 ft.), Bennaunmore (1,490 ft.), Eskduff and Stoompa (2,281 ft.); then Mangerton (2,756 ft.) long believed to be Ireland's highest mountain — observe the flow from the Punch Bowl near the summit;

and Torc (1,764 ft.). Then there is the great cutting in which the Upper Lake lies. Then to the right begins the barony of Dunkerron North ranging from the right hand shore of the Lower Lake to encompass the great line of the Reeks, comprising the Eagle's Nest (1,103 ft.), Shehy (1,827 ft.), Tomies (2,413 ft.) and Purple (2,739 ft.). Then just to be discerned is the deep cut of the Gap of Dunloe, and to the right of this the Mac Gillacuddy's Reeks, with five peaks of over 3,000 ft., including the highest peak in Ireland, Carrantuohil (3,414 ft.). Behind the hotel one can see more of the flat stretch of Magunihy and stretching off to what is now one's left, the great line of the Dingle mountains, rising to Brandon (3,127 ft.) the second highest mountain in Ireland, but seldom to be seen. From these mountains to those one has been observing was once a great glacier. When it was melting it retreated back through the two great gaps at Glenflesk and Dunloe. This action played a special part in forming the Killarney lakes.

Continue on this road. At the T junction turn left, with on one's right the youth hostel, formerly *Aghadoe House*, (I.93.93.c.) home of Lord Headley. At this junction one can buy good German delicatessen at the shop on the right; but in true Irish fashion one may have to go round the back to get service.

At the bottom of the hill turn left again and go past the crane factory until one comes to the entrance to the golf club. Drive in here through the magnificent scenery, and enjoy the intimate view of the Lower Lake from *Mahony's Point*, (I.93.91.b.) just beyond the car park.

Back to the road and through the town to the Muckross road and take the first turn right to *Ross Castle*, (I.95.89.b.).

This is an inlet of the lake facing mainly back the way one has come. To the left is the peninsula of Ross 'Island' where in pre-historic times, and again in the early 19th century, copper was mined. Above this towers the near end of the Reeks — Shehy, Purple and Tomies mountains. Before one is Inisfallen where there was a monastery for a thousand years, and behind it, on the far

Ross Castle, Killarney

shore, where one has been, the white shape of the Hotel Europe with its two monstrous lines of red-roofed bungalows that ruin nearly every view in Killarney. To the right is the Kenmare estate, now owned by an Irish-American.

When there is no breeze here this place sums up Killarney at its best, its tranquility disturbed only by the movement or cry of a water bird, or the appearance of a row-boat. It is here that many of the boats land after the voyage down the lakes.

The most prominent feature is, of course, Ross Castle itself. This beautifully placed castle was built by O Donoghue Mor in the 16th century building revival. The O Donoghues had intruded into Killarney in the 11th century, eventually overcoming the Eoganacht kingdom established there about 100 BC. In the local lore O Donoghue has become confused with the ancient lake god. O Donoghue took the losing side in the Desmond rebellion, and lost his life and his

lands in consequence. The castle, by a bit of sharp practice, came into the hands of Donal Mac Carthy Mor, 1st Earl of Clancarre, in the 1580s but he, being chronically short of money, even to pay interest on a mortgage, mortgaged it to Sir Nicholas Browne. In the collapse of Mac Carthy fortunes that followed Clancarre's death in 1596 the castle came into Browne's hands and, with much litigation, remained the Browne residence until after the cromwellian and williamite wars; it gave the family their secondary title, Castlerosse. In the seventeenth century it became a permanent military post. The building attached to the castle was the Browne home built towards the end of the century and converted after 1688 into a barracks. When the barracks was abandoned in 1815 Lord Kenmare had the square windows narrowed to match the style of the castle.

Ross castle was the last significant stronghold to surrender in the cromwellian wars. It was held by a strong force under Lord Muskerry, and was invested by Ludlow and Sir Hardress

204 Waller. To attack it from the water Ludlow had pre-fabricated ships built in Kinsale, brought up the Laune, assembled and launched. The story is that the defenders, seeing this, remembered an old saying that Ross would never be taken from *land,* and immediately surrendered. In fact, Muskerry, realising the war was for all practical purposes over, had opened negotiations for surrender. These had been broken off, but were resumed about the time the boats appeared. The castle capitulated on 28 June, 1652, Muskerry being granted the usual terms of being permitted to ship his men to serve with the army of any European country not at war with the commonwealth.

Return to the Muckross road and turn right. Shortly after one has crossed the Flesk Bridge there is, right, the entrance to the Lake Hotel. Drive in here in front of the hotel and walk around the far end of it and out onto the causeway jutting into the lake. This was the entrance to the old Mac Carthy castle of *Castlelough,* (I.98.89.c.). One is now on another inlet of the lake, with Ross Island on the right dividing one from the Ross Castle inlet. To the left is the Muckross estate and before one the narrow neck of land separating the Lower from the Middle lake. Further on to the left is the shapely form of Torc mountain and, before one, on the skyline the way to Moll's Gap and Kenmare.

This is a limestone outcrop and dotted about the lake are other remnants of limestone — often formed into fanciful shapes — the last vestiges of a deep layer that covered the whole countryside now almost wholly eroded by the weathering of more than 200 million years.

Castlelough, now wholly ruined, was one of the great, and beautifully situated, castles of Mac Carthy Mor. The first (and last) Earl of Clancarre (who died in 1596) was given to mortgaging all of his inheritance and he mortgaged for £400 or £500 this castle and lands to Florence Mac Carthy Reagh, who married his only daughter Ellen. Warham St. Leger wrote, after the marriage, in 1589: 'it is the strongest situation of a castle that is in Ireland . . . The castle stands in a great Lough, where there is a great store of orient

Castlelough Bay, Killarney

pearls found'. The Lady Ellen lived here with their children for a few years until the disasters of the O Neill wars when Florence went back to the Tower, and, she followed him to London. Four years later, in 1605, her bastard brother, Donal, and his son Donal 'borne before marriage' were granted Castlelough and 5,000 acres, but probably for Ellen's use — the four children stayed with their father. Florence Mac Carthy of Castlelough has been confused with the

governor of Kerry in the Irish interest after the revolt of 1641. This was Florence Mac Finneen Mac Carthy of Ardtully (Captain Sugan) killed in action near Cork in April, 1642. So, in 1663, Dame Sarah Mac Carthy, widow of Ellen's son, Donal, and sister of the Marquis of Antrim, and her son, Florence, were declared 'innocent papists', and the lands of Pallas, Muckross, Cahirnane, Castlelough and other places were restored to them. Cahirnane is directly to

Castlelough, with ruined castle, left

one's left as one looks out the lake, and this Florence sold it to Col Maurice Hussey in 1684 who sold it to Arthur Herbert. Florence disposed of Castlelough to his cousin whose grandson sold it in 1745 to Colonel William Crosbie. Twenty-five years later the last Mac Carthy Mor died unmarried and Muckross went to his mother's people, the Herberts, who gave such loving care to it. It is not clear how Pallas, the principal residence was disposed of. Fuit Ilium.

Go back to the Muckross Road and turn right. A little further on, right, is the *main entrance* (I.98.88.b) to the Bourn-Vincent Memorial Park, a national park. One cannot bring a car in here; but it is worth while leaving the car and walking through the gates for the short period the lake is in view, and then turning back.

Then, in the car, continue along the main road and pass the Muckross Hotel on the left, and just beyond it, also left, a road signposted 'Mangerton'. About a mile further on is an unposted forestry road, left. Take this.

About a mile up this road, shortly before *Torc Old Bridge,* (I.97.84.b), there is a fine view of the Lower and Middle Lakes.

Return to the road and a little further on is the signposted entrance to *Muckross House,* (I.97.87.d), on the right. Go in here, and park. Walk around to the front of the house and observe the view of Muckross Lake. There are magnificent gardens here and a museum of sorts, but leave these for another day.

Back to the road again and turn right. The road runs along by the Muckross lake, and beneath masses of rhododendrons on the left. In May-June these are in magnificent bloom.

Follow this road for about 6 miles to *Ladies View,* (I.91.81.b). This is the famous panorama of the Upper lake. There are two stopping places here, one in front of the souvenir shop, the other about half a mile further up. It is worth going to the second of these, especially for the view of the Reeks and of the road from the Gap of Dunloe winding through the bottom of the Black

Valley to the head of the Upper Lake. Above these is the mass of Carrantuohill. Below is the long stretch of the Upper Lake with its islands. Just to be discerned is the Middle Lake and below it the white shape of the Lake Hotel at Castlelough. Directly beneath one are the woods of Derrycunihy, which are of such interest to botanists.

Return the way one has come. Stop just short of the *'Tunnel',* (I.92.82.b), the bridge of rock across the roadway about two miles from Ladies View. Walk up right just short of this, and there is an easy way up onto the top of this bridge. It gives a splendid view of the setting of the Upper Lake and of the Long Range (or Reach) which connects it with the other lakes. Many people think of the Upper Lake as the most beautiful of the three and it is easy to believe that here. The Upper Lake is a sandstone one and note how the sandstone has been smoothed and rounded by the passage of the glaciers.

Drive towards Killarney, for a mile until one comes to *Five Mile Bridge,* (I.94.84.b). Leave the car just beyond this and walk back to the parapet of the bridge. This gives another splendid view of the Upper Lake, perhaps especially with a stormy winter's sunset.

Then back to Killarney. The total driving distance is 35 miles. Allow as long as you wish to stare, and remember that this is only a quick introduction; but the journey and 'Killarney' can be done, at a pinch, in half a fine day. If time is very tight, settle for Aghadoe, Ross Castle, Castlelough, Ladies View and, if at all possible, the Tunnel view of the Upper Lake.

2. Knockacullig

When the mountains are clear, perhaps especially in the early evening, there is an extensive panorama, quickly obtained from Knockacullig. (Strictly, the peak to which this directs one is *Knockatagglemore,* (I.100.100.d), but it is not marked on the ½ inch map: *Knockacullig,* (I.102.99.d), *is* marked, is a short distance away, and does not give as good a view). From this those unable or unwilling to walk can enjoy a prospect as good as any earned by the hardest

Upper Lake, Killarney

mountain climber. From Killarney take Lewis Road (between the Franciscan Friary and College Street) and follow it past the Mental Hospital. Just four miles from Killarney at the second cross roads turn right. On this road take the fifth turn to the left up a rough road (not marked on the ½ inch map). One mile up this road, after one has been driving through open bog for a half mile, take the first turn left, and a few hundred yards later, the first turn right up a steep hill. Do not be daunted by this. There is a short run to the summit, where the car can be easily turned. The view here of the Lower Lake, of the east-west spine of mountains, and of the mountains of the Iveragh and Dingle peninsulas is striking indeed.

Coming back, turn left (instead of right) at the bottom of the mountain road and take the third turn on the right. This brings one back to Killarney by the Cork road.

Total distance 16 miles. Time about one hour.

(III) THE MUCKROSS AREA

Once one has got the 'feel' of Killarney perhaps the next best thing is to explore the Muckross area. This has so much to offer that one could spend a long time on it alone. The major difficulty to be overcome is that the Bourn-Vincent Memorial Park does not admit cars, except to Muckross House itself. The circuit of the main part of the demesne

206 can be made by jaunting car, by bicycle or by walking. The whole circuit is about eight miles from the main entrance gate and back again; but this can be cut by the three miles of the public road if one can be picked up at the Dinis entrance.

It consists of two main overlapping parts — Muckross village and surroundings and Muckross demesne. The following five trips cover the area fairly well (1) Killegy—Muckross 'Abbey'—Torc Waterfall, (2) Muckross Demesne I, (3) Muckross Demesne II, (4) Muckross Demesne III, and (5) Torc Mountain.

1. Muckross Village — Killegy — Muckross 'Abbey' — Torc Waterfall.

A pleasant short run is to *Muckross Village* (formerly called Cloghereen) (I.98.88.d). Leave the car at the village green. Underneath the high stone cross, somewhat to the right of it, is an old roadway leading up to *Killegy* (I.99.88.c) churchyard. The high cross is over the grave of Henry Arthur Herbert, the most magnificent of that family, who built Muckross House, was (briefly) Chief Secretary for Ireland, and entertained Queen Victoria and her family. Notice the mistake made by the stonemason, and its remedy, testifying to the 'virtue' of the late Mr Herbert. Close by is the grave of Arthur Rose Vincent who received Muckross Estate as a wedding present from his father-in-law, William Bourn and who, after his wife's death, presented the estate to the Nation in 1933. It is said that the late Mr Vincent was buried here standing, looking out over the lakes he loved.

There is an old reconstructed church, over the grave of Col Maurice Hussey, with an interesting tablet inside, if one can see it. It reads:

> This church of Killegy was built
> As a family mortuary chapel
> By Maurice Hussey of Cahirnane
> Late colonel in the army
>   of King James II
> At his death in 1714
> His body was borne here by his
>   4 sons.
> And buried at midnight by torch light.

This was in accordance with Hussey's will, which also provided that he be buried in the habit of St Francis. He bought Cahirnane from the Mac Carthy family in 1684, and represented Tralee in King James's parliament. He was a lieutenant colonel in McElligott's regiment in the subsequent fighting. When that war was lost Hussey survived here, a noted trimmer, (and perhaps a spy) though he was imprisoned, with many other local worthies, in 1708 for refusing to take the oath abjuring the Stuart succession.

Also buried in this graveyard, but no one knows where, is Rudolf Erich Raspe, the author of the *Travels and Surprising Adventures of Baron Munchausen.* As professor of archaeology and keeper of the national library of one of the petty states of Germany, he made away with some of the valuables in his care. In England he became an honorary member of the Royal Society, and published a work of very high standing, on mineralogy. In Scotland he got into trouble for salting minerals. Later he came to Ireland and managed the copper mines on the Herbert Estate. Here he died in November 1794 from typhoid, after he had been in Killarney about one year. (It is possible that he was buried, not in Killegy, but in the grounds of St Mary's Killarney).

Beside Muckross green, in the grounds of the Church of Ireland church, is a stone cross also to the memory of Henry Arthur Herbert in the same form, but smaller than that over his grave. This was 'erected by Harry his valet'.

Drive up the short distance to the Muckross Hotel on the left. *Muckross 'Abbey'* (I.98.87.b) is best approached on foot from the entrance gate opposite the Hotel, one of the oldest in Killarney. The Halls stayed there about 1840 at a daily charge for full board for two, including a pint of wine, of 12s 6d (62½p).

This friary was known as the Monastery of Irrelagh (Oir-bhealach) or Eastern Way. It was built on the site of a church destroyed by fire in the 12th century.

The Four Masters say that this friary was founded in 1340, but this was a mistake in one of their sources. In fact it was founded by Donal Mac Carthy Mor in 1448 for the Observantine Franciscans, probably the second of their houses in Ireland, as part of the movement of renewal then going through the church. The friary was not completed for 50 years, when the south transept was added. The changes in building style during this period are to be noted, strikingly in the cloisters. It was built more or less on the standard Franciscan plan, but the tower is more square and squat than, say, Quin — it resembles the Dominican style of tower rather than the Franciscan. It is one of the finest examples we have of a Franciscan friary.

The Friary seems to have had no history until 1588, and to have long been unaffected by the reformation. In that year, at midnight, Ellen, heiress daughter of Mac Carthy Mor, Earl of Clancarre, was married here to Florence Mac Carthy Reagh, an event that landed both into endless trouble. In 1589 a party of English soldiers raided the monastery and captured and tortured to death two of the friars, Fr Donagh O Muirhily, the sacristan, and a companion who, after the flight of the community, hid chalices and other church valuables on one of the islands of the lake. In 1595 the Queen granted the Abbey of Irrelagh, Co. Kerry, with appurtenances, containing four acres of lands, two orchards, and a garden, at a rent of 13s 4d Irish to Captain Collum. A year later Donal Mac Carthy Mor, first and last earl of Clancarre died and was buried in the choir where the large O Donoghue tomb stands. His grave slab lies against the wall with his arms showing his Irish crown above his English coronet. The O Donoghues intermarried with the Mac Carthys and came to possess their tomb. It seems that the friars never went far from Muckross and were back, perhaps only briefly, in 1602. Sometime after 1612 the place was repurchased and restoration began. The work was completed by 1626 under Father Thaddeus O Holen, as a tablet in the far left corner of the choir commemorates. The chimneys in the housing quarters upstairs were probably put in at this time. There was a sharp persecution in 1629-30 and the friars had to flee, but it is to be assumed that they were soon back and in possession until the cromwellians took over in 1652. A year later Piaras Ferriter was hanged in Killarney and, according to tradition, he was buried somewhere in or near the abbey. The 'Hidden Ireland' is literally buried here. In the nave, in the far right hand corner is a plaque with a verse by Fr Dineen commemorating the four great Kerry poets. To read the quatrain one stands on the gravestone of the O Rahilly family, under which that Jeremiah of the end of the gaelic order, Aodhgan, now one hopes after life's fretful fever sleeps well. The other two poets, as became aristocrats, are buried in the choir — Seafraidh O Donoghue in the obtrusive O Donoghue tomb, and Eoghan Rua O Suilleabhain under the third slab out from the arched O Sullivan Mor tomb recess in the right hand wall. Back in the nave spare a thought for the virtues of Lucy Gallwey remembered on the south wall.

From the days of Restoration down to 1873 there was a guardian and community of Irrelagh, but not ever, it would seem, in residence here. A wild place above Torc waterfall is called the Friars' Glen where, when times were hard, they fled for shelter. In the eighteenth century they moved into Killarney and opened a school in College Street. It seems to have been a friar of the community, an O Sullivan, who wrote the *Ancient History of the Kingdom of Kerry* about the year 1750. The last friar to be identified officially with the abbey was Father James Fitz Gerald, a native of Dingle who founded a classical academy for boys in Killarney and who died in Clonmel in 1881.

The present Franciscan community in Killarney was brought by Bishop David Moriarty from Belgium via Gorey in 1859.

Muckross Friary:
Ground floor plan

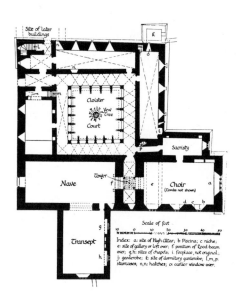

Muckross Friary:
Upper floor plan

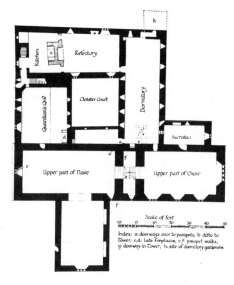

The buildings of Muckross are of considerable interest, a fine example of the late Irish gothic style. They were mainly erected between 1448 and 1475. The tower is the only wide Franciscan one now standing and was crowned originally with battlements; it went up in the last quarter of the century. The south transept was the last to be built, about 1500.

In the left hand wall of the choir, east of the sacristy door, are two rather crude tomb recesses. These occupy the place usually reserved for the tomb of the founder. Perhaps this Donal Mac Carthy, who died in 1468, is buried in the less elaborate of the two. The sacristy, just off the choir, may have been the site of the earlier church.

The east and south windows are very fine; but the most famous feature is the cloister. The south and west arcades, lower and with more numerous and rounded arches, may be the later. The whole is much overshadowed by the famous yew tree which, superstition says, it is fatal to cut. The tree is rooted in the eighteen inches of debris in the court and is thus much younger than the building.

208

Upstairs one gets some idea of life in the monastery — for example, the fine fireplace in the Guardian's room, signalling the first evidence, from the 1620s, of the arrival of the chimney in Kerry, and the marks on the floor of the main dormitory that show where the friars' cubicles were.

The building is worth walking around from a little distance, the imagination filling in the now fallen battlements that were such an oddly attractive feature of fifteenth century church building, and the roof of grey stone slabs.

Burial in and around the monastery is now controlled and one is not affronted here as in other places in Kerry. In the early decades of the last century the horror of the place apparently beggared description, but several writers were vivid enough in what they managed to describe. The building was unable to contain all those to be buried there, and the recently dead were dug up to make room for the recently living, so that decaying bodies and great heaps of bones lay all over the place. Skulls were arrayed in lines, and visitors wrote their names and *graffiti* on them. At length, in the 1830s Mr Herbert cleared the place. According to the Halls, he had dug a large pit and had transported to it the human remains in the place. This occupied four men for five weeks and between 700 and 800 cartloads were taken away.

Return to the car. Just beyond the hotel there is a road signposted 'Mangerton'. This leads up into open country above the plantations in the Torc area, but the trees are now so high that there is no special view of the lakes — and it is not a very good way of approaching Mangerton. So it can be ignored. Carry on the main road for one and a half miles. One passes, left, the farm buildings of Muckross where there are prize Kerry cows, and on the right the car entrance to Muckross House. Stop at the car park, left, at *Torc Waterfall* (I.97.85.b). Walk up here by the tumbling river, if possible up to the top and turn right for Torc Old Bridge. Then return to the car and Killarney.

Total driving distance: eight miles. Allow a half day.

2. Muckross Demesne I

Muckross demesne is part of the national park of 10,000 acres, virtually all the land one can see from the demesne. The owner, prior to Mr Bourne and Senator Vincent, was Lord Ardilaun, a Guinness who married a descendant of the Herbert family. (She is said to have induced him to give up the vulgar trade of brewing). He bought the estate in 1899 after the Herbert family had run into severe financial trouble in 1889 and the house and estate had been in the hands of the Standard Life Assurance Company. The Herberts had owned the place since 1770 when they inherited it from the last Mac Carthy Mor, whose mother was a Herbert. They had leased it for some time before that. They were descended from a Herbert of Castleisland, agent of the Lord Herbert who had held that estate in the 17th century.

The Herberts lavished loving care on the estate and were criticised by the extravagant county families for wasting their money in this way. They were also criticised from another quarter. In 1807 Weld wondered whether the improvements had not gone too far and quoted Bishop Berkeley as saying that one could build another Versailles, but never another Muckross. However, the improvements continued, to our benefit and delight. They had a passion for building houses, and the great one now close to the lake was their third, in different locations, in little more than two generations. It was built in 1843 in the neo-tudor style — the then Mrs Herbert was a Balfour — and faced in imported Portland stone. Here Queen Victoria, with her family and a train of 100 was entertained in 1861, shortly before her husband's death. The iron staircase from her groundfloor bedroom is a fire escape specially built because of the Queen's fear of fire. The house is now a folk museum.

Drive to the Muckross Hotel and walk into the demesne by the gate opposite and pass the 'Abbey' and the T junction into a fairly rough place until one comes to a track along by the ledge of the Lower Lake. Follow this until Muckross House appears on the left. To the right is an inlet of the lake, a harbour where the many Herbert ships could lie safely at anchor. The lake was once a major thoroughfare and boats could reach the sea laden with copper and cobalt ore from the mines by sailing down the Laune to Killorglin. Go up to the house and inspect the museum. Internally, the house is not striking. Note the antlers of red deer on the walls, with the names of those who shot them including Balfours.

There are also antlers of the Great Irish Elk, extinct these 8,000 years. They are some eight and a half feet wide and were found in a bog on Tomies mountain.

In the house is a reputed portrait of the famous countess of Desmond who died, aged 140 (or 162), from falling from a tree where she was collecting cherries. On the portrait is written:

Catherine Countesse of Desmonde. As she appeared at ye Covrt of our Soureigne Lord King James in thys preasant AD 1614 and in ye 140th yeare of her Age. Thither she came from Bristol to seek Reliefe ye House of Desmonde having been ruined by Attainder. — She was married in ye Reigne of King Edward IV and in ye covrse of her long Pilgrimage renewed her Teeth twice. — Her Principal residence is at Inchiquin in Munsteir whither she undavntedlye proposeth, (her Purpose accomplished) incontinentlie To Return. Laus Deo.

The Inchiquin referred to is near Youghal. It is unlikely that the portrait, itself a copy, is an actual painting of the indomitable old lady.

Outside, there are most magnificent gardens. If one is lucky enough to be there between mid-April and mid-June when first the azaleas and then the rhododendrons are in flower the place is superb.

But at any time these are magnificent and almost inexhaustible gardens. There is a fine rockery in an outcrop of limestone in the peaty soil. Push across the lawns across the little artificial stream (where in Spring trout can be seen spawning) to the walks on the far side, some of them aromatic walks. Keep bearing left until one comes out onto a tarred roadway, turn left anf follow this to a huge Cedar of Lebanon and then turn right by a boathouse onto a headland. About half way out on this there are souterrains, some partly excavated. Wander back through the gardens.

Perhaps one can arrange to be picked up at the car-park at the House. Otherwise walk back much the same way as one has come. This is a walk of about three miles, plus the amount of walking one has done in the garden. Allow about three hours in all.

3. Muckross Demesne II

Take the car to Muckross House. Walk down the path to the inlet of the lake. There is a track bearing right into the woods which gives a very attractive walk, called Jacko Boy's Walk. (Windele calls him Jackey Bwee). After a short time one emerges from the woods onto another inlet of the lake and there before one on the far side of the inlet is Jacko Boy himself fishing. The track comes out, after about a mile, on the tarred road. Turn left here. About half a mile further on, between the road and Muckross lake, there are old disused *Muckross mines* (II.95.86.a) for copper and cobalt, reopened in 1750 and flooded later in the 19th century. These mines date, from copper halberd discoveries, to about 2000 BC. Close to the shore here there is a large jagged rock. This is called the Colleen Bawn's rock, where the Colleen Bawn, in Boucicault's play, *The Colleen Bawn,* and Benedict's opera, *The Lily of Killarney,* was pushed into the lake and drowned. This has now become part of the synthetic folklore of Killarney. It is based on a well-known 19th century novel by Gerald Griffin, *The Collegians,* itself based on a famous murder in Limerick. The facts, as given by Begley are that a young protestant gentleman called Scanlan pretended to marry a young peasant girl, Ellen Hanley before a purported priest in Limerick, who was a henchman of his called Sullivan, having already tricked the girl of some money taken from her uncle. After some weeks of 'marriage', Scanlan persuaded Sullivan to row the girl out into the Shannon from Tarbert,

Old Weir Bridge, Killarney

tie a stone around her neck and throw her overboard. Sullivan did this, and disappeared. Through the efforts of the Knight of Glin and a Spring Rice, later Lord Monteagle, Scanlan was arrested, defended by Daniel O Connell, and hanged, protesting his innocence to the end. Sullivan was found in the course of a year. He had fled to Castleisland and married the proctor's daughter with whom he was promised money. It was not paid, so he stole it and was lodged in Tralee gaol. Here he was recognised, brought to Limerick, tried and hanged, having confessed the whole story.

A walk of just a mile brings one to *Brickeen Bridge* (I.94.86.b). As the peninsula narrows one has fine views of both the Muckross and the Lower Lakes. At Brickeen note the vigorous growth of the dark green arbutus on one's right as one looks down the Lower Lake. Under the bridge is a chain to help boatmen to bring their big boats up against strong

currents at flood time. One crosses the bridge onto Dinis Island. Note the boats tucked away on the right. One of the passions of Killarney people is fishing. When the fish are rising the boats hidden in these little coves come out and the Lower Lake especially is dotted with them.

Walk on from here to the cottage at *Dinis* (I.94.86.d) and right behind it by the tropical shrubs to the so-called *Meeting of the Waters* (I.94.86.d) (it is a parting but nonetheless beautiful), with the Old Weir bridge framed up-river. There are some fine arbutus trees here. The channel to the right goes directly into the Lower Lake behind Dinis Island, the channel to the left into Muckross lake. Follow this left channel and turn right at the bridge. It is a walk of just under a mile onto the main road. There are sometimes red deer to be seen here. If the car is not waiting follow the road for a mile and go in the gate short of Torc waterfall and go back to

210

Muckross House that way. In the first case the walk is of about three and a half miles, in the second five and a half miles.

4. *Muckross Demesne III*

This can be amalgamated with the previous walk if one is sufficiently energetic. Bring the car five miles from Killarney to the branch right labelled *Dinis* (I.95.85.b), where one has emerged from the previous walk. Take the path and 50 yards short of the bridge over the channel into Muckross lake there is on the left a track through the rhododendrons that may be much overgrown. In one can get through here there is a pleasant outlet at *Old Weir Bridge* (I.94.86.d) i.e. the bridge that can be seen from the Meeting of the Waters. It is possible to cross this bridge and wander up around the river, keeping close to the bank. It is drier at the river's edge (unless the river is very high) than it is further inland. It is worth climbing up on to one of the reaches of the rocks, close to the river here and getting an impression of the Eagle's Nest and the wild mountain and woodland which are the continuation of the Reeks. Given ideal conditions — such as, oddly, a sleety day in Winter — the colour effects here are really stupendous. Unless one wants to tackle more of this very rough country, return over the Old Weir Bridge and back to where the car has been parked. The distance to the Old Weir Bridge and back again is about two and a half miles. To this should be added any walking done on the far side of the bridge.

5. *Torc Mountain*

The other main activity in the Muckross area is to climb *Torc Mountain* (I.96.84.b), a not too strenuous but rewarding experience. Torc means a boar, from an enchanted boar killed here by Fionn Mac Cumhail. Drive to *Torc Old Bridge* (I.97.84.b). (One can leave the car at the car park at the bottom of Torc Waterfall and walk up to Torc Old Bridge. But why walk where one can drive?). Follow the old Kenmare Road beyond the stile on that road until one passes the rain gauge within its square of wire where remarkable rainfalls have been recorded. Immediately

above one, right, is the peak. Contrary to appearances it is easier to climb the mountain if one keeps the peak to the right of one. The mountain is not high but it is very steep and is often very wet. The panoramic view of Killarney, of the three lakes and of the mountain ranges from the top of Torc is, as the guide books say, worth the effort. Torc is 1764 feet. Time: two to three hours from and to Torc Old Bridge. The walk is three miles and the total driving distance is ten miles.

(IV) THE DERRYCUNNIHY AREA

The second main area of Magunihy that should be explored is the Derrycunnihy — Gallwey's Bridge area. This involves four trips) (1) Derrycunnihy — Looscaunagh; (2) Cromaglan Mountain and Cascades; (3) Torc Old Bridge — Gallwey's Bridge; (4) Old Kenmare Road.

1. *Derrycunnihy and Looscaunagh*

Take the Muckross road for eight miles from Killarney. *Derrycunnihy* (I.92.82.c) is not sign-posted and is difficult to find. After one has passed the Tunnel and as one twists up this road after the Upper Lake has been lost from view there is a signpost on the left showing that the road serpents. Just beyond this, on the right, ¾ mile from the Tunnel, there is a fairly broad untarred roadway with a rough surface, leading down into the rhododendrons. Follow this with the car for about half a mile until one comes to a rickety wooden bridge. Leave the car and cross over the bridge and on to the flat green mound beyond it where a cottage was built for Queen Victoria. Look back here and see the effect of the cascade, especially if there has been heavy rain. Then follow the flow of the stream by walking down a pathway to a very pleasant waterfall. Salmon can be seen jumping this. The pathway leads down through the woods to the shore of the Upper Lake but this journey is hardly worth making. It is extremely wet and uninteresting. Instead, turn up left from the waterfall and just underneath the cottage will be found a

narrow pathway; follow this over a stile and then a roadway (usually very wet) through the woods. Derrycunnihy woods which have survived here for over 4,000 years, when the other woods of Kerry were being engulfed by peat, are botanically very rich, especially in mosses and liverworts. They are in prolific and perpetual decay. Eventually one comes out in open country above the Upper Lake. If one is energetic, it is possible to cross around the top of the Lake over to the Black Valley, but this is rough going. Alternatively, it is possible to climb up through the woods, up to Ladies View. The journey from where one has left the car, out to the open country and back again is about two miles. Take the car back to the road and turn right up to the attractive *Looscunagh Lough* (I.89-90.80). This is just outside the southern limit of Magunihy.

Total driving distance: 23 miles. Walking distance and overall time to taste.

2. *Cromaglan Mountain and Cascades*

Take the Muckross road and leave the car at the *Tunnel* (I.92.82.b). Walk along the road, towards Derrycunnihy, for 200 yards. Here there is, on the left, what looks like a ride, with a pronounced deer track up the mountain side. For the Killarney area this is an unusually dry place. Follow the track through the various deer shelters, bearing a bit left until one comes on open ground. From here there is a splendid view of the Upper Lake. As one climbs higher the Middle, and then the Lower, Lake come into view. For a short walk and no real climbing effort, this gives one quite the finest aspect of Killarney. Walking distance (depending on the height climbed): something over two miles. *Cromaglan mountain* (I.93.82.d), which has a flat top, is 1,226 ft. Allow an hour to an hour and a half.

Turn the car and about a mile along the road stop just at the *Tower Lodge* (I.93.83.b) — the tower was a look out point for poachers — on the right at a river that runs into the lake. On the lodge side of the river there is a path that eventually leads up to the Old Kenmare road. Travel this path for about 10 minutes and one sees through the trees a small but engaging cascade. There are others to be seen further up this river, but the going is rough. In wet weather slender cascades also fall down the cliffs on the Killarney side of Cromaglan mountain and can be seen from the road.

Total driving distance: 14 miles. Allow two and a half hours — longer if one wishes to be more energetic.

3. Gallwey's Bridge — Torc Old Bridge

This calls for either two cars, or a driver willing to deposit and collect at the terminal points.

Drive to the small dark Pugin church·at *Gallwey's Bridge* (I.92.81.c) beyond Derrycunnihy. The church is now abandoned since worshippers in the Black Valley got their own church. Turn left. Leave the car here. Follow this rough roadway for just ½ mile. At the left of the road is a rough sheep-pen. Leave the road here and climb up through the woods until one sees the remains of the old Kenmare road before one. Turn left here and stick to the remains of the old road even where they are very wet. This road, connecting Killarney with Kenmare, was one of the improvements made in the mid-18th century by the 'Good Lord Kenmare', who was, indeed, a distinguised man and the man who got the economic development of Killarney under way. Follow this road through Esknamucky Glen and by the well-known *Cora's Cascade* (I.95.82.c) back to Torc Old Bridge. This goes through country much favoured by red deer; it could be worth while bringing glasses to view them.

Total walking distance: four miles. Driving distance for one car: 18 miles. If a second is used, it will travel 10 miles. Allow three and a half hours.

An alternative is to start from Tower lodge, instead of Gallwey's Bridge. This does not much affect either distance or time.

4. Gallwey's Bridge — Old Kenmare Road

This calls for a higher degree of co-operation.

Drive to Gallwey's Bridge and walk up along the road, past the sheep-pen, and through a ford. Here, on the left, is a very good 'rocking stone'. Continue along this road until it joins the *Old Kenmare Road* (I.92.80.b) from the left. Continue over the Windy Gap for three and a half miles to that part of the Old Kenmare road still in use.

The driver, or the second car, will have continued along the main Kenmare road to *Moll's Gap* (I.87.78.a). He will then, after 3½ miles from Moll's Gap take the first tarred road to the left, and then, a short distance later, the first turn to the left. He will follow this road for about a mile and a half to a *cross roads at Gowlane* (I.92.76.d), and leave the car here. The old road is that crossing from left to right.

Total driving distance for one car: 42 miles, and for a second, if used, 18 miles. Allow about three hours.

Lower Lake, Killarney

(V) LOWER LAKE   211

The third main area is the Lower Lake itself.

The Lower Lake will have been sampled from Aghadoe, Mahony's Point, Ross Castle and Castlelough but there are some other experiences. These are — (1) Kenmare Estate and the Golf Course, (2) Reen and Ross, (3) Ross Island, and (4) Inisfallen.

1. Kenmare Estate and Golf Course

The Kenmare estate was formerly that of the earls of Kenmare (a place in Limerick) direct descendants of Sir Valentine Browne, an 'undertaker', who arrived after the crushing of the Desmond rebellion, whose son, Nicholas, married the daughter of O Sullivan Mor. The family became and remained catholics and survived — at one time amongst the greatest landowners in Ireland — into the middle of the present century. The main part of the estate has since been held by a series of Americans.

212   The family first lived in Killarney in Ross Castle. In the 18th century they built a not very distinguished house here in the estate with famous gardens, and, when that burned down in the last century, the present, not very exciting Kenmare House. Unlike the Herberts the Kenmares never seemed to make much of their surroundings until the superb golf course was laid out by the last earl who. as Viscount Castlerosse, was a well known journalist.

A spectacular walk is to enter the Kenmare estate opposite the *Cathedral* (I.96.91.b). Follow the track, right, up the hill and across by the Castlerosse Hotel to the golf course — surely one of the most beautiful in the world. This is a distance of two miles. If one does not want to walk back, it is easy to get a lift back to the town.

2. Reen and Ross

This walk can be combined with the foregoing. If not, enter the estate in the same way but take the road straight before one and stay on this roadway until after ¼ mile one crosses the Denagh river. The dark japanese (or sika) deer can often be seen here. About ½ mile further on there is a right turn off the road overgrown with grass. Follow this, bearing right, for ½ mile. This brings one to *Reen Point* (I.95.90.a) (the two words mean the same thing) from which there is a fine view of the Lower Lake, especially in the evening. Follow the track around the point until it rejoins the roadway one has left. This eventually brings one out at *Ross Castle* (I.95.89.b) from which one can return to the town either through the Estate, if one keeps to the right, or around the public road. This is a walk of about four miles.

3. Ross Island (I.94-5.89-90)

Drive to Ross Castle and enter the gate on the left, taking the lefthand branches of the roadway until one comes to the *Ross copper mines* (I.95.89.d) at the edge of the lake. These have been worked since perhaps 2000 BC. They reopened in 1804 but were abandoned after four years. Part of the trouble was to keep the lake water out of

them -- for this purpose a steam engine was erected. Further trouble came from the quantity of rock to be extracted. Bad management may have contributed to the failure. Nonetheless, the ore was rich: in four years £80,000 worth was sold in Swansea. Some 500 people were employed. The mines are now manifestly very flooded. Stone hammer heads have recently been found near them. Carry on out to the very tip of the island (it is not an island, it is a peninsula) from which a good view of Inisfallen can be obtained. There is a nature conservancy on *Governor's Point* (I.94.90.d), a bleak and exposed part of the peninsula, with the remains of a yew wood. Coming back, bear again to the left. In this way one can cover the complete island. The strong smell that may meet one comes from a herd of wild goats in the place. This is a walk of about three miles.

4. Inisfallen

It is a delightful row of a mile from Ross Castle out to *Inisfallen* (I.94.90.c). A little firmness will get a boat without a boatman, if that is desired. The island is much neglected and the ruins are not very evocative.

The island monastery was founded by a leading member of the Eoganacht Locha Lein, Faithliu, whose uncle and father had both been kings of West Munster. The father, Aed Daman, died in 633 AD. The monastery, like that at Aghadoe, was dedicated to St Fionan. Faithliu was no doubt, a disciple of the saint. Between the landing stage and the main monastery there are the vestiges of a beehive hut, conceivably dating from the first foundation. In 869 a noscomium, or hospital, presumably for lepers, was built by the monks. The monastery became a major seat of learning and it is said that Brian Boramha studied there. His friend, Maelsuthain O Carroll, was its most famous monk.

There survives an 'Inisfallen crozier', dredged from the river Laune in 1867 and now in the National Museum; it dates from 1000 AD, a good example of the period. The *Annals of Inisfallen* is one of our major sources of Irish history. It does not seem to have been

begun here, but most probably at Emly and migrated here, possibly via Killaloe, Limerick and Lismore, after 1159. It was continued here until the early 14th century and remained on the island until, probably, early in the 17th century. By 1624 it was in the library of Sir James Ware in Dublin. After his death it was sold several times until in the middle of the 18th century it was bought by the great English collector, Rawlinson, and left by him to the Bodleian library, Oxford. One of the earliest extant Irish historical manuscripts is known there as Rawlinson B 503. A fine edition and translation appeared in 1953.

The little romanesque church overlooking the landing place dates from the 12th century.

In the general disorder of that century Inisfallen was several times raided and plundered, and there is a vivid entry in the *Annals* bewailing the anarchy of the times. Inisfallen itself was plundered by the O Donoghues in 1180.

With the general reform of the church in the twelfth and thirteenth centuries, the old monastic settlement was taken over by the Augustinian canons some time after 1197 and became the priory of St Mary. Thereafter, it seems to have sunk into steady mediocrity and, later, worse. Early in the 14th century the recording of the *Annals* came to an end.

It is clear from such ruins as remain that from this period at least the monastery was an extensive one; but little remains in the main buildings of architectural interest — one good pilaster, and another of some interest.

At the end of the 15th century the monastery was in a really bad way. In 1461 the prior, John Olyden, was said to be living with a concubine, to have children and to be residing elsewhere. The place was in the charge of William Osega, son of a priest. In 1478 the office of prior was said to have long been void and Donal Osega had held it for four years without any title. Osega (O Shea) was said to be living in *partibus montanis* and his canons in private houses outside the monastery, and altogether neglecting divine worship in their church. Donal O Sullivan, canon of Ardfert, is given charge *in commendam* in the hope of removing O Shea and reassembling the scattered community. It is doubtful if he made much of this charge beyond raising the value of the office from 24 marks to 30 in 1494 when it is taken over by John O Moriarty, a notable pluralist, who already held a number of diocesan offices, including four parishes.

It was not until a century later that it was to feel the effects of the reformation. About 1589 the island of about 120 acres, with garden etc., was given to R. Collum. In 1613 it was granted to Sir Valentine Browne of Molahiffe. Was it from this source that Ware acquired the manuscript of the *Annals*? In 1633 the monastery seems to have been still alive, but in all Kerry there were, to staff five priories, only 12 Augustinian priests and, three years later, only eight. It was finally abandoned in 1652 when the cromwellians came, and a thousand years of monastic life on this island came to an end, never to revive.

A century later, about 1750, Killarney began to be developed as a tourist centre and Sir Valentine Browne's descendant, Lord Kenmare, caused many improvement to be made. He arranged for boats and boatmen on the lakes and laid out a roadway around Inisfallen. The little romanesque church he had roofed and turned into a 'banqueting hall'; the gap in the wall is where he inserted a bay window. Excursions to Inisfallen became one of the principal attractions of Killarney. Around the turn of the 18th century Inisfallen was full of the sound of merrymaking parties. Thomas Moore wrote his charming 'Inisfallen fare thee well' after a visit in the 1820s and is reported to have said that if Killarney was Heaven's reflex then Inisfallen was Heaven itself. About 1840, tastes having changed, the little church was restored to its present state of picturesque ruin.

In 1973 the owner, Mr John McShain, gave the island to the State and it is now part of the National Park.

If one is energetic and the day is calm it is a

Inisfallen, Killarney

pleasant row of two miles from the island to *O Sullivan's Cascade* (I.92.89.d). A further row of four miles will bring one as far as *Glena* (I.93-94.87), a beautiful spot readily accessible only from the lake.

(VI) THE MANGERTON AREA

A fourth main area to explore is that of Mangerton, Lough Guitane and the wild mountains behind it. There are five main trips here – (1) Mangerton, (2) to the Horses Glen, (3) to Lough Guitane and Cappagh, (4) to Lough Nabroda and Aughnanus Bridge, and (5) the Queen's Drive and Tooreencormick.

1. Mangerton

There are two main approaches from Killarney to *Mangerton* (I.99.81.a) (2,758 feet). One is from Torc Old Bridge, as for Torc Mountain. Shortly beyond the stile on the old roadway is a *wooden bridge*

(I.97.84.d) across the stream on the left. Cross this river and stick by its tributary that flows down from the Punch Bowl, a lake near the top of the mountain. At the outflow bear right and follow the track right up to the top. It is possible to do a full circuit of the Punch Bowl in this way gaining a view of the wild Horses Glen to the right as one returns to the mouth of the Punch Bowl. Mangerton, except at the top, is a very wet mountain indeed. The total walk is five miles.

The alternative, a less good one, is to follow the roadway, beside the Muckross Hotel, with the signpost 'Mangerton'. Leave the car at the *bridge* (I.99.85.a) on the left of the road, where the road begins to bend right away from the mountain. Try to follow the remains of the old pony track, now largely washed away, up to the Punch Bowl. This track goes by *Tooreencormick battlefield* (I.98-9.84-5) on one's right. This is very wet indeed, and in the early stages steep going. The total walk is six miles. The total driving

214   distance is eight miles.

Either way allow about four to five hours from the time one leaves the car until one comes back to it.

2.   The Horses Glen

One can get to the Horses Glen by following the Muckross road until, just beyond the Muckross Hotel, one takes a turn to the left labelled 'Mangerton'. Drive up this road, but do not turn to the right where the signpost again says 'Mangerton'. Carry on straight through rough country until after just over a mile on this rough road one comes out at the Lough Guitane road (one could have taken the Lough Guitane road in the first place) beside a stream; cross *the bridge* (I.101.86.b) and take the first turn to the right. Follow this roadway past a bridge on the right. Shortly afterwards there is again on the right a gateway up to a farmhouse; drive through the gateway, leave the car at the farmhouse. There is a very rough turf-cutter's road up to the lowest of the lakes, at the *mouth* of the *Horses Glen* (I.100.84.b). There are two further lakes inside the Glen. This is a very wet and savage place, a striking example of one of the coums, or cirques, left by the ice age in its final agonies. Return the way one has come. Total driving distance: 12 miles.

3.   Lough Guitane and Cappagh

Take the Muckross road as far as the signpost labelled 'Muckross Church' which is to the left a short distance beyond the first entrance to the Muckross estate. There is *Muckross church* (I.99.88.d) designed by Rupert Boyd-Barrett, about one mile up this road on the right. This is well worth a visit. Note particularly the stations of the cross, by Ian Stuart. They are no more than suggestions for meditation. This is perhaps the most successful of the large number of very well, and plainly, designed churches that have been built in Kerry since the end of World War II, very many of them by the same architect.

The lake is about two miles beyond the church. *Lough Guitane* (I.102-104.84-86) is very

attractive and gives striking views of Mangerton and Torc mountains, and the tortured volcanic shapes of Stoompa, Bennanmore and Crohane, as well as the Cork mountains, especially in the afternoon and evening. Where the road pulls away from the lake, and begins to climb again, just six miles from Killarney, one will see on the right, a very wide tubular steel *gate* (I.104.86.a) painted (1964) green. On entrance tridents are crudely inset. Drive the car along this road by the east end of the lake, through the first farmyard, and leave it at the end of the roadway, about a mile and a half around the lake. Here the roadway parts near a ford. One branch of the road runs to the right, where there are two farmhouses, the other runs to the left about half a mile to a further farmhouse. (If the ford is too deep, there is a precarious foot-bridge somewhat to the left of it).

Go through the yard of the *left hand farmhouse* (I.104.84.a) and follow the turf cutter's road to the right of the volcanic mass of Bennanmore (1,490 ft.). Keep this on one's left, and, when the roadway peters out at the turf banks make way down to the bank of the river, by which there is an excellent sheep track almost the whole of the way. At one stage at the neck of the valley, this becomes rough but do not lose heart.

The coum here is *Cappagh* (I.103.82.b,d) pronounced Keppoch). The scenery here is savage indeed. Allow about two and a half hours of walking time to and from the ford at the edge of Lough Guitane. Return the way one has come. One could turn right at the public road and left at the main Cork road, but it is not an interesting route. Total driving distance: 16 miles. In all, allow about three and a half hours.

4.   Lough Guitane — Lough Nabroda — Lough Crohane — Aghnanus Bridge

This is best as a two-car trip, but if there is only one car it can also be managed.

Take the first car to the ford by Lough Guitane as described for the Lough Guitane — Cappagh trip. Go to the

farmhouse on the left. About half a mile beyond it, where the turf cutter's road begins to rise, there is a *branch left* (I.104.83.b). Follow this, keeping both Bennanmore (1,490 ft) (the mountain between the two coums) and the volcanic wedge to *its* right constantly to one's right, and Crohane mountain (2,162 ft) and the stream on one's left. Observe the basalt cliffs, with their organ pipe effects, high up on Crohane, the remnants of convulsions of more than 200 million years ago when the great weight of the sandstone deposits forced molten rocks through the earth's crust at this place. About 1½ miles from where one has left the car is *Lough Nabroda* (I.104.82.b), and less than ½ mile further on is Crohane Lake. From here it is one and a half miles to *Aghnanus Bridge* (I.105.79.b), following the line of the outflow from Crohane Lake. This makes a total walk of about three and a half miles. If, however, there is not a second car, it may be well to turn back at Crohane Lake. This would give a total driving and walking distances similar to the Cappagh trip.

If there is a second car it should set out on the Cork road and through the spectacular Glenflesk. Eight miles from Killarney branch right. This is a beautiful winding road — brilliant with birches in early winter — that leads one onto the main road to Kenmare. Travel right along this main road for two miles to the sharp bend at Aghnanus Bridge. There is a substantial wood here. The cleft containing Crohane Lough is almost due north of one here. Follow the stream that issues from it.

For this car the total driving distance will be: 24 miles. The total walking distance for each party will be three and a half miles.

5.   The Queen's Drive and Tooreencormick

Take the Muckross road, and the road labelled 'Mangerton' from the Muckross Hotel. Three miles from Killarney the road takes a sharp turn to the left. Leave the car here and branch right into the forest. This is the *Queen's Drive* (I.98.87.d), built by the Herberts for Queen Victoria. Follow this road, which is pretty rough going, bearing left until one comes out on to open country, from which a splendid view of the Middle and Lower Lakes will be obtained. Carry on until one comes to Torc Old Bridge. This is a walk of about two miles. There are many tracks through the mountainside here, most of them involving walks through the woods with occasional striking views of the countryside. To return follow the roadway about a mile down towards the main road, then turn right. This brings one back through the Queen's Drive. Back to the car and drive it up the hill and turn right at the top following the 'Mangerton' sign. Follow this road as far as it will go. In the wild land just to the south of one is the battlefield of *Tooreencormick* (I.98-9.84-5). This battle was fought in 1262, a year after the decisive battle of Callan Glen, on the far side of Mangerton when the victor of Callan, Fingen Mac Carthy, was already dead. The battle of Tooreencormick was an attempt by the anglo-normans to stop the overrunning of Glanerought, Dunkerron and Magunihy by the victors of Callan. The battle here was indecisive, and this represented a last failure of the anglo-normans below the line of the Maine. The battle is named after Cormac Mac Carthy who was killed here. He was Fingen's brother. Also killed here was Gerald de Roche, brother in law of John Fitz Thomas the ancestor of the Desmonds who was killed at Callan.

Return the way one has come. Total driving distance: eight miles. Total walking distance: four miles. Allow two hours.

(VII) SLIABH LUACHRA – MOLAHIFFE

What is left of interest in Magunihy is less dominated by Killarney and can be covered in two trips – (1) Lissyvigeen – Killaha – Sliabh Luachra, and (2) Molahiffe – Ballymalis – Pallis.

1. Lissyvigeen – Killaha – Sliabh Luachra

Perhaps one should first get into the mood for this trip which is to travel the area where gaelic culture staged its last real stand.

First, stand in front of the Franciscan Friary in Killarney. It is built on a place known as Gallows Hill. Here, in 1653, Piaras Ferriter,

poet and leader of the siege of Tralee castle, was hanged, with others. On his death a nameless poet wrote an elegy beginning:
 Do chonnac aisling ar maidin an lae ghil'
(I saw a vision on the morning of the bright day). This vision of Ireland as a young woman — a recollection of ancient days when she embodied the idea of sovereignty — now bewailing disaster was to haunt the imagination of gaelic poetry until it died at the end of the 18th century. Just behind where one stands is a not very distinguished sculpture of the aisling or speir-bhean (sky-woman) erected through the efforts of Father Patrick Dinneen to commemorate the four great Kerry poets — Ferriter, O Donoghue, O Rahilly and O Sullivan. Well, here they are.

But first, a diversion into antiquity.

Take the Cork road and, just two miles out, the third turn to the left outside the town, at

the small shop. About a quarter of a mile up that road there is a turn to the left. Leave the car there, at the junction, and walk up to the first farmhouse on the left. Walk through the yard and right across the front of the house, through a field and a gap, (closed by a rickety gate) on the right. At the top of the next field, there is the *Lissyvigeen circle* (I.100.91.b) of standing stones, and, most unusually, a henge, as well as two outliers. Note the neolithic scribings at the back and to the side of one of these. This may be a remain of an open-air temple of the Beaker folk, who colonised Britain and elsewhere and survived in Ireland into the Bronze age. These circles are also called 'henges' from the great circle at Stonehenge. Croker records an old story that the two outliers and the seven internal stones were two giants and their seven children who were turned into stones in a dispute with a magician at Ross. He also records a significant story that one May day the big stones were seen as giants again and

Glenflesk, Killarney

216
the seven children dancing round and round in the middle of the fort, so supporting the theory that dancing in a sunwise way, the deisiol, was one of the ceremonies carried on at these places. Unusual views of the lakes can be got from here.

Continue along the Cork road for four miles. On the right, a mile short of, but guarding the entrance to, Glenflesk are the gaunt remains of the late tower house of *Killaha,* (I.105.87.b), the home of the O Donoghue of the Glens. They were a branch of the invading O Donoghues at the 11th-12th century, living wildly in this wild place. The most famous member of the family was Seafraidh (Geoffrey) who lived from c. 1620 to 1677 and is buried in the great O Donoghue tomb in the chancel of Muckross Friary. He with his father and two brothers were 'out' in 1641, at the siege of Tralee castle, but even the cromwellians did not dare to punish people in these wild parts, so he wrote his poetry and threw great parties and continued to live as his ancestors had done. He wrote a good deal of verse, much esteemed in its time, but of not much modern appeal. This wild place though so close to Killarney, was during the 18th century a noted haunt of rapparees and outlaws.

If one has not been through *Glenflesk* (I.107-8.84-6) it is worthwhile taking this detour. After one and a half miles through the glen — which floods badly in very wet weather — turn left and take the winding road until it reaches the main road to Kenmare. Turn left here for the Cork road and cross *Loo Bridge* (I.109.82.d) with the tortured volcanic mountains on one's left until one reaches the Cork road to *Cloonkeen* (I.112.83.a). Here, right, is a rather pleasant Boyd Barrett church. One is here just on the Cork boundary. Turn back through Glenflesk. This is a detour of some 10 miles, but worth it.

At the entrance to the Glen turn right for Barraduff. Just two miles up this road, on the left, is *Headford Junction* (I.108.89.c) where, formerly, there was a branch railway line for Kenmare. Here, on 21 March, 1921, was fought the most considerable military action of the war of independence in Kerry

where a party of 30 British soldiers from Kenmare, waiting for a train to Killarney, was attacked, with 26 casualties before the Killarney train full of soldiers arrived. Two volunteers, Dan Allman and Jim Bailey were killed, and a memorial has been erected to them.

At *Barraduff* (I.109.91.a) go right across the Mallow road into the *Sliabh Luachra country.* (One may well ask how so unattractive a place bred two of Ireland's greatest poets). Follow this road for two and a half miles, turn right at the cross roads, and just two miles further on turn left. Follow this road for just over ½ mile until one comes to a T junction. This is *Scrahanaveal* (I.111.97.c) and somewhere here Aodhgan O Raithile was born about 1670. He lived most of his life in this area. Bear right here and right again at the T junction and across the crossroads. One mile after a schoolhouse on the right is a branch left to Stagmount where O Raithile spent most of his life with his two daughters. As one takes this road one turns one's back on an empty, barren area — *Knockdoorah* (I.110.93). Aodhgan O Raithile died in his daughter's house, according to the texts, at Knockdurath, Tomies; but this is the only place in Kerry with that name. So he must have died, within a couple of miles of the two places where he was born and where he lived much of his life, epitomising in that life the ruin, the degradation, the tenacity and the beauty of that gaelic world he bewailed.

Turn back from *Stagmount* (I.111.93.d) and turn right to the schoolhouse, now on the left. Stop at *Meentogues* (I.111.94.b) and it was here that that Burns-like character, Owen Rua O Sullivan, was born in 1748, twenty years after O Raithile's death.

Carry on to the cross-roads and go right and then, at 5 point cross-roads, take the second of the two left turns. This brings one into *Gneevegullia* (I.113.97.b) where Owen opened his first school, and wrote one of his most beautiful poems when a young girl publicly presented him in school with his child. At Gneevegullia turn right and go across the Blackwater (and into Cork) to *Knocknagree* (I.118.98.c). After a stormy life teaching, labouring, womanising, in the

navy and the army, all the time composing poetry, he died here in a fever hut, aged 36, from a blow received in a tavern brawl in Killarney. Then turn right for *Rathmore* (I.117.94.d) (Pop. 1971: 437).

Born in Rathmore was the celebrated priest, Patrick Dinneen (1860 to 1934) who is best remembered for his Irish-English dictionary, indispensable and (unconsciously) amusing. Amongst other works he edited the poems of Ferriter, O Donoghue, O Rahilly and O Sullivan. He was responsible for getting erected the monument facing Ferriter's place of execution in Killarney and for a plaque commemorating the four poets in Muckross friary. It is said that his little book *Muintir Chiarraidhe Roimh an droch-shaoghal* (1905) was a major influence on Daniel Corkery's famous book *The Hidden Ireland;* if so, it is difficult to see why. The Dinneens were a hereditary learned family in the service of Mac Carthy Mor.

From Rathmore take the road due S from where one has entered the village. This winds for 5 miles until, at a cross roads at a school, there is a road left and then a boithrin, leading towards the Paps (2,273 and 2,284 ft) of Anu or Dana, each with a cairn for nipple. She was the great mother goddess of the Tuatha De Danaan. A ninth century tract says that Munster owed its fertility to Anu, goddess of prosperity. She was also known as the Mor Rigu, the Great Queen, a demon of the battlefield.

The boithrin, after a short stretch, comes to an end at the *City* (I.114.89.d), a stone ringfort called Cahercrovdarrig, the fort of Crobh Dearg, or Red Claw, before which is a well at which rounds used to be made all night on May eve. Crobh Dearg (whose name came to be associated with one of three sister saints venerated in the district) may perhaps be related to Badb (which means carrion crow) one of the two sisters of Anu. The well, the rounds, and the coincidence of the two sets of three sisters — one lot pagan goddesses, the other christian saints — vividly suggest the survival of ancient religious practices.

It has been suggested that this place was

217

Teamhar Luachra, or Luachar Dedadh, headquarters of the Erainn of West Munster, which figures in many stories of Curoi Mac Daire and the Fiana. It was also held to be the burial place of Clann Dedad. It is not clear whether any such place existed — T. F. O Rahilly says it was a purely literary invention. But a number of other places contend for this hypothetical honour. It has been located in the townland of *Ballahantauragh* (I.105.101.d) (Beal Atha na Teamhrach) not far from Scartaglin or another place of the same name near Dysert, Castleisland. Here, it is claimed, there is a ford over a small stream; perhaps the road to Teamhar Luachra crossed this ford. Traces of it have been claimed to lead to Taur Hill, over the Cork border. Ballydesmond and two places in Co. Limerick (Coshlea and Portrinard, near Abbeyfeale) have also been suggested as the site of Teamhar Luachra.

More than a mile south of the City, by what is presumably *Lough Glannavreaghaun* (I.115.86-87), lived Crede, the daughter of the local, wealthy king in the time of Fionn. She loved to have her home praised and said she would marry whomever did so fittingly. Cael, one of Fionn's men, and son of the king of Leinster, did this — there is a lovely 12th century poem purporting to give his praises — and won her. The poem says she lived beside Loch Cuirre 'north east of the mountain'. This can only be Lough Glannavreaghaun. Crede then went with Cael to the battle of Ventry where, in the final struggle he lost his life and she, lying beside his dead body, died of grief.

Then back to the schoolhouse and go due N, turning left at the main road for Barraduff and Killarney.

Total driving distance: 34 miles. Add seven miles for the Glenflesk — Loo Bridge detour. Allow two and a half hours.

2. Molahiffe — Ballymalis — Pallis

A trip for the historical minded is to take the Limerick road and the second turn (after the New Road) left out of the town to Firies. This is a straight, dull road, one of the several 18th century roads built between Killarney and Tralee. As one passes the second junction, left, one is going through the townland of *Knockasarnet* (I.95.94) where a copper hoard dating from perhaps 2000 BC was found. Carry on the straight road until, one has travelled on it for in all four miles, one comes to a cross roads. Turn left here. After just under a mile one comes to a junction on the left. Stop here. On one's right is an iron gate. Go through this and through the field before one (very muddy in winter) and into the next field rising above it. Here there is an alignment of four stones and, in the next field on one's right, a great gallan. The alignment may have been a, not very accurate, a signpost to it, marking, it would seem, a very important burial of the early bronze age. This is the townland of *Ballynacarrig* (I.91.99.b). Crawford says there is a crutched, or potent, cross here, but I could find no-one who knew where it was.

Turn here and go back along the road one has been on, turning left for *Firies cross roads* (I.91.104.d), two miles further on. Here, turn right for Firies village, a not very exciting one. Go straight through the village, then keeping left until, after a mile, one comes to a large farm on a sharp left hand bend of the road.

Just in front of the house are the rather scanty ruins of *Molahiffe castle* (I.92.105.a), built as an outlier across the line of the Maine by the anglo-norman intruders in 1215-16. After Callan it seems to have fallen into the hands of O Donoghue Mor, whose eventual successor forfeited it (with his life) in the Desmond revolt. It was then acquired by Nicholas Browne who resembled the early anglo-normans in his avidity for land, a trait shared with two brothers. Nicholas had also acquired Ross, but was partly tricked out of it by Clancarre, who however mortgaged it to him and engaged to him Clancarre's only daughter Ellen, destined to be his heiress. However she tricked him by marrying secretly Florence Mac Carthy Reagh, and Nicholas spent many long years writing to Queen Elizabeth intriguing, litigating and fighting hard against Donal Mac Carthy, Clancarre's bastard son but by Irish law his rightful heir. Other planters, notably Sir William Herbert of Castleisland, coveted the extensive and beautiful properties of Mac Carthy and aimed

to move to the more attractive neighbourhood of Killarney. This castle of Molahiffe was severely attacked in the O Neill wars and captured after a spirited struggle. But in the end, Sir Nicholas Browne of Molahiffe won through and established in Killarney, by means of Florence Mac Carthy Reagh's jilted financee, Julia O Sullivan, the line that was destined to become one of the greatest landholders in Ireland, Perhaps his natural cupidity and ability were sharpened by the dullness of this place.

Carry on this winding road for another mile until one comes to a T junction. In the flat land facing one was built another of these geraldine castles, advanced posts along the River Maine, at *Cloonmealane* (I.89.105.d); but it does not figure in subsequent history. Here turn left along the Killarney—Tralee road one had been on. Follow this for a mile and a half and at a sort of cross roads take the second of the two roads to the right. After three miles turn right at the cross roads and go through *Faha* (I.89.96.a). Turn right at the cross roads here and, after just over a mile, left. This brings one down to the Killorglin road. Turn left here and a little further on, to the right, is a boithrin with a

Wall 'Bartizan', Ballymalis Castle

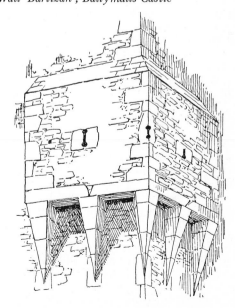

218 sign for *Ballymalis castle* (I.85.94.a). Leave the car here and walk down to the banks of the Làune. The castle was first built by the anglo-norman intruders, and after the Callan disaster they staged a rally here in 1270 by, with Mac Carthy help, routing King Donal Rua Mac Carthy here. However this was not a decisive defeat. The present building is a fine example of a 16th century tower house, built at the end of the century for the Ferris family, guardians of the line of the Laune. An interesting and unusual feature are the two bartizans built at a second storey angle to prevent undermining by hostile forces. There are some carvings in the stonework of the castle.

Return to the car. About a mile further on there is a boithrin to the left. A short distance up this there are the remains of *Kilbonane parish church* (I.86.94.b) which had a long ogam stone with complex inscriptions. It is now removed to Coolmagort across the river, and is the recumbent there.

Return to the main road. One passes, left, the townland of *Lower Laherard* (I.88.94) where, in the famine of 1740, most of the tenants died.

A little further on one comes to *Beaufort Bridge* (I.89.93.a), a pleasant place by the Laune. Just beyond the bridge there is a road left, and just beyond that a gateway up to McKay's farm. Just behind this farmhouse are the nettle covered vestiges of *Pallis* (I.89.94.c) (or the Palace) the principal seat of Mac Carthy Mor for about 300 years. However, an English observer, Fenton, with Pelham on his incursion in the Desmond wars in 1580 was not impressed: 'the Palace, a name very unfit for so beggarly a building not answerable to a mean farmer's house in England, and his (Clancarre's) entertainment much like to his dwelling'. It seems to have been a long, low thatched building. However, there was some sort of castle for the cromwellians to destroy, and in the end, in 1837, the stones from it went into making the roadway one has been on, and into piggeries at Beaufort House. This is what is left of the great families of Ireland who flourished 'before Christ died'. The view

from here is staggering.

In effect the dynasty came to an end when Donal Mac Carthy Mor, first and last earl of Clancarre, died in 1596, though the family continued until 1770. Clancarre possessed some sort of title to 500,000 acres from here almost to Cork city; but he was always chronically hard up, and mortgaged what he could, including his daughter to the Brownes. He was dissolute and a drunkard, but a poet in the refined gaelic medieval tradition. Some of his poetry was religious, some secular. Frank O Connor has translated one of his poems, written perhaps in this wonderfully beautiful place. Here are the last two stanzas:

> *I am a ghost upon your path,*
> *A wasting breath,*
> *But you must know one word of truth*
> *Gives a ghost breath —*
>
> *In language beyond learning's touch*
> *Passion can teach —*
> *Speak in that speech beyond reproach*
> *The body's speech.*

Windele says the green field before the Pallis is Pairc an Crochadh, the gallows field, where Mac Carthy executed delinquents.

Back to the road and a short distance further on, to the left, is the modern church of *Fossa* (I.91.93.c), a neat example of the church building of the nineteenth century catholic renaissance. It is unusual in Irish catholic churches in that it has a number of military memories of the O Connell family, collateral descendants of Daniel O Connell, who live at Lakeview close by.

Continue toward Killarney. Just as one enters the built up area, and before the sharp turn right, there is at *Ballydowney* (I.96.92.a) a pleasant,and recently restored, georgian house on the left, the home of a respected 18th century smuggler in Killarney, James Mason, whose daughter, Elizabeth, was the mother of Robert Emmet.

Total driving distance: 29 miles. Allow two and a half hours.

(VIII) OTHER ACTIVITIES

The golf courses (there are two side by side) are in splendid surroundings; one is a championship course. As they are about four miles from the town, a car is likely to be necessary.

For Killarney people, perhaps the greatest interest is in fishing. Fishing on the Lakes for salmon and trout, and for coarse fish, is free, and one gets the impression that nearly everyone in Killarney has a boat nestling away in some small creek of one or other of the Lakes. When the fish are rising, large numbers of boats can be seen fishing on the Lakes. For visiting fishermen it is necessary to hire boats and boatmen. This is because, mainly, some skill and knowledge are needed in knowing where to fish in the varying weather conditions of the Lakes.
Salmon fishing begins on 17th January and trout fishing on 17th February. They go on to 12th October.

Fishing is available on the Flesk River, and the fishing there is usually good after a flood. The River Laune is a fine salmon river. For both of these rivers a fee has to be arranged with the Lough Leane Anglers Association. This applies also to *Kilbrean Lake* (I.101.94). Fishing is free on Lough Guitane. There are innumerable small mountain loughs that can be freely fished.

The other main activity in Killarney is shooting and deerstalking. Shooting is mostly free. Deerstalking, which can be engaged in from mid-August to end-September, must be arranged for the Bourn-Vincent Park through the Office of Public Works. This should be done through the Estate Office in Muckross Village.

Killarney has a *race course* at *Bunrower* (I.96-97.90) (near Ross Castle) and two meetings are held each year—for two days in the fourth week of April and for three days in the fourth week of July.

DUNKERRON NORTH

The western boundary of this barony runs

SW from the river Laune just east of Killorglin through *Lough Nafanida* (I.77.92.a) and then due south through the southern half of Caragh Lake along the Caragh river to the spine of the Dunkerrons due north of Sneem. It follows this spine east along a line south of Ballaghabeama and north of Lough Brin and its outlet the Owenreagh, to the Upper Killarney lake and then along the western shores of all three lakes. Its southern boundary is the river Laune almost to Killorglin.

It consists of only one complete parish—Knockane—and part of Killorglin.

The name comes, of course, from Dunkerron, the castle near Kenmare in the barony of Dunkerron South which for four hundred years was the seat of O Sullivan Mor. O Sullivan power fanned in two main directions in Kerry—west along the seaboard, and north to include the wild country of the Reeks, named after a sept of the O Sullivans, the Mac Gillacuddys. There seems to have been only one stronghold in this barony, at Dunloe, a castle established by the anglo-normans in 1207, but in the hands of O Sullivan Mor for just four hundred years from 1261. In earlier times this was one of the great hunting areas of the Fiana. Earlier still the Lugaid, whose fort was at the north of the great pass of Dunloe that still bears his name, was the god who killed Cuchulain.

The place is still overwhelmingly wild mountain; it reaches over 3,000 feet in several places. Carrantuohil (3,414 ft) is the highest mountain in Ireland. There is, in effect, only one significant road in the barony, and that is not complete. Fortunately, this enables one, with considerable difficulty, to make a circuit of nearly the whole barony. A major defect is that there is no road along the southern shores of the lakes, although there is a forestry road along part of the Lower Lake.

There is no town, or even village, in the barony, although there are some places to stay. For this reason, and because it plays such a part in the scenic effects of Killarney, that is taken as the starting point for what follows.

(I) BLACK VALLEY

Perhaps the best way to get the flavour of this barony is to do a circuit through the *Black Valley* or *Cummeenduff* (I.79-87.80-83). Because there is no road round the barony this cannot be done wholly by car, but if two groups will do it in opposite directions with two cars a fair attempt can be made. This involves one car going to Moll's Gap, taking the Sneem road and, then, the first turn right. At the T junction turn right again and then, at the end of this long road, after one has crossed a bridge just before a T junction, the left turn up into the Black Valley. One passes an attractive little Boyd Barrett church on the left and the road up to the Gap of Dunloe on the right. Then bear up Cummeenduff (the Black Valley) taking (notwithstanding what the map shows) the next turn left below the two visible lakes. Follow this to the top of the second lake and leave the car at a wide fork on the roadside just beyond the lake. It is possible to drive further, but turning is difficult higher up. Here in the twisted valleys and the little lakes high up on the hillsides are relics of the ice age in its final retreat from the Killarney plain through the Gap of Dunloe and up into its defeat in this valley. To one's right, as one faces up the Valley, are the steep flanks of *Carrantuohil* (I.81.85.c), and to one's left the spine of mountains along which the boundary runs between the baronies of North and South Dunkerron.

Bearing right, walk up the roadway to the head of the valley past a couple of shepherds' houses in this remote place. There is a track right over the *Pass* (I.80-81.83) at the top, and this drops down to join the other roadway. This is a walk of about three miles, but allow two hours for it. On this pass are, in season (late April to early July) many examples of the most beautiful of wild flowers, the Large-flowered Butterwort (*Pinguicula grandiflora*) with its flowers of Parma blue rising six to nine inches from a light green starfish base, usually in very wet places.

On the road below should be the other car.

(This will have taken, at Beaufort, the road to Kilgobnet and, at the next cross roads, turned left for Lough Acoose. After the lough it will have consistently borne left until it reaches the head of the *Brida valley* (I.73-80.81-82)).

The task of the other party in crossing this pass is a bit more difficult because the track is harder to find at that side. It climbs over the top of the second hill from the left. It is worth going to a little trouble to find it. Follow this track almost to the head of the valley. There it seems to disappear, but follow the line of boulders and then it reappears winding over the steep, wet head of the pass. At the summit it is necessary to cross a wire fence. Given that the rendezvous has succeeded, take the other car back keeping to the right until one runs by *Lough Acoose* (I.76-77.85-86). Just after one leaves the lake is a hill to the left, *Derryfanga* (I.76.87), a favourite hunting spot of the Fiana. For four and a half miles after one has left the lake take no turn until one comes to a cross roads. Turn right here for Beaufort and Killarney. In this way one does a complete circuit of the Mac Gillacuddy Reeks.
Let the other party return the way one has come.

This is a drive of 44 miles for one's own car, and 48 miles for the other. Allow one and a half hours for driving and two hours for walking.

(II) GAP OF DUNLOE

The *Gap of Dunloe* is a most striking one. If the famous Gap-Lakes tour has been taken from Killarney, that is enough. But if one has not taken this for any reason there are two possible ways of using one's car. There are also severe restrictions. The road is nerve-wracking. During the tourist season the road is full of nervous and inexperienced tourists riding the most unprepossessing ponies. A car passing is liable to upset them. Finally, the entrance from *Kate Kearney's Cottage* (I.89.89a.) is frequented by pony men who much resent motorists.

Nonetheless, in the off season it is possible, with some anxiety, to bring the car down

220

the route from Moll's Gap and down through the Gap of Dunloe without evoking more than scowls.

When one enters the Black Valley, after crossing the little bridge, instead of turning left, go right. This brings one down to *Lord Brandon's Cottage* (I.89.82.a) where the boat trips down the Lakes begin. Return along this road. After one has passed the little *Black Valley church* (I.87.83.a) take the turn right for the Gap of Dunloe. Where the road winds back above the little church, stop and observe the really striking view. Then through the Gap, and back to Killarney. Total driving distance: 38 miles.

An alternative, when there are two cars, is for one car to be left at the head of the Gap of Dunloe, and the other at Kate Kearney's Cottage and for both parties to walk the Gap, a distance of three miles. Allow one and a half hours for walking. The distance from Killarney to Kate Kearney's Cottage is only seven miles while that by Moll's Gap to the head of the Gap is 28 miles, so make allowance for this difference. Total driving distance: 35 miles. Allow four hours in all.

(III) DUNLOE–COOLMAGORT– KILGOBNET–KILCOOLAGHT– BALLAGHABEAMA–CLOON LOUGH

Take the road for the Gap of Dunloe. After one has crossed the *Laune Bridge* (I.90.92.c) leave the car and walk left along the Laune until, if there is no flooding, one comes out at the bottom of Lough Leane. This is a notable stretch of salmon fishing. Pearls were often taken from this river. Return to the car and go into the grounds of the Dunloe Hotel to the right and bear left. On the banks of the Laune are the remains of *Dunloe castle* (I.89.92.d), much altered in the 19th century, perched on its motte. This was first built as a wooden prefabricated castle in 1207 by the first anglo-norman main intruders into Kerry and was a stronghold of O Sullivan Mor for 400 years. It was damaged by Ormond in the Desmond wars and severely 'slighted' by the cromwellians whose confiscations ruined O Sullivan Mor, who had played a prominent part in the fighting in South Kerry. About 1665 it came into the possession of John

O Mahony, who had married an O Sullivan, and it was restored for use. His son was the the redoubtable Donal O Mahony who, although a catholic, maintained in the 18th century his feudal state with a private militia of 4,000 men. As Froude said, the Viceroy might be supreme in Dublin castle but (in the first half of the eighteenth century) Daniel Mahony was supreme in Kerry.

Return to the road and immediately bear right down the hill, and right again. Here are set up, to the right above the road, the seven *Coolmagort* (I.89.92.c) ogam stones found in a cave near here, and a recumbent stone from Kilbonane, now the central one. They are deciphered elsewhere. One of them commemorates the son of a man called Ttal who was buried within sight of the mountain that seems to bear his name. They are very good examples of their kind.

Return to the road for Dunloe and follow the signposts for Carrantuohil until one reaches *Gortboy school* (I.84.89.c). From the school follow the road down by the river and take the first turn left. Follow this to a cross roads and again turn left. Just up this road, beside a substantial farmhouse, is *Lispadrickmore* (I.81.90.b), a fine bivallate ringfort with a five chamber souterrain cut in the hard ground.

Go back to the cross roads and go straight on. At the junction turn right and, at the next cross roads, left. There is a junction a short distance down this road. Stop here. On the right is *Kilgobnet* (I.83.92.a), an old church site with a cross pillar. Miss Mac Neill indicates that Puck Fair may first have been held here but was moved to Killorglin in the middle ages.

Due N of here, and west of an angle described by the river Laune is *Whitefield* (I.84.95) where the O Sullivan sept with the splendid name of Mac Gillacuddy of the Reeks established themselves. In this townland, as well as that of Coolmagort, were found ogam stones with crosses on them used in the construction of a souterrain.

Turn here and take the first turn left. Then,

after ½ mile, the first turn right and, almost immediately, another turn right. Just up here us the fine ringfort of *Lisnagullaun* (I.83.90.b) with three rings and a three chamber souterrain. From here back to Kilgobnet. Keep left until one goes through a cross roads. A mile further on, leave the car and follow a boithrin to the right, to reach the *Kilcoolaght* (I.80.93.b) ogam stones. There are eight of them, some much damaged. There was probably a cemetery here, now encroached upon for farming needs.

Back to the car. Follow this road to a T junction and turn left, crossing a main road from Killorglin. Follow the minor road one is on—it runs almost along the boundary of the barony—bearing left at the next junction, and continuing to bear left until one comes to a cross roads. Go through this and shortly afterwards one comes, on the right, to *Glencar hotel* (I.73.86.a), a famous fishing hotel. If one wishes to explore the island in *Cloon Lough* (I.70-71.78-79) ask the obliging Mr Daly for the key of his boathouse there. Continue on this road and go straight through the next cross roads. At the next junction bear left for *Ballaghabeama* (I.75-76.79) and, after two miles, bear right. Go through this striking pass—particularly so in dark weather after heavy rain—and look out into Dunkerron South on the far side. Turn and go back the way one has come. After one has left the pass for about two and a half miles there is a narrow road to the left, over a bridge. Follow this road until one comes to Cloon Lough. Here, despite appearances, follow the left-hand road up behind the head of the lough to a farmyard. Leave the car here and walk down a boithrin beyond the farmyard, bearing left. Follow this as far as possible and make for a lone ash tree. One comes upon, after about 10 minutes' walk, in the middle of the 'slough', the most interesting, if wetly sited, anchoritic settlement of *Cloon* (I.71.78.c). The little standing cross slab has been broken with the years; but the carving on the pieces – of swastika and maze design – is most striking and unusual. Graves saw and illustrated towards the end of the last century, this and another similar cross in this place. Go back to the car and follow up the boithrin until one is close to other farmhouses, a bit above one. Bear right along a track and, after a few moments, one is in an ancient farming settlement, with ruined clochans and terraced fields. A short distance further on there is,

O Sullivan's Cascade, Killarney

in the coum in the usual way another lake, *Lough Reagh* (I.70.71.76-77). The fold of mountains above it separates three baronies— Dunkerron North and South, and Iveragh.

Back to the car. The island in the lake is

surrounded by a caher; this is most unusual; but there is no trace of building inside. The island is so overgrown with rhododendron as to make a journey over hardly worth while even if one has borrowed the key of the boathouse in Glencar. Stephen Gwynn

222

has a chapter on a memorable day spent fishing here.

Turn left when one meets the main road again, then, at the crossroads, if one has borrowed the key left for Glencar, (at the next crossroads right, and at the T junction left) otherwise straight by Lough Acoose to Killarney. Total driving distance: 63 miles. Allow in all: six hours.

(IV) O'SULLIVAN'S CASCADE

Take the Killorglin road to the bottom of the Lower Lake, and turn left at the first sign for Kate Kearney's Cottage, over the bridge over the River Laune. Shortly beyond this bridge the road takes a sharp bend to the right, with a hideous piece of local architecture facing one; turn sharp left along the bad road. To one's right here was *Tomies House* (I.90.91.c) where the last O Sullivan Mor died in 1762. It is necessary to go through three gateways taking, whenever a decision has to be taken, the right turn until the third gateway has been passed through. Then take the left fork through a fourth gateway (which may be locked, so requiring one to leave the car), and go a mile along a very rough road as far as the river, over which there is a footbridge of sorts. About seven and a half miles from Killarney, and shortly before one comes to this river, the roadway widens out considerably. Leave the car here. There are often red deer in the woods here. A little further on there is a track down through the woods to the edge of the Lake. Follow this, and when one has got one's views of the Lake, turn back along the edge of the stream, along another track on the bank, to *O'Sullivan Cascade* (I.92.89.d).

It is necessary to retrace steps here, and, if one wishes, walk along the edge of the lake for some distance. If one has crossed the stream by the stepping stones at the Lake edge, climb up through the woods up to the forestry road again. Turn right and back across the footbridge. After one has crossed along the footbridge, turn left along the edge

of the stream and climb up through a most attractive wooded and mossy place, where the stream tumbles over shelves of blackened rock. There is a further forestry road some distance higher up. The glen through which this river tumbles in innumerable cascades, goes up some considerable distance up the mountainside. A climb of about half a mile brings one to the top of the wooded place.

The whole is a very attractive trip. From this place one can climb *Tomies Mountain* (I.90.87.b). This is a fairly easy, if wet, climb giving a round trip of about three miles and takes about two hours. If one is energetic one can push on from Tomies to *Purple Mountain* (I.89.86.d) adding another three miles and another two hours to the trip. If the forestry gate is closed add another two miles of walking. The maximum driving distance is 15 miles.

(V) CARRANTUOHIL

The more energetic walker will want to climb *Carrantuohil* (I.81.85.c) (3,414 feet), the highest mountain in Ireland. This is a mountain with which no liberties should be taken and one should not attempt it except in clear settled weather. There are a number of ways of tackling this mountain but for the climber who is not fully experienced a choice can be made of the following three routes. For all of them take the Killorglin road from Killarney and turn left at Beaufort towards the Gap of Dunloe.

The normal tourist route is signposted. Follow this route until, after four miles from Beaufort the road turns sharp right from the river at the schoolhouse at *Gortboy* (I.84.89.c). Leave the car here and take the second track on one's left through several farm gates that runs parallel to, but above, the river. Follow this track through the Hag's Glen to the two lakes of *Gouragh* and *Callee* (I.82.85.a,b). Keeping the summit severely to the right cross the moor to the *Devil's Ladder* (I.82.84.a) to the Saddle. The Devil's Ladder is an extremely disagreeable climb, as the name suggests. It can be avoided by

climbing the ridge to the left of Lough Callee. This brings one to the summit of the ridge above the Gap of Dunloe and gives a splendid ridge walk to the *Saddle* (I.81.84.b), but at the price of losing some of the height so hard gained. From the top of the Ladder turn right and up the slope to the summit. If there is time and the day stays settled there are a number of ridge walks before one.

A second route is to take the road from Beaufort to Lough Acoose (nine miles) and to turn left up the boithrin just beyond the lake. Bring the car to a *farmyard* (I.76.85.c) one and a half miles on and leave it. Climb the ridge before one to the south west, keeping the river that runs into the lough on one's left. At the *saddle* (I.77.83.d) bear left, and follow the spine of the mountain to the summit. This is an easy, steady climb. There are variations of the route from Lough Acoose for the more experienced.

Perhaps the easiest way up Carrantuohil is to take this spine from the other side. Continue on the road past Lough Acoose and, at the cross roads two miles further on, turn left.

Follow this road and after two and a half miles bear left. After a further two and a miles (and one mile from the end of the road) stop just short of a *farmhouse* (I.78.82.a). At this point there is (but it is difficult to find) on the left a track rising to the spine of the ridge to the left. Once one reaches this spine, follow it, right, to the summit.

The first of these routes involves a drive of 20 miles from and to Killarney, the second 34 miles, and the third 45 miles. Allow seven to eight hours for the walking and climbing.

(VI) LOUGH ACOOSE

A milder version of the second or third expeditions above is to take two cars, one to the second starting point, the other to the third, and to walk over the spine of the mountain exchanging keys on the *ridge* (I.77.83.d). This is a walk of four miles, and allow two hours for it.

Chapter 13

The Desmond Lands: Trughanacmy and Corkaguiney

When the geraldines, who became earls of Desmond, overran Kerry they established themselves principally in the rich barony of Trughanacmy and also in its continuation, the Dingle peninsula.

TRUGHANACMY

The barony consists of a belt of land about 20 miles wide spreading east from a line drawn from Barrow Harbour to Cromane and running a little north of east to the Cork border. It loses a stretch of land to Magunihy where the Maine becomes its southern border and bends towards the north and inserts two narrow salients north west of Fieries. It comprises the rich mainly flat limestone country north of the Maine and some fairly wild highlands along its northern and eastern boundaries.

The barony name comes from Triocha Chead an Aicme Chiarraighe, the barony of the people of the Ciarraige. It was the original base of the tribe, the Ciarraige Luachra, which gave Kerry its name. In early christian times the Ciarraige began to overwhelm the neighbouring tribes and to establish their power in the whole of northern Kerry. They were named after the Sliabh Luachra mountains to the east of the present barony where they had their seat. The barony consists of rich, limestone land and, by Kerry standards, big farms. When the anglo-normans overran north Kerry it was in Trughanacmy they had their principal base and the Desmonds held there their two great castles of Castleisland in the east of the barony and Tralee in the west. It is not surprising that the principal town in the county should have grown up here.

(I) TRALEE

Tralee (II. 84-85. 115) comes from Traigh Li, the strand of the (river) Lee. This is the capital of Kerry (pop. 1971: 13,263). It is a thriving town, elegant in places, an urban district, with a number of factories, substantial commercial business, a newspaper *(The Kerryman)* and the largest festival in Ireland, the 'Festival of Kerry', where each September a Rose of Tralee is chosen from 'Roses' of Kerry descent from all over the world. A four

Trughenachme Barony, after Petty

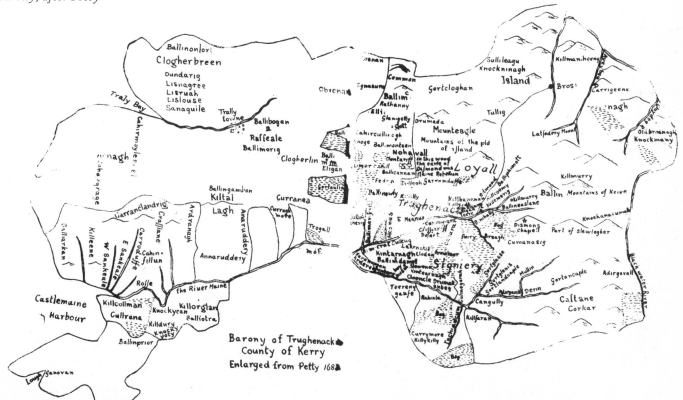

Barony of Trughenack
County of Kerry
Enlarged from Petty 1681

224 day race meeting, amongst other festivities, is held at this time. There is also a good golf course.

The town grew up around the major geraldine castle from the 13th century. The castle was destroyed by the Desmonds against Ormond's advance in 1580. In 1587 it, together with a seignory of 6,000 confiscated acres of Desmond lands, was granted to Sir Edward Denny, knighted for bravery at the massacre of Smerwick. The Dennys were to be the leading family here for over two centuries. The town became a borough in 1613, returning two members to the Irish parliament in the Denny interest until 1800, and then one until 1840 when it lost its borough status, but with a limited form of local government until it became an urban district in 1878. The Dennys rebuilt the castle in the 1620s. It was besieged by the Irish in 1641-2 under Piaras Ferriter. According to the Ordnance Survey Letters it must have stood on the west side of Denny street. From this, upper and lower Castle Streets obtained their name.

The town was abandoned by the jacobites in 1689 and destroyed when they later retreated before the williamite forces. It was then rebuilt with something of georgian grace, helped by the very red local sandstone. There is a fine classical courthouse built in the 1830s of local limestone and designed by Sir Richard Morrison, (d. 1849) a pupil of Gandon's. An attractive building is the Thomas Ashe Memorial Hall, the headquarters of the Kerry county council, built when the old county hall was burned down in 1920 when, for eleven days from end October, the town was in siege by the British army seeking to have two kidnapped policemen released.

There are two good catholic churches — St John's, spoiled by a pretentious baldacchino, and the Dominican church. St. John's has two interesting medieval sculptures. Over the south door of the baptistery is a wedge shaped slab with effigies of two children in swaddling clothes, or chrisoms, one of only two in Ireland, dating from the 13th or early 14th century. Built into the north wall of the nun's chapel is a fine carving of the Assumption, dating from the 15th century. The Dominican church was built in 1871, designed

by the firm of Ashlin and Pugin. In the sacristy is some fine work by Michael Healy — five painted pieces and some glass panels. In the grounds, built into a rockery, are a few remnants of the original 13th century Dominican priory, now otherwise wholly disappeared. These are the sculptured figures of a knight (or, possibly, a gallow-glass) a dragon or basilisk, and, probably, a virgin and child. This priory was founded in 1243 by the founder of the Kerry geraldines, John of Callan who with his son was buried in the priory in 1261. Many of the earls of Desmond were buried in the priory — one was a lay brother there. The priory was suppressed in 1580 in the Desmond wars. However, the friars were back in 1622. In 1633 there were 12 Dominicans in Kerry, presumably based on Tralee: they ran a school there at that time. The priory was finally suppressed in 1652 when the cromwellians arrived and destroyed it and the community fled to Castlemaine. There, according to the story, surprised at a mass rock in Killaclohane wood, the prior, Thaddeus Moriarty, was arrested, lodged in Ross castle and hanged in Killarney on 15 October, 1653, with his brother, Piaras Ferriter, and two others. The best known of the Dominicans of this time was Dominick O Daly, born near Tralee of the famous bardic family. He wrote a history of the Desmond geraldines, founded a priory and a convent for Dominican nuns in Lisbon, was ambassador of the king of newly independent Portugal and died bishop-elect of Coimbra in 1662.

The Dominicans were back in Kerry after the Restoration. In 1691 Fr G. FitzGibbon was put to death in Listowel. In 1702 Fr Dominic Mac Egan was arrested on entering the country — the informer was paid £11 0 1½d — and lodged in Newgate jail in Dublin. Notwithstanding this he was elected prior of Tralee in 1703. He died, still in jail, in 1713. During this period Fr Arthur Mc Geoghegan was hanged in London. The community seems to have been restored about 1740, but at Knockanure, Moyvane. In 1756 there were two fathers in Tralee, aged 54 and 50. Later, the community dispersed, at the bishop's request, to do parochial work, and the last of them, Fr Shine, died as parish priest of Brosna in 1827. In 1861 Bishop Moriarty asked the

Dominicans to set up a new priory of Holy Cross, and in 1871 the present church was opened.

Tralee was twice the seat of the bishop of Kerry: from 1720 when the catholic see was restored until the 1780s when Lord Kenmare coaxed the fifth 18th century bishop, Francis Moylan to Killarney; and between 1111, from the synod of Rathbreasail, to 1152, at the synod of Kells, when Ratass lost its primacy to Ardfert.

Ratass (II. 86. 115. c) is the most interesting antiquity in Tralee. It is a mile from the centre of the town, on the main road to Castleisland and Killarney, in a cemetery to the left.

What remains now is a little church, much altered with the years, now ruined and cruelly and disgustingly neglected. It may have been linked with the settlement at Rattoo in the north of the county (from *theas,* south, and *tuaidh,* north). At the synod of Rathbreasail it was called Rath Mhaighe Deiscirt, that is, of the southern plain. The nave may comprise part of a church first erected in stone in the 7th or 8th century; this may possibly be deduced from the large stones incorporated in the walls. Curiously, the church is built mainly of sandstone, even though this is limestone country. There is a fine trabeate west door with a huge stone for lintel. Observe the antae projecting at each side of this gable recalling (as at Kilmalkedar) the construction of wooden churches. A chancel was added in romanesque times; the late romanesque east window has, unusually, internal moulding. The settlement of which this church was no doubt the heart suffered much in the disorders of the 12th century. It was burned in 1136 by the O Briens; cracks may be seen in the stones that could have been caused by fire. It is possible that it never fully recovered from this disaster and this may be one reason why it lost to Ardfert its place as the seat of the bishopric. It continued as a parish church and lost all claims to eminence when the geraldines established the Dominicans in Tralee in 1243 and chose that priory as their burying place. Nonetheless it survives even as a ruin when all traces of the Desmonds and

Windmill at Blennerville, Tralee

225

their foundation have disappeared from Tralee. It was much restored around 1700.

(II) BLENNERVILLE — ANNAGH

Take the Dingle road. *Blennerville,* (II. 82. 113. b) is just outside Tralee. It is a decayed village named after the Blennerhassets, but previously called Tramore. It was at one time the port of Tralee. Then, in the 1830s, the now abandoned and silted canal was built to bring ships of up to 300 tons from Blennerville to Tralee to facilitate the export of grain and the import of coal and timber. After one crosses the bridge over the canal take the boithrin right parallel to the canal towards a ruined windmill. This is one of the few windmills in Ireland. This brings one out to a view of the sand and mudflats of Blennerville which reach out into Tralee bay. This is one of the finest bird-watching centres in Ireland. To be seen here are many kinds of tern, which breed in the bay, as well as many varieties of waders, duck, geese and swans.

Just a mile along the Dingle road is (signposted) *Annagh church* (II. 81. 113. c). One can open the gates on the boithrin on the right and drive in to the church if one wishes. The church is one of St Brendan's many disputed birthplaces around the bay — Fenit has the strongest claim. To be seen now are the rather pleasing ruins of one of the parish churches built in the 12th-13th centuries when the parochial system was being finally established in Ireland. There is an unusual carving of a horseman on a small stone in the church wall. The carving may date from the first half of the 14th century.

There is a splendid beach just below the main road as one leaves Annagh. Exactly four and a half miles from Annagh, just over the border of Corkaguiney, at *Derrymore* (II. 75. 112. c), recalling the great oakwoods that covered this place in the 16th century, there is a roadway leading the half-mile from the main road to this beach. Here there is a fine stretch of sand and sandhills, and very good views.

Total driving distance: 14 miles. Allow about two and a half hours.

(III) TRALEE — CASTLEMAINE — MILLTOWN — KILLORGLIN — CROMANE

Take the road due south of Tralee over the mountains towards Castlemaine to *Glanaskagheen,* Scotia's Glen (II. 84. 110. b). Near the summit there are fine views north over Tralee. Just below the last house on the right near the head of the glen and across the stream is a deeper part of the glen. Here is a huge slab carved with innumerable names. It is said to mark the grave of Queen Scotia. She was the widow of Milesius and daughter of the Pharaoh. There are two accounts of her death. One is that she was killed in the great battle of Sliabh Mis nearby between the Tuatha De Danaan and the invading Milesians, fought in the year 1695 BC. The other is that she used jump across this glen until one day, being pregnant, she fell and was killed.

Above the glen the road becomes pretty rough, but passable. As one begins to descend on the far side one has splendid views to the south. After a steep fall turn right at the cross roads along a narrow road for about two and three-quarter miles and turn sharp left at *Boolteens* (II. 81. 105. c). Follow this road for one and one-quarter miles. Then, on the right, there is a national monuments sign for the *Ardcanaght* stones (II. 82. 103. b).

They require a walk of a half-mile along a boithrin, through a farmyard and, bearing left, over a stile into a field. There are fragments of ogam stones that may not be genuine. Of greater interest is another stone in the group covered with cup markings and other scribings.

Return to the car and drive on to *Castlemaine* (pop. 1966: 170) (II. 84. 104. d).

226

In this town where, according to the song, Jack Duggan, the Wild Colonial Boy, was born, there are two pubs facing each other, one labelled Day, the other Knightly. It is worth while pausing on the new bridge over the river Maine. To the right as one looks towards the sea were until recently the traces of the old castle — Castell Magne — that spanned the river and, many times, the whole world between the anglo-normans of North Kerry and the gaels of South Kerry. John and Maurice Fitz Gerald, the main geraldine invaders of Kerry, built this castle on a rock in the centre of the river in 1215 as part of a line to defend the marches between their newly acquired territory and that of Mac Carthy. It remained a Desmond castle — one of the strong places of Munster — until the revolt of James Fitz Maurice. In 1571 Perrott besieged it but failed to take it. In the following year he besieged it again and took it after 12 weeks. At the end of 1573 the earl of Desmond, now out of jail, took back his ancient castle, but was persuaded to give it up within a year. It remained a royal stronghold until the O Neill wars when it was besieged, October, 1598 by the Sugan earl of Desmond, but held out for 13 months. A year later it was yielded up to the Queen's earl of Desmond, and again became a royal fortress. In 1641, after a short siege, it fell to one of the Mac Carthys, and in 1649 it surrendered to Inchiquin. Then, like castles generally, it was 'slighted' by Ludlow's cromwellians in 1652 and came to an end after over 400 years. Queen Elizabeth had appointed a constable of her castle and the post continued, as a sinecure, up to 1832 when its last holder died.

Castlemaine gave the title of earl to Roger Palmer, husband of Charles II's mistress, the Duchess of Cleveland. James II commissioned him to reconcile England with the Holy See which he did with such lack of success that the Pope sent him packing.

The Commissioners for Woods took over the place when the last constable died. In 1839 Castlemaine was a village of 31 'thatched Cabbins of the poorest description and one small slate house'. Three of the houses were occupied by publicans, two by tradesmen, and the rest by labourers. The quay was built in 1839 by the Commissioners. They assisted a number of families from here to emigrate to America in 1848, 1849 and 1851. The population in 1966 was 170.

That the line of the Maine was but a temporary limit to Desmond power is shown by the fact that this barony that they especially ruled now runs south of Killorglin to Cromane so that they could command the two harbours on this side of Dingle Bay — Castlemaine at the mouth of the Maine and Killorglin at the mouth of the Laune.

Over the bridge and turn right for *Milltown* (II. 83. 101), a very decayed place with a 1971 population of 260. On the right, in the town, is the ruined 'big House' Kilcolman 'Abbey', former seat of the Godfreys. The first of them was a cromwellian, Major John Godfrey, who acquired the lands of Killagha priory. It was a Sir John Godfrey of the 19th century who, taxed with his habit of rising from bed only at lunch-time, replied: 'The fact is, I sleep very slow'. In Milltown occurred in 1920 a decisive sign of the crumbling morale of the Royal Irish Constabulary when, under intense pressure by republicans, a number of constables 'resigned'.

Turn left onto the Killarney road. Almost immediately (just below the protestant church) turn left. Follow this narrow road for 1.2 miles until one comes to a sharp right bend with an old whitewashed house on the corner. Go left through the barred gate here and over the wooden gate just beyond into *Killaclohane wood* (II. 85. 102. d). Follow the principal forestry road for seven or eight minutes until one comes to a forestry workers' hut on the right. Just beyond this, on the left, is a narrow track down into the wood. After about a minute one comes on a rock with an arrow pointing to a track on the right. Follow this for a short period until one comes to a great rock, a mass rock. Here Thaddeus Moriarty, prior of the Dominican house in Tralee, was arrested by cromwellian soldiers and carried off to Killarney to be hanged on 15th October, 1653. He and some of the community had taken refuge in this wood to carry on their ministry for a while.

Return to Milltown and take the Killorglin road (signposted) for a half mile. At the Killagha signpost turn right for a mile to where the road bends sharply to the left. Go through the gateway facing one. This brings one to the fine, transitional style ruins of *Killagha Priory* (II. 82. 102. d), founded for the canons regular of St Augustine in 1215-16 by the anglo-norman justiciar, Geoffrey de Marisco, Strongbow's nephew. Geoffrey provided that no Irishman should be a member of this community. It may have been founded on the ancient site of the Irish monastery of *Kilcolman* (II. 83. 101) which had probably become, by then, extinct. Certainly the Godfrey house between Milltown and Killagha is called Kilcolman Abbey.

Killagha was the richest foundation in Kerry and one of the richer ones in Ireland. It was one of 223 Augustinian houses for men in Ireland and of five in Kerry, all of these canons. Nine Augustinian priors were lords of parliament, including the prior of Killagha. This was the most important in Kerry and in the papal taxation of 1302 ranked third (after the bishop and a church called Ecclesia Nova) with an income of £4. The priory was called, somewhat surprisingly, De Bello Loco, of the beautiful place. The canons from the beginning established a leper house somewhat to the west of the priory, but where has not been determined.

The monastery is basically of the transitional style but substantial rebuilding, as elsewhere, took place in 1445. The fine east window and some ogee windows and doors date from this time. See them from the outside. Only the church and a few indications of the priory now remain.

At the dissolution the priory was found to have most extensive possessions — considerable lands in the area, and many rectories — those of Killagha, Dingle, Killorglin, and Kilmakilloge and half of twelve others, including most of those in the Iveragh peninsula. The rectory of Dingle led the priory into severe trouble in 1391. Presumably because they had acquired the rectory at an earlier time the community refused to admit the pope's nominee, John O Mochlehayn, to be priest there and the prior, Thomas Scarleg,

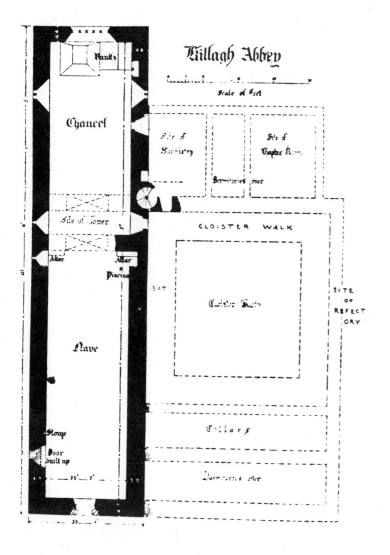

Killagha Priory:
Ground plan

Notwithstanding this, in 1411 Alan Olongsygh of the Limerick diocese, 'a student of canon and civil law at Oxford' is dispensed to be made prior. In 1476 the prior, John Fitz Gerald, is deprived, to be succeeded by Florence Mac Carthy, himself to be deprived eight years later. It is clear the Killagha was suffering from a decline similar to that afflicting the augustinian monasteries in Kerry.

The last prior in Elizabethan times was an O Moriarty, who laicised. It would seem that the Augustinians returned in the 17th century. Two first cousins, Maurice O Connell and James O Mahony, (who may have been Kerrymen — they were in the county in the 1630s), both prominent Augustinian *friars*, played an active part in getting a papal decision in 1643 that the Augustinian friars take over the houses and properties of the Augustinian canons. The friars had not hitherto had a house in Kerry, but as a result of this took over Killagha, the richest of the canons' Kerry houses. They came to an end after 1653.

Notwithstanding the exemption of ecclesiastical property from secular taxation Mac Carthy Mor enjoyed an income of £4 a year from Killagha. Grants of Killagha and of its extensive possessions — from Dingle to Tuosist — were made in 1576 and 1583, but the effective grant seems to date from 1588 to Captain Thomas Spring. The Springs forfeited after the cromwelliam wars and Killagha came into the possession of the Godfreys.

Where the boithrin to Killagha joins the roadway there is another boithrin left. This leads after a short distance to, on the right, a ruined parish church, a pleasant enough example of the type of church being built in the late romanesque period.

Back to the car. Where the road rejoins the Killorglin road there is, facing one, a gateway. Walk up to an old farmhouse and bear sharp right up the hill and parallel to the road. Some little distance up are, right, the ruins of a house in a three-ringed fort, with fine views of the valley of the Maine. This is *Fort Agnes* (II. 82. 101. c). There is a souterrain under

and the community were excommunicated, suspended and placed under interdict. However, in the same year the bishop of Limerick was authorised to lift these sentences.

The trouble did not end there for the prior, Thomas Scarleg, was in 1397 deprived of his post for his 'faults and demerits' and William Macyldroma was appointed from Rome. William seems to have enjoyed real influence for, in the following year, the vicarages of

Kilcrohane, Kilmaniheen, Dingle and Killorglin are appropriated to Killagha and three years later the vicarage of Cahir. There seems to have been a limit to William's skill as a diplomat. His name suggests him to have been an Irishman of old stock; but when he and the canons in 1403 petitioned Rome for the lifting of the founder's rule against the profession of Irishmen they received a papal rebuke and an instruction that 'they shall not admit any one contrary to the said ordinance'.

228

the inner ring. Beneath the fort is a deep hole, Poll na Ratha, from which it is said were quarried the stones for Killagha.

Return to the road and take the next turn right. At the second cross roads turn right out to the mouth of the Maine. Here, early in the 13th century, the geraldines built the advanced castle of Callanafersey to command the mouth of the river that became the effective boundary for many centuries between their world and the old gaelic one. Then back along the straight road until one turns right on the main road to *Killorglin*. (pop. 1971: 1150) (II. 78. 97). Here one crosses the Laune so entering the odd salient of Trughanacmy stretching along the coast to Cromane.

Over the Laune turn right immediately and up the hill past the sandstone catholic church. There is from here a fine prospect of the river, the swans and the Reeks behind. Go straight on with the church on one's left and go for two miles to *Ballykissane pier* (II. 78. 99. b). On Good Friday, 1916, two cars were speeding to Cahersiveen to raid a radio school of its transmitting equipment so as to set up near Tralee a radio contact with the arms ship *Aud* (which had no radio). One of the cars took the wrong turn in Killorglin and shot over the pier into the water, and three (including the radio operator from England) of the four occupants were drowned. They were the first casualties of the 1916 rising.

There is a monument to them at the pier.

Return to Killorglin and turn right at the catholic church and then, almost immediately, turn left. Between the little protestant church and the National Bank is a wicket gate that leads into the garden at the back of the bank. At the end of the garden is all that remains of the Castle.

Killorglin is south of the river Laune, itself a few miles south of the Maine, and thus in the Mac Carthy sphere of influence, who had ousted the Moriartys. However, there was an anglo-norman castle on this site, from 1215, built by the notorious Geoffrey de Marisco, that came into geraldine hands about the middle of the 13th century. It came to be

held by the Knights Hospitallers, whose general function was a policing one; but when they ceased to hold it is not clear. In any event it seems to have reverted to the Desmonds and was confiscated when they fell. This may well have been a convenient neutral area through which trade could flow. The castle is now called Castle Conway: from the planter, Jenkin Conway, who acquired it after the Desmond confiscation. In the 18th century the Blennerhasset family (who descended from Conway) had famous gardens going down to the river. It was sold in 1796 to Thomas Mullins, later 1st Lord Ventry. The castle was occupied up to 1830. The last tenant, according to Windele, was the parish priest.

The most notable feature of the town is the three day Puck Fair, held between 10th and 12th August, now being extended into a week-long tourist festival. This is basically a fair in which horses and cattle are sold, but it is the great entertainment of the whole countryside and an occasion for heroic, non-stop drinking. This fair, its dates altered by the calendar reform of the 18th century, was originally held around 1st August, and thus can be associated with the cult of the celtic god Lug. Its original site may have been Kilgobnet nearby.

On the evening of Gathering Day a wild puck (male) goat is crowned king of the festival and is hoisted onto a platform high above the ground in the square, where he presides over the festivities until Scattering Day, 12th. The formal explanation is that a herd of wild goats warned the townspeople of the approach of cromwellian soldiers and saved their lives (or stock); but one would deduce that the goat represents the survival of a cult even more primeval than that of Lug. Miss Mac Neill, in her remarkable book *The Festival of Lughnasa* (pp 289-300) discusses the issues at length. She tentatively concludes that a blatantly pagan symbol would not have survived christian opposition; but this would be more convincing if there were not other pagan survivals. However, she suggests that the goat may be of anglo-norman origin. It seems to have been a practice of theirs to hoist above a festival an emblem (sometimes an animal) of amnesty and enjoyment. Some such emblem

would be particularly important during its principal fair in a town along the marches as here, which also enjoyed a significant role as a centre of trade on a navigable river. At least in the eighteenth century, we learn from Arthur Young, goats played the part in mountain grazing that sheep do now. Sam Hussey says that the goat was formerly attached to the flagstaff of the castle.

Go down through the town and take the road east and south of the river towards Caragh lake. After a mile the road forks. Go through the gateway here on the left and follow the boithrin along the edge of the river back towards the town. About halfway back is a tin hut and, a little to the left of it over a wet way, is the recumbent rock, with a syrian (three crosspiece) cross carved on it, a degenerate chi-rho, and other embellishments, of *Farrantooreen* (II. 79. 97. c). This is one of very few of these crosses in Ireland and is another example of coptic influence on the early Irish church.

Then take the main road towards Glenbeigh and after about a mile branch right for *Cromane*, (pop. 1966: 316) (II. 70. 98. d) There is a pleasant new church. Continue on by a small beach until one comes out at *Cromane Point* (II. 70. 101. d). Here one is behind the Rossbeigh and Inch sand spits to the west and one gets fine views of the Dingle mountains across the water. A little beyond the beach at Cromane is a state mussel purification farm and the big, black boats with their grids are used for mussel fishing hereabouts. Castlemaine harbour and its mudflats that lie here before one are a main centre in Kerry for bird life. The Point extends for about half a mile beyond where the road ends. This is a pleasant walk and gives an extensive view of Castlemaine harbour and its bird flocks.

Because of the peculiar nature of the Trughanacmy salient one must go back the way one has come as far as Castlemaine. Here there is a choice of taking the rather pleasant main road to Tralee, or of branching right in the town above the valley of the Maine. After three miles one turns left at the cross roads onto the fabulously straight 18th century road from Killarney to Tralee. Follow this road for another three miles and then, at the cross roads, turn right. A mile later turn left. One is now going through the rich farming land of Kerry, marked by the big farmhouses. After a mile up this road one comes, left, to *Ballyseedy House,* (II. 88. 113. b) now a hotel. John Blennerhasset, who was for long father of the Irish House of Commons, built this house in 1760. There were later, early 19th century additions. It is one of the very few examples in Kerry of an extant 18th century house; but it is a puzzling example. Close by, according to Lewis, are some fine limestone caves.

From the house turn left and this brings one out onto the main Killarney-Tralee road. Here there is a very fine war memorial done in recent years by the Breton sculptor Yann Renard-Goulet, who also did the memorial at the Custom House, Dublin. It commemorates those Kerrymen who died in the war of independence and the subsequent civil war. It is erected on the place, *Ballyseedy Cross* (II. 89. 113. a), where as a reprisal in the civil war nine men were tied to a landmine, eight of them being blown to pieces. But it transcends old bitternesses.

Turn right towards Killarney and then, almost immediately, left up the hill. After a mile, at the T junction, turn right. This brings one along by *Chute Hall* (II. 89. 116. c) on the left , now in ruins, but splendidly sited under its tree-covered hill. In the 19th century enthusiasm for antiquities many ogam stones were collected from the Dingle peninsula and erected here. They are (I think) all now in museums. The Chutes were one of the principal families in Kerry during the 18th and 19th centuries. All along this rich limestone country beneath one these families — Blennerhassets, Chutes, Days, Dennys and the rest — settled in post-Desmond and post-cromwellian times, as the Desmonds did before them in the 13th century. Also like the Desmonds they survive now only in the scattered relics of surnames and the ruins of their once great estates.

One is here on the edge of the old parish of O Brennan, commemorating the tribal name of earlier, also scattered, inhabitants of this place.

Memorial at Ballyseedy, Tralee

Then, back to Tralee. Total driving distance: 56 miles. Allow 6-7 hours.

(IV) TRALEE – GLOUNAGEENTHA – CASTLEISLAND – BROSNA – CORDAL

Take the main road towards Castleisland. Two miles after the fork for Killarney take the fourth turn left after that fork (thus turning one's back on the sign that says 'Edenburn'). At the end of this road, is the church in *Ballymacelligott* (II. 94. 114. c), named after the Mc Elligott family. O Donovan quotes an old source saying that they were originally Mac Leods of Skye who came to Kerry with Geoffrey de Marisco. They played some part in the cromwellian and williamite wars, and in the 18th century a number of them served with distiction in the Austrian army.

After the church turn sharply left and, shortly afterwards, ignoring a boithrin, take the first turn right for the hills, from which a fine view can be had. This brings one through *Glounageentha* (II. 95. 115. d). Stop at the first roadway that drops into the glen. This is an historic spot.

When, by the summer of 1583, the Desmond rebellion was broken, Gerald, the 16th earl, lived for some months a hunted life in these hills. Eventually, some of the earl's few remaining supporters raided the cattle of an O Moriarty from the Maharees. In the process they ill-treated O Moriarty's sister by stripping her naked in the fields. One of the leaders of the earl's raiding party was Shane

230 Daly (called Cornelius by his nephew, the historian Dominic O Daly). O Moriarty went to the garrison at Castlemaine and was given four soldiers to supplement his own 18 kerne. On the morning of Martinmas, 1583, before the cattle raiders had arrived with their loot, O Moriarty surprised the earl on his own in a hut farther up the glen. The earl in being captured was wounded so severely that he could not walk. One of the O Moriartys carried him along the glen but was unable to bring him up the side of the glen, and none of the others would do so. O Moriarty, fearing that the earl's followers would arrive, and notwithstanding that the reward for him alive was twice that for him dead, ordered one of the soldiers, O Kelly, to strike off his head — he got a pension of £20 a year for this. Throwing the body down they fled with the head. The earl's body was temporarily buried in this spot. A ledge about 120 feet down and three feet above the level of the present roadway, on the left hand side as one descends, is pointed out as Desmond's grave. After eight weeks he was disinterred and re-buried at *Kilnanama,* (II. 107. 108. a) at Cordal, east of Castleisland. O Kelly, notwithstanding his pension, was long after hanged at Tyburn for highway robbery. In the O Neill wars O Moriarty was hanged at his own door by Lord Kerry. Glounageentha means the glen of the mourning, and the wind wailing through it is said to mourn the last palatine earl of Desmond.

Beyond the head of the glen turn right and, at the next junction bear right. This brings one to *Castleisland* (pop. 1971:   1929) (II. 100. 110) for long the centre of Desmond power in Kerry. The castle was originally built in 1220 by Geoffrey de Marisco who was so attached to Ireland that, dying in France, he directed that he be buried in Co. Limerick. Of the castle there remain now only a few blocks of masonry and a gaunt tower. This was the famous Castell of the Island — an island formed by turning the waters of the Maine into a moat around the castle. The castle was inherited by Geoffrey's daughter Eleanor, and came into geraldine hands. It was deemed impregnable but the royal forces took it in a fortnight in 1345 in the time of the unruly first earl of Desmond. Its seneschal, Sir John Coterel and two other

leading defenders were hanged, drawn and quartered before the castle. In the Desmond wars Desmond and his countess narrowly escaped being captured in the castle, 'a huge, monstrous castle of many rooms, but very filthy and full of cowdung'. It was forfeited when the last earl palatine fell and came, with 12,000 acres, as part of the seignory of Castleisland into the hands of Sir William Herbert. It was destroyed by the Irish in 1600, but was later restored, at least in part. In 1661 Thomas Herbert was living in it. It is to be seen as one leaves the town by the Killarney road, just behind Dwane's garage on the left. Here amid the back-gardens and the children playing is what is left of the power of those ungovernable Desmonds. Castleisland was the centre of considerable disorder during the Land War and of much bitterness during the Civil War. During the Parnell split the travelling trouper, Johnny Patterson, author of *The Garden where the Praties Grow* and other popular songs, pitched his tent here and sang a song urging peace between Parnellite and anti-Parnellite. This provoked a riot in which Patterson was so badly injured that he died.

There is not much of interest in the town. Off the main street, left as one heads for Killarney, is a fine gothic style church designed by Ashlin and Pugin. On the opposite side of the main street are the ruins of the old parish church with an interesting 12th (?) century head, human or sphinx, on the south wall of the roofless part of the church.

Near here are red marble quarries that supplied the marble for the Honan chapel in University College, Cork. About a mile due east of the town is *Ballymacadam* (II. 102. 111. d) where lived Robert Madgett who originated the famous and ferocious breed of Kerry Blue terriers.

From Castleisland take the main road for Abbeyfeale. Four and a half miles up this road observe the straight road on the right, the now largely superseded 18th century road for Abbeyfeale. Four miles further on, at Headley's Bridge, it is worth turning left at the signpost and then right for the pleasantly sited hilltop village of *Knocknagoshel* (II. 107. 121. a). It was near here that an

atrocity in the civil war unleashed the terrible reprisals at Ballyseedy, Countess Bridge and Cahersiveen. But Knocknagoshel is best to be remembered for its splendid banner displayed to Parnell just before his death in 1891: 'Arise Knocknagoshel and take your place amongst the nations of the earth'. Coming down from the village, turn left for the main road. After three miles one comes to the river Feale and the Limerick border. Just short of these, almost opposite the pub on one's left, is the site of the now vanished church of *Kilmaniheen* (II. 110. 123. a), a vicarage of Killagha priory. Then, take the road right for three miles along the valley of the Feale. Then turn sharp right for *Brosna* (II. 114. 119. b).

This is a pleasant little town (pop. 1971: 250) perched on the side of a hill. At the bottom of this hill take the unmarked road: it is the continuation of the approach road to Brosna. Continue along this road, deviating neither to right nor left. It follows an attractive route over the shoulder of *Mount Eagle* (II. 110. 111. a) and through some pleasant forestry plantations. After eight miles it joins a better road. Bear left here. Just less than a mile further on, in a field on the right, is an interesting ruin, *Kilmurry Castle* (II. 105. 110. a), a 16th century tower house to which was added a now much ruined fortified house of the early part of the 17th century. This is one of only two 17th century fortified houses I know of in Kerry — the other was attached to Ross Castle in Killarney. Close beside Kilmurry Castle is an attractive early victorian house, Kilmurry House.

Just beyond here, at the cross roads, turn left and, for a mile bear right, leaving the old church and graveyard of *Kilmurry* (II. 105. 110. c) on one's left. At the main road from Castleisland turn left through the hamlet of *Cordal* (II. 106. 109. c). About a half mile further on there is a turn left between two houses. Leave the car here (because of turning difficulties) and walk along this road left for a quarter mile. By the road, left, is a burial ground with some vestiges of a church. This is *Kilnanama* (II. 107. 108. a), where the 16th earl of Desmond is buried, brought here, headless, from his temporary grave in

Glounageentha. From here one can look out over the rich plain his marauding ancestor overran in the 13th century, and a good part of the palatine lands in which he and his forbears held virtually undisputed sway for three and a half centuries.

Return to the car and, at the cross roads at Cordal turn left for *Scartaglin* (II. 104. 105. d). Follow this road along the edge of the uplands for three miles and turn left at the T junction. After two miles one comes upon this rather attractive village (pop. 1966: 156), tucked (like Brosna) in off ·the road. Continue on the road over the Brown Flesk river and turn right along the valley of this river, a pleasant run. After five miles from Scartaglin turn right over the river and after a mile on this road left for *Currans* (II. 95. 106. a). After a further mile and a half, at the T junction, turn left. This is *Crag* (II. 95. 106. b). Just beyond the turn there is, left, a farmhouse. Walk right across the front of this farmhouse and, in a field on one's left, is a remarkably large ogam stone. A couple of fields due west of this is another great irregular stone marked in ogam 'LEGUTTI VELITAS', (the stone of) Leguttos the Poet. It is not known who Leguttos was or what his works, but in the fourth or fifth century AD, Macalister argues, his works must have been considered to be of great importance. If Macalister is to be accepted, and some do not, this is the oldest and greatest memorial to a poet in northern Europe.

Follow the road through Currans and turn right onto the main Killarney-Tralee road. One and a half miles later turn off right and cross the railway line at *Gortatlea junction* (II. 94. 110. c). It was here that in April, 1918, the first attack on a police barracks was made, nine months before the anglo-Irish war began.

Follow this road until one reaches after two miles a T junction. Turn left along this road for Tralee. However, if one turns to the *right* along this road for a mile to just beyond the next cross roads at *Woodville* (II. 96. 112. c) there are to be found no less than six ringforts reasonably close together, four on the right hand side and two on the left. Some

of these have souterrains and are linked to a cave.

Turn back along this road by *Edenburn hospital* (II. 94. 112. a), an ugly house where Sam Hussey once lived. A mile further on is *Arabella* (II. 91. 113. d), a house named after the brilliant Lady Arabella Denny.

Total driving distance: 65 miles. Allow, apart from ringforts, four hours.

(V) TRALEE — FENIT — BARROW

From Tralee take the Fenit road through the old watering place of *Spa* (II. 79. 116. c) (pop. 1966: 165) to *Fenit* (II. 73. 116. b) (pop. 1971: 360), the harbour of Tralee. From the harbour wall there is a good view of Tralee Bay and of how a wide circle of limestone has been eaten by the sea. It is generally accepted that St Brendan the Navigator was born here in 484 AD; but amongst other claimants is Annagh just across the bay. This is the country of the Alltraige from whom St Brendan came, later to be annexed by the Ciarraige. Stretching west is the fine sweep of the Dingle peninsula with Mount Brandon, Ireland's second highest mountain, at the western end. From there St Brendan is reputed to have sailed for America.

It was at Fenit that the German guns were to have been landed at Easter, 1916 and the *Aud* came nosing in here on the night of Holy Thursday — Good Friday looking for the signal lights that did not shine. Fenit is an important sea angling centre. There are oyster beds. It is the one developed sailing centre in Kerry.

The road north from Fenit round *Barrow Harbour* (II. 73-75. 117-8) gives a pleasant run especially when the tide is in. At the top of the hill on this road, right, at *Church Hill* (II. 75. 117. b), just two miles from Fenit, is the parish church of Ballynahaglish, restored in the early 17th century with a belfry added in 1798, but now in ruins. Go down the hill and, after the bridge, take the road left through two gates. At the end of this is a bumpy grass track to *Barrow Point* (Ceann Bearra) (II. 73. 119. d), the most westerly of

the diocese as defined at the synod of Rathbreasail in 1111 AD. The round castle of Barrow at this place is similar to that at Aghadoe: there are these two in Kerry and only a few in the whole of Ireland. It was built, probably in the 13th century either by Fitz Maurices or the de Clahull family. Note the murdering hole inside the entrance. The square castle opposite on Fenit island was a Fitz Maurice one.

Back to the tarred road. At the T junction turn left and then, after a short distance, turn left up a hill to a farmyard. Through a field, bearing left, one finds the remains of the great *rath of Barrow,* one of the reputed residences of the King of Cashel, Aenach na mBearrain (II. 75. 119. a). It had three rings and two (still deep) fosses. Close by, it is said, is an ancient burial ground where the aenach or assembly was held; but I could not see it. This is the land that was given to Maen of the mighty deeds, the first barber of the milesian invaders. He may have used one of the large, two-bladed instruments believed to be razors and now to be seen in the National Museum, Dublin.

Go back to the bridge and turn right for Tralee. A striking feature of this area is its lightsomeness.

Total driving distance: 20 miles. Allow two hours.

CORKAGUINEY

This barony consists of the Dingle peninsula east of a line drawn south to Glanbrack mountain, over Bartregaum and Caherconree south to Aughils.

The peninsula as a whole is very beautiful and very varied. The barony of Corkaguiney is geologically perhaps the most interesting in Kerry and it is extraordinarily rich in archaeological remains. This is particularly true of the area west of Dingle. There are rich concentrations of remains in the Ventry, Fahan-Glenfahan, Smerwick, Ballyheabought, Gallerus-Kilamlkedar, and Ballynavenooragh areas. There are also less crowded sites of some interest in other parts of the peninsula.

232 In what follows it is possible to mention only some of the sites of special interest. This peninsula, unlike others, has many magnificent beaches.

The peninsula is about 40 miles long and a circuit of it gives a run of some 100 miles. If this is to be done in one day choose a brilliant one. On such a day the peninsula gives the best return of all the Kerry peninsulas; but if the day is dull, postpone the run: of all the peninsulas this is the most weather-moody. If one takes Dingle as base, as is recommended here, the run should be west by Slea Head to Ballyferriter and back to Dingle; then over the Connor Pass to Camp and over the rough road to Aughils; then back by Inch to Dingle.

To see the peninsula in some detail one should give it a few days. For that purpose Dingle is quite the most convenient centre and it is an attractive place in itself. Those who wish to be in an Irish speaking area will stay on the western seabord. The accommodation west of Dingle is as a rule fairly (often very) simple.

The barony name comes of course from the Corcu Duibne, the people who, according to their legend, were the descendants of Corc and (the goddess) Duben, or Dovvinias, his daughter or sister. Their territory comprised the southern side of the peninsula and the northern and much of the western sides of the Iveragh peninsula. They seem to have been a branch of the Earna, or Erainn, themselves a branch of the Fir Bolg, or Belgae, who came to Ireland in the period 500 to 300 BC. They were pre-goidelic, but part of their territory, now mainly that west of Ventry, is one of the few remaining gaelic speaking areas. They were, in early historical times, subject, and paid tribute, to the Kings of Cashel.

It is amongst the Corcu Duibne that, it seems, writing first arose in Ireland. This was the clumsy ogam script based on the roman alphabet that was invented about 300 AD. This peninsula is a major area for ogam stones.

An important tribe of the Corcu Duibne, in later times at least, seems to have been the Aes Iorruis, the people of the peninsula. Around 1200, perhaps earlier, they peopled both sides of Dingle bay, and the land was divided into Aes Iorruis Tuaiscirt (northern) and Aes Iorruis Deiscirt (southern). They seem to have been the people who established the town of *Fahan* (III. 34. 98. d), which was flourishing in early christian times. They received a violent raid from the fierce Ceallachan, king of Cashel around 940 AD.

The other main tribe of the peninsula was the Ui Fearba, who peopled the northern part, between Brandon and Annagh. In medieval times it supported the deanery of Offerba.

There was another ancient division of the barony, Letteragh, from leath trioca (chead) the half barony. This seems to have been the northern part of the barony between the Maharees and Mount Brandon.

Corkaguinie Barony, after Petty

There was a norse kingdom of Limerick from 922 AD which seems to have had a settlement at *Smerwick* (III. 35-39. 105-109), from the name 'smoer' (butter) and 'vik' (harbour). *Blaskets* (or Blasquets) (III. 18-29. 91-102) also seems to be a name of norse origin.

The Corcu Duibne lost their power in the Iveragh peninsula from the incursion in the 11th and 12th centuries of the Mac Carthy and O Connell families, and in the Dingle peninsula from about 1200 from the incursion of the anglo-normans. The peninsula became part of the territory of the earls of Desmond and thus was within the medieval county of (North) Kerry. The Fitz Geralds were the principal settlers here, and a cadet branch of the family of Desmond, the Knights of Kerry, had several castles in and around Dingle. There remain, in surnames, traces of the other settlers of that time — Ashe, Prendeville, Bowler, Landers, etc. Other prominent families from that time are Ferriters, Husseys and Rices. Perhaps from norse times, certainly from anglo-norman times, Smerwick was one of the principal harbours in Munster; but from the 14th century Dingle became the principal harbour: in 1322 Raymond Fitz William and John Fitz Raymond were appointed Receivers and Collectors of Customs there. In the same century Spanish traders had settled there. Dingle may have had an early charter from the local magnate, the Knight of Kerry. It certainly was the first town in Kerry to be incorporated by royal charter in 1585 after the Desmond wars in which the whole peninsula was utterly devastated. The peninsula saw the first invasion of Ireland by foreign forces aiding Irish attempts at independence in Smerwick in 1580. In the 1840s it saw the most sustained effort made by the Church of Ireland to win over the ordinary people. In the present century writers from this peninsula have made notable contributions to literature in Irish.

(I) DINGLE

Dingle (III. 45. 101-102) (pop. 1971: 1401) is the principal town of Corkaguiney and, in a sense, all roads of the barony lead to and from it. This is, basically, because, unlike other peninsulas, no road circles Corkaguiney — the huge bulk of Brandon is not surrounded on the sea side by a road. For seeing the barony of Corkaguiney, Dingle is thus well placed. There are, generally, four areas to be covered: Letteragh, the area from Connor Pass to Killelton; the rest of the area east of Dingle and south of the mountains; the area around Slea Head; and that west of Brandon.

Dingle (Daingean Ui Chuise, which probably means Hussey's Haven, hence Dingle i Couch) has a population now about one-third of that of 135 years previously. It is, plainly a town that does not economically progress; only recently has it, the centre of a wonderful tourist area, been equipped with modern hotels. It is one of the principal fishing harbours of the country; but that enterprise is still in a small way.

The Husseys, after whom the town was named, were an anglo-norman family (possibly called de la Cousa) that settled here in the 13th century under the patronage of the future Desmonds. Their castle was behind the present market house. Already, by the end of that century Dingle had an extensive export of wool and hides, yielding perhaps 1% of the national revenue from the export tax on these items in the years 1287 to 1292. In quantity, a revenue of this size could represent some 1,800 stone of wool *or* over 4,000 hides.

In the 14th-15th century Dingle took over from Smerwick the place of the leading port in Kerry. From this period, at latest, it carried on an extensive trade with Spanish ports. Its church was, unusually, named after St James, the patron of Spain. In the 18th century Dingle was the centre of extensive smuggling.

For something over two centuries — up to the end of the 18th century when they concentrated on Valentia — the leading family in the town was a cadet branch of the Desmonds, the Knights of Kerry. Another prominent anglo-norman family here were the Rices.

Dingle became a chartered borough — the only one in Kerry — in 1585, for the purposes of the parliament of 1586 that attainted the last palatine earl of Desmond. Queen Elizabeth, who did not throw money around, gave £300 for walling the new borough. The borough corporation was under a 'sovereign'. The borough status was confirmed by a charter of James I in 1608, and Dingle remained a borough until 1840 when it lost its local government. As a borough Dingle returned two members to the Irish parliament up to 1800 when the owner of the two seats, R.B. Townshend (heir of the Knight of Kerry) was paid £15,000 compensation for their abolition. The Dingle corporation built the pier in 1765 with the aid of £1,000 parliamentary grant; the pier was later enlarged. Dingle had a coinage of its own, at least for a period, and there is extant a 'Dingle Penny' of 1769. In 1750 Dingle exported large quantities of linen, as well as butter, eggs, hides and cattle. The linen weaving industry throve here until the early 19th century. In the 1760s the town was in decay, but travellers commented on the stone houses with balconies and oval windows that gave it an exotic and 'Spanish' character, like Galway. As late as 1830 the road between Tralee and Dingle was very bad and the post was exchanged between a runner from each town at the half way mark.

It was here that James, 11th earl of Desmond, received the emissary of Charles V in 1529. The emissary was Gonzalo Fernandez, the emperor's chaplain who spoke english well. The earl had opened negotiations by sending to Charles at Toledo a gift of hawks and greyhounds, and asking for aid against England. Fernandez had landed first at Cork, then was driven into Berehaven, where he was asked to meet the earl at Dingle. Here he was hospitably received. He would not, however, join the earl in one of the local sports — an expedition to a harbour 'a few miles off' to capture some French and English vessels there. Gonzalez describes the earl's great possessions, but says: 'He has some allies, but not so many, by a great deal, as he has enemies'. He goes on to say:

The earl himself is from thirty to forty years old, and is rather above the middle height. He keeps better justice throughout his dominions than any other chief in Ireland. Robbers and homicides find no

234

Dingle

mercy, and are executed out of hand. His people are in high order and discipline. They are armed with short bows and swords. The earl's guard are in mail from neck to heel, and carry halberds. He has also a number of horse some of whom know how to break a lance. They all ride admirably without saddle or stirrup.

Desmond asked for four large vessels of 200 tons, six pinnaces well provided with artillery, and 500 Flemings to work them. Fernandez said that 'such a demand was out of all reason' and persuaded him to reduce his demands which he did to 'especially cannon available for land service and fit for breaching castles.' In fact he got nothing — the Turks were at the gates of Vienna — and he died in Dingle two years later.

It was here also that James Fitz Maurice Fitz Gerald first came in July 1579 with his

little band that touched off the final Desmond revolt. They disembarked with some solemnity. Two friars first, followed by a bishop with mitre and crozier. Then Sanders, the papal legate, bearing the banner given by the pope. Finally, Fitz Maurice followed by his men. They immediately marched to the little port of Smerwick. A month later, Fitz Maurice was dead, killed in a senseless squabble.

A month earlier, in June, Patrick O Hely, bishop of Mayo, Conn O Rourke, son of the prince of Breffni, and a third, landed here — another story says it was at Smerwick. They were apparently picked up and handed over to the earl of Desmond who caused them to be delivered to the English. At Kilmallock they were cruelly tortured and hanged by Drury.

The many-gifted David Duffe Fitz Gerald, so

praised by Stanihurst, seems to have come from Dingle. He was killed in the Desmond wars at Aghadoe in June, 1681, and his property in Dingle was confiscated.

During the O Neill wars the town, held by the Knight of Kerry, was in 1600 burned by the Sugan earl of Desmond.

O Donovan says that the present protestant church stands on the site of an old monastery. This is probably wrong. The rectorship of Dingle became attached to the Augustinians of Killagha in the early 15th century after a struggle during which the severest papal penalties — excommunication and interdict — were applied to the community for sticking to their claim to the parish.

Where the catholic presbytery now stands on Main Street was a Rice house, 'the highest house on the hill'. James Rice, count of the Holy Roman Empire, planned in the French revolution to rescue Marie Antoinette and, it is said, bring her here, the house having been fitted up for her.

The catholic church is worth a visit. As one turns down Green Street from Main Street one can see, left, on the upper storey of a house a relic of the rebuilding of the town after the Desmond wars, a stone with the date 1586.

In Dingle there was a British army post. In the year 1793 there was a major agitation against excessive rents by tenants of the Mullins estate. At a big demonstration in Dingle in June, 1793, the soldiers, on Mullins' orders, opened fire, killing fourteen and wounding many others.

Dingle was a notable centre for smuggling not only in the 18th century but, so far as at least tobacco was concerned, well into the 19th. Miss Hickson and Foley have a number of stories of the struggles between preventive men and the local traders.

Dingle was the centre of an extensive linen industry fostered from about 1760 by the Knight of Kerry with public help from the (national) linen board. Flax was extensively grown in the peninsula (and on Valentia), spun at home and woven in a Dingle factory. At the end of the 18th century there was a considerable export to Cork but the industry died away in the general depression of the 19th century.

At Dingle began in 1831 the one successful protestant missionary effort in the history of Kerry; this spread to a number of the surrounding areas. The curate in Dingle, Rev T. Goodman, played an active part in this. By energetic efforts, preaching in Irish, establishing schools, and with the active support (and pressure — large numbers of tenants were cleared off his hands) of the local landlord, Lord Ventry, a notable number of people were won over from catholicism. The most notable of these was a Dingle man, Thomas Moriarty, who later became dean of Ardfert. In 1840-42 a 'colony' of 25 houses was built to house those converted. The centre of this effort became Ventry village, where an Englishman, Charles Gayer was rector. Schoolhouses were erected in Dunquin, the Great Blasket, Ventry, Kilmalkedar and Dunorlin. In 1844 a catholic priest stationed in Kilmalkedar, named Denis Brasbie, became a protestant, and this caused a great stir. By the following year, 700 - 800 men, women and children had been enrolled. In January, 1848, Gayer died of famine fever: he had done notable work to relieve distress. It was only then that a vigorous catholic counter-attack was made with the holding of great parish missions — this movement had begun generally in 1842. In 1846 the Vincentian fathers held a seven week mission in Dingle. Catholic schools were established by nuns and christian brothers — this latter in 1848. In consequence, the protestant mission fell away. Goodman's son, James, also a clergyman, became one of the great collectors of Irish music.

In the main street is a great bullaun, lying at the side of the road.

There is a golf course and a race course. The harbour is an important fishing base.

At the east end of the harbour, near the entrance and rather less than a mile beyond the Hotel Sceilg, is a small *raised beach*

(III. 45. 100. b) with a scattered midden of mainly oyster shells.

(II)   DINGLE – CONNOR PASS – CLOGHANE – FAHAMORE – KILLELTON – INCH

This is a day trip. Take the Connor Pass road left out of the town. There are magnificent views both ways from the top of *Connor Pass* (III. 50. 106. a). To the right, at the Pass, is a track. Follow this on foot until it degenerates into a stream. Climb to the ridge on one's left. This brings one out on a typical 2,000 foot peneplain. There are fine views here. Follow this until one comes over a steep and startling coum. Bear right here through the eroded peat mounds until one comes to the head of a coum with three lakes. This is *Coumanare* (III. 52. 106. d), the coum of the slaughter. There is a vague tradition of an old battle here reinforced in recent years by the finding of many yew objects that may have been arrows. There is a very fine view from here. Return to the boithrin one has left. This walk will take about two hours.

Below the Pass the first road left is for Cloghane. Pass this and continue on the main road for two-fifths of a mile. Then take a boithrin, right. Follow this to a farmyard, walk through a gateway and follow the deteriorated boithrin to a second gate. Go through this and follow the track for a similar distance to a stream and ford. From here, in the direction of the stream's flow one should see a gallan, sharply pointed, and, to the left of it, another, parts of a three gallan alignment that may have contained two or three others. It was clearly a pointer to the fine wedge tomb of *Ballyhoneen* (III. 53. 109. c). What may be the ruins of two smaller tombs are nearby. Some distance further on there is a ruined caher. The coum itself is striking with, further on, two lakes and an island, but the going is rough and wet. Allow an hour for the antiquities and at least as much again for exploring the coum.

Turn back to the branch, now on one's right, for *Cloghane* (III. 51. 112. d) (pop. 1966: 68). This is a pleasant run if the tide is in. Within not much more than living memory the pattern here was the year's great assembly

of the peninsula. It was held on Domhnach Chrom Dubh, the last Sunday in July. It was associated with a fair in Dingle on the preceding Saturday and a pilgrimage to the 3,127 foot summit of *Mount Brandon* (III. 47. 112. a). This set out from Kilmalkedar and followed the Saints' road to the summit, a comparatively easy climb in clear weather. The pilgrims then took a hazardous path down the eastern side of the mountain to Cloghane to the patron. This was ostensibly held to celebrate the conversion to christianity of a local magician, Crom Dubh. As Miss Mac Neill has shown it was the continuation of a festival of the god Lug, and Crom Dubh represented another god over whom Lug staged a temporary victory to celebrate the harvest. In the wall of the chancel — which is a good deal older than the rest — of the protestant church, now in ruins, of Cloghane there is the stone carving of a head that is said to represent Crom Dubh. If so, this is one of the very few pagan idols that have survived and possibly the only one in Kerry. It has the typical apoplectic, yet amiable, look of a celtic god. Crom Dubh is said to have lived here. The head was kissed as a cure for toothache. The church is up a boithrin at the middle of the village to the left as one enters from the Camp side. The head is on the right hand wall of the chancel of the church, the nave of which, now in ruins, was rebuilt in 1828 during the Church of Ireland revival in Kerry but which in Foley's time (1907) was already dismantled. The view from here of mountains and sea is very fine, if one ignores the usual hideous strong box vaults about one, in which the dead are (barely) shut off by loose flags.

On the pattern day in July 1918, a school of porpoises were stranded at Cloghane, and in November 1965, a school of no less than 63 pilot whales.

Carry on from Cloghane and, at the signpost, take the road to *Ballyquin strand* (III. 53. 114). This is one of the many attractive beaches in the area with striking views of Brandon and the other mountains. The notable feature of this beach is that it is red, unlike the Castlegregory beaches. Here one can see that last vestiges of the limestone and, after it, the assault by the sea on the old red

235

236

Head of (?) Crom Dub, Cloghane

sandstone reducing it once more to its state of 400 million years ago.

If the day is clear it is worth one's while to continue out through Brandon village to where the road ends at *Brandon Point* (III. 53. 117. b). The views here of Brandon Bay and, further on, of Tralee Bay are magnificent. Brandon Point has been identified with Srub Brain where Bran and his companions touched land after their voyage amongst the magical western islands, including a presumed year spent on the Island of Women. Here one of the crew, Nechtan, sprang ashore and immediately collapsed in a heap of ashes. Then Bran and his companions, realising the length of their voyage, turned again for the ocean and were never heard of again. So it was that Bran gave his name, according to one account, to the great Mount Brandon above the point.

Return to Cloghane and bear left around

Brandon Bay (III. 53-62. 113-120). The road runs parellel to splendid beaches to which there are numerous roadways. Take the left fork through *Stradbally* (III. 60. 113. c) and *Killiney* (III. 61. 113. b). Behind the protestant church, right, with its curious square tower, are the remains of a parish church built in the elegant style of the 15th century — an unusual feature. Beside it are the remains of a square tower, curiously solid for a belfry. There are here a high, crudely carved stone cross of the 8-9th century, and a small cross, with one arm broken of perhaps the 7th-8th century.

From here there are fine views of *Lough Gill* (III. 60-62. 114-115), a noted centre for water fowl. Just before one enters Castlegregory there is a short road left to this lake. This is one of the not numerous places in Ireland where one can see large quantities of Bewick's swan. With the mute and whooper swans this makes up the three types of swan to be found in this country. Bewick's swan breeds in Siberia and winters in Ireland.

Castlegregory (III. 62-63. 114) (pop. 1971: 216) is a tidy village with, close to it, a most beautiful white strand. There is now no trace of the castle. There are two reputed origins of the name Gregory. The first is from Pope St Gregory the Great (590 — 604) who, despite his admiration for the English, enjoyed an extraordinary reputation in Ireland. He was called Gregory Goldenmouth and was claimed to be of Irish origin, being of the Corcu Duibne of near these parts. Hence Synge's description of 'the bay of Gregory of the Golden mouth' in *Riders to the Sea*. In fact he seems to have been confused with a Gregory of probably the same period who was the patron of a church near Glenbeigh but whose feast day (March 12) was celebrated on the same day as Pope Gregory's.

The second origin is Gregory Hoare who built the castle about 1550. There was a Montague-Capulet relationship between him and a neighbour called Moore. When Hoare's son, Hugh, married Moore's daughter old Gregory died of a fit in 1566. Fourteen years later a party of Lord Grey's army heading for Smerwick lodged at Hoare's castle. They are said to have included Spenser, Raleigh and

Denny. Hoare's wife, rather than give hospitality to the Queen's men, opened the cocks of the wine barrels and emptied them. Hugh Hoare, in a rage, stabbed her to death and, the following day, himself died suddenly.

The castle descended to Walter Hussey of Dingle, a supporter of the Knight of Kerry in the cromwellian wars. He escaped from here to Minard castle and was blown up with it. Castlegregory was 'slighted' at this time in the usual way, and its stones were used in the building of several houses in the village.

Castlegregory is at the neck of a spit of land that divides Tralee and Brandon Bays. Its tip consists of a survival of limestone rock as yet unconsumed by the sea in the action that has made the two round bays. Beyond this tip are the Maharee islands, themselves isolated survivals. Sea and wind to their best to cut through the sand that links the limestone tip to the mainland. The trip out along this spit is well worth while. There are beautiful strands and views.

Branch off the road to Kilshannig. A short distance along, and close to the road on the right, is an enormous gallan, perhaps 3,000 years old. *Kilshannig* (III. 63. 120. b) is not a thriving place. On a limestone bluff, defying the sea, stands an old parish church that gives the place its name. Inside is a 7th century cross pillar that shows that this must have been a religious settlement many centuries before the parish church was built. A sharp contrast to the battered fishing village is the tomb inside the gate with its suburban type red brick facings and pebble dashing.

Go back to the fork and on to *Fahamore*, (III. 61. 119. a), where there is a little pier. From here it is possible, given a wholly unlikely coincidence of opportunities, to get a boat to take one to the Maharee islands. The significant one is *Illauntannig* (III. 62-63. 122) on which there are the remains of an early christian settlement, surrounded by a remarkable cashel, rude and 18 feet thick. The settlement of Oilean tSeanaig is half demolished by man and undermined by the sea. Inside there are two oratories, three clochans, three 'leachts' or burial stones. One of the oratories is mostly in the sea. There is a cross of rounded white stones over the doorway. There is a rude cross six feet high near the leachts. 100 yards from the cashel, near a low cliff, is a bullaun and incised cross with small circles at the end of the arms. Seanach is said to have been a brother of Senan of Inis Cathaigh, but may have been he.

To one's left, on the quay of Fahamore, is *Inishtooskert* (III. 60-61. 123) where Spindler and the *Aud* made their side of the rendezvous on the night of Holy Thursday — Good Friday in 1916 with the rifles that might have decisively enlarged the scale of the 1916 rising. There are accounts that the *Aud* cruised up and down both sides of the sandy spit looking for the signal that should have come from this spot. Here one can see that most distinctive mark of the peninsula, the canvas covered canoe, or *naomhog* being made. To this countryside, about 1830, came a family from Clare called Hartney and introduced tar-covered canvas as a substitute for animal skins. This seems to have made much more popular this remarkable craft.

Take the road back for Castlegregory. Just before one comes to the bridge at the limit between the cultivated land — onions are grown extensively here in the Maharees — and the beginning of the sandhills there is a track towards the sea at Brandon Bay. Here amongst the high sandhills are to be found faint traces of the (Castlegregory) *sandhill settlements* (III. 61. 116) — to be known by the accumulations of sea shells — with occasional finds. Here, at the end of the last century, Knowles found, amongst other things, a bear's tooth, suggesting a very old occupation of the place by perhaps a mesolithic people. Other finds are relics of a small horse and of red deer.

After Castlegregory go left until one reaches the main road from Dingle.

For a view of a coum from the bottom up it is worth turning right for a quarter mile then left for three miles up to *Glanteenassig* (III. 60-62. 108-109). Just above the end of the road is *Lough Slat* (III. 61-62. 108) in which there is fishing and, a mile further along the stream running into Lough Slat, a

complex of lakes beneath a steep cliff. This is a striking coum.

Turn back to the main road. About one and a quarter miles along it one reaches *Meenascorthy* (III. 67. 111. c) townland where in June, 1919, one of the first incidents in the war of independence in Kerry occurred when two policemen were disarmed. Continue along the main road until it is joined right by the other main road to Dingle. Carry on for one mile by the old railway line towards Tralee to *Killelton* (III. 73. 111. c). This little ruin is, right, up an overgrown boithrin just beyond a modern bungalow and facing a boithrin leading to the sea. It is a short walk up the boithrin until it meets another in a T junction. Turn left for some 30 yards. Climb the bank on the right. Some yards inside, buried in bracken and ivy, is a tiny rectangular church, much ruined, but clearly from its size and simplicity one of the earliest stone rectangular churches built in Ireland, but with some mortar in its construction. It dates probably from the 7th or 8th centuries. The base of the east window is finely shaped. The west door is dressed and shows the Staigue-type batter. Some sort of building was erected west of the church. There are to the north the remains of an oblong structure. West is a pillarstone, but without the usual inscribed cross. The whole is enclosed in a caiseal. It looks as if this church were abandoned at an early date — otherwise a 9th - 10th century chancel would have been added. Apart from those on the Skellig and at Templenacloonagh this church is unique in Kerry as an untouched example of the earliest type of rectangular, mortar-built church. Lynch says that it is the remains of an even earlier oratory, but in this he was clearly wrong. It is a great pity that this most valuable site is so neglected.

This little church is in the parish of Kilgobban. Gobban and Elton were, with Sedna, sons of Erc married to Mor, supposed sister of St David of Wales. She lived at Alltraighe Cliach (Knockannish, across Tralee Bay). David's mother was Irish and he was a major influence on the early Irish church. David died about the middle of the 6th century. All three nephews settled and died in Kinsale, and Elton, victim of a succession of diminutives

and of anglicisation came to be known at St Multose.

The church is built on a curbed mound, traditionally the grave of Fas, wife of one of the Milesian leaders. She was killed in the great battle of Sliabh Mis in which her mother-in-law, Scotia, was also killed. This is another example of a christian site being associated with a pagan one. The glen here is called *Glenfash*, (III. 72. 110) after her. Scotia's Glen, Glanaskagheen, is a few miles to the east, in Trughanacmy, near Tralee.

West, in the farmyard beside the bungalow on the main roadside is a supposed ceallunach and cross pillar. Neither is correct, but there are ruined clochans there. Along the low land here, right back to Tralee, was in the 16th century Derrymore, the great oak wood.

Return along the Dingle road and at the branch off for Castlegregory bear left. Then at the sharp bend take the signposted road left for Caherconree. After two miles this road crosses a steep stream where a small dam for a waterworks has been made. At the top of the short track along this stream, left, is a splendid place to picnic in. This is the *Finglas* (III. 71. 109. d) river.

One is here beneath the great mountain of *Caherconree*, (III. 74. 108. a) named after the most striking inland *promontory fort* (III. 73. 107. b) in Ireland where Curoi Mac Daire had his fortress high on the mountain. It is one of the most famous of the places mentioned in the Red Branch cycle of legends. Close to the summit, at about 2,000 feet is a neck or promontory of mountain, sheer on three sides, with a large stone wall preventing access across the neck. Here, in this unlikely place, Curoi had his mist enshrouded fortress. It is said he spent much of his time abroad (presumably to dry out) but that every night, no matter where he was, he was able to set the wall of the fortress spinning so that no-one could get at the gateway until morning. Curoi was, formally, head of the Deaghaid, or Earna, a tribe of the Firbolg, but he seems to have been a god, with some perhaps totem relationship to a hound, like the more famous Cuchulainn. Curoi was friendly with the Ulster heroes, amongst whom he appeared in

237

238 often grotesque forms. When the great dispute between the three Ulster champions — Laegaire, Conall and Cuchulainn — as to which was the bravest could not be settled locally it was to Curoi at his fortress that they came for a judgement. As usual, Curoi was away but each of the champions was set in turn to guard the fortress alone at night. Here Curoi in terrifying forms attacked them, throwing Laegaire and Conall back over the wall into the fort. Only Cuchulainn fared reasonably well against the demons. Thinking however that Laegaire and Conall had jumped the wall he tried to do this too. In the end he barely got over. Later, in Emain Macha in Ulster, Curoi (again in grotesque form) was to demonstrate beyond doubt that Cuchulainn was entitled to pre-eminence and his wife to precedence.

Nonetheless it was Cuchulainn who killed Curoi here over a woman, Blathnaid, and the plot was hatched between them somewhere near this spot on the Finglas river. Blathnaid was the daughter of a Manx chieftain whose heavily defended fort was besieged by Cuchulainn and his friends in pursuit of booty and Blathnaid. Curoi, as usual in disguise, showed the baffled raiders how to take the fort, on condition that he had first pick of the jewels it contained. When the party got back to Ireland and the loot was being shared Curoi picked Blathnaid. Cuchulainn refused to let her go. Curoi retaliated by taking all the loot — jewels, magic cows, Blathnaid and all — and disappeared with them. Cuchulainn pursued him and, near Cashel, caught up with him. However, Curoi, still disguised, overwhelmed the famous little man, buried him up to his armpits, shaved his head and rubbed cowdung on it.

After this humiliation Cuchulainn went into retirement for a year until his hair grew. Eventually he was led by strange birds to this place at the Finglas river where he met Blathnaid, no doubt by now thoroughly fed up with life in the clouds and mists. Here they plotted to kill Curoi some time later, on 1st November. Cuchulainn turned up on this date with his men and, when the river ran white with the milk of the captured Manx cows (Blathnaid's sign that the way was clear) Cuchulainn and his men began to climb up to the fortress.

In these later times it is better to climb from a place further on, and only if the day is clear and settled. About half a mile further along the roadway there is a *deserted farmhouse* (III. 71. 108. d). Turn left by this and begin to climb. The fortress is directly above one. Follow a fence on the right until it takes a right angle. Here one must decide whether to go straight for the fortress, or to reach it obliquely. The former calls for stiff climbing. If the easier way is chosen bear gently right along the flank of the mountain above the glen on the right. There are many steep tracks along this flank and they bear right across the higher part of the glen making it easy to reach the saddle at the top of the glen. From there the walk to the fortress, (on one's left) is straightforward. There are magnificent views as one climbs.

Blathnaid had cleared the fortress by persuading Curoi that his place should be the most magnificent in Ireland. For this much larger stones were needed. The menfolk were sent over Ireland to collect large stones. When they were gone, and there were only a handful left in the fort she gave the sign. She had Curoi in the gateway combing his hair. He noticed people coming up the mountain but she reassured him, brought him inside, gave him a bath, put him to bed and took away his sword. When Cuchulainn and his men burst in, killing Curoi's son, their prey gave a good account of himself with his bare hands and feet, but Cuchulainn eventually killed him, set fire to the buildings in the fort and carried off Blathnaid to Ulster. With them went Curoi's old druid Feircheirtne. As he was speaking to the Ulster King, Conor, on a cliff point above the sea, Feircheirtne suddenly grasped Blathnaid in his arms and jumped over the cliff, so that they were both smashed on the rocks beneath.

One can picture the hair-combing as one stands in the entrance of the now partly ruined fort. The stones of the wall *are* small and the argument that bigger ones would be more impressive was sound enough. The wall must have been higher once if even the redoubtable Cuchulainn could not readily jump it. This is the wall that spun furiously round each night as the sun set. The enclosure is large. Perhaps once a considerable group lived here almost 2,500 years ago. It is a strong and impressive place.

There were other stories, too, about this place, but they are now lost. There is an old reference to the seven battles around Caherconree and to the plundering of Curoi with the seventeen sons of Deaghaid.

The rocky promontory is much eroded and the stones of the wall have been worn off it. They are a striking example of the famous Inch conglomerate. The gneisses and the schists embedded in its hardened mud, now raised so incongruously high, are amongst the oldest stones in Ireland, dating from the pre-cambrian period of between 600 million and 2,000 million years ago.

The descent is easy. It is possible to continue on the road to *Aughils* (III. 73. 103. c) and Inch. The views of the Iveragh mountains, and of Carrantuohill in particular, as well as of Castlemaine harbour, as one drops down from the summit are something to remember.

Otherwise go back to the main road and turn left for Dingle. A little later is the village of *Camp* (III. 70. 110. d). Just before the village, at Curraduff viaduct over the Finglas river to one's left, the Dingle train in 1893, speeding down towards Camp, ran out of control and fell over the viaduct, killing the crew of three and injuring 13 passengers. Turn left at the cross roads in the village. After about half a mile, just beyond a house on the left, and before one comes to another cross roads, there is in a field, left, within a few yards of the road *Naisi's Grave* (III. 70. 109. b). This is a fallen gallan with a male point. The ogam reads 'Conunett moqi Conuri' and, in script, 'Fect Conuri'. What is interesting is that this should have been called after Naisi, the lover of Deirdre in the great Ulster tale. There are unusual memories here of the Ulster stories — Curoi and Cuchulainn at Caherconree; Cuchulainn again near Anascaul; Naisi here, and the account in the same tale that, when Deirdre eloped with Naisi, her nurse, Lavarcham, came to Brandon. This shows something of the unity of the Erainn people north and south, even when they had been overrun by the goidels.

It is better to turn back here and go up the main road with splendid views of Tralee bay on the right. The road then turns inland by *Gleann na nGealt,* (III. 68. 108-109), the madmen's glen, where afflicted people came to drink at the well, Tobar na nGealt, and eat the cresses that grow by the stream, and so get relief — a foreshadowing of present-day drug treatment. One of the most famous of these visitors was Mad Sweeney, the hero of the great medieval tale.

After the glen take the first turn left and stop at the first house left. In the haggard of this house is a fine example of a wedge shaped grave, with cup markings on a displaced capstone to the side. Below this and below the road are the remains of a megalithic cemetery — a wedge tomb fairly well preserved, what seems to be a second — in poor state and partly overgrown with peat; upright stones that seem to be part of other tombs, and a larger recumbent slab. This is presumably the 'altar' in the name *Maumnahaltora* (III. 69. 107. a) (mam means a gap or pass). Nearby is a well, Tobar na hAltora, to which pilgrimages were made each year between the feasts of St John and SS Peter and Paul. Unusually, there does not seem to be a specifically christian settlement nearby. This is an important site.

Return to the main road and at the signpost turn left for *Inch* (III. 66. 102. c). About a mile east of Inch on the hillside, left, just before one comes to a stream, is *Ballingroun* (III. 67. 102. b), former house of the Godfrey family and a remarkable collection of quern stones. In this townland one of the Kerry lunulae was found. One of the finest views in Kerry is to be had at *Inch Strand* (III. 65. 101. a), a mile west of Inch. The strand itself is magnificent, often used it is said in the 18th century for wrecking ships from the West Indies. In the wild west storms a horse with a lantern on its head would be put to graze here and the harassed mariners would take this tossing light for another ship ahead unaware of the great bar of sand before them.

A mile along the strand — one can drive to it — in the middle of the sandhills of *Maghaglass*

Inch Strand

(III. 66. 100. c) is a valley between high sandhills with in places stretches of water. High above one, to the south is a raised beach with shell middens of primitive shore dwellers. Charcoal and other traces of fire are visible. There are 'hammer stones' and 'grain rubbers', broken and whole, sandstone 'knives' and axes, bones, traces of iron smelting. This is an extended site of great interest.

A further midden of great size is about half a mile away, *Gubranna* (III. 67. 100. a). On the eastern shore where it first strikes out into the bay is a midden about 600 yards long by about 60 yards wide, making a small cliff of five or six feet high where some of the midden has been washed away. Here also are to be found hammers and 'rubbers'. Middens of this kind are relics of very primitive times, but it seems that in this place, up to 1911 at least, shellfish were being taken along here, shelled, boiled and taken away for sale or

home use, so adding to the great midden.

Follow the coast road until it comes out on the main road to Dingle. This goes through the famous *Dingle Beds* (III. 60-64. 101) with their extremely ancient small stones of gneiss and schist lodged in the conglomerate rock.

Then on to Dingle. Total driving distance: 90 miles. Allow the whole day.

(III) DINGLE — LISPOLE — ANASCAUL — MINARD — KINARD

Take the road for Tralee. A mile along this road, close to the top of the hill, take the branch road right. Take the left fork and, after 0.7 miles, where the road begins to drop sharply, stop and go into a field on the left. About 50 yards above one is the ceallunach of *Ballintaggart* (III. 47. 100. a). It is surrounded by a cashel with earth bank inside. The burial

240

ground is unusual in having a number of rounded ogam stones, some with simple incised cross, lying flat in a rough circle over some of the graves. The stones, rounded by the sea, seem to have come from Minard some five miles away almost as the crow flies. The ogam writing and the crosses suggest that this burial ground dates from the transition from pagan to christian times. One of the stones has a cross with three triple ends and commemorates the three sons of Mailagnos. The readings on the stones are given elsewhere. This is an important site. Back to the car. The road leads downhill to the rather simple Dingle golf course. The ceallunach can also be reached from the main road, where it is signposted. But this involves a longer walk.

Back to the main road. Just before one enters the village of *Lispole* (III. 52. 102. d) one passes a schoolhouse on the right. Half a mile further on, just before one crosses the bridge to enter the village, is a sharp turn left. Take this turn and, at the cross roads, turn left. Just 0.1 miles from the cross roads leave the car at a gateway on the left. Two fields below one is an early christian church, *Temple Martin* (III. 52. 102. c) set in a large ringfort. This is an interesting building, important for the early stages of Irish church architecture, but it is, alas, much ruined. However, the ruins give one a chance to study the early use of mortar in these buildings and the development from the simpler structure at Killelton. The large stones, inside and out, were set without mortar, and the interior filled with rubble grouted with mortar. The west door is of well dressed stone, with the usual slanting jambs, but trabeated, the first setting back of doorway within doorway that was to receive such development in Irish romanesque; but here, of course, the lintel is still flat in the traditional style. Compared with Killelton this church is large. It is not clear whether this was so from the beginning or whether a chancel, now disappeared was added on. No doubt, this church dates from the late 8th century.

Turn the car and, through Lispole, head for *Anascaul* (pop. 1971: 236) (III. 60. 102. a). Anascaul is said to take its name from a woman, Scal ni Mhurnain, who drowned herself in the lake, Loch an Scail, two miles

north of the town. The story is that a giant came to take her away. She sent to Cuchulainn for help. He stood upon Dromavally mountain to the east of the lake and hurled defiance at the giant who was on another mountain to the west. They began throwing boulders at each other. After a week of this Cuchulainn was hit, gravely wounded, and gave a great groan. When Scal heard this she thought he had been killed outright and she jumped into the lake and was drowned. On the top of the mountain on which Cuchulainn stood there are three stone cairns called Leaba, Tigh and Uaigh Cuchulainn (the bed, house and grave of Cuchulainn). There is another tigh Cuchulainn on another part of the same mountain, in *Ballynahunt townland* (III. 62. 107). The story of Scal and these reputed remains may hark back to a very primitive, pre-literary connexion between Cuchulainn and this peninsula.

In the village there is the South Pole bar named by Tom Crean who went to the South Pole with Scott. The distinguished sculptor Jerome Connor was born here: he did the Lusitania memorial at Cobh and a Robert Emmet statue: a replica of the Washington original is in St Stephen's Green, Dublin, facing Emmet's first home.

Turn the car, cross over the bridge and turn right. Follow this road north for one mile until one comes to a cross roads. Turn right here and a short distance later follow the short road to the left. At the top of this, on the right, are the remains of the multiple cist cairn of *Knockane* (III. 58. 104. d). Some of the cists are exposed and the remains of an earthen circle around the cairn itself still remain. South of, and just beneath, the cairn is a bank on the far side of which is a large stone that may have come from the cairn with a well cut greek cross with a slight ornament suggesting a chi-rho. Turn and, at the T junction, turn left. At the cluster of houses bear left towards the lake. *Lough Anascaul* (III. 59. 105-106) is a typical coum lake, dark and forbidding, the mountainside around it littered with boulders. Here one can easily understand how the story of Scal secured belief. There is fishing in the lake. At the far side of the lake is *Dromavally* (III. 60. 106) where O Connell located a most

unusual souterrain with a side passage leading to a chamber cut off by a porthole that can be closed by a moveable stone; I have not identified this.

Return to Anascaul and follow the Tralee road for a mile and a quarter to a cross roads. Turn left here and, at the T junction, right. Keep bearing right until, after about a half mile, there is a sharp bend left. Here, on the right is the old graveyard of *Rathduff* (III. 62. 104. a) filled with strong box tombs. A fair distance in, on the west side of one of these, is propped the little Rathduff cross pillar, with its circled greek cross, the scutum fidei, the shield of faith. Back to the car. A short distance further on the road turn right for the main road and again right for Anascaul.

From Anascaul follow the main road towards Lispole for half a mile. Take a sharp turn right up a hill north and bear left at the bend. Follow this road for half a mile until one comes to a railway cottage, right, where the now disused railway crossed this road. Walk along the disused railway line for about 100 yards. In the field south of the line is *Dun Claire* (III. 58. 102. b), a fine three-ringed fort, a 'royal house' as the Ordnance Survey letters call it. Return to the main road.

Take the road back for Lispole. After the second of the bad bends one comes to *Ballynasare* (III. 56. 101. a) cross roads one mile further on. Turn left here and follow this road for about a mile. Turn left at the T junction and follow the principal road until it comes out at the sea. Here is a beach of sorts littered with curious long, rounded stones that were used for the Ballintaggart ogams. To one's right are the ruins of *Minard castle,* (III. 56. 100. c) a stronghold of the Knight of Kerry. In the cromwellian wars it was garrisoned by Walter Hussey from Castlegregory and the cromwellians succeeded in blowing it up with all its garrison. Beyond the castle is a well dedicated to St John the Baptist and, as usual, close by the scanty remains of the ruined church of *Kilmurry* (St Mary's church) (III. 56. 99. a).

Return and, at the T junction where one has come from Ballynasare, continue on straight for a mile until one comes to a sharp turn left. Take this and after half a mile one comes to the little settlement of *Aglish* (III. 54. 100. a) where there is a cross pillar with two swastikas. Reverse here and take the branch sharp left up a narrow twisting road until one comes, after about a mile, to a television mast. Just beyond this there is, left, a very rough boithrin. Leave the car here and follow the boithrin until one reaches the ditch of the field on one's right. Just beyond the summit above one is Puicin an Chairn at *Doonmanagh* (III. 53. 100. a), a wedge shaped tomb, little damaged with some of its covering of stones, the cairn, still in place.

Back to the car and follow the road for exactly two miles until one comes to a road right and, immediately after it, another left. Take this road up the hill until at the top one comes to a graveyard. This is *Kinard* (III. 50. 100. b). This was the birthplace in 1885 of Thomas Ashe, after whom the fine county building in Tralee has been named. In Easter Week, 1916, he commanded the largest action outside Dublin — at Ashbourne, Co. Meath. He was the acting head of the IRB when it was reorganised in 1917 and died in that year from medical neglect after he had been forcibly fed while leading a hunger strike in jail. What is now the concrete-roofed outbuilding of the most southerly of the three houses was his birthplace. This was the home base of a famous smuggler, Sean Mor Griffin, who ran many cargoes into Trabeg below. The Ashes were an anglo-norman family — d'Esse — who came to Kerry from Kildare and, later, married into Kinard. In Thomas Ashe's childhood this was still an Irish speaking area and it was here Ernest Blythe came to live as a labourer while learning Irish.

In the graveyard, at the western end, in front of a strong box tomb is a rounded stone, half buried, with, facing east to the tomb, a complex set of greek crosses set in a square grid. This is also an ogam stone that reads 'Mariani'. There is another ogam stone in this graveyard, lying flat, that I did not find. Macalister says it is exceptional in reading from the top down the left hand side. West of the new graveyard is an iron gate. In the second field above this, to the left of the gap,

is a scribed stone with cup marks, circles and grooves. In the same field are to be seen what seem to be the remains of megalithic tombs. As is usual hereabouts the christian site either occupies or was close to a pagan one.

The area is often called Tearmon Fhionain, St Fionan's sanctuary. It is said that he and St Michael landed at Trabeg below from the Skellig in thick fog. They were thristy, and two wells opened at their feet. The Virgin then appeared and a third well opened. Pilgrimages used to be made to those wells which are about half a mile due south of this place. The Fionan pilgrimage was on 12 February. The ordnance map has it wrongly St Fintan. This is, I think, the only reference to Fionan on this peninsula.

The road winds round the graveyard down to *Trabeg*, (III. 49. 99), the little strand, a

Gallan at Ballyneetig, Dingle

pleasant place where there is a narrow inlet of the sea that opens into a fair sized lake. Continue on the road as it winds back, bearing right. At the cross roads go straight on. Half a mile further on take the branch left. This drops down to a bridge. It is reported that in a *field* (III. 51. 101. b) 300 yards above one, south, is a scribed stone and, 50 yards above the road above this, another, but I did not find them. Follow the road over the bridge. This lands one, after a short journey, onto the main road. Turn left for Dingle. Just a quarter mile along this road, 100 yards south of the road, is the *Ballineetig* (III. 48. 101. b) gallan, the most remarkable in the barony, with its crudely pointed (male) tip.

Total driving distance: 36 miles. Allow nearly a full day.

(IV) DINGLE — MILLTOWN — FAHAN — BALLYFERRITER

On a clear bright day the journey around Slea Head is perhaps the finest in Kerry, but it is essential to choose a suitable day. On a gloomy or misty day take another trip.

Just outside Dingle to the west is a junction, signposted. Take the left junction for Slea Head. After about 200 yards, at the top of a rise in the road, just beyond a modern burial ground at *Milltown* (III. 43. 102. d), are the remains of an ancient burial ground inside a field gate to the right. Here are two large gallans, 'the gates of glory'. Beside one of them is a smaller gallan. Between the 'gates' are what look like two ruined dolmens. On one of these are typical scribings — deep cup marks, circles and other marks.

Exactly one mile further along this Slea Head road is a narrow road to the right. Follow this across a cross roads three quarters of a mile further on and take the first turn left. Follow this road left around a farmhouse and, at the T junction immediately after this, turn right. A short distance along this road is a farm. Leave the car here. Just beyond the farm climb into a field on the left. Above one, at the far side of the field, are the ruins of *Temple Manachain* in Ballymorereagh

241

242   (III. 41. 103. a). It is also called *Temple Geal* from the bright lichen that grows on the stones of the oratory. This place is well preserved and cared for. On top of the oratory has been placed a finial carved out of the soft conglomerate rock. This does not seem to belong at all to this type of tower, architecture; but it is not clear where it can have come from; in any event it seems to be a later addition. Inside the oratory is a grave slab, suggesting that the place may have been used in the 8th or 9th centuries. There is no ceallunach, so this place may have been abandoned around 800 AD. This is unusual. One can still see on the internal walls the remains of pointing or plastering: this seems to have been a feature of these well-built oratories. (Indeed Gallarus, the best of them, may have been pointed or plastered also on the outside). Beside the oratory is the usual cross pillar with ogam that reads: 'Queniloci maq maqi -ainia muc (defaced)', so that this christian settlement must date from 600 AD or so. It also has a latin inscription 'Fect Queniloc'. Above the oratory are other cross inscribed stones, and remains of a chamber tomb. So here again we see a christian settlement associated with, and clearly intended to supersede, an older pagan shrine. There is a splendid view from here.

Go back to the main road by the way one has come. Turn right along the main road and after a quarter mile turn left along a road that skirts the Burnham estate. This belonged to the Mullins family — who came to Kerry in 1666 and *bought* land. They later changed their name to de Moleyns. They became Viscounts Ventry in 1800. They had extensive lands here and they acquired the Blennerhasset lands at Killorglin, including the Hospitallers' castle, later Castle Conway. The family were a main support of the attempt to win the local people to the Church of Ireland in the first half of the 19th century and the wife of their agent, Mrs D.P. Thompson, has left a vivid account of this. *Burnham* (III. 43. 100. a) is now a convent school. The place was formerly called Ballingolin; before 1641 the Rices had a castle where the house stands. The road comes out into open country that gives fine views of Dingle and its harbour. To one's right is *Ballymacadoyle hill* (III. 43. 99. d) (Baile

mac an Daill, son of the blind-man) also called Harperstown in elizabethan times. O Beolain says that it was from one of these harpers — O Conors pardoned in 1585 and 1601 — that Piaras Ferriter received that gift of a harp that prompted one of his most accomplished poems. South of this hill is a beacon tower — a famine relief work organised by the Rev Charles Gayer — from which there are magnificent views. Continue along the road until one has come two miles from the main road. From here there is a fairly easy climb to the *tower* (III. 44. 99. d) which is hidden from this spot. At the top there is, apart from the beacon, the remains of a World War II look out post for belligerent aircraft, and below this, two remarkable promontory forts. The view here on a fine day is one of the best in the peninsula.

Back to the main road and turn left. This brings one to Ventry, which comes from Fionn Traigh, the bright strand. There is a turn left for part of the strand called *Cantra* (III. 40. 100. b) where one can get a good view of the circuit of *Ventry harbour* (III. 38-41. 98-101). This inlet was crowded with invading ships for the famous battle of Ventry (q.v.). In early days, before the rise of Dingle, it was a significant port. Here, in the Desmond wars, Admiral Winter kept his fleet, a competent and, for those days, an astonishingly humane sailor who protected the refugees that came crowding here from the merciless military commanders who had driven them before them. Ventry was the main focus of the Church of Ireland missionary effort. From Ventry west one is in an Irish speaking area. From the strand return to the main road. A little further on turn right up the hill. Take the first turn left. After 0.4 miles along this road stop at a quarry. Climb up around this and go left to the wall running up the hill. There are many remains of beehive huts. On the brow of the hill are the remains of a very ruined wedge grave, *Leaba an Fhir Mhuimhnigh* (III. 40. 102. c), the munsterman's bed. There may be another grave here, and there are the remains of several more beehive huts. There are fine views over to the Reeks and the Skelligs. Go back to the car. The road one is on is the beginning of the Saints' Road, but it soon peters out for cars. So, turn here and go back

to the main road. Along the main road, beyond the catholic church at the signpost, turn left. (On a second trip turn right at the church and take the left fork near the summit. The views of the Blaskets as one drops down to Dunquin are very fine). Follow this road left at the church until one comes out at a little pier and a ruined coastguard station, at *Pointanskoh* (III. 39. 99. c). Along the strand to one's left are to be found considerable numbers of large scallop shells that children love to collect and that adults use for ashtrays. To the right, intermittently out to *Parkmore Point* (III. 40. 98. a) are the remains of a pre-glacial raised beach. Champneys refers to an 11 chamber souterrain in the Ventry area. South west of the pier, that is, well outside the harbour and to the west is a rock in the sea called *Leekeel,* (III. 38. 98. c) Leac Chaoil, near where Cael, in one of the most touching of the sub-stories of the battle of Ventry, was drowned.

Go back to the main road and at a schoolhouse on the right stop at the boithrin sharp right over a stream. A short distance along this there is a boithrin left that brings one up through the fields. Here amongst great boulders in the fields is a ceallunach, with a cross pillar. Here again one sees a christian settlement of sorts — for there are now no traces of buildings — close to a ruined chamber tomb. This is *Kilvickadownig* (III. 36. 98. b). Here it was said was buried Daire Donn, the king of the world, who led the invasion at Ventry. From here he sacked three of the cahers to the west. He was finally killed by Fionn mac Cumhail. This seems to have been a shrine of Daire (or Donn), perhaps the principal god of the Earna. Above one, north, is the townland of *Caherbullig* (III. 36. 99), that is, of Bolg. (No caher remains). Bolg was the god of lightning and tutelary god of the Fir Bolg, or Belgae, of whom the Earna were a branch. Daire and Bolg are aspects of the same deity. All along this peninsula one feels that pagan religion has been buried in a light covering of earth.

Back to the car. The next road right leads up to the village of Fahan. Here, at the end of the road, left, are the remains of a christian church, *Teampall Beag,* (III. 36. 98. b), the small church, with a barn built on and practically unrecognisable. There is a small cross-inscribed pillar here. There is an old road that continues through the ancient village of *Fahan* (III. 33-36. 97-98); but go back to the main road.

Along the main road, between here and Coumeenole, is the greatest concentration of archaeological remains in Ireland — and that is no small thing.

Macalister did an intensive survey of the area — in TRIA for 1899 — and found over 500 remains. There were over 400 clochans, 30 standing and inscribed stones and crosses, 19 souterrains, and a number of miscellaneous remains, including two promontory forts, several cahers and the church we have seen. The settlement extends over some three miles west, mainly north of the present road, on the steep slopes of *Mount Eagle,* (III. 34. 99. a), in a beautiful situation facing south.

Along the road is, signposted, *Dun Beag* (III. 36. 98. d), perhaps the most striking and complex of the promontory forts. It is about five minutes' walk from the road and well worth it. The defences include fosses and ditches; but the striking feature is the enormous stone wall behind them that cuts off the promontory, the outer part of the wall being an addition. Inside are the remains of a large house and a beehive hut. There is a souterrain under the entrance. Most of the fort is now, however, fallen into the sea.

A little further along the road is *Cathair Connor* (III. 35. 98. d), marked by a wooden notice. A little further on again is, similarly marked, *Cathair na Mairtineach* (III. 35. 98. d), often wrongly written na Mactireach (of the wolves). They are in fact named after the owners of the land who make a small charge for viewing. The ruins lie in clusters along an old road that runs a few hundred yards parallel to and above the modern road. They are of considerable interest. Within each cathair are many complex clochans. These have single, double and treble chambers, often with a small chamber for the dog.

Travel along the road over the ford at

Glenfahan (III. 34. 98. c). About a quarter mile further on, again marked, is *Cathair Murphy* (III. 33. 97. b) with more curious buildings inside and a complex ogam stone with a crude version of the risen Christ. A little further on is *Cathair-fada-an-doruis* (III. 33. 97. b), with a remarkable triple clochan. Du Noyer, who first brought this settlement to public notice in 1858, illustrates a number of the most interesting of these clochans.

Who were the people who so unusually established this crowded town, this exceptional reliquary of the Irish past, in late pagan times? Were they invaders from some tradition other than that of the celts who colonised Ireland in earlier centuries? Were they invaders from the Atlantic trade routes who landed here and, after their fashion, prospered? As one stands here one can see the main part of the land skirting Dingle bay. This land was called in historical times Aes Iorruis, that of the people of the peninsula. We are standing on Aes Iorruis Tuaiscirt (northern) and facing us is Aes Iorruis Deiscirt (southern). Presumably these people fanned out from here along both shores of the bay. Here, in the middle of the 10th century, the ferocious king of Cashel, Ceallachan, defeated them and took their king prisoner. At the beginning of the 13th century Meiler Fitz Henry got a grant of 'Ossuris'. Presumably, these people were the Corcu Duibne in historical times known to be settled on both sides of the bay; but their building here a town in a manner unique in celtic Ireland requires more study than it has had. One is reminded again that the mountains to the north were the real barrier and that the stretch of water for a fishing or sea-faring folk was, geographically and politically, a unifying factor.

The whole settlement covers several square miles and must have accommodated 1,000 to 2,000 people at a time, comparable to Dingle at the present time. The existence of the early christian church at one end and of gallans at the other suggests that the settlement dates from late pagan — early christian times. If this is an Irish — instead of an intrusive — settlement it suggests that something approaching town life *did* exist in

early Ireland: in places where buildings were not of stone — as here — there would be no obvious remains. On the other hand, if the settlement were not Irish in the traditional sense then it has a unique interest. Here is a place that cries out for a major scientific excavation. Two things are obvious even to the unpractised eye. First, this was not an organised community in the sense we would think of as now constituting a 'town'. Secondly, the people must have been small, from the size of the clochans and souterrains, but strong, from the size of the stones used in building.

According to Macalister one can see in the remains a steady evolution of house dwellings over time. First, there are caves. Secondly, there are rock shelters, that is, artificial caves made of stones and by some excavation of natural rock. Third, there are D-shaped houses, an evolution of the rock shelter. Fourth, these evolve into rectangular and oval houses. Fifth, there are the regular rectangular buildings. Sixth, there is the aberration of the cuspidate structure. If Macalister is right the people here must have been at first very primitive cave dwellers who were capable of fairly rapid development and of adaptation to Irish conditions. If they were invaders does the story of the great invasion of Ventry embody some memory of this? And were they, for example, assimilated via Daire Donn into early Irish mythology?

The road, as it winds round *Slea Head* (III. 32. 97. b), drives such speculations out mind as the striking views of the Blaskets are revealed. There is a fine strand at *Coumeenole* (III. 32. 98. a) but bathing there is dangerous. In the little village of *Coumeenole* (III. 32. 98. b) one can see, beside the farmhouses, modern clochans used as sheds. In the high land above one are many similar buildings but these are relics of the practice of booleying, huts to shelter those herding cattle sent up in the summer months to graze. The practice of booleying continued to the middle of the 19th century.

A little further on is *Dun Mor* (III. 31. 99. d), a large promontory fort but, notwithstanding the name, it is not as striking as Dun Beag. It

243

244

Coumeenole and Great Blasket

has a deep ditch and wall. It has been suggested that this was a sanctuary of the goddess Dovvinias, or Duben, who gave her name to the peninsula. One of the markings on the ogam stone now erected in the centre of the fort was (erroneously) read as '[A] nme Dovinia' and thus held to personify the goddess. But Macalister gives the reading as being without doubt 'Erc maqi maqi-Ercias mu Dovinia'. The Mor in the name of the dun has been held to be that of Mor, daughter of the sun and wife of the sea god, Lir, who lived here. Just a mile along the road, on the right on the side of Mount Eagle, about half a mile from the road, in the townland of Vicarstown, is a major megalithic tomb, called *Tigh Mhoire,* or Mor's Grave (III. 32. 100. b).

Just before Dunquin turn left for the little *Dunquin harbour* (III. 32. 100. a), that is the point of departure for canoes for the *Great Blasket* (III. 24-29. 95-99.), deserted since 1953-4. Here the peasant remnants of gaelic culture flickered brightly before the end. Three good autobiographies came from here: *An tOileanach,* (The Islandman), *Fiche Blian ag Fas* (Twenty years a-Growing), and *Peig,*

all translated under those titles. The first of these is a masterpiece of its kind. Two of the islands, the shapely *Tiaraght* (III. 18-19. 95), the most westerly, and *Inishvickillane* (III. 21-22. 91-92), the most southerly, are notable breeding grounds for seabirds, including many thousands of pairs of storm petrel. The small flat island in the foreground is Beiginish in the lee of which the ships of the Spanish armada sheltered before the *Santa Maria de la Rosa* broke away to her doom and the *San Juan* was overwhelmed by the terrible seas. The northerly island, with its striking volcanic outcrop is *Inishtooskert* (III. 23-24. 101-102). The remaining island is *Inishnabro* (III. 21-22. 93-94.).

The friendly donkeys here have a well developed taste for sugar lumps. The coloured silurian rock in these cliffs is striking. It dates from some 400 million years ago, and along the coast it contains many forms of fossils, of coral and of early forms of shellfish, the brachiopods.

A striking sight here, as in the other little harbours along the coast is fishermen launching their black canoes — upended, like great beetles, with three or four pairs of legs beneath. These boats are of tarred canvas over a light frame and must be the direct descendants of the hide covered boats of St Brendan's time. They are very seaworthy. They resemble the currachs of the Galway coast but they are bigger and have high stems out of the water. Here the canoe is called a *naomhog.* The word comes from the Old Irish *noe,* having the same stem as the latin *navis,* a ship. *Naomhog* is the diminutive. They were re-introduced to the area about 1830 by a family from Co. Clare who settled near Castlegregory and replaced the hide covering by tar-covered canvas.

The strange rock shapes one sees on the headlands (e.g. *Clogher head* (III. 31. 103. a) and Inishtooskert) and the scattered rocks in the sea, are the tortured remains of the greatest volcanic area in the British isles. They are the debris of a vast volcanic explosion. One can see stretching from Brandon in the north, along by Smerwick, the landward side of Sybil head, and between Inishtooskert and the Great Blasket a sunken

and partly drowned valley of those times.

About two miles beyond Dunquin there is a turn left for the beautiful and dangerous *Clogher strand* (III. 32. 104. c). Beyond the strand take a left turn off the main road and bear left until, after about half a mile, there is a cluster of houses. Go through the yard of the first farmhouse, right, and diagonally across the field behind it. Over the fence is an eremitical site, *Ballincolla* (III. 33. 105. b), with a fine cashel, two portals, a cross pillar, and a laura. Almost beside it, to one's right, is another, smaller site, less impressive, with a number of simple cross pillars. A twin site like this is, I think, unique in Kerry. Continue on this road until it comes to an end just beyond the small strand at *Ferriter's cove* (III. 33. 106. d). At the cove take the boithrin left. It is a pleasant, moderately stiff walk to *Ferriter's castle* (III. 33. 106. a), or Castle Sybil. Ferriter, or le Fureter, was an early norman settler in these parts, a tenant of the Desmonds, from some time before 1290. In 1574 the Ferriters were pardoned after the Fitz Maurice rising, and forfeited after the Desmond rebellion. But they survived here. The most famous member of the family was the poet, Piaras Ferriter, a leader of the insurgents of 1641, hanged in Killarney by the cromwellians in 1653, and one of the four leading Kerry poets who wrote in Irish. His son, Major Dominick Ferriter, was in exile with Charles II and after 1660 had the Ferriter lands restored to him. Castle Sybil is said to be named after Sybil Lynch of Galway who eloped with a Ferriter. When her father sought her out she was hidden in a cave beneath the castle and was drowned by the rising tide. The name Sybil on *Sybil Head* (III. 31. 106. b) seems, however, to be older than the time of the Ferriters, so there must have been a compression of legends. Indeed, about Piaras Ferriter himself many folk legends have grown up.

Above the castle is *Doon point* (III. 32. 106. d), a promontory fort with, near the tip, the remains of dwellings. Fossils may occasionally be found in the friable silurian rock here. The views are very fine. There is a modern hotel here, and a golf course.

On the way back from Ferriter's cove bear left at the cross roads and take the next turn right to *Beal Ban* (III. 35-36. 106-107), or White Strand, a splendid stretch along which one can walk to Ballyferriter. There is a fine view of *Smerwick Harbour* (III. 35-39. 106-109). The tiny village of *Smerwick* (III. 35. 108. b) is on the western heights overlooking the harbour. There is some discussion as to what Smerwick means. It was sometimes called St Mary's Wick, but the most likely origin is from two norse words, *smoer*, meaning butter, and *wik*, meaning harbour. It was presumably a place for exporting that famous Kerry product, butter, to the norse kingdom of Limerick. Smerwick itself seems to have been a norse settlement — nearby is a place called Clochan na Lochlannach, the village of the norse. Near the eastern entrance to the bay is *Baile na nGall* (III. 38. 107. a) (Ballydavid), the town of the foreigners. It is likely that Smerwick was the principal Kerry port at least from the 9th century. It so continued during the early years of the norman occupation. In 1311 the customs of Kerry were farmed out to Toraldus de la Papa, a merchant of Florence, for one year for 10 marks. In 1312 Reginald Broun, the sheriff of Kerry, was required to swear James Henry of Wynchelsee to answer to the king why he carried hides from the port of 'Shemery-wyt' without paying the customs due thereupon, as Toraldus de la Papa, the keeper of the customs, can show. It was not perhaps for another century that Dingle took over from Smerwick as the principal port of Kerry. Even still, Smerwick is a notable place of refuge for storm bound foreign trawlers.

Return to the road one has left. Close to the junction is a signpost pointing over a field to *Dun an Oir* (III. 36. 107. a), Forte del Oro, the Golden Fort, a name that once rang through Europe. The fortress had a brief and tragic history.

In 1578 a Dingle merchant, Piers Rice, built a fortalice on the little headland (probably in a promontory fort), ostensibly for trading with fishermen but really, it was believed, as a preparation for Fitz Maurice's coming. About the same time a ship of Frobisher's, laden with pyrites from north America, was driven aground there and had to shed its cargo.

Because of the golden colour of the dumped pyrites the fortalice was called Dun an Oir. When James Fitz Maurice arrived here from Dingle in July, 1579, he seized and strengthened the fort against the promise of substantial foreign aid. He then left to rouse the country, but was killed shortly afterwards.

Over a year later, on 13 September, 1580, the foreign aid at length arrived at the fort, some 600 men — mainly Italians, but some Spaniards and Irish — with substantial supplies of arms and some cannon, the first of all the ill-fated foreign landings. The leader was Sebastiano di San Giuseppe of Bologna. The newly arrived soldiers further strengthened the defences, lingering there, against advice, hoping for further foreign aid. The space inside was very constrained for so large a garrison, some 350 feet maximum in length and about 100 feet wide. Water came from two streams half a mile off on either side.

The Lord Deputy, Lord Grey, with 800 men reached Dingle at end October and this place on 7 November. With him were Edmund Spenser (Grey's secretary), Sir Walter Raleigh and Edward Denny (Grey's cousin), who was knighted by Grey for gallantry in attacking the fort and who founded a leading family in Tralee. Two days earlier Admiral Winter's fleet had arrived in Smerwick. On the 7th heavy guns were landed from the ships and at night a trench was made cutting off the fort from the land side. From this guns could play on the fort from 240 yards. Half way through the 8th the defenders' guns were silenced and that night a further trench was made to within 120 yards of the ditch of the fort.

On the 9th the defenders, showing little stomach for further fight, began to parley. During this the interpreter, an Oliver Plunkett from Drogheda, by misinterpretation, tried to set the two sides at issue but he was discovered. There is much dispute as to what was agreed. The defenders yielded to Grey 'at discretion'. How he chose to use that discretion is set out, in Spenser's beautiful hand, in Grey's letter of 12th to the Queen:

I sent in certain gentlement to see their weapons and armures layed downe and to gard the munitions and victaile there left for spoile: Then putt I in certeyn bandes who streight fell to execution. There were 600 slayne; munition and vittaile great store, though much wasted through the disorder of the Souldier, which in that furie could not bee helped. Those that I gaue life vnto, I have bestowed vpon the Capteines and gentlemen . . . . . So hath it pleased the Lord of hostes to deliver your enemies into [your] Highnes handes.

The Irish in the garrison, some 50 of them including women, some pregnant, were hanged. Three special victims — Laurence Moore, a priest; Oliver Plunkett; and an Englishman, William Wollick, had their arms and legs broken in three places at the forge, and were hanged a day later. Edward Denny was one of the officers in charge of the butchery and so, it was said, was Walter Raleigh; but there is some question as to this.

The Queen was well pleased with what had been done with the deliverance: 'I joy that you have been chosen the instrument of His glory'; but she censured Grey for sparing anyone. 'Fides Greyi' became a by word in Europe and a grim warning to all who should attempt to invade the Queen's dominions.

The road runs up to the dilapidated hamlet of Smerwick. Just beyond the houses there is a track to the left that leads to the top of the Three Sisters. On the exposed side of the chief of these peaks, *Binn Diarmada* (III. 36. 109. a), is a ledge in a terrifying spot where Diarmuid and Grainne are said to have slept during their hunted years. Another derivation is that it was from here that Diarmuid mounted his watch during the battle of Ventry. There is here a fine view of the ocean.

Go back to the road and take the second turn left and then, at the main road, left for *Ballyferriter* (III. 36. 105. c). This small town has a tourist business, much of it from people who wish to speak Irish with native speakers. It is the headquarters of a parish the natives of which, over the past 60 years, have published some 60 books of all sorts, some in

246

English, but most in Irish. They have also yielded vast manuscript collections of local folklore.

The history of this parish illustrates the resurgence of the catholic church in Ireland in the latter part of the 19th century. In a space of 16 years from 1855 the three churches of the parish were built, the desperately poor people of the area giving some money — to pay for skilled masons — but prodigally of their labour, to draw timber from Killarney, lime from Killorglin, and stones. In addition, they helped with the actual construction. Ballyferriter church was begun in 1855, and the two outlying churches of Dunquin and *Carrig* (III. 40. 108. a) in 1857 and 1866 respectively. These were all to replace old and decrepit buildings. Dunquin church was roofed with timber cast up by the sea. Something like this was happening all over Ireland.

As one goes out of the town east there is a rough road right, up a hill. Follow this. Near the top of the hill, in a field just below the road, are two fine gallans, a male and a female one, now linked by a wall. There are fine views here. Follow this road beyond a junction, left. A little further on the road runs through the corner of the early christian settlement of *Reagleis,* Ballywiheen (III. 36. 104. c).

There is a large, carved cross in the ditch on one's right. The settlement was enclosed by a caiseal of considerable diameter. There is a ruined oratory. There is, as at Kilmalkedar, a so-called sundial, but more crudely incised, with holes on both sides, but it is not perforated. This is the first of a large number of christian sites dating from about the 7th century to be seen in this neighbourhood.

Turn the car and take the next turn (now) on one's right. At the T junction turn left. Immediately on one's left is a gateway into *Ballineanig church* (III. 37. 104. a). This is a typical medieval parish church. Inside there is an early, incised cross pillar and a quern, suggesting that this site dates from a date similar to that of Reagleis, but was promoted to parish status in the 12th-13th centuries. Close by the church, south, is an unusual

stone with a cross and knicks on the top.

Follow this road until one comes to a (more or less) T junction and bear right. Shortly afterwards there is a sharp turn right by a filling station. Almost immediately after this there is another turn right. A short distance up this road there are, left, the pillar stones of *Reask* (III. 37. 105. d) and, right, now being excavated, the remains of the eremitical settlement. The principal stone here is a very fine and well known example of a well developed, but still early, christian cross pillar. One of the few finds so far has been considerable quantities of iron slag. Similar finds have been found on the Skellig and elsewhere. Why was iron smelting carried on in these places? It is now clear from the excavations that this was a big settlement inside a large caiseal. There are the remains of the usual clochans, but also of larger houses, including one of considerable size that must have been thatched. This place has quite a different atmosphere from that of the Skelligs and seems to resemble the typical monastery of the 7th and 8th centuries and, no doubt, later.

Turn the car and retrace one's steps by Ballineanig church. Follow this road for a further mile and a half. After a double junction on the left there is, in a field on the right, the remarkable tower house of *Rahinnane* (III. 37. 102. b). This belonged to the Knight of Kerry, head of a cadet branch of the Desmonds, and was built in a great ringfort mentioned in the account of the battle of Ventry. The fosse here between the two rings is remarkably deep; perhaps the normans deepened it and kept it so. The castle was taken in 1602, and was destroyed in the cromwellian wars.

This road brings one back to Ventry and along the main road to Dingle. Total driving distance: 45 miles. Allow the whole day.

(V) DINGLE – TEMPLENACLOONAGH – GALLARUS – KILMALKEDAR

Just after Milltown take the straight road left. After a mile and a quarter one comes to a bridge over a stream. Climb over the ditch, right, staying on the Milltown side of the

stream. Follow the green road here through three fields. On one's left is the eremitical site of *Kilfountain* (III. 43. 104. c), much ruined, but showing all the classical signs — caiseal, laura, quern, ruined oratory, clochans (the buildings very ruined) and a fine cross pillar with a greek cross with the circle or *scutum fidei*, as well as, most unusually, the founder's name, Finten, incised on it, and a formalised chi-rho. Back to the car. Continue on the road. Three miles after Milltown, at the cross roads, turn left and, immediately, left again. After three quarters of a mile this road turns sharp right. At the cross roads just after this turn right along a rough road by a school. On this road, after 0.4 miles there is a cross roads, barely discernible. Just before the cross roads there is, left, divided between two fields, the interesting early christian site of *Templenacloonagh* (III. 40. 105. c). There are the remains of the caiseal that surrounded it and of a very early church (as distinct from an oratory) built almost wholly of dry stone with a scanty grouting of mortar. This must be one of the earliest churches in Kerry, built in the style of the oratories and of almost the same dimensions (c.15 feet by 11 feet). Compare with Killelton. West of the church are two fine cross pillars: that on the south has a curiously developed syrian cross with a small greek cross beneath; that on the north is boldly and well incised, with a greek cross on top running into a circle enclosing another greek cross with finials, all above a latin cross with finials rising out of the anchor motif.

On the back is a rather rough latin cross. In the next field, north, are the remains of what was probably an oratory, but could be another early church. Around it one can just discern the mark of the *laura,* the raised part of the enclosure where the founder had his special site. If so, this ruin is most likely that of an oratory. There are some remains of what may have been beehive huts.

Return the way one has come back to the main road to the first cross roads where one had turned off it. Here continue across the main road and, following the signposts through this confusing place, turn right and right again for *Gallarus* (III. 40. 105. b).

Gallarus Oratory — entrance

This name does not, according to An Seabhach, refer to a foreign settlement but to a rocky headland (Gall-iorrus). This is the only perfect oratory on the mainland (there are two on the Skellig). It is the best example of dry rubble masonry in Ireland and, probably, anywhere else. It is as dry as when it was first erected. It was clearly built by men who had achieved a mastery of the form and is thus likely to be later than the other ruined ones in the neighbourhood and on the Iveragh peninsula. This is borne out by the fact that it has a rounded east window unlike the ruined one at Kilmalkedar or those on the Skellig. It is a true arch scooped out of soft conglomerate stones (common in this neighbourhood), a number of which are used in the rest of the building. The flat entrance has also been made of this stone, carefully dressed. Inside one can see how the other stones were roughly dressed by, presumably, being hammered square after they had been laid. It seems clear from the thin remains of mortar between the courses that the building was internally pointed, perhaps plastered, but whether at the time of building, or later, is

not clear. There are other signs of superficial mortar outside that suggest that it, too, was pointed or plastered. There is on the roof at the east gable a conglomerate stone that may have been cut into a cross, but looks more likely to have been a finial. All of these marks suggest to some observers that the building may have been erected some centuries after the usual 7th-8th century date. But the cross pillar, with greek cross, beside it is typical of 7th century settlements. Teampall Geal, at Ballymoreeagh, also had internal pointing or plastering and has a finial (clearly, I think, added later) but is otherwise a typical 7th century settlement. At Kilmalkedar is an oratory with a square window; so it is likely to be earlier than Gallarus. We have a date to 636 AD for Mael Cathair's death. It seems that the arch was introduced to Ireland about the 8th century, so a date not later than about 750 AD is not implausible for Gallarus. Whatever the date, it is a masterpiece of its kind. Note, inside the door, the two projecting holed stones — the door was hinged from these. Whether it was of leather or of wood is not clear; but, given the strength of the west winds hereabouts, a wooden door would have been more serviceable. Apart from the cross pillar there are no other signs of early eremitical settlement; but excavation, as at Reask, might reveal these.

From the oratory one can see below one, west, the ruins of *Gallarus castle* (III. 39. 106. d), a Fitz Gerald tower house. Miss Hickson tells the story of the last Fitz Gerald

Gallarus Castle

Chancellor's House, Kilmalkedar

to live there, a man whose fierce pride was above work but not, it seems, occasional smuggling. In extreme old age he was on his deathbed for some days unconscious when at night a great storm arose. In the morning he revived and commanded that he be brought to the window. There for hours he watched the magnificent fury of the ocean tearing at the broken landscape. His last words were: 'Tis just the day for a Geraldine to die'.

Follow up the road by Gallarus oratory to the signposted cross roads. Turn sharp left. Just half a mile along this road, on the crest of the hill, right, is a complex *alignment* (III. 41. 105. a). There are three stones in the principal alignment, with another stone to its end, and three more stones some little distance away.

Continue on this main road to *Kilmalkedar* (III. 41. 107. c). Here are to be found examples of many stages of Irish building from pagan to medieval times. The name comes from the church of Mael Cathair who, as we have seen, died in this place in 636 AD.

The *Martyrology of Donegal* claims that he was the grandson of the king of Ulster and of the race of Fiatach, monarch of Erin. He was thus clearly a missionary to Kerry at a period much later than other missionaries and when, indeed, missionaries from Kerry were at work in north Munster. This is a further indication that paganism made a last determined and not wholly unsuccessful stand in this remote area.

248

But, first, the *Chancellor's house* (III. 41. 106 a), on the left, just after a cross roads. Kilmalkedar was an important benefice in the diocese of Ardfert and the chancellor of the diocese was entitled to half the tithes; perhaps he was rector from time to time; hence the name of his house. The ruin is interesting for being the remains of one of the few dwelling houses that remain to us of, probably, the 15th century. There is another beyond the church.

A little further on, right, is the church, the remains of one of the finest second rank romanesque churches in Ireland. It had a corbelled stone roof, a development of the Gallarus style in imitation of Cormac's chapel at Cashel. When the roof was intact the whole must have been beautifully proportioned. The nave was built in the mid-12th century; the chancel, less pleasing, was added a little later. The influence of wooden churches is to be seen in the antae protruding at each end of the west gable and the winged finial, like protruding slanted cross beams, on the top of that gable. Inside the church note the half columns and the classic style entablature, the heads grotesquely truncated inside the tympanum and the round headed windows. Note how the chancel was later added, spoiling, I think, the proportions of what must have been a little gem of a church.

Inside the church is the abcedarium stone, with latin alphabet crudely carved and with a simple cross. This suggests a relic of an early 7th century school where the local children were taught to write — reminding one that a special, and continuing, feature of Irish missionary effort is to found schools.

We are reminded of another continuity in Irish life by the holed stone also in the church.

There is another outside, with ogam. These recall the Indian *yoni* stones. In India, if the hole is big enough, people pass through it to be regenerated. If the hole is too small, as here, a hand or foot through it will serve the same purpose, but the east window of the church is known as cro na snathaide, the eye of the needle, through which one must squeeze to be saved. Wakeman says of the holed stone: 'some 50 years ago' (i.e. about

Kilmalkedar Church

1850) 'the virtue of this stone was famous — persons afflicted with chronic rheumatism, falling sickness and some other ills might, by passing three times round it' and 'offering certain prayers', be cured. He refers to the Stennis stone in Orkney where the oath to Woden (or Odin) was sworn by persons joining their hands through the hole in the runic stone. On Easter Sunday, 1970, many people could be seen squeezing through cro na snathaide, and making clockwise rounds, this last the continuation of the bronze age practice of the deisiol. Outside, west of the west door, half hidden amongst the mounds of graves — the place was so crowded, as a burial ground that people were buried above ground with the earth heaped about their coffins — is the so-called 'sundial.' This is a very well carved, holed — but not perforated — stone, round above a plinth. The face is divided diagonally, each segment — on the sundial theory — to represent three hours, the gnomon projecting at right angles to project the shadow. A moment's reflection will show this theory to be nonsense. The stone is on a vertical, not horizontal, plane, faces east, and shows complete ignorance of the geometrical principles of setting out hour angles. The back is ornamented with intersecting arcs of circles, the sides and pedestal with incised lines terminating in a greek fret pattern. This is a very sophisticated piece of work and is, almost certainly, from a date long before christianity reached this place. There is another similar stone, but much more crudely carved, at Ballywiheen, Ballyferriter. There is what well may be a sundial to be seen on the

Skellig; but it is quite different from this at Kilmalkedar. We have seen that many of the christian settlements are associated with what must have been pagan places of worship of the dead. Here, no doubt, we had a major centre for the worship of the principle of life.

This, clearly, proved more tenacious than the other — did it get re-inforcement from the viking settlements of the harbour below? That this stone, the *yoni* stones and the deisiol should have survived at what was an important christian settlement — clearly intended to appropriate pagan religious practices to its own ends — for over a thousand years is quite astonishing. About a quarter of a mile due west of the church is a holy well.

In the church grounds, also, are a large, crudely made cross — one of few in Kerry — and a number of smaller ones.

North of the church is a roadway and, where it forks, is, left, 'St Brendan's House', a relatively well preserved 15th century house, one of very few, no doubt a presbytery for the church.

Bisecting the angle made by the fork here ran the old Saints' Road, running from, it may be, Ventry by way of *Ballybrack bridge* (III. 43. 110. c) to the top of Brandon. A large number of christian sites were established on both sides of this road. Parts of the road are now lost, but much of it is marked on the 1 inch ordnance map. At Curanly Hill, on the Kilmalkedar side of *Ballinloghig*, (III. 43. 109. c), there are, according to Foley, 'over 36 flag-steps' to be found of the old road. It was along this road that the great pilgrimages to St Brendan's shrine at the top of the mountain were made. The most famous of these pilgrimages was a relatively recent one when on 28 June, 1868, on the initiative of the redoubtable Fr (later Canon) Brosnan, an estimated 20,000 people attended Mass on the peak celebrated by David Moriarty, bishop of Kerry. The bishop and the pilgrims from Tralee climbed the mountain from the Cloghane side. The present bishop of Kerry, Most Rev Eamon Casey, has revived the practice.

Kerry crosses, in quality of stone, sculpting and proportion. There is incised on it a cross with double circle. There are some other crosses here, very crude. The site is very ruined. Back to the main road.

Ballyheabought (III. 44. 104. b) (Baile Ui Sheaghdha Bocht) is some three quarters of a mile along the road to Dingle. This townland is the only place in the peninsula named after the O Sheas, once a ruling family of the Corcu Duibne. There is here, about 100 yards east of the road, a bivallate rath of some interest. It is made of stones, lightly covered with earth, the inner rampart being 12-14 feet thick. It contains the remains of a rectangular structure and of two beehive huts with a souterrain linking them. One of the beehives is of interest in that it is in fair preservation and contains a flying wing inside, a sort of curved, partial partition.

Total driving distance: 23 miles. Allow a half day.

(VI) MOUNT BRANDON

One may feel tempted to come to terms with the great, brooding bulk of Brandon that commands the western part of the peninsula. This is not easy because the summit is so often covered with mist. It is, of course, at 3,127 feet, the second highest mountain in Ireland. Experienced climbers may attack it from the Cloghane side; but, given a settled day, those without much experience or gear will find it a relatively easy climb if it is tackled by the Saints' Road on the west side.

Take the Brandon Creek road from Dingle for six miles. Shortly after one has crossed the Feohanagh river there is at *Ballybrack* (III. 43. 110. c) a road right. Take this and bring the car up as far as one thinks prudent. This is the Saints' Road. The walk to the summit, which may be wet in places, is about three and a half miles. On a clear day the views from Brandon are magnificent.

At the top is an oratory dedicated to St Brendan, and a set of 'rounds' long christianised, but harking back to an older tradition. On top of this mountain was

St Brendan's House, Kilmalkedar

About a quarter of a mile along the main road, on the right, two fields above the road, are the remains of *Kilmalkedar oratory*, (III. 40. 107. d), perhaps Mael Cathair's original settlement, but now called St Brendan's oratory. This is a ruined, Gallarus style building, shored up by the Office of Public Works. The masonry is cruder than Gallarus and the east window has a flat lintel. It is clearly an earlier building than Gallarus. Close by is a bullaun stone, called 'St Brendan's Keelers'.

From here one can follow the pleasant (but bad) road through *Murreagh* (III. 39. 107.c) by the little church of *Carrig* (III. 40. 108. a) the building of which in 1866, with the others in the parish, is so vividly described in an tAth O Ciosain's book, *Cead Bliain*, and on to *Feohanagh* (III. 40. 110. a), turning left here

for the attractive inlet of *Brandon Creek* (III. 43. 112. a). From here St Brendan set off on his voyage.

Come back along the main road to Dingle and, after three quarters of a mile, turn left at the schoolhouse and right at the T junction. This is *Ballynavenooragh* (III. 43. 111. b), where there are many cahers with clochans, rather like Fahan, but not so numerous. Macalister says he saw in one of these, known as 'The Baker's Hut' 'something like an oven.'

Just three miles along the main road to Dingle there is a cross roads. Turn right here and, a short distance further on, right again, and then up the first boithrin right into a farmyard. Two fields above one is *Reenconnell cross* (III. 43. 107. a), now set in concrete. This is quite the best of the shaped

250

celebrated within close to living memories the latter day forms of the festival of the pagan god, Lug, and his temporary triumph over his adversary Crom Dubh. This struggle became christianised in the victory of St Brendan over the same adversary. It will be recalled that Brendan's father was Findlug, and that Find (or Fionn) and Lug were synonymous. What is more, this mountain now so associated with St Brendan and his voyage seems to take its name from an earlier mythical voyager, Bran.

There are two other walks in this area that can be conveniently done with two cars or a driver willing to deposit and pick up.

The first is to drive through Cloghane to Brandon Point. The driver will return and get on the road from Dingle to Brandon Creek, but a mile short of the Creek, he will turn right at the cross roads and then at the T junction he will turn left. He will follow this road as far as he dares. From Brandon Point the climbers will get up to the 1,000 ft peneplain and keep broadly to this height parallel to the sea. There are magnificent cliffs. The substantial mountain between Brandon and the sea is *Masatiompan* (2,509 ft.) (III. 47. 115. b). Keep north of this for the views; but the side of this mountain is very steep. South west of this mountain one eventually comes to a roadway where, sooner or later, depending on his resolution, the driver should be found. The walking distance is about seven miles.

The other walk is through the Pass of *Mullaghaveal* (III. 46. 107. b). Take the road for Cloghane. Just short of the catholic church there is a sharp turn left by a house gable right. Follow this road for two miles to where there is a boithrin right. About 300 feet above one is *Lough Avoonane* (III. 49. 109. a), under a cliff, about half a mile from the road. North of this, half a mile away, is the much larger *Lough Cruttia* (III. 48-49. 110-111). A mile further on, above a steep cliff, is *Lough Nalacken* (III. 48. 111. b). Three loughs nestling under cliff faces in this way are very typical of Kerry coums. Back to the car. There are on the left as one travels to the end of this coum several loughs with high above them the road over the Connor Pass.

At the Pass of Mullaghaveal it will be necessary for the driver to go back to Dingle and get on the Brandon Creek road for four miles, turn right at *Glin cross* (III. 44. 106. a) and follow this road as far as it will go. Those left behind will take the old road over the col which, bearing north west, after less than two miles, brings them onto the road where they should meet the driver. There are fine views all the way. The total walking distance will be about two miles for this and about four miles for the earlier one by the lakes.

St Brendan's Oratory, Kilmalkedar

Chapter 14

North Kerry: Clanmaurice and Iraghticonnor

CLANMAURICE

This barony runs in a wedge from, in the west, the mouth of the Feale to Barrow Harbour to a point on the Limerick border some three miles south west of Abbeyfeale. Its northern line is the river Feale and its southern one, at the eastern end, the Stack and Glanruddery mountains.

The barony takes its name from the Fitz Maurice family, the lords of Kerry, descendants of the geraldine Maurice from Shanid who overran it in 1215. The great centre of their power was the ecclesiastical city of Ardfert, but their castles lay along the line of the Feale, from Listowel to Ballybunion, against the surviving power of O Conor Kerry in the barony of Iraghticonnor to the north. The Fitz Maurices survived in this barony until the 18th century, and then linked with the Pettys, to become the Petty-Fitz Maurices still surviving as Marquesses of Lansdowne, with a seat near Kilmakilloge. The Fitz Maurices, who in their hey-day

Ballyheigue Castle

continually married Irish, were fairly consistently disloyal to the Crown and, from the 16th century, their power was gradually taken over by the Crosbies who, beginning as reformed bishop of Ardfert, lasted there until the end of the 19th century. Now, the abiding historical memory there is of the tragedy of Casement and the *Aud*.

(I) BALLYHEIGUE

Clanmaurice has, at its eastern end, good farming land, but flat and rather dull, and the mountains to the east are not much to boast of; but the barony has its own attractions. Perhaps the most agreeable centre is *Ballyheigue* (pop. 1971: 450) (IV. 75. 129. d), set at the head of most magnificent strands with splendid views of the Dingle peninsula and the Maharee islands. Very plain is Inishtooskert where the *Aud* was to have been picked up by the local pilot who saw, but ignored, her because she was two days too soon. The area around here enjoys the driest and brightest weather in Kerry.

Ballyheigue is dominated by a neo-gothic castle built by the Crosbies about 1812, but not completed for some years. It was designed in 1809 by William Morrison, then aged 15, son of Sir Richard Morrison. It was in Ballyheigue that the Danish ship, the *Golden Lyon* ran aground in 1730 and in the

Clanmorris Barony, after Petty

252

then low thatched house of the Crosbies that the bulk of her crew with their bullion were lodged, giving cause for one of the most notorious of 18th century crimes and scandals. This is discussed in detail elsewhere. It was here the Cantillons (originally de Cantelupe) settled in early norman times. They were a prominent family before the rise of the Desmonds overshadowed so much. They remained catholics and suffered with the Desmonds in the 1580's, but managed to survive until the time of James II. One of them, James, emigrated to France in 1690 and a descendant became Baron Cantillon de Ballyheigue in the French creations of Louis Philippe. Another of the family was Richard, a wealthy banker in Paris, a founder of the science of economics, who was murdered in London in 1734. Ballyheigue castle itself — its ruins are close to the neo-gothic ruins — came into the hands of the Crosbies by marriage.

(II) ARDFERT — BANNA — AKERAGH

Quite the most important site in north Kerry is Ardfert. From Ballyheigue take the main road through the flat, strangely luminous land to Ardfert. One can reach *Kilmoyley North* (IV.79.126) townland, where a great gold hoard from bronze age times was found, by taking, a half-mile outside of Ballyheigue, the road left for two miles. Due south of one is the townland. Return to the Ardfert road.

Ardfert (IV. 79-80. 121-122) is a decaying little town (pop. 1971: 286) with a long history. It was here that Bishop Erc, one of St Patrick's assistants, established a missionary post in the mid-fifth century. Here St Brendan was educated about 500 AD and founded a monastery. From him it was known as Ardfert-Brendan. It seems to have no recorded history until the 11th century. In 1046 the stone church was destroyed by lightning and, in 1111, shortly before the Synod of Rathbreasail, by warring factions.

Perhaps this is why the synod chose Ratass as the seat of the new bishopric. However, Amchad O hAnmchada died as bishop of Ardfert in 1117. Mael Brenainn O Ronain attended the Synod of Kells in 1152 when

Ardfert was the chosen see for Kerry. He died in 1166 and was buried in Ardfert. The bishop of Ardfert was amongst those who did fealty to Henry II in 1172. Ardfert remained the seat of a bishopric until 1660 when, on the restoration of the protestant episcopacy, it was joined to Limerick. When the catholic episcopacy was restored in 1720 the bishopric was seated first in Dingle, then in Tralee, and then in Killarney.

Ardfert was also the main centre of the Fitz Maurice family, lords of Kerry for four centuries from the 13th to the 17th. They had a castle here but no remains of their power survive here. The founder of the family fortunes and father of the first Lord Kerry founded the Franciscan friary in 1253, and the second Lord Kerry, who died in 1332, built a leper or lazar house here. After the eclipse of the Fitz Maurices their power here for the next four centuries was taken over by the Crosbie family, founded by John Crosbie, second reformed bishop of Ardfert. A description of the 'Countie of (North) Kerrie' of 1598 lists Ardfert, 'Dingley and Traley' as the three 'Principall townes' of the county. It seems to have become a borough of sorts before the parliament of 1613, though it never seems to have had a charter, and, it is claimed, returned one member to it. From 1639, at latest, it certainly returned two members to subsequent Irish parliaments. It remained in the pocket of the Crosbies until it lost borough status in 1800 under the Act of Union. It was a classic example of a rotten borough. The Crosbies were paid £15,000 compensation which helped their members to vote for the Union with good conscience.

The most striking features of the town are the cathedral, with its associated ruins, and the remains of the Franciscan friary.

The cathedral site illustrates a feature of Irish ecclesiastical cities, the proliferation of churches, three of them almost side by side — the cathedral, Temple-na-Hoe, and Temple-na-Griffin. It also illustrates a good part of the development of later Irish church architecture at one of its finest periods. That the city was populous about 1250 can be seen from the size of the cathedral. It has no

tower: that function was discharged by a round tower — one of four in Kerry — which was 120 feet high and fell suddenly in 1771. This was built with an earlier romanesque church, part of which survives in the west wall of the cathedral and part in the north wall. Note the use of large stones. The cathedral is of course a fine example of the harsh early English style. Temple-na-Hoe (i.e. of the Virgin) to the north of the tower site, illustrates the next period of norman, or transitional, architecture: observe the norman row of beads on the cornice outside. The blending of romanesque and transitional styles can be seen in the window enclosed in a border of flowers and other decorations outside the splay. Temple-na-Griffin is an example of the style of the 15th century, and incorporates in a window jamb inside the north wall two wyverns with crossed necks (mistaken for griffins, hence the name of the church) representing evil devouring itself. This represents an old tradition but unusually depicted in this way in the 15th century style.

The triangular heads of the piscina recall the style of some of the very earliest churches, and the two trefoil-headed lights of the east

Ardfert Cathedral

window under a segmented arch imitate 13th century work.

But the main feature is, of course, the cathedral itself. The principal part of the building was erected about 1250 in the early English style adopted almost entirely from England. It will be appreciated that from about this date on Ardfert was the centre of anglo-norman ecclesiastical influence in Kerry. There was virtually no building in the 14th century but in the 15th the south transept and the north east chapel were added to the cathedral. These represent the late Irish gothic style, a very distinctive adaptation of the general style. Probably from the 16th century date the acutely pointed ogee arch in the north side of the cathedral and the distinctive Irish feature of battlements was added about this time. It is not clear whether the usual dividing wall between nave and chancel ever was built here. The cathedral was destroyed in the 1640 wars. The south transept was turned into a protestant parish church in 1670.

Set into the wall of the cathedral inside is

Stone carving, Ardfert Cathedral

an effigy, sometimes said to be of St Brendan, sometimes of a Bishop Stack, three of whom were bishops of Ardfert in the 15th century. It is usual, but there are many exceptions, for a bishop's crozier to point outwards, stressing his external jurisdiction, as against an abbot who, because his jurisdiction is limited to his own community, has his crozier pointing in, as has this figure. So it may represent St Brendan or one of his abbot successors; it is in fact a late 13th century carving.

Under the great east window is a tomb with an inscription that, according to the *Kerry Magazine,* was legible in the 1850's:

> Orate P..............
> ....is Diony Moriarty et Evgeny
> O Sullivan
> Episcopus Kerrienses
> ....us Scups
> Johannes Roach, 25 Martii, An. Dni, 1762.

Denis Moriarty was the first, and Eugene O Sullivan the second, bishop of Kerry in the 18th century. They died in 1737 and 1740 respectively. It is a sign of declining religious tension that they should have been re-buried here in 1762. In the same tomb was buried the fourth 18th century bishop of Kerry, Nicholas Madgett, who died in 1774. (The third bishop, William O Meara, became bishop of Killaloe, having swapped dioceses with Madgett!).

At the entrance to the south transept is another tomb, the inscription on which is quite clear. it reads:

> This tomb was erected by Br Anthony Kavenagh for ye Revs. Frs. Der. Falvey Decd, Aug 22, 1750. Aged 68.
> John Shea, May 3, 1751. Aged 62.
> I. Goggin, Decr. 1st, 1765. Aged 40 years.
> And for the rest of his Brethren, 1773.

These were presumably Franciscans, survivors of the community at Ardfert friary, another example of the great tenacity of the friars in Kerry.

In the south transept itself lies Anne Petty, countess of Kerry, who died in 1737. She was the daughter of the great Sir William

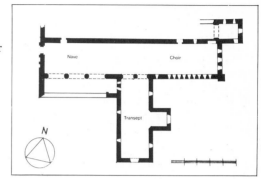

Plan of Ardfert Cathedral

Petty and ancestress, by her Fitz Maurice husband, of the Lansdowne family. Also buried here are many members of the Crosbie family.

Observe the usual megalithic strong boxes in which more recent burials have been made.

Across the road to the right, in the grounds of Ardfert house, are the ruins of Ardfert friary, a house of conventual Franciscans, founded by Thomas, 1st Lord Kerry, in 1253. He died in 1280 and was buried in the 'founder's tomb' to the left (as one faces it) of the altar. There are two other Fitz Maurice tombstones of interest in the centre of the chancel. One is a much worn coffin shaped lid with the remains of a figure, which Miss Hickson identified as Sir Gerald Fitz Maurice, Grand Prior of the Knights Templars in Ireland when they were abolished in 1307-12. Behind this is the beautifully decorated tomb lid which Miss Hickson identified as that of Edmund Fitz Maurice, 10th Lord, who between 1530 and 1540, resigned in favour of his son and became a lay brother in the community. He died in 1543. This friary was unusual in that in 1325 it contained both Anglo-Irish and Irish friars — it seems that the Irish friars had taken the Bruce side in the recent wars.

The buildings were much altered over the years, but the fine gothic chancel is original, with its 'second pointed' gothic windows. The Knights Hospitallers had some rights in the town of Ardfert and there is a record of a dispute between them and the

254   Franciscans in 1325 about the market cross and pillory. As was general at the time the friary was largely re-built in 1453 when the beautiful cloister with unusual four centred arches, the rather unusually located tower at the west gable, and the south transept were built. In the south transept we see the late Irish gothic feature of round headed windows and an inscription that Donald Fitz Bohan completed it in 1453. The friars became Observantine Franciscans — joining those at Muckross and Lislaghtin — in 1518. They were driven out in the Desmond wars, but seem to have been back again in the 17th century, perhaps after the death, in 1621, of John Crosbie, reformed bishop of Ardfert who lived here. The community remained in existence in the neighbourhood until the 1800s. We have seen in the cathedral the tombstone of a number of friars of the second half of the 18th century. The last friar was Timothy O Sullivan who entered the Sorbonne in 1768.

In the Desmond wars the tower became the barracks of the soldiers of the hated Captain Zouch and then the residence of the reformed bishops Nicholas Kenan and John Crosbie.

When the protestant chapel was being constructed in the cathedral in 1670 the window of the south transept of this friary was taken down and inserted in it. However, the last earl of Glandore restored the status quo.

John Crosbie, second reformed bishop of Ardfert, was an Irishman, Mc Crossan from Laois, who conformed, had a large family and many catholic connexions. He acquired extensive properties around Ardfert and built a house near the friary. In the next century Sir Maurice Crosbie built a pleasant georgian house, the ruins of which among the dead trees are above the friary. The house was considered small for the late 18th century taste of the last countess, a Sackville, sister of the last duke of Dorset. But her husband would not allow it to be touched, or the bowling green behind it.

John Crosbie's son, Col David Crosbie, played a prominent part against the insurgents in 1641 and was later appointed by Cromwell governor of Kerry. As we have seen, the Crosbies owned the pocket borough of Ardfert and through this, their influence in the county at large and in the two other

Kerry boroughs, usually commanded three or four votes in the Irish parliament in the 18th century. The head of the family, Sir Maurice Crosbie, became first Baron Branden, first Viscount Crosbie, and first Earl of Glandore. In Vol II of the *Kerry Archaeological Magazine* there is an interesting account of a tenants' gala given in 1793 by the third earl's agent. These festivals were usually held after the gala (gale) days, March 25 and September 29. This one was held on a Sunday in mid-April, 1793. All the tenants, and two priests, a doctor and two other catholics not tenants but 'specially attached' to the landlord, were invited. There were three levels of guests — 22 in the parlour (who drank 34 bottles of claret); the second rate who were entertained in the breakfast parlour with port wine and rum punch; and the third rate in a tent pitched on the avenue near the Abbey. Here were drunk 'above 80 gallons' of whiskey punch and 'plenty of Beer besides'. 'Pipers and Fiddlers enlivened the intervals between the peals of ordnance, The Maymen and Maids with the hobbyhorse etc. danced most cheerfully'. 'An ox was roasted whole to great enthusiasm and six sheep were also consumed. A fine serene evening favoured happily the glee and hilarity of the meeting'.

Ardfert Friary

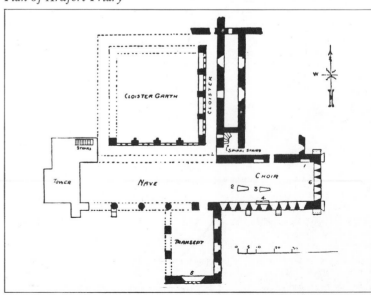

Plan of Ardfert Friary

Cloister of Ardfert Friary

The earldom became extinct when the third earl died childless in 1815. The name was carried on by his nephew, John Talbot; hence the Talbot Crosbies from that time. The nephew commissioned Sir Richard Morrison, who designed the fine courthouse at Tralee, to build some distance away from the georgian house a neo-gothic castle. This building was burned down during the troubles in May 1921. The fine gateway is in the centre of the village.

Take the road to Fenit for about a half-mile and turn sharp right at the signpost 'Casement's Fort'. About a half-mile along this road there is a further signpost. In the field to the right is a bush-surrounded ringfort of impressive size once called *'Mc Kenna's Fort'* (IV. 78. 121. d). Here it was that Sir Roger Casement was arrested on Good Friday, 1916, by police from Ardfert, alerted by reports of the landing of three men early that morning on Banna strand nearby. They had come by German submarine and their rubber dinghy and hastily buried pistols had been found. Casement was ill and could not walk further. He hid in this fort while his companions went to Tralee for help. By the time they had got a car and had missed their road back Casement had been captured and lodged in Tralee on his way to being hanged as the only 'traitor' of the 1914-18 war. He had come to try to put off the rising planned for Easter Sunday 1916.

The mishandling of the arrangements in Tralee and the Maharees that morning for landing arms from the German ship *Aud* had in any event ensured that the rising planned to be a considerable and national revolt would be no more than a local and forlorn gesture — if a highly effective one. The fort itself is an interesting example. The fosse around it must once have been very deep if one allows for the levelling effects of the centuries.

Continue along this road and, undismayed, along a sandy track over a little stream until at length one comes to a lightly tarred road. One goes by substantial sandhills and these contain a great variety of wild flowers, one of the leading botanical areas in the county.

Follow the tarred road until one comes to a junction and turn left until one comes to the main access to the splendid strand at *Banna* (IV. 75. 123. d). Near here Casement and his two companions landed, their dinghy having overturned and Casement being dragged out of the waves more dead than alive. Close by there is a memorial of this landing. Casement's principal companion was Captain Robert Monteith who was not captured and the unnamed one was Sergeant Bailey (or Beverley) who was captured, and turned King's evidence at Casement's trial. There is a haunting song about all this.

Turn back this road for rather less than a mile and at the T junction turn left for Ballyheigue. After two miles turn left and follow the road to the sea. Here one is at the outlet (with a lock) of Lough Akeragh. Return to the road for Ballyheigue. After about a mile one reaches, off the road left, *Lough Akeragh* (IV. 76-77. 126-127), one of the principal places in Ireland for winter birds, especially American ones. They are attracted by an unusual mixture of brackish and fresh water, the shelter and plentiful feeding. In winter the place is full of many varieties of water bird. Many of these move out beyond the sandhills into the sea.

Then back to Ballyheigue. Total driving distance: 15 miles. Allow a half day at least.

(III) KERRY HEAD

At Kerry Head we run into exposed sandstone and conditions comparable to some of the best of the sandstone areas further south.

Some three and a half miles along the road from Ballyheigue there is a signpost left for the old church of *Cill Mhic a' Deaghaidh* (IV. 70. 130. d), reputedly founded by Bishop Erc, St Brendan's mentor. This is at the very end of that road, about a half mile down, behind a cluster of farm buildings. The church, which is relatively well-preserved, is clearly not as old as its reputed founder and is not of great interest. Erc is named in this connexion as the son of Deaghadh who was it would seem the tutelary god of this area — Curoi MacDaire, the slightly grotesque hero of Caherconree across the bay, is variously given as the son and the grandson of this god and North Kerry was often called after him.

Back onto the main road and, at the fork, bear left for just under a half mile. Stop outside a yellowish one storey farmhouse facing the road on the right. A little beyond this, but on the left, is a gateway to a boithrin. Follow this boithrin down almost to the cliff edge. Three fields down, on the right, are the remains of bee-hive houses and the marks of souterrains. At the sea end of the sixth field, directly under where one has entered, is the entrance to a remarkable souterrain which can be explored without too much trouble. These are the well-known *Glenderry* souterrains (IV. 69. 130. d). Old clothes and a torch are essential, children a help. There are a number of chambers — six or seven I am told; I got no further than four because our clothes were not *that* old — joined by small tunnels through which one must crawl. The chambers are in effect corbelled bee-hive houses, of fair size and splendidly preserved. From the outside, in the field next above the cliff, one can discern the marks of the chambers and of the connecting tunnels, perhaps exposed by erosion — otherwise they must have lost most of their point. The exit is almost at the top of the cliff. There are a number of souterrains in this area. They are unusual in not being associated with a ringfort. What turned people in pre-atomic times to take such pains to scuttle underground if events

255

256

were harsh? The small tunnels put any intruder at a grave disadvantage. The views from here are very fine. Plentiful hereabouts are the translucent rock crystals known as Kerry diamonds.

Continue on the road one has come and take the next turn left. This brings one close to the point of *Kerry Head* (IV. 68. 127). Here there are two small promontory forts, *Cahercarberybeg* (IV. 68. 131. b) and *Cahercarberymore* (IV. 69. 133. d), the latter about a mile north of the former. These also seem to have been places of refuge for the inhabitants of the Head — they are not accessible from the sea. They seem from their appearance to be of greater age than the great stone forts, dating no doubt from the early iron age.

Close to Cahercarberymore, nearly a mile from the cliff edge, begins a curious earthwork, the Cleeroe (Cladh Ruadh) or Red Ditch. It is about four feet wide and deep at this place. Smith says it runs from here across to the hill at Knockanure (that is, the one between Listowel and Athea) and reappears at Athea. From there it is said to link up with the Cladh Dubh (or Black Ditch) that runs to Rath Luirc. Here, at Kerry Head, it runs for under a mile east south east up the hill. It then disappears in the bog. It reappears north east of the summit of the hill, *Maulin* (IV. 73. 131. c), and runs east south east across the road as it goes along the north side of Kerry Head. There are in Ireland a number of these curious linear earthworks, but nothing is known of them. In early times they were most probably defensive earthworks. In later times they may have become roadways.

Back onto the road and continue round the Head. Here the mouth of the Shannon and the Clare coast come into sight. This is a very different, but impressive, prospect. Four miles further on there is the little church of Teampall Daithlionn at *Glendaghalin* (IV. 75. 132. b). The church can be discerned left after a group of houses, also left, about 400 yards from the road and 200 yards from the sea. It can be easily reached over the fields; but there is, further on, a signposted road left. Leave the car at the end of this road and walk

down and up to the church. There is also a well for sore eyes.

Daithlionn was reputed to be the sister of Erc whose church we saw at the other side of the Head. The church is much ruined, but it is of considerable interest and some charm. (For one thing there have not been burials around it for centuries past). It seems to be a good example of the second period of ecclesiastical architecture, that is from the 7th or 8th century. It is small, consisting only of a nave with dressed, flat lintelled but unornamented doorway. This doorway, unusually in early churches, is in the south wall. The east gable fell some time before Westropp wrote about it (c.1912); it is clear from the Ordnance Survey Letters (which give a sketch) that it had a fully arched window, as in the chancel at Ratass. It is just possible that the tradition is correct and that this was the foundation of a nun of the early sixth century — but the church seems to be a century or two later — even if she was the reputed daughter of a god. (It will be recalled that the famous St Brendan himself had an even more distinguished divine parentage, having a father called Findlug).

About a mile further on one comes to a cross roads where one turns right. Just beyond this, left, are reputed to be the remains of the Red Ditch on its way from Kerry Head to the Cork-Limerick border. It is difficult to be sure of this location because, while the tradition of the Ditch lives on, there is little precision in the accounts.

From here continue on the road: it doubles back to Ballyheigue.

Total driving distance: 20 miles. Allow up to three hours.

(IV) BALLINGARRY — RATTOO — LIXNAW — ABBEYDORNEY

Take the second (i.e. the coast) road towards Ballyduff.

Two miles after one has turned right onto this road there is an un-signposted road left that after a mile and a quarter brings one past a wonderfully decorated farmhouse close to the

sea at *Ballingarry* (IV. 77. 134. c). Leave the car at the last farmhouse. A few minutes' walk along the track brings one to what is known locally as 'Ballingarry Leap'. This is a promontory fort that survived into historical times. Apart from the isthmus, defended by a gateway, there is a narrow chasm between the promontory and the mainland. They were in former times joined together by a drawbridge. Here the Cantillons built a castle in 1280. The castle was besieged by land and sea in 1602-3 and capitulated. In what came to be known as the cromwellian wars Colonel David Crosbie held out with 100 men for four years — including a period of truce — in the parliamentary interest. He also gave refuge for a time to a large number of those freed from the siege of Tralee castle. After Tralee fell this was the only loyalist stronghold in Kerry. He and his people were supplied from the Clare coast by the earl of Inchiquin. Eventually, in February, 1646, three of the garrison betrayed the castle by letting down the drawbridge over the chasm. Crosbie was ill. His life was saved because his Mac Gillacuddy niece alerted two of his nephews on the Irish side, Colonels Mc Elligott and Mac Gillacuddy. He was released in 1647 and took command of Kinsale in the parliamentary interest. Cromwell made him governor of Kerry.

There are in these cliffs extensive subterranean passages.

Back to the road to Ballyduff. This is comfortable land, heavily colonised in anglo-norman times. Note the farmhouses with hip gables, fully or half thatched, a stage in the evolution from the oval, and the earlier circular, houses. After four and a half miles there is a boithrin left leading to the *Clashmealcon caves* (IV. 82. 137. b), scene of a grim incident in the civil war. After the last farmhouse on this boithrin leave the car and climb over the ditch into the field above the sea. A memorial stands over the spot. Back to the road to Ballyduff.

At *Ballyduff* (IV. 88. 135. a) (pop. 1971: 406) turn right down the main street in the direction of Tralee. (If one had gone on straight one would have reached after two miles *Ballyhorgan* (IV. 89. 136. c). The

Stoughton house here — they had acquired the lands of Rattoo monastery — was the first of the Kerry 'big houses' to be destroyed, after the third attempt, in the troubles of 1920. However, go unflinchingly through Ballyduff and through the cross roads at its end. A little further along the Tralee road there is a turn left, signposted, for *Rattoo* (IV. 89. 134. a).

Follow this rather rough road to its end. At the right are a few relics of the almost obliterated monastery. Inside the wall facing one are the remains of a church built or rebuilt in the 15th century. It is not of great interest and (1966) was in a most disgusting condition. Outside this enclosure is the round tower, the only complete one in Kerry. At 92 feet it is not as high as others, but it is one of the finest in Ireland. It is of the third style, that is probably earlier than that at Aghadoe which was begun in 1027 AD which was of the fourth and final style. The difference is in the elementary style of arch in the windows and the absence of romanesque ornament. There were six floors inside, and the top storey has windows facing the cardinal points. This marks the existence of a substantial monastery in Gaelic times, perhaps from its name associated with the 9th-10th century Ratass (Rath Theas), Tralee. About the year 1200 there was founded here by Meiler Fitz Henry a preceptory of the Knights Hospitaller of St John of Jerusalem; but before 1207 it came into the hands of the Arroaisian Augustinian canons under the tutelage of SS Peter and Paul. From here the Arroaisian canons spread to Ballinskelligs. Some hundreds of yards east of the tower are the ruins of a fine 15th century priory church. The prior of Rattoo was a lord of parliament. On the suppression of the monasteries the formal grant of Rattoo (as of O Dorney) was given to the earl of Desmond who, it is to be assumed, did not disturb the canons. On Desmond's fall the ownership passed through the hands of several planters. The monastery was finally destroyed by the Irish in 1600 on the approach of the English under Wilmot. Early in the 17th century it was held by Anthony Staughton in whose family it remained.

It is better to return to the Tralee road and

Round Tower, Rattoo

turn right. At the cross roads turn right again, and again right at the T junction. After just over a mile turn left across the river Brick for Lixnaw.

Lixnaw (IV. 91. 130. c) (pop. 1971: 219), was a principal seat of the Fitz Maurice family. Although the weather between here and Listowel is the driest and brightest in Kerry, Lixnaw is a watery place and the Fitz Maurices used have channels and water access to their castle, of which little now remains. The castle was, as part of a general Irish policy, undermined and propped with timber to be demolished should the English appear; but Wilmot took it by surprise in 1600, whereupon Lord Kerry is said to have died of grief. Early in 1601 his successor was pardoned and the castle was restored to him but when, later in the year, the Spaniards landed at Kinsale, the new Lord Kerry revolted in company with nearly every one of the Irish and old English in Kerry. In 1602 Wilmot again took the castle, a woman having told him that the Irish in the castle — which was a pike's length from the river — had not bothered to bring water inside. When the supply was cut off they surrendered and Wilmot for once spared them all. There is now no trace of the castle. Smith in the 18th century spoke very highly of the taste and culture of the house, Old Court, later built here. It was a Lady Kerry, thinking of the water parties here, who said there were only two places in the world, London and Lixnaw. There was a monument on the nearby hill of East Clogher that dominated the scene around; it was the tomb of the first *earl* of Kerry and it possibly of his successor, but has now been demolished. The marshes here are of special botanical interest. Just four miles along the road to Listowel from here is the little village of *Finuge* (IV. 96. 132. b), with its new folk-theatre workshop.

Take the road for Ardfert. After just over three miles, at *Tonaknock* (IV. 85. 127. b), at the church site of Killahan, is for Kerry an unusual monument — a 10 ft high cross, plain, with one arm broken off, another unsuccessful Kerry attempt to achieve the transition from the eremitical cross pillar to the carved high cross. Shortly after this take the road left for Abbeydorney some four miles away.

Abbeydorney (IV. 86. 123. a) (pop. 1971: 188) is of interest because it is the site of the cistercian abbey of Kyrie Eleison at O Dorney (from the Ui dTorna, a local tribe whose *tuath* was here and who, with another tribe, the Ui Flannain, gave their name to the rural deanery of Athorna and Offlanan). The

258

abbey was founded in 1154, only 12 years after the cistercians first came to Ireland. The mother house was at Croom, Co. Limerick. The foundation although small was a rich one and the abbots were lords of parliament. Here died in 1186 Christian O Connairche, first abbot of Mellifont, trained by St Bernard at Clairvaux, later bishop of Lismore, president of, and papal legate at, the synod of Kells in 1152 and the synod of Cashel of 1171-2.

The community here were, it seems, soon in decline. In the visitation of 1227, the abbot of O Dorney was, with four other abbots, deposed. Later the community came under the influence, if not control, of the Fitz Maurice family. They travelled a long way from the reforming days of St Malachy. It was reported that towards the end of the 15th century Dublin and Mellifont were the only cistercian abbeys where the monks followed the rule and wore the habit. In 1450 the prior complained to Rome against James, 7th earl of Desmond, and Patrick Fitz Maurice who had brought the monastery under their secular jurisdiction and gravely interfered with the abbot and his subjects, compelling the monastery to pay taxes and forcing its subjects into wars. Three years later very serious charges are made against the abbot, Maurice Fitz Maurice. In 1472 we learn that Edmund Fitz Maurice had held the abbey *in commendam* without any title for between eight and fourteen years. It was then given to the representative of another local family, successful collectors of ecclesiastical benefices, Philip Stack, who became bishop of Ardfert in 1488. The last pre-reformation bishop of Ardfert was James Fitz Maurice, son of a priest, appointed in 1536 at the age of 25 and already abbot of Abbeydorney.

In 1576 the abbey was granted to the earl of Desmond. It was effectively suppressed after the Desmond wars and in 1589 it was, with other grants, given to John Champion (or Chapman) of Dingle. He sold it in 1599 for £100 and two years later it was bought for £130 by one of the Crosbies. At that time the property consisted of 'one chancel, one churchyard, one steeple, one cloister, with it was doctor's chambers and other chambers, built with lime and limestone; one watermill

with course of water; the town of Odorney, consisting of twenty four tenements and gardens; ten ploughlands of 120 acres arable with parsonages, rectories and tythes of Odorney, Mollahiffe, Dysert in Clanmaurice, Aughnamanna, and the moiety of the parsonage, rectory and tythes of Moylagh'. The great enemy of Strafford, Sir Piers Crosbie, sold these lands, with others, to his cousin David Crosbie of Ardfert in 1638 to finance his defence of a libel suit brought against him by Strafford.

The cistercians did not die out completely for a considerable time. In 1633 there were only one or two cistercians in the county; but after that they disappear from history.

From Abbeydorney one can reach *Banemore* (IV. 96. 128) townland where three of the five extant gold lunulae of Kerry were found. Take the road for Kilflynn. Turn right there for the main Listowel-Tralee road. Turn left here. After one has travelled five miles one is in Banemore townland. The detour is 16 miles.

Otherwise, from Abbeydorney take the Ardfert road by the fine new church for two and a half miles. At the cross roads turn left for a half mile. Just beyond a thatched farmhouse on the left is a wicket gate. The owner of the farmhouse expects a fee for the passage over his land. About 200 yards from the road is a large, shallow well, *Wethers' Well* (IV. 82. 121. d), so called because when St Brendan was baptised there three wethers leaped out of the well. Pilgrimages are still made there. Special days are the Saturday before 1st May; Saturday before St John's Day, June 15; and Saturday before 1st August. Observe these dates and all the rags on the bushes about and marvel at the ancient survivals. The altar has three, rather crude panels — in the centre a corpse, on its right an abbot or bishop, and on its left an unfinished figure of a woman with a book. It has been suggested that the panel is from a tomb in Ardfert friary, with a representation of the corpse (unique in Ireland) of St Brendan and of his foster mother, St Ita. The story is that a cromwellian settler tried to take this panel to his home near Tralee, that the oxen were able to draw it no farther than

a neighbouring hill (now called Bullock Hill), that it was left for the night and found in the morning in its usual place at the shrine.

It is easy to return to Ballyheigue by way of Ardfert. Total driving distance: 42 miles. Allow about half a day.

IRAGHTICONNOR

This barony is the most clear-cut of the nine. It is bounded by the Shannon to the north and west, by the Feale (which becomes the Cashen at its mouth below Ballybunion) on the south, and by the Limerick border east of Tarbert. The name comes from Oidhreacht Ui Choncubhair, O Conor's Inheritance. The O Conors were the ruling family of the Ciarraige which from the seventh or eighth century came to dominate all North Kerry. The family played a very vigorous part on land and on water in the disturbed times of the 11th and 12th centuries, but it lost its power and became confined to this barony when the geraldine invasion occurred.

Keating's description of the diocese of Rath Mhaighe Deiscirt at the synod of Rathbreasail puts the northern boundary of the diocese on the Feale, so this barony may have been excluded. If so, when it came to be included in the diocese of Ardfert is not clear; it was part of the diocese in 1302.

The Fitz Maurices had a major seat at Listowel at the south of the barony and a number of other castles along the western shore of the Shannon. Nonetheless, O Connor Kerry held out here, based on Ballylongford. He survived between Fitz Maurice on the south and the Knight of Glin on the east because, as Sir Nicholas Browne was to point out in 1597, 'by reason of his woods and bogs he was wont to hold his own in spite of them both'. This continued until cromwellian times when, in 1653, the last prominent O Conor Kerry, Teigue, was hanged in Killarney.

(I) LISTOWEL

The principal town in the barony is *Listowel* (IV. 99-100. 134) (pop. 1971: 3,021). It is an urban district, and is pleasantly situated on

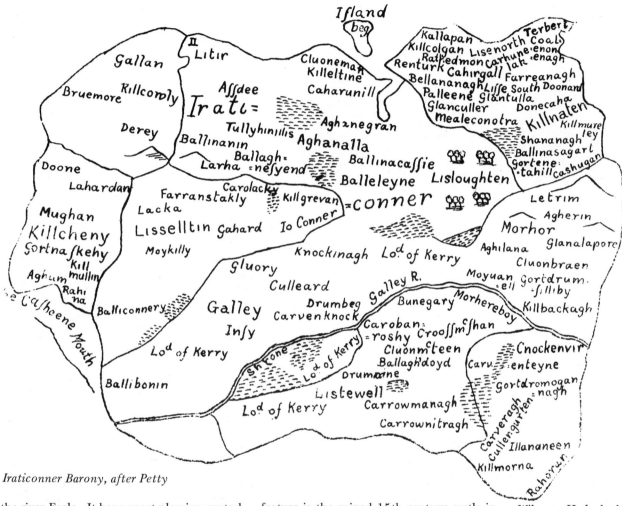

Iraticonner Barony, after Petty

the river Feale. It has a most pleasing central square with two gothic style churches peering at one another. The sites for these were given by Lord Listowel in 1814. The Church of Ireland church was built in 1819; the catholic church was begun 10 years later and took its final form in 1910. There is a wonderful piece of sunbursery — 'The maid of Erin' — on the Central Hotel at one corner of the square. This was done by a local worthy, Pat Mc Auliffe (1846-1921). There are many other examples of his work in the town and in Abbeyfeale. There is a pleasant bridge over the river Feale (built by Richard Griffith in 1829 for just under £2,500). A striking

feature is the ruined 15th century castle in the square; it shares with Bunratty castle the unusual feature of two turrets joined.

The Fitz Maurices, Lords of Kerry, showed themselves consistently disloyal to the crown in both the Desmond and the O Neill wars. Their principal seats were at Ardfert and Lixnaw but an important one was here at the marchland of Listowel. Although Lord Kerry was an active and determined leader in the Desmond wars these castles do not seem to have been stormed. In the O Neill wars Listowel castle, his last stronghold, was besieged in November, 1600, by Sir Charles

Wilmot. He lacked artillery. One attempt to undermine the castle so as to blow it down with gunpowder was prevented when the digging unearthed a substantial spring; however, a second tunnel was more successful. The garrison of 18 men surrendered; all but one of them were despatched. The women and children were let free. One of the children was the five year old eldest son of Lord Kerry, carried off by his nurse. In return for his life a priest, Dermot Mac Brodie, discovered the child and handed him over.

The Lord Kerry of the time was in 1641 made governor of Kerry in the King's interest.

260

The Square, Listowel

Listowel Castle

Having commissioned a number of captains who promptly showed their disloyalty he retired to England. The only Kerry action — a skirmish — of the williamite wars took place close to Listowel in September, 1691, as the English resumed control of the county. In the process they killed here a Dominican priest. Parnell's third last public appearance before his death was in Listowel in 1891, when he spoke from a window of the Listowel Arms Hotel. Three weeks later he was dead.

Two distinguished writers live in Listowel — Bryan Mac Mahon, short story writer, playwright and schoolmaster, and John B.

The Maid of Erin, Listowel

Keane, playwright and publican. The early Abbey playwright, George Fitz Maurice, and the novelist, Maurice Walsh, also came from Listowel. The town's literary tradition is each year fostered at a notable Writers' Week. A distinguished Listowel family were the O Rahillys, relatives of the 1916 leader — Alfred, Cecile and Thomas — who made notable contributions to Irish intellectual (and polemical) life. All three were professors — Alfred of mathematical physics, Cecile and Thomas of celtic studies. Alfred became president of University College, Cork, and, after his wife's death and his retirement, a priest and a monsignor. Thomas was the author of the great book *Irish History and Mythology*.

There is a title, earl of Listowel, borne by the Hare family. A Cork businessman, of English descent, Richard bought in 1783 the Listowel properties of the earl of Kerry, and of the Knight of Kerry in 1796. He and his son were members of the Irish parliament and voted for the Union, and he became baron Ennismore (from the Knight of Kerry's property) in 1800, viscount Ennismore and Listowel in 1816, and earl of Listowel in 1822. The family have been absentees, concerned with English politics. The first earl's grandson was the central figure in the tragic scandal of 'Hare's election' in 1826.

The famous monorail, the Lartigue railway, ran between Listowel and Ballybunion. There is a four day race meeting in Listowel.

(II) BALLYBUNION — BALLYLONGFORD — TARBERT

Take the straight flat road for Ballybunion. After two miles one crosses the Galey river and, a little further on, at the cross roads there is, a short distance along the road on the right, the ruined medieval parish church of *Galey* (IV. 96. 137. b), apparently named after a local tribe, a relic of one system of parish formation in the 12th-13th centuries.

Back to the main road and, two miles further on, at *Lisselton cross* (IV. 94. 139. a) turn left. After four miles on this road take the narrow rough road left until it takes a sharp turn right at the sandhills of *Ballyeagh* (IV. 87. 140. c). There is a boithrin directly opposite one through the sandhills to the sea. Along this boithrin near its end are, right, to be seen the signs of sandhill dwellers — shells, broken stone tools, bones, etc. Over the ridge on the left more are to be found. These relics may date from neolithic times. Early iron age pins and roman coins have been found, as well as seventeen stone lined long cists with skeletons.

Out to the beach. At the races here on St John's day, 24 June, 1834, took place the famous faction fight between some 1,200 Cooleens on the one hand and about 2,000 Lawlors and Black Mulvihills, the victors, on the other. Perhaps 20 Cooleens were drowned when the boat they tried to escape in south over the river Cashen was overturned and they were mercilessly beaten under the water. The Lawlors were descended from the Laois clan transplanted here early in the 17th century and the Mulvihills came from Clare in the middle of that century. The Cooleens, no doubt still resenting these intruders, were from south of the river Cashen and the loss of life came when they were driven back over the river. The deaths caused great scandal and determined the government to put down with a firm hand further faction fighting.

The beach is, of course, a magnificent one and the walk of a mile or so to the Cashen is worth the effort. Return to the car and follow the road one has been on for a further mile to Ballybunion (IV. 87. 142) (pop. 1971: 1,287). The place is named after

Ballybunion

retainers of the geraldines, the Bonyons, who date from 1290 at least, so showing the squeeze on O Conor Kerry. Ballybunion is a gay holiday town with a fine golf course and cheerful night life in the pubs. There are in the cliffs a number of striking caves, some related to the Fitz Maurice castle overhead, destroyed in the Desmond wars. There is a legend of one of these caves that the seven daughters of a local chieftain attempted to elope with seven Norsemen, his prisoners. When they were discovered their father ordered them to be thrown one fearful night through the hole in the roof of the cave, now known as the cave of the Seven Sisters. To the north east is *Knockanore* (IV. 92. 143. a), three miles away. This comes from Cnoc an Air, the hill of the slaughter, where Fionn and the Fiana, with great killing, attempted to protect a greek princess fleeing from husband and father.

Take the coast road to Ballylongford. A number of the headlands here have promontory forts. Just three miles along this road, left, is the old church of *Kilconly* (IV. 88. 146. b). Nothing is known of Conla except that he killed (or was killed by) a huge serpent that lived at *Lisnapeastia* (IV. 89. 146. a) about a quarter mile east of the church — another indication that serpent worship was one of the enemies that christian missionaries may have had to fight.

Five miles from Ballybunion is Beal. There is a school on the right and on the left a boithrin to Beal point. About a half mile along this is *Beal castle* (IV. 91. 149. b),

another Fitz Maurice strongpoint. The castle figures in history. During the O Neill wars a small, brave and energetic soldier was a renegade Kerryman, Maurice Stack. He was also the unscrupulous accomplice of such major, and fraudulent, land-grabbers as Richard Boyle, later earl of Cork, and Sir Patrick Crosbie. These proclivities may explain his fate. Lady Kerry (who was sister to the loyalist earl of Thomond) invited Stack in August, 1600, to dine at Beal castle. After dinner, having spoken privately with Stack, she cried out to her guard for help. The guard stabbed Stack and threw him into the courtyard below. Lord Kerry, to show his solidarity with this behaviour, when he heard of it next day, hanged Stack's brother, Thomas, long his prisoner. The fortifications of this castle were destroyed by Lord Kerry himself, presumably to deny their protection to the English.

Back to the main road. Three miles further

Carrigafoyle 'slighted'

on is *Astee* (IV. 95. 146. a), which used be the headquarters of Diarmaid Sugach O Conor Kerry. Here in 1146 he built those ships that, four years later, he brought 'on wheels' to Loch Lein. There, however, they did not meet with much long-term success. Three miles further on, just before one reaches Ballylongford, there is, at a bend in the road, a sharp turn left (signposted) to *Carrigafoyle castle* (IV. 99. 148. b). A short distance along this road on the right are the ruins of a big parish church that seems to have been built in the 15th century and crudely shortened in protestant times. Just two miles along the road one comes to the castle, a tower house built about 1490 by Conor Liath O Conor Kerry. It is now severely 'slighted' but is nonetheless in unusually good condition. It is built of thin pieces of limestone, used almost as bricks. There are some attractive windows. This is a very fine example of 15th century building. The surroundings are now silted and overgrown, but the illustration in *Pacata*

262 *Hibernia* shows the unique feature of this castle. It was completely surrounded by water from the channel of the Shannon cut off by Carrig island opposite. The walled defence now standing between the castle and the mainland shielded the castle on three sides, protecting it from the mainland and enclosing a stretch of water in which boats — apparently of up to 400 tons — could be moored. Within that was a further wall, now disappeared, that surrounded the castle on four sides. Carrigafoyle was the main stronghold of O Conor Kerry, the principal chieftain of this barony named after him, descendant of the ruling family of the Ciarraige, tracing his ancestry back to Ciar, the triplet son of the fabulous Medb and Fergus Mac Roigh. From here O Conor Kerry was able to intercept ships going up the Shannon to Limerick, board them and take a part of their cargoes. This little practice continued to the middle of the 16th century.

In the Desmond wars this castle saw the first effective use of artillery in Kerry and a neat combined naval and military operation under Sir William Pelham. Guns were taken from naval vessels and mounted on the mainland where the road now runs. In addition, ships from the Shannon bombarded the castle over Carrig island. After two days the castle was breached and taken on Palm Sunday, 1580. The survivors of the defenders — the Italian commander, 16 Spaniards, and 50 Irish (including women) were either put to the sword or hanged.

The castle was in the wars again in 1600 when O Conor Kerry surrendered it to the Lord President, Carew, so giving him his first foothold in Kerry and a headquarters for his campaigns. This was in return for 13 ploughlands in Clare given to O Conor Kerry by the earl of Thomond. However, when a party of Spaniards arrived in the following year, about the time of the Kinsale landings, O Conor Kerry re-took the castle and slew the whole English garrison. In 1649 the castle was finally destroyed by the cromwellians.

Bring the car up to the bridge and cross over to *Carrig island* (IV. 98-99. 148-149), turning left for fine views of the Shannon and the 19th century battery. The Map of Monastic

Carrigafoyle Church

Ireland shows an 'abbey' on the island with 'order and period doubtful'. It is more than doubtful if the ruin on the highest point of the island (hardly worth a visit) is that of a church at all; but O Donovan, in the Ordnance Survey Letters, says it is.

On the mainland by the bridge and opposite the castle is a church built in the sophisticated style of Carrigafoyle and at about the same date. It may have been a parish church, or else an outlying church of the nearby Franciscan friary of Lislaghtin founded by John O Conor Kerry in 1478.

Back this road and turn left for *Ballylongford* (IV. 101. 145. a). This is a pleasant little village (pop. 1971: 504) with a solid house where The O Rahilly was born in 1875. His

father seems to have made enough money here in his short life to enable his son to lead the life of a gentleman and to use a self-acquired title. He was one of the founders of Sinn Fein and of the Irish Volunteers. He was at the Howth gun-running in July, 1914. He loyally supported Mac Neill's attempts to cancel the 1916 rising and travelled to Kerry with the cancellation order. When, nonetheless, the rising took place he hastened to the Dublin GPO. At the evacuation of the burning building he led a party up Henry street but was killed nearby. He was a gay, talkative, loyal and gallant man.

Out of the village turn left onto the coast road for Tarbert. About 0.8 miles along this road, at a series of sharp bends, is left a gateway and boithrin. From this one can

263

readily see the ruins of *Lislaghtin Franciscan friary* (IV. 101. 147. c) founded by John O Conor Kerry in 1478. He was the father of the builder of Carrigafoyle. Here again we see a nice use of masonry, and some very good carving on the windows. This was a large friary, although not as much of it has survived as of Muckross. In particular, the tower and the cloisters are gone. Nonetheless the ruins are imposing. These Franciscans, like the Muckross ones, were Observantines, members of the great 15th century reform movement that received such support in the gaelic parts of Ireland. It is believed that the friary was built on the site of an early monastery founded by St Lachtin, a Corkman from Muskerry who also founded a monastery in Freshford, Co. Kilkenny, and who died in 622 AD.

When one considers the nature and extent of this building, of the nearly contemporary Carrigafoyle castle, and the churches close to it, one can note what seems to have been a great access of wealth to the O Conor Kerry family towards the end of the 15th century. This growth of wealth must have been general at the time and must have contributed greatly to the ecclesiastical and building revival of the time.

At the time Carrigafoyle fell in April, 1580, this friary was raided and three aged friars had their throats cut by English soldiers.

In 1629 the Franciscans were again in the building, and, although the cromwellians sacked it in 1652, they survived around

Lislaghtin until the 1860s when the bishop of Kerry founded a new Franciscan house in Killarney from Belgium. There is a list of the guardians (superiors) of this friary from 1629 to 1860, with only a few short breaks, given in the second volume of the *Kerry Archaeological Magazine*. A fine processional cross from Lislaghtin, known as the 'Ballylongford' Cross, which dates from 1521, is in the National Museum.

From Lislaghtin it is four miles to *Tarbert* (IV. 107. 148. b) (pop. 1971: 485) a seaport on the Shannon, with a power station and an hourly car ferry to the Clare coast. On a fine day this is a pleasant trip. John Crosbie's brother, Patrick, settled large numbers of turbulent Laoismen in the Tarbert area in 1607-9.

Take the road for Listowel but after two miles branch left for *Newtownsandes* (IV. 108. 140. a) (pop. 1971: 268) and through it. Just over three miles further on turn sharp left up a steep hill for about a half mile to the new Michael Scott church at *Knockanure* (IV. 108. 136. a). Architecturally, but not liturgically, this is an uncompromisingly modern church. There is a fine Oisin Kelly carving of the Last Supper to be seen through the glass gable (especially if one approaches in the morning). Inside, there are striking stations of the cross by Lesley Mac Weeney. If one feels that this little church is not a complete success go down the hill again and turn back to Newtownsandes. In the village turn right for the new parish church, of an ugliness

indescribable.

The village was named after the local landlords, the Sandes. In the 1880s, during the land war, George Sandes, both landlord and land agent, made himself so odious to the local people that in 1886 they changed the name to Newtown Dillon, after John Dillon. This name did not stick, so in 1916 it was renamed Newtown Clarke, after the 1916 leader. Again the new name did not stick, and in 1939 it was changed to Moyvane with more, but not complete, success. From here turn back onto the main Listowel road.

A pleasant run is, just before one reaches Listowel, to take the Abbeyfeale road along the valley of the Feale, the boundary between the baronies of Iraghticonnor and Clanmaurice. Just three miles along this road one passes right, in the valley of the Feale, the site of *Kilmorna house* (IV. 106. 133. c) where Sir Arthur Vicars, sacked as Ulster King of Arms after the theft of the crown jewels in Dublin, was shot as a spy in 1921. The house belonged to his relatives the Gun Mahony family and is now totally destroyed. The site was through the second of two gateways on the right, each faced on the left hand side of the road by an imposing lodge.

About a mile and a half further on one can turn across the river to the village of *Duagh* (IV. 106. 130. b). Turn right back to Listowel.

Total driving distance: 56 miles. Allow six hours.

Chapter 15

The Iveragh Peninsula: Iveragh and Dunkerron South

This peninsula is much the biggest — it is up to 30 miles long and 20 miles broad. It contains three of the nine Kerry baronies — Dunkerron North, Dunkerron South and Iveragh; but it is more convenient to take Dunkerron North with Magunihy.

It is bounded at the top — to the north east — by the long line of the Mac Gillacuddy Reeks, rising to over 3,000 feet, along the seacoast to the north west by a line of mountains mainly over 2,000 feet, and, somewhat in from the seacoast, to the south west by a range of the order of 2,500 feet. Two roads traverse its length by the seacoast, and a third runs through its middle, while it is crossed by only two roads. The roads were built at the end of the eighteenth century and in the first half of the nineteenth. Before that the accounts are eloquent on the impassability of the countryside and its inaccessibility because of the mountains and the extremely wet bogs. Much of it is still inaccessible except on foot.

The road from Killorglin, through Cahersiveen and Sneem to Killarney is the famous 'Ring of Kerry' and is a must for the tourist. It is not so demanding of brilliant weather as the Dingle run; but there is no use attempting its 100 odd miles unless visibility is good. It is better to take the run anti-clockwise because the marvellous views between Killorglin and Glenbeigh, Mountain Stage and Cahersiveen and, in particular, at Coomakista are better seen in that direction.

The other long run is between Waterville and Ballaghisheen, which is better taken in that direction so as to get the full view of the Reeks as one descends from the gap at Ballaghisheen.

IVERAGH

The barony of Iveragh is bounded by the sea to the north and west. The southern line runs from the outlet of Lough Currane, through the lake, along the spine of the Dunkerron mountains to a point due north of Sneem. It then runs north along the Caragh river and part of Caragh lake. It then meets the Trughanacmy boundary west of Killorglin and reaches the sea just west of Cromane. The

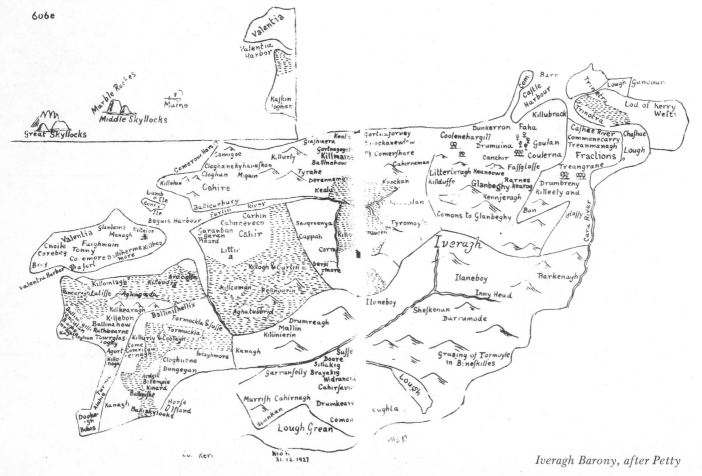

Iveragh Barony, after Petty

barony consists of seven parishes: Glenbeigh, Killinane, Cahir, Valentia, Killemlagh, Prior, Dromod; it also contains a bit of Killorglin parish.

The settlement pattern in early times was determined by ease of access. So the mountain ridges in these peninsulas divided the various tribes, and the bays united them. The Corcu Duibne occupied the strips of land north and south of Dingle Bay — those on the north side were called the Aes Iorruis Tuaiscirt, and those on the south the Aer Iorruis Deiscirt — respectively the Northern and Southern Peninsular People. The kingship of the Corcu Duibne was shared between the families that came to be known in the north as O Falvey and in the south as O Shea. The latter were centred on Ballycarbery (O Shea), near Cahersiveen. When the Mac Carthy invasion occurred in the 11th-12th century they overran the barony of Iveragh and, forced back by anglo-norman pressure, in the thirteenth century maintained their headquarters there until the end of the fourteenth century when they made Killarney their headquarters. They seem to have begun by settling in Ballycarbery, and it remained an important centre of their power until the end. However, in the 13th century at latest they moved to Eightercua, technically in Dunkerron South, on the south bank of Lough Currane. The English did not get to Iveragh until the end of the 16th century when Donnell Mac Carthy Mor, first (and last) Earl of Clancarre, mortgaged the magnificent Ballycarbery castle — of which the O Connells were seneschals — to Sir Nicholas Browne.

There are three main towns in the barony of Iveragh: Glenbeigh, Cahersiveen and Waterville.

(I) THE GLENBEIGH AREA

Glenbeigh comes from Gleann Beithe, the glen of the birch tree. The river Behy that runs through it is similarly named. *Glenbeigh* (V.67.92.d) is a village of (1971) 266 souls with promise (as yet unfilled after over a century) as a tourist centre. It is close to good bathing (at Rossbeigh and Kells Bay);

golfing (at Dooks); fishing (in many rivers and lakes); bird watching (in Castlemaine harbour); and a great range of mountains.

A big body of Fiana legends centres around here — in Glencar where the Fiana were so often hunting; in Glenbeigh itself where Diarmuid and Grainne spend some days hiding in a cave in the valley of the Behy, since destroyed when the railway line was laid; at Drung Hill, where Diarmuid achieved such exploits against his pursuers; at Rossbeigh where Oisin and Niamh took to the sea on their white horse to live in the land of youth; at Ballaghisheen where Oisin, returned, sought his kin now long dead, another Irish revenant linking the pagan and the christian times. Relics of old religion survive at Puck Fair in Killorglin and at the pattern of Drung Hill, where, also, St Fionan is said to be buried. At Rossbeigh was one of the great, magic, roaring waves of Ireland, the Tonn Toime against which Aodhgan O Rathile, in his last years, so strongly inveighed. Glenbeigh was the last outpost of civilisation to travellers in the eighteenth century, appalled by the terrors of the track along the precipitous sides of Drung Hill, until at the end of the century the modern road was built to Cahersiveen and Waterville. Almost a century later came the short-lived railway.

The startling ruin of Glenbeigh Towers recalls the landlords of this place — the Winns, Barons Headley. The title dated from 1797 and in the early nineteenth century Lord Headley, a wealthy man managing his estate with benign but aloof intelligence, engaged in extensive improvements in laying out roads; improving farms by breaking up the rundale system and 'striping'; building a rampart against the sea, so enclosing 500 acres — £5,000 of the cost being taken in labour for arrears of rent, and rents reduced. It was also hoped to develop the tourist trade — an inn was built and manned by Mr Wales — it is now the Glenbeigh Hotel (then a very simple inn indeed if Lady Chatterton is to be followed) — and those attractive retreat lodges on the way to, and at, Rossbeigh, some of which are now being re-conditioned.

Headley Towers, Glenbeigh, c. 1900

The fourth baron built the Towers from 1867. The architect was W. E. Godwin who during the years of building had Ellen Terry as mistress, and the baliffs as visitors. Lord Headley took legal action against him because the costs exceeded estimate, and the walls and roof leaked. The affair was settled in 1875 when Godwin's partner, Crisp, agreed to finish the job. Headley tried to set himself up as a feudal baron. In the 1880s, following legal disputes in the Winn family 70 tenants in the Glenbeigh area got into serious arrears of rent. This led to large-scale and brutal evictions — notorious as the 'Glenbeigh evictions' — during the Plan of Campaign in 1886-7.

The fifth baron, who succeeded in 1913, became a mohammedan in that year and, having made the pilgrimage to Mecca, used the title Al Hadj. He said in 1925 that he had three times been offered the throne of Albania. The Towers were burned down in 1922. The view from the site is superb.

Synge spent a number of spells at Mountain Stage, close to Glenbeigh, early this century and has some vivid, laconic accounts in his little book *In Wicklow and West Kerry*. In more recent times there was a famous, and financially prudent, parish priest here, Father Jones, about whom hilarious tales are told. The two hotels here are very well known: they have a number of paintings including early Jack B. Yeats.

266

1. Mountain Stage and Rossbeigh

Rossbeigh (V.65.92.c) is only a mile and a half away: but on a clear day the more intrepid driver may care to approach it in a memorable way. Follow the main road of the Behy valley for about three and a half miles. At a public house on the right, at the old *Mountain Stage* (V.63.90.c) railway station, turn right. Over the old railway line turn right again and at the cross-roads a half-mile further on bear left. After a short distance one drops down a very steep, bad road onto Rossbeigh. On a clear day this is a splendid sight: if, in addition, there is snow on the Dingle mountains, it is unforgettable.

Rossbeigh is a spit of sand two miles long running out into Dingle Bay. From Inch, on the other side of the Bay, there is a comparable spit. These have been built up by the wild western Atlantic storms. On these in the eighteenth century many West Indies ships, flying before the storms, were beaten to pieces; and there are stories of deliberate wrecking. Between them the great waves roar, giving the booming sound of Tonn Toime. From the end of this strand Oisin and Niamh galloped over the sea on their white horse to Tir na nOg, and here again, 300 years later Oisin came back from that paradise. On this strand is held, in July or August each year, the two-day Rossbeigh races, an immensely popular local event that shows that the Ireland of Somerville and Ross still survives. There is firm sand under the high

Rossbeigh

water mark almost to the beacon at the end of the spit and the less energetic can drive on it; but leave at least an hour before high tide.

2. Dooks – Caragh Lake – Ballaghisheen – Glencar

Take the Killorglin road and, just two miles on, where the road crosses the Caragh River and turns right, take the left turn and follow this road as it skirts *Dooks* (V.68-69.95) golf links on the left. This is one of the oldest in Ireland – the club dates from 1889. Just beyond the links there is a rough road left that brings one down to the channel of Castlemaine Harbour. This is the habitat of Ireland's unique toad, the natterjack.

Turn back to the Killorglin road and turn left for two miles. Then turn right. Follow this road for a short distance to *Ard na Shee Hotel* (V.74.92.b). The view from the gardens of *Caragh lake* (V.71-74.89-93) from here is very fine. A mile or so further on there is a complex of small lakes on both sides of the road, most of them overlooking the main lake. About another mile along this road there is a boithrin to the right that brings one to a *farmhouse* (V.73.90.d). There are fine views of the lake and, in good circumstances, of the Dingle mountains.

Return to the road and after a mile take the right fork. Follow this until one comes to the Caragh river, a famous early (and preserved) salmon river, at the aptly named *Blackstones* (V.71.87.d). Petty had an iron mine and smelting works here until all the trees about had been felled and burned. The ruins are still to be seen. A very pleasant trip, if one has a boat is to launch it in the pool below the rapids here. There is a delightful journey along the river and out onto Caragh Lake. Fishing on the river is preserved but on the lake it is free. Return here and take the next turn right and then right again by the Glencar hotel. Then keep bearing right until one is out into the heart of *Glencar* (V.71-72.81-85) and climbing up to *Ballaghisheen* (Oisin's Gap) (V.67.80.d). It may be worth while driving through the Gap as far as *Lissatinnig Bridge* (V.63.77.b) at the fork right five miles on. The rest of this road is covered in other trips, so turn here. As one comes down from

Ballaghisheen there are magnificent views of the Reeks, and of Carrantuohil in particular. Here Oisin, back from his 300 years in the Land of Youth, reined his white steed and peered keenly for his companions of the Fiana so often to be found hunting in Glencar. It was from here that the first (and last) Earl of Glencar took the title from Queen Elizabeth, forsaking the old gaelic one of Mac Carthy Mor. (The title is also written Clancarre, from Clann Charthaigh, the Mac Carthy family. This valley was part of their property).

Go back to Blackstones and follow the road by Caragh Lake, at its end turning left for Glenbeigh. A striking variant of the run along Lough Caragh on the main road is to take, after Blackstones, the second turn on the left up a rough road. Where this passes through a gate and forks at a hairpin bend, bear right and follow this road. It gives splendid views of the lake. After three miles on this road, at the cross roads, carry on straight.

Total driving distance: 54 miles.

3. Coomasaharn – Drung Hill

A striking run on a good day is to take the road between the catholic church and the Towers hotel and follow it until it peters out at the substantial, if temperamental, fishing lake of *Coomasaharn* (V.63-4.84-5) (The odd name may be Cum-fhos ath-fhearainn – the coombe stance of the reclaimed land). There is a special kind of char – a small freshwater type of salmon – in this lake known as the 'Coomasaharn char'. There are seven lakes here and a magnificent ridge walk. A whole day would not be misspent about here.

However, turn the car and, where a mile or so back, a road branches left at a small plantation of pines leave the car and walk towards the sharp turn. About half-way up, in a field to the right, some yards in from the road, is a large flat stone with neolithic style concentric circles and other scribings, one of the *Coomasaharn scribed stones* (V.64.86.b). This, and the old field system that can just be discerned, were uncovered by turf cutting. There are other scribed stones in the neigbourhood, five in all. One of these links the usual cup and (single) circle into a complex tree-like system.

Back to the car and make for the next turn left. This brings one out at the main Ring of Kerry road short of Mountain Stage. Turn left along this road and, after one has passed the crossing at the old Mountain Stage station on the right, keep left on the old road and stop outside the third house on the left, a bungalow with a parking space just off the road. Above one under the flower bed in the extreme right hand (from the house) corner, is the famous *Coolnaharrigal scribed stone* (V.63.89.a). Unless one wishes to enlist (as I did) the help of a friend of the owner (who has recently levelled his new garden) to dig down over a foot to uncover the stone, horseman, pass by. (There is a photograph of it in O Riordain). A little further on is a roadway right that goes over the old railway and turns left sharply. A short distance further on one turns sharp left over a stream and then, very sharply right. Here the roadway broadens and one can turn the car. It is a very short walk to a shingly and rocky beach on the edge of Dingle Bay, where one can bathe and enjoy splendid views. There is sand only at very low tide.

Back to the main road and one is now coming to the famous *Drung Hill* (V.61.88.a) and the roadway that so terrified the women visitors to Derrynane in the 18th century. Smith refers to the doggerel rhymes that travellers along this road had to make to avert misfortune. Stop the car at the first turning on the left. This is the abandoned road that after about a half mile, beyond a farmhouse, finally peters out. Here veer sharp right, and follow the old road, now a track. If one is energetic and someone can be induced to bring the car around to the other side of the hill to the end of the old road (turn left after the branch off to Kells Bay, and follow up the road for a mile until one meets the old road on the left; but do not attempt to drive further along this neglected old road to Cahersiveen) a striking walk and climb may be had — the walk and climb come to some 5 miles. The road starts from a little above the 600 foot contour and crosses the shoulder at the mountain above the 1,200 foot

contour. Here are St Fionan's *penitential station and well* (V.60.89.d), where pilgrimages were made on the last Sunday in July. It is the special quality of the well to cure cattle. A fair used to be held on the hill. The summit of the hill is at 2,100 feet and is surmounted by a remarkable monument, called *Leacht Fhionain* (V.61.88.a) where St Fionan is reported to be buried. This cairn is 100 feet in diameter and five feet high. On top is a standing stone with worn ogam which reads only *MAQI R*. A cross is scratched on the eastern face. If this is indeed Fionan's burial place it is an historical spot, because he was perhaps the greatest of Kerrymen. However, the place is also called Leacht an Daimh — Ox's cairn. It was a Lughnasa site. There was a kingdom of Drung; perhaps the hill marked its western boundary. In the *Book of Rights* the tribute of Drung to Cashel was 30 oxen. There is a folktale that says the King of Spain invaded Ireland and forced the King of Ireland to yield the whole country to him except that point west of Leacht Fhionain. The views from the summit are striking. It was on the slopes of this mountain that Diarmuid performed three bloody feats of dexterity that so weakened the mercenaries that Fionn had hired from overseas to catch him and who had landed nearby. Back to the car and to Glenbeigh.

Total driving distance: 14 miles. Add 12 if one is picked up at the end of the old road.

(II) THE CAHERSIVEEN AREA

Cahersiveen (V.47-48.80) (Cathair Saidhbhin — Sabinia's stone fort) (pop. 1971: 1,547) is virtually one long street between *Bentee mountain* (V.48.79.d) and Valentia river, reflecting its origin in the road built between Glenbeigh and Waterville at the end of the 18th century. The communications were so bad that the town, 'having some intercourse with America, the Dublin newspapers and letters used sometimes to arrive there via New York'. In 1815 there were only five houses: but twenty years later the population had risen to about 1,200. The name comes from a now vanished caher near the old hospital. Nothing is known of Saidhbhin. The quay was built in 1822, and some fishing is carried on. From 1893 until 1960 it was

Cahersiveen

the terminal of a railway branch line from Farranfore. There is a small hospital, a state meteorological station (called, from its first site, 'Valentia'), and a couple of small factories. On the other side of the town is another state enterprise — an immensely uneconomic electricity generating station for burning sod peat. There is a small tourist trade. Otherwise, the town is, simply, a market town. Lady Chatterton, referring to to the Irish fancy for shop signs cites the tailor here in the 1830s who painted under his name 'From London', so forcing his rival, to redress the balance, to paint above his shop: 'Never was in London'.

Cahersiveen figured in history by being the centre of the premature and only Fenian rising in Kerry, in February, 1867. Perhaps it was the frustration of failing to capture the leader of the Fenians, O Connor, that led the English army colonel Curzon to report in March, 1867: '. . . . Caherciveen I have seen and I have no hesitation in saying that I never saw so vile a spot . . . . The appearance and the manner of the people of that place stamp it as a den of mischief.' It was certainly the centre of much disturbance in the civil war of 1922-3. Here, on 12 March, 1923, was perpetrated one of the most shocking incidents of the time: five men were tied by the military to a landmine and blown to pieces, having first been shot in the legs. This explains the tone of the monument near the church, and its commemoration of those who died in the struggle for

268 Irish freedom "1916 to 19   "; but it does not excuse the hideous limestone hominid on the high plinth.

Cahersiveen's most famous son is Daniel O Connell born, in 1775 before the town existed, at *Carhan* (V.50.81.c), about a mile along the Glenbeigh road, which bends sharply left after crossing the Carhan river. Only a couple of ivy covered walls now survive — the house was already in ruins in Lady Chatterton's time. The large catholic church in the town is the O Connell Memorial Church, designed by George Ashlin. Inside the porch of the church are interesting relics of its stormy birth. The parish priest, Canon Brosnan, wished to erect a church to commemorate the centenary of O Connell's birth. The bishop of Kerry would not permit this; neither, on appeal, would the Archbishop of Cashel. The canon went to Rome and in 1883 got the approval of the pope, Leo XIII, who had a great admiration for O Connell (but perhaps less grasp of the financial strength of Iveragh), sent a stone from the catacombs to be the corner stone of the church, and ordered the Archbishop, Croke (one of the founders of the GAA) to lay it, which he did in 1888.

The church, far from being built in the local sandstone, was built in Newry granite. After great financial troubles (including the bankruptcy of the builder) the church was built. The uncompleted spire is the memorial of these later difficulties.

1. Cahersiveen – Killobarnaun – Ballycarbery
Leacanabuaile – Knockadobar

There are many antiquities to be seen in the neighbourhood. An interesting short trip is to cross the bridge over the Valentia river. The striking building one sees short of the bridge is the ruined police barracks. Its curious style of architecture is explained locally, as in so many other places, as the result of a mix-up of architectural plans so that a fortress intended for the north western province of India was built here — presumably a building for Cahersiveen is to be found in that province. The barracks was to have been captured in the first Fenian rising of February, 1867, but this attempt was

abandoned when it became clear that the police were alerted. The barracks met its end, as did so many others, in 'The Troubles'.

Cross the bridge. A little way up, to the right, is an old graveyard and in it the remains, much overgrown, of an anchoritic oratory of the Gallarus type. This is *Killobarnaun* (V.47.81.d), one of the very many such sites at the tip of this peninsula. Follow the road from the bridge a little way. At the T junction turn left.

After about a mile, at Kimego school, turn left for *Ballycarbery castle* (V.45.80.b), the ruin of what was once a magnificent fifteenth century castle of Mac Carthy Mor in, as usual, a splendid setting. This seems to have been the seat of the ancient kingdom of the Corcu Duibne that comprised both sides of the Dingle Bay — all of the Dingle peninsula, but also that part of this peninsula comprised by the modern barony of Iveragh. The name comes from Cairbre, a ruler of the O Sheas who alternated with the O Falveys as kings of Corcu Duibne. When the southern part of that kingdom was overthrown by the Mac Carthys, the usurping family established a principal seat here. The O Connells, who had been driven from the Killarney area by the incursion of the Mac Carthy, O Sullivan and O Donoghue families in the twelfth century, were, from about 1350, the hereditary wardens of this castle and its predecessor. They were not unduly submissive vassals. There is a story that when Mac Carthy Mor sent a cradle to

Birthplace of Daniel O Connell,
Carhan, Cahersiveen

O Connell as a sign to send for a Mac Carthy child to foster, O Connell cut off the head of the messenger and sent it back in the cradle. Friar O Sullivan has a more civilised story. Two O Connell brothers, bachelors and unfriendly, divided the castle into two flats, the older living below. Mac Carthy and his lady came to visit the castle. The elder brother entertained them the first night. The younger brother wanted the distinguished guests for dinner on the second night, but the elder objected. The lady said they would dine with whichever had a meal ready the earlier. The elder brother thereupon sealed off the upstairs flat to cut off the younger brother from water and fuel. But the younger cooked in Spanish wine and used 'liquorish' for fuel and won. O Sullivan tells the story to illustrate how plentiful things Spanish were in times past. He says that at the beginning of the 17th century at Templenoe, near Kenmare, a fresh salmon would buy a gallon of Spanish wine. A distinguished member of the O Connell family, Richard, was born here in 1575 and was, as usual educated and ordained in Spain (Two of his brothers also became priests). He had administrative charge of the Kerry diocese, in one shape or another, for over 40 years, becoming in 1643 the only bishop appointed in Kerry in the 17th century. He died in Killarney in 1653.

The first, and last, Earl of Clancarre was given to pledging the family property for cash. He pledged Ballycarbery towards the end of the 16th century for £80 to Sir Nicholas Browne. Florence, the husband of Clancarre's daughter, extinguished the pledge in 1630, but it seems to have remained in Browne's hands. The last O Connell seneschal, Maurice, was transplanted to Clare in the cromwellian confiscations. At length the O Connells restored their fortunes at the other side of the peninsula, at Derrynane. Morgan O Connell, Daniel's father, came back to Carhan nearby, and prospered in a business not dissimilar from that carried on at Derrynane. In the middle of the nineteenth century, Sir James O Connell, Daniel's brother, who had settled in Killarney, bought the ancient property at Ballycarbery.

Turn back to the school and turn left. At the next cross turn right for Cooncroin. After about a quarter of a mile there is a boithrin on the right. This is almost at the foot of a caher — *Leacanabuaile* (V.45.81.b) — placed on a splendid outcrop of rock. Inside this are the remains of houses, some on top of earlier ones. The fort was excavated in 1939-40, and partially restored. The excavators dated the occupation to the early christian period of 500 to 900 A.D.; but Mr E. Rynne suggests that the construction may be later than 1200 A.D. The excavation yielded meagre results and the finds were poor — iron knives and pins, bone combs, whetstones and querns. They showed a comparatively well-housed, but primitive, community fed on the products of their land and the neighbouring sea-coast, but poor in articles implying trade or other connections with the outside world. Inside the ruined clochan room is a souterrain by which children and smaller adults (in old clothes) can get outside the caher.

The run up to the little inlet of *Cooncroin* (V.45.82.a) is short and pleasant. There is a fine promontory fort — *Duneaniv* — at this place. There seem to be no further ones up this side of Dingle Bay. Turn back towards Cahersiveen. A short distance beyond the cross roads is a boithrin.

This leads up to another caher, *Cahergal* (V.45.81.b), which can be seen from Leacanabuile. Cahergal is much dilapidated and has ruins of a clochan and of a rectangular house; but it is an interesting contrast to Leacanabuaile in clearly presenting the construction of these cahers. Observe the great skill with which the unmortared stones of the walls were matched together. The caher is named *geal* presumably from the light colour of the stones. Neither of these — nor a third in the neighbourhood, Caher na gat—compares with Staigue fort, but they give interesting examples of the style, including the internal stairs.

Go back towards Cahersiveen, but instead of turning right to cross the bridge carry on straight. After a further mile take the road bearing left. Follow this for just under a mile to a T junction. Tun left for just under a quarter of a mile. Here, a little way in to the right is a well — really a pool, but called in

Irish *Glaise Chumhra* (V.49.83.a), the fragrant stream — dedicated to St Fursa. He spent his childhood amongst his people's kin in south Munster and was one of the notable Irish missionaries in Europe. He died in 650 at Peronne. His visions of heaven and of hell, deriving from the Irish literary genre (of which another branch fathered St Brendan's *Navigatio*) had a profound effect on the medieval world; it set a style that culminated in the Dante masterpiece. His feast is held on January 16th. The 2,207 foot mountain above one is called *Knockadobar* (V.51.85.b) (Cnoc na dtobar—the hill of the wells). The redoubtable Canon Brosnan revived the devotion and had erected stations of the cross up the two mile track to the top of the mountain, surmounted by a great cross. There is an ancient tradition of holding a festive gathering at the top of this mountain on the last Sunday of July: and Miss Mac Neill lists it as a Lughnasa site like Drung, six miles away. There are five standing stones on the south slope of the mountain; they are now much defaced. South of the stones can just be traced an oval platform. It is suggested that they are an alignment.

Total driving distance: about eleven miles.

2. Killoe—Killogrone—Kilpeacan—Keeldaragh

The Cahersiveen area is, thanks to the remarkable researches of Mlle Francoise Henry, a major centre for the study of ancient anchoritic sites. No less than five of these can be seen south of the town, one of which *Ceallurach* (? V.47.77.b) I could not find.

For *Killoe* (V.49.77.c) take the high road out of the town through the very old and decaying houses. There are fine views. Keep to this road for three miles until, at a farmhouse, it swings sharp left. Here, at the right of the road, is a very ruined eremitical site with little of interest except a lintel stone with distinctive scribings along a narrow edge, no doubt re-used from some ancient use. There is also a simple quern.

For *Killogrone* (V.51.77.b) follow this road until, after a half-mile, it is joined by another road from the right. Just after this it goes through a shallow pass. When the scene

Scribed lintel at Killoe, Cahersiveen

opens out again there is a boithrin to the right leading to a farmhouse. Follow this to the farmhouse. Killogrone, is a short distance beyond the farmhouse on the flat ground below it to the left. There are a number of ruins in the enclosure and a cross inscribed ogam stone that is now upside down. There are two beehive huts set into the enclosing wall, and the remains of two large oblong houses in the centre of the enclosure lie north of these. There are also the obscure remains of what may have been two other oblong but smaller houses. This was clearly a well populated settlement.

Turn back along the road one has come and take the first turn left. Follow this until one reaches the main road and turn left. One and a half miles further on there is an undistinguished cross roads. Turn up the little road to the left. This brings one, after about a quarter-mile, to *Kilpeacan* (V.48.74c). This enclosure is unusual in being rectangular and like Killogrone, having the ruins of two rectangular houses, but no beehive one. It has the usual cross-pillar with ogam and what seem to be the remains of several coptic-style shrines.

At the cross roads carry on the road from the main road, for a quarter-mile until it hits the main road again. Here take the broad road left off the main road to the site of *Keeldaragh* (V.50.73.b), Cloghanecarhan. Follow this road for one and a half miles until it crosses a bridge over a stream. The site is in the field to the right, through an iron gate. This is an old, crowded burial

270

ground inside a ringfort, with an ogam stone, and the remains of structures, souterrains and a cross slab.

Continue on this road until it comes to a T junction, and turn left. This brings one along the valley of the Inny until the road again bears off left. Follow this until one comes to a signposted road seven and a half miles from Keeldaragh, turn left and carry on this road back to Cahersiveen. Two miles along this road, bearing left, one comes to the ruined parish church of *Killinane* (V.54.80.a), on the left. This parish, now incorporated in that of Cahersiveen, was dedicated to St Fionan (Cill Fhionain) who was probably the great inspiration of the anchorites whose sites we have been visiting. The church is a typical, undistinguished medieval parish church. Catholic burials still continue here, and it is not unlikely that it continued to be in use during penal times. Above the road (on one's right) about half a mile from the church in a direct line north east in a secluded part of the steep hill, is *Maum-an-Affrin* (V.54.80.b), two pieces of a single rock which according to tradition was used as a mass-rock when the church below was denied to those who kept to the old faith. On the lower rock is a large circle about 30 inches in diameter: it is not clear what its purpose was. A little further along the road, in a field on the left, is a very large gallan. Some distance further on, again to the left, is the abandoned workhouse at *Bahaghs* (V.52.81.c), used as a barracks during the civil war. The road comes out on the main Ring of Kerry at Carhan, Daniel O Connell's birthplace.

Total driving distance: 25 miles. Allow two hours.

3. Ballynahow Beg—Caherlehillan—Kells Bay

Take the road for Glenbeigh for about two and a half miles. Where it turns left, just at the power station, carry on straight. Follow this road for just a mile until, just short of a bridge, at *Foilmore* (V.53.83.a), over the river, one turns sharp right. At the cross roads, a quarter-mile further on, turn left and carry on until, less than a quarter-mile further on, one comes to a narrow boithrin on

the right, the first of two. Beside this boithrin there is a recently built county council cottage. Just behind the ditch directly behind this house, but a little to the left of it, beside another ditch on the left of the field is a large stone, the famous *Ballynahow Beg scribed stone* (V.54.83.c) covered with moss and brambles, which when lifted reveal a really striking example of rock scribings in their various shapes and forms.

Return to the car and follow the road one is on for two miles, until one comes to a T junction. Turn left here and three-quarters of a mile further on, after one has crossed a bridge over a river, turn right up the hill. Stop at the farmhouse on the roadside on the right, after one has travelled about half a mile.

This is *Caherlehillan* (V.58.84.a). Just off the roadside to the right, and a little below the the farmhouse, is an interesting ceallunach with the graves piled up in a congested place. In the ceallunach are two cross pillars, one with, most unusually, a maltese type cross in a circle on a stand with two curious squiggles under the cross, and a bird raised above the cross. The other is a latin cross with the usual expanded finials, above a circle. A little above the farmhouse, just under 300 yards due north of the ceallunach, off the roadway to the left, is the ruined caher that gives the townland its name. The views here are very fine. Just over 300 yards north west of the caher—a bit more by the boithrin, as it has now become—and to the left is a good example of a wedge shaped grave with cup marks on the top slab. It is as well to inquire in the farmhouse for precise directions. About 300 yards up the mountain side in a direct line from the caher and the gallery grave, across three fences is another more ruined example. Continue up the mountain on this straight line for some 700 yards. At about 1,200 feet is a large scribed rock with cup and circle and the usual complex patterns. This is the *Gortnagulla* (V.58.85.b) scribed stone.

Return to the ceallunach. Go back towards the road, and up the second boithrin is another scribed rock—with the usual cups and

circles and, quite exceptionally for Kerry, a neolithic style spiral. There is also a cross with two cross-pieces, the triple or syrian cross, (another coptic influence). Some of the scribings have scaled off because fires were lit on the stone according to the accepted version; but the presence of the cross suggests another reason for the scaling. A triple cross is very rare in Ireland. The upper cross piece represents the title board that bore the inscription. Usually, there is a third cross piece, a foot piece, but the rock seems to have broken off here. There is a complete triple cross on a rock at Farrantooren, Killorglin. It is striking that both examples in this area should be on rocks, not pillars or slabs. On the Skellig there is a slab with what looks like a syrian cross.

Behind the hills here are the seven lakes of Coomasaharn and its fellows. These hills make a splendid ridge walk.

Follow the road one has been on until the Ring of Kerry road appears. Turn right here and, a short distance later, turn left off it for Kells Bay and Roads. At *Kells Bay* (V.56.89) there is excellent swimming and provision for boating. The coastguard station here was attacked in the Fenian Rising of February, 1867. This is commemorated in a well known ballad. Beyond Kells Bay there is a rough road to *Roads* (V.53.88.d) with, on a suitable day, fine views of Dingle Bay. From Roads—that is rather before the road itself comes to an end—there is a track of three and a half miles over the shoulder of

Scribed rock, with syrian cross, Caherlehillan, Cahersiveen

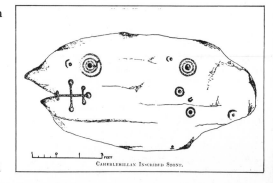

CAHERLEHILLAN INSCRIBED STONE.

Knocknadobar that rejoins a road near the
old railway line overlooking the great valley
towards Cahersiveen: but this involves an
arrangement with the driver who has, in any
event, to turn here and retrace his tracks to
the main road.

Nearby is Foilmore, where Daniel O Connell
was in fosterage. Directly below the saddle
of the mountain, close to the old railway
track about one and a half miles south west
of the former Kells railway station, is the
townland of *Lisbane* (V.53.85). Windele
suggests that here was Lisbane-na-Cahir (or
Lisbanagher), where Mac Carthy Mor was
inaugurated.

Total driving distance: 26 miles. Allow,
depending on the time spent at Caherlehillan,
three to four hours.

4. Portmagee—Valentia

Take the Waterville road and after four miles,
at a creamery, the road right for Portmagee.
Portmagee (V.38.73.a) itself has little to
offer: it is the site of the new bridge to
Valentia island. It is named after a famous
smuggler from the north of Ireland who
died in Lisbon in 1724. His business was
carried on from here by his redoubtable
widow, a Crosbie, and her family, one of
whom married the Archdeacon Lauder who
achieved fame as (probably) the ring-leader
of the Danish silver robbery in
Ballyheigue.

Valentia (V.33-43.73-79) comes from Beal
Inse, the Irish name for the Portmagee
channel. The name of the island is in Irish
Dairbhre, that is the oak-wooded; sometimes
it is Dairinis, the oak island. It is about
seven miles long. Over the bridge turn right
and go through the minute village of
Chapeltown to the island's little 'capital',
Knightstown. It is beautifully situated
on the splendid harbour.

A very pleasant approach is to take the ferry
from *Reenard* (V.44.78.a) to Knightstown.

The island is notable in legend as the home
of the famous, or infamous, druid Mogh
Roith, the Servant of the Wheel, who is said

Valentia Harbour

to have beheaded John the Baptist. One of
the petty kings of the Corcu Duibne had his
seat here. It was raided by the vikings and, as
we shall see, they left some remains behind.
Mac Carthy Mor, when he became Earl of
Clancarre in the 1560s, had a secondary
title Viscount Valentia, borne by his only
legitimate son who pre-deceased him. The
cromwellians built two forts here, one at each
end of the island, but these were dismantled
later in the 17th century. The harbour was
in the seventeenth and eighteenth centuries
a favourite rendezvous of French privateers
who raided the surrounding country until
it was impressed on the French king that the
resulting losses were taxed on the catholic
people. Thanks to the enterprise of the
Magee family and others the harbour was a
famous smuggling port in the same period,
even when British naval vessels were anchored
there: the benevolent effects of an anker
or two of brandy were considerable. The
famous American privateer, Paul Jones, was
often here. The island once had a big export
of its excellent slates—used, amongst other
things, for billiard tables—but that is finished.
Knightstown (V.43.78.d) (pop. 1971:236)

received the first cable messages across the
Atlantic on 16 August 1858, after struggles
of over a year to lay the cable: but that,
too, is ended since 1966. It lives now on a
small tourist business and the usual
small-scale fishing and farming: and on the
expectation that the new bridge will prevent
its further decay. In June, 1883, as part of a
government scheme to assist emigration to
America, two ships came into the harbour.
The *Belgravia* took on board 800 men,
women and children and, a fortnight later,
the *Furnessia* took another large group.

The local magnate, at Glanleam, was formerly
the Knight of Kerry. The disinherited 17th
Knight—the Dingle properties having gone to
his relatives, the Townsends—settled here in
1780. His son, the 18th Knight, represented
Kerry in parliament for 37 years, from 1794
in the Irish parliament, and then at
Westminster. Disgusted by corruption, he
voted for the Union and was a strong
advocate of catholic emancipation. He died
in 1849. His grandson, the 20th Knight,
supported Carson and joined the Ulster
Volunteer Force in 1913. In 1936 Lord

272

Monteagle, of the Spring-Rice family long settled in Dingle, came into short-lived possession of the property. The first Lord Monteagle was chancellor of the exchequer in the 1830s. His successor's cousin was British ambassador in Washington during World War I and disseminated knowledge about Casement's diaries to defuse the movement there to have him reprieved. Ironically, a member of the family, Mary Spring-Rice, was one of the gun runners who helped to bring German guns landed at Kilcoole, Co. Wicklow, in 1914 for the Irish National Volunteers. At least one of those condemned to death in 1916 probably owed his reprieve to the intercession of a Spring-Rice.

J. J. O Kelly (Sceilg) (1878-1957), born in Valentia, was minister for education in the republican government of 1921.

The most attractive harbour contains two islands of some interest—Beiginish and the tiny Church Island. They make a pleasant trip from Knightstown, where a motor boat and boatman can be easily and cheaply hired.

The wind has blown away much of the sand that had accumulated on *Beiginish* (V.41-43.79-80) and revealed the remains of eight houses set, without enclosures in the small fields. One gets the impression of what a farming and fishing community was like in early medieval times. There are on the island clinkers from early iron smelting. At the eastern end of the island are the remains of a large circular house with a later lean-to attached. This house was excavated by Professor M. J. O Kelly. The house clearly had a thatched roof supported by wooden poles resting on the wall. The house was found to be full of shells of the fish that must have constituted a major part of the food of the people. Used as a construction pillar in the house was the runic stone referred to elsewhere, one of the very few in Ireland. It is dated to the 11th century so the house must be of later date. Found along the strand were the remains of a stone Scandinavian bowl. It may be that there was, for a while, a settlement of norsemen in the place. However, the houses that remain are not

viking ones. There is a record of the landing of norsemen in Caomh-Inis-Obhrathach in 815 with sixty ships, and the pillaging of Inis-Labhraine and Dair Inis. Then, later, some of them may have settled here, as at Smerwick, the harbour at the end of the Dingle peninsula.

Beside Beiginish is the little *Church Island* (V.43.79.b) with its caiseal all around it. The main monument is a now collapsed, perhaps 8th century, oratory built of the local slate; it was a good deal bigger than the standard oratory, so there must have been a community of say a dozen or so. It was built on the site of a small wooden church, by which there were 33 burials. There are a few other remains: a ruined round house, that may have had a thatched roof, built on the site of a wooden house and outside the caiseal a rectangular house. Now in the Cork museum is a very fine cross slab found here with a maltese cross and ogam markings later than the cross. As ogam is believed to have gone out of use by 700 AD we have a late date for the full development of that very distinctive Kerry monument, the cross-pillar. Perhaps the community here survived longer and thrived better than most. Again there are remains of iron smelting. The island was raided by the vikings in the middle of the ninth century, so the community may have been still there at that time.

In the harbour there is fishing for scallops and sea urchins when there is an 'R' in the month.

To the right as one climbs up out of the town is the unmetalled road to *Glanleam* (V.41.78.d), formerly the home of the Knight of Kerry. The place is exquisitely sited and surrounded by lush gardens with many rare South American trees. Back this road and right and right again to the old *slate quarries* (V.39.77.c). These were opened in 1883 and are now abandoned; but they have been turned into a most impressive religious grotto.

Back along this road and turn right along the main high road of the island. There are a number of gallans and small antiquities

to be seen as one goes along but perhaps special interest can be paid to the townland of Tinnies Upper which one reaches after a mile along this road. Beyond a most impressive set of farm buildings on the left there is just beyond a brightly painted cottage on the right a number of antiquities. There are, almost on the roadside on the right, a rath and souterrain, a pillarstone and some early graves. *Tinnies* (V.39.76) is said to be where Mogh Roith lived and to be named from the fires he used to light. There were copper deposits here and the name may recall ancient smelting.

About a half-mile further on, just short of a roadway down to the left—itself just short of another gallan—is, on the right, just short of a new farmhouse, the anchoritic site of *Kildreenagh* (V.38.76.c). This is one field in from the road, a roughly circular enclosure, with the ruins of four circular buildings and four rectangular ones, an ogam pillar stone and the remains of a coptic style shrine. As one might expect, about 130 yards north west of this site, over some rough ground, is a fine wedge grave with cup marks on the top and what has been described as traces of a gutter at the eastern end.

The road from the left continues across to the right but becomes pretty rough. It is not marked on the ½ inch map. This leads to a gate at a farmhouse. Walk just below the farmhouse towards the sea. A short distance further on there is a small gallan. Between one and the sea, but to the left and beneath one, is another. They point, roughly, to the promontory fort of *Cooseenadagallan* (V.37.77.c). However, continue directly towards the sea and the impressive cliffs. A short distance below one to the left is the fort with three ramparts and the remains of stone portals. Nearer the sea within this enclosure and in a windy place are the remains of two clochans. An odd place, but with striking views of the Blaskets to the north.

Back to the crossroads and turn right. Just a mile along the road take the second of the two roads right. Neither is marked on the ½ inch map. This second road has a signpost, but no sign. Follow it for a mile or so until it peters out at a farmhouse. Just beyond this is another anchoritic settlement with, unusually, three crudely shaped stone crosses with lightly incised crosses on them. There is little more to suggest the settlement, but perhaps it has been engulfed by the bog which has nearly swallowed one of the crosses. In the deep bog is *St Brendan's well* (V.36.76.a) with modern remnants of devotion. Turn and, on the main road, go right. This winds pleasantly back to the bridge and Portmagee.

Total driving distance: 34 miles. Allow four and a half hours.

(III) THE WATERVILLE AREA I

Waterville (V.51.66-67) village (pop. 1971: 547) depends entirely on tourism which itself is largely based on fishing. The village is at the short outlet of Lough Currane to the sea. This lake is famous as a place for fishing salmon and sea trout. Back towards Cahersiveen is the Inny, another famous fishing river. Amongst the mountains skirting Lough Currane are many mountain lakes, fruitful sources of brown trout. It is worthwhile to go into the hallway of the Butler Arms hotel any evening during the fishing season to see the day's catch laid out for inspection. Just outside the village, on the road to Caherdaniel, the lake waters take their short run to the sea. Here was a famous net fishery beside a handsome eighteenth century house of the Butler family. The Butlers supplied a number of the Customs and Excise officers who tried (usually unsuccessfully) to cope with the extensive smuggling all along the Kenmare river. A little further on, to the left, is the Waterville Lake hotel, from which there is a magnificent view of Lough Currane and its circle of mountains.

This village, with its English name, given it by the Butlers—has roots stretching back into history and legend. It was in Ballinskelligs Bay, possibly hereabouts, that Cessair, her forty-nine women, and three men, companions landed just before the flood, having lost here the other two ships of their convoy—presumably they would have restored the balance between the sexes. Here, too, the last legendary invaders of Ireland—the Milesians—landed and there are reported memorials of their coming and of their dead about this place. There are christian remains dating back to the sixth century St Fionan Cam, and the twelfth century reformer St Malachy. On the south side of the Lake the Mac Carthy family had their inaccessible retreats while they were fighting for their lives against the Anglo-Norman intruders. Through here, in later times, passed the O Connells to their even more inaccessible retreat at Derrynane. Many of the houses date from the setting up here of an Atlantic cable station in 1870, now obsolete.

Some of the good things of living can be got in this place. A shop close to the post office sells really excellent farmer's butter (made from sour cream and salted, at its best capable of giving a wholly new dimension to the word). Nearby one can occasionally—if one is very lucky—buy a sea-trout, the most delicious of fish. One can come across lobster and crayfish: but these are now expensive. Back on the river bank at the *Inny bridge* (V.51.70.a)—two miles on the Cahersiveen road—one can buy during the salmon netting season when the tide is reaching its height (except on Saturdays and Sundays) netted salmon fresh from the water at wholesale prices. Very occasionally, and only in early summer, one can get a sea trout.

Loafing around the village one can see brown and white beagle dogs. In winter beagling is a great sport in the whole of south Kerry. In summer the dogs are sent racing in teams over a dragged scent for some 12 or 15 miles over mountain and valley. It is well worth attending one of these contests, with teams entered from far and near. The whole countryside turns out to these races. Bring glasses.

There is a new, splendid golf course.

However, the primary sport here is fishing. This is one of Ireland's leading fishing places. But it is also a splendid centre for sightseeing.

Between the village and the lake is a great number of ancient remains—stone forts, beehive huts, souterrains, old road systems, all, but the last named, now much ruined.

1. Spunkane—Beenbane—Termons—Church Island (Lough Currane)

Take the inland road for Cahersiveen for about a mile, ignoring two roads to the right. About a third of a mile beyond the second of these stop at a big farmhouse, right, set amongst some well grown trees. Go through the farmyard and two gates beyond following the fence on one's left over the brow of the hill. There is at least one scribed rock to one's right just below the brow. Follow the fence to a gap and take a diagonal right to the far end of this field. Here is the fine *Spunkane* (V.52.69.c) slab with a little greek cross. There is no sign of an eremitical settlement. The views here are superb.

Turn the car and take the first turn left and, at the T junction, turn right. After a short distance there is a roadway left leading to the lake. It will be necessary to leave the car at the farmhouse and walk along the old road to the lakeside. At the end of this roadway there is the very ruined caher of *Beenbane* (V.52.67.c) with little of archaeological interest except a system of souterrains. But the site is beautifully situated. Back to the main road, turn right and, after a short distance, up a hill, left. This gives a very fine view of the whole countryside. After a half-mile, just short of a little lake deep on the right, is a gateway left and a rough boithrin leading up the hill. In a thicket of thorns a little way up is, left, the eremitical site of *Termons* (V.53.69.a) with a rather primitive greek cross. Return to the road and turn. On the way down admire the colour scheme of the house at its end.

Turn left at the main road. After about two miles there is a signpost, right, for *Church Island* (V.54.67.a). A boat may be hired at the first house on the left of the boithrin. On a clear, calm evening the trip over to the island is most agreeable. Church island in *Lough Currane* (V.51-57.66-68) is to be distinguished from the Church island in Valentia harbour. The island is flat and

274

featureless. It has been partly submerged by the rising waters of the lake caused by the growth of vegetation at its outlet. At one time the island must have sheltered a large community: traces of a considerable settlement still remain. This foundation is also attributed to St Fionan, the remains of whose life-work are still so evident in South Kerry. There is a well dedicated to him on the mainland nearby at *Caherbarnagh* (V.54.69.a). At the western end of the island is a not-too-ruined oratory-shaped building of curious construction—the stones are large and irregular and the structure, longer than usual, seems to have been designed and put together in a spirit of primitive brutalism (It is known as St Finan's Cell but Mlle Henry suggests it may have been a barn). Its construction is vastly different in tone from the carefully pieced clochans on the Skellig and the oratory at Temple Cashel; but its shape, a transition both inside and outside, from the round to the square puts it plainly in the line of evolution between them and so, by way of Gallarus oratory to St Kevin's church and King Cormac's chapel. There is another link. The other structure of interest is the romanesque church at the eastern end of the island. This is a relatively simple church, with a fine west door ruined by incompetent restoration.

Was this built by St Malachy after his expulsion in 1127 with 120 'monks' — not only clerics but almost certainly tenants of monastic lands — from his monastery of Bangor, Co. Down? He went first to Lismore where he made friends with a fellow exile, Cormac Mac Carthy, temporarily deposed from being King of Munster. Cormac gave him a grant of land in 'Ibracense' and helped him to build a church. Cormac was the main thrust in the Mac Carthy intrusion into Kerry at this time, where they were to rule for nearly five centuries. They were also to live in Eightercua, beside Lough Currane. Two questions arise. Was 'Ibracense' Uibh Rathach (or Iveragh), Co. Kerry? There is much dispute about this. It has also been identified with Ibracken, near Cashel. We know that Cormac used come to inspect the progress of the work; so a site near Cashel is likely; but there are no monastic remains in Ibracken.

St Fionan's Church, Church Island

If it was Uibh Rathach where was the monastery built? Here also there is dispute; but if it was in Uibh Rathach, then Church Island is the most likely place. (A claim is made for Ballinskelligs, but this is not convincing because there is no obvious 12th century building there). Here was a long-standing monastery in an area that the Mac Carthy family were newly acquiring as mensal lands. It is not improbable that Cormac would come to inspect work on Church Island in full view of Eightercua. The monastery had extensive property and the island buildings were really extensive.

Here, perhaps, was a run down monastery requiring the kind of reform that St Malachy was preaching. Here was built a church of the period, complete with round tower, in the style that Cormac Mac Carthy was to raise to its highest peak in his 'Chapel' at Cashel. There is nothing of this kind in Ballinskelligs, or elsewhere in Iveragh.

St Malachy was not of course to stay long

here — he was to leave reluctantly to become bishop of Armagh in 1132, aided by Cormac Mac Carthy as king of Desmond and O Brien as king of Thomond. His church in 'Ibracense' was not to be completed until 1134. Ironically, for a friend of the Cormac of Cormac's chapel, he was to be the single greatest influence in destroying the Irish romanesque style, in that he later imported the cistercian order with their very different conceptions of architecture, and the Arroaisian Augustinians, who seemed to have no special conceptions of architectural style, at least in Kerry.

As one looks down the lake, on one's left is Eightercua where in the generations of struggle with the anglo-normans the Mac Carthy wives and children were to find secure shelter along the southern shores of this lake.

The island was known as Inis Uasail, the noble island, and of enough importance in the fifteenth century to give its name to the whole parish now called Dromod. Built in the wall of the church is a worn stone showing a man playing with a stringed instrument, not a harp, one of very few representations of its kind from early Ireland. There are eight cross-slabs, with varying styles of cross, two with inscriptions of the 9th-10th centuries. One reads: *Beannacht F (ar) Anmain Gille in Chomded I Buicine Adbur Ri Ciarraide* (A blessing on the soul of Gille in Chomded O Buicine, Royal heir of the Ciarraige). The other reads: *Beannacht F (ar) Anmain Anmchada* (A blessing for the soul of Anmchad). One of the cross-slabs shows a crozier of a bishop/abbot. A bishop's crozier is to be known because it is turned outwards, showing the outward bent of his jurisdiction. An abbot's is turned inwards because his jurisdiction is limited to his community. But there are numerous exceptions to this rule.

These cross slabs are of several distinctive kinds, discussed elsewhere. One of the four round towers of Kerry stood here, but no longer. There are the remains of oblong houses.

Total motoring distance: about 10 miles. Allow about three hours. Lough Currane is, of course, one of the most famous (free) salmon, sea trout and brown trout fishing areas in Ireland. It offers most agreeable boating, and sailing — except at the northern end. It is liable to sudden, and occasionally disagreeable, squalls.

2. *Caherbarnagh — Dromkeare —Cahersavane — Loughs Isknamacteery and Nambrackdarrig*

This trip can be conveniently combined with the Church island one if time permits. Go back to the Waterville road, turn right and about a half-mile further on, just before the right turn, there is, at the edge of a little wood, left, a gateway. One can walk or drive up the steep roadway. Just under the first farmhouse is the well-kept St Finan's well at *Caherbarnagh* (V.54.69.a), in a stone circle with three big ash trees. This has the marks of modern devotion. Above the well is set a stone with a very primitive greek cross, no doubt rubbed deep by pious fingers. If this was the state of cross sculpture at St Finan's time he clearly was at the very beginning of the eremitical movement and it is likely to have had its origin in Kerry in this area. The views here are superb. Back to the main road, and immediately bear right at the fork. About 0.6 miles along this road just before one crosses the bridge of the little Dromkeare river is the open gateway of a former mink farm on the shores of the lake. Some 200 yards inside this entrance, just before a branch in the entrance road, walk due left through high bracken and brambles to a line of holly bushes just short of the river. Here is a cross pillar with well marked latin cross and partly obliterated ogam, evidence, no doubt of the struggle between pagan and christian worlds. What is left reads: *TIDONN(A) MAQ DOMNGINN*. This is one of the most interesting and best known of the early christian cross pillars, the *Dromkeare cross* (V.55.69.a), partly incised and partly pocked. There is a partly obliterated ceallunach about the cross.

Continue on the public road up the hill for about a mile until the road turns sharply to the left. Leave the car here, and, a short distance above one on the right is *Cahersavane* (V.57.70.c), an interesting and splendidly

sited caher. There is a small outside rampart, a deep inside ditch and an inside rampart. There are a number of clochans outside the caher. Inside can be seen the remains of stepped galleries on the Staigue model. In some ways this is an interesting if not well preserved caher because it gives one some idea of what defended farmsteads of persons of consequence must have looked like when they were in occupation.

Continue on this road until one comes, after just a half-mile, to a T junction at a school. Turn sharply right here along a rough road and follow this road until one crosses a bridge and comes to rising ground from which *Lough Isknamacteery* (V.60-61.70) can be seen. A boithrin runs from a gateway here through the ruins of an ancient village of clochans—they are scattered all over the hillside. Keeping well above the lake and the stream that flows into it penetrate along the glacial debris into the deep glacial coum in which is *Lough*

Cross at Dromkeare, Waterville

Nambrackdarrig (V.62.70.c). This is a remarkably typical Kerry coum, with its two lakes connected by a stream and surrounded by glowering cliffs. These lakes are attractive on a bright day, but memorable on a threatening one.

3. *Loughnamona — Cloonaghlin and Derriana Loughs*

It is necessary to go back to the school and there bear right for the main road from Waterville. At this, turn sharp right and follow the road for just two miles until one comes to a cross roads. Turn right. Follow this road as it winds along, very picturesquely, by *Lough Namona* (V.60.71-72) and *Cloonaghlin Lough* (V.61-62.71-72).

Turn back to the main road and about a mile further on, just short of a school, turn right for *Derriana Lough* (V.61-63.73-74). This is a rough road that gets worse, but not impossible. It gives a splendid view of the lake. At the end of this road there is a ford, or stepping stones. Here there is the opening of another coum, *Coumavoher* (V.64-66.74-75). This contains a number of lakes — the nearest about a half-mile from the road's end, and the next about a half-mile above that, with several smaller ones strung out higher still. There is a pleasant road from the ford along the river. After a short distance it crosses the river at another ford and stepping stones.

There is reported to be good fishing for brown trout in all these lakes, but some at least of them are preserved.

Turn and go right at the T junction. This leads back to the main road to Waterville. Turn left here. After five miles along this road, above the Inny river, there are two cross roads close together. A half-mile after the second of these, just beyond a boithrin and a farmhouse, left, is on the high ground above one, but close to the road, the *Doory* (V.55.71.a) alignment. This consists of four gallans, with a fifth farther away. There were others, now fallen. Did these point to some now lost major monument? Back to the car and to Waterville.

275

276

Total motoring distance: 26 miles; in addition to the Church island run. Allow three hours.

4. *Ballinskelligs — St Finan's Bay — Portmagee*

Take the Cahersiveen road. This crosses the Inny River, a famous salmon one. From June to October (except Saturday and Sunday each week) there are netting rights on this river. If you pass when the tide is coming in it is possible to buy salmon (and occasionally sea trout) on the bank to the seaward side of the bridge at wholesale prices from the netsmen. Turn left to Ballinskelligs, through a dull foreground giving splendid views. Three miles along this road there is a branch left of a half-mile to *Reenroe* (V.47.69.c-d) where there is a hotel and a magnificent strand, with some surf-bathing; ponies may be hired.

Back to the Ballinskelligs road and turn left at the junction. Less than a quarter-mile along this road there is a bye-road on the left. Almost immediately opposite this is a farmhouse. In the fourth field behind this is a damaged but interesting sample of a wedge shaped gallery grave, that of *Meelaguleen* townland (V.45.69.c).

Rather more than a further quarter-mile along the main road take the second of two boithrins to the left until one comes to a T junction, above the sea. Leave the car here. Take the boithrin left along by the sea until it ends. Facing one is *Garrai (or Traigh) na Sasanach,* or the *Englishmen's Garden (or Strand)* (V.46.69.c) which commemorates one of the few actions in Kerry of the cromwellian wars. At the end of May, 1642 an expedition of two ships was mounted from Youghal to relieve the siege of Tralee castle. On the way they put in to Ballinskelligs and, as a reprisal for the disarming of some of the party, burned the town and the surrounding country. Then, having had a hot welcome in Dingle, they came back on 3rd June, 1642, and 80 men landed to raid for cattle. By this time, O Sullivan Mor, who had been at Glanbeg, divided his force in two, some of them going to Sneem and Poulnanuragh, and four companies under Captain Owen O Sullivan

towards Ballinskelligs. The raiding party fell in with O Sullivan's forces and were wiped out close to the sea, only three of them, including a much wounded Captain Vauclier, escaping by swimming until they were picked up by a boat from the ships. The dead English were buried here. The Irish suffered some 30 dead and a like number wounded. It was this action, it is claimed, that later led to the stationing of garrisons at Valentia and Nedeen.

Return to the car and, at the cross roads, turn left. This brings one into the dilapidated village of *Dungeagan* (V.45.68.c). Less than half a mile beyond the village, after one has rejoined the main road is, beside a small stream, another boithrin left which brings one to the sea and the very fine *Ballinskelligs strand* (V.44.66-67).

A short distance further on is the struggling village of *Ballinskelligs* (V.44.66.a). This is an Irish speaking area much favoured by nuns. There is an old cable station. There is a rather pleasant small hotel above the beach.

There are the ruins of a 16th century Mac Carthy Mor castle or *tower house* (V.44.66.a) which is of some interest: it was built on the isthmus to defend the place from pirates.

Close by is *Ballinskelligs Abbey* (V.44.65.a), a ruined sea-eroded (and disgustingly

Coastguard Station, Ballinskelligs

neglected) Augustinian priory. This seems to have been built as an offshoot of the settlement on the Skellig — possibly originally, after an interval of some two or three centuries. Archdall says it was after 885 — as a base for the island. It has been argued that it was to this part of 'Ibracense' (not Church Island, Waterville) that St Malachy came in 1127 and built a monastery with the aid of King Cormac Mac Carthy. But there is nothing about the buildings here to suggest the sophistication and charm of King Cormac's period, as there is on Church Island. The Arroaisian Augustinians took it over, it seems, in the 13th century (about 1225). Already before this time it would seem, from Giraldus Cambrensis, the Skellig community was withdrawn to the mainland. It may be that other Augustinian canons had taken over before the Arroaisians and that they had wound up the Skellig community sometime during the 12th century.

The buildings in this monastery singularly lack charm. The place seems not to have benefited from the great building revival of the 12th century and, although the remaining buildings seem to date from the 15th century they show little of the grace of that century either.

A considerable part of the monastery, including the east window of the church, has fallen into the sea. For the papal taxation of 1302-6 the prior of Ballinskelligs was the collector for the Archdeaconry of Aghadoe. Ballinskelligs itself was assessed at an income of only £2.13.0 — either the influence of the collector was helpful, or the pilgrimages to the Skellig had fallen off, or had not begun.

One gets tantalising glimpses of how these houses were run. In the fifteenth century this monastery seems to have become a perquisite of the O Mulchonry family. They had been imported from Connacht to be bards to the Mac Carthy family. In 1411 Alan O Mulchonry is made prior. In 1455 Maurice O Mulchonry was prior; we read that he had studied canon law in Oxford for over two years — an interesting sidelight on this heart of the gaelic world. In 1476 John O Mulchonry is prior, but he is ordered to be deprived because of serious charges made

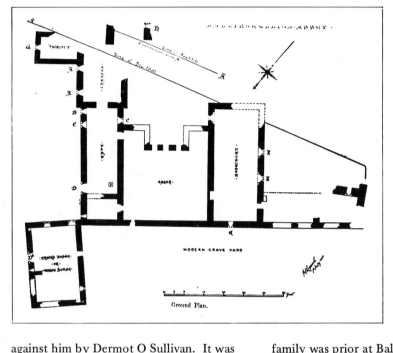

Ground Plan.

against him by Dermot O Sullivan. It was alleged that he is 'an open and notorious fornicator, that he has abandoned and miserably dilapidated divers immovable goods of the said monastery and converted these to his evil and damnable uses'. These charges O Mulchonry completely denied, but eleven years later he is forced to resign and O Sullivan resigns the living of Kilcrohane to a namesake to take over the office of prior. However, the O Mulchonrys were not to be easily dispossessed. It was a provision of canon law that a son could not directly succeed his father in an ecclesiastical benefice, so a member of the community, Robert O Cuynd (? O Cuinn, or Quinn) is nominated for the office. Within weeks he was superseded by John O Mulchonry, junior, who takes over and, at the same time, secures the newly erected prebend of Killemlagh. One may reasonably deduce from this that the younger John was the elder John's son. It is not clear what became of that foolish man, Dermot O Sullivan. In 1506 another O Mulchonry, Thaddeus, succeeds John junior and acquires the prebend of Killemlagh. During the greater part, it not the whole, of 100 years a member of the O Mulchonry

family was prior at Ballinskelligs.

In 1578 the priory is granted to Jyles Clinsker and later to others. It is possible that some or all of the community survived in Killemlagh during the whole of the penal times. That there was continuity in Killemlagh is probable; but whether it was Augustinian continuity or not is not clear. In 1633 the community seems to have been in existence, but not necessarily in this building. There is some indication that the Augustinians also held the parish church of Killinane at Srugreana. The modern parish of Ballinskelligs is still called 'Prior'.

It may be possible to get to the Skelligs from the little harbour nearby, but leave time for organising this. Shell and other fish can be bought here. The views from *Ballinskelligs pier* (V.44.65.c) are splendid. From here take the road right up the hill and take the second turn left. This road stops at a farmhouse, but there is an ancient road beyond it winding up the hill to the south. Near the summit is, left, the *Kildreelig alignment* (V.42.64.a) of four standing stones. This is the reputed burial place of the milesian

leader Erannan, allegedly matching and in line with the alignment at Eightercua across the bay; but it is not.

If there is a driver to bring the car round the hill (turn and take the first turn right and then right again and after about three and a half miles stop shortly after the semi-ruined fishing hamlet) one can continue down this old road. On the far side, a little above the metalled road is, left, a caher with a souterrain. A few yards north is a fallen gallan. A few yards further on is, right, a not too ruined clochan.

A short distance west along the metalled road there is, on the left, by the side of the road the much ruined but rather substantial exquisitely placed *Kildreelig eremitical site* (V.41.64.d) with a fallen-in boat shaped oratory, the ruins of several clochans, two inscribed pillars, and a substantial but crudely built caiseal. One of the cross pillars has an elongated latin cross with double circle. The other has basically a greek cross in a circle, with segments cut within the circle, and other adornments. Both suggest a spare elegance much at variance with the crudity of what otherwise remains. North of the cashel are the ruins of a rectangular building without mortar but with large stones, one nine feet long. This may have continued as a church attached to Ballinskelligs until the late 16th century — at least so Lynch suggests. About 36 yards west of the caiseal is a ruined

Ballinskelligs Priory

278

dolmen and in the next field a holy well. So, we see here three different levels of religious experience.

Carry on this road. Below the farmhouse on the left, a couple of hundred yards from the road, is a caher. The road ends in a farmyard. From this it is a walk of about a mile to *Bolus Head* (V.40.64.b). Fine views are to be had. This is the nearest land point to the Skellig.

Return this road and, after two and a half miles, just after the waterworks on the left, turn left at the school for St Finan's Bay. Above one, right, is *Reigleish* (V.43.67.c), meaning an abbey church (no doubt from Ballinskelligs). It is said there was once a round tower here, but the whole is now so ruined as not to be worth a visit.

After just over a mile, after a group of houses, turn down a bye-road on the left and, two fields down, just at the bottom of the valley, in *Coom* (V.61.66.b), is a wedge shaped gallery grave with forecourt. If one continues across the river and turns right at the T junction, on the left is a gallan in *Leabaleaha* (V.41.46.a) (pronounced 'Lybalayha'). Beside it are the ruins of another wedge shaped gallery grave, about 700 yards west of the other.

Turn here and go back to the road to *St Finan's Bay* (V.39.69). Just before the bay — bathing in which can often be dangerous — on the right is *Killemlagh* church (V.40.69.d). This place is known as the Glen. The church was built on the site, it is said, of St Fionan's original settlement. The old church here was a 12th-13th century Irish romanesque structure, but the west doorway has been walled up. There are a couple of well-carved windows. Attached to it is a later parish church, said to have survived, in this remote area, in penal times. This parish came to be attached to Ballinskelligs priory in the later 15th century. It is just possible that when the priory was suppressed in the late 16th century some vestige of the community survived here, a return, as it were, to St Fionan. 150 yards south of the church is the *'Pagan's Grave'* (V.40.69.d), an unusual enclosure of standing stones 18 ft.

by 11 ft. The pagan Maolmorna tried to have St Fionan murdered, but himself was killed in error. Killemlagh Church has more recently been replaced by the little church of *Glen* (V.39.69.b) a few hundred yards away, the gift of Irish-American donors to their old parish, and designed by Rupert Boyd-Barrett. It is worth seeing. Directly behind the new church is a farmhouse with a gallan, with ogam markings, in the field above it. In the field immediately above this is a ringfort with a good example of a three-chamber *souterrain* (V.39.70.d). There is a stone man-hole in the centre of the fort, but entrance is easier just outside the ring, in the direction of the house. This needs very old clothes, a good torch and some agility.

From the new church and facing it, take the right turn up the hill for exactly one mile. At a narrow gateway at the left hand side of the road stop and climb up the hillside on the left to *Killabuonia* (V.41.70.a). This is a most interesting eremitical site to which pilgrimages are still made, though no one knows who this Buonia (recte Buaine) was, whether man or woman. A little to the west of the settlement

Cross Slabs, Kildreelig, Ballinskelligs

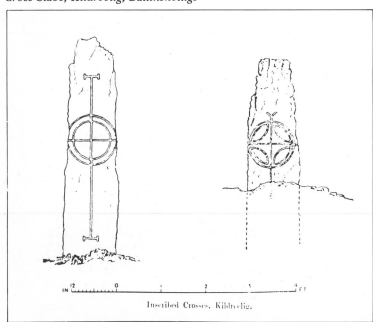

Inscribed Crosses, Kildreelig.

Wedge grave, Coom, Ballinskelligs

is a well dedicated to St Buonia. Note the greek crosses rubbed into the stones including an (?) 18th century one with a representation of the saint's face. Here again, as at Kildreelig, one sees a christian settlement on a pagan one devoted to the cult of life (the well) and of death, the great tomb. The site gives the best general impression on the mainland of what the Skellig settlement is like, but it is greatly ruined while the Skellig settlement is almost intact. There are two collapsed boat-shaped oratories, the ruins of a number of clochans, graves, and a coptic style grave shrine. There is the usual cross pillar but with a latin cross with expanding finials above a diamond enclosing another latin cross. There is also a crudely shaped stone cross. This in spite of its ruinous state is an important site.

Unless one chooses the alternative offered below, turn on the road and return to the church and then take the signpost for Portmagee. At the wicked turn right (also signposted), bear left and stop at the gateway to the first farmhouse on the left. Walk down the boithrin past the farmhouse to a field, at the bottom of which are the remains of the very early convent of nuns at *Temple Cashel* (V.37.69.b). All that can be readily seen now is the boat-shaped oratory, perhaps the best preserved of the ruined ones. This is almost square inside (12' 6" by 10' 8") and the east and west walls have slightly curved batter. It is the natural link between the square clochans on the Skellig and the intact rectangular Gallarus oratory. Inside are the same holed stones for a hanging door, as at Gallarus. The foundations of the caiseal around may be just discerned faintly. This is well worth the visit. The walled enclosure to the left was a garden of a branch of the O Connell family who lived nearby.

Return to the car and for about a mile follow the road, past the farm gate, up to open country. From here there are fine views of *Puffin Island* (V.37-38.68-69) and the Skelligs. Return and, if one has good nerves for a bad, but just passable, stretch of road, turn left at Portmagee. At the top of the hill, at the T junction, it is worth turning right for a mile and three-quarters to the TV mast. From around this splendid views

are to be had. Turn here and go straight for Portmagee. Back then towards the Cahersiveen road. Just four miles along this road take the signposted road right. After 0.3 miles along this road, after a farmhouse, right, is a field entrance, also right. Just inside this is the eremitical site of *Killoluaig* (V.44.73.a), much rearranged and neatly laid out as a ceallunach. The notable feature is a coptic style shrine, with the end pieces missing. There is also a boomerang shaped stone, presumably a failed shaped cross.

Carry on this road through a cross roads. About a quarter-mile beyond this just beyond the brow of the hill there is, left, beside the roadside, the ruined small caher of *Fermoyle* (V.44.72.c) with the remains of clochans inside. This is not very exciting in itself but it does illustrate the small farming settlement, as opposed to those in the more imposing cahers, and also the secular model of the smaller eremitical settlements. Follow this road, and turn left at Reenroe for Waterville. Total motoring distance: 30 miles. Allow four hours.

As an alternative to the Temple Cashel — Portmagee run continue up the hill from Killabuonia for just three miles until one comes to signposted cross roads. Turn left here for just a mile until, after a bend left, one reaches, now on the left, the eremitical site of Killoluaig referred to above. Turn the car here and continue up the hill as previously described.

5. Skelligs

A journey to the *Great Skellig* (V.25.61.b) is a high point of a visit to Kerry and is not to be missed if a suitable day offers — this is not often. The island covers some four acres and is about eight miles west of Bolus head, but the journey by sea from Portmagee is about twelve miles, takes about one and a half hours, and is suitable only for a fairly calm day when the wind (unless it is very light) is *not* from the east. Should such a day offer it is worth the sacrifice of other plans. There are now regular services by motor boat from Portmagee, Reenard, Cahersiveen and Derrynane. It may also be possible to arrange

trips from Ballinskelligs. The regular services have a fixed fare per head; others will need some preliminary organisation. Allow about three hours for the island: thus, at least six hours from Portmagee, and longer from most other mainland places of departure. It may also be possible to take a helicopter from Killarney.

There are two main rocks that impress their personalities on travellers along the south western tip of the peninsula, and a small one called *Lemon Rock* (V.31.64.b). The large ones are Skellig Michael, or the Great Skellig, and the Lesser Skellig.

It is almost impossible to land on the *Lesser Skellig* (V.27.62.b). It is now a bird sanctuary and is one of the three gannetries around Ireland. It is the largest of their haunts. The masses of white one sees as one approaches the rock are the 20,000 pairs of gannets perched on their rock galleries. Gannets have to nest on precipitous rocks because their wings are so much longer than their feet that to set into flight from land they have to throw themselves, as it were, into the air. The more inquisitive of the birds are impressive as they circle the boat, with their six foot spans of black-tipped wings. When they are fishing they make a striking sight as they plunge vertically into the sea. The population of gannets has fluctuated over the years. Their breeding here was first mentioned in 1700. In 1748 there were 'an incredible number nesting', in 1828 there were 500 pairs, in 1880 about 30 pairs, in 1906-8 some 15,000-20,000 pairs and over the past 30 years about 10,000-20,000 pairs. On Bull Rock, a little to the south, there are 1,500 pairs, rather more than the number at the turn of the century. Gannets were first seen on Bull Rock in 1853.

The Great Skellig is host to kittiwakes, guillemots, puffins as well as petrel and some shearwater and fulmar. Lewis says that, at least early in the last century, these birds were captured by people from the mainland. Because they fed on fish they were held to be suitable for eating on fast days.

On a calm day the sea is covered with groups of these birds. In the calm waters can be

280   found the great basking sharks — often 40
feet long — and the sluggish sun fish.

One lands on the Great Skellig at a little cove
facing east, Blind Man's Cove. Directly above
this landing place one can see leading upwards
the steep steps to the monastery, just to be
discerned. These steps originally led straight
up from the Cove, but the bottom ones were
cut away in the last century when the new
road was made to the lighthouse. A walk of
some ten minutes brings one to the beginning
of the steps now in use — the 'smooth and
elegant stairs', led from Cross Cove, east.
Here in rough weather, one can now land
and leave — by derrick. Right across the
island, in Blue Cove, is another landing place
from which another set of steps used lead
to the monastery. These three landing
places meant that in former times one could
land on the island, whatever the point from
which the weather came.

A short distance up from Cross Cove there
is an ancient, worn cross. This is a suitable
place to picnic. One can believe that the
Gulf Stream really does reach these parts, the
place is so warm. Frost is believed never to
fall on the island. The view is breath-taking.

To the right are the Bull and Cow rocks and
one is reminded by this, the cross and the
steps of the three periods of Skelligs history
— the pagan, the monastic and the time of
pilgrimages.

Bull Rock in early Celtic mythology was
Teach Duinn—the House of Donn—the
abode, perhaps paradisal, of the dead. There
the ship of one of the Milesian invaders was
lost, and here at the Great Skellig another
one of the sons of Milesius—Ir—was drowned
and buried on the saddle, above, where a
dolmen once was supposed to stand. Here
the great fleet of King of the World, Daire
Donn, gathered momentarily before, piloted
by a renegade Killarney man, Glas Mac
Dreamhain, it choked the harbour of Ventry
at the end of the Dingle Peninsula, to the
north. This was the host that took a battle
of a year and a day for the Fiana and their
allies to destroy.

The first historical reference to the Skelligs is

Approach to Skellig

The Lesser Skellig

from the end of the fifth century when, we
read, that Duach, king of the Eoganacht Locha
Lein and of West Munster, when pursued
by Oengus, king of Cashel, fled to 'Scellec'.

A monastery in these parts would be unusual
if it were not sited on an existing site of a
pagan cult. There is some echo of the
struggle between christianity and the pagan
worship of serpents which, according to
Brash, was carried on on this island.

St Patrick, notoriously, never got to Iveragh,
but there on the Skellig, if the thirteenth
century German chronicler is to be believed,
the last great battle between the power of
the saint—holding his arms aloft in prayer like
Moses — and the evil things and venomous
serpents was fought with the aid of St Michael
and his angels. Up these steps the battle

raged until the devils and serpents were driven to the top and over the 700 feet of sheer cliff to perish in the sea. St Michael is perhaps more easily reached on such high rocks in the sea, as in Cornwall and in Brittany.

In any event, we toil up the steps and, where they divide, take the right fork for the monastery on the north summit. Behind one is the perilous point at the highest peak of the south summit, 715 feet, where pilgrims climbed out on a narrow ledge above the sea. There are some vestigial ruins on this south summit—of a rectangular building with slabs lying prone. On one's left is the way down to the landing place at Blue Cove. But the place of greatest and most accessible interest is the monastery on the north summit. Here we can, almost literally, step into the sixth century. In this monastery the remarkable St Fionan—whose works are all over this peninsula—established his little hermits' settlement towards the end of the sixth century. For some six centuries life continued here in simple austerity just 600 feet above the sea on a tiny patch of cultivable (or probably made) ground. Probably for long after individual hermits lived here.

How beautiful it is here on the fine mild days: how terrifying in the wild Atlantic storms! One wave is recorded to have damaged the first of the lighthouses at 175 feet above sea level. One gets here a sense of immediacy with the early stages of Irish christianity. Here is a typical eremitical settlement, almost perfectly preserved. Here is the clochan complete, the most ancient form of our houses. Here it is evolving into the boat shaped style that was so successfully achieved at Gallarus. The five surviving huts are crowded together inside their surrounding wall—a late medieval construction—as we see in countless ruins on the mainland. The two outlying huts are probably of later date than the others. All but one of the huts is round outside but, unlike the mainland huts, square inside, the first step to the boat shaped oratory. The largest of the huts is oval, containing a rectangle, the second step to the oratory. There are also two oratories.

The protruding stones on the outside of the buildings probably acted as a scaffolding for the construction and then, perhaps, held a wind-covering of sods, or of the sea-pink that grows so luxuriantly. Those stones protruding inside were used to hang the leather satchels in which the precious psalm books—the basic necessity of old Irish monastic life—were stored.

We read that when Longarad Whitefoot of Ossory, the Augustine of the Gael—'a master in theology, in history, in the Brehon law and in poetry'—died 'all the book-satchels of Ireland fell down'. These inside stones may also have supported a floor (to make the houses two storied) hanging from a central pole. Inside each hut are wall cupboards. The buildings crowding together on the slope about the *two* wells are almost like the older ones in the little village on the Great Blasket, inhabited a generation ago. There is a small concession to artistry in the skilful gallery on the outside of one of the large buildings, in the greek cross picked out in white quartz over the entrance to that cell, the latin cross, also in white quartz, over the entrance to the main oratory, in the framing of the Little Skellig in the window of St Michael's church, and in the fine stone roof of the (much later) garderobe. There are the remains of other huts; perhaps the stones were used for the later walls. There are the two boat-shaped oratories. There is the cluster of graves of monks long dead, with their simple crosses, and in the medieval church of St. Michael the pathetic, incongruous tomb of the lighthouse keeper's two children. About the island are five crude crosses—at best the stone here did not lend itself to good work—and three cross slabs—two with simple roman crosses and one with what seems to be a syrian cross—with three cross members—in a double circle. There is also a perforated stone that is, most likely, a sundial. Lady Chatterton recounts the finding, by workers on the lighthouse building, of an extremely crude bronze figure of Christ, about four inches high, and a clay figure of the Virgin. Iron slag has also been found. There is the terraced monk's garden, and perched on the northern cliff two other terraces; but it is hard to see that these would provide food. Of course, the seas

about are full of fish, and perhaps sea-birds were taken for food.

This was the ultimate practicable retreat from the world and, perhaps on occasional fine days, gave some taste of that paradisal place that, in accordance with ancient Irish myth, inspired the other saint from Kerry, Brendan, to voyage to the western world. Primitive, simple, a blind alley no doubt, but marvellously affecting.

Perhaps it was this remoteness that saved it, so that the great plagues of 664-67 and 682-83 that seem to have finished off the settlements on the mainland, did not reach this place.

The second historical reference to Skellig is in the *Martyrology of Tallaght*, written at the end of the 8th century, which on 28 April mentions Suibni of the Scelig, commemorating the feast day of a holy man.

The souterrain reminds us that here the vikings came in 812, again in 823 or 4, and again in 838, when Eitgal was carried off and died of hunger and thirst. What gain they can have got here, God knows. Perhaps on some wild night a monk here may have penned, or recalled of one of his ninth century brothers, this quatrain (in James Carney's translation):

Is acher in gaith innocht,	*Bitter and wild is the wind to-night,*
fu-fuasna fairrgae findfolt;	*tossing the tresses of the sea to white,*
ni agor reimm mora mind	*On such a night as this I feel at ease,*
dond laechraid lainn o Lothlaind.	*Fierce Northmen only course the quiet seas.*

It may be that the settlement was abandoned for a time, but was restored in 860, and in 882 we read of the 'repose' of Flann, son of Cellach, abbot of Scelec, and in 950 of Blathmac Sgeillice. About 993, the story, is, Skellig had its revenge on the vikings because here was baptised King Olaf Tryggvason of Norway, born in Iveragh after his father was killed. He met on the island a hermit whose knowledge of coming events so

282

impressed him that he asked to be baptised. He went back to Norway, won back his kingdom in 995 and lost it with his life in 1000. He was one of the christian predecessors of St Olaf and is credited with introducing christianity to Norway. There are some who say that the islands were not the Skelligs but the Scillies.

Given the number of dwellings and the degree of overcrowding acceptable in early communities, there would have been, at least on occasion, a considerable community here. This must have raised formidable problems of supplies. Giraldus Cambrensis explains how one crucial problem was solved. Outside the porch of the church, on the right hand, there was, he says, a stone partly fixed to the wall. In the hollow of this St Michael arranged that there would be each day enough wine for the Masses of that day. More prosaicly, the monastery at Ballinskelligs was an offshoot of the Skelligs community from the mid-ninth century: no doubt it acted as a supply centre. While the Abbot of the two communities had his headquarters on the island, it may be that—as was the practice elsewhere—many of those in the island community were members of the mainland one who volunteered for longer or shorter periods for the more anchoritic life of the island. But we have few hard facts. The annals tell us of Eitgal, and of the death of three abbots—Flann in 882, Blathmac in 950 and Aed—'the chief of the Gael in piety'—in 1044. St Malachy, the great church reformer, is said to have visited here during his exile in 'Ibracense' in the 1120s. The end of the island community probably came when as a result of St Malachy's reforms the Augustinians took over the Ballinskelligs monastery as part of the general winding up of the old Irish monastic system in the twelfth and thirteenth centuries, and the island community, as an extreme example of the Irish form of spirituality, was closed down. Giraldus Cambrensis, writing towards the end of the twelfth century, tells us that 'the situation of this abbey being found extremely bleak, and the going to and from it extremely hazardous, it was removed to Ballinskelligs on the continent'. It is likely that, as elsewhere, occasional hermits lived on the island in later years.

The third period in the life of the Skelligs is that of pilgrimages that began, probably, some time around 1300. That these were extensive in late medieval times is clear from the amount of building from that period— the garderobe and the fine retaining wall are of that date—the old buildings were kept in repair and, most likely, the three sets of steps from the three landing places were made. The nature of these works show that the pilgrimages to the island—which continued at least intermittently until the 19th century— were of considerable numbers of people. But we know tantalisingly little about them. There is a tradition that a boatload of monks was lost in Cross Cove: this may have been a boatload of pilgrims. In 1543 a man in Armagh, Heneas Mac Haill, who had murdered his son and had been given as penance to visit all the Irish penitential stations, mentions in the list of those he had visited, Skellig Michael. A pilgrimage to Skellig Michael is recorded in the life of William Tirey, bishop of Cork, 1623-45, and from the same period Keating says it

Way of the Cross, Skellig

was visited by great numbers of people since the time of St Patrick. Smith says that up to 20 years before his time (1756) large numbers used go on pilgrimages to the island. Foley says the pilgrimages lasted until after 1850—that pilgrims came for Holy Week and bad behaviour made it necessary for police to clear the rock.

Possibly because this isolated community maintained the ancient form of calculating Easter—which could be up to three weeks later than by the official method—and thus Lent did not begin there until later than elsewhere, there grew up the practice of drawing up 'Skelligs Lists' of young people who, in the opinions (sometime malicious) of the compilers ought to have married before Lent began. This practice continued until recent times in Kerry and West Cork.

The venturesome can, as they return from the monastery to the Saddle, try doing the stations up the steep 'smokestack' of the island out to the last point where one crosses a cleft onto an arm of rock, hanging 700 feet above the sea.

There is a story of an English soldier who went out on the point to mock the devotions and fell into the sea. He was heard to cry out, as he was falling, 'what a long way it is to fall!'.

In 1826 the first of the two lighthouses built here was erected, but it was later wrecked by storm. The wall above the monastery seems to have been built by the early lighthouse men.

Here for days in the September gales of 1588 tossed the great stricken ships of the Armada in terror of being driven on the cruel rocks between Dursey and the Blaskets. By here, on many occasions, sailed the privateer Paul Jones on his way to and from Valentia. Eighteen miles west of the Great Skellig Karl Spindler's arms ship the *Aud* was captured on the evening of Good Friday, 21st April, 1916, after he had fruitlessly attempted to seek aid from the shore to land his precious cargo for the impending Rising.

A fascinating problem in natural history is

pointed out by Lloyd Praeger. There are on the island no less than thirteen molluscs, some nine snails and four slugs. Some at least of these would not have got mixed up with vegetables brought from the mainland. Could they be here since the island was attached to the mainland? That too, is unlikely.

DUNKERRON SOUTH

The western line of this barony runs from the outlet of Lough Currane along the sea east to the south of the Finnihy river at Kenmare. It runs almost due north from there to the Lower Killarney lake and then west along the Owenreagh, but north of Lough Brin and south of Ballaghabeama then along the spine of the Dunkerron mountains above Sneem until it plunges into Lough Currane and emerges at its mouth. It is a narrow strip of very poor land, a few miles wide, but 30 miles long. It consists of three parishes— Kilcrohane, Sneem, and Templenoe. The principal town is Sneem, but Waterville or Caherdaniel are suitable centres for seeing the southern part of the barony. The coast along the Kenmare River, being sheltered by the line of mountains of the north has a very mild climate, sub-tropical in the Sneem area. The coastline is also very beautiful. The coast line from Currane to Sneem is called Bord Eoghainin Fhinn (or Boardeen); but who this fair-haired Owen was or why the coastline was named after him is not known.

Another version is that the name is 'Bord Uamhan Duinn'—the coast facing Donn's Cavern (to the otherworld)—that is, from which Bull Rock is visible.

The early history of this coastline is obscure, although the coast from Ballinskelligs Bay to Glanbeg Strand was the arrival point of many of the mythical early invaders of Ireland, and certainly the mountains above Caherdaniel saw substantial mining in the copper and bronze ages. As we have seen with Dingle Bay, the Kenmare River linked the land on both sides, and after 1185 AD the O Sullivans overran the land on both sides of the River, spilling over, on the far side, to Bantry Bay. Their head, O Sullivan Mor, had his seat at Dunkerron, south of Kenmare, and this gave its name to the barony. After the cromwellian wars nearly all these O Sullivan lands—virtually all the wild land one can see from the Kenmare River—were acquired by Dr William Petty.

The intriguing question is—who was here before the O Sullivans? In the earliest gaelic times these lands were part of the kingdom of West Munster. After it collapsed, about 834, these lands, may have continued to be part of the territory of the Eoganacht Locha Lein. Their power, in turn, was collapsing at

the time the O Sullivans were driven—by O Brien and anglo-norman power— from Tipperary. The O Sullivans were, of course, an Eoganacht family, and their ancestress, Mor, was a daughter of Aed Bennan, after whom was named the fort of Ardea across the River. She was wife of Fingen, king of Cashel. Both Aed and Fingen died in 619 AD. The great fort of Staigue, near Castlecove, may have been Cathair Meathais, a rig-port where the king of Cashel was, according to the *Book of Rights,* entitled to stay. The founder of the Eoganacht, Eogan Mor, invaded Ireland either through the Kenmare River or Bantry Bay, and his wife, Bearra, gave her name to the peninsula to the south. This territory may have remained, therefore, in Eoganacht hands. There seems to have been no record of an intervening power in these parts. What more likely, then, in the great uprootings of the 12th century, when the local Eoganacht were reeling from the attacks of the O Donoghues around Killarney, for the O Sullivans, senior family of the Cashel Eoganacht, now driven from their home, to seek to return to what was left of

Dunkeron Barony, after Petty

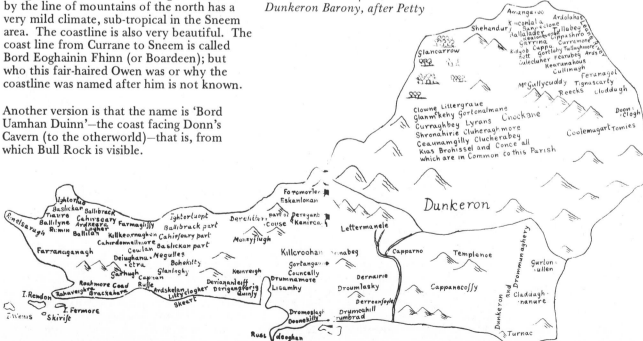

284 the first conquests of their ancestors in Ireland?

The MacCarthys also took a foothold in this barony—at Eightercua where, in the thirteenth and fourteenth centuries, they had their principal settlement.

(I) THE WATERVILLE AREA II

1. *Glenmore—Eightercua—Baslickane—Loher —Coomakista*

From Waterville take the Sneem road and just after the Waterville Lake hotel, turn left. This gives a pleasant run along the southern shores of Lough Currane. Exactly five miles from the main road, just before a little bridge, is, right, a boithrin leading to two houses. Stop at the second of two gates. Across two fields, right, is the little, totally ruined eremitical site of *Inchfarranagleragh* (V.59.66. d), with a tall cross pillar with an elegant latin cross rather like that at Dromkeare, but with an expanding finial at the base and a tiny greek cross at the back. A little further on, at *Glenmore* (V.58.65.a), the road becomes very rough. Return and turn left along the Sneem road.

About a quarter of a mile further on one sees on the hilltop on the left an alignment of four pillar stones. Stop here and cross the field on the left to the very ruined church of *Templenakilla* (V.52.65.a)—this might be a seventh century church because despite its relative size it uses no mortar and there is evidence of a cyclopean—large stone— construction; but it is too ruined for one to be sure. South is a ceallunach. On the brow of the little hill of *Eightercua* (V.52.65.a) are the four pillar stones—one of two such small alignments: the other is at Kildreelig on the far side of Ballinskelligs Bay on a line just south of due west from this place which marks the reputed grave of another of the Milesian invaders, Erannan, and it is claimed that the two alignments are in a direct line. (They are not). The Eightercua alignment is the reputed burial place of Scene, the wife of Amergin, the magical and poetic leader of the Milesian invaders who landed near this spot. The Irish name for the great inlet of the Kenmare

River is Inbhear Scene. The alignment can be seen to be part of a stone circle; they are on the north west side of a platform. There is an entrance south east leading directly east to Lough Currane, but what its real significance is is not clear. There is a stone at right angles to the second stone (from the east of the alignment). West of it there is a stone lying on the ground. If it were standing, the two would support an altar table, with the alignment as screen. This is Lynch's persuasive suggestion. The views here are magnificent, overlooking towards Lough Currane the place where MacCarthy Mor had his home in the 13th and 14th centuries, before he moved to Killarney. From the hill one can just see the shape of the Ballybrack dolmen in the field between the Finglas river and the sea. This is reputed to be the tomb of Fial, the wife of another of the Milesian invaders, Lugaid. From the dolmen was, it is said, a line of boulders to this place.

In the direction of Waterville there is a neighbouring small hill also in *Eightercua* (V.51.66.d). It is worth while going back onto the road and walking back to this hill, because it too must have been an important site. At the top is what appears to be an overthrown dolmen, savagely mutilated, and surrounding it a number of circles of large stones, some of the circles now disturbed. If these observations are correct this looks as if this were an important pagan site—the mutilation and the setting up of the little church close by suggest something of *odium theologicum*. Wakeman says the custom of building a stone circle round a dolmen stretches as far as Syria and Arabia.

Back to the road and travel about half a mile over the sharp bridge over the Finglas river. Just beyond this, on the right, is an old roadway. It is possible to bring the car along here; but on the whole it is better to leave it. All along the way, on one's right, between this ancient roadway and the river are dotted cahers. This must have been an important farming area in early christian times. About one-third of a mile along, the roadway suddenly broadens out to the left. Just here, above one on the left, through a barricaded gateway, is the very early christian site boasting the name *Baslickane* (V.51.64.d),

apparently from basilica. This is not a very clear site, but it shows, with some effort, the surrounding cashel of large stones, the remains of an oratory and bee-hive huts, and early cross pillar with a crude attempt to broaden the top for a cross.

Turn back to the car and continue towards Sneem. Just under a half-mile up the road, on the right above one before a *ruined house* (V.51.64.b) in Ardkeragh, are two stone pillars apparently the entrance pillars to a stone circle. They are unusual in being two, in being so small, and in being so clearly portal. Perhaps they are no more than the surviving portals of a now vanished clochan.

Continue along the main road to the church on the right. Below this is a farmhouse. Halfway, in a line between the two, is the very ruined eremitical site of *Ardkeragh* (V.51.64.c) with a simple cross in circle, or scutum fidei, on a small pillar. Then up the hill for a mile and a half. At the last farmhouse on the right below the top of the hill, stop, cross the ditch and the two fields below it, and onto the old roadway below the field. Just off this, on the Waterville side and a little below it, in a large patch of bracken, is the famous early christian site of *Loher* (V.51.62.b). Here the layout of these sites can be seen at its clearest, with the oratory in the raised platform, or laura, inside the cashel, and the cross-incised pillar—a simple latin cross with alpha and omega under the wings in merovingian style—probably marking the grave of the founder. There are two other smaller pillars beside it. Underneath is the line of cahers that shows that this was a farming area of probably early christian times. Some of the ruins are clearly older than others, so that it is probable that this place was occupied by farming and fisher folk from perhaps earlier than the christian era.

Go back to the car and finish the climb to Coomakista. Note the continuation of the old road one has been on straight up the hill, disdaining the craven winding course of the present day nineteenth century road, and forming a deterrent to those who might think of interfering with the O Connell domain and smuggling business over the hill.

The culmination of this trip is the pass of *Coomakista* (V.51.61.c) which on a fine fresh day yields one of the finest views possible to imagine. The name comes from the coum of the cash, from the money hidden there by shipwrecked French privateers in the eighteenth century and still there when they came to reclaim it long afterwards.

Back then to Waterville. Total distance: 32 miles. Total time: about three and a half hours.

2. Loher—Hog's Head

From Waterville take the Sneem road and, just outside the town turn right into the grounds of the pleasant eighteenth century Butler residence, Waterville House. Regard the salmon fishery here, one of the most famous in Ireland. On the road again take the first turn right. About a quarter of a mile along this road just short of a cross roads climb over a wall to the right. In the middle of this field is the partly ruined but fine *Ballybrack dolmen* (V.51.65a), a relic of the neolithic age (but it could also be a ruined wedge grave, with some of the cairn stones still remaining; but if so its orientation—just west of north — is quite wrong). It is said to be the grave of (the much later) Fial, wife of one of the invading Milesian princes who had landed in Waterville. She was running naked from bathing in the river below when she met her husband, Lugaid, also naked at this spot, and dropped dead of shame. The dolmen is north west of the alignment at Templenakilla, which can be seen on the ridge above the main road. There was said to be an avenue of boulders from Templenakilla towards the dolmen. South south east of it, the avenue continues—from a large boulder near the road fence there is an irregular avenue of small boulders running south and west ending at another boulder near the boundary wall of the field to west south west; this leads to pillar stones on the edge of the cliff above *Pouleragh* (V.50.66.d).

Follow this road, which becomes bad but not impossible. When it reaches the tarred road turn left and, immediately, right, through *Loher* (V.50-51.62-63), a rather grim place,

Dolmen at Ballybrack, Waterville

where Irish is still, in some degree, spoken. Where the houses thin out there is in a field on the right a caher with, beneath it, the unusual feature (for these parts) of a chevaux de frise. There are a number of other cahers here and, above them, the early christian site of Loher. It is possible, by turning right, to continue on to Hog's Head. If courage fails, turn back and take the turn left on the tarred road. Follow this until it finishes before a farm house. Take the green road through the abandoned hamlet and cross a couple of stiles. Where the green road divides, take the higher road which degenerates. It is easy going to the highest point. From here, at *Hog's Head* (V.47.61.b), there is one of finest views in Kerry, with Waterville Bay on the right and Kenmare River on the left.

Go back and bring the car to a branch to the right, now fenced off. Walk up this roadway to the ruined look-out tower at the top, relic of the Napoleonic wars. From this there is quite a good track bearing left around the headland in the direction of Derrynane, until one comes to a ruined *farmhouse* (V.49.61.d) where the track greatly deteriorates. There is an air of great seclusion about this place. Return and, where the track forks, take the right fork and then turn left at the roadway to where one has left the car. On the way back follow the tarred road until one turns left on the main road to Waterville.

Total motoring distance 9 miles. Total walking distance 4 miles. Allow two and a half hours.

(II) THE CAHERDANIEL AREA

285

1. *Caherdaniel and Derrynane*

Caherdaniel (pop. 1966: 80) (V.55.60.b) is a tiny village that grew up in the shadow of the O Connell big house at Derrynane. It has an attractive catholic church built by the O Connells in 1825 when, it may be, that Kilcrohane (or Coad) was finally abandoned. The village takes its name from a not too ruined caher—there is a more ruined one and an old road system—a little distance to the north-west.

Branch from the Ring of Kerry road on the sea side through the village and follow the narrow, winding road to Derrynane. About a mile along this road, on the left, is an ogam stone rescued from the encroaching sea.

A little further on one comes to the gates of *Derrynane* (V.53.59.b). The road left leads to the splendid Derrynane beach. At the car park are leaflets for a short nature trail showing the evolution, rise and fall of the (not very impressive) sand dunes above the beach.

Doire Fhionain—St Fionan's oakwood— is now a national monument and museum of Daniel O Connell (1775-1847) who created Irish democracy, won the legal emancipation of catholics and, for the first time in history, gave the plain people of Ireland some voice, however inadequate, in the way they were governed. John O Connell, brother of the Maurice who had been transplanted from Ballycarbery to Clare in the 1650s got a lease of land here from Lord Cork about 1680. The principal part of the house, a wanly appealing georgian house, was built by O Connell's grandfather, Donal Mor, in the mid-eighteenth century—'the first slated house in South Kerry'—but this did not survive the recent re-conditioning and what remains are the ugly victorian additions of O Connell's time. This house was once the great gaelic centre of south Kerry. O Connell's long-lived grandmother, an O Donoghue, Maire ni Dhuibh, kept a great state here in the old gaelic style. Apart from being the mother of 22 children, many of them gifted, she was a natural wit and

286

excelled in the much esteemed art of versified repartee in Irish. Her son Maurice, called Hunting Cap, in his long life of minding his own business (largely smuggling and money lending) created a substantial fortune. There are many stories of his encounters with unduly zealous customs men. One of his brothers, Andrew, was hanged in Cork for such activities, and another lost at sea. A third brother, Count Daniel O Connell was the last Colonel of the Irish Brigade. A sister, Eileen, wrote a wonderful poem in Irish on her murdered husband. He (Maurice) was childless and left his house and much of his fortune to his nephew, Daniel, who, four years later, when he entered parliament, forsook his great practice at the bar, and devoted himself wholly to politics. O Connell, when he was in Derrynane—not in the nineteenth century quite as remote as in the 18th: in 1795 it had taken him 11½ days of travel to go from Derrynane to London—maintained the old gaelic traditions of open and indiscriminate hospitality, and there are many folk memories of people who travelled long distances to him with their legal troubles. His practice was to hold these consultations in the mornings on the green before the house. The museum has its own hideous interest.

One of his proteges was Tomas Ruadh O Sullivan (1785-1848), born at Banard near Coomakista, and buried at Aghavore, a poet in Irish, a schoolmaster, a fiddler and story-teller, maintaining in some way the ancient bardic tradition. He lived in the houses of his patrons and taught school in various spots between Caherdaniel and Portmagee. It was on a voyage to the latter place that a boat sank in Derrynane harbour with all his books. His poem bewailing this calamity gives us an idea of the library of a schoolmaster at the time. In another poem he confesses that his fee was sixpence a quarter. His poems have been published by another Caherdaniel man, Seamus Fenton, who wrote a book of reminiscences *It All Happened*. A third literary figure was a local schoolmaster Domhnall O Suilleabhain who wrote a good book in Irish on local historical topics, *Seanchas na Deasmhumhan*.

It is possible to drive behind the house and

to come out on the roadway one has been on. Turn sharp left here and this brings one out onto Derrynane beach, a most attractive bathing place. The beach is separated by a neck of sand from *Derrynane harbour* (V.52.59), well concealed from the open sea, that was the source of Hunting Cap's fortune. From here, all during the eighteenth century, sailed the little boats to France, the Low countries, Spain and Portugal, with their precious cargoes of young men going for education and, later with the wives they came back to claim. They became soldiers in all the armies of Europe. One of them, Hunting Cap's brother Daniel, the 'last Colonel of the Irish Brigade' of the French Army, ended as a General and as a Count. It was another of them, Arthur O Leary, from the Austrian army, who married Eileen O Connell (so causing her to be banished from the family), who wrote one of the most

famous Irish poems about him and his death. Many of the young men became priests and came back through here to minister to their people in great poverty. There was a substantial export trade in hides and cattle products, and an import of wines, brandies, silks, furniture for the richer households of all Kerry. To here, from Couliagh Bay opposite, often came the great Dan O Connell on his way to Derrynane from Cork assizes. Along the neck of sand, easily accessible except at high tide, is *Abbey Island,* or *Aghavore* (V.52.58-59).

Here are the remains of a monastery reputedly founded by St Fionan, but probably a ninth century foundation of Flann Mac Ceallach. The present, rather undistinguished buildings, several times altered, are clearly not so old, but in part at least date from about the 10th century.

Aghavore Priory

DERRYNANE ABBEY. 2783. W.L.

They remind one of the monastery at Ballinskelligs. The monastery was called Aghavore and was staffed by Augustinian canons in the 12th-13th centuries. It was a subsidiary of Molanah Abbey near Youghal rebuilt by Raymond le Gros, who is buried there. In 1479 we read of a petition to Rome by Donald Y sulibayn (O Sullivan) Canon of Molanah that the monastery is over sixty miles from the mother house in Molanah and is served from there but neglected. The other side of the story is that the chapel of the monastery and its fruits have been held by O Sullivan for several years against the will of the 'Abbot'—presumably of Molanah. O Sullivan represents that if the chapel and its fruits are collated to him he would do his best to restore the same. In spite of this plea he is ordered to be deprived. It looks from this as if the community were already largely dispersed. However the priory seems to have been in existence in 1633.

Molanah was part of the immense possessions acquired by Sir Walter Raleigh in the Desmond confiscation and, with it Aghavore. They were bought by Richard Boyle, first Earl of Cork in 1602 and that is how, later, the Boyles became head landlords of the O Connells at Derrynane. How long the monastery survived under Boyle is not clear, but its remoteness seems to have saved it until cromwellian times.

Buried in a large tomb in the church are Hunting Cap, his mother and father. Inscribed on the tomb of the old man (he died at 96) is the just statement that the 'chief ambition of his long and prosperous life was to elevate an ancient family from unmerited and unjust oppression'. Also buried in this tomb is Daniel O Connell's wife, Mary, a distant cousin, whom he married in 1802, who died in Derrynane in 1836. Contrary to the (much later) rumours, they were a most devoted couple. She bore him seven children. In the graveyard is a white glazed brick tomb which, even for Kerry tombs, is memorable. It is quite an experience to see a funeral procession walk across the sands headed by a dark-suited man with a white sash.

Back to the car, and turn back, taking the

first turn left. This brings one back onto the Ring of Kerry road. About half a mile up this road, on the left, just before one comes to a house on the right, there is behind steps over the wall of the roadway, the fine *Boardeen dolmen* (V.54.60.a). The original burial mound has been largely dug away to reveal this tomb and, before it, a much smaller one. The burial mound was surrounded by two stone circles.

Take the next turn left and, going down a very twisting road, keep left until one reaches another part of Derrynane harbour, at *Bunavalla* (V.52.60.c). This can be very pleasant in the evening. Return the way one has come and take the first turn left. This brings one at its end to the lobster and crayfish tanks of a Waterville firm at *Coumatloukane* (V.50.60.a). It may be possible to get permission to inspect these: children find them fascinating. Walk a little further on and one comes to some inlets of the sea. One of these is full of the coloured shells of sea urchins.

Come back and return to the uphill road. A little further on there is another road left that soon ends in a track. A walk of a mile or so brings one out onto a typical wild Kerry headland, hard on unprotected feet, because of gorse.

Back to the car and back to the Ring of Kerry road. Just a half-mile farther on there is, right, a little glen, with, above one, the built up side of the old road from Derrynane to Waterville. At this point, just above the old road, is a wedge shaped tomb at *Farraniaraigh* (V.52.61.c). It is a pleasant walk from this along the old road up to the old pass leading to Loher on the other side. Back to the car. A few yards below the main road, amongst the boulders, are two more wedge-shaped tombs. In line with these but about a half-mile below, beside a gigantic boulder, is a fourth wedge shaped tomb. Lady Chatterton says one was destroyed in making the main road. So there seems to have been a beaker folk cemetery in this beautiful place.

It is another half-mile to Coomakista. This on a clear, fresh day gives perhaps the finest

view in Kerry. Then back to the village.

Total driving distance: 26 miles. Time depends on that spent in Derrynane and on the beaches. It would be wise to allow a whole day for this trip.

2. Scariff and Deenish islands

Scariff island (V.44-46.55-56), which was inhabited until recently, is worth a visit. The boat journey from West Cove is a splendid one. The island is cliff bound, but there is a fair landing place with steps up from the water cut into the rock. There is a superb view on a clear day from the 840 foot summit of Scariff, on the spine of the island as one climbs to the summit. Again, as one might expect, there was an anchoritic site on the island, some very ruined remains of which survive close to the route to the summit. There are pagan remains close by. Just below the christian site is a wedge-shaped tomb, and below this again the oval remains of what may have been a bronze age house. There seems also to have been a very old field system here.

Froude (in *A Fortnight in Kerry*) describes a shipwreck here in the time of Richard II at the end of the fourteenth century. A Cornish knight, Sir John Arundel, recruited a band of wild youths to make an expedition to Ireland. Windbound either at Penzance or St Ives they made a raid on a neighbouring convent and there followed scenes of 'unrestrained and frightful debauchery'. The wind then rising they carried off the wretched nuns to their ship. A gale arose off the Kerry coast and the women were thrown overboard to propitiate the demon of the storm. Nonetheless the ship was driven on the rocks. A handful were saved. Arundel himself emerged from the sea, only to be hauled back by an enormous wave.

A Franciscan Friar, Father Francis O Sullivan, born in Tuosist, who according to the local story had been an emissary of Ireland to the court of Spain, was hounded down on this island by the cromwellians, and decapitated there on 23rd June, 1653. He had been provincial from 1650 of the 62 Franciscan houses in Ireland. Before that he had been

288

guardian (or head) of the Franciscan Friary at Ardfert. He was buried on the island, but a portion of his skull became an important relic of the O Connells and, in Hunting Cap's time, oaths were sworn on it. There is a tradition that Irishmen are lax about keeping oaths taken on a bible, but scrupulous about those taken on a holy relic. The skull was said to have been returned from Winchester in England to Derrynane in 1931. It was the practice of the local fishermen to invoke his aid in these stormy and dangerous seas. There is a nasty race between Scariff and the neighbouring island, *Deenish* (V.47.56-57). This also is now uninhabited. Unlike Scariff it has a beach.

Trench, in his *Realities of Irish Life,* gives a most interesting account of a seal hunt in 1856 in a deep cave facing Scariff island which can only be entered by boat at exceptionally low tide.

Allow 4-5 hours for this trip.

3. Caherdaniel—Coomnahorna—Tullig

Take the road for Coomakista and, a short distance outside the village, where the road bends and becomes broad, leave the car. On one's left, on an outcrop of rock, is *Caherdaniel caher* (V.55.60.b) from which the village takes its name. There is a gateway off the road and an old road system going down to, and under, the caher, which is in a fair state of preservation. Between it and another outcrop of rock is a stream with a little bridge over it. On the other outcrop is a much more ruined caher, presumably, a much older one. Here one begins to fret at the lack of excavation. If Caherdaniel itself would seem to be a contemporary of Leacanabuaile, which seems not to be older than 6th century, what about this other caher? They are both firmly placed on what seems to be the old route from the copper mines at Coad to the harbour at Derrynane. Who exacted tolls on the copper that was presumably exported from there? Did this exporting and toll gathering go on until christian times? What is the relationship of these small, but strongly placed, forts to

a great military one like Staigue, nearby, and the copper workings at Coad to the scribings—supposed to be made by copper miners—on the rock a mile below Staigue? What is the relationship of all this to the philological evidence that suggests these cahers were built by the Firbolg, or Belgic, invaders? Why, even in stony places, did they feel the need to build so strongly, especially in christian times when this countryside seems to have been so peaceful?

Leave these perplexities and back to the road. A short distance further on there is a road on the right up through *Coomnahorna* (V.56.61-62) (improbably, of the barley). Follow this, keeping generally to the left. If one's car is small and one is reasonably intrepid it is possible to drive some distance along a bog road leading to the top of the mountain. A short walk brings one to the peak of *Tullig* (V.55.63.c), over 1,200 feet. From here, on a fine evening, there is a magnificent view over Lough Currane, Ballinskelligs Bay, Valentia and the rest.

Come back the way one has come; but when the choice offers half way down the coum bear left to *Garrough* (V.56.61.b). A short distance on, where this road bears left there are on the right, two gallans in a field. A little further on turn left and through a gateway on the road. Just short of the farmhouse is, right, a most interesting site. Here we have the still striking remains of a six gallan alignment, presumably a signpost from Derrynane harbour to the copper mines at Coad. Beside the alignment is an old beehive hut, and close by what seem to be the remains of a chamber tomb. The whole site is enclosed in what seems to have been a stone circle (but this may have been a natural freak). Below this, a little to the east, is what seems to be a small stone circle. Because of the amount of glacial debris around one cannot be sure that these are artificial circles—but if the main one is such a circle we have a most striking site in this place. Return to the car and go straight down the valley to the village itself.

Total driving distance 6 miles: Allow about three hours.

4. Lamb's Head—Rath—Kilcrohane—Staigue—White Strand

Take the Sneem road and, just outside the village, at a bad bend of the road, turn right. A short distance on one's right are the ruins of the tower house of *Ballycarnahan* (V.55.59.b), that was the stimulus for the much better preserved one at Castlecove. There is a strong tradition along this coast of atrocities by cromwellians. One of the worst offenders was a Captain Barrington who kept a bloodhound that he let loose on women and children. It was a Brennan from Ballycarnahan who, when the dog was savaging a group of them, seized it with his bare hands and tore its jaws apart. This Captain Brennan played a distinguished part in the forces raised by O Sullivan Mor in these wars.

About a mile along this road there is a curious conceit of a house built in concrete as a *ship* (V.54.58.a) in great detail, jutting out of the cliff, with splendid views. The road goes on to the little fishing pier of *Lamb's Head* (V.53.57.a). On either side of this part of the road are to be seen the attractive creeping rock juniper tree. Beyond the harbour are the remains of a small copper mine. Back to the main road and, less than a mile further on, there is a bad road right. This, if one bears left on all possible occasions, leads one to *Rath strand* (V.55.58.d), with another pier and a salmon fishery. It was on the Rath strand and the nearby Glanbeg strand that on Tuesday, 14 May, 2680 BC the second of Ireand's legendary invaders, Partholon, landed after the long journey from Greece. The party was 1,000 strong, and Partholon was fleeing from the guilt of having killed both his parents.

A little further along the main road is *Glanbeg strand* (V.57.59.c). In summer this is covered with caravans. At Glanbeg O Sullivan Mor (Brennan's uncle) kept the forces that were engaged in the battle at Ballinskelligs in 1641 and in that at Castlecove in 1644. Gibbons, governor of the garrison at Nedeen made a foray with some 180 men. He landed near Castlecove and drove as far as Lough Currane, and then returned driving cattle before him. The Irish attacked them near the present ruined castle, at Bunaneer (or West Cove), and killed, wounded or captured the whole English party at the cost of some forty casualties to themselves. It was this exploit that led the government to order the evacuation by the natives of the whole peninsula south of the Laune and west of the Finnihy, on penalty of death. It was this that gave Barrington and his bloodhound their chance. Friar O Sullivan says Barrington slaughtered a large party of refugees near Glencar, and another party near Sneem.

It was on the latter occasion that Brennan killed the dreadful bloodhound. There was a later slaughter by the Nedeen garrison at Derryquin, near Sneem. For about 30 years to the 1880s a patron, with boat races, was held here, transferred from Kilcrohane. The races have recently been revived.

A short distance from Glanbeg is *West Cove* (V.59.60.a). There is the little *harbour* of West Cove (Bunaneer) (V.59.60.b) to the right, with splendid views.

At West Cove a road runs about a mile north to *Coad* (V.58.61). At a T junction there is to the right the abandoned parish church of *Kilcrohane* (V.58.61.b). It is of little architectural interest, and is much overgrown. Beside the church is another ruined building, presumably a presbytery. These seem to be evidence of the continuity of religious practice in this remote place in the 16th and 17th centuries. It was attached to Killagha priory. In the 1470s and 80s the vicar here, Dermot O Sullivan, made determined attempts to unseat the prior of Ballinskelligs and get the office: but failed. He was succeeded here by another Dermot O Sullivan. Since the early part of the last century the parish church has been at Caherdaniel. The parish is extensive, running from east of Castle Cove almost to Waterville, and north from the sea to a line that touches the southern shore of Lough Currane.

Kilcrohane is the church of St Carhan or Crohan (Criomhthain). There is no record of him. It has been suggested that he was St Kieran of Saiger who composed his monastic rule in the hermitage nearby. St Kieran came of a pre-gaelic family of

west Cork who are said to have been christians before St Patrick's mission.

Up to the last century a three-day patron was held beside the church, between July 29 and August 1. Maire Mac Neill suggests it descended from a festival of the god Lug. A pilgrimage was made to the well, just north of the church, called *Tobernavila* (V.58.62.d) (or the well of the sacred tree), suggesting the even earlier form of animistic religion. St Crohan is said to be buried under the tree. A second *well* (V.58.62.c) is about a half-mile to the north west, up the mountain and a third at *Windy Gap* (V.60.64.c) to the north east. This pilgrimage continues to be made on July 30. The patron suffered first a change of venue and then extinction. It was moved a mile west by the old (now much overgrown) road to Caherdaniel. In the fifties of the last century a man was killed at the patron and it was replaced for some 30 years by boat races at Glanbeg strand. The patron has recently been revived.

If one follows the old road — which was the old coach road to Sneem that Daniel O Connell had to take before the present main road was built in his fortnight long journey to London — west for nearly a mile one comes to another leading up the mountain to the right. Near the top of the mountain there is a branch left. Follow this until it crosses a stream by a bridge. Follow this stream to the right for a short distance to where one comes across old diggings of *Coad mines* (V.58.62.c). These are the remains of the copper mining operations of Petty and his successors from the seventeenth century, and explain the existence of this roadway which leads down to the harbour at Derrynane. The mine was re-opened briefly in 1808. In a rock above the stream is a cave. This is an older mine-working, dating back to about 2000 BC when copper was first mined here. O Riordain reports that nearby are the foundations of an old circular house where these men may have lived. It may be that the ceremony at Tobernavila may be a living remain of their religious practices. Here in this cave St Crohan is said to have lived as a hermit. The shape of his back is said to be seen in the cave. The stalactites of this cave were prized for their magical qualities. The

origin of the stream is the second of the wells of pilgrimage. The third well brings one back to the mountain road running north east to Windy Gap, by which worshippers in the most remote part of the parish came to Kilcrohane church.

Return to the main road. A little way along this road is, on the right, a curious group of buildings, part of them a ruined coastguard station, others intended by an eccentric aristocrat, the Hon Albinia Broderick, as a tuberculosis hospital. She took, however, an extremist republican line at the time of the civil war and did not get official approval for her plans. She left the property to the 'Second Dail', and legal and political difficulties have since prevented any action in relation to the ruins.

Just before the village of Castlecove there is a turn left, signposted for Staigue Fort.

A mile and a half from the main road one comes, on the right, on *Staigue bridge* (V.61.62.b), an elaborate stone bridge clearly leading nowhere. For those interested, it is worth crossing the bridge. On one's right, about 50 yards away (but over several fences) just beyond a wet boithrin is a large exposed rock on a slight hillock. This has some striking scribings. They are best seen (at the southern end) if one brings some chalk and traces out the designs. There are other stones in the neighbourhood.

A mile further along the road is *Staigue Fort* (V.61.64.d), a large caher, the best of its kind. There is a caretaker who lives a little above and to the left of the carpark at the road's end. There is a fosse around the fort, and an ancient road leads from it. The entrance, square topped with sloping sides, shows a typical early Irish building form; it faces almost due south. Note the 'batter' of the walls outside, that is, as they rise they slope inwards. The quality of the dry-stone building — this was built before mortar was used in Ireland — is very high indeed. Note on the north west side, just at the 'cellar' are two vertical lines in the wall making a blunt wedge. It is likely that it was here that work began, extended south to the present entrance and then, the circle completed, ended with

290

the filling of the 'wedge'. I think, from the nature of this 'divide', the only one in the structure, that those commentators who say the work was done in sections were mistaken. On the wall at the entrance is an uncommunicative statement about the fort from one official body — in short, it might date from any time you please from the bronze age. Nearby is a minatory and wholly uncommunicative notice from another official body. Formerly, inside the entrance in an uncomfortable spot, was another communication indicating that the structure may be an iron age (from 5~~00~~ BC to 500 AD) or early christian (from 500 AD to 1000 AD); but this is now removed.

The striking feature of the fort is how well preserved it is — so unlike so many of our monuments. Perhaps not more than four to six feet are missing from the highest point of the wall. The nine — originally ten, but insensitive restoration has obliterated one — sets of steps from the ground up to a now lost rampart at the top suggests that this was clearly a defensive building (a similar feature can be seen in the much more dilapidated Cahersavane, Waterville), but defences constructed with an architectural *style* that is unusual in such monuments. Here, perhaps, is the beginning of Irish secular architecture on a splendid scale, with considerable grace and obvious delight in the mastery of dry-stone building.

There are, unfortunately, no surviving direct historical or literary references to this place. In the *Book of Rights* one of the privileges of the king of Munster was to maintain royal residences in a number of the sub-kingdoms. They included stone forts of this kind. O Donovan says that Cathair Meathais, referred to in this context, is, in fact, Staigue Fort. If so, this would make it a royal residence during part at least of the latter half of the first millenium AD. It is very similar to the Grianain of Aileach, near Derry, an existing fort captured by the northern Ui Neill in the fifth century AD. Earlier than this there is reference to the building of forts of this kind — such as the famous Dun Aengus at Aran — by the Firbolg when they were under pressure from later invaders. This suggests that this type of fort may date from

Staigue Fort

about 300 BC. It is clearly the work of skilled workers; this may mean that this type of fort was being built from an earlier age. A piece of negative evidence underlines its importance. Because there are no remains of buildings to be seen — the interior seems to have been levelled by the Office of Public Works in the last century—it seems likely that it contained wooden houses—probably the makings of a significant village. Wooden houses were the marks of the nobility in iron age times at least, as we know from the sagas. So its very emptiness now illustrates its one-time importance. Lesser forts contain the remains of stone houses, used by the poor. But this must be speculation until the place is excavated.

The only stone fort in this area to have been excavated was Leacanabuaile, Cahersiveen; this was occupied in the early christian period, and we may assume that this is the period of most of the stone forts one sees around this coast. But Staigue is on a

different scale. This is a place where one feels most acutely the backwardness of Irish archaeology and the lack of excavation. To the left of the entrance is, as usual, in the wall the kennel for the guard dog. There is another similar one where the work on the structure commenced. The fort is, of course, beautifully placed, like so many other cahers, built close to the head of a valley running down to the sea. It is a centre for a really splendid, rewarding and not too exhausting ridge walk. Allow three to four hours for this.

Castlecove (V.60.61.c) takes its name from a little harbour to one's right and an unfinished castle built on the sea's edge. The story is that a seventeenth century wife in her husband's absence and envious of her neighbour's castle at Ballycarnahan, Caherdaniel — began the work. When he came home, he forbade further work. Whether the story is true or not, the clearly unfinished castle at Castlecove is in much better condition than its supposed exemplar at Ballycarnahan. The bay here is splendid for fishing mackerel and pollack. Seals are plentiful here and all along the coast.

Half a mile beyond Castlecove, on the right, is a branch off the road to *White strand* (V.61.60.a). This is the first good strand on the Kerry coast as one moves up from Cork. It tends to be covered at high tide, but at other times it provides a splendid place and safe bathing for children. It also gives shelter from the wind which Derrynane does not always do.

Just over two miles along this road — from which there are splendid views — there is a series of wicked bends. At one of these is a (very) rough roadway, left. This, after a few hundred nerve-wracking yards, leads to a small lake, *Glan Lough* (V.62.63.d), set in a pleasant place. There is some brown trout fishing here.

Back to the main road and turn left. After a few hundred yards, where the road straightens out, there is a road, right, at an acute angle. This is just before a small shop and a little church converted from a schoolhouse. At the junction there is, right, a decrepit wooden gate. If one goes through this and walks at right angles to the road one comes after about 200 yards to a small river crossed by a wooden footbridge. Cross this and, on the other bank, climb directly up the small hill facing one. From the top of this, about 100 yards away, somewhat to the left, one can see a gallan. This is one of three of an alignment — the other two have fallen. The alignment seems to have pointed south. Behind the alignment is, north, a very ruined *gallery grave* (V.64.63.c). In principle, it would seem to be a wedge gallery; but this one seems to have been circular. It is a most unusual monument.

Half a mile along the main road there is a road, right, signposted, to *Gleesk Pier* (V.67.63.a). Follow this road, without being diverted, to its end. To the left of the pier, after a short walk, is a tiny, but genuine, coral strand.

Total driving distance: 25 miles. Time: this depends on how long one wishes to spend on the beaches, on Coad mountain, and on the coum above Staigue. Allow a full day, or more.

(III) THE SNEEM AREA

Sneem (V.70.67.a), (which unlikely name comes from snaidhm, a knot or twist, from its snaky river) is a village of 285 (1971) inhabitants. It possesses two village greens and its houses are painted an engaging variety of colours. It has an attractive, italianate catholic parish church, dating from 1865 presented by the third earl of Dunraven, who formerly owned Garinish at the mouth of the Sneem river. He compiled a magnificently illustrated book on early Irish architecture, edited by Miss Margaret Stokes, who herself produced a useful book on the subject. The priest of the parish was Father Michael Walsh, who was an expert in Irish music and was an important early influence on the young David Moriarty, who was to become a notable bishop of Kerry. Walsh was the model for the Father O Flynn who figured in the famous song of Alfred Perceval Graves, father of a distinguished family and son of Dr Charles Graves, protestant bishop of Limerick and Ardfert, who lived at what is now part of the Parknasilla hotel nearby. Graves, with Lord Dunraven, did much to focus attention on the neglected antiquities of Kerry.

There is a tiny, attractive protestant church, recently renovated, which looks as if it might date to elizabethan times; but this is so improbable that it has been suggested that it was designed by an 18th century architect with original ideas of what a contemporary church should look like! Smith says the parish churches of Templenoe and Kilcroghan were in ruins, and would certainly have commented on Sneem church had it been in existence then. Note the weather vane, appropriately a salmon. The Sneem river is a famous salmon river which is, of course, preserved; but for those who like to eat, rather than catch, salmon there is also net fishing in the estuary and fish can usually be bought, after high tide, in the village up to early August.

Hussey tells the story of two local families in the faction-fighting days of the nineteenth century, who had a remorseless feud. One day a solitary member of one of the families was so foolhardy as to venture into the village and was surrounded and beaten up by members of the other family. One of these, with a wooden leg, hobbled up, late, shouting: 'Boys, for the love of mercy, let a poor cripple have one go at the black-hearted varmint'.

From outside Sneem came the all-in wrestling family of the Caseys, famous in the 1930s, and the backbone, in a later generation, of much notable sporting prowess in the village.

The mountains around present splendid opportunities for ridge walks. There are many lakes where trout fishing is free.

The village is a couple of miles in from the sea and at high tide an evening trip up the river to the pier is worth taking. Just below the bridge, the river falls over a big jumble of rocks. When there has been really heavy rain and the river is in one of its brief, tempestuous floods, the sight from just below the bridge is impressive indeed. At the west end of the village is a road leading towards the sea that soon peters out, but is agreeable when the tide is full.

There is not a great deal of interest along the road towards Caherdaniel, apart from that already noted, except the remarkable rate of growth of trees at the forestry plantation below the pass of Beal some two miles from the town and the quarry at the same place with its various colours (and ages) of sandstone.

1. Sneem — Dromtine — Tullakeel

North of the town, from the western village green, leads a road that rapidly divides. Take the left branch and drive into the coum for just under two miles when one crosses the Sneem river. About half a mile further on the road worsens and branches left. It is as well to leave the car here. Follow this left branch over a bridge, past a farmhouse and, just short of a second, turn right. A short distance further on there is a rough track through a gateway. This is a very old

292

roadway that goes through a boggy patch and then rises on a small hill. Just here, to the right a little way in are circles in the soft ground. Whether these are the foundations of old houses, or places where the rough herbage of the slough was dried, or both, is not clear. There are many more of them hereabouts. Back to the track and a few yards further on, to the right, is a large rock with scribings. This is *Dromtine* (V.67.70.b). The track leads up to a ringfort, and in it a very tall (and thus, presumably, bronze age) gallan, leaning sideways. Whatever its original purpose, it seems clear that this unusually placed gallan was used as a signpost. Below one, towards the left, the track leads towards places with traces of bog-iron, and an ancient circular house. Perhaps this was the purpose of the community on the hill, with its notable signpost. If one travels a little further into the coum — on the higher drier ground one is in the townland of *Glorach* (V.67.72), well named from the tremendous echoes given by the surrounding cliffs.

Back by the old road through the gate to the roadway one has left. From here climb the low hill on the right. This brings one up above *Dromtine Lough* (V.67.70.b), the source of Sneem water supply. All along this hill are dotted the remains of ancient farming settlements — clochans and old field systems. There is a boithrin here that leads under the two farmhouses back over the river.

This place presents one with the opportunity for splendid ridge walks. The most straightforward of these can be begun by driving straight to the end of the road one is on. However, these call for not inconsiderable exertion, strong boots or shoes (this place tends to be extraordinarily wet), settled weather and a good ration of time.

If these conditions are not satisfied, simply drive up into the coum, and return to the fork in the road near the village and turn sharp left, past the village cemetery and dump, and follow this road until, two miles from the fork, there is a rough road on the left that rises steeply. Follow the road one is on for a quarter-mile until, on the left, one sees a barred up gateway. Leave the car here and

follow the overgrown roadway to a line of bushes. A little below one to the right under a big holly tree is the well known *Tullakeel scribed stone* (V.70.71.b). This is like the Dromtine one, but smaller. It is of interest to trace out the patterns in chalk. Were they simply doodlings, as most of the framework might lead one to suppose; or had they a real purpose? The similarity in the patterns — for example, at Staigue, Dromtine, here and on the most interesting of them at Derrynablaha, Ballaghabeama — suggest that they were not doodlings. Alas for the backwardness of Irish archaeology!

Back to the car. The road one is on penetrates into another coum, and it is of some interest to do this but, as with all these coums, one must return the way one has come.

Total driving distance: 16 miles. Allow (apart from ridge-walking) three and a half to four hours.

2. *Sneem — Coum — Temple Dermot — Mullaghanattin*

The mountains all about Sneem are full of scooped out glacial hollows, called coums, from the Irish word bent. The place called by local people *Coum* (V.73-4.76-7) simply is one of the most striking of these. On the map it is labelled *The Pocket*. This trip needs a good day.

Take the Killarney road from Sneem for seven and a half miles until one comes to the cross labelled Ballaghabeama. Take this road for a mile until it forks just beyond the ridge over the Blackwater. Bear left here and follow this road until, shortly after one has opened and shut a gate, it ends in a farmyard, surrounded by fuchsia, with the usual geranium pots on the windows. Leave the car here. The main objective is to climb *Mullaghanattin* (V.74.78.c), the mountain just facing one. It is 2,539 feet, and the highest in the peninsula. The immediate objective is the old monastic site of *Temple Dermot* (V.74.77.a) which is on a ledge of the mountain, at just under 1,000 feet. One can see, directly before one, a stone wall leading up part of the mountain. It points directly at Temple Dermot, the ledge of

which is just above where the wall ceases. Temple Dermot, it must be confessed, is, even as Irish ruins go, a disappointment: it shows barely the shape of some beehive huts. The view here is splendid, but the exposure and the damp must have been cruel for Dermot and his disciples.

As one is up so far, it is worth attempting the rest of the mountain. The climb is straightforward, safe and dry; but it is severe. However, the view from the top is superb. One can see right across the peninsula — from the Dingle to the Beare mountains; the Reeks (with Carrantuohill); and the jumble of mountains and lakes to the west. Directly beneath one is Glencar and the entrance to Ballaghabeama.

When we had returned from this climb we were told of one of the young local sheep farmers who had climbed the mountain to watch his sheep, saw a fox at the top, ran down the mountain to his house for his gun, and ran up the mountain in time to shoot the fox.

Total driving distance: 23 miles. Allow five hours.

3. *Sneem — Derrynablaha — Graignagreana — Lough Brin — Lissaree — Dunkilla — Derryquin*

Take the Killarney road for seven and a half miles and turn left for Ballaghabeama. Do not branch off this road, as for the previous run, but carry on for three and a half miles from the Killarney road until one comes to a bridge over a stream and a sharp bend right. This is *Derrynablaha* (V.77.77.a). Leave the car here and climb left by the south bank of the stream and then of a tributary to it that joins it some yards above the bridge. About half a mile above one — 20 minutes of middle-aged climb — some 50 yards from the south bank of this stream, on the third of the natural ledges of the mountainside, are, together, the two most interesting and most elaborately scribed of the rocks in South Kerry. The smaller of the stones, which may have been moved into the company of the scribed rock, has elaborate decorations, like a shield. There has been some excited discussion as to whether or not it is of the same period as the rock. The rock itself is elaborately scribed. In addition, it is covered with pock (or peck) marks that show just how the scribing was done with a pointed stone chisel.

There are many more stones in this area, but none to compare with those just mentioned. For example, directly beneath this stone, about a quarter-mile beneath the road, on the same side of the river, where it takes a significant bend, are two large, very red rocks, with simple scribings.

Across the valley is *Lough Brin* (V.79.78), a noted (and preserved) fishing lake. It is said to be named from Fionn's great hound Bran, which pursued an enchanted stag into the lake, and both of them were lost. However, sometimes a great creature like a white greyhound has been seen on the banks of the lake and a local cow calved an animal half calf and half hound.

Back to the car, and through the very impressive gap of *Ballaghabeama* (V.76.79.c) the only route across the peninsula between Killarney and Waterville. A famous hunting expedition of the Fiana is named after this place. In a drive from the Reeks to Ballaghabeama they killed many deer. But over to the right, in Derrynafeana above Lough Acoose, they roused a wild sow which they pursued for two days when she escaped, having killed many of the hunters and hounds.

(If one has not had a chance of seeing Cloon Lough from the Glenbeigh side, this is an opportunity of doing so).

Back through the gap and back to the Killarney road.

Turn left here and drive towards Killarney for six miles. Then, just after *Barfinnihy lake* (V.85.77.b) on the left, take the steep, and winding road left down into the valley and, over a bad road, through *Graignagreana* (V.81-84.79). This is a very fine drive, perhaps especially in early evening. Go along by Lough Brin on the right. This road brings one back again to the Sneem road. Turn right. After four and a half miles it branches

left for Parknasilla. Take this branch and a short distance along it, is a small shop on the right and a boithrin, also on the right. Leave the car here and walk up a short distance to a well-preserved ringfort, *Lissaree* (V.74.69.b), the liss of the king. Normally a king's liss has two vallums, or moats; this has only one. Perhaps it was a summer retreat.

Follow the road down to the main Ring of Kerry road at *Tahilla* (V.75.66.a) church. Just after the church, on the Sneem side, turn left and follow this narrow road for half a mile until one passes a shop on the right. Immediately beyond this is a boithrin on the right. Leave the car and climb up this. At the ridge, bear left towards a clump of trees surrounding the diminutive hillfort of *Dunkilla* (V.74.66.c). The views here are probably the best in the whole district — and that is saying a great deal. The hillfort is not of special interest, except in relation to the strength of its position and that — even though it is small — it is the only one of its kind that I have found in Kerry.

Back to the car and continue on the road one is on for a mile until a road branches left. This leads on a short distance to *Rossdohan* (V.72.62-64), a magnificent garden which contains a remarkable collection of trees and shrubs, notably Australasian ones. Permission to view these can be obtained. Back to the branch. Observe the effect of Dunkilla on the sky line. Bear left. Almost immediately, on the left, is the entrance to *Derryquin* (V.72.65.c) castle. The grounds are now the Parknasilla golf course. The castle itself is now demolished because dangerous. It was built by the Blands, the local great family. It is a victorian castle, built in the current fashion, burned down during the Troubles. This was a favourite occupation when there was no fighting. The story is that the arsonists came to burn down the neighbouring Parknasilla hotel, but were deflected to Derryquin by the eloquence of one of the hotel staff who explained how much local employment would be lost with the hotel. The founder of the family in Kerry was the Rev James Bland who came to Ireland in 1692 as chaplain to the Lord Lieutenant. He married Lucy Brewster, heiress of Sir Francis Brewster, a former Lord Mayor of

Dublin, who had acquired extensive forfeited lands near Killarney. Bland became vicar of Killarney, archdeacon of Aghadoe and dean of Ardfert. His eldest son succeeded him as vicar of Killarney — a Bland was vicar there for a century.

His second son, Nathanael, who died in 1760, was a doctor at law and became a judge in Dublin. He acquired extensive lands around Sneem and built a summer lodge between the two rivers there. He is the Dr Bland, described by Smith as an improving landowner, in that agriculturally not rewarding area. By 1758, when Pococke called, he had moved house to something approximating the present site of Derryquin. His third son, Captain Francis Bland, forsook the army and in Dublin in 1758 fell in with a Welsh actress, Grace Philipps, by whom he had six or seven children and himself became an actor. In 1774 he married a rich Miss Mahony, of Killarney (? of Dunloe); he died in France in 1778 and is buried in St Mary's, Killarney. His second child by Grace Philipps was born in London in 1761 and became Dorothy Jordan the famous actress. After Bland's death the mother and eldest children came to Dublin from Wales, and seemed to get support from Bland's widow. The two eldest girls began their acting career in the Crow street theatre. In 1791 Dorothy Jordan became the mistress of William, Duke of Clarence, later William IV, to whom she bore 10 children—the Fitz Clarence family— before he pensioned her off, after 20 years, in 1811. She died at St Cloud in 1816.

Carry on through the golf course and emerge on the Ring of Kerry road. Turn left for Sneem.

Total driving distance (excluding Cloon Lough): 46 miles. Allow four and a half hours.

4. Sneem—Oysterbed—Parknasilla

Take the Kenmare road for a mile. Then turn right at the signpost for a mile to *Oysterbed pier* (V.70.64.a) (because oysters grow here). This gives very fine views. Just opposite one to the right is *Garinish* (V.69-70.63-64), the former island home of

294

the Earl of Dunraven which contains a heronry and another splendid garden similar to Rossdohan, but not as well developed. Permission may also be obtained to see this. To the right is the Sneem river. It is occasionally possible in the village to hire a motor boat here. This is well worth doing.

There is often good mackerel fishing between the islands, and amidst charming scenery. The trip up the river at high tide towards Sneem is memorable. In general, this is a most attractive boating place.

Back to the main road and turn right for another mile to *Parknasilla* (V.71.64.b) hotel, beside a former home of the Graves family. The views here are delightful. There is a cruiser that sails around the bay. Some boats and horses may be hired. There is a pleasant 9-hole golf course.

Total driving distance: six miles.

5. Sneem—Blackwater—Dunkerron

Take the Kenmare road for just over four miles, as far as Tahilla. Directly beyond the church on the right is a boithrin leading down to the neglected *Tahilla pier* (V.75.66.b) with pleasant views. Back to the main road. Less than a mile further on, is, on the right of the road, the long, narrow lake of *Lough Fadda* (V.76.67.d), with its rocks rounded and scraped by glaciers.

Three miles further on, just before one comes to Blackwater bridge, there is a boithrin to the left that leads under the main road down to the little *Blackwater harbour*, or *Lackeen Pier* (V.80.68.b). Salmon can, on suitable occasions, be bought here from the net men.

Back to the main road and admire the view of the river from *Blackwater bridge* (V.80.69.d)—not at the viewing points made in it now overgrown. Short of the bridge and the post-office there is a road left that brings one pleasantly up to the Killarney road. Then turn and after less than a mile, right again by the church. About half a mile along take the more southern of the two left turns. This brings one up onto high ground

with pleasant views behind one and, later, a striking view of Kenmare river. After one has been on this road for a mile and a half turn left. Eventually one comes out on the main Kenmare road again at *Templenoe* (V.84.70.b), the new church, established by O Sullivan Mor, for this was the centre of the family's power.

Less than half a mile west of this, between the road and the sea, are the ruins of *Cappanacush castle* (V.84.70.c), the last O Sullivan owner of which was Col John O Sullivan, the companion of the Young Pretender in 1745. He was sent to Paris to school at the age of nine, and later to Rome. He had a very successful career as staff officer to a number of French generals. He enjoyed the esteem and confidence of both Old and Young Pretenders, even after the failure of the '45; indeed the Scots held that in that adventure Charles relied too much on O Sullivan's advice and blamed on him the failure of Culloden. This branch of the family were known as the Vera-O Sullivans because the founder of the family had married a slavonic lady called Vera.

Return towards Kenmare. After a mile and a half, at the cross roads, turn left and go for exactly two miles. Stop at Mrs Downing's a new cottage, left. Just short of this, through a wide gap, left, is the *Poulacopple* (V.85.74.d) scribed stone. Turn here. On the way down note the great quantities of flowering currant in the hedges. At the cross roads, turn left. About a mile and a half along the road towards Kenmare is *Dunkerron*

Bridge at Blackwater, Kenmare

castle (V.89.71.c), the seat of the O Sullivan Mor for some 400 years; before that an anglo-norman castle; and before that probably (from the name) a pre-gaelic fort. The castle itself, a short walk from the road, on the right as one faces towards Kenmare, is now wholly in ruins: it was built in Tudor times. From here the head of the most senior, the most numerous of all Munster families could survey the two beautiful, if unprofitable, peninsulas his people acquired by conquest early in the 13th century. They lost them again by conquest in the seventeenth century; Owen O Sullivan Mor was a main leader of those who revolted in Kerry in 1641. It was near here that the last of the skirmishes of the war took place. O Sullivan attempted to break out past the fort at Nedeen but was driven back and staged a stand near here, where he was finally defeated. Although it was Petty who acquired the ownership of the land, in practice it was a family older in these parts than the O Sullivans, who occupied the land, as tenants in chief of Petty, the O Mahonys.

One is now close to Kenmare: but if that is not on the agenda, turn back the main road for three and a half miles. This brings one to the entrance to *Dromore castle* (V.82.69.c), an O Mahony seat. The family was founded by Denis O Mahony, elder brother of the remarkable Donal O Mahony of Dunloe. These O Mahonys became protestant, like many other big landholders, in the 18th century. The famous 'Captain Dan' O Mahony, the hero of Cremona, was of this family. The castle is an undistinguished 19th century affair, notable for two things— that it is not in ruins and for a haunting song written about it, *The Castle of Dromore*. A little further on is the curious notice "car park". This is a viewing point made in the forest from which a fine view of the Kenmare river can be had.

Back then along the main road.

Total driving distance: 35 miles. Allow three hours.

GLANEROUGHT

The western line of this barony runs from close to Moll's Gap just west of the Kenmare road along the Finnihy River to its mouth at Kenmare. It then runs, on the far side of the Kenmare River, from a point just west of Kilmakilloge Harbour south to the spine of mountains south of Glanmore, then east along mountains and then north. Just north west of Morley's Bridge the line goes west to the summit of Mangerton and then to Moll's Gap. The barony was once, with the rest of South Kerry, and with West Cork, part of the County of Desmond, but it went with Kerry when Desmond ceased in 1606.

The name is Gleann Ui Ruachtaigh—the Glen of the Roughty (River) which runs along the road from Loo Bridge, gaining strength from many tributaries as it goes, to the sea at the head of the so-called Kenmare River. But, as we have seen the barony also incorporates about half the northern side of the Beare peninsula.

Presumably this area was part of the territory of the Eoganacht Locha Lein, for one version of the legend says that it was at Kenmare that Eogan Mar (or Mug Nuadat), the legendary leader of the Goidels, first landed in 150 BC and peacefully took the sovereignty from the two local kings because he had supplies in a time of famine. Part at least of this barony was overrun by the O Sullivans at the end of the 12th century and, a little later, when the anglo-normans

from Cork drove down the valley in 1215 and established the two castles of Ardtully and Dunkerron. Here near Kilgarvan, at Callan Glen, in 1261, was fought one of the decisive battles in Irish history that baulked the invaders for over 300 years, and Mac Carthys occupied Ardtully and O Sullivans Dunkerron. Up this valley came Rinuccini in 1645, and after the wars much of the barony came into the possession of Sir William Petty, whose descendants still have a house here, at Derreen. Some of the greatest suffering in the Great Famine of 1845-7 occurred here. Kenmare was the scene of some vigorous fighting in the civil war in 1922-3.

(I) KENMARE

Kenmare (VI.91-92.71) (pop. 1971: 903) is the principal town of the barony of Glanerought, which boasts of only one other town, Kilgarvan. Kenmare comes from Ceann Mara, the head of the (inlet of the) sea, and there is reference in the Papal Taxation of 1302 to 'Eccia de Keynmara'. The modern Irish name is, however, An Neidin, the little nest. This recalls the town of Nedeen founded just to the north of the

present town by Sir William Petty in 1670. Petty's descendant, the first marquis of Lansdowne, (who was prime minister when Grattan's Parliament got its independence) had the present town laid out in 1775, as was common with other improving landlords of the time. He instructed that the town 'may be begun by laying out the capital streets 50 feet wide at right angles'. In fact, it was laid out in an 'X' plan. The town has thus a pleasant shape, enhanced by a number of houses built in the local limestone. Lansdowne thought Nedeen meant 'nest of thieves' so he revived an older name for the place to honour his friend, Lord Kenmare, whose title, however, came from a *Limerick* property.

Near here the great goidelic invader Mug Nuadat (or Eogan Mar) landed at about the beginning of our era and fought the battle of Carn Buide. This is probably almost due south of Kenmare on the southern slopes of the mountains north of Glengariff.

Near here Rinuccini landed in late 1645 after his exciting chase from France, and made his way to Ardtully, a few miles up the Roughty valley. Beside the town are the remains of a

Glaneroghty Barony, after Petty

296

seventeenth century castle, the oddly named Cromwell's Fort (he never got to Kerry), in fact a garrison post established during the cromwellian wars but abandoned later in the century. Petty opened the Glanerought Iron Works on the right bank of the Finnihy river, a half-mile along the Killarney road where slag still remains. The iron was smelted with charcoal; as a result the surrounding thick woods were devastated. At one time Petty's colony numbered 810 souls. Coins struck by the ironworks in 1667 and 1669 are extant.

In the williamite wars the colony under Richard Orpen took refuge at Killowen but was driven out. With great hardship they sailed to Bristol in two ships supplied by James Waller, son of Petty's patron, the regicide Sir Hardress Waller. They returned after the war.

The Lansdownes, a descendant of whom still has a seat at Derreen, near Lauragh, through the centuries contributed liberally to works of public improvement—roads, bridges, piers, schools etc.

Near Cromwell's Fort, most awkwardly fenced off, is a fine dolmen and stone circle—just after one has, approaching from Killarney, crossed the bridge turn right at the ballroom and then right again.

According to O'Donovan in the Ordnance Survey Letters there was one furlong east of the modern Protestant church (on the road to Glengariff) a remarkable gallan—Gallan na Cille Bige—surrounded by an irregular group. If so it has fallen. If what is there now constitutes the remains of an artefact at all —the place, just in front of a bungalow, is woefully overgrown—then it is the remains of a remarkable gallery grave. Between it and the modern church are the remains of what may be an earlier church, again perhaps an association between christian site and pagan tomb.

On the south side of the Roughty, above the suspension bridge in *Kenmare Old* (VI.93.71.d), is an old church and well dedicated to St Fionan. The suspension bridge—which was replaced in 1932—was the first in Ireland—its foundation stone was laid in 1838. The cost of £6,000 was borne jointly by Lord Lansdowne and the Board of Works. The pier is the result of similar collaboration.

The town was connected by a good road to Killarney only in the 1820s and to Glengariff and Bantry in the 1830s.

There was great distress in this area during the Great Famine. Through incompetence or heartlessness—there is some evidence of both—the Lansdowne estate, which had some reputation to lose, did very little to succour the victims of starvation and disease and there was terrifying mortality in the area, centred on the newly opened workhouse. After the Famine, in order to clear the workhouse— which was maintained by rates paid in large part by the estate—large parties of emigrants were shipped off to New York. About this, too, there was some controversy. Trench, the estate agent responsible for this emigration scheme, wrote a book, *Realities of Irish Life,* which deals, in part, with this and other local happenings. Trench was also an active magistrate and the object of great local hatred. The local ribbonmen formed plot after plot against his life. These he circumvented by judicious bribery, informers, and his own extreme courage.

There is a pleasantly sited golf course beside the Great Southern Hotel. The little pier is attractive when the tide is in. Here the well known composer, E. J. Moeran, was drowned.

Froude, the English historian, spent periods in the 1870s at Derreen. His *English in Ireland,* his *Essays on Great Topics,* Series II, and his novel, *Two Chiefs of Dunboy,* have much local colour. He was, perhaps, more gifted as a writer than as an historian.

In the town is a fine catholic parish church. Inside are really striking roof timbers.

Attached to this is the convent of Poor Clares, founded in 1861. This branch of the Poor Clares—of which there are several in Ireland— is not of the really strict observance because its purpose is teaching. One of the founding sisters in 1861 was Sister Mary Frances Clare Cusack, born in Dublin an evangelical protestant. She became a catholic in England. From Kenmare she published many books— devotional and historical—(from which she apparently earned a lot of money) under the title of the 'Nun of Kenmare'. One of these was her *History of Kerry,* a standard work, published in 1871. She formed a fund for the relief of the severe distress caused by the famine of 1879 and was the centre of, especially for a nun, a quite remarkable public controversy. She left Kenmare in 1881 and, after a couple of years as a nun in Mayo, founded a new order of nuns in Britain in 1884. In the same year she went to the United States to spread her new order. Amongst her many gifts was, supremely one for falling foul of bishops and priests, and in 1888, she ceased to be a nun and returned to the evangelical fold. In the following year she published in America *The Nun of Kenmare: An Autobiography,* which must be amongst the bitchiest of books.

The Poor Clares, on the basis on an existing centre for crochet work, established with their other schools a centre for needlepoint which achieved some fame. A tabernacle veil, designed by members of the convent and carried out by the Misses Leahy, is described by Mrs Boyle as 'the single most beautiful object of applied art' produced in Ireland for a hundred or more years.

A short distance east of the town is a small hospital.

During the civil war of 1922-3 the town changed hands a couple of times. One of the most curious incidents during the civil war was when a British sloop, HMS *Barrington,* landed some marines—presumably for peaceful purposes—at Lackeen Pier, in September, 1922. The local IRA garrison got reinforcements from Killarney and opened rifle fire on the sloop, manifestly to its surprise. After a while, recovering, the *Barrington* retorted with its guns, before pulling off and returning to Berehaven. No real harm seems to have been done.

(II) ROUGHTY VALLEY

Take the Kilgarvan road. After just over a mile one comes to *Killowen* (VI.93.72.a), where Petty's agent Orpen had his siege. Just a mile further on one comes to a hamlet with a monument on the right. Turn left here and drive up a narrow boithrin until one comes to a disused railway line. Leave the car here and turn right along the line for about a quarter of a mile. There is a rusty wicket gate on the left and just inside this is the geological joke of *Cnoc a Cappeen* (VI.94.73.d). This is a stone mushroom some ten feet high with a large block of sandstone resting on a plinth of limestone, reversing the order of nature and, no doubt, fallen from some ancient glacier. Along this valley one is on the edge of the limestone country. On the other side of the valley, almost due opposite, there is a huge block of limestone resting on sandstone, a last vestige of the limestone that has elsewhere on that side been stripped away. Inevitably there are local stories of giants throwing stones at each other. As one walks back note the sandy shore of the great ice age lake that once stretched from Kilgarvan to Kenmare.

Back on the main road turn left to Kilgarvan. Less than a mile further on one crosses *Cleady Bridge* (VI.95.73.c) and skirts the townland, left, of *Kilpatrick* (VI.95.73), the only townland in Kerry named after the patron saint of Ireland. Just two miles beyond the bridge there is a boithrin to the left and a few yards up this behind a farmhouse to the right, is a disused lead mine and a little further on a copper mine, both opened in the 30s of the last century, but neither successful. Half a mile along the main road there is, right, the entrance to *Ardtully house* (VI.99.73.b). One can drive in here. This was the home of the Orpens, agents to the Lansdowne estate. The founder of the family was the Rev Richard Orpen, established at Killowen in Petty's time; and leader of the Nedeen settlers when they were besieged in 1689; he left us a striking account of the adventure. A descendant was Goddard H. Orpen who wrote *Ireland under the Normans,* a fine history. Another recent descendant was Sir William Orpen, the painter, who designed the Irish currency notes.

Ardtully castle once stood here, but was destroyed by the cromwellians. Ardtully

297

Cnoc an Cappeen, Kenmare

Ardtully Castle, Kenmare

castle was one of those built by the first anglo-norman invaders. A couple of miles away is Callan Glen where Mac Carthy power asserted itself over the geraldines in 1261. This castle then became Mac Carthy property. It was for long held by Mac Fineen Mac Carthy, direct descendants of that Diarmaid Mac Carthy killed at Tralee assizes in 1325. One of the family was Florence Mac Finneen known as Captain Sugan, one of the leaders of the 1641 Rising in Kerry. He was Governor of Kerry from 1641 but was killed near Cork, in 1642. His elder brother Donagh, gave princely hospitality to Rinuccini and his entourage when they stayed here for two days in 1645. A third brother was killed in action in 1652. Donagh's son, Donal, defended the Ford of Slane, at the battle of the Boyne, with the loss of 300 Kilgarvan men. He himself fell at the battle of Aughrim in 1691.

298   The maps also show the old monastery of
Monasternoriel here (apparently very close
to the house) but no vestige of it remains.
Below the house is a bridge across the
Roughty overlooking a very famous salmon
pool.

One and a half miles further on the main road
is *Kilgarvan* (VI.102.74.c) (pop. 1971: 228),
not a very exciting village. As one drives
through it one takes a sharp turn right into
the centre. Just facing one at the bend is
a little shop where delicious farmer's butter
is sold.

Turn at the village and almost immediately,
from the Kenmare road, turn left.
Immediately after one has crossed the bridge
over the Roughty turn right and some
hundreds of yards further on, right again.
Wind through the valley for about half a
mile until one comes to a steeply climbing
boithrin on the right. This brings one back
along the top of the valley. At the last
farmhouse stop and walk along the track
that begins to bear down again into the valley.
One is now looking down over *Callan Glen*
(VI.101.73.a) (pronounced Cullen) where
the one decisive battle ever fought in Kerry
was won by the Mac Carthys over the
geraldines in 1261, and south Kerry was
kept free from the invaders for over 300
years. This was the time when Hanmere's
record had it that 'the Carties plaied the
Divells in Desmond'. In the battle were
killed John Fitz Gerald, his son Maurice,
eight barons, five knights and countless
soldiers. They were aided by a grandson of
Dermod Mac Carthy, king of Desmond when
the anglo-normans came. Maurice, son of
John, married the daughter, or more likely
the grand-daughter, of Geoffrey de Marisco
the Justiciar who had established
Castleisland. Their child Thomas an Apa
(from the monkey who saved him as a baby
from fire) was the founder of the great house
of Desmond. John and Maurice were buried
in the Dominican priory in Tralee, which
John had founded. A little distance down
the boithrin on the left almost in the ditch is
a huge stone said to cover the grave of one of
the Mac Carthys. The victor of this battle
was another grandson of King Dermod
Mac Carthy, Finghin Ranna Roin. In the

Roughty Bridge, Kenmare

following year 1262 a sequel to this battle
was fought on the far side of Mangerton,
at Tooreencormack, but it only confirmed
the results of the battle of Callan. At this
time the anglo-norman castles erected in the
second decade of the century separating
north from south Kerry, of which Ardtully
was one, were captured and destroyed.

Turn back and, when one meets the road at
the bottom of the valley, turn right. After
one mile take the left fork and, after a further
one and a half miles, the right one. This
brings one up through some rough, but quite
passable country from which there are fine
views. After one and a half miles one comes
to houses and a T junction. Turn left here for
some hundreds of yards. A couple of
hundred yards from the road, on the right,
is a great block of limestone, already referred
to, known as *Iron Rock* (VI.94.74.d). This
has been identified as Cloch Bearraidhe (or
Cloghvaragh on the 6-inch map) in

Gortalinny. Here Mug Nuadat, in full retreat
after his first invasion of Ireland, and hotly
pursued by Goll Mac Morna, was rescued by
the goddess Etain, who turned this stone into
Mug's likeness so that Goll hacked it. She
turned, also, the stones around into the
likeness of soldiers. While Goll's men
attacked these Mug was able to escape to
Etain on Beare island, and then to Spain.

Turn here and drop down into the valley
but, before the Roughty is reached, turn
right and follow the left bank of the river
for about a mile until one comes to a boithrin
leading to a farmhouse above one on the
right. On the hill above the house is the
interesting three gallan alignment of
Dromtouk (VI.96.72.c), with ogam markings
on the central one.

Turn the car and go back along the road by
the river. One can, at the right state of the
tide and of the time of year, see salmon

netting going on here and, if luck is in, buy a salmon from the fishermen at a reasonable price. Shortly after one crosses the Sheen river—there are fine views from the bridge—there is, on the right, an extensive cemetery. Between it and the Kenmare river is the old St Fionan's church and a well to which pilgrimages are still made. (I am assured that they are there but was not able to find them).

Back to the road, and turn right at the main road to Kenmare. Total driving distance: 14 miles. Allow: two hours.

(III) DRUMOUGHTY–MUCKERA–LOHART–CLONEE LAKES–ARDEA CASTLE–LAURAGH–GLANMORE–DROMBOHILLY

Take the road south from Kenmare and after the suspension bridge, turn right. This run is one of the most attractive in all Kerry.

About a mile and a half along this road, is *Killaha East* (VI.89.69.b), where close to the road, on the left, a hoard was found dating from very early in the copper age (1800-2000 BC). It consisted of axes, a halberd and a dagger. Just one mile further on along this road is *Dawross Bridge* (VI.88.68.b); turn left here. (If one overshoots, there is, a little farther on, another road left at a church that winds back left to the Drumoughty road). Just over a mile and a quarter from the bridge take a fork right and, a little further on, after a bridge, a boithrin right. Take this until it forks at a shed. Leave the car here

Sheen Bridge, Kenmare

and walk up by the farmhouse on the right. Beyond the farmhouse follow the boithrin, each time taking the right fork. After some ten minutes, near some scrub trees on the left side of the boithrin, one comes on the interesting *Drumoughty* (VI.89.66.a) recumbent stone circle. In the middle is a small dolmen with cup marks. Instead of outliers, there are two inner portals, one fallen. Unusually, there seem to be the remains of two low circles some distance outside the main circle. The whole shows a clear overlap between neolithic and bronze age cultures.

As one goes back one can see a low hill up the valley about a mile. Here is, at *Drombane* (VI.90.65.a), a ceallunach and a very ruined church, (they are so ruined that one has to take this on trust). They are hardly worth the journey. This involves, at the T junction a right turn, instead of return left, and a journey up the hill just over a mile. Immediately after a bridge there is a branch, right, through two substantial gate pillars up to a farmyard. Walk right along a track by a ruined shooting lodge to a low hill, beside which are the ruins. The views here are fine. Back to the road. The way, right, leads over a pass onto the Glengariff road, but is quite impassable from this side.

Back to the main road from Kenmare. A mile further on is the attractive island of *Dinish* (VI.86-87.68), where there are the much ruined remains of a medieval monastery. At the landing stage on the mainland the road cuts through a great pile of oyster shells, which may have been a midden heap. In much later times, about 1800, an extensive oyster trade was carried on from here to Kinsale, Youghal and elsewhere.

One mile further on there is a turn left to *Muckera* (VI.85.66.b). The road climbs steeply for rather less than a mile and gives really splendid views of the Kenmare river and the mountains across it.

Back to the main road. Just about a mile and a half further on there is a short road left. Just beyond this is a bridge over a small stream, and just beyond this again a house on the right with, beside it, the well known

stone circle and chamber tomb of *Lohart* (VI.83.67.b), modernised and improved in recent times.

One and a half miles further on along this road one comes to a misleading signpost on the right which points to Inchiquin Lough, and straight on for Clonee Lakes. Nonetheless, turn left and one travels along a narrow, trying road, keeping to the right; but one is rewarded by striking views of the *Clonee Lakes* (VI.80-83.64-65), until, at the head of the coum some three miles up, one comes to the real end of the road (there are several apparent ends to the faint-hearted) at *Inchiquin Lough* (VI.83-85.63-64). This road goes through one of the most attractive places in all Kerry and one that is, in its own rough way, one of the most accessible to the motorist. The neighbourhood of these four lakes is also one of the most important botanical areas in Kerry where the special treasures of the county grow freely—the saxifrages, *pinguicula grandiflora,* the Irish spurge, arbutus and the rest. *Uragh wood* (VI.83-85.63), overlooking Inchiquin and facing one from the road, is a remnant of native forest.

Return to the main road and shortly after the little hotel on the right, take the second road right and, almost immediately turn right again up a steep hill. Again almost immediately, at a cross roads, turn left and follow this for a mile until it begins to drop sharply just after a farmhouse on the left. Leave the car here. A couple of hundred yards from the farmhouse there is on the right an overgrown boithrin to a deserted farmhouse. Beyond this, over a stile, there is a faint track up a low hill, bearing right. A short distance along this are the ruins of *Ardea castle* (VI.78.63.a) perched on a cliff above the sea. The site is exposed, but the view on a fine evening is breath-taking.

There is some history associated with this place. Ardea means 'Aed's Height'. The castle is built on the site of a fort of Aed Bennan, King of West Munster, who died in 621, of the Eoganacht Locha Lein. He was, clearly, a man of some ability and made an unsuccessful bid for the kingship of Munster as a whole. He had 12 sons and

Keating says one of them was St Fursa. It was Faithliu, a son of his successor and brother, Aed Daman, who died in 633, who founded the monastery of Innisfallen. O Donovan quotes a source who says Aed Bennan was ancestor of the O Moriartys who in historical times ruled, on occasion, the Eogantacht Locha Lein. Aed Bennan had a daughter Mor who married Finghen, King of Cashel; from her sprang the most senior and the most numerous of all Munster families, the O Sullivans, (in 1890 there were 43,000 of them). At the end of the twelfth century the anglo-normans drove the O Sullivans south from Tipperary and they settled in this countryside again. As far as the eye can reach it rests on O Sullivan territory. In this peninsula the main O Sullivan sept was O Sullivan Beare, and Ardea became the home of the tanist of the family. It commanded the nearby harbour and its possessor gained great profits from the constant traffic of ships with Spain— exporting provisions, wool and hides, importing wines, brandies and clothes. About 1553 it was reported that Mac Finghin Dubh of Ardea 'received £300 per annum from the Spaniards for liberty to fish in the river of Kenmare and the head of this sept had several deeds signed and sealed by his ancestors in connection with the said fishery'. Towards the end of the sixteenth century Sir Owen O Sullivan Beare surrendered his territories to the crown, and was re-granted them to hold according to English law. His nephew, Donal, challenged his title. The dispute ended in a royal partition in 1593. Donal got Beare, Sir Owen got Bantry, and his younger brother, Sir Philip, got Ardea.

In the O Neill wars a party of Spaniards landed at Ardea, and even while Dunboy was besieged in June, 1602, a Spanish ship arrived at Ardea with the bishop of Ross, Owen Mac Egan, some money, munitions and wine. However, Ardea, submitted without a fight in the following January.

The O Sullivans of the sub-sept of Mac Finghin Dubh held it for the next 50 years. It was again in the wars in cromwellian times and here, or close by, the papal nuncio Rinuccini landed on 21-22 October, 1645, hotly pursued by a pirate ship commanded

Inchiquin Lough, Kenmare

by a renegade Irishman, Plunkett, anxious to serve the English interest. He gave up the chase only when his cookhouse went on fire. Rinuccini spent his first night in Ireland in a shepherd's hut nearby. In 1652 the cromwellians finally 'slighted' Ardea so that part of the castle fell into the sea. The O Sullivans generally lost their lands in the subsequent confiscation and the new owner of virtually all that the eye can see was Sir William Petty, whose descendant, the Marquess of Lansdowne, still has a property at Derreen a few miles away. Mac Finghin Dubh continued on as tenant of the new owners. Weld has a story that in 1802 an old man of the name, living nearby and now sunk in great poverty could give his descent from Sir Philip O Sullivan and could produce the deeds of the adjudication of 1593, just over two centuries before. This must have been the Mac Finghin Dubh O Sullivan who died in 1809 and is buried at the old church

at Kilmakilloge.

It is inadvisable once one is back on the road, to drive down to the house at the edge of the sea, to turn. But it is worth the short walk down. Back to the cross roads, turn right and right again for a pleasant run along the coast.

As one travels on this road and turns inland along *Kilmakilloge harbour* (VI.73-77.59-61), there are, on the right, ruins of *Kilmakilloge church* (VI.75.61.d) of the romanesque and earlier periods, where the last Mac Finghin Dubh O Sullivan, who died in 1809, was buried. There is a monument over his grave. It seems to have been an old church adapted —by being widened and lengthened—to the standard form of parish church in the 12th-13th centuries, but is of little interest.

A little further on, close to a sharp bend on

the road, is *Lough Mackeenlaun*
(VI.76.61.c) whose floating 'islands' (really
tussocks) so excited Smith. The lake often
dries up in summer. By the east shore of the
lake are the remains of an eremitical site.
Here it was that St Killian spent a period
before he set out as a missionary to what is
now Germany and to martyrdom in Wurzburg
in 697. When the early Irish church had to
claim a martyr St Killian was the one claimed
because none had been martyred in Ireland.
Both Makilloge and Mackeenlaun are said to
be affectionate forms of Killian.

It is worth pausing at the pier at *Lauragh*
(VI.76.61.c) in Kilmakilloge harbour.
Massari, the dean of Fermo (Rinuccini was
bishop of the place) has left us a vivid account
of his own welcome at this place the day after
Rinuccini's landing—of the friendliness of
very poor people, and of how well instructed
they were in their religion—there was not one,
he says, who could not repeat the Our Father,
the Hail Mary, the Creed and the
commandments of the Church.

From Lauragh continue on the road past
the Lansdowne estate at *Derreen*
(VI.78.59.a). The gardens here are open to
the public three afternoons a week from
April to September. They are remarkable
for rhododendrons, tree ferns, camellias,
bamboos, eucalyptus. At the T junction turn
right and, almost immediately, left. Follow
this very narrow road along the lovely
Glanmore lough (VI.77-78.55-56) into the
striking *Glanmore* (VI.76-78.52-54) for just
under six miles to near the top of the valley.
The Kerry boundary is along the top of the
mountains bounding this glen.

Under a yellow farmhouse, right, by a little
stream, stop. Just before this, about half way
between the road and the river, left by a
ditch, somewhat overgrown by hollies, is a
most interesting *monument* (VI.77.53.a), but
rather ruined. It may be two wedge graves,
but if so of unusual construction, and facing
to the north. Maddison O Brien suggests
that what is here are the remains of a portal
dolmen, with two large stones leaning
together and the capstone cast down between
them. If so, this would be a most exciting

monument because portal dolmens have not
hitherto been found in Kerry nor any other
clear relics of neolithic inhabitants. He
suggests that the long, unusual stone lying on
others nearby may be a fallen gallan. This
does not seem to match the portal dolmen
suggestion. If this long stone is not the
capstone of a second wedge (if that is what
the first one is—for one thing the
orientations are wrong) then it may be the
capstone of the portal dolmen.

Back again by the Lough. Below this, after
a sharp turn left, there is a bridge and shortly
after it a road left. Take this into a really
savage coum called the *Pocket* (VI.75.55).
Near the head of the glen, along the top of
which the Kerry boundary runs from the sea,
there is a gate across the road. A little
beyond this, clearly visible in a field to the
right, is the small *stone circle* of *Shronbirrane*
(VI.76.56.c) of rather tall stones, the highest
being a male pointed stone. Back along this
road to a T junction on the main road. Then
right (and, later, left) for Lauragh.

From Lauragh take the rough road right up the
hill. This gives magnificent views on both
sides of the summit. On the far side, beyond
a school and some houses, turn right
immediately before a bridge. At the next
two T junctions turn right, and then, almost
immediately after the second, turn left. A
short distance further on take the first
boithrin right. Stop at the farmhouse here
and follow the boithrin on foot. Turn off
it at the first little wooden wicket and pass
through two more. Almost above one, a
little to the right, is the notable *stone circle*
of *Drumbohilly* (VI.80.61.a), consisting of, as
it were, gallans, with two portals. There are
magnificent views. Back to the farmhouse,
turn left out of the boithrin and right at the
T junction. Follow this road until one comes,
at a cross roads, to a main road, with a parish
hall and calvary on the right. Follow this
road back to Kenmare.

Driving distance: 60 miles. Allow: four
hours.

All the other road trips from Kenmare involve
forays into County Cork.

(IV) GOUGANE BARRA—KEIMANEIGH— COOMHOLA—BORLIN—SLAHENY

301

This, because of the high ground travelled, is
a most striking trip; but for the same reason
the cloud ceiling must be over 1,200 feet.

Take from Kenmare the Cork road through
Kilgarvan. Four miles after Kilgarvan is
Morley's Bridge (VI.105.76.d) where the
Roughty comes tumbling down from the
right. Take the steep road up to the right.
After five miles one reaches the Cork border,
at 1,000 feet. Just after this take the right
fork, and three miles further on, again turn
right. After two miles turn right again. This
is a winding, difficult road but it gives one a
splendid approach view of *Gougane Barra*
(VI.110.67.c), with the Kerry border along the
ridge to the right. Leave Gougane Barra by
the main road. After a mile turn right
through the pass of *Keimaneigh*
(VI.111.63-65) for *Ballylickey* (VI.101.54),
on Bantry Bay. Here turn right towards
Glengariff and, two miles further on, turn
right at *Snave Bridge* (VI.100.55.b) for
Kilgarvan. A mile along this road again turn
right at *Coomhola Bridge* (VI.100.56.b).
(Do not be tempted to go left for Priest's
Leap: the road, about two miles from the
summit, gets virtually impassable from this
side). Follow the right road up the *Coomhola
valley* (VI.100-104.57-60).

Along this road from Snave, some
commentators say, O Sullivan Beare led his
retreating people. Imagine old people,
women, children, impedimenta, being brought
over the ridge on the right near the head of
the valley, in mid-winter, to reach Gougane
Barra where they certainly made their first
stop. Other commentators, more merciful,
would have them go by Keimaneigh.

However, there was one clear historical
passing here. Almost exactly eight miles from
Snave bridge, where the ridge at the head of
the valley turns left, there is a bridge over a
stream coming from the ridge on the right.
At the close of the war of independence,
in late May, 1921, Tom Barry's famous West
Cork flying column was hard pressed by a
major British Army effort. Thousands of

302 troops forced the 100 odd men of the column further and further west. Landings were made at the head of Bantry bay to press them from the south. Other landings were made at the head of the Kenmare river. A line of troops stretched from Kenmare to Headford to prevent their retreat west into Kerry. Barry's men went up the Coomhola valley and, with a local guide leading them on a long rope climbed at night over this ridge and down a treacherous pass into Coomroe and Gougane Barra, thus foiling, but barely, a major military effort to capture or destroy them.

At the top of the valley skirt across the *Borlin valley* (VI.105-106.62-66) on the left, passing back to Kerry at a height of almost 1,200 feet, and then down through the *Slaheny valley* (VI.102-103.67-73) to Kilgarvan. Three miles short of Kilgarvan is, left, *Bird Hill* (VI.102.69.b) rising steeply above the road. Here there lived in the first half of the 18th century a family of

O Sullivans, three brothers and a son, all poets of some quality in Irish, their poetry collected and published by Risteard O Foghludha.

The run is better taken in the order shown because of the spectacular approach it gives to Gougane Barra and because the Slaheny valley gives a better view going down than does the Coomhola valley.

Total driving distance: 60 miles. Allow three and a half hours.

(V) TEMPLE FIACHNA–PRIEST'S LEAP– GLENGARRIFF

Take the Glengariff road. Exactly four miles from Kenmare turn left, across *Drumassig Bridge* (VI.102.69.b) and then right, up the valley of the Sheen River. (If one misses this turn one of the subsequent ones in the next couple of miles will do). After four miles from Drumassig Bridge one comes to the very ruined church of

Temple Fiachna (VI.97.65.d), on the left. In a field above the road, on the Kenmare side of the church and outside the churchyard enclosure, is a notable bullaun, with round stones for grinding the grain still in place. (There are many stories of what happens when attempts are made to take them away).

At the cross-roads just after the church turn right and follow as much as one can of the two and a half miles of road to the top of *Priest's Leap pass* (VI.99.62.d), at over 1,500 feet on the Cork border. Here it is worth walking over to the summit on the right for fine views of Bantry Bay. *Priest's Leap* (VI.100.62.a) is named after the feat of a priest, surprised saying Mass in penal times, who jumped his horse as far as Bantry. There a stone can be seen with the hoof-marks, and even the mark of the whip that fell from his hand when he landed.

If one can coax the car up to the pass it is possible, with careful driving, to go down the Cork side to Coomhola Bridge and Snave Bridge. (The reverse journey is not feasible). Turn right here for Glengarriff and Kenmare.

Total driving distance: 36 miles. Allow two and a half hours.

BEARE

(I) GLENGARIFF – GARINISH – ADRIGOLE – HEALY PASS – LAURAGH

Take the tunnel for Glengariff. This is an example of Board of Works road building in the early 19th century. Just eight miles from Kenmare at the turn left for *Bunane Bridge* (VI.95.64.c) one goes through the townland of *Milleens* (VI.94.64) where a fulacht fiadha has been excavated. Continue along the road and, just before one enters the topmost tunnel (and leaves Kerry), it may be worth looking at the surrounding rocks rounded and grooved by the great glacier that passed this way. To the left of the tunnel opening, less than a half-mile away (but through wet ground), is the peak of *Turner's Rock* (VI.92.61.c), which is particularly well marked.

Gougane Barra, Co. Cork

Garinish, Glengariff

In *Glengariff* (VI.93.57.d) (pop. 1971: 244) do not fail to cross to the gardens on *Garinish* (VI.94.55-56) in the harbour. These are public property, a gift from Roland Bryce, the last of the family who in the early years of this century transformed an island as bare as anything in the harbour into a paradise. The gardens are splendid at almost any time of the year. The trip will take about an hour and a half and involve expenditure on toll and boat fares. Boats tend not to be available in the evenings. At the highest point on the island is a Martello tower. This was the first of a genre built around the British isles against the expected Napoleonic invasion of 1804-05. As might be expected after the near miss of the Tone invasion, two others were built on Beare island.

In season bathe in the Poul Gorm beside the hotel of that name.

Then take the road to Adrigole.

As one leaves Glengariff harbour behind one passes through, for most of the journey to Adrigole, a territory between the road and the sea formerly inhabited by a curious race of people called the 'Ranties'. They seem to have survived as a separate people up to the middle of the 19th century. They were very small, and kept themselves entirely to themselves. The first written record of them is from 1629 in Sir John Burghley's *Relation*

of the State of the Church in Ireland. He says that 'they practise Judaism, for every Easter Day in the morning before sunrise they eat a lamb roasted, head and appurtenances, as prescribed to the Jews in the Levitical law; and the poorest sort make lamb pies on Good Friday, and bring them to the priests, who set them on the altar and sprinkle them with Holy Water; and these are called the Holy Lamb, and are eaten on Easter Day as the other roasted'. They spoke a dialect of Irish that required an interpreter, and always intermarried. The women wore distinctive red cloaks dyed from small shellfish. Their own tradition was that they came from the North in perhaps the 16th century and at first were robbers and plunderers. It is not clear what was the origin of the name; but it is suggested that a similar race of people came from Togher Rann, near Lahinch, Co. Clare.

At *Adrigole* (VI.82.51.c) turn right up to the *Healy Pass* (VI.79.54.b), from which there are magnificent views. The pass is named after Tim Healy, the first governor-general of the Irish Free State when it achieved independence as a dominion in 1922. He was a member of the 'Bantry Gang' and was a most bitter opponent of Parnell when the Irish parliamentary party split in 1891. After one has gone through the Pass and the boundary of Kerry there are fine views of Glanmore Lough below one, left. The road drops down to Derreen. Here turn right for Kenmare.

Total driving distance: 110 miles. Allow about seven hours.

Cromwell's Bridge, Glengariff

(II) HEALY PASS — CASTLETOWNBERE ALLIHIES — EYERIES — ARDGROOM

303

The Healy Pass is worth approaching from the Kerry side if only for the splendid views of Bantry Bay as one drops down to Adrigole. Here turn right for Castletownbere. The road is dominated by the lean, well-named *Hungry Hill* (VI.77.50), the most southerly point of Kerry.

Just over four miles along the Castletownbere road is, at the foot of a short road left, *Bank Harbour* (VI.76.47.b). Here are the barely distinguishable ruins of Sod Fort, the house of the redoubtable French Huegenot, the Rev James Fontaine, who started a fish curing and exporting business here early in the 18th century. The coast was infested by French privateers who were assisted by the Irish. Fontaine, a justice of the peace, tried to prevent this, and made himself so unpopular that he had to build a fortified house. In June 1704 a French privateer attacked the house, at first with armed men and then with cannon. Fontaine armed his wife and children and some retainers and with great courage, they beat off the attack after eight hours of continuous firing. This exploit, thanks to Fontaine's energy and flair for publicity, became known throughout Europe. Fontaine was granted a pension of five shillings a day. He strengthened his fortifications, and mounted several cannon, for which the government gave him 500 cannon balls and four barrels of powder. In October, 1708, Fontaine was again attacked. This time his garrison consisted of his five sons, his wife and four servants, and he was heavily outnumbered. After a long fight, in which he was wounded, he capitulated, and was carried off by the privateer. His dauntless wife, armed with a speaking trumpet, early next day hailed the ship as it passed Dursey island, and made a deal for the release of her husband on payment of £100. She could raise only £30, her second son was taken as a security for the balance, and Fontaine released. Eventually, the boy was released by the captain in Stᵗ Malo, and the £70 was *not* paid. From the government and from the Cork grand jury Fontaine received in all £900 for the losses he had suffered. Fontaine wrote

304

a vivid account of the affrays.

Castletownbere (VI.69.47.c) is a decaying village (pop. 1971: 812) that grew up when the copper mines at Allihies were opened in 1812 and maintained a living once when the British Navy — until 1938 — used Bantry Bay as a base. The bay is extraordinarily deep and the largest possible ships can come close to land. Hence the huge oil tankers that unload at Whiddy Island at the heart of Bantry Bay. It is now being developed as a fishing centre.

Here O Sullivan Beare had his great castle of Dun Baoi, or Dunboy, beside the sea, in the shelter of *Beare Island* (VI.68-77.42-46). A few traces of the castle now remain. There was a regular shipping service from Dun Baoi to Spain. Baoi was the wife of Dinioch, a druid, and she cleansed Corc, the incestuous son of Duben from his sin — the guilt being washed into a cow (or bull) which became Cow (or Bull) Rock, off Dursey. This Corc became the ancestor of the Corcu Duibne. Baoi may have been the wife of the god Lug, whose descendants settled at Beare.

Castletownbere is the centre of the hungry barony of Beare, as lean a place as there is in Ireland. The great family of the southern Gaels were the Eoghanachta, from a Goidelic invader Eogan, otherwise known at Mug Nuadat. He first landed at Kenmare and as part of his diplomacy, married a princess (or goddess) Etain, from Beare Island. His first expedition was a failure and he only narrowly escaped to Spain thanks to Etain's magic. He married a spanish princess, Beara, and when he invaded Ireland once more, nine years later, he landed here and named the island after his wife.

It was here, that the raiders from Fresen, near Spain, too, landed and carried off the wife of Tadg Mac Cein as well as his two brethren, so that Tadg set out from here to rescue them. This was one of the magical voyages of Irish literature, with strange islands where he met Cessair and other of the early invaders of Ireland, as well as other famous people before he achieved his task and returned.

Close by (but where precisely I have not found) are the remains of the old celtic nunnery of Killaconenagh. It recalls one of the most famous of Irish poems: the lament for old age of the Nun of Beare. The peninsula is unique in that it shows the remains of no less than four celtic convents of nuns, all within a radius of fifteen miles of this place — in all Kerry there is but one, and they are very few elsewhere in Ireland. She calls herself Baoi the Hag of Beare so that it was probably here at Castletownbere close to Dun Baoi that the famous poem was set. She was the foster-mother of Corc, the ancestor of the Corcu Duibne. She passed into seven periods of youth. The version we have is of the early ninth century, but Frank O Connor, who has published at least three translations of it, says, in the latest (*The Little Monasteries*, 1963): 'As I see it now the poem is really a series of lyrics from a lost eighth century romance dealing with the Goddess of Munster and St Cummine. In the romance, the Goddess, regarded as an Irish Mary Magdalen, must have invited Christ to spend the night with her and been fully converted only on his appearance.' The old nun, not fully regenerate, bewails her life in the convent (O Connor's translation):

I who had my day with kings
And drank deep of mead and wine
Drink whey-water with old hags
Sitting in their rags and pine.

St Cummine (or Cuimine), (596-662) called Fota (or the tall) was St Brendan's most distinguished seventh century successor as abbot of Clonfert. He answers her in the orthodox way:

May my cups be cups of whey,
May thy will be done, I pray,
And the prayer, O living God,
Quells the madness in my blood.

But her pining is intense as she watches with her one failing eye from her convent the tide swirl around the island of Beare:

Ebbtide is all my grief;
Bitter age has sucked my blood;
But though I get no relief
Merrily returns its flood.

Happy island of the main
To you the tide returns again,
But to me it comes no more
Over the blank deserted shore.

About a mile along the main road west from the village one comes to an inlet of the sea, and about half a mile along the west side of this — beyond the large victorian ruin — at the tip of the spit of land — one comes to a famous site. Here beside the sea, was the great castle of Dun Baoi, or *Dunboy* (VI.67.45.d). The present ruins are of the castle built c. 1470 to 1500. This was the main settlement of O Sullivan Beare, the second main branch of the O Sullivans, who moved here from the Cashel area in the thirteenth century. The principal branch, that of O Sullivan Mor, occupied the main part of the next peninsula in Kerry. What became of the earlier inhabitants we do not know. The lordship of O Sullivan Beare covered virtually the whole peninsula, as well as the north of Bantry Bay around Bantry and Whiddy island. In the 1580s a great dispute arose between Sir Owen O Sullivan and Donal Cam O Sullivan, each claiming to be O Sullivan Beare. They both appealed to Queen Elizabeth and the lordship was divided between them. Donal was granted Dunboy and most of the peninsula. He became the principal gaelic leader in the O Neill wars in Munster, and, indeed, one of the most famous men in Irish history. Here at Dunboy there was a constant trade with Spain — said to be worth in shipping dues to him £500 a year.

Also at Dunboy, 'of the incredible strength whereof much was noysed', was fought the most tenacious struggle of the whole war. A party of the Spaniards who landed at Kinsale in 1601 came here, hotly pursued by the English ships which themselves were driven off by the O Sullivans. After the defeat at Kinsale and the surrender Donal O Sullivan did not yield up the castle. At length in June, 1602, it was invested by land and sea. Under the command of its hereditary warden, Richard Mac Geoghegan, it held out heroically for over a fortnight until it was battered to pieces. The garrison offered to surrender on terms but during the parley someone fired a cannon at the English camp. The envoy was hanged and the siege resumed. Mac Geoghegan was mortally wounded. As the English came to the last, ground floor stronghold, Mac Geoghegan struggled to his feet, grasped a candle and was about to ignite a barrel of gunpowder when an English officer seized him, and he was killed. Almost all the remnants of the garrison were immediately put to death. *Pacata Hibernia* says:

> The whole number of the Ward (garrison) consisted of one hundred and fortie three selected fighting men, being the best choice of all their Forces, of which no man escaped but were either slaine, executed, or buried in the ruines, and so obstinate and resolved a defence had not bin seene within this Kingdome.

It asserts that a substantial Spanish expedition, which had been prepared and was confidently expected, was put off because of the fall of Dunboy.

There was much slaughter throughout the peninsula until at last Donal O Sullivan, despairing of victory, but determined not to give in, gathered his people, over a thousand strong, at Glengariff at Christmas, 1602, and determined to march them to Ulster where O Neill still held out. So in mid-winter, without food or protection, they set out, men, women and children. They made first for Gougane Barra, probably by way of Keimaneigh; but it is also argued that they went from Snave up the Coomhola valley and climbed up the savage ridge at its head. Either way it was a grim beginning to a terrible journey. Along the whole terrible journey they were dogged by enemies, cold, wet and hunger. To cross the Shannon they had to make two boats out of the skins of their horses, whose flesh they were glad to eat. One boat sank with all its occupants in the swollen river. The other ferried the party across. At last they reached friendly territory, O Rourke's, in Leitrim — all that was left of a party of over a thousand, were thirty four men and one ageing woman. A relative of Donal's, Philip O Sullivan, wrote a Latin account of this journey.

Donal O Sullivan went to Spain where Philip III gave him a handsome pension and created him Count of Dunboy. In 1619 he was killed in a brawl by a fellow Irishman, his valet.

From Dunboy set sail for Corunna, Spain in 1607, Muiris Mac Dhaivi Dhuibh Fitz Gerald in a ship of Donal O Sullivan's. He wrote a famous poem in Irish about the parting and the voyage.

After the cromwellian wars the lands on this peninsula were all acquired by William Petty.

In 1689 a French fleet landed supplies here for James II with complete success — unlike that of a century later.

The Dunboy property came into the hands of the Puxley family which attempted to maintain the English presence and English laws in this area. They fell foul of Morty Og O Sullivan Beare referred to below. They were also responsible for the development of the Allihies mines in the 19th century. The ruins of their home, burned down in 1921, are close by.

In the 18th century the famous member of the O Sullivan Beare family was Morty Og (1712-54). The cause and occasion of his death make a dramatic story.

One of the English planters who was in possession of Dunboy was John Puxley. He was also a customs officer who took the unusual (and highly unpopular) course of attempting to stamp out the smuggling that was rife along this wild coast. With his cutter he harried the exporters of wool and of recruits to France, and the importers of wine, brandy and silks to all the best families in the area. In this task he received no help from the Dublin government. His zeal was such that, on Easter Sunday, 1754, while he was going with his wife to church at Castletownbere, he met the chief of the local smugglers, Morty Og O Sullivan Beare, with two companions. Morty shot Puxley dead. His companions urged Morty also to shoot the wife, lest she identify them, but he did not.

Puxley Hall, Castletownbere

Morty had been educated in France and had been an officer in the Austrian Army. He had fought with the Irish Brigade in their great victory of Fontenoy in 1745 and again at the great defeat of Culloden in 1746. He had settled down near Eyries, some four miles due north of Castletownbere. Below his house, inside Coulagh Bay, was a harbour so intricate that no outsider could approach it. Here he anchored his brigantine, a formidable vessel armed with eight guns, more than a match for a naval cruiser. She had sunk many naval ships and was mistress of these seas. With this vessel Morty did a regular trade with France, and was a major recruiting and transport agent for the Irish Brigade there.

Prompted by the brothers of Puxley's widow the normally inert government decided not to tolerate this killing and forces were sent from Cork to Dunboy. On one wild night in May 1754 an expedition set out for Morty's house and surrounded it. Morty had just returned from France, and his ship was at anchor beneath the house. The house was bravely defended, but not until it was in flames around him could Morty be discerned. As he stayed shooting away in the blazing house he was killed by a shot. The ship was then sunk. Morty's body was brought to Dunboy and then, after some days, dragged behind a ship back to Cork. His two companions in Puxley's murder — one of them an O Connell from Derrynane — were taken in the blazing house and hanged in

306 Cork. Froude has a vivid account of this in his *English in Ireland* and based his novel *Two Chiefs of Dunboy*, on it.

Off Beare Island was played out another of the tragi-comedies of foreign aid for Irish nationalism. Froude gives a memorable account. Wolfe Tone persuaded the Directory to send a strong French force to invade Ireland. It consisted of 43 ships, 15,000 of the best of French veterans, artillery and vast quantities of arms to arm the Irish people who were expected to rise in revolt. The invasion was under the command of Hoche, second only to Bonaparte as a general, assisted by Grouchy. The invasion set out from Brest on 16 December, 1796. Five days later 35 of the ships were off Cape Clear; but Hoche's frigate was missing and Grouchy hesitated to invade on his own authority. The next day a gale got up and 16 ships with difficulty made Bantry Bay and anchored at Beare Island, Tone's ship *Indomptable* and Grouchy's *Immortalite* amongst them. The rest were blown to sea. A fierce storm of wind and snow immobilised them on 23rd. Next day, on Tone's urging, they tried to make the shelter of Whiddy Island, to land near Bantry, and push on to Cork then only lightly defended. But so fierce was the storm from the east that after eight hours of desperate effort they had not gained a yard. Christmas Day was wilder still, and the next day one of thick fog. On 27th the tempest was furious and the ships dragged their anchors, and then, one by one, cut their cables and were swept, under bare poles, to sea. Eight ships, with four thousand men, remained. The chance of surprising Cork was lost, and they stood out to sea intending to make for a landing on the Clare coast. But when they were off Dursey the wind turned west and a wild sea got up. This was too much for French seamanship and the ships turned for Brest. The great expedition was a total failure, without one English vessel being sighted. Two ships were lost and two, crippled by the storm, were later picked up by English cruisers. For six days a really formidable invasion force was within almost touching distance of Irish land here at Beare Island, and had met the most cruel luck.

From Castletownbere take the coast road for

Dursey, but it is hardly worth the trouble to turn left for *Dursey sound* (VI.51.42.b) and *Dursey island* (VI.45-51.39-42) which can be reached, on occasion, by cable car. Off Dursey island are the three isolated rocks, the Calf (VI.45.38.a), the Cow (VI.43.40.c) and the Bull (VI.41.40.b) Rocks. The last named is also called Teach Duinn because on that rock the ship containing Donn, one of the joint leaders of the milesian invasion of Ireland, was wrecked and he and his people buried. Donn was also the god of the underworld and to go to Teach Duinn (Donn's house) was to die. This was one of the entrances to the isles of enchantment that constituted part at least of the gaelic conception of the world after death.

Take the road for *Allihies* (VI.59.45.b) whose ancient copper mines — reopened by the Puxleys in 1811 who also mined lead and barytes — employed in 1851 no less than 1,200 people, a third of them miners from Cornwall. They lived in a separate settlement, known as the Cornish village, close to the mine. Competition from that ancient rival, Spain, brought hard times to the mines in the 1850s, and they eventually closed down in 1886. At peak production, £2,000 a month was, it is reported, paid in miners' wages, and Puxley's profits for many years ranged from £30,000 to £37,000 per annum. Some attempts have since been made to revive the mines. Daphne du Maurier, using Puxley family papers, has written a novel, *Hungry Hill,* about these mines. (The real Hungry Hill is, of course, some 12 miles east of Allihies).

Allihies, Co. Cork

Then go on to *Eyeries* (VI.65.51.b). About three miles beyond Eyeries turn left for the splendid Beara ring. After about a half-mile turn left for Ballycrovane harbour, a very pleasant spot. On the way back one can see on the high ground to the right the notable *Ballycrovane gallan* (VI.66.54.d). A boithrin and track lead up to it. It is remarkably high — 17½ ft — and most likely was first erected as a beacon for bronze age mariners approaching the hidden harbour. It was, much later, appropriated as an ogam memorial.

Back onto the road and continue left. About two miles further on there is, right, *Kilcatherine church* (VI.64.54.d), a typical medieval parish church. Catherine is an unusual name for these parts, and it has been argued that the name comes from Cat iarainn, the iron cat, an ancient object of worship, or totem, with which christianity had to come to terms. Over the south door of the church is a stone head on a long neck that may indeed be a cat's head, but there is no trace of iron. Another derivation is said to be from Caitigern. Here, in ancient times, was a monastery of both monks and nuns. However, one does not have to be too fanciful about this. There was in Ireland in medieval times an extensive cult of St Catherine, and effigies of her and her wheel are common in the eastern part of the country. Perhaps the name here replaced, at the time of the building of the parish church, an older dedication of the former monastery.

Follow the winding road, with splendid views along the coast, to *Ardgroom* (VI.59.56.d) and around Kilmakilloge for Kenmare.

Given a good day the run from Allihies to Derreen is one of the most striking in Kerry and West Cork. It is better to take the circuit in the order shown: on the whole, the Healy Pass is more striking taken from north to south and, certainly, the vistas on the north side of the peninsula are better from west to east.

Total driving distance: 150 miles. Allow six to seven hours.

Select Bibliography

A bibliography of Kerry has been prepared in typescript (1968) by Miss Margaret Stack and can be seen in the Kerry County Library, Tralee. It contains almost 2,000 entries.

Kerry has had a good book to itself since 1756, Charles Smith's *Antient and Present State of Kerry*, republished in 1969 and still full of interest. This was updated in 1871 by Miss M.F. Cusack's *History of Kerry*. In this century appeared various editions of a curious, but curiously indispensible, book, J. and E. King's *History of Kerry*, 1917 to 1931. The volume O Flanagain, M: *Ciarraighe* in the official county history series, published in 1941, is very useful but tails off at the end of the 17th century. Pleimonn, P: *The Story of Kerry*, 1935, is an account for younger readers. Richard Hayward's *In the Kingdom of Kerry* (1946) is readable but sketchy. Since Smith's time a great deal has been uncovered about the county and its past, but little attempt has been made to bring this together in narrative form or to use it to throw light on Irish life as a whole. There have been a number of books dealing with parts of the county, the most notable being Fr J.A. Gaughan's big book *Listowel and its Vicinity* (1973).

The position about guidebooks is not good. The only good guidebook devoted to the county is C.P. Crane's *Kerry* (1907), long out of print. Crane did much of his travelling by bicycle. No comparable work has been produced for the age of the motor car. There is a small modern guide: *Kerry County Guide* (nd) but its scope is limited. Of the national guides, Killanin, Lord and Duignan, M.V.: *The Shell Guide to Ireland* (2nd edition 1969) is indispensable, but difficult to use for an area such as a county. Another useful general guide is S. Jennet (ed): *Traveller's Guide to Munster* (1966): but it has to cover six counties in 120 pages. The Bord Failte Eireann guide, *Illustrated Ireland Guide* (nd) covers the county in 27 pages.

The county has a good weekly newspaper, *The Kerryman*, survivor of many papers since the 18th century.

The first periodical specially devoted to the antiquities and history of Kerry was the *Kerry Magazine* published monthly in Tralee for the three calendar years 1854-56. It was edited by Archdeacon A.B. Rowan. The second was the *Kerry Archaeological Magazine*, journal of the Kerry Archaeological Society founded 1907. This appeared annually between 1908 and 1920. Miss Charlotte Hussey was editor for the first six issues, Mr S. Trant Mac Carthy for the remainder. The *Annual Reports* of the County Kerry Society of London appeared between 1922 and 1940. The *Journal* of the Kerry Archaeological and Historical Society edited to 1971 by P. de Brun and since by Fr K. O Shea has appeared annually since 1968. These, in their entirety, are essential sources. For that reason individual articles from them are not listed in what follows.

Other important periodical sources are the *Journal* of the Cork Historical and Archaeological Society (JCHAS), the *Journal* of the Royal Society of the Antiquaries of Ireland (JRSAI), *Archivium Hibernicum*, and, of course, the *Transactions* (TRIA) and the *Proceedings* (PRIA) of the Royal Irish Academy. I give references to what seem to me to be the most important papers in these, so far as they are relevant to Kerry issues.

There is a large number of books and articles that give a background to the Irish scene, with perhaps only incidental references to Kerry; that deal with Kerry as part of a larger subject; that are devoted to a part of Kerry or to some aspect of the Kerry scene. I have listed those I have found most useful; they appear, normally once, under the chapter headings I have considered most relevant; but many of them will not be confined by such bonds.

Any local history must be seen in an overall framework. For the history of Ireland as a whole, perhaps the best short outline is: Moody, T.W. and Martin, F.X. (eds): *The Course of Irish History*, 1967; in more detail, Lydon, J. and Mac Curtain, M.: *The Gill History of Ireland*, 11 vols, 1972-75.

The present book aims to assemble in convenient and readable form what can be known about the county of Kerry from printed sources and personal observation. Because so much material had to be synthesised, detailed references would have overloaded the text, so footnotes have been eschewed; but every effort has been made to ensure that factual statements can be supported, and this bibliography lists all the principal printed sources. Nonetheless some matters may have been unwittingly misstated or misunderstood; corrections would be welcomed.

308 **Part 1** **Memories**

Chapter 1 Legends and Folk Tales

LEGENDS

Boswell, C.S.	An Irish Precursor of Dante (1908)
Comyn, D. (ed)	Keating, G.: History of Ireland, Vol I (1902)
Dillon, M.	The Cycles of the Kings (1946)
Dinneen, P.S. (ed)	Keating, G.: History of Ireland, Vols II and III (1908) and IV (1914)
Jackson, K. (ed)	Cath Maighe Lena (1938)
Joyce, P.W.	Old Celtic Romances (1914)
Macalister, R.A.S. (ed)	Lebor Gabala Erenn, 5 vols (1938-1956)
Mac Neill, E. (ed)	Duanaire Finn, Vol I (1908)
Murphy, G. (ed)	Duanaire Finn, Vol II (1933) and Vol III (1953)
Murphy, G. (ed)	The Ossianic Lore and Romantic Tales of Medieval Ireland (1961)
Murphy, G. (ed)	Saga and Myth in Ancient Ireland (1961)
Ni She, N. (ed)	Toraiocht Dhiarmada agus Ghrainne (1971)
O Cadhlaigh, C.	An Fhiannaidheacht (1937)
O Cadhlaigh, C.	An Ruraiocht (1956)
O'Curry, E. (ed)	Cath Mhuighe Lena (1855)
O Floinn, T. and Mac Cana, P.	Scealaiocht na Rithe (1956)
O'Grady, S.H. (ed)	Toruigheacht Dhiarmada agus Ghrainne (1857)
O'Grady, S.H. (ed)	Silva Gadelica (1892)
O'Rahilly, C. (ed)	Cath Finntragha (1962)

FOLK TALES

Croker, T.C.	Fairy Legends and Traditions of the South of Ireland (1825)
O Duilearga, S. (ed)	Leabhar Sheain I Chonaill (1948)
O Duilearga, S. (ed)	Irish Folk Tales collected by Jeremiah Curtin (1956)
O'Sullivan, S.	Folk Tales of Ireland (1966)
Sayers, P.	Peig
Sayers, P.	Machtnamh Seana Mhna (1939)
Sayers, P.	Scealta on mBlascaod (1939)
Sayers, P.	An Old Woman's Reflections, trans Ennis, S. (1962)

Chapter 2 The Celtic Invaders

Chadwick, N.	The Celts (1970)
Dillon, M. and Chadwick, N.	The Celtic Realms (1967)
Jackson, K.H.	The Oldest Irish Tradition: A Window on the Iron Age (1964)
Joyce, P.W.	A Social History of Ancient Ireland (1903)
Filip, J.	Celtic Civilisation and its Heritage (1962)
Henry, F.	L'Art Irlandais, 3 vols (1963-4)
Hogan, E.	Onomasticum Goidelicum (1910)
Mac Neill, E.	Phases of Irish History (1920)
Mac Neill, E.	Celtic Ireland (1921)
Mac Neill, E.	'The Pretanic background in Britain and Ireland' JRSAI 63 (1933)
Norman, E.R. and St. Joseph, J.L.	Early Development of Irish Society (1969)
O'Rahilly, T.F.	Early Irish History and Mythology (1946)
Powell, T.G.E.	The Celts (1958)
Raftery, J. (ed)	The Celts (1964)

Chapter 3 The Christian Invasion

Bede	History of the English Church and People (1955)
Bieler, L.	Ireland, Harbinger of the Middle Ages (1963)
Bieler, L.	St. Patrick and the coming of Christianity (1967)
Byrne, Francis J.	Irish Kings and High-Kings (1973)
Carney, J.	Medieval Irish Lyrics (1967)
Carney, J.	Early Irish Poetry (1965)
Dillon, M. (ed)	Early Irish Society (1954)
de Paor, M. and L.	Early Christian Ireland (1958)
Duignan, M.	'Irish agriculture in early historic times', JRSAI 74 (1944)
Flower, R.	The Irish Tradition (1947)
Greene, D.	The Irish Language (1966)
Hogan, J.	'The tricha cet and related land measures', PRIA 38 (1928-9) C
Hughes, K.	The Church in Early Irish Society (1966)
Hughes, K.	Early Christian Ireland: Introduction to the Sources (1972)
Hull, V.	'The migration of the Ciarraige', Speculum 25 (1950)
Kenney, J.F.	Sources for the Early History of Ireland: Ecclesiastical (1929)
Lehane, B.	The Quest of Three Abbots (1968)
Little, G.A.	Brendan the Navigator (1945)
Mac Niocaill, G.	Ireland before the Vikings (1972)
O Buachalla, L.	'Contributions towards the political history of Munster, 450-800 AD', JCHAS 56 (1951), 57 (1952), 59 (1954) and 61 (1956)
O'Connor, F.	Kings, Lords and Commons (1961)
O'Connor, F.	The Little Monasteries (1963)
O'Connor, F.	The Backward Look (1967)
O'Donoghue, D.	Brendaniana (1893)

Phillips, W.A. (ed)	History of the Church of Ireland, Vol I: The Celtic Church (1933)
Plummer, C. (ed)	Vitae Sanctorum Hiberniae (1910)
Plummer, C. (ed)	Bethada Naem nErenn (1922)
Ryan, J.	Irish Monasticism (1931)
Ryan, J. (ed)	Feil-sgribhinn Eoin Mhic Neill (1940)
Webb, J.	Lives of the Saints (St. Brendan, etc) (1965)

Chapter 4 The Gaelic Nation 800 - 1200

Bugge, A.	Caithreim Cellachain Caisil (1905)
Dunning, P.J.	'The Arroaisian order in medieval Ireland', Irish Historical Studies 4 (1945)
Gwynn, A.	The Twelfth Century Reform (1968)
Henry, F.	L'Art Irlandais, Vols II and III (1964)
Kelleher, J.V.	'The Rise of the Dal Cais' in E. Rynne (ed): North Munster Studies (1967)
Knott, E. & Murphy, G.	Early Irish Literature (1960)
Lucas, A.T.	'The plundering and burning of churches in Ireland, 7th to 16th century' in E. Rynne (ed): North Munster Studies (1967)
Mac Airt, S. (ed)	Annals of Inisfallen (1951)
Martin, F.X.	'Augustinian friaries in pre-reformation Ireland', Augustiniana 6 (1956)
Meyer, K.	Ancient Irish Poetry (1913)
Murphy, G.	Early Irish Lyrics, 1962
Nicholls, K.W.	'Rectory, vicarage and parish in western Irish dioceses', JRSAI 101 (1971)
O Corrain, D.	Ireland before the Normans (1972)
O Cuiv, B.	Literary Creation and Irish Historical Tradition (1963)
O'Donovan, J. (ed)	The Book of Rights (1847)
O hInnse, S. (ed)	Miscellaneous Irish Annals AD 1114-1437 (1947)
O'Meara, J.J. (trans)	Giraldus Cambrensis: Topography of Ireland (1951)
O'Meara, J.J.	Eiriugena (1969)
Ryan, J.	'The historical content of "Caithreim Ceallachain Caisil" ' JRSAI 71 (1941)
Walsh, T.J. and O'Sullivan, D.	'St. Malachy . . . . and the rule of Arrouaise', JCHAS 54 (1949)

Chapter 5 Feudalism 1200 - 1500

Archdall, M.	Monasticon Hibernicum (1786)
Begley, J.	Diocese of Limerick, 3 vols (1906) (1927) (1938)
Bolster, E.	History of the Diocese of Cork (1972)
Curtis, E.	History of Medieval Ireland, 1086-1513 (1923)

	Calendar of Papal Letters, 1198-1484, 14 vols (1893-1961)
Dodd, M.J. de C.	'The manor and fishery of Killorglin', J. Galway Arch Soc. 21 (1944)
Dolley, R.H.M.	'The 1834 Bantry find and the battle of Callan' JCHAS 70 (1965)
Fitz Gerald, B.	The Geraldines, 1169-1691 (1951)
Gwynn, A. and Gleeson, D.	History of the Diocese of Killaloe (1962)
Gwynn, A. and Hadcock, R.N.	Medieval Religious Houses in Ireland (1970)
Jennings, B.	'The abbey of Muckross', JCHAS 45 (1940)
Knott, E.	Irish Classical Poetry (1960)
Leslie, J.B.	Ardfert and Aghadoe Clergy and Parishes (1940)
Lydon, J.	Ireland in the Later Middle Ages (1973)
Mac Niocaill, G.	'Duanaire Ghearoid Iarla', Studia Hibernica 3 (1963)
Mac Niocaill, G.	'The origins of the betagh', Irish Jurist 1 (new series) (1966)
Mooney, C.	The Church in Gaelic Ireland, 13th to 15th centuries (1969)
Nicholls, K.	Gaelic and Gaelicised Ireland in the Middle Ages (1972)
O'Connell, J.	'15th century diocesan organisation in Kerry', Proc Irish Catholic Historical Cttee (1956)
O'Connell, J.	'Obligationes pro annatis diocesis Ardfertensis', Archivium Hibernicum 21 (1958)
O Cuiv, B.	Seven Centuries of Irish Learning (1971)
O Mahony, J.B.	'History of the O Mahony sept', JCHAS 16 (1910)
O Murchadha, D.	'Battle of Callan, AD 1261', JCHAS 66 (1961)
O Rahilly, T.F. (ed)	Danta Ghradha, AD 1350-1750, 2nd edn (1926)
Orpen, G.H.	Ireland under the Normans, 1169-1333, 4 vols (1911-20)
Otway-Ruthven, J.	History of Medieval Ireland (1968)
Phillips, W.A. (ed)	History of the Church of Ireland, Vol II (1934)
Sayles, G.O.	'The rebellious first earl of Desmond' in Watt, J.A., Morrall, J.B., and Martin, F.X. (eds): Medieval Studies Presented to Aubrey Gwynn, 1961
Sayles, G.O.	'The legal proceedings against the first earl of Desmond', Analecta Hibernica 23 (1966)
Sweetman, H.S. (ed)	Calendar of Documents relating to Ireland, Vol V (1302-7) (1886)
Watt, John	The Church in Medieval Ireland (1972)
Ziegler, P.	The Black Death (1969)
—	'Pobal Ailbe', Cashel and Emly Atlas (1970)

Chapter 6 Conquest 1500 - 1700

Bagwell, R.	Ireland under the Tudors, 3 Vols (1885-90)

310

Bagwell, R.	Ireland under the Stuarts, 3 vols (1909-16)	
Beckett, J.C.	The Making of Modern Ireland (1966)	
Brady, W.M.	The Mac Gillycuddy Papers (1867)	
Brady, W.M.	Episcopal Succession, Vol II (1876)	
Buckley, J.	'Munster in 1597', JCHAS 12 (1906)	
Butler, W.F.T.	Gleanings from Irish History (1925)	
Byrne, M.J. (ed)	P. O'Sullivan Beare: Ireland under Elizabeth (1903)	
Caball, J.	'Siege of Tralee, 1642', Irish Sword 2 (1956) and 4 (1960)	
Cullen, L.M.	'Population Trends in Seventeenth-Century Ireland', Economic and Social Review 6 (1975)	
Denny, H.	Handbook of Co. Kerry Family History (1923)	
Dineen, P.S. and O'Donoghue, T.	The Poems of Egan O'Rahilly, 2nd edn (1965)	
Dunlop, R.	Ireland under the Commonwealth, 2 vols (1913)	
Edwards, R.D.	Church and State in Tudor Ireland (1935)	
Fanshawe, A.	Memoirs (1907)	
Fitz Maurice, E.	The Life of Sir William Petty (1895)	
Flood, W.H. Grattan	'Dr. Richard O'Connell', Irish Ecclesiastical Record 13 (1903)	
Fuller, J.F. (ed)	Orpen, R.: The London Master, or the Jew Detected, JCHAS 8-9 (1902-3)	
Hardy, E.	Survivors of the Armada (1966)	
Hayes-Mc Coy, G.A.	'Gaelic society in Ireland in the late 16th century', Historical Studies IV (1963)	
Hickson, M.A.	Old Kerry Records, 1st series (1872)	
Hickson, M.A.	Old Kerry Records, 2nd series (1874)	
Hickson, M.A.	Ireland in the Seventeenth Century (1884)	
Hull, C.H. (ed)	The Economic Writings of Sir William Petty, 2 vols (1899)	
Jennings, B.	'Priests in the diocese of Ardfert and Aghadoe, 1636', Archivium Hibernicum 14 (1949)	
Jones, F.M.	The Counter Reformation (1967)	
Kilfeather, T.P.	Graveyard of the Spanish Armada (1967)	
Lansdowne, Marquis of	Glanerought and the Petty-Fitz Maurices (1937)	
Larcom, T.A. (ed)	The Down Survey of Dr. William Petty (1851)	
Mac Carthy, D.	Life and Letters of Florence Mac Carthy Reagh (1867)	
Mac Curtain, M.	Tudor and Stuart Ireland (1972)	
McCracken, E.	Irish Woods since Tudor Times (1971)	
Mac Lysaght, E.	Irish Life in the seventeenth century, 2nd edn (1950)	
Martyn, A.	Fr. Thaddeus Moriarty (1954)	
Massari, D.	My Irish Compaign', Catholic Bulletin 6-10 (1916-25)	
Meehan, C.P. (ed)	D. O'Daly: The Geraldines (1655) (1847)	
Murphy, M.A.	'The royal visitation, 1615: Dioceses of Ardfert and Aghadoe', Archivium Hibernicum 4 (1915)	

Mooney, C.	The First Impact of the Reformation (1967)
O'Brien, G.	Economic History of Ireland in the 17th century (1919)
O'Connell, W.D.	'Franciscan re-organisation in Munster during the early 17th century', JCHAS 44 (1939)
O'Connell, D.	'Dr. R. O'Connell and "new religion" in Kerry, 1603-53', Irish Ecclesiastical Record 13 (1903) and 14 (1904)
O'Doherty, J.F. (ed)	John Lynch: De Praesulibus Hiberniae, 2 vols (1944)
O Duinnin, P.S. (ed)	Danta Ph. Feiriteir (1934)
O Duinnin, P.S. (ed)	Danta Sh. Ui Dhonnchadha an Ghleanna (1902)
O'Rahilly, A.	The Massacre at Smerwick (1938)
O Suilleabhain, D.	Seanchas na Deasmumhan (1940)
Pielou, P.L.	The Leslies of Tarbert (1936)
Pochin-Mould, D.D.C.	The Irish Dominicans (1957)
Prendergast, F.J. (ed)	Friar O'Sullivan: The ancient history of the Kingdom of Kerry, JCHAS 4-6 (1898-1900)
Prendergast, F.J. (ed)	Franciscan Annals on Kerry History (1888)
Quinn, D.B.	'The Munster plantation: problems and opportunities', JCHAS 71 (1966)
Ranger, T.O.	'Richard Boyle and the making of an Irish fortune, 1588-1614', Irish Historical Studies 10 (1957)
Reidy, D.A.	'The diocese of Aghadoe, (Kerry)', Irish Ecclesiastical Record 49 (1937)
Renwick, W.L. (ed)	E. Spenser: A View of the Present State of Ireland (1934)
Sainthill, R.	The Old Countess of Desmond (1861 and 1863)
Smith, W.J. (ed)	The Herbert Correspondence (1963)
Stafford, T.	Pacata Hibernia (1633)
Strauss, E.	Sir William Petty (1954)
Walsh, T.J.	'Through Kerry, Cork and Limerick with Rinuccini', Capuchin Annual (1963)
Wood, H.	'Sir William Petty and his Kerry estate', JRSAI 64 (1934)

Chapter 7 Death and Rebirth 1700-

18th CENTURY

Bromwich, R.	'The keen for Art O'Leary . . .' Eigse 5 (1945-7)
Buckley, J.	'The parish priests of counties Cork and Kerry in 1704', JCHAS 6 (1900)
Burke, W.P.	The Irish Priests in Penal Times, 1660-1760 (1914)
Collins, J.T.	'Arthur O'Leary, the outlaw', JCHAS 54 (1949)

Connell, K.H.	The Population of Ireland 1750-1845 (1950)
Corcoran, T. (ed)	Selected Texts on Educational Systems in Ireland (1928)
Corkery, D.	The Hidden Ireland (1924)
Cullen, L.M.	'The smuggling trade in Ireland in the 18th century', PRIA 69 (1968) C
Cullen, L.M.	'The Hidden Ireland: Re-assessment of a Concept', Studia Hibernica 9 (1969)
Day, E.B.	Mr. Justice Day of Kerry (1938)
Dowling, P.J.	The Hedge Schools of Ireland (nd)
Froude, J.A.	Short Studies on Great Subjects, 2nd series (1871)
Froude, J.A.	The English in Ireland in the 18th century', 3 vols 2nd edn (1881)
Hutton, A.W. (ed)	Arthur Young's Tour in Ireland (1776-9) (1892)
—	Irish Catholic Directory (1842)
James, F.G.	'Irish smuggling in the 18th century', Irish Historical Studies 12 (1960-61)
Johnston, E.M.	Ireland in the Eighteenth Century (1974)
Lecky, W.E.H.	History of Ireland in the 18th century, 5 vols (1892)
Mac Lysaght, E. (ed)	The Kenmare Manuscripts (1942)
Maxwell, C.	Country and Town in Ireland under the Georges (1714-1830) (1940)
O'Brien, G.	Economic History of Ireland in the 18th century (1918)
O'Connell, M.J.	The Last Colonel of the Irish Brigade (1892)
O Foghludha, R. (ed)	Eoghan Ruadh O Shuilleabhain, 1748-84 (1937)
O Maidin, P.	'Pococke's tour of south and south-west Ireland in 1758', JCHAS 63-4 (1958-9)
O'Sullivan, D.	Irish Folk Music, Song and Dance (1961)
O Tuama, S. (ed)	Caoineadh Airt Ui Laoghaire (1961)
Reidy, D.A.	'A pastoral instruction in the Irish language', JCHAS 44 (1939)
Wall, M.	The Penal Laws 1691-1760 (1961)

19th CENTURY RESURGENCE

Chatterton, G.	Rambles in the South of Ireland in 1838, 2 vols (1839)
Cousens, S.H.	'The regional variation in mortality during the great Irish famine', PRIA 62 (1963)
Cullen, L.M.	Life in Ireland (1968)
Cullen, L.M. (ed)	The Formation of the Irish Economy (1969)
Curtis, L.P.	Coercion and Conciliation in Ireland (1963)
Cusack, M.F.	(The Nun of Kenmare): An Autobiography (1889 and 1893)
Doheny, M.	The Felon's Track (1914)
Donnelly, J.S.	The Land and People of Nineteenth Century Cork (1975)
Edwards, R.D. and	The Great Famine (1956)
Williams, T.D. (ed)	
Evans, E.E.	Irish Folkways (1957)
Eager, I. ff.	The Nun of Kenmare (1970)
Hall, S.C. and A.M.	Ireland, Vol I (1841)
Harmon, M. (ed)	Fenians and Fenianism (1968)
Hussey, S.M.	Reminiscences of an Irish Land Agent (1904)
—	Index of Surnames of Householders in Griffith's Primary Valuation of 1824-1860: Kerry (1963)
Jerrold, C.	The Story of Dorothy Jordan (1914)
Kennedy, T.P.	'Church building' in Corish, P.J. (ed): The Church since Emancipation (1970)
Lee, J.	The Modernisation of Irish Society, 1848-1918 (1973)
Lewis, S.	Topographical Dictionary of Ireland (1837)
Lyons, F.S.L.	Ireland since the Famine (1971)
Mac Intyre, A.	The Liberator: Daniel O Connell and the Irish Party, 1830-47 (1965)
O Brien, G.	Economic History of Ireland from the Union to the Famine (1921)
O Cuiv, B. (ed)	A View of the Irish Language (1969)
O Donovan, J. and others	Ordnance Survey Letters: Kerry, 1841 (unpublished)
O Faolain, S.	King of the Beggars (1938)
O Neill, T.P.	'Fever and public health in pre-famine Ireland', JRSAI 103 (1973)
Ordnance Survey	Name Books: Kerry. 6 vols (unpublished)
O Tuathaigh, G.	Ireland before the Famine, 1798-1848 (1972)
Phillips, W.A. (ed)	History of the Church of Ireland, vol III (1934)
Radcliffe, T.	Report on the agriculture of Kerry (1814)
Ryan, D.	The Phoenix Flame (1937)
Ryan, D.	The Fenian Chief (1967)
Smith, C. Woodham	The Great Hunger (1968)
Thompson, A.M.	Brief Account . . . . of Religious Opinion in Dingle, etc. 2nd edn (1847)
Trench, W.S.	Realities of Irish Life (1861)
Weld, I.	Illustrations of the Scenery of Killarney and the Surrounding Country (1812)

20th CENTURY INDEPENDENCE

Bourke, M.	The O Rahilly (1967)
Coogan, T.P.	Ireland Since the Rising (1966)
Crane, C.P.	Memories of a Resident Magistrate, 1880-1920 (1938)
Fenton, J.	It All Happened (1949)
Fitz Gerald, D.	Memoirs (1968)
Industrial Development Authority	Regional Industrial Plans, 1973-77: South West Region

Select Bibliography

312

Ireland, J.C. de C.	The Sea and the Easter Rising (1966)
—	Irish Catholic Directory, 1970
Kerryman, The	Kerry's Fighting Story (1947)
Lennon, J. and others	'Survey of Catholic Clergy and Religious Personnel, 1971', Social Studies 1 (1972)
Macardle, D.	Tragedies of Kerry (1924)
Mac Coll, R.	Roger Casement (1956)
Mac Giolla Choille, B.	Intelligence Notes, 1913-16 (1966)
McGlade, J.	The Missions: Africa and the Orient (1967)
Monteith, R.	Casement's Last Adventure (1932)
Murphy, J.A.	Ireland in the Twentieth Century (1975)
Neeson, E.	The Civil War in Ireland (1966)
O Connor, S.	Tomorrow is another Day (1970)
O Donoghue, F.	'The failure of the German arms landing at Easter, 1916', JCHAS 71 (1966)
O Lochlainn, C.	'A night in Kerry', Dublin Magazine 24 (1949)
O Luing, S.	I Die in a Good Cause (1970)
Robinson, H.W.	Church of Ireland Population of Ardfert (1971)
Ross, M.	Further Data on County Incomes in the Sixties (1972)
Ryle, M.P.	The Kingdom of Kerry (1902)
Spindler, K.	The Mystery of the Casement Ship (1965)
Stephan, E.	Spies in Ireland (1963)
Younger, C.	Ireland's Civil War (1968)

Praeger, R. Lloyd	The Way that I Went (1937)
Praeger, R. Lloyd	Natural History of Ireland (1950)
Scully, R.W.	Flora of County Kerry (1916)
Webb, D.A.	An Irish Flora, 4th edn (1963)

LIVING THINGS

Evans, P.G.H. and Lovegrove, R.R.	'The birds of the south west Irish islands', Irish Bird Report, 1973 21 (1974)
Gresson, R.A.R.	'Pilot whales stranded at Cloghane, Co. Kerry', Irish Naturalists' Journal 15 (1966)
Gresson, R.A.R.	'White sided dolphins stranded at Ventry Harbour', ibid 16 (1968)
Gresson, R.A.R.	'White sided dolphins stranded at Brandon Bay', ibid 16 (1968)
Irish Specimen Fish Committee	Report (1971)
Mac Dougald, T.J.	'Notes on the habits of the natterjack toad in Kerry', Irish Naturalists' Journal 8 (1942)
Moriarty, C.	Guide to Ireland's Birds (1967)
Moriarty, C.	Natural History of Ireland (nd)
Moyles, M.G.	'Kerry cattle, a brief outline', Dept of Agriculture Journal 53 (1956-7)
O Rourke, F.J.	The Fauna of Ireland (1970)
Redlich, A.	Dogs of Ireland (1949)
Ruttledge, R.F.	Ireland's Birds (1966)
Whitehead, G.K.	The Deer Stalking Grounds of Great Britain and Ireland (1960)

CLIMATE

| Bilham, E.G. | The Climate of the British Isles (1938) |

Part 2 Things

Chapter 8 The Physical Scene

SHAPES

Bryant, R.H.	'The pre-glacial beaches in south west Ireland', Irish Geography 5 (1966)
Charlesworth, J.K.	The Geology of Ireland: An Introduction (1953)
Charlesworth, J.K.	Historical Geology of Ireland (1963)
Coleman, J.C.	The Caves of Ireland (1965)
Whittow, J.B.	Geology and Scenery in Ireland (1974)

PLANTS

Freeman, T.W.	Ireland, a General and Regional Geography, 3rd edn (1965)
Hyams, E. and MacQuitty, W.	Irish Gardens (1967)
Mc Cracken, E.	'The Woodlands of Ireland c. 1600', Irish Historical Studies 11 (1959)
Orme, A.R.	The World's Landscapes: Ireland (1970)
Praeger, R. Lloyd	The Botanist in Ireland (1934)

Chapter 9 Pre-Christian Remains

Allen, J.R.	'Notes on antiquities in Co. Kerry', JRSAI 22 (1892)
Anati, E.G.	'New Petroglyphs at Derrynablaha', JCHAS 68 (1963)
Armstrong, E.C.R.	Catalogue of Irish Gold Ornaments (1920)
Borlase, W.C.	The Dolmens of Ireland (1897)
Carmody, W.P. and Wilson A.G.	'Kitchen Middens in [sandhills] in Dingle Bay', JRSAI 42 (1912)
Cooke, J. (ed)	W.F. Wakeman: A Handbook of Irish Antiquities, 3rd edn (1903)
Daniel, G.	The Megalith Builders of Western Europe (1963)
Dawson, G.W.P.	'The frequencies of the ABO and Rh(d) blood groups in Ireland . . . .', Ann. Hum. Genet. London 28 (1964)
Evans, E.E.	Prehistoric and Early Christian Ireland (1966)
Fahy, E.M.	'Recumbent stone circle at Drumbeg, Co. Cork', JCHAS 64 (1959) and 65 (1960)

Hackett, E. — 'Two main racial components in the Republic of Ireland', Irish Medical Assn Journal 42 (1958) March

Harbison, P. — 'Mining and metallurgy in early Bronze Age Ireland', North Munster Antiquarian Journal 10 (1967)

Harbison, P. — Guide to the National Monuments of Ireland (1970)

Harbison, P. — 'The earlier bronze age in Ireland', JRSAI 103 (1973) 93

Harbison, P. — The Archaeology of Ireland (1976)

Hooton, E.A. and Dupertuis, C.W. — The Physical Anthropology of Ireland (1955)

Jackson, K. — Language and History in Early Britain (1953)

Knowles, W.J. — 'Remains from the sandhills of the coast of Ireland', PRIA 22 (1900-2)

Lucas, A.T. — Sacred trees of Ireland, JCHAS 68 (1963)

Macalister, R.A.S. — Ireland in pre-celtic times (1921)

Macalister, R.A.S. — The Archaeology of Ireland, 1st edn 1928

Macalister, R.A.S. — The Archaeology of Ireland, 2nd edn 1949 (a new book)

Macalister, R.A.S. — Corpus Inscriptionum Insularum Celticarum (1945)

Mac Cana, P. — Celtic Mythology (1970)

Mac Neill, M. — The Festival of Lughnasa (1962)

Mac White, E. — 'A new view on Irish bronze age rock scribings', JRSIA 76 (1946)

Mahr, A. — 'New aspects and problems in Irish pre-history', Proceedings, Prehistory Society 3 (1937)

O'Connell, D.B. — Letters to the *Kerryman*, 1936-8, 1939

O'Connell, D.B. — 'A hoard at Killaha East, Kenmare', JRSAI 69 (1939)

O Danaghair, C. — 'The holy wells of north county Kerry', JRSAI 88 (1958)

O Danaghair, C. — 'The holy wells of Corkaguiney', JRSAI 90 (1960)

O'Kelly, M.J. — 'Excavations and experiments in ancient Irish cooking places', JRSAI 84 (1954)

O Riordain, S.P. — Antiquities of the Irish Countryside (1964)

Raftery, J. — Prehistoric Ireland (1951)

Raftery, J. — The Celts (1954)

Raftery, J. — 'A matter of time', JRSAI 93 (1963)

Thom, A. — Megalithic Sites in Britain (1967)

Westropp, T.J. — 'Promontory forts of the County Kerry' JRSAI 40 (1910), 42 (1912), 50 (1920), 51 (1921)

Wood-Martin, W.G. — Pagan Ireland (1895)

Wood-Martin, W.G. — Traces of the Elder faiths of Ireland, 2 vols (1902)

Chapter 10 Christian and Other Buildings

313

Aalen, F.H.A. — 'The evolution of the traditional house in western Ireland', JRSAI 96 (1966)

Aalen, F.H.A. — 'Clochans as transhumance dwellings in the Dingle peninsula', JRSAI 94 (1964)

Andrews, J.H. — 'Road Planning in Ireland before the railway age', Irish Geography 5 (1964)

Brash, R.B. — The Ecclesiastical Architecture of Ireland to the Close of Twelfth Century (1875)

Carson, Edward — The Ancient and Rightful Customs (1972)

Champneys, A.C. — Irish Ecclesiastical Architecture (1910)

Conroy, J.C. — History of the Railways in Ireland (1928)

Crawford, H.S. — 'A descriptive list of early Irish crosses', JRSAI 38 (1907)

Crawford, H.S. — 'A descriptive list of early cross slabs and pillars', JRSAI 42 (1912)

Danaher, Kevin — 'Old house types in Oighreacht Ui Chonchubhair', JRSAI 68 (1938)

Danaher, Kevin — Ireland's Vernacular Architecture (1975)

de Breffny, F. and ffolliott, R. — The Houses of Ireland (1975)

du Noyer, G.V. — 'Early stone built fortresses etc', Archaeological Journal 15 (1858)

Graves, C. — 'On similar forms of the Christian cross found on ancient monuments in Egypt and Ireland', JRSAI, 21 (1891)

Graber, A. — Christian Iconography: a study of its origins (1969)

Hadcock, N. — Map of Monastic Ireland (1964)

Harbison, Peter — 'How old is Gallarus oratory? A reappraisal of the role of Gallarus oratory in early Irish architecture, Medieval Archaeology XIV (1970)

Henry, F. — 'Early Irish monasteries etc . . . . (Gallarus, Kilfountain, Kilmalkedar)', Co. Louth, Archaeological Journal 11 (1948)

Henry, F. — 'Early Irish monasteries etc . . . Caherciveen and Waterville', PRIA 58 (1957) C

Henry, F. — L'Art Irlandais, 3 vols (1963-4)

Hunt, J. — Irish Medieval Figure Sculpture (1974)

Jope, E.M. (ed) — Studies in Building History (1961)

Leask, H.G. — Irish Castles, and Castellated Houses (1941)

Leask, H.G. — Irish Churches and Monastic Buildings, 3 vols (1955-60)

Lionard, P. — 'Early Irish grave slabs', PRIA 61 (1960)C

Macalister, R.A.S. — 'An ancient settlement in Corkaguiney', TRIA 31 (1899)

Meghen, P.J. — Roads in Ireland (1965)

Mooney, C. — 'Franciscan architecture in pre-reformation Ireland', JRSAI 85-7 (1955-7)

O Lochlainn, C. — 'Roadways in ancient Ireland', in Ryan, J. (ed): Feil-sgribhinn Eoin Mhic Neill (1940)

314

O'Kelly, M.J.	'An island settlement at Beiginish, Co. Kerry', PRIA 57 (1956) C
O'Kelly, M.J.	'Church Island near Valencia, Co. Kerry', PRIA 59 (1958) C
O Riordain, S.P. and Foy, J.B.	'The excavation of Leacanabuaile stone fort near Caherciveen', JCHAS 46 (1941)
Pender, B. and Richards, H.	Irish Railways Today (1967)
Roe, H.M.	'The Irish high cross: morphology and iconography', JRSAI 95 (1965)
Rynne, E.	'Some destroyed sites at Shannon airport, Co. Clare', PRIA 65 (1964) C
Stalley, R.A.	Architecture and Sculpture in Ireland, 1150-1350 (1971)
Stokes, M. (ed)	Notes on Irish Architecture, by Edwin, 3rd Earl of Dunraven, 2 vols (1875 and 1877)
Stokes, M. (revised by G.N. Plunkett)	Early Christian Art in Ireland, 1911
Sutcliffe, Sheila	Martello Towers (1972)
Taylor, G. and Skinner, A.	Maps of the Roads of Ireland, 2nd edn 1783 (Reprinted 1969)
Wakeman, W.F.	'On the earliest forms of inscribed christian crosses found in Ireland', JRSAI 21 (1891)

Part 3 Places

A number of the references given above relate also to special places. What follows is a list of references of more local topographical interest, including some already given above. It should be stressed that the bulk of the more local periodical references are in the special Kerry periodicals referred to above and are *not* detailed here.

Chapter 12 The Killarney Area: Magunihy and Dunkerron North

Collins, J.T. and Quinlan, J.	Castles and Monasteries in Killarney (nd)
Coleman, J.C.	The Mountains of Killarney (1948)
Corkery, D.	The Hidden Ireland (1924)
Croker, T.C.	Legends of the Lakes (1829)
Dinneen, P.S. and O Donoghue, T. (eds)	The Poems of Egan O Rahilly, 2nd edn (1965)
Everett, K.	Bricks and Flowers (1949)
Fehilly, J. and Shipman, P.	Killarney Valley Survey (1966)
Gwynn, A.	'Were the Annals of Inisfallen written at Killaloe?', North Munster Antiquarian Journal, 8 (1958)
Gwynn, S.	Duffer's Luck (1924)

Hilliard, F.M.	Guide to Maps and Prints at Muckross House (nd)
Jennings, B.	'The abbey of Muckross' JCHAS 45 (1940)
Leask, H.G.	The Friary of Muckross (nd)
Lewis, Frank	Muckross House Folk Museum (1975)
Mac Lysaght, E.	The Kenmare Manuscripts (1942)
O'Cahill, D.	Killarney, Land and Lake (1931)
O'Cahill, D.	Legends of Killarney (nd)
O Duinnin, P.S. (ed)	Danta Sh. Ui Dhonnchadha an Ghleanna (1902)
O Duinnin, P.S. (ed)	Muintir Chiarraidhe roimh an droch-shaoghal (1905)
O Foghludha, R. (ed)	Eoghan Ruadh O Shuilleabhain, 1748-84 (1937)
O'Rourke, K.	Old Killarney (nd)
Praeger, R.L.	The Way that I Went (1937)
Prendergast, F.J.	History of Muckross Abbey
R[owan], A.B.	Killarney Lake Lore (1853)
Ward, Lock and Co.	Killarney and South West Ireland (nd)
Weld, I.	Illustrations of the Scenery of Killarney and the Surrounding Country (1812)
Whitehead, G.K.	The Deer Stalking Grounds of Great Britain and Ireland (1960)
Windele, J.	Handbook to Killarney (1844)

Chapter 13 The Desmond Lands: Trughanacmy and Corkaguiney

TRUGHANACMY

Carmody, J.	'The abbey of Killagha', JRSAI 36 (1906)
Casey, A.E.	O Kief, Coshe Mang, Slieve Lougher and Upper Blackwater in Ireland, 13 vols (1952-67)
Coleman, J.C.	The Caves of Ireland (1965)
Donovan, T.M.	A Popular History of East Kerry (1931)
Doyle, J.J.	'Teamhar Luachra' JRSAI 57 (1927)
Mac Dougald, T.J.	'Notes on the habits of the natterjack toad in Kerry', Irish Naturalists' Journal 8 (1942)
O'Donoghue, D.	Brendaniana (1893)
Ryan, I.	History of the Dominican Priory of Tralee (1961)
Seabhac, An (O Siochfhradha P.)	'Ainmneacha bailte fearainn . . . i dTriuch an Aicme', Bealoideas 20 (1950)
Smith, W.J. (ed)	The Herbert Correspondence (1963)

CORKAGUINEY

Aalen, F.H.A.	'Clochans as transhumance dwellings in the Dingle peninsula, Co. Kerry', JRSAI 94 (1964)

du Noyer, G.V.   'Early stone built fortresses etc',
                 Archaeological Journal 15 (1858)

Flower, F.   The Western Island (1944)

Foley, P.   The Ancient and the Present State of the
                 Skellig and Blasket Islands etc (1903)

Foley, P.   History of the County Kerry in Baronies:
                 Corkaguiney (1907)

Harbison, P.   'How old is Gallarus Oratory?' Medieval
                 Archaeology 14 (1970)

Hardy, E.   Survivors of the Armada (1966)

Henry, F.   'Early Irish monasteries . . . (Gallarus,
                 Kilfountain, Kilmalkedar etc)', Co. Louth
                 Archaeological Journal 11 (1948)

Hickson, M.A.   'Killelton in Glenfas', JRSAI 28 (1898)

Hill, A.   Ancient Irish Architecture: Kilmalkedar
                 (1870)

Lynch, P.J.   'Notes on Dunbeg fort', JRSAI 28 (1898)

Lynch, P.J.   'Caherconree, Co. Kerry', JRSAI 29 (1899)

Macalister, R.A.S. 'An ancient settlement in Corkaguiney', TRIA
                 31 (1899)

O Beolain, A.   'Piaras Feiritear', Comhar 28 (Feabhra, 1969)

O Ciosain, M. (eag) Cead Bliain, 1871-1971 (1973)

O Conchuir, D.   Corca Dhuibhne (1973)

O Criomhthain, T. Allagar na hInise (1928)

O Criomhthain, T. An tOileanach (1929)

O Criomhthain, T. The Islandman, trans Flower, R. (1937)
(O Crohan, T.)

O Criomhthain, T. Dinnsheanchas na mBlascaodai (1935)

O Criomhthain, T. Seanchas o'n Oilean Tiar (1956)

O Danachair, C. 'The holy wells of Corkaguiney, Co. Kerry',
                 JRSAI 90 (1960)

O Danachair, C. 'Some primitive structures used as dwellings',
                 JRSAI 75 (1945)

O'Donoghue, D.   'Mor, sister of St. David . . . mother of Kerry
                 saints', JRSAI 21 (1891)

O Dubhda, S.   Duanaire Duibhneach (1933)

O Duinnin, P.S. (ed) Danta Ph. Feiriteir (1934)

O'Rahilly, A.   The Massacre at Smerwick (1938)

O'Rahilly, C. (ed) Cath Finntragha (1962)

O Suilleabhain, M. Fiche Blian ag Fas (1933)

O Suilleabhain, M. Twenty Years a-Growing, trans by Davies,
                 M.L. and Thomson, G. (1933)

O'Sullivan, T.F. Romantic Hidden Kerry (1931)

Sayers, P.   Peig. i. A Sceal Fein (1936)

Sayers, P.   Machtnamh Seana Mhna (1939)

Sayers, P.   Scealta o'n mBlascaod (1939)

Sayers, P.   An Old Woman's Reflections, trans Ennis, S.
                 (1962)

Sayers, P.   Peig, trans by Mac Mahon, B. (1974)

Seabhac, An   Trioca Cead Chorca Dhuibhne (1939)
(O Siochfhradha, P.)

Seabhac, An
(O Siochfhradha, P.) Cath Fiontragha (1925)

Shearman, J.F.   'Loca Patriciana IX' JRSAI 14 (1876-8)

Synge, J.M.   In Wicklow and West Kerry (1912)

Thompson, A.M.   Brief Account . . . . of Religious Opinion in
                 Dingle, etc 2nd edn (1847)

Westropp, T.J.   'Promontory forts: III and IV, Corkaguiney',
                 JRSAI 40 (1910)

Chapter 14 North Kerry: Clanmaurice and Iraghticonnor

Brunicardi, Mrs. 'The shore dwellers of ancient Ireland', JRSAI
                 44 (1914)

Byrne, M.J.   'Rattoo', JCHAS 16-17 (1910-11)

Danaher, K.   'Old house types in Oighreacht Ui
                 Chonchubhair', JRSAI 68 (1938)

Gaughan, J.A.   Listowel and its Vicinity (1973)

Hickson, M.A.   'Ardfert friary and the Fitz Maurices, Lords
                 of Kerry', JRSAI 25-27 (1895-7)

Hickson, M.A.   'Round Tower of Barrow', Royal Historical
                 Assn Journal 16 (1883-4)

Hill, A.   Ancient Irish Architecture: Templenahoe,
                 Ardfert (1870)

Nunan, F.   Kerry's Ancient See and Shrine Ardfert —
                 Brendan (1950)

O'Connor, S.   Tomorrow is Another Day (1970)

O Danachair, C. 'The holy wells of north county Kerry',
                 JRSAI 88 (1958)

O Donnell, Patrick The Irish Faction Fighters of the 19th
                 Century (1975)

Quane, M.   'Banna School, Ardfert', JRSAI 84 (1954)

Westropp, T.J.   'Promontory forts: I, Iraghticonnor, II,
                 Clanmaurice', JRSAI 40 (1910)

Chapter 15 The Iveragh Peninsula: Iveragh and Dunkerron South

Anati, E.G.   'New petroglyphs at Derrynablaha', JCHAS
                 68 (1963)

Crawford, H.S.   The early cross slabs and pillar stones at
                 Church Island, near Waterville', JRSAI 56
                 (1926)

de Paor, L.   'Survey of Sceilig Mhichil', JRSAI 85 (1955)

Fenton, J.   Songs of Tomas Ruadh O Suilleabhain,
                 1785-1848 (1922)

Fenton, J.   It all Happened (1949)

Graves, C.   'The croix gammee, or swastika . . . Glencar
                 and Inisvicillane', JRIA 27 (1878)

Henry, F.   'Early monasteries, beehive huts etc . . .
                 Caherciveen and Waterville', PRIA 58 (1957)
C

316

Lych, P.J.   'Some antiquities around Ballinskelligs Bay', JRSAI 32 (1902)

Lynch, P.J.   'Some antiquities around St. Finans Bay', JRSAI 32 (1902)

Lynch, P.J.   'Antiquities of Caherlehillan', JRSAI 36 (1906)

Lynch, P.J.   'Inscribed Stone at Poulacopple, Co. Kerry', JRSAI 36 (1906)

Lynch, P.J.   'Some notes on Church Island, Lough Currane,' JRSAI 38 (1908)

Macalister, R.A.S.   'A monument with bronze-age scribings in Co. Kerry', PRIA 45 (1938-9)C

Mahony, P.   The Truth about Glenbeigh (1887)

O'Connell, M.J.   The Last Colonel of the Irish Brigade (1892)

O Duilearga, S.   Leabhar Sheain I Chonaill (1948)

O'Kelly, M.J.   'An island settlement at Beiginish, Co. Kerry', PRIA 57 (1956)C

O'Kelly, M.J.   'Church Island near Valencia, Co. Kerry', PRIA 59 (1958) C

O'Kelly, M.J.   'A new group of Rock-scribings in Co. Kerry', JCHAS 63 (1958)

O Riordain, S.P. and Foy, J.B.   'The excavation of Leacanabuaile stone fort near Caherciveen' JCHAS 46 (1941)

O Suilleabhain, D.   Seanchas na Deasmumhan (1940)

O Suilleabhain, D.   Seanchas Bhoirdoinin, Bealoideas 15 (1946)

Quane, M.   'Zelva School, Valentia Island', JCHAS 72 (1967)

Rynne, E.   'Some destroyed sites at Shannon Airport, Co. Clare', PRIA 65 (1964) C

Seabhac, An (O Siochfhradha, P.)   Ui Rathach, Bealoideas, 23 (1954)

Shee, E.A. and O'Kelly, M.J.   'The Derrynablaha 'Shield' Again' JCHAS 76 (1971)

Westropp, T.J.   'Promontory forts: V, Iveragh', JRSAI 42 (1912)

—   Sneem: The Knot in the Ring (nd) (?1976)

Chapter 16 The Kenmare Area: Glanerought and Beare

Bigger, F.J.   'Lake and church at Kilmakilloge etc', JRSAI 28 (1898)

Boyle, J.A.   The Irish Flowerers (1971)

du Maurier, D.   Hungry Hill (1943)

Froude, J.A.   'A fortnight in Kerry' in Short Studies on Great Subjects, 2nd series (1871)

Froude, J.A.   Two Chiefs of Dunboy (1889)

Fuller, J.F. (ed)   Orpen, R.: The London Master or the Jew Detected, JCHAS 8-9 (1902-3)

Lansdowne, Marquess of   Glanerought and the Petty-Fitz Maurices (1937)

Lynch, P.J.   'Kilmakilloge', JRSAI 28 (1898)

Mawhinney, K.A.   'The Allihies copper mine, Co. Cork', Technology Ireland 3 (1971)

O Brien, D. Maddison   'A list of some archaeological sites on the Berehaven peninsula', JCHAS 75 (1970)

O Connell, D.B.   'A hoard at Killaha East, Kenmare', JRSAI 69 (1939)

O Donoghue, J.   In Kerry Long Ago (1960)

O Foghludha, R.   Cois na Ruachtaighe (1938)

O Suilleabhain, S.   Diarmaid na Bolgaighe agus a Chomharsain (1937)

Somerville-Large, P.   The Coast of West Cork (1972)

Trench, W.S.   Realities of Irish Life (1861)

Westropp, T.J.   'Promontory forts: VI. Beare and Bantry' JRSAI 50 (1920) and 51 (1921)

Note on Place Names

The placenames used in this book are, in general, in the form left us by the Ordnance Survey of the 19th century. The spelling used then was an attempt to reproduce the names as given by Irish speakers, where that was appropriate. Thus, the townland of *Riasc* in Irish became that of Reask, that of *Beitheachan* became Behaghane, and so on.

It is usually difficult to give the full meaning of placenames: much work has yet to be done on them. So far as Kerry is concerned, the field is virtually untilled. The difficulties come from phonetic errors, corruptions of sounds over the years, allusions now lost, and the incorporation in the names of pre-celtic words, such as for mountains and rivers.

However, there is a constant repetition of some suffixes, and an account should be given of these so far as the most common of them appear in the index of places that follows. A large number of the names describe some significant feature of the place.

Ard-, bar-, binn-, can- (or ken-), croagh-, drom- (or mullagh), knock-, all relate to rising ground, respectively, height, top, peak, head, ridge, hog-back, hill.

The very common *ballan-, ballin-, bally,* relate either to town, townland (baile), as does *farran-,* or ford (beal atha).

Caher-, lis-, rath-, and *dun- (or doon-),* all refer to forts — the first to stone forts, the second and third to earthen ones, and the fourth to all kinds.

Clon-, cloon-, gort-, park-, all mean a field.

Coom-, coum-, glan-, gleann-, glen-, mean much the same thing.

Derreen-, derry, refer to oak woods, now often vanished, but also to any kind of wood.

Illan-, illaun-, inis-, inish-, mean an island, and *inch-* a place by water.

Keel-, kil-, kill-, meant originally a cell, hence a church of some sort, as does the affix *-aglish* (e.g. *Ballinahaglish*, Churchtown).

Leac-, is a flagstone, and *loch-, lough,* a lake.

Reen-, and *ross-,* mean a point.

Index of Places

General Index